BORN INTO A WORLD AT WAR

Edited by

Maria Tymoczko and Nancy Blackmun

St JEROME
PUBLISHING

First published 2000 by

    St. Jerome Publishing
    2 Maple Road West, Brooklands
    Manchester, M23 9HH, United Kingdom
    Tel +44 161 973 9856
    Fax +44 161 905 3498
    stjerome@compuserve.com
    http://www.mcc.ac.uk/stjerome

ISBN 1-900650-23-1

© Maria Tymoczko and Nancy Blackmun 2000

All rights reserved, including those of translation into foreign languages. No part of this publication may be reproduced, stored in a retrieval system or transmitted in any form or by any means, electronic, mechanical, photocopying, recording or otherwise without either the prior written permission of the Publisher or a licence permitting restricted copying issued by the Copyright Licensing Agency (CLA), 90 Tottenham Court Road, London, W1P 9HE. In North America, registered users may contact the Copyright Clearance Center (CCC): 222 Rosewood Drive, Danvers MA 01923, USA.

Printed and bound in Great Britain by
T.J. International Ltd., Cornwall, UK

Cover design by
Steve Fieldhouse, Oldham, UK (+44 161 620 2263)

Cover Photograph: Coventry Cathedral ruins after the bombing
of 14 November, 1940

British Library Cataloguing in Publication Data
A catalogue record of this book is available from the British Library

The copyright on this volume does not apply to the photographs commissioned by the Agencies of the Government of the United States of America. These are in the public domain.

BORN INTO A WORLD AT WAR

Steven Kilston, 1946.

*For our parents,
and our children*

Was du ererbt von deinen Vätern hast,
Erwirb es, um es zu besitzen!

If you would possess what you have inherited from your forebears, take it and make it your own.

Goethe
Faust, part 1, scene 1

TABLE OF CONTENTS

Born into a World at War   13

Prologue   19
   Nancy Blackmun and Maria Fleming Tymoczko,
   "Recorded on the Body, Etched on the Heart"   21

Paradox   35
   Julie E. Coryell, "Legacies of the Manhattan Project"   37
   Eva Botstein Griepp, "Growing Up in the Shadow of the Holocaust" 45
   Deborah Lucas Schneider, "Shape Up, Kid"   51
   Nancy Blackmun, "Falling through a Wrinkle in Time"   55
   Robert G. Sakai, "From Poston to Palau"   65
   Matthew W. Stolper, "Their Happiest Ten Years"   77
   Maria Fleming Tymoczko, "War Babies"   87

Parable   103
   Anthony Graham-White, "Bombs and Brambles"   107
   Klaus Peter Katzlberger, "Life Goes On"   111
   Ursula Oppens, "Silence"   123
   Christine Tanz, "Hiding in the Open"   127
   Francis L. Zebot, "Out of Slovenia"   153
   John Dundas, "The Worm in the Apple"   159
   Margaret deBeers Brown, "Reflections on a Quaker Father"   165
   Kazuko Iwasawa Ihara, "Of Our Life in Japan during the War"   169
   Mathea Falco, "Childhood Memories of Postwar Germany"   173
   Hugh Field, "Trolling Along at the Bottom"   181
   Max Gitter, "Born in Samarkand"   189
   Goh Cheng Teik, "A Baby of the Japanese Occupation"   195
   Howard Gardner, "Dissolving Repression: A Half-Century Report" 201
   William M. McConahey III, "My Father, Battalion Surgeon"   207
   Charles Styron, "War Stories, Past and Present"   215

Parallax   225
   Marina Sulzberger Berry, "Home Is Abroad"   229
   Steven Kilston, "Glory Remembered Is Hope Preserved"   237
   Betty Chang Sun, "Chinese Girls Don't Wear Hats"   247
   Laurel Strange Hayler, "Wartime Separation"   261
   Helena Worthen, "XXOO"   265
   Andrew D. Cohen, "The Holocaust by Marriage"   275

Sarah Niles Kafatou, "My Flier" 281
Kevin Lewis, "Innocence and Experience" 285

Epilogue 297
Nancy J. Chodorow, "Individuals in History
and History through Individuals" 299

Notes on Contributors 315

Acknowledgments 323

Glossary 327

Notes 339

Sources and Works Cited 349

Bombing of the destroyer USS *Shaw* at Pearl Harbor, December 7, 1941.

War brides and war babies in the summer of 1944; Maria Fleming Tymoczko with her mother, center

BORN INTO A WORLD AT WAR

Hugh Field and his mother (left) with friends.

Born into a World at War

January 8, 1940: Anthony Graham-White, born in Tolworth, Surrey, England
    Mother: Kathleen Adela Korts, born February 9, 1916, in Kingswood, England
    Father: Peter Joseph Dominic Graham-White, born August 18, 1914, in Sarawak (now Malaysia)

June 30, 1942: John Dundas, born in Perth, Perthshire, Scotland
    Mother: Ruth Northrup, born September 24, 1907, in Minneapolis, Minnesota, U.S.A.
    Father: John George Lawrence Dundas, born November 3, 1893, in Anderby Hall, Yorkshire, England

October 23, 1942: Kazuko Iwasawa, born in Kamakura, Kanagawa, Japan
    Mother: Aiko Kaneko, born October 2, 1919, in Tokyo, Japan
    Father: Kenkichi Iwasawa, born September 11, 1917, in Kiryu, Gunma, Japan

November 11, 1942: Klaus Peter Katzlberger, born in Lorch, Württemberg, Germany
    Mother: Irene Bauer, born January 12, 1919, in Lorch, Württemberg, Germany
    Father: Anton Katzlberger, born April 15, 1917, in Oberdorf, Mettmach, Austria

January 10, 1943: Deborah Lucas, born in Evanston, Illinois, U.S.A.
    Mother: Mary Husted, born July 31, 1913, in Toledo, Ohio, U.S.A.
    Father: William Ernest Lucas, born May 30, 1910, in Walhalla, South Carolina, U.S.A.

March 10, 1943: Laurel Strange, born in Los Angeles, California, U.S.A.
    Mother: Phyllis Jean Swanson, born April 20, 1917, in Chicago, Illinois, U.S.A.
    Father: Robert George Strange, born January 25, 1910, in Denver, Colorado, U.S.A.

April 24, 1943: Sarah Niles, born in New York City, New York, U.S.A.
    Mother: Helen Louise Beccard, born November 12, 1903, in St. Louis, Missouri, U.S.A.
    Father: Walter Wheeler Niles, born September 14, 1909, in Olathe, Colorado, U.S.A.

April 27, 1943: William M. McConahey III, born in Philadelphia, Pennsylvania, U.S.A.
Mother: Adrienne Parsons Magness, born May 7, 1916, in Pittsburgh, Pennsylvania, U.S.A.
Father: William M. McConahey, Jr., born January 20, 1920, in Akron, Ohio, U.S.A.

June 16, 1943: Hugh Field, born in New York City, New York, U.S.A.
Mother: Kate Margaret Thornycroft, born August 8, 1912, in London, England
Father: Hermann Haviland Field, born April 13, 1910, in Zurich, Switzerland

July 8, 1943: Nancy Blackmun, born in Minneapolis, Minnesota, U.S.A.
Mother: Dorothy Eugenia Clark, born December 12, 1910, in Cloquet, Minnesota, U.S.A.
Father: Harry Andrew Blackmun, born November 12, 1908, in Nashville, Illinois, U.S.A.

July 11, 1943: Howard Gardner, born in Scranton, Pennsylvania, U.S.A.
Mother: Hilde Weilheimer, born September 15, 1911, in Nuremberg, Germany
Father: Rudolph Gaertner (later Ralph Gardner), born April 14, 1908, in Nuremberg, Germany

July 13, 1943: Kevin Lewis, born in Asheville, North Carolina, U.S.A.
Mother: Phebe Ann Clarke, born November 2, 1914, in Lake Forest, Illinois, U.S.A.
Father: Burdette Gibson Lewis, Jr., born June 4, 1912, in Bronxville, New York, U.S.A.

September 24, 1943: Margaret deBeers, born in Washington, D.C., U.S.A.
Mother: Marianna Hurd Hill, born November 26, 1912, in Buffalo, New York, U.S.A.
Father: John Sterling deBeers, born July 7, 1914, in Evanston, Illinois, U.S.A.

October 11, 1943: Francis L. Zebot, born in Ljubljana, Slovenia, Yugoslavia (now Slovenia)
Mother: Ivana Korun, born May 1, 1922, in Ljubljana, Slovenia, Yugoslavia (now Slovenia)
Father: Cyril A. Zebot, born April 8, 1914, in Maribor, Slovenia (then Steiermark Province of Austria-Hungary)

October 16, 1943: Goh Cheng Teik, born in Bagan Dalam, Straits Settlement of Penang (now Malaysia)
  Mother: Ooi Kim Khuan, born January 1, 1923, in Bagan Dalam, Straits Settlement of Penang (now Malaysia)
  Father: Goh Soon Tit, born April 11, 1921, in Kebun Sirei, Bukit Mertajam, Straits Settlement of Penang (now Malaysia)

October 19, 1943: Robert G. Sakai, born in Minneapolis, Minnesota, U.S.A.
  Mother: Sady Kitaoka, born March 19, 1921, in Fullerton, California, U.S.A.
  Father: Robert Kenjiro Sakai, born April 3, 1919, in Riverside, California, U.S.A.

October 22, 1943: Helena Worthen, born in Cleveland, Ohio, U.S.A.
  Mother: Eleanor Goddard, born June 10, 1908, in Evanston, Illinois, U.S.A.
  Father: Eugene Mark Worthen, born April 10, 1909, in Plymouth, New Hampshire, U.S.A.

October 29, 1943: Charles Woodrow Styron, Jr., born in Raleigh, North Carolina, U.S.A.
  Mother: Ellen Devereux Joslin, born September 17, 1914, in Raleigh, North Carolina, U.S.A.
  Father: Charles Woodrow Styron, born November 6, 1913, in New Bern, North Carolina, U.S.A.

November 17 or 18, 1943: Manes Giter (Max Gitter), born in Samarkand, Uzbek, U.S.S.R. (now Uzbekistan)
  Mother: Paula Nissenbaum, born December 10, 1917, in Międzyrzec (Mezrich), Poland
  Father: Wolf Giter, born September 17, 1916, in Uvnów, Poland (now Ukraine)

December 15, 1943: Maria Anne Fleming, born in Providence, Rhode Island, U.S.A.
  Mother: Anne Figuly, born January 8, 1926, in Klenovič, Czechoslovakia (now Slovakia)
  Father: Robert La Follette Fleming, born June 17, 1924, in Cleveland, Ohio, U.S.A.

December 22, 1943: Chang Zung Wei (Betty Chang), born in Shanghai, China
  Mother: Lee Yen Yuen (later Irene Chang), born August 4, 1916, in Peking (Beijing), China
  Father: Chang Cheng Teh (later Leo Chang), born January 3, 1913, in Nanking (Nanjing), China

December 24, 1943: Julie E. Coryell, born in Oak Ridge, Tennessee, U.S.A.
   Mother: Grace Mary Seeley, born September 14, 1914, in Colorado Springs, Colorado, U.S.A.
   Father: Charles DuBois Coryell, born February 21, 1912, in Alhambra, California, U.S.A.

January 20, 1944: Nancy J. Chodorow, born in New York City, New York, U.S.A.
   Mother: Leah Ruth Turitz, born September 9, 1909, in New York City, New York, U.S.A.
   Father: Marvin Chodorow, born July 16, 1913, in Buffalo, New York, U.S.A.

February 2, 1944: Ursula Oppens, born in New York City, New York, U.S.A.
   Mother: Edith Hirsch, born September 25, 1910, in Kluges (Clausenburg), Hungary
   Father: Kurt Franz Heinrich Oppens, born April 7, 1910, in Hamburg, Germany

March 1, 1944: Matthew W. Stolper, born in Philadelphia, Pennsylvania, U.S.A.
   Mother: Martha Vögeli, born February 21, 1912, in Zurich, Switzerland
   Father: Frederick Wolfgang Stolper (later Wolfgang F. Stolper), born May 13, 1913, in Vienna, Austria

March 14, 1944: Andrew D. Cohen, born in Washington, D.C., U.S.A.
   Mother: Rena Alpert, born July 4, 1917, in New York City, New York, U.S.A.
   Father: Harold J. Cohen, born February 2, 1913, in Indianapolis, Indiana, U.S.A.

September 3, 1944: Steven Kilston, born in Hollywood, California, U.S.A.
   Mother: Ellen Hoschanger, born September 21, 1921, in Berlin, Germany
   Father: Benjamin Cohen (later Benjamin Kilston), born November 11, 1914, in Los Angeles, California, U.S.A.

September 11, 1944: Marina Sulzberger, born in Cairo, Egypt
   Mother: Marina Tatiana Ladas, born May 1, 1919, in Athens, Greece
   Father: Cyrus Leo Sulzberger, born October 27, 1912, in New York City, New York, U.S.A.

September 27, 1944: Krystyna Maria Szwienczicka (Christine Tanz), born in Warsaw, Poland
   Mother: Regina Wiernicka, born February 4, 1913, in Cracow, Poland
   Father: Henryk Tanz, born January 29, 1911, in Cracow, Poland

October 15, 1944: Mathea Falco, born in Montgomery, Alabama, U.S.A.
    Mother: Kathleen Fream, born April 11, 1909, in Innisfair, Alberta, Canada
    Father: Maceo Falco, born July 4, 1893, in Santiago, Cuba

December 3, 1944: Eva Botstein, born in Zurich, Switzerland
    Mother: Anna Wyszewiańska, born August 30, 1912, in Lodz, Poland
    Father: Chaim Botsztejn (later Charles Botstein), born January 18, 1911, in Uman, Ukraine

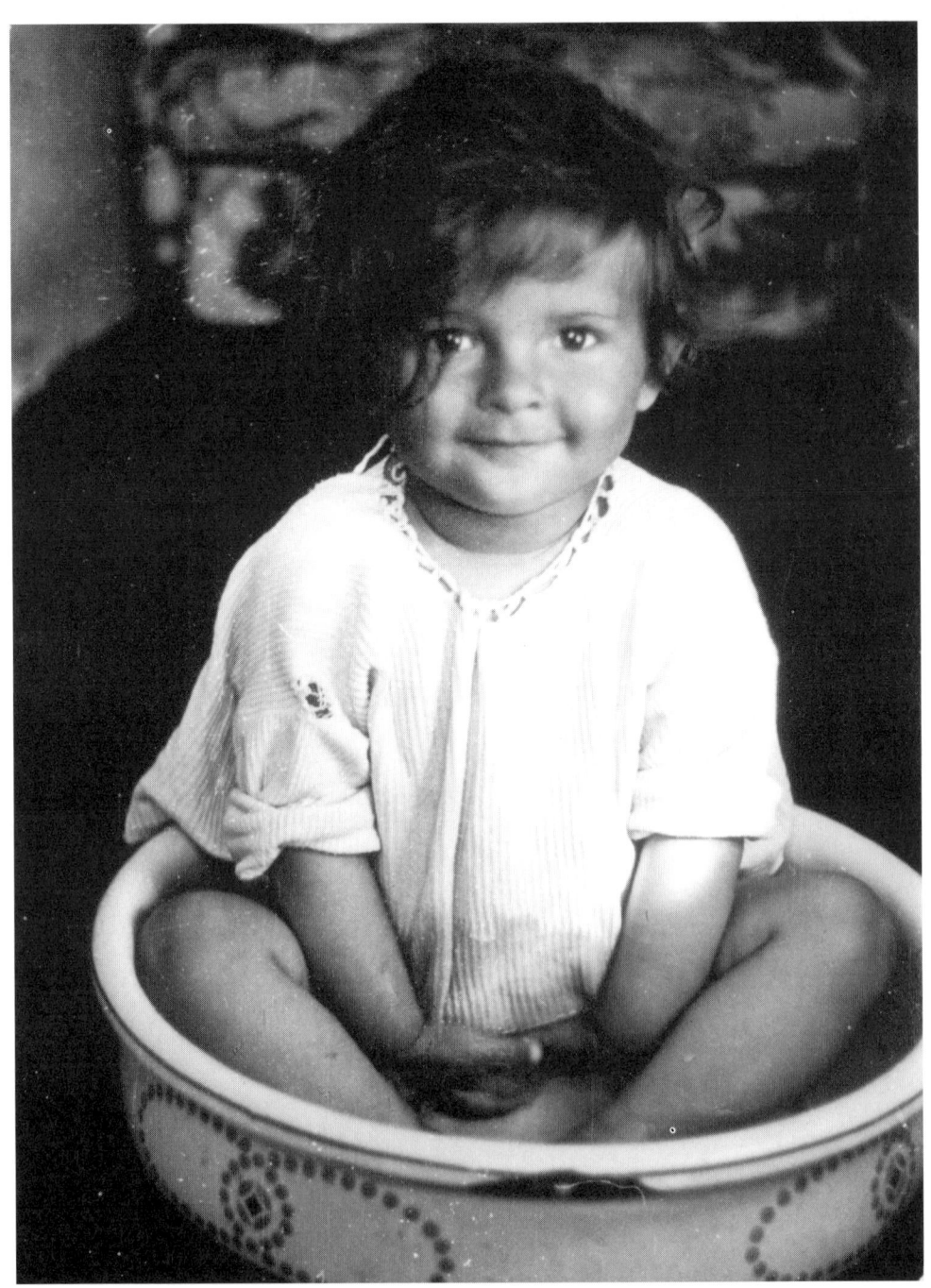

Christine Tanz, Gdansk, 1947.

Prologue

Hugh Field (center) and other war babies in 1946.

RECORDED ON THE BODY, ETCHED ON THE HEART

Maria Fleming Tymoczko and Nancy Blackmun

What do any of us really know about our lives when we were babies? What do we know about that time before our first conscious memories, that time when we could already walk and talk, climb and jump, run and play? We could already understand what was spoken to us. We could practically smell pleasure and safety, sorrow and fear. Yet, very little remains to us of those first years that shaped our characters, our values, and our choice of life's work. And if we were babies when the world was shaken and overturned by war, when the world was chaos, when a new order was taking shape, how did those things affect us? How does history stamp and shape us, whatever the era of our birth?

The stories collected here have been written by people who set out to answer just such questions, people born during World War II, the historical event that has most pervasively shaped modern life. Turning to that period when memories were recorded on the body, the writers in this book engage in an archaeology of the self, trying to recapture the connections between self and family, self and time, self and history, that elude the knowing mind. Those writing here explore the forces that shape the conscious self as well as the unconscious. Although these explorations are engaging in themselves as small-scale biographies, giving glimpses into varied and interesting lives, often they are more. Many of them are courageous acts, testimonials to events and interactions that families have, tacitly or deliberately, carefully hidden away for years.

These are stories about the impact of war on the lives of children and families. War touches the young in profound ways that obliterate adult categories: victory and defeat, allies and enemies, winners and losers, "us" and "them." War from this perspective is not primarily about nations, nor does it entail the official construction of history by the winners. It is about the seismic effects of the most terrible of human conflicts on the lives of the smallest and most vulnerable members of the human community. Children have no part in choosing the chaos of war, nor in being able to shape and change the warring communities they are born into, but they, too, suffer the effects of war. War sets the foundations of their personalities and their relations to life. As the essays collected here indicate, the impact of war is not inevitably or solely trauma. War breeds heroism, courage, resilience, determination, resistance, and compassion as well, even in the very young.

Unlike many other child narratives about World War II, particularly the narratives of children who survived concentration camps, these stories do not bear witness primarily to brutality and injury. In most cases they are stories about growth and vitality, about the irrepressibility of babies and young children even in the midst of deprivation and disaster. The varied voices recorded in this book exist because they and most of their parents lived to tell the tale. They are the lucky ones who survived World War II and who, in general, ended up with secure and satisfying lives. For the most part, though not always, the trauma narrated here is not personal to the writers or personally remembered, but is the legacy of their families. These are stories about the way life and the world went on even in the midst of chaos, about the price paid for the war, and about reparation of damages. At the same time the collection asks for alternatives less destructive than war, demonstrating the long effects of war and expressing hopes for other solutions to conflict that will avoid a heritage of trauma.

There is more here than the individual stories. Sketching out related and partially overlapping figures, together the writers create a portrait of a generation linked by experiences shared around the globe – the generation born into a world at war. Fully conscious only of the new world that emerged after the war, but formed psychically by the war itself, these authors are at the same time the immediate heirs of the prewar era. This generation forms a bridge between the prewar world and the world taken for granted by the Baby Boomers. Our essayists tell the stories of children whose lives are touched from the start by global events, whose world is marked by radical change and even instability, whose experience often includes loss at an early age. The accounts illustrate the persistence of history into the present. They show history shaping a generation that, half a century later, is now itself shaping history, revealing the lingering long-term impact of war on subsequent generations. The collection indicates how history can reproduce itself, even as it bears witness to change and evolution, reflecting shifts of values and life patterns, including patterns of gender and class.

These essays grow out of presentations made to the thirtieth reunion of the Harvard-Radcliffe Class of 1965. When planning for the reunion began in 1994, the world was beginning to commemorate the fiftieth anniversaries of the final events of World War II: D-Day and the other bitter and costly battles of the last year of the war in both Europe and Asia. Nancy Blackmun, therefore, organized a symposium to honor the fiftieth anniversary of the end of World War II, in which Class members would talk about the impact of the war on their families and themselves. By the time we met in October 1995, the world had commemorated V-E Day, the bombing of Hiroshima and Nagasaki, and V-J Day. It was beginning to look backward on the postwar period of change that set the terms of our adult lives.

About a quarter of the essays gathered here were presented in a preliminary form at the reunion. Julie Coryell described her father's work on the Manhattan Project and the way her family was reduced to rubble in the aftermath of the bombings. Robert Sakai told of his family's incarceration in the so-called "relocation camps" for Japanese Americans, incarceration ordered despite his grandparents' active and energetic attempts to build understanding between

Japan and the United States. Holocaust survivors recounted their stories, notably Christine Tanz, whose parents survived extermination by hiding in the open in Warsaw, undertaking whatever dramatic measures were necessary for survival. The symposium was electrifying. It became the centerpiece of the reunion, triggering memories of the war and its effects in the audience. The moving nature of the presentations and the reaction of the listeners made it clear that the stories would touch others as well, and so this project was launched. As editors we decided to open participation to our college Class as a whole, so as to add perspectives not represented at the reunion, but to limit contributions to members of the Class, thus creating not primarily a birth or an age cohort, but a cohort that entered adult life at the same time in the same place.

Although in some ways a narrow band, the Harvard-Radcliffe Class of 1965 is an international group of people who were born during World War II. In a less global era, with extended travel more difficult than today, such groups were less common than they are now, and few places in the world attracted as many students from around the globe as did Harvard in 1961, when most of the essayists entered college. In addition, unlike some institutions that had an international appeal, Harvard in 1961 was no longer the exclusive bastion of wealth and station that it had been before the war. Committed to a diverse student body and to financial aid for those in need, Harvard and Radcliffe were attracting young people from many ethnic traditions and socio-economic strata. The voices in this book, therefore, come from a variety of backgrounds. They include the children of wealth, privilege, and fame, but there are also children from uneducated and working-class families. There is wide geographical representation as well: the writers were born in a dozen different nations on four continents, including both Allied and Axis powers. When the far-flung birthplaces of parents are taken into account, the stories reflect an even greater number of nations and a broader geographical range.

A generation's experience or identity can be defined only by partially overlapping characteristics, not by a common denominator shared by all. There are many ways to tell the story of a generation, just as there are many ways to tell the story of any one person. In the United States the generation born during World War II has had other formative experiences besides the war. We were in primary school when the Korean conflict heated up and Senator Joseph McCarthy polarized the nation, in junior high school when *Sputnik* was launched and the priorities of American education were radically altered, in high school when John F. Kennedy was elected President of the United States, and juniors in college when he was assassinated. We were of draft age during the Vietnam War and many of us served in the military in that conflict. We were the youths involved in the civil rights movement and the antiwar protests. In our mid twenties Martin Luther King, Jr., was assassinated, and the cities of the United States went up in flames. During the same decade the feminist movement swept America and revolutionized our lives. We lived all these things before we were 30. In other nations of the world, our generation was shaped by equally momentous times and similar social upheavals. Not each of these events has marked every member of our generation, yet their overlapping influences delineate us as a group. Nonetheless, of all the influences which have been so important to our generation, we see World War II as dominant.

The stories speak to the impact of war on children and families, but also to the meaning of the past as it is encoded in different ways. The essays show how personal memory, collective memory or tradition, and official or public history intersect in giving meaning to the past. Individuals perceive the past through their own primary experiences, yet at the same time those memories are conditioned by collective memory – by family traditions, by the definitions and views of the past specific to the ethnic or tribal or political groups to which the individuals belong. Differences in familial traditions despite shared collective memory are immediately apparent in the accounts of the families who fled the Holocaust: the reticence and caution Eva Botstein Griepp describes, the denials and engagements of Matthew Stolper's family, the silence Ursula Oppens grew up in, the repression of Howard Gardner's family, and the "Zip-a-dee-doo-dah" cheer Steven Kilston records. Such familial traditions and collective group memories in turn intersect with official or national histories. The meaning of the past to an individual emerges from the interaction of these levels, and it changes as one's own perspective on events shifts, whether through increased knowledge or understanding, or through changes in the larger world. Sometimes the different levels are integrated and amalgamated. At other times they do not cohere and there is interference. In the latter case, a person works against the grain of the history as told by the family, the group, or the nation. William McConahey illustrates the coherence of the various levels of history, but interferences are apparent in many of the other essays, and one sees the writers struggling to construct new ways to talk about the past that will incorporate individual experience and personal memory, correcting family and national history alike with new perspectives. Thus, for example, World War II is taught in American schools as primarily a European event, but our Asian classmates remind us that such an official history is a partial one, needing radical expansion. Similarly, official history or family tradition may be at odds with the memory of a child, as we see in Mathea Falco's essay, where her powerlessness as a child provides a very different perspective on the position of the "victors" of World War II.

Editing this collection has been a privilege. We have learned many things about our writers and our generation, and we have had the opportunity to reflect on the essays in a detailed way. Clearly it was not always easy for the contributors to write about private family matters or personal ones. Despite the dramatic events during the first three decades of our lives, it has taken more than 50 years for us to develop enough perspective to see ourselves and our families within the context of history. We had so little grasp of shared historical experience when we were in college that even classmates whose families were refugees from the Holocaust never talked about their common past. Such an ahistorical viewpoint is endemic for young people who, in separating themselves from their families and in forging their own identities, need to feel they have invented themselves. It has taken us a long time to appreciate the circumstances that have shaped our lives. In writing these essays we wish to share that appreciation, honoring and commemorating the impact of historical events on the lives of our grandparents, our parents, ourselves, and, now, our children and grandchildren.

The process of writing the essays energized and galvanized the writers. Almost all undertook some reseach, if only to master basic facts about the war. Some contributors seized the opportunity to read old family letters and journals, often by people now dead. Others visited the places they write about or sought out people far away who could contribute more information. Almost everyone talked to relatives, particularly members of our parents' generation – those who were young adults during the war, who fought as soldiers and served as civilians, and who were our caretakers in our infancy. Some of the conversations and interviews were recorded on tape, others saved in written form, still others etched on the heart. In almost every case such conversations proved to be precious opportunities to talk about important things once more – or even for the first time – before the older generation is gone. In some cases this final opportunity to speak before dying provided our elders with an incentive that had not been present earlier, when what there was to say had felt too uncomfortable to remember, let alone to reveal. More than one of these essays began in conversations with a parent and ended as a memorial to that same parent.

When the essays began to arrive, as editors we found it exciting and sometimes stunning to see the cross-currents emerging among them – to realize, for example, how geographically close some of the parents or families had been in the past. Peter Katzlberger's father fought in the German Wehrmacht and disappeared near Warsaw, even as Christine Tanz's parents were escaping the same city. The fathers of Charles Styron and Helena Worthen were both part of the landing on Saipan. Mathea Falco and Peter Katzlberger were both children in southern Germany, raised on opposite sides of the victory line, with bittersweet childhood memories that have some remarkable similarities, while nearby Max Gitter waited with his parents in a displaced persons camp for the visas that would permit them entry to the United States. Sibling rivalry is looked at from the perspective of both older and younger children, all affected adversely by being born during a father's absence, birth order notwithstanding. Fate is seen playing its tricks on the young: for one American baby raised in the United States, German became the language of love and understanding; for another, attached to the occupying forces in Germany, it became the language of power and reprimand.

In World War II it was the men who went off to fight, the women and children who were left on the sidelines and inherited the wreckage. Perhaps because the war was seen so paradigmatically as a male enterprise, fathers are the focus of many of these essays. Many of the writers speak about the loss of fathers physically, emotionally, and spiritually, and many talk about the quest to find the father. There is the theme of the long-hoped-for reunion, which almost always dissolved in disappointment. And of course there is the common connection to mothers, some of whom rose to meet extraordinary challenges during the war, showing courage and resourcefulness, becoming a tree of life to their children. Other mothers proved unequal to the tasks their strange fates required, and the children 50 years later record the anguish that resulted. As might be expected, for babies and young children, the lines drawn by history – the lines, for example, between victor and vanquished – are blurred by other, more immediate, aspects of childhood experience. The writers speak as well about the ways that the boundaries of time are different for children and adults. For many the experience of war did not end in 1945, but persisted on into the 1950s, blending imperceptibly into the Cold War. Such connections linking essays and essayists are everywhere.

In part because of different ways the past is encoded, a central feature of these stories is their complex layering of perspectives. Their origins in the writers' earliest experiences are evident: many of the memories are coded in things other than language, recorded in sensory and physical terms – in sights and images, in sounds, in smells and tastes, and in feelings. The stories are moving not only because of the grand sweep of world events they embody, but because of their intensity – the power and immediacy associated with preverbal childhood memories, rooted in the body, charged with the strong fears and desires of young children. Because of this basis in infant and toddler ways of remembering and perceiving, the essays are often striking for their concreteness and luminosity of detail. Such details evoke whole scenes viewed from the perspective and understanding of a child – for example, Anthony Graham-White's absurdist vision of Coventry with the fronts of its houses neatly sliced away by bombs. At times even the prose seems to circle back to the language associated with those early visions of the world, and the reader can almost hear a child's voice speaking, as when Peter Katzlberger's native German shows through his English sentences. In other cases the sentences shorten, the vocabulary becomes basic, paragraphs are discrete and disconnected, as the authors call back early experiences that are themselves discrete, disconnected, fragmentary, or stored in the simple language of the very young.

Many of the essays concentrate on the writers' parents, the principal actors during World War II. It's a strange thing to have the most important events in one's life happen before one was born, as Christine Tanz suggests, but when that is so, the stories of times before one's birth must be told. As William

Faulkner said, these are the stories of "the people in whose living blood and seed we ourselves lay dormant and waiting" (80). A young child's grasp of a parent's inner life, however, is nonverbal and inchoate, bounded by a lack of experience and a limited understanding of things beyond what is known. Such characteristics are clear in some of the essays. Often the writers attempt to supplement that childhood view of the world, in order to present the wartime feelings, motivations, beliefs, and actions of their parents from their parents' points of view, thus offering another perspective on the impact of war and history on families and individual lives. As many of the essayists consulted with their parents and relatives in the process of writing their own stories, they came also to represent the older generation's lives with a doubled vision, that of their childhood memories and their parents' views at the time, set in counterpoint with the parents' more recent views of the same events.

Finally, there is a third perspective, born of wisdom gained from the developmental process and knowledge of the full circle of life. We are now the age of our grandparents during World War II. We look back on our baby selves and our parents alike during the war after nearly a lifetime's experience – the experience of being young adults and parents, of caring for and knowing our own babies, many of whom have now reached the age of our parents during the war. This mature perspective is a more severely tested one – few come half a century without themselves meeting adversity and acknowledging failure – and it enables a depth of understanding that was impossible to attain earlier in life, as well as a new appreciation of paradox and irony. Thus, the immediacy of childhood memory is enriched with the comprehension of age.

It is no accident that these essays emerged during the fiftieth-anniversary commemorations of the war's end. Anniversaries, especially major anniversaries, have the power to reactivate issues that lie dormant, to elicit memory, and to compel review. Compounding the impact of the fiftieth anniversary of the war's end was the impact of another major, if more personal, anniversary for our group – the thirtieth anniversary of completing college, a formal marker for the entrance into adult life. We found ourselves standing exactly halfway through the current life expectancy of 60 years of adulthood. In addition we had celebrated our own fiftieth birthdays not so long before and were conscious of having lived half a century. The anniversaries triggered both childhood recollection and adult comprehension, resulting in a multiple consciousness about war and history and time in these stories: things loved, desired, and suffered are seen now in several lights. The writers narrating their own stories understand in ways they never could have as infants, children, or even young adults. In judgments about the past, they are capable of a spare, uncompromising truthfulness, but there is a new capacity for compassion and forgiveness as well.

The essays are not merely the result of recollection: they are shaped by the narrative skills of storytelling. These are artistic constructions, framed by the authors' purposes, by the rationale of the book itself, and by the companion essays. They are given form by conscious and unconscious decisions about what to reveal and what to conceal, what to tell and what to keep silent. Some of the writers had trouble telling their stories because of all the associations created by the outward spiraling of their lives, making it difficult to decide where to stop, what to leave out. Yet finally each essay has an unspoken border, with things on the other side of that frame. The reader instinctively perceives those edges and has the tantalizing sense that there might be more to be seen: siblings not mentioned, the divorce of parents, the remarriage of a widow, the rifts and fracturings of lives not fully articulated.

Although not universally the case, there is some disparity in emotional style between the stories of the men and those of the women. The women in general have been more willing and able to address feelings and to concentrate on them, while the men have been more inclined to focus on facts. The difference is epitomized by the way one woman and two men deal with early separations from their mothers. The woman builds her entire essay around the separation, while neither man moves beyond a brief reference to a much more profound separation from his mother. While this gender difference fits cultural stereotypes, as editors we were still surprised by its strength and prevalence in our writers. The difficulty of connecting with the child self must not be underestimated: that self is a vulnerable self and in most of the world the definition of manhood still excludes vulnerability. In editing the essays, we have come to wonder whether men are culturally encouraged to seal off the man self, the adult self, from the child self – the time of vulnerability – making emotional memories of childhood less accessible to men than to women. It is worth noting that a number of the men whose essays have the greatest emotional intensity are those whose connections with their mothers were exceptionally strong.

Curiously, this project returns the writers and readers to some major questions of the modern age. Since the beginning of the twentieth century and the reaction to positivism, inquiry in all spheres – science, philosophy, linguistics, literary studies, history – has rejected the view that there is a simple objective truth about things or that experience is an unmediated given, instead embracing the fundamental premise that reality is constructed. The essays here indicate how all levels of history are constructed. The very terms used for childhood memories in these essays are set by the material and social environment of each individual writer. At the same time, a child is born into a family, and each family has its own ways of construing reality, which in turn affect a child's perceptions. Such constructions are based partly on affiliation with larger identity groups that build their own structures of perception about the past. Thus, the primary memories of a child are conditioned by family traditions and the collective memories of the larger groups to which the individual belongs, and such collective memory shapes and even at times overrides or obliterates individual perceptions and memories. Operating on yet another level, official histories are constructed in accordance with a culture's dominant values. But if these levels – personal memory, collective memory, and national history – are constructed, they can also be deconstructed and reconstructed. All these processes are apparent in this collection of essays.

Awareness of the ways that memory, tradition, and national history are constructed, as well as recognition that there are alternate versions of history, leads some of the writers in this collection to be concerned about the instability and uncertainty of memory. Max Gitter does not know the date of his own birth, and he confronts his false recollections, which he maintained well into adulthood. Kevin Lewis examines his earliest memories, contrasting them with the stories he has been told and the carefully preserved letters from the time of his infancy. Anthony Graham-White is uncertain where to draw the line between personal memories and newsreels he may have seen, and he is unable to map his fragmentary memories onto the timeline of history. Francis Zebot wrestles with inconsistent accounts about the family's past, wondering how to square them with his own visceral feelings about his childhood. These writers remind us of the larger uncertainties of history: if it is not always possible to be certain about the events that immediately affect our own families, how can we be certain that we fully understand larger historical events, including Hitler's rise to power, or the gas chambers of Auschwitz, or the Allied armies' invasion of Europe, or the bombing of Hiroshima and Nagasaki? How is it that we construct the histories of our selves, our families, our nations, our world?

In telling any story we construct a reality, but in telling our own stories, we construct ourselves. Indeed psychoanalysis, so germane to the conceptualization of this book, has been compared to storytelling, to learning how to tell the story of the self. One can even ask whether we know what our lives have been until we are able to tell the stories of our lives coherently. For the writers of these essays, constructing the story to tell has been a powerful process. It has involved delving inside the self, bringing to light things that have been buried and forgotten but that are formative, making meaning of them, and putting a framework on the results. As in cases governed by Heisenberg's uncertainty principle, the observation has changed the situation. Those who have written these essays have rewritten their families' histories. As they have rewritten those family histories, they have rewritten themselves, and they have become changed. We have heard repeatedly from the authors about what a powerful and even liberating experience it was to write their stories.

For some of the contributors, writing became part of the assertion of our own standing as "elders," those who are acknowledged as repositories of the past, who define the past, who are the historians of the family or the tribe. In writing our stories, we seize history, we presume to "tell it like it was," to make normative judgments not merely about our own lives, but about the lives of our parents and grandparents as well. In so doing there is an added power in writing for and witnessing to strangers. Inevitably this led to conflict with some members of the older generation, with parents and relatives who did not welcome these new versions of their own past. In one case the conflict was so disruptive that the writer withdrew from the project after submitting a completed essay that was the fruit of much labor.

Memory is a contested site not just for families but for nations, and national constructions of history play a role in these essays also. Indeed, in the stories told here, childhood memories, finally, are not solely or perhaps even primarily personal – they are familial and cultural as well. As such they enter into the discourse about how to write national and world history. Memory transcends the personal and becomes political. The intensity of childhood memories in these stories often points directly to interpretations of world events and world history. The prime mover behind these stories is the war that was sweeping across much of the globe during the infancy of these writers, the war that shaped and configured not just the lives of the babies born into it, but the world we all now inhabit. The stories ask implicitly and explicitly how that war is to be understood, thus interrogating all levels of history about the war. Consequently, the essays in this collection take their place among other contemporary documents and studies having to do with the politics of memory and the memorializing of history, even though they deal with memorials preserved in the body and the psyche and the heart, rather than in wood or bronze or stone.

We have traced here some threads connecting the essays and tried to show their bearing upon larger cultural questions. These are some of the things that can be said *about* the stories that follow, but in the end the stories tell themselves. Each is an encounter not just with an individual, but with a family – and not just with a family, but with one of the faces of that hydra-headed event we call World War II. Ultimately the essays open onto enigmas and even mystery. Behind the personal memories of babyhood, behind the narratives of family and relatives, there is the war. The stories suggest that although we are born into the flow of time and shaped by it powerfully before our conscious memories are formed, we can never fully know our place in world events. Yet life has meaning only when we make the attempt to understand.

Maria Fleming Tymoczko and a friend, 1946.

Sergeant Robert Kenjiro Sakai in the Palau Islands, September 1944.

Paradox

" ... a seemingly contradictory statement that may nonetheless be true ...
... a situation exhibiting inexplicable or contradictory aspects ...
... an assertion that is essentially self-contradictory, although based on valid deduction from acceptable premises ..."

from Greek paradoxon, *'conflicting with expectation'*

The destruction of Nagasaki by the atomic bomb,
August 8, 1945.

PARADOX

Each of the essays in this first section presents a paradox revealed in the experience of these children born into a world at war. Sometimes the paradox is a result of contradictions within family attitudes and actions. At other times there are ironies of history, or ironic and unforeseen effects of complex causalities. Each story in some way challenges a presupposition, an expectation, or a general premise about the impact of war on children and families. A child in the United States comes to feel that German is the language of love. A Japanese American family that worked to build cross-cultural understanding is interned in a "relocation camp." For one family fleeing Nazi Germany, the years of the Holocaust and the war become "their 10 best years."

The opening essay looks squarely at the atom bomb. Julie Coryell, a child of Oak Ridge, gives a dramatic and stark account of how the invention of the bomb literally and figuratively devastated her own family, causing it to implode in the aftermath of Hiroshima.

Eva Botstein Griepp writes a densely factual account of her family that is at times hard to follow, but this very condensation becomes a signpost. The facts are virtually the only grave markers for relatives murdered in the Holocaust. It is not just relatives who are lost, but whole communities, cultures, and ways of life. One result is intense parental anxiety, such that demands are placed on the next generation to prepare for portable professions that are not dependent on the language of the country in which one happens to find oneself. Juxtaposed with this inability to feel safe is a fervent patriotism for the new country, the United States, that offers tangible if not psychically secure refuge.

Matthew Stolper's story complements Eva Griepp's. The Nuremberg Laws force both families to emigrate, but for the Stolpers investment in the present and the future becomes more compelling than war losses. Matthew Stolper introduces a continuing theme of the book: a child's difficulty in grasping the meaning of a parent's life, the inner experience that would help explain a parent's actions. His story raises thorny questions about familial avoidance and denial of disaster, at the same time that it portrays remarkable levels of public responsibility and engagement. Though the losses suffered during the war are seen as manageable by his family, another loss, a medical one, becomes the displaced center of trauma, functioning in ways analogous to the Holocaust.

For Nancy Blackmun and Deborah Lucas Schneider in the United States, there is the wartime safety of Minneapolis and Chicago. One father is drafted and the other exempt from service, but neither is very present for his toddler daughter. Both stories illustrate the way that external realities connected with the war are taken inside the self and imbued with intensely personal meaning, and both focus on early childhood distress.

Deborah Schneider is the first of many writers in the book to grapple with the feelings of disconnection between the fathers, who went away to war, and the toddlers left at home with the women of the family. From various angles and with varying tonalities, this theme reappears in many subsequent essays.

Racial prejudice completely overturns the lives of Japanese Americans during World War II, tainting the idealized picture many Americans have of their nation as "the land of the free." Robert Sakai's essay about U.S. racial attitudes and actions toward its citizens during the war etches an eerie parallel to the Nazi treatment of Jews. But the Sakai family vigorously counters such discrimination through a renewed commitment to their nation, with Robert Sakai's father resolutely seeking to serve in the United States Army, undeterred even by his failure to pass the physical, and achieving a distinguished service record that stands as a benchmark for values in the family for half a century.

This first section closes with Maria Fleming Tymoczko's account of her own and other American working-class families, immigrants and native-born alike, tracing the revolutionary social changes wrought by World War II. She examines the ways that the formative childhood experiences of war babies can be connected with their later actions during the 1960s and the 1970s – from protest against the Vietnam War to involvement in the feminist movement. She discusses ironic disjunctions between the experiences of women and men, as well as long-term casualties inflicted by the war, even on its "victors." Her dislocation when the return of the soldiers broke up her multigenerational wartime household of women reverberates with Deborah Schneider's feelings of disconnection from her father. What was a temporary, make-do household for their mothers during the war was the only reality of home these war babies had ever known.

LEGACIES OF THE MANHATTAN PROJECT

Julie E. Coryell

>Born: December 24, 1943
>Oak Ridge, Tennessee, U.S.A.

The Manhattan Project formed as a consortium of scientists, civilian contractors, and the United States Army, to build atomic weapons fueled by plutonium and uranium. Fear that the Nazis would develop and use such deadly weapons mandated deep secrecy and unremitting work. Recommended by his thesis adviser, Linus Pauling, my father joined the project early in 1942 in Chicago. About September 1943, my parents moved to the muddy town of Oak Ridge, still under construction, restricted, segregated, and located in *dry* Anderson County, Tennessee. My father was a section leader in the Clinton Labs, where research on the products of nuclear fission was the chief task.

Conceived in Chicago, I was born to Charles DuBois Coryell and Grace Mary Seeley Coryell on Christmas Eve of 1943, a child of the Manhattan Project, the first baby of the Clinton Labs, soon after the new hospital in Oak Ridge opened. Taking a red pencil to my father's exuberant suggestions, my mother named me Julie Esther Coryell: Julie for her friend Julie Stitt, Esther for her

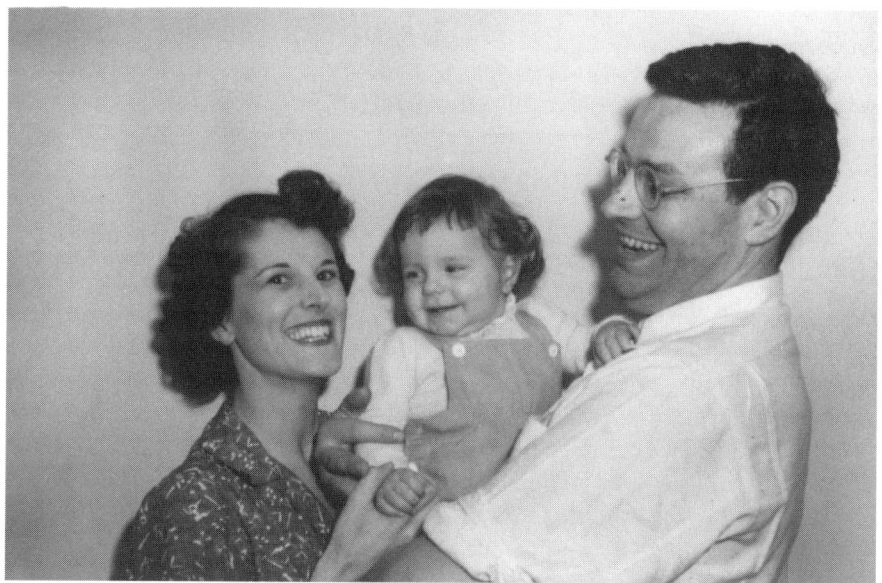

Julie Coryell and her parents in 1944.

gynecologist Esther Davies, a neat rhythmic pattern to her poet's ear. Because his first wife had divorced him, my father had left his church. For marrying a divorced man, my mother also had experienced separation from her religion, so I was not baptized as a baby. But my mother's joy at hearing "Hark! The Herald Angels Sing" after her delivery and the special expectation and spirituality of my Christmas Eve birth have endowed my life with a deep sense of love and faith. We three celebrated my tenth birthday in Bethlehem.

In retrospect, I feel the pressures of the Manhattan Project, the secrecy, the racism of segregated life in the new town, the fearfulness and magnitude of the project further contributed to my parents' vulnerability and alienation from their familial roots.

Because of the history of secrecy, to this day I do not have a clear intellectual idea of the work my chemist father did, aside from its having to do with the study of nuclear fission. Two of his students discovered a new element produced in fission. He always gave them credit for the discovery and they always honored my mother for naming it. As she was a poet, they went to her with their story and request for a name. Her response was, "I got a 'D' in high school chemistry. Refresh my memory, what's an element?" And to their explanation that an element is irreducible matter, she said, "Name it after Prometheus. You have stolen fire from the gods, and mankind may suffer for it." And so element 61, a rare earth, came to be known as promethium, abbreviated Pm.

As my father's daughter, I have visited reactors, labs both aromatic and stinking, and even sat at a desk in Marie Curie's Institut du Radium at the Sorbonne in Paris, where the creaky lift reputedly ran on radium rays. Nevertheless, when I was growing up and really wanted to know about The Bomb, my father never divulged secrets. I formed a particular jealousy for the daughters of deuterium and other isotopes, affectionately called *isodopes*, and cushioned myself against the pain of being excluded from understanding by uneasily persuading myself that what he did was unknowable. I observed my parents closely and derived comfort from my father's principled advocacy of Linus Pauling's Scientists' Petition, the World Federation of Scientists, Peaceful Uses for Atomic Energy, and SANE; from the enormous love and caring of people like Eugene Wigner, Leo Szilard, Hans Bethe, and Victor Weisskopf; and from my father's sheer energy applied to teaching and research. I witnessed that music consoled my father and found healing for my own jealousy in Beethoven's *Tochter aus Elysium*.

I have spoken with other children of the Manhattan Project who have also affirmed that the secrecy affected them as children, in part inhibiting us from becoming scientists ourselves. In *Sexual Politics* Kate Millett describes a division between men, who benefit from patriarchal power and create the world, and women, who are often left with cleaning up after disasters while feeling helpless. As a child I worried that, if the atomic bomb ever went off and destroyed my world and I somehow survived, failing to understand how things are built and work, I would not be able to reconstruct the world. Millett's analysis voiced my unspoken fear and placed it in a powerful and clear context. It also explained my childhood observation that women scientists were scarce, particularly American women chemists.

After the war my father moved to MIT as one of three full professors appointed in 1946, he in chemistry, Ted Martin (now my father-in-law) in mathematics, and Jerrold Zacharias in physics.

Julie Coryell and her parents, Christmas, 1958.

My mother's postwar pathway anguished me. With the move she stopped driving. In the heady, more class-conscious university community centered in Cambridge, Massachusetts, she suffered for her lack of a college education as a child of the Depression. With a little more money available, she began to drink beer, Manhattan cocktails, and, in honor of her naming the element Pm,

PM whiskey. Perhaps she was self-medicating mood swings, but from the time I was five years old, she was a serious binge drinker with recurring periods of angry dysfunction. At other times, particularly when we traveled, she was clear, witty, and creative, a storyteller, poet, letter writer, and cook *par excellence*. My father boasted that at the time of their meeting, she had more poems in print than he had scientific papers. After their marriage she stopped publishing, but continued to write poetry.

Our home was filled with wonderful visitors, international friends, students, piles of papers, photographs – and worries. In 1946 my mother completed a poem based on the photograph by Jack Aeby of the Trinity bomb blast at Alamogordo on July 16, 1945.

A Picture

On my mantel is a picture of the atomic bomb
Taken in the first second after the first explosion.
I don't quite know where to put it, though it's been there
Nearly a year.
It attracts the attention
Of everyone who comes into my house.

Perhaps it is just as well that I can't quite find a place for it.
Everyone reads the personal note on the back of the picture.
Once a comment was made about its similarity to a Japanese print.

What should I do if an English friend
Or a Russian, Chinese, French or Spanish friend
Came into my house?

That can't happen just now because I still live
In a restricted area.
But suppose they did come
Should I hide it?

I can't take down one picture and replace it
With my photograph of the bomb.
I can't throw it out
Because it has a personal note on the back of it
To me.

It is on the mantel like a cablegram which has just arrived.
Nearly a year is a long time for it to stay unanswered.

This is a new thing
Which came into my house and my thoughts
Just after everything else was in place.

> The coming of the atomic bomb to the world
> Has shattered all thoughts and ideas of the past
> As dramatically as it crystallized the sand of New Mexico
> Into a film of pale green glass.
>
> And I don't know where to put it.
> Neither do the Army and the Navy, or the U.N. or the Russians.
>
> The rocket bomb does not move slowly like thoughts in the past.
> It takes into consideration and into calculation
> The curvature of the earth and the winds of the stratosphere.
>
> My thinking must become geared to rocket speed
> And to the size of the earth.
> The rocket and the atomic bomb can come from any land overseas
> To destroy the mantel where I have my picture.
> You have your own fireplace and a mantel.
> And, you, too, have a picture.
> If you reflect, you will find
> It bears a note
> Which is very personal.
>
> Grace Mary Seeley Coryell

My mother's poem touched many of the fears and ironies of life in Oak Ridge. She grasped intuitively the emotions and visions of a new world. For example, during the civil rights movement and the Vietnam War, my father told how he had been ordered at gunpoint in his own laboratory building in Oak Ridge not to enter the door labeled "Colored" even though he would be late for an important scientific meeting if he used the door for "Whites." The military ruled over a quirky alliance with ironic goals: to make discoveries to shorten the war using science, ideally without boundaries, under conditions mandating secrecy and pressure, and in circumstances far from egalitarian, all at unknown cost to humanity.

Looking back, my husband and I think the war labors and burdens conditioned my father to an impossible work pattern. My father was known for his "boundless energy" (A. Smith, 102). The weekend that President Kennedy was shot, my father experienced the first of three severe manic breakdowns. Meanwhile my mother was obviously worsening. In the spring of my senior year of college, she died after taking every pill she could find in the house and lingering for 10 days in a coma. My husband Seelye and I married on June 24 of that year. The next winter my father developed giant-cell bone sarcoma. Courageously he announced, "A rare form of cancer means no one knows what to expect." He lived five and a half vigorous years, relatively untouched by debilitating mood swings. Without doubt his work on the Manhattan Project promoted his developing cancer. Without doubt the field of nuclear medicine that grew from studies of nuclear fission resulted in radiation treatments that prolonged his life. My father felt he had lived three lives' worth in one and did not fear his death.

In *American Mom* Mary Kay Blakely (71) quotes Tillie Olsen as follows, "For myself, 'survivor' contains its other meaning; one who must bear witness for those who foundered; try to tell how and why it was that they, also worthy of life, did not survive. And pass on ways of surviving; and tell our chancy luck, our special circumstances." Blakely's descriptions of modern motherhood resonate with the griefs and glories of my mother's life and the frustrations and delights of my own. Reading her book and reflecting on Olsen's words about survivors encouraged me to embrace the fiftieth anniversary of the end of the war as an opportunity for mourning and reflection.

So, during that anniversary year, I began reacquainting myself with my parents in my heart. Learning the words of the ancient prayer, "Almighty God, to you all hearts are open, all desires known, and from you no secrets are hid ... ," gave me courage to ask long-suppressed questions. Although I have not seen Hiroshima or Nagasaki, I have, as a result of several trips to Japan, nurtured friendships with numerous Japanese people and devoted myself to studying the Japanese language. I treasure my father's copy of Alice Kimball Smith's *A Peril and a Hope: The Scientists' Movement in America 1945-1947*. I carefully read Richard Rhodes's *The Making of the Atomic Bomb* and eagerly awaited publication of *Picturing the Bomb: Photographs from the Secret World of the Manhattan Project* by Rachel Fermi and Esther Samra.

One way I keep my mother's kindness and mothering close to my heart now is by having house rabbits. When I was a toddler in Oak Ridge, the four children across the street lost their mother to breast cancer. They wanted me to have their big white rabbit, Peter, stuck him in our mailbox, and rang the doorbell. I still remember my mother gingerly releasing Peter and tenderly guiding the children to take Peter back to his home, where I could visit any time and they would not be losing another loved being.

I believe that making connections offers the best healing and safeguards against further wounding. Listening honors the dead and strengthens survivors. Perhaps there is a metaphor in the explosive power of atomic fission: that with enough loving connections around the world and among all life, we need never unleash such terror again. Geared to the atomic age, this Promethean message remains both global and very personal.

Self Portrait: Julie Coryell with Jack Aeby's photograph of the Trinity bomb blast, 1974.

Eva Botstein at age six or seven.

GROWING UP IN THE SHADOW OF THE HOLOCAUST

Eva Botstein Griepp

>Born: December 3, 1944
>Zurich, Switzerland

It would be hard to overestimate the impact of the Holocaust on my family, and therefore, inevitably, on me.

My parents both grew up in Lodz, Poland, although my father was actually born in what was then Ukraine. My mother's great-grandfather had been the chief rabbi of Moscow, but my mother grew up in a relatively assimilated milieu, with piano lessons and French and German governesses. My father was raised in a more orthodox and Zionist environment, speaking Yiddish at home and Hebrew in school. Both my grandfathers were in the textile business, but they were barely acquainted with one another and generally traveled in different social circles. Because it was very difficult for Jews to obtain higher education in Poland, my father started medical school in Prague in 1930. Then in 1932, when "Poles" became unwelcome because of a border dispute with Czechoslovakia, he transferred to Zurich. Shortly after arriving in Switzerland, my father asked my mother, who had already completed her first year in medical school there, whether he could borrow a textbook. My parents soon became nearly inseparable. They both graduated from medical school in Zurich in 1935, were married in 1936, and were still in the midst of postgraduate medical training in Switzerland when the war broke out. When Poland was invaded, my father, who had served as an officer in the Polish army, went first to the Polish consulate in Bern and then to the recruitment office for the Polish foreign legion in France to try to join the war effort, only to be told that no Jewish officers were wanted. Thus, my parents remained in Switzerland during the war, and it was in Zurich that my two brothers and I were born.

But at the outbreak of the war, both my parents' families were still in Poland. My father's father had died shortly before the war, and his mother, afraid to go far from home, perished in the ghetto in Lodz. My father's younger brother, who had just finished medical school in Bratislava, died of typhus at the age of 26, while trying to alleviate as best he could the suffering of others under the appalling circumstances of the Warsaw ghetto. My mother's older brother Leon, a gifted chemist, relinquished opportunities to escape to Switzerland early in 1939 and in 1942, and elected to stay to try to protect his parents and younger brother. It was Leon who realized in time the danger of remaining in the Warsaw ghetto once the deportations began to increase in early 1943. He managed to bribe an SS officer to allow him to escape with his parents and younger brother only three weeks before the Warsaw Ghetto Uprising began in April 1943. Leon arranged to have my grandparents hidden in Warsaw by a lady who revealed only after the war that she was a converted Jew. Through this same woman, Leon arranged for my Uncle Samuel to be hidden outside the city by a Polish farm girl, whom Samuel married after the war. Both the lady who took in my grandparents and my aunt (the Polish farm girl), as well as her sister, are among those "righteous gentiles" for whom a grove of trees has been planted as part of the Yad Vashem memorial in Israel. Just before the Warsaw Uprising led by the resistance in 1944, my grandparents were sent to a work camp in Parchim, in northern Germany, where they were liberated by the Russians in 1945. But my Uncle Leon, who had supported his parents and brother in hiding by illegally distilling vodka, was caught and killed by the Gestapo in December 1943, at the age of 32.

When the war ended, my parents were able to bring my surviving grandparents and Samuel (my sole surviving uncle) and his wife temporarily to Switzerland, thanks to considerable help from friends with influence in the Swiss government and the Red Cross. From Switzerland these four family members went to Mexico, one of the few places to which it was possible to

Eva Botstein and her family
just prior to leaving Switzerland for the United States in 1949.

obtain a visa, to try to build a new life. Despite their Swiss medical training, remaining in Switzerland was not an option for my parents, either. Every six months, even during the war, the Swiss authorities had summoned them to ask about their plans to leave. So it was with enormous relief that my parents learned that they had been granted permission to emigrate to the United States.

My first memories are of the transatlantic journey on the SS *America*, a huge ocean liner complete with swimming pool. We arrived in New York in May 1949, when I was four and a half years old. A cousin of my mother's, who had come to the United States before the war, met us at the pier and took us to our first apartment. Within a few days of our arrival, my father called an uncle whose name he had found in the Brooklyn telephone book. Although they had not previously met, my grandfather's brother responded with chicken soup, advice, and furniture. My parents never forgot the welcome they received as immigrants, much of it from virtual strangers, and there is a long list of distantly related or unrelated immigrants whom my parents subsequently helped in one way or another.

I grew up with a strong immigrant appreciation of the United States. By the time I entered junior high school, some of my fellow classmates, who came from homes in which parents were disillusioned because of the McCarthy hearings, refused to stand for the Pledge of Allegiance, which was still recited at the start of each school day. Such an attitude was utterly unthinkable for me. My parents had come with very little money and very rudimentary and heavily accented English, and yet within several years we were living in a nice house in a lovely neighborhood and my father had been appointed a full professor in one of the best medical schools in the country. In our family it was considered a great privilege to have been granted United States citizenship. I can still remember the giant swearing-in ceremony we attended at Yankee Stadium to celebrate the occasion. Even now my eyes fill with tears whenever the national anthem is played.

Although my parents felt little real nostalgia for Poland, the loss of so much immediate and extended family made them cling to whatever remnants of the Polish-Jewish community of their youth had survived. Throughout my childhood, an assortment of vaguely connected "uncles" and "aunts" with whom my parents had grown up became a kind of surrogate extended family. Into this reconstructed family my parents also adopted Schwester Frieda, a Swiss nurse who had come to take care of us when I was a toddler. She was an unsung "righteous gentile" who had helped a young Jewish widower and his daughter survive the war in Vichy France before she came to work for us. When my parents decided to come to the United States, Frieda came with us and eventually herself became an American citizen. She died in my parents' home long after all the children were gone. She was like a beloved honorary grandmother. An exceptionally fine cook, she even learned to concoct various Eastern European Jewish specialties which my father remembered fondly from his youth.

My parents treated not only my uncle and grandparents but also the other old and often lonely people within our extended family with almost infinite patience and considerable generosity. Differences of values and taste, as well as affronts of various sorts, were frequently overlooked in relatives and in old friends, especially in those who had helped us when we first came to the United States, in order to preserve peace within the small community that remained. I think my parents sought to compensate, by their solicitude toward surviving relatives and friends, for the enormous guilt they felt for having suffered comparatively little during the war. They been spared when so many had been cruelly annihilated or had been forced to endure much greater personal hardship and losses and to witness unspeakable horrors.

Perhaps because of this communal history, there was always a clear distinction in my parents' house between minor aggravations and real *tzores*: between the very few things that really matter and everything else. Real sympathy was reserved for serious illness or unequivocal personal tragedy. My father enjoyed telling anyone who would listen that he considered it a privilege to pay taxes in return for an environment of social stability and political freedom. In response to pecuniary setbacks of various kinds, he would invariably respond, "It's only money." My parents' outlook was indelibly colored by memories of friends and relatives who lost their lives or compromised the lives of others by clinging to the familiar comforts of their middle-class prosperity until it was too late to escape.

Although there was only occasional direct discussion of the worst aspects of the Holocaust as I was growing up – a hush would come over adults when we children entered the room during such conversations, because the subject was considered too obscene to be discussed in front of us – the shadow of its presence was frequently felt. The war had clearly been a time in which character had been tested. My parents knew many individuals who had risked their own lives and those of the people they most loved in order to help friends and even strangers, while others had stood by silently, averting their eyes. Some people had behaved with courage and dignity throughout horrible ordeals, whereas others had been unable to rise above selfishness and pettiness. I remember countless tales of various sorts about friends and relatives of my parents who had survived and had subsequently thrived, and others who could never quite put together the broken pieces of their lives. There was inspiration to be drawn from those who had reconstructed productive lives despite terrible disillusionment, the loss of spouses and children, and the need to find another home, learn yet another language, and acquire new skills. But there were also important lessons to be learned from the unhappiness of those who had failed to rebuild their lives after the war. Some were unwilling to sacrifice immediate comfort for later security and fulfillment, and others were unable to reconcile themselves to the loss of an imagined future of much greater promise and prosperity that the war had destroyed – and they were therefore unable to appreciate whatever joys and comforts were still within their reach.

One important lesson, as far as my parents were concerned, was that the idea of true assimilation was a dangerous delusion which should forever be laid to rest, given the fate of the Jews in Germany. Even the apparent freedom and acceptance of Jews in the United States they considered somewhat illusory. My parents' life experience had taught them that a Jew must accept the fact that he would always be identified as a Jew first and foremost and that anywhere but Israel would always be the diaspora. They felt strongly that those who had fared best during and after the war were those with a strong positive identification with Judaism. My brothers and I were brought up to be prepared for the inevitable next wave of anti-Semitism, likely to be followed sooner or later by the need to flee. This view of the future made it highly desirable to be fluent in several languages and to have a concrete, portable, international skill, preferably a scientific one. But we were also imbued with the idea that the miracle of our having escaped while so many others perished placed upon us the obligation to make something worthwhile of our lives. The first step was to get an education that would enable us to do something truly useful.

With this background I came to college knowing that it would not be acceptable for me to be what my parents called a *Luftmensch*, regardless of whatever talent or inclination I might have shown for various aspects of the humanities. Thus I never really questioned my choice of medicine as a profession until long afterward. Although there were many options theoretically open to me, many of them would have made me vulnerable to criticism for being either impractical or self-indulgent, and enough survivor guilt had permeated my upbringing that I felt compelled to choose a profession easily defended as being of humanitarian service. I trained first in pediatrics, then in pediatric cardiology, and subsequently in cell biology, and my professional efforts have been divided among patient care, teaching, and research. (My younger brother Leon, also destined in the eyes of my parents for a medical career, was reluctantly permitted to abandon this path only by concurrently demonstrating an inability to master inorganic chemistry and by so impressing several college professors with his extraordinary gift for scholarship in the humanities that they pled his case with my parents.)

In addition to influencing my choice of profession, another legacy left to me by the Holocaust has been a lifelong preoccupation with issues of moral choice. I have always felt and still feel a need to reassure myself that I have the courage to do the right thing: that I will make whatever sacrifices and take whatever risks are necessary to speak out against injustice, however minor. I trace this compulsion to be scrupulous in even small matters involving right and wrong to a need to convince myself that, translated to a different time and place, I would have been among those who resisted complicity with Nazi evil. In retrospect, this need to feel justified in condemning those who participated in the atrocities of the Holocaust probably explains my heightened fear of being actively complicit – or even simply silent – in situations which violate my notions of honesty or fair play. Although an almost hysterical insistence on abiding by strict scruples has occasionally been counterproductive in my professional life, it has succeeded in preserving my peace of mind.

Apart from the shadows cast by the losses of the Holocaust, my parents' lives turned into an immigrant version of the American dream once they reached the United States. My mother's academic career was compromised by the gradual onset of an untreatable form of nerve deafness, but she was supported in her desire to continue working despite her handicap by the administrators of the innovative health plan for which she became the director of pediatrics and by her many devoted patients. My father, too, was a committed and idealistic physician who loved his work and was revered by his patients. The honor and recognition accorded him for his contributions to the emerging specialty of radiation oncology far exceeded his expectations. In addition to their professional success, my parents were touchingly proud of their three modest homes and one hundred acres of abandoned farmland. More important, they were in a financial position to fund the higher education of nephews, nieces, daughters-in-law, and more distant relatives, in addition to that of their own children.

When my older brother David applied to college, my father insisted that Harvard be among his choices, because of its international reputation. Eventually my parents saw all three of their children awarded various Harvard degrees. David started doing research while still an undergraduate, and, as I write this essay, is the chair of the Department of Genetics at Stanford. Leon, named after the uncle who bribed his family's way out of the Warsaw ghetto, is the president of Bard College and music director of the American Symphony Orchestra. He was recently awarded a medal by Harvard's Graduate School of Arts and Sciences. My mother, now writing her memoirs, has come once again to appreciate how much immigration to the United States expanded what it was possible for her to achieve and what has subsequently come within reach of her children. My father, who died in 1994, also felt that he had lived a life far more wonderful than anything he had ever imagined before the war. When asked on his eightieth birthday, he could think of nothing – with the possible exception of yet more grandchildren – that might further have enriched his life.

SHAPE UP, KID

Deborah Lucas Schneider

>Born: January 10, 1943
>Evanston, Illinois, U.S.A.

So my early childhood wasn't ideal. It wasn't exactly the Bataan Death March either. Quit whining and shape up, kid. As my father said to my mother when he saw the mountain of luggage she had assembled on the station platform for a cross-country trek to his new posting, "Good Lord, Mary, don't you know there's a war on?" Or, in Rick's more familiar lines to Ilsa in *Casablanca*, "It doesn't take much to see that the problems of three little people don't amount to a hill of beans in this crazy world. Some day you'll understand that."

I discover a deep sense of shame attached to the idea of writing about my early experience and presenting it to others as if they could or would share my view that it contained multiple calamities. But that is an adult perspective. Shift it back to the time when you were knee-high to grown-ups and your little neural circuit boards were being wired for life, and trivial events on the grand scale of things loomed hugely. Each story matters to only one child, but when that child is yourself, it matters a lot. The details have a way of cropping up for the rest of your life. The circumstance of being wartime babies resonates in different ways with all of us and each story overlaps in bits and pieces with others, making the experience of a generation. In this context it seems possible, perhaps even useful, to tell my story.

I was born in January 1943. Four months later my father signed up with the navy. This was the first calamity for me, for I am convinced my father and I never had a chance to develop the bonds he had with his other daughters, born into settled peacetime routines. The lack of such bonds plagued our relationship from then on.

The second calamity was my mother's inability to cope. Never robust or confident to begin with, she was not up to life on her own with a toddler and a new baby. She moved back in with her own widowed mother to get some mothering herself. Grandmother was an imperious woman with servants and daily life was comfortable even in wartime. There are family snapshots taken at my grandmother's house in Florida: Dad on leave in a crisply pressed uniform, Mom smiling and relaxed in a bathing suit on a chaise longue, my older sister in a paper hat blowing a toy horn, friends and visitors on the lawn and the dock. One of them has lifted me out of my infant seat and holds me up for the camera – I have no idea who this woman is.

The third calamity was my sister's reaction to these events. She was furious at losing her adored father and her home, at losing part of our mother to depression, and at having to share what remained of Mom's attention with me. As three-year-olds have only limited data from which to deduce cause and effect, she held me responsible for America's entry into World War II, or at least she took out on me her distress over the war's disruption of our immediate family. Perhaps she concluded that while she hadn't been particularly happy at the arrival of a new baby, our father was so upset over it that he left home. I was the enemy, the cause of this disaster, and I learned I was horrible long before I learned why. We suffered together through the next few years, she in her distress and I the ever-present reminder of her losses. How well I remember my fear of arousing her anger. Once after some small mishap at a neighbor's house that incensed my sister, I fled home in terror and was ringing the bell frantically, hoping to be rescued, when she caught up with me and punched my head through the glass panel in the front door. Today I wonder about the intensity and sources of such rage.

About this time I developed a hysterical fear of birds. All attempts to con-

Deborah Lucas Schneider with her parents and older sister, Florida, 1944.

vince me that the backyard robins were cute, friendly little creatures failed. Wasn't there another little creature that adults thought was cute, but who attacked me all the time when no one was looking? As far as I was concerned, adults had no clue about the deadly hostility lurking in the one and they were pretty likely to be wrong about the other also. My fear of birds was replaced for several years by attacks of paralyzing pain in the gut, which Mom and Dad dismissed as irrelevant once the hospital staff reported that my digestive system looked tiptop on their x-rays. In my case the growing process obviously involved a lot of involuntary internalization of my own hatefulness. Physical symptoms expressing inner hurts gradually disappeared when I went to school, where I was eager, curious, engaged, and – it turned out – able to learn quickly. School started the exact opposite of a vicious circle, where first successes led to self-esteem and friendships in which I felt valued. At college I made bright, kind, and caring friends who have been a source of much comfort and happiness throughout my adult life.

It was also at college that I began learning German. Today I understand the reasons behind this decision far better than I did at the time. I see how clearly my fascination with this language grew out of early childhood experiences. As the war was coming to an end, my parents bought a house north of Chicago. We moved there even before Dad was discharged from the navy. Chance decreed that our next-door neighbors in Evanston were German. Thus, the first man I encountered who lived at home with his wife and family was Werner Leopold, a professor of linguistics at Northwestern, who was then engaged in research on children's acquisition of language, with an emphasis on bilingual environments. The study was based in large part on his own daughter Hilde. Hildy. As a toddler I registered that he was kindly and approachable, paid unusual attention to children, and listened to what we said more attentively than most grown-ups. When Dad returned from the war, he became absorbed in rebuilding his legal practice, a different form of nonpresence for me. Has nature programmed us all to be little investigators from birth, drawing hilarious inferences from our tiny samples? It would seem I concluded that while American fathers went off to fight wars, German fathers did not. When it came time to choose a father for my own children, I picked a man who would stick around and maybe even show an interest – a German academic – and I moved to Germany. Since I was already identified with the enemy, perhaps I also figured I might as well go whole hog.

There was another reason, though, for my hopes of finding lasting bonds of affection among the people my father had joined the navy to fight. After the war the Leopolds became involved in helping refugees, displaced persons, and immigrants. Through their urgings, my parents acquired a nanny when my younger sister was born. This nanny became my second mother. She was a sturdy German girl as cheerful and accustomed to surviving disasters as my real mother was diffident and depressed. Uta's family was scattered around the Chicago area, trying to make a new start, and her sister lived as a nanny with another family nearby. I remember their amusement as they tried to carry on a conversation in German on our back porch and I pummeled Uta's stomach with my fists, shrieking, "Talk so I can understand you! Talk so I can understand you!" For some reason – possibly because I thought this language contained the secrets that allowed family members to be loving together – I have devoted most of my adult life to mastering German. Come back, Uta! I have a big surprise for you!

Deborah Lucas Schneider with her two sisters and Uta, spring 1950.

FALLING THROUGH A WRINKLE IN TIME

Nancy Blackmun

>Born: July 8, 1943
>Minneapolis, Minnesota, U.S.A.

With increasing relentlessness, I found myself haunted by World War II. The war became a preoccupation steeped in sadness, eventually reaching depths that looked almost perverse, a fascination with tragedy and horror.

My preoccupation with the war seems to have begun in 1960, when at 17 I spent a semester in Germany as an American Field Service exchange student. It was only 15 years after the war had ended and reminders were everywhere. Eighty percent of Würzburg, where I was sent, was destroyed in an American bombing raid that lasted only 20 minutes. There is a mass grave for the 3,000 people who were killed. Terrible damage was done to the town's architectural jewel, a Baroque palace featured in the textbook used in many introductory art history courses during the era when we were in college. I asked, but no one seemed to know, why the town had even been a target. It was clear that it was not good manners to interrogate one's hosts about their problematic past. But I could see without having to ask that fully a third of my classmates at the *Gymnasium*, born as I was in 1943, had no fathers, all dead in the war. Most disturbing during this semester in Germany was a conversation with the one teacher in the Gymnasium who spoke fluent English and took an interest in me. His eyes glittered behind his wire-rimmed glasses as he said, with a chilling insistence, that it was essential to have an elite. He would have been just old enough to have been inducted as an adolescent into the desperate defensive efforts at the end of the war and just the right age to have had all his years of formal education up to that point controlled by the Nazis.

A favorite American Field Service friend from Berlin, whom I had admired and respected at 17 for his honesty, commented more recently on the mysteries that had disturbed me in Germany in 1960. He said that you can tell the politics of the parents of children born during the Nazi era by what they named their children. His name, *Jörg*, for example, is a made-up "Scandinavian" name, meant to sound even more Aryan, more elite, than anything in German. He was yet another of the Germans born in 1943 with a father lost in the war. His earliest memory is of watching the firebombing of Dresden in February 1945 from a hilltop on his grandmother's estate outside the city. He was just two years old.

A second impetus to my preoccupation with war occurred during sophomore year in college, when an instructor said, "If you're interested in reading more about war, here are the titles of three excellent books, all firsthand reports." This single comment precipitated a long read, as I tried to imagine my way into what wartime was like in both world wars, on the battlefield and off. With my reading spread out thinly over decades, for a long time I did not see that I was trying to research something. The real subject of the research was even less visible.

The third chapter in the genesis of this gathering preoccupation unfolded in my office. I am a clinical psychologist. In the spring of 1988, a new patient concluded his first session by saying, "By the way, my parents are Holocaust survivors." Without connecting the time with the symptoms that had brought him in for therapy, this patient had arrived on the fiftieth anniversary of the Anschluss, which is when the Nazis simply walked into Austria unopposed and took it over. If your family is from Hungary, as his was, Austria is right next door. He finished therapy six years later, after the fiftieth anniversary of his grandfather's deportation to Auschwitz. And he was not the only one with such exquisite timing. Eight other people in my small private practice surfaced during those anniversary years, all of them with significant traumatic early childhood histories connected with the war, or with someone in the immediate family who had such a history. There were, for example, adult children of camp survivors who were barely able to let their own children out of their sight and who kept the family passports up to date and in the top drawer of the desk, should a fast escape become necessary.

When my Hungarian patient finally saw that he needed to explore his family's history, he did a lot of it through reading. Somewhere between Helen Epstein's *Children of the Holocaust* and Art Spiegelman's *Maus*, which I read, too, I took off on my own, for more than a year devouring nothing but Holocaust materials, mostly memoirs by survivors. My reading was amplified by films like *Shoah*, *The Pawnbroker*, and *Hanna's War*. These materials were about people who had been from Poland, Hungary, France, Italy, Czechoslovakia, Holland, Denmark, Germany, and Greece, people of both genders, who had been various ages during the war, who had had various roles – member of the resistance, child in the Warsaw ghetto, physician, daughter in a deported family. I was consumed by urgent questions. What were these events like? How and why did they happen? Who survived? Why and at what cost? What could the bystanders see? Why didn't they see it? Or did they see and yet do nothing? If so, why? And, finally, what made it possible for some rare souls like Oskar Schindler, a whole town like Le Chambon in France, a nation like Denmark, or the Jews trapped in the Warsaw ghetto, to fight back? Out of my preoccupation with war a single issue, the Holocaust, had now emerged.

The members of my household were disturbed. Holocaust books were all over the house. My husband, struggling with his own demons, experienced this reading as a purposeful personal affront. The children, deeply attuned like most children to a parent's feelings, joined me and became curious, too. One undertook Holocaust research of her own. The other read everything ever published by Stephen King, then moved on to Thomas Harris and *The Silence of the Lambs*, descending finally into Dante's *Inferno*. The three of us, the children and I, were all hunting in the heart of darkness.

In 1992, in the middle of the six-year stretch of fiftieth anniversaries of the war, after my year of Holocaust immersion reading, my parents invited me to travel with them in Europe. The trip was to end in Berlin and that generated some irresistible options. One was to see the fiftieth anniversary exhibit at the Wannsee villa, the place where the highest Nazi officials and leading German industrialists had met in January 1942 to plan how to implement the Final Solution. The Wannsee villa is an elegant house, the kind of dignified, white, classical place you might find in the expensive old residential areas of any big American city. The exhibit was set up very much like exhibits on the Holocaust everywhere. Whatever the special feature of the particular exhibit, they are all the same, because they all have the same story to tell. In every exhibit different rooms are set up to address various aspects of the Holocaust.

In the Wannsee villa the centerpiece in the room devoted to deportation was an enormously enlarged photograph of Jews being marched through city streets by armed guards toward – one knows, although they did not – trains that would take them to death camps. I had seen many versions of this photograph in other places, but this time there was a shock. The caption said that this particular photograph had been taken in Würzburg – my Würzburg, a quiet Catholic river town known for its beautiful Baroque palace, home to a famous brewery and a university dating from the Middle Ages, and not much else. For 32 years, in a lacuna of information, without ever noticing it, I had not thought about Würzburg as a city that had had Jews. Here was the proof.

My parents, both in their eighties, had come with me to this exhibit. They moved through it in slow motion, their eyes huge, their faces ashen. Somehow, despite having been adults in the United States during the war, despite reading the papers and hearing the news on the radio, despite all the information about Nazi Germany that came out in the Nuremberg Trials – one of whose prosecutors was a law school classmate of my father's, they hadn't known either. And that has something to do with my detailing all of this here. Despite having lived in Germany, despite all of my reading, there was still an area of my mind that assumed this nightmare hadn't gone on in Würzburg.

Getting as far as Berlin also made it essential to drive to Poland, where the vehicles on the country roads looked comfortingly familiar, right out of the Forties. In Poland I immersed myself in a place where, without knowledge of a Slavic tongue, it was almost impossible to function in language – where I was thrown back to a psychic era before language. I went to Cracow looking for William Styron's Sophie. I went to see Auschwitz itself, to do something about my ashamed discovery a few years before that there had been not just Auschwitz, but five more camps in Poland devoted to death *en masse*, and that four of them had names I had never even heard of. I went to face the reality about us, human beings, that these places constitute, for the Nazis didn't have the franchise on evil. And I went to pay my respects, to bear a kind of witness, which I do here, for Poland is not a popular destination. Here are the things that I can't get out of my mind.

Auschwitz is vast, exhausting. During the war it was a place without a blade of grass. Now, for a midsummer traveler, it is awash with wildflowers that grow right up to the edges of the barracks that are still standing, wildflowers that blossom among the railroad ties of the infamous tracks leading to and through that familiar gaping entrance in the red brick guardhouse, the mouth of death. Until the frenzy of killing in the final years of the war, when quantity meant more than keeping meticulous records, the Nazi SS took photographs of prisoners: right profile, left profile, full face. In a museum room devoted to children at Auschwitz, some of these sets of mug shots are enlarged to poster size, larger than life. There are two girls, 13 years old, kerchiefs tied over their shorn hair, their eyes frightened and pleading. Their photos don't have the dated look of snapshots from the Forties. They are as fresh as if they had been taken last month. These could have been the daughters of any of us. This could be now.

Bełzec is one of the camps I had never heard of. It is where the Nazi SS first experimented with the insecticide Zyklon B, which killed people faster, in greater numbers, than had been possible with carbon monoxide. It is a place that was bulldozed by the Nazis themselves in 1942, because by then the geographical area it was designed to serve had been emptied of Jews. There is nothing left now but a vastly reduced number of acres and some haphazard statues made of something cheap that looks like plaster of Paris, something that won't hold up over time. At the entrance there are two objects, a house where a family lives – how can they sleep at night? – and a large bronze plaque, perhaps five feet by three, reading, in Polish, "In this place the Nazis killed 600,000 Jews gathered from many places in Europe and 1,500 Polish political prisoners." And that is all. So many people – 601,500 human beings murdered and bulldozed – and nothing to mark the place but some crummy sculptures and a big metal plaque.

After Auschwitz, the second-largest death camp was Majdanek, which the map shows as very near Lublin, the largest city in eastern Poland. But Majdanek is not just near Lublin, it is *in* Lublin. Auschwitz during the war was surrounded by a no man's land of three kilometers, further hidden by a dense band of poplars. But the old heart of Lublin, like any ancient city from an era when ease of defense against attackers meant survival, is built on a hill, commanding a view for miles around. The entire layout of Majdanek and anything that went on there out of doors – endless hours of roll calls, beatings, hangings, the infamous selections of who would live and who would die – would have been visible to anyone with a pair of binoculars in the old part of Lublin. In Lublin the question of whether people knew what went on in the camps is moot. The whole city would have had to know what happened at Majdanek.

But knowing is not as simple as it might sound. The history of the Polish people in World War II cannot be reduced to anti-Semitism run amok. If my family were Jewish and had been wiped out in the Holocaust, perhaps it would not have been possible for me to go to Poland, curious and interested, to go backstage so to speak, behind the Western Europe that is more familiar. Like the characters in Tom Stoppard's play *Rosencrantz and Guildenstern Are Dead*, I was a kind of Nancy Rosencrantz or Guildenstern. A nucleus of deeply hospitable English-speaking Polish families welcomed me to Poland, where I was fed, housed, ushered into tiny apartment bathrooms for delicious hot baths after long days of driving. I was escorted wherever I wanted to be taken, sometimes even without having to ask. My endless and increasingly personal questions were answered respectfully and in depth, despite the invariably puzzled question, "You aren't Polish, you aren't Jewish, why are you here?"

Every few kilometers on the roads in eastern Poland, there is a memorial marker to members of the resistance killed in the war, the graves in the woods as well tended as if the deaths had just happened. With the exception of Cracow, all the major cities and many minor ones were mashed flat by fighting. School above third grade was canceled from September 1939 to the war's end, because the "subhuman" Poles weren't thought worthy of something as privileged, as "Aryan," as education. Every family had war deaths and war traumas. I can't begin to list the number of people I met who, when I asked how they had learned the rusty German we were conversing in, answered by saying, "As a prisoner of war."

In the town of Przemyśl, where Helene Deutsch, a famous protégée of Freud's, had grown up, the small municipal museum with its polished parquet floors had displays from the eighteenth century – two rooms of exquisite antique furniture, a series of lovely watercolors of the local surround, and small, dignified portraits of area gentry – a sudden glimpse of what had been lost in 1772. This was when Poland ceased to exist as a nation, carved up by Russia, the Austro-Hungarian Empire, and Prussia. In the United States we all learned in elementary school history that a Polish general, Thaddeus (*Tadeusz* in Polish) Kosciusko, came to the American colonies to help George Washington fight the British in the American Revolution. He needed battle experience to take back home for the struggle against the invaders of his own country. Chopin's haunting music expresses the Poles' inconsolable sadness over the loss of their nation. The juxtaposition of beauty and tragedy everywhere in Poland is staggering.

But it was not Chopin or the Holocaust that I was researching with all this travel and with the long read about World War II, triggered by my college instructor's comment about war memoirs. It was my own early history in my family that I was trying to find. I wasn't Polish and I wasn't Jewish, so why was I hunting in Poland? Why was I painstakingly sorting through the Holocaust, so far from the wartime safety of Minneapolis, where my father had been drafted after Pearl Harbor, only to be declared 4F, ineligible because of a heart murmur?

In our small apartment a domestic disaster began in the final weeks of the war, when I was just short of two. In March 1945 my mother's mother, then living in another part of the country, had a major stroke. After an anxious and distracted month of waiting for her mother's medical condition to stabilize so that the extent of neurological damage could be determined, my mother spent all of April traveling out by train to bring my broken grandmother back to Minnesota. My father was opposed both to my mother's making the trip and to her determination to have my grandmother live with us. Why my mother felt she had to take on these responsibilities is another story, but in the disagreement between my parents and in the strained period that followed, the loving heart of their romantic relationship collapsed permanently and could not be recovered.

My father would not have had the means to connect his upset and depression over this event with a catastrophe in his own family when he, too, had been a toddler and his mother had become depressed over the loss of a full-term baby. Nor could he have connected it with a worse catastrophe in *his* father's life when his father was also a toddler. Four of the six children in that family had died in an epidemic of diphtheria in a period of a few weeks. This made three generations of loss in our family – in 1882, 1911, and 1945 – all hitting parents and toddlers, each successive loss a blow upon a bruise. In the spring of 1945, with no one at home to make him dinner, my father avoided the emotional reminder his stunned and distraught toddler daughter embodied, working late in his office and eating dinner downtown. For me, this left both parents "gone."

Nancy Blackmun and her mother in February 1944.

Watched over by a familiar but perfunctory baby-sitter, I wandered lonely in their absence through the rooms of our apartment, devastated with longing, unable to understand how my mother could be missing and yet present behind the glass of the framed photograph of her with me as a baby in her arms. To my adoring eye she looked as lovely in this picture as a famous portrait by Vermeer that I realized decades later exactly caught the turn of her head and her happiness as a new mother. Over and over I opened her closet to slide my hands into her shoes, searching for her feet, holding the soft fabric of her dresses against my face, trying to find her body in the familiar fragrance of her garments. But even when she finally returned, she was not the mother I had known. She had become someone who was distracted and exhausted by caring for her disabled mother, someone puzzled and hurt by the disappointment of my father, who withdrew even more than usual into his work. And I had become someone else for her, too. With the telephone call that had announced the news of her mother's stroke, a balance suddenly shifted. I was transformed from being the cherished center of my mother's existence to being more than she could manage. On top of her worry and fatigue, on top of the nursing care her hemiplegic and incontinent mother required, a toddler was now a maddeningly childish nuisance. It was not lost on me that if being a nuisance was bad, being childish was worse. Both became something to avoid. The exasperated impatience that went with these words still rings in my ears: "Don't *be* that way," "You're being *childish*," "Oh, *don't* be a nuisance."

All through these weeks, before my mother left and while she was away, the radio was on. Interspersed with the popular songs of the era were news reports. Cologne was captured and the American army crossed the Rhine. The Russian army took Gdansk. U.S. troops successfully encircled a huge contingent of German troops in the Ruhr. Hanover fell. And then, most shockingly, on April 11 Allied troops liberated Buchenwald, on April 15 Bergen-Belsen, and on April 29 Dachau. General Eisenhower went in person to see the camps. He had a group of United States senators flown over to see them as well, because he knew that without extensive documentation and eyewitness viewing by himself and other high government officials, denial of what the Allied armies found there would prevail. General Patton, a member of this group of top brass, had to retire behind a building to vomit. Edward R. Murrow, after visiting as the pre-eminent American radio newsman, wrote and delivered for all of the radio listeners in the United States to hear, the single most remarkable piece of broadcast journalism ever given on American radio. All of this I heard.

A fog descended in subsequent years over the family war in our apartment. It was not a hot war like the one just ending in Europe and the Pacific, but more like the Cold War that developed between the Soviet Union and the rest of the Allies, a tense, unspoken, and silent war. Forty-five years later, in my mind's ear, a thread of lovely melody by Mendelssohn, with its German words veiling their English meaning, heralded the first thinning of this fog:

> Ich weiss nicht, was soll es bedeuten,
> Dass ich so traurig bin;
> Ein Märchen aus alten Zeiten,
> Das kommt mir nicht aus dem Sinn.
>
> I don't know what it means
> That I am so sad.
> There's a story from long ago –
> I can't get it out of my mind.

The story is of the Lorelei, whose beauty, as she sits on a cliff above the Rhine, combing her golden hair and singing an irresistible melody, distracts a boatman into disregarding the rocks at the base of the cliff, so that he crashes into them and drowns.

Since I had been a baby, my mother, who loved music and loved to dance, had quieted me for sleep by putting records – the old 78s – on the Victrola and dancing with me in her arms. She especially loved Bing Crosby. Like bits of biology caught in amber, the songs he sang, usually waltzes, many of them by Irving Berlin, evoke for me how badly I missed her while she was gone. They are mostly war songs about love and separation. Their lines echo in my memory: "Where the blue of the night meets the gold of the day, someone waits for you," "I'll be loving you always," "What'll I do when you are far away and I am blue, what'll I do?" "I'll be seeing you in all the old familiar places," "Smile the while I kiss you sad adieu ... So wait and pray each night for me till we meet again." My favorite ends with these words: "When you return you'll find me waiting here."

But I couldn't wait. I was too little, and this intimate domestic disaster and its *sequelae*, which no one understood at the time, or was able to acknowledge later, went on for too long. Unendurably long absence for a small child is abandonment.

In my mind's eye I see the black-and-white newsreel logo from the Forties, used in a television series called *The World at War*. It shows a spinning globe being engulfed in flames, a nightmare that swallows everything. That's how it is to be a toddler whose world collapses because of her parents' absence and her own rage. I was crazed with sorrow and anger, and we weren't a family that knew what to do with either feeling.

When my own children were toddlers, I fled too – not to the office, staying downtown for dinner as my father had, but to graduate school to earn a doctorate, with no more idea of why that was so compelling right then than my father had had about staying late at the office when my mother was gone and I was almost two. As a tiny child, precocious and very verbal, invariably praised for being a smart big girl and wanting badly not to be "childish," I severed my body and my feelings and retreated into my head. I became such a very good, very smart girl in school that the eventual reward was admission not just to a fine college, but to what was then considered the best women's college in the country. At such places there are many people who retreated early into their heads because some part of their experience was unbearable. It is visible in their faces, the brittle intellectualism camouflaging a gray pall, years of childhood depression.

Early memory takes peculiar forms, lacing its fingers into apparently unrelated events, reverberating in our bodies when there are no words, especially when it comes from a time before words. Distilled to its essence, it can echo in melody, hover in fragrance, reside in a starving hunger to see, live in longing for a touch, a caress from the past. It seeps through in moods preserved from another era. At moments in the present we fall through a wrinkle in time.

I offer this précis as an example of how major historical events affecting millions of people and changing whole civilizations can become entwined and confused with domestic events on the smallest of family canvases. All of the questions that drove my relentless war research and all of the haunted discoveries in Germany and Poland that I have felt essential to detail here were translations of undigested toddler experience, translations into "German," or even more obscurely into "Polish," of events that had been untranslatable in my family, not just for me, but for the two generations before me.

In the historical Holocaust, the Holocaust that belongs to the Jews, I found an enormously compelling event that captured unmanageable and unaddressed pieces of my own early internal experience. The real Holocaust was of unassailable importance and legitimacy. It felt far more valid than the invisible tragedy of a toddler. The Holocaust – and Poland and Germany – were there, as anything external is, to be brought inside, to become a vehicle for something else, something more private, more personal, more interior. And in becoming that vehicle for me they ceased, of course, to be the historical Holocaust, or Germany and Poland. They became another entity.

That other entity may make what I want to say in conclusion sound presumptuous to readers who own the real Holocaust, especially those whose families suffered terrible losses at the hands of the Nazis. This is an unbridgeable chasm. I want to say that it has been surprisingly, disturbingly easy for me to understand the rage of Hitler, who was willing to bring all of Germany and most of Europe down in flaming ruins around his head, as well as to feel, almost as if they were my own, the terrible suffering and losses of the Jews in the Holocaust, and the plight of an impoverished, maligned, forgotten – and defiant – country in central Europe. This statement is not about Hitler or the history that belongs to the Jews. It is not about Germany or Poland. It is about events that became metaphors in subsequent decades for the feelings of a very little girl who, unnoticed, lost her mind and did her utmost to murder all memory of her beloved and loving mother when that mother left her as the war was ending.

But perhaps concluding on such a note is asking too much of those whose families were devastated by the Nazis. What right have I to use the Holocaust, which does not belong to me, as a metaphor in my own small history? The impatient voice of one of my children underscores this objection: "I've had it, Mom, with the Holocaust as metaphor." And so instead I will end by saying something else. Without understanding why until recently, I have been drawn to listening for cries from childhood, sounds from a time before language, feelings without words, from wars that may or may not be recorded in history books, but are engraved on the souls of the people who sit in my office.

Nancy Blackmun with her parents, February 1944.

FROM POSTON TO PALAU

Robert G. Sakai

> Born: October 19, 1943
> Minneapolis, Minnesota, U.S.A.

Growing up I didn't have any doubts that I was an American. I didn't perceive that my interests or cultural behaviors were any different from those of anyone else. The *Lone Ranger* was my favorite radio program. My friend Mark and I would eat pieces of freshly baked bread his mom gave us while we listened to *Sergeant Preston of the Yukon* at his house. I saved my allowance to buy Superman and Donald Duck comic books. I was thrilled when my father took me to my first major-league baseball game and I got to see Sam Jethro steal second base for the Boston Braves. I collected baseball cards. In the empty lot on Sheridan Street near my house in Lincoln, Nebraska, I hit the longest home run anyone knew of.

But every now and again I was reminded that others didn't perceive me the same way that I viewed myself. Out of the blue people would say, "Where did you learn to speak such beautiful English?" or "What country are you from?" When we were teenagers discussing girls, one of my best friends once told me, "Don't worry, Bob, you'll marry one of your own kind when you grow up." I was too surprised to tell him that I didn't think "my own kind" was any different from his. At other times the comments contained more than curiosity, such as "Why don't you go back where you came from?" or "Japs killed my uncle on the Bataan Death March." On each one of these occasions, but particularly when people could not distinguish me, a third-generation American citizen, from the Japanese Imperial Army, it was a great comfort to be able to tell others that my father had fought for his country against the Japanese military.

Some people have said that the *nisei*, the second-generation Japanese Americans born in the United States, such as my parents, have been hesitant to talk about their wartime relocation experiences because of a sense of shame. This doesn't seem to have been the case with my mother and father. They spent a fair amount of time during and after the war speaking about the Japanese American situation to church congregations and other public groups. They were not activists, but, when someone asked them to speak, they did so willingly. My mother in particular made a number of appearances to introduce herself, to discuss civil rights, and to try to help dispel misconceptions about Japanese Americans.

My father was never timid about speaking out when something was wrong. On one occasion, when I was 22, he became angry at a bus-line employee in Lincoln, Nebraska, who gave my seat on a full Greyhound bus to someone else. Since we had arrived early, bought my ticket, and asked several times about the departure of the bus, I should have been the first to board from Lincoln. When several later arrivals were given seats on the bus and I was denied a seat because it was full, my father became very angry. In a loud voice he asked for an explanation for this clear act of racial discrimination and later he filed a written complaint. Afterward we talked about the importance of standing up and speaking out for one's rights.

So it is surprising that my parents did not tell their children much about their wartime relocation experiences. Although they don't really have a clear explanation for this silence, they may have felt that the past is the past and sometimes it does not help to dwell on it. Certainly, in the years following the war, the family had plenty of economic concerns without expending additional emotional resources on the injustices of the immediate past. For this reason, as a child I had a somewhat vague concept of the relocation camps. It wasn't until the late 1950s, when I was 15, that I realized the "camp" where my family had stayed had been surrounded by barbed wire and machine-gun towers. As we cleaned out my grandfather's attic after his death, I found a handkerchief that someone had made in the camp. It looked like a tourist souvenir, but in the corner was a hand-painted picture of a guard tower and barbed wire. Underneath was the inscription, "Poston, 1943." It wasn't until then that I realized the extent to which the word *camp* meant *imprisonment*.

I was also not very perceptive about why my parents chose to live where we did as I grew up. Fresh out of graduate school, my father had taken a position as an assistant professor at the University of Nebraska instead of a higher-paying post at the Air Force War College in Alabama. My mother and father had decided against raising their children in the segregated South, despite the fact that his salary at Nebraska was less than that of an elementary school teacher. Eventually my father took a position at the University of Hawaii. After I moved to the San Francisco Bay area for graduate training and my sister and her family moved to Irvine in Southern California so they could pursue their academic careers, my mother commented on how ironic it was that both her children had ended up living in California. Until that moment I hadn't realized that my parents had made a conscious decision not to live or seek employment in California. In part because the bulk of Japanese Americans had settled in California before the war, it was there that the most virulent wartime racism against Japanese Americans was played out.

My parents were not the only ones with strong feelings about that period of California history. One summer vacation during junior high school, when our family was visiting relatives in Southern California, I found an article in the newspaper of the Japanese American Citizens' League about a lawsuit against an insecticide company that had referred to "Jap beetles." I thought this was overreacting and said so. Suddenly the conversation of eight or nine relatives stopped and all attention focused on me. No one was angry, but there was a solemnity I can still remember as I was told it was a big issue that I didn't understand. My mother, my father, and several aunts and uncles explained the intense wartime hostility that had been associated with the term *Jap*. It was a calm but very serious discussion, with all the adults in agreement.

Over the years my parents have visited California often. They have maintained friendships with non-Japanese Californians who were sympathetic and supportive during the war period and the relocation experience. They often talk about the sacrifices some of these friends made during the war to help them out. One of my mother's friends went so far as to save enough precious gas-ration coupons to drive from Fullerton, California, to Poston, Arizona, to bring wedding clothes, shoes, fresh flowers, candy, nuts, and a wedding cake for my parents' wedding ceremony in the relocation camp.

Nevertheless, my parents still feel strongly enough about the hysteria in California at that period and about the role the Hearst newspapers played in stirring up anti-Japanese sentiment that they have never considered returning to live in California, and they do not want to be buried in the state where they were born. To be fair, it was not just Californians who succumbed to the hysteria. The relocation of Japanese Americans was authorized by Executive Order 9066 signed by President Franklin D. Roosevelt. It was upheld by the Supreme Court. Not until 1952 – a full 50 years after my grandfather came to the United States – were my grandparents and other Japanese Americans of their generation able to vote or own property. But it was in California that my parents most directly experienced the worst of the hysteria and irrational hatred of that period.

Little by little I learned what had happened during World War II and how my parents felt, but there weren't many occasions when the topic came up naturally. Thus, I welcomed the opportunity this essay provided to revisit these issues at a time when my parents could consider those events with more historical perspective and I could view them as an adult.

Although there had been rumors and warnings circulating in the Japanese American community, it was still a shock in May 1942 when my parents and their families were actually ordered to go to the relocation center at Poston, Arizona. How could the United States government do something like that, especially to its own citizens? A sense of what that period must have been like emerged during the wartime reparation hearings in the early 1980s in San Francisco. Reference was made during the testimony to FBI documents, indicating that every report of Japanese sabotage had been thoroughly investigated and that no evidence could be found to support any of the charges. Nevertheless, General John L. DeWitt defended his actions in relocating Japanese Americans from the West Coast. He testified before the commission that in contrast to the Italian and German communities, which had turned in some of their members for spying activities, not one Japanese had been turned in by the Japanese community. When the late Senator Edwin Brooke asked, "Just what, exactly, did you make of that?" General DeWitt, who had argued during the war that the Japanese *race* was a threat, replied that it indicated the problems they had with the "cliquishness" of the Japanese.

My father's father came to California from Japan in 1902 and my grandmother followed in 1912, both with the intention of making this country their home, but this did not mean that they cut off communications with relatives in Japan. Each grandparent made a trip back to Japan in the 1930s in order to ensure that all their American-born children would have an opportunity to meet uncles, aunts, and cousins in Japan. As tensions between the United States and Japan grew in the decade before the war and as Japanese propaganda against the U.S. became more strident, my grandfather demonstrated his allegiance when he felt compelled to set the record straight while traveling in Japan. In public gatherings he told about his own experiences in the U.S. and testified that the Sakai family had been treated well in America. Because of his activities, the Japanese secret police began to follow him and to disperse those who wanted to hear what he had to say. My grandfather's response was to buy train tickets to one destination and then get off at the next station to go to a different destination.

My grandmother also did her part to try to improve relations between the U.S. and Japan. She visited churches around the Coachella Valley in Southern California, where the Sakai family had settled as farmers, and she tried to tell the community about Japan. She would sing folk songs and tell stories in her accented English to try to break the ice with her neighbors. She and her generation had enrolled their children in Brownies, Cub Scouts, Girl Scouts, and Boy Scouts. They made sure their children studied English and learned about civics and democracy. My mother relates how her mother encouraged her to work as an *au pair* during college to learn more from the inside about how American families do things. It is no accident that both my parents have a professional command of English grammar and vocabulary and that my mother is sensitive to proper American etiquette.

Unfortunately, the "yellow journalism" of California newspapers and the wartime paranoia swept away any progress that had been made to increase understanding. My mother's father was one of the first to be incarcerated as a dangerous alien. He had been a civil engineer for a large orange ranch in Southern California, so he had a collection of aerial maps. He used the maps to help him plan the best pattern for locating trees so that each could receive the proper amount of sunlight and water. At the outbreak of the war, sensing that the maps would be a problem, he immediately turned them in. Ironically, that probably hastened his incarceration. He was taken away by the authorities in early March as a security risk. Eventually, however, everyone in the Japanese American community on the West Coast, including small babies, the sick, the old, and the infirm, was incarcerated in the relocation camps.

The experience at the Poston relocation camp, where my family was sent, was not pleasant. Located in the middle of a desert near Parker, Arizona, in the middle of the Colorado River Indian Reservation, Poston was divided into three

Relocation camp, Manzanar, California, 1942.

sections of hastily built barracks for a planned population of 20,000. By fortunate coincidence both my parents, who had been dating each other in college but were still single at the time, and their families were assigned to Poston I. Even within the barracks there was little protection from the 120° desert heat and the dust storms. Finding ways to keep the dust out of the rooms was a major preoccupation in the first months. My father recalls suspicions that the first two babies born at Poston died of dehydration because the hospital had no air conditioning. Each room, approximately 20 feet by 25 feet, was supposed to house exactly six people. This meant that families were often split up. There was little privacy in any case. My parents say that three married couples had to share one of the rooms. Initially, the toilet seats were arranged ten in an open row. Eventually some partitions were devised. Although there was enough to eat, the food was unpalatable for most of the internees, who were used to an Asian diet. Sauerkraut was inedible for them and, unaccustomed to dairy products, many of the first generation could not stomach cheese. Bottled drinks, when they were available, often contained bugs or other contaminants.

The relocation involved monetary loss, as well as physical hardship. The evacuees were allowed to take only what they could carry with them. Everything that could not fit into two suitcases had to be sold for a loss or given away. Since the relocation order came just before the harvest, farmers like the Sakai family lost an entire year's investment in their crops. The financial assets of Japanese American families had been frozen except for funds to provide minimum subsistence and to pay laborers. No one knew how long relocation would last or when they would return to their houses, but the Japanese Americans knew they would lose their land if they abandoned it. For that reason three pieces of the Sakai family farm were given to a Caucasian friend with the understanding that he could live there and farm the land for free. All he was asked to do was give it back when the family returned. Fortunately he was an honorable man and those three pieces of land were returned. Unfortunately another 20 acres owned along the highway in what is now downtown Palm Springs were lost because there was no way to pay taxes while the family was in the relocation camp.

At a family reunion in 1995, however, my older relatives agreed that the physical hardship and financial losses were not the primary insult. I think particularly about the story my 77-year-old Aunt Alice told. Just before leaving for the camp, she and her family were hosting a last party for her friends when the police came to take her father away. The arrival of the police caused worried parents to come and collect their children. At that moment all the efforts her family had made to be good citizens and to gain the respect of the surrounding community came to mind. With emotion and indignation still filling her voice even after 53 years, she recalled thinking, "How dare they do this to us!"

The anger was rooted in believing so firmly in the principles of American citizenship and then seeing the government itself casually strip away the most basic human rights, colluding with racial hatred directed at Japanese Americans. The anger of my family comes from having been humiliated and betrayed. It wasn't merely that they had committed no wrong. It was knowing they had tried harder, studied more, and taken being "American" more seriously than their Caucasian friends. A country that promised equal opportunity and civil liberties had arbitrarily revoked that promise for Japanese Americans.

One particularly serious problem for the social organization of the camps was that before 1952 federal law had not allowed the *issei*, or first-generation Japanese Americans, to become American citizens. This meant that the authorities treated them as enemy aliens. The authorities gave the second-generation nisei more authority, as citizens born in the United States, but because the vast majority of nisei were under the age of 20, this created serious rifts in the Japanese American community regarding leadership.

Born in the United States, my father was one of the older second-generation nisei who took a leadership role in the camp. He served on the community council, chaired the education committee, and taught in the senior high school. Ironically, the theme of the curriculum for that year was "democracy," sparking many impassioned debates. In the spring of 1943, when army recruiters appeared in Poston seeking volunteers, the discussions about politics got even more heated. Some of the draft-age nisei argued that because the government was not permitting them the privileges of citizenship, they had no obligation to fight. Many of my father's generation did volunteer, however, and distinguished

The parents of Robert Sakai at the Poston Relocation Center on their wedding day, October 24, 1942. The barrack in the background (100 feet by 20 feet) had four rooms with six persons assigned per room.

themselves by their heroism. By the end of the war, the 442nd Regiment, made up almost entirely of Japanese Americans from Hawaii and the mainland – the mainlanders volunteering from relocation camps – became the most honored and most decorated military unit among all the United States armed forces.

Wartime circumstances forced my father and his generation to make a decision that second-generation Americans normally do not have to make. The government required them to state in writing whether they forswore allegiance to the emperor of Japan. There was great resentment from those who already considered themselves to be Americans because if they answered yes, it implied that they had sworn allegiance to a foreign emperor in the first place. In response to this demand of the U.S. government, a few of the Japanese American community decided to go to Japan. A few others, proclaiming their American identity, answered *no* to the government's allegiance question and were sent to jail. Decades later they were exonerated.

My mother and father were married at Poston in October 1942 and my mother shortly thereafter became pregnant. My parents were determined that I should not be born in an internment camp so they began exploring ways to leave. Beginning in the spring of 1943, some of the internees were allowed to leave the camp if they could find outside sponsors. Permission was granted at first on a temporary basis to do field labor. Gradually it was expanded to students attending school and then to those who could find sponsors who would employ them away from the West Coast. Thanks to the church community in Minneapolis, my maternal grandfather, the civil engineer, found a sponsor who could use his drafting skills. This enabled my mother's family to leave the relocation center in time for me to be born in Minneapolis in October 1943. At the same time my father had been accepted for military intelligence training at Camp Savage in Minnesota, so my parents were able to move together. My father greeted his newborn son a few months before being sent overseas. While he was in the army, my mother and I lived with her parents in St. Paul, and she went back to college, finishing her degree at the University of Minnesota.

My father wasn't required to fight in the war, but was determined to do so. At age 24 his poor eyesight and flat feet had disqualified him when he tried to volunteer to be an army paratrooper early in 1943. He was accepted for army intelligence training only when a superior officer spoke on his behalf, because of the importance of his Japanese language ability. Since the Berkeley draft board delayed in clearing his papers, my father was accepted for military intelligence training before he was accepted into the army. Consequently my mother and father had to pay their own expenses to get to the army language-training school and to subsist while my father attended classes as an unpaid "civilian volunteer." Only through frugal living were they able to make the meager $200 that friends and relatives had pooled for them when they left the camp stretch to cover expenses for the four months that it took my father's papers to clear.

About a month before the end of the language training, the papers appeared and my father had to take two weeks off to report to the induction center for a physical. Again he flunked the physical and passed only after the intervention of his superior officer. When he returned to language class, he tried to make up for what he had missed by studying after "lights out" under the blankets with a light shielded by his army helmet. After several days the strain made it impossible to focus his eyes and he lost another week of classes. Fortunately he had done so well prior to his leaving for the induction center that he did not have any difficulty graduating with his class. However, his eyesight almost derailed his military career yet again. He was allowed to go overseas with the other interpreters only when his superior officer intervened for a third time.

My father's determination and persistence resulted in his playing an active role in the war. As a reward he was allowed to join General MacArthur's forces, participating in combat as the troops island-hopped their way to Japan. From Guadalcanal to the Palau island chain in the South Pacific and finally to Japan, my father saw combat – storming beaches, avoiding snipers, encouraging Japanese troops to surrender, and always being wary not to get shot by his fellow soldiers. As an intelligence officer, he had many duties, from interrogating prisoners to entering dark caves thought to harbor Japanese troops in order to encourage them to surrender. He never knew whether he would stumble onto mangled corpses or a hail of machine-gun fire or both. For years afterward he had nightmares about some of these experiences.

Because of my father's dedication, he was promoted in the field from sergeant to lieutenant. Before awarding him his field commission, the commanding officer asked, "Sakai, why are you fighting this war?" My father replied that he was not fighting the Japanese people, he was fighting the Japanese military government. Apparently his commanding officer was satisfied. In my father's mind there was no question about his duty as an American citizen. He did not fight in spite of the discrimination experienced in the relocation camp. Instead, he felt that he was being further discriminated against by not being allowed to defend his country.

Robert Sakai's father is promoted in the field to 2nd Lieutenant in June 1945.

After the war my father became a professor of Japanese history, teaching American students about the period just prior to the arrival of Commodore Perry in Japan in 1853. Although he retired from teaching in the United States in 1984, he continued to teach Japanese history and topics in American history at a Japanese university for another 13 years, until he reached the age of 78. He also served as president of the Japan America Society in Honolulu and was one of the main organizers of the first international conference of Japan America Societies in both the United States and Japan. He is a member of the panel that selects recipients of the Crown Prince Akihito Scholarship, an award that sends American students to study in Japan and Japanese students to study in the U.S. He also screens native speakers of American English for an English conversation program sponsored in Japan by the Ministry of Education.

Recently my father also put together a museum exhibit to highlight the history of Manjiro and Joseph Heko, two Japanese who in separate nineteenth-century maritime accidents were rescued by American ships prior to the opening of Japan by Commodore Perry. Following their rescues, both men were taken to the U.S. and educated there, before they returned to Japan and played important roles in helping to open Japan to the West. The exhibit toured Hawaii in 1997 and was shown in Japan and the continental United States as well. In recognition of a lifetime of promoting better understanding between the U.S. and Japan, my father received the Third Order of the Sacred Treasure, one of the highest awards bestowed on foreigners by the Japanese government.

In view of my father's belief in standing up for one's rights, and also in view of the strong negative feelings he and my mother still have about wartime California and the relocation, it is easy to imagine his doing something other than volunteering for the army. The injustice of relocation might have deterred him. A desire not to fight against relatives could have softened his resolve. When asked about his decision to serve in the army, he says that in some ways he wishes he had taken a stand against the relocation laws, but then he would have been jailed and that would have created even greater hardship for his parents.

In the complex environment of World War II, where a number of injustices were committed, my father established priorities and focused on fighting the greatest injustices. His parents supported his decision to join the U.S. Army and go to war against Japan. In fighting the Japanese military government, he fought a system of government he did not believe in to preserve one he did believe in – even though the principles of the government he believed in were not being observed in his particular case. Knowing the ambivalence I felt before serving in the military during the Vietnam War, my initial reaction is to think I would have reacted differently from my father, given the same circumstances.

The fact that my father and other nisei conducted themselves as they did, however, created entirely different circumstances for their children and grandchildren. When people accusingly tell me that a relative was killed by the Japanese during the Bataan Death March, I sympathize and tell them my father was a U.S. Army lieutenant who fought as part of MacArthur's troops in the South Pacific. Because of my father and his generation, there is now a body of facts that contradicts General DeWitt's racism and hatred.

My parents have passed on to their children and grandchildren a belief that everyone in the United States has an equal opportunity to succeed. Whatever their motivation for not telling their children more about the relocation, the effect was to nurture a family culture relatively free of the bitterness experienced by their generation. The legacy of nisei actions during World War II is that my 18-year-old son does not have to defend or excuse his ancestry. It is fortunate, but ironic, that because of my father's actions my son is so secure in both his ancestry and his American identity that it is hard for him to understand his grandfather, who at roughly the same age was so anxious to fight for the country that had imprisoned him and his family in the middle of a desert.

Robert Sakai and his parents in 1943.

Frankfurt-am-Main in ruins, 1945.

THEIR HAPPIEST TEN YEARS

Matthew W. Stolper

    Born: March 1, 1944
    Philadelphia, Pennsylvania, U.S.A.

In late September 1933 a young Swiss woman, Martha Vögeli, came to a hotel in London to find a young German, Wolfgang Stolper. He had received a letter earlier the same day advising him not to return to Germany because it was likely that he would be arrested there. He was surprised to see her. He thought she was in Switzerland. Now, just when his prospects had plunged into uncertainty, she had come, as he puts it, "to accept him." In his view it was the turning point of their young lives and the beginning of their happiest 10 years, the same years that saw the Depression reach its depth, fascism triumph across Europe, and the war break out, spread, and turn. He was 21, she was 22. They were to marry and become my parents.

    Wolfgang's father, Gustav Stolper, my grandfather, was a former Reichstag deputy, the editor and publisher of a financial weekly, the *Deutsche Volkswirt* (*German Economy*), and a nonobservant Jew. After the Nazis took power in early 1933, he concluded that even a civilized country could fall into the grip of ruinous lunatics. He sold his weekly to ungenerous Aryans and sold his other property as well. He sent the younger son of his first marriage to finish secondary schooling in Vienna and went with his wife – my father's stepmother – and their two young children to London. They would sail for New York at the end of September of that year. My father, the oldest of his children, had come to see them off. Before the letter arrived warning him not to return to Germany, the plan had been that when he finished his undergraduate studies in Bonn and his brother finished Gymnasium in Vienna, they would follow the others to America.

    In Bonn my father had been studying law, which he hated, and economics, which he loved. He had begun under the tutelage of a family friend, the economist and social philosopher Joseph Schumpeter. Schumpeter was called to a chair at Harvard in my father's second year at university. The plan laid out for my father had been that he was to finish the *Referendariat* (the legal diploma at the undergraduate level) in Bonn, compete for a Rhodes scholarship to Oxford, continue on to Chicago for a Ph.D., and return to Berlin to be groomed for the editorship of the *Volkswirt* and for the entire niche of privilege and engagement, opinion and influence, that his father had created in the Weimar years. Now the plan was changing. My father was Austrian by birth, German by circumstance and choice but soon no longer by law, liberal by political conviction, sincerely Protestant by faith, and a Jew under the Nuremberg Laws. It seems absurd to give such flat labels to a young man still being formed, but at the time they were the labels that determined one's fate. They precluded him from finishing his legal studies and compelled him to embrace economics, brought him under the scrutiny of student fascists and the protection of principled friends, and now they prevented him from returning to Bonn and to the university in the autumn of 1933.

Before the warning not to return to Germany reached him in London, my father had taken advantage of being outside Germany to write a long letter to the young Swiss woman, my future mother, for whom he harbored a desire that seemed both unshakable and futile. They had met almost exactly three years earlier, in September 1930, at a vacation language class in Grenoble (it was the same day that brought the news of the Nazis' unexpected success in the 1930 election). When they returned to their own countries, he tried to pursue their romance from a distance, and she tried to pull away from it. Now his letter to her from London not only gave an account of life in Germany under the fledgling Nazi regime, but also explained that he would soon be the last of his family in Europe and not there for long, and it pleaded with her to spend some days with him before the tides of history swept them apart to uncertain prospects on different continents. At about the same time, she wrote him a letter, explaining why she thought they could not have a future together and why that made her treat him coldly in a way that troubled her. She wrote of differences in nationality, culture, education, and upbringing, of his Berlin existence as the heir of a privileged family and her placid upbringing in Zurich, and of the staid conditions of her life as a village teacher. Perhaps she implied more than she said about how his love pressed upon her, seemed to confine or suffocate her. When he wrote his letter, he did not know she was working in England as an *au pair*, teaching French to the children of an English family. When she received his letter, forwarded by her family in Zurich, she put her letter away unsent and went to see him.

She came from a Swiss family that for 500 years had been farmers and schoolteachers. They were civil, decent, warm, genteel, and upright without self-righteousness. She had completed teacher training and now took up a series of assignments, some in rural communities that were so closed and mean that they could depress even someone brought up in the midst of legendary Swiss parochialism. Once she was rejected outright by a village that would not tolerate the idea of employing a female teacher of marriageable age at a time when men needed jobs. While she struggled to teach the children of families who seemed to embrace ignorance, she exchanged letters with my father about Mozart, Karl Barth, and Ortega y Gasset. But the conditions of his life – divorced parents, a change of nationality, political activity – must have seemed antithetical to hers, and the pressure of his affection must have been fascinating and frightening and not quite proper. Now events overwhelmed these differences. His exile meant that the outward social and cultural differences between them were no longer good reasons for her retreat from the pressure of his love. Perhaps she felt that she had to respond by putting away what seemed like ungenerous inner reservations.

But she eludes me and always will. She died 25 years ago. While she was alive, I was not inclined to ask about these things, imagining that I knew what needed to be known. I think she would not have been inclined to answer. It would have meant exposing feelings that she wanted to control or deny, and the inquiry might have been experienced as more intrusive than affectionate. I have read some of her letters to my father, but I have her history mostly as it is embedded in his, and her younger personality as it is memorialized by him.

And so, instead of a Rhodes at Oxford and a Ph.D. at the University of Chicago, my father began graduate study in Zurich, her family's home, and the two of them shared a happy year there. In 1934 he joined his parents and siblings in America, and she stayed in Switzerland. He had no diploma from Bonn, no graduate degree from Zurich. He spoke scanty English, but thanks to Schumpeter he came to graduate school at Harvard with a fellowship. He could travel on an Austrian passport until 1938. He wrote occasional encyclopedia entries to raise money for freighter passage to Europe. Each summer he spent some time with her in Switzerland. The steps ahead were again no longer open to question. He would complete his Ph.D. in the United States and declare himself economically and professionally independent of his family. Then he would marry her and begin a family of his own.

He finished his Ph.D. in 1938 and sent for her to come to America. She hesitated, he pressed, she came on the liner *Normandie*, and they married in New York. Why did she hesitate again? Was it that he and his family had become as glittering and alien in America as they had been in Berlin and it was no longer a question of accepting him, but of acceding to him? Was it that she was happy with the ambiguity of their life on two continents, nothing of her own background lost, no future possibility excluded by drastic choice? Are love and honor enough to explain her choice? Was something in her own life, reflected in her sometimes gloomy and withdrawn letters, simultaneously holding her back and pushing her toward him?

My father had ceased to be an exile very quickly. He and his parents were concerned with the affairs of Europe, but they rapidly became Americans in their commitments and hopes. They had arrived at the height of the Great Depression, and after the politics of Depression-era Europe, they were astounded by the apparent social cohesion and the success of liberalism in America. They became citizens as quickly as possible and enthusiastic backers of Roosevelt even before that. At Harvard, where my father's position as an instructor allowed a life without poverty – a life rich in music, literature, art, and the exercise of intellect – my parents were surrounded by students and colleagues who had every reason to consider themselves the best and the brightest. In New York my grandfather was achieving financial success and political connection. In a way, the plans for my father were not far from their original track, however derailed the rest of the world was. While the world was crushed by the Depression and Europe slipped into despotism, atrocity, and total war, my parents had an existence so charmed that it has always amazed me that the rest of their lives was not poisoned by longing for the loss of those golden times.

In the introduction to a book, my grandfather wrote that Germany had gone from a pinnacle of economic and political success at the end of the nineteenth century through five episodes of catastrophe, those of 1914, 1918, 1923, 1933, and 1939, "and the next, most dreadful and possibly final catastrophe already looms on the horizon – defeat in the present war" (Stolper, 3). The book is copyrighted in 1940 and its preface is dated May 1941 – a time when the German army was victorious on all fronts, a month before the German invasion of Russia, seven months before Pearl Harbor. Who could have such implacable confidence at such variance with the apparent course of events? It is not the voice of an exile or even of a refugee.

The year that book was published, 1941, was a turning point for my parents in several ways. My father collaborated with Paul Samuelson on a theoretical article that would make him celebrated, at least among people who deal with international trade. Even 50 years later, during the North American Free Trade Agreement debates of the early 1990s, the *New York Times* could publish charts showing the effects of NAFTA under "Stolper-Samuelson" assumptions without feeling obliged to tell readers of the business pages what that meant. That fall, my father began teaching at Swarthmore College. And their first child, my older brother, Thomas, had been born at the beginning of the year. Months passed before doctors diagnosed the cause of the baby's problems as hemophilia.

Although this young couple had been driven to another continent, the life they found there would have been enviable to anyone. Their experience left them with their youthful vigor and confidence undiminished, and they must have assumed, at least tacitly, that being humane, involved, attentive, and civilized would allow one to master the brutality of the world. Now the X chromosome hit them where Hitler and the Depression had not touched them. The preludes to the war, emigration, the war itself, and its aftermath had deep effects on my family's social values, but Tom's hemophilia shaped its emotional dynamics.

The physiological effects of hemophilia are simple and brutal: the blood does not clot. Small cuts cause great blood loss. Small bruises cause massive hemorrhaging. Joints swollen with blood require long periods of bedridden convalescence that interfere with the growth of muscle and bone mass. Crises need transfusions. Threats too mundane to imagine have consequences beyond sane expectation. A bite on the inside of the cheek while chewing leads to a swelling that threatens death by suffocation. A playground mistake costs an eye. During Tom's childhood, medicine had no remedy beyond transfusions of whole blood. The science was not much better than what it took to refill a leaky radiator. The use of cryoprecipitate or of isolated clotting factors was decades away.

The new parents were helpless and frustrated. They could nurture, but they could not protect. They could share sleepless nights, but they could not offer respite. Love was alloyed with suffering, joy with fear. And, because the disease was inherited, they had to face guilt and anger, or deny them.

Hemophilia is a sex-linked characteristic, transmitted by a gene on the X chromosome. About 25 percent of cases arise from genetic mutation; otherwise, the disease is inherited. Men have a single X chromosome, women have two. Men have the disease, as my brother does, or they do not, as I do not, but women can transmit it without having it. My mother was a carrier.

She said she did not know she was a carrier, although her sisters said they knew. I think some sense of being a carrier of hemophilia had contributed to her hesitation and her choices up to the point of finally marrying my father. I know that with Tom's diagnosis the emotional burden on my mother became damaging and the strain on the relationship between my parents became intense. I am certain that they withstood despair. Now that they knew she had the gene for hemophilia, they saw the risks and the consequences with perfect clarity, but they still chose to have another child. I was born in 1944.

By then the war had turned and the coming defeat of the Axis was clear. What was in the balance after the U.S. became a combatant was how long that defeat was to take, what it was to cost, who was to bring about the victory, who was to suffer and who to profit, and what the postwar conditions of Europe and America were to be. These issues are not retrospective historical abstractions. At the time they actually engaged my father and his family, especially my grandfather.

Many people perhaps grow up thinking of their formative years not as part of historical time, but as a matter of things simply becoming as they were meant to be. Many people of my age are apt to suppose that World War II simply led to the Marshall Plan, without considering how implausible it would be for any nation to fight a total war for such aims. During the war and in its immediate aftermath, explicit American policy was entirely different. No terms but unconditional surrender were acceptable. The Morgenthau Plan, mostly forgotten in America but recollected by an older generation of Germans, called for the deindustrialization of Germany, rendering it forever harmless by reducing it to an almost premodern society, barely a nation. It was an effective ideology for wartime sacrifice, but it offered a prospect of catastrophe for victors who would be politically and economically exhausted by the costs of winning the war – not to mention the even greater catastrophe for the vanquished – and my grandfather opposed it with whatever influence he had acquired. He and his children had long since ceased to be German-Jewish refugees and had become Americans who believed that America was to be closely connected to Europe and that Europe was inevitably bound up with Germany. So, as the war came to an end and soldiers were ready to come home, Stolpers went to Germany.

My father's two younger brothers had joined the U.S. Army and served in Europe. The one who had gone to Vienna to finish Gymnasium in 1933 stayed on in Military Government in Germany. My grandfather took part in the Hoover Mission to coordinate food supplies during the hard winter following the war. My father, who had been exempted from the draft as the head of a household with infant children, joined the Strategic Bombing Survey. He got a uniform and a token rank – he called it being a "chocolate soldier" after the character Bluntschli, the "chocolate cream soldier" of Shaw's *Arms and the Man* – and he arrived in Paris in time for V-E Day in May 1945.

In Paris he found his own mother and her second husband. Unlike her first husband, my grandfather, she was a Jew who had converted to Christianity. Nonetheless, by the standards of German race laws, she was just a Jew, so they had fled Vienna for France after the Anschluss in 1938 and had survived the German occupation of Paris. Later she made her experience sound almost like a television cartoon when she talked cheerfully to my brother and me about knitting in the Tuileries while the Gestapo and the Resistance chased each other around the park snapping their pistols. But the realities of getting food and shelter and help with hiding in the crowd had been much harder. And her youngest son by her second marriage, my father's half-brother and a child when the Stolpers left Germany, had been caught by the Gestapo while he was still in his teens and had disappeared into the camps. My father searched for him across Germany. Eventually it became clear that he had died in Auschwitz.

The Strategic Bombing Survey was an academic triumph and a political farce. Its aim was to assess the effectiveness of strategic bombing on German war production and on civilian morale. It confirmed the failure of strategic bombing, finding that arms production had increased during the bombing, that despite many raids on ball-bearing factories and storage facilities, for example, there was a two-year supply of bearings at the end of the war. On the other hand, the design of the survey was a milestone in the development of modern survey research methods, so its effects are still felt indirectly with every advertisement of a new product and every election campaign. The commanders of the survey – including John Kenneth Galbraith, George Ball, and Paul Nitze – were men who made policy 20 years later. The foot soldiers of the survey were people like my father, youngish men who spoke German and had some training in the social sciences. For six months immediately after the war, my father traversed Germany with more freedom than most soldiers or civilians.

My father's letters are a moving counterpoint to my uncle's memoir of his experience in Military Government. Together they depict what most histories of wars downplay or ignore – the moment after the end, when blood and iron and violent lunacy give way to grief and need, awareness of ruin and the consequences of stupidity, the dislocation of the most fundamental social norms and the eerie persistence of shreds of culture, art, and music where society – even subsistence – has collapsed. While released prisoners, conscripts, bombed-out civilians, and others shambled around Germany looking for their places, my father had opportunities to find old family friends, to search for clues to his lost half-brother, and to visit monuments. A momentary gap in the not-quite-yet Iron Curtain, for example, allowed him to go to the Thomaskirche in Leipzig, where J. S. Bach had been *Kapellmeister*. There he met an American army master sergeant who was a church organist in civilian life and who turned on the organ and performed an all-Bach recital. My uncle, the young regular-army lieutenant, took on the responsibilities of seeing an occupied town of 25,000 through the winter with inadequate food and medicine, coping with the prohibition on employing former Nazi party members when the only doctor in town had been a Nazi. My father, in uniform but not a proper soldier, had uncomfortable experiences of being among the victors – being quartered with fearful civilians, for example, or occupying the house of a local Nazi party official who had killed himself and his children rather than surrender. In a slightly more subtle way, he had the experience of being arbitrarily separated from his own past as a German national by the nonfraternization rules of the early occupation. A reconciliation with Germany marked some of his later academic career. During the "Economic Miracle" of German reconstruction in the 1950s, a number of German students came to Michigan, where he had begun teaching in 1949, to do their Ph.D.s with him. Late in his life some of them arranged a medal in lieu of a festschrift, to thank him for treating them as students and colleagues, not as survivors of a defeated enemy.

There was never a question of my family returning to Germany. All of them had become thoroughgoing Americans. Nor were my brother and I brought up to think of Germany as a second homeland or even as the place where our European roots were. After my grandfather's death in 1949, my step-grandmother would spend long visits in Germany with people who were still close to her, but my father had only a few intimate friends left there from his days in Berlin and Bonn. All of my mother's family were still in Switzerland. In 1933-34 they had embraced my father with a familial warmth different from the atmosphere of the political and intellectual household in which he had grown up. He responded in kind, showering his in-laws with affection and loyalty, and developing a Swiss chauvinism that would be comical to many Germans. When he received a fellowship and a sabbatical in 1948, he took us with him to Zurich for the year and brought us back for the summer of 1952. It was Switzerland, not Germany, that my brother and I experienced as our European roots, the home of our European family.

We grew up in Michigan, as the memory and effects of the war tailed off. But not really quite in Michigan. We saw little of the country that was immediately in front of us. Landscapes were sought not in northern Michigan but in northern New England, where my parents looked for a summer home, eventually buying a place in Vermont. Far from being embarrassed by my parents' accented English, I was conceited about having traveled in Europe and being part of a family that I thought of as more cosmopolitan and sophisticated than those of my schoolmates. I was more familiar with Boston and Zurich than with Detroit. It was only when I took up fishing in my thirties that I began to learn the Midwestern landscape and to feel anchored in it.

My family's experience of the outward events of the war, its prelude and aftermath, was extraordinarily fortunate. Some of its effects can be described as an absence of effect. I did not grow up with a consciousness of holes in the family, missing cousins, uncles, and aunts. Instead of fear and rancor at the monstrous race that perpetrated the Holocaust, I learned to suppose that people of perfectly ordinary character and intelligence could find their lives ruined by being caught up in monstrous acts through stupid but ordinary choices. My family had none of the exile's mourning for a lost world, all of the immigrant's patriotic zeal, but not much chauvinism for the old country or the new. That Europe and America were a single society did not seem a new condition, as it did to some native-born Americans – in the borderlessness of the academic world, it seemed natural. If my family had a muted sense of the atrocities of the past, perhaps we had a heightened sense of the danger of the present as it appeared, for example, in the McCarthy years.

Despite the terrible fact of Tom's hemophilia and its emotional tolls – for my mother, growing reticence and isolation, for my father, powerlessness over the circumstance that was shaping his family – my parents tried hard to offer me a lovingly ordinary family life. Tom was my big brother, the one who told the stories, the one who chose the movies, the one whose opinions were to be emulated and whose friends were to be envied, and who was more interesting than most big brothers because he had an exotic condition that did not diminish or daunt him. I was the fortunate one who could do best by standing aside and looking after myself. There was no conscious neglect, but in the nature of things I was bound to get less attention than my brother and to get attention of a different sort. My father would sometimes tell me that my brother would become a responsibility to me (which has not been true), but I was "protected" from taking part in the troubles that might prepare me for responsibility. My mother formed a view, of which I have only a dim notion, that Tom had a spiritual quality that should affect the world's relationships to him. My task was to do well at the things that everybody esteemed, avoid making disturbances, avoid taking risks, offer reassurances that I would be all right.

When I reflect now, I dwell on how the traits my family brought to their responses to outer events and to each other persist in me. I see my mother's emotional reticence in my own history of painfully ambiguous long-distance relationships. I see my father's importunate need and desire in my eventual clumsy efforts to remedy my detachment and blunder into undefended intimacy. The specific consequences of the historical events themselves seem modest, not only because my parents were privileged and lucky, but also because they had traits that allowed them to turn privilege and luck into success. They escaped with the knowledge that wickedness and brutality were deadly earnest, but without wounded bodies or tortured souls. They transmitted a view of the world that was largely optimistic. If the life built on that view seems placid and ordinary, the preservation of the view is a hard-won small miracle.

What the Depression and the war were to many other families – an arbitrary, crushing catastrophe – hemophilia was to mine. It had a great deal to do with our separation into emotional lives that were ever more different. Now, when my brother and I have passed the horizon of middle age and my father is very old and we all need reconciliation, we remain similar but have grown apart, appallingly ignorant of one another, insensitive to how we have shaped one another, with suppositions about feeling, language, self-knowledge, and understanding so different that they resist reconciliation. I suppose that is a truism, a recognition of the general experience that, in the words that Norman Maclean (104) puts in his own father's mouth, "It is those we live with and love and should know who elude us."

Still elusive to me are the connections between the outer world and the inner world, between history and the lives of individuals. I still puzzle over the link between the ways in which the events leading to the war brought my parents together and the ways in which my family has been disturbed and divided by hemophilia. Perhaps there are connections of this sort: when my father's forced exile overwhelmed my mother's reasons for keeping away from him – whether or not they included some denied knowledge that she was a carrier of hemophilia – she could only make the "good" choice of accepting him. The "good" choice had apparent risks, but it soon led to safety and relative prosperity. So when the hemophilia appeared in Tom, it was a cause for deep anger in both of them, that the good choice also led to such an unfair, terrible outcome, that in fact their lives had not escaped the catastrophe of history unscathed. But it was an anger that they could not permit themselves to indulge or express. And perhaps there is a negative connection as well. Their comparative good fortune in evading the most brutalizing forms of wartime trauma – their ability to look terrible times in the face perceptively, but from a safe vantage, not from captivity behind barbed wire or from a hunted existence – left them without some emotional facility as well. Without that strength they could not come to terms with the hemophilia as something terrible and arbitrary that must be faced – like war itself – in the here and now by controlling guilt, anger, and denial. So they were left to rely upon love and hope, both absolutely essential but not sufficient.

But I have come to the troublesome boundary of personal privacy here. I speculate about how these things were connected for my mother, now long dead. I speculate about how they were connected for my father, who still reflects on the same questions, and how they continue to affect my brother. But I can assert my speculations only at the price of hurting deeply held feelings about things that my father and brother are obliged to see very differently.

After Church: supporting the boys in uniform.
Maria Fleming Tymoczko with her parents and
members of the congregation, spring 1945.

WAR BABIES

Maria Fleming Tymoczko

>Born: December 15, 1943
>Providence, Rhode Island, U.S.A.

In thinking about the extraordinary political activism of Americans of my generation, I had always assumed that it could be traced primarily to the radicalizing experience of the Vietnam War as we were coming to political consciousness: the impact of moral horror and outrage, the apprenticeship in resistance and demonstrations, the lesson in political and social analysis, the fear of the draft, the trauma of serving in the war, and so on. To be sure, those experiences can scarcely be underestimated, yet I found myself significantly revising my views when I belonged to a women's political group that met weekly for a year or so in the early 1980s in Amherst, Massachusetts. Our meetings had some aspects of a support group – that is, we were willing to try to be very honest and personal with each other – but we were interested in directing our energies outward to the world rather than inward to ourselves. We wanted to explore what political action meant to each of us, why we felt a sort of compulsion to be engaged, and how those sensibilities could best be harnessed to effective action. So we talked, and we talked about ourselves.

Nearly all of us were age-mates, as it happened, born in 1942 or 1943 like most members of the Harvard-Radcliffe Class of 1965. From civil rights activism to the antiwar era to the second wave of feminism, we were veterans of marches and movements, we had put our energies and bodies and money on the line, and some of us had even spent time in jail. Yet, to our surprise, we found ourselves talking repeatedly about the way in which our political identities were rooted in the impact of world politics on our birth families, the way that World War II had profoundly shaped our early years. I have come to feel that what my women's group discovered is to a great extent true of all of us born in the war.

As infants, most of us in the Class of 1965 were called "war babies." We were regarded as somewhat different, marked out as anomalous – precious life springing from death, little lives created and salvaged out of the peril and rubble that were consuming half the world. There weren't a lot of us and we were cherished accordingly. We were the affirmation of the fecundity and endurance of the species, even in the face of the chaos that wrenched our fathers and mothers apart. We were seen as the epitome of the future for which the fighting was engaged, the hope held in the hearts of all the adults whose lives were being ravaged. We came to awareness of ourselves with the label *war baby* in our ears, with a subliminal sense of the price paid for our lives and our future. That price included sacrifice by those who held us most dear and sometimes the wounding, disabling, or even death of our own relatives. For American war babies those relatives at risk were usually fathers and uncles, though there were some grandfathers involved as well.

World War II brought an early politicization to my life. My family was working-class and none of my grandparents had completed a high school education. My father's parents were both factory workers, my grandfather having come as a child from Scotland. My father's mother was from British Isles stock that had been settled in America a long time, long enough at any rate for her great-grandfather to have starved to death in the Confederate prison at Andersonville. As the oldest child of six, she had a hard life, particularly after her father was killed in an accident working on the railroad. Because of her father's accident, my grandmother dropped out of school at the age of 12 to help support the family. In 1941 the aspirations of my father and his siblings were bounded by the prospects of their own parents' lives – factory work, or bartending, or manual labor of some sort. Or maybe the exotic: in the case of my good-looking Aunt Louise, a stint in the chorus line of the Roxy, the local burlesque house on the national circuit, which she tried for a short time, until her career was cut short by her mother's adamant opposition. Louise retaliated by marrying a minor member of the Mafia, but that's another story.

My mother's family were immigrants from Czechoslovakia, the sort of immigrants who were doing their best to be upwardly mobile. My grandfather was a shoemaker, a small-scale entrepreneur who had dreams of becoming landed gentry in Slovakia by buying land there with profits from his American shops. My maternal grandmother had nowhere to go but up. She was the daughter of peasants who lived in one room in a farm complex owned by a landlord, peasants whose only possessions were household goods and a clutch of geese. Like my father's mother, this grandmother also began to work at the age of 12, when she was sent to the small city nearest her village to be a servant for a rich Hungarian family. It was an experience that made her determined to seek a better life in America, where she aspired to freedom, equality of a rudimentary sort, and flush toilets.

My mother's family moved back and forth across the ocean and in fact my mother was born in Slovakia in 1926. All my grandfather's hopes of becoming gentry were curtailed by the Depression (perhaps fortunately so or else the family would have been in Europe during World War II and behind the Iron Curtain thereafter, suffering as most of our relatives in Slovakia did). When my mother's family returned to the United States in 1930 to monitor their business in America, they came to settle for my grandmother's benchmarks, the flush toilets and a little respect, or respectability anyway. My grandmother followed her own leadings even in America. Throughout most of the 1930s, to the embarrassment of her assimilationist children, she fattened the Christmas goose herself, harboring it in her kitchen, even plucking its down for pillows while it was still alive. The aspirations of my mother and her siblings were not unlike those of my father: a working-class American life (without geese), a steady job, and your own home, if you were lucky.

My parents met initially in a junior high school in Cleveland, Ohio, and they married in 1942 shortly after Pearl Harbor. My father had graduated from

Maria Fleming Tymoczko with her parents in 1945.

high school but my mother dropped out of tenth grade to marry just after she turned 16. Both were fresh-faced, bright teenagers, with aspirations molded by the Roosevelts and images of stability from the 1930s. My father had led a somewhat wayward and wild youth, which probably was attractive to my mother, who came from a strict and pious Baptist household. She also liked the fact that he was "a real American" – he didn't have the faintest trace of ethnicity.

The 1930s were very hard on people like my parents' families. Survival was the paramount concern and it tightened people's focus on themselves. Both my grandmothers slaved to keep their children alive, one on the assembly lines, the other washing floors. The stories my father told of his youth were not political. They were about living in foster homes so his mother could earn a livelihood, and forays to the library for amusement, and going (with a suitcase of history books) to summer camp for poor children, and hitchhiking cross-country, and minor theft, and local bootlegging. My mother told about wanting to be American, and refusing to speak Slovak, and being hungry, and stealing green tomatoes from vines, and yearning for a Shirley Temple doll. World War II shattered that emotional isolationism bred of economic impoverishment.

During the war and afterward, the world became the context of our lives. What happened elsewhere mattered in a new way. It had a connection to us and to our daily doings in Cleveland. All the men of my parents' generation were caught up in the war, except my father's brother Bill, who was a quadriplegic, and my mother's brother Johnny, 13 years old when I was born. My father's older brother Jack joined the marines and became leader of his platoon by virtue of being able to beat all the other men in the group in hand-to-hand fighting. He had been decathlon champion of his high school and a semi-pro boxer before he joined up. My mother's brother Paul had been in the Civilian Conservation Corps during high school and he joined the army with a band of buddies just after war was declared. I was born in December 1943 and my 19-year-old father enlisted in the army shortly thereafter. Even the men who stayed at home did so because they were part of the war effort. Uncle Joe worked at a foundry in Cleveland, casting parts for bombers, a valuable part of war work that earned him an exemption month after month.

The world became somewhere family members might be sent and, later, after the war was done, it was somewhere uncles or friends or neighbors had been. We learned that what happened elsewhere mattered. It had connection. You couldn't ignore it, because what happened in the world, in politics, might come home, catch your own life up, and change you forever. Because his eyes were so weak, my own father was never shipped out, but he was terrified that he might be during the big buildup before the Normandy landings. So Normandy was close to us. My father might have been there, part of that desperate scramble through the waves, under fire, to gain a beachhead. The Pacific islands were where Uncle Jack was landing with his marines, and, later, the place where he rescued one of his men hit in a Japanese ambush, and, later still, the place he was machine-gunned himself and pulled to safety by his loyal and grateful men. Australia was the place where one uncle had a brief marriage and a war bride who wouldn't return to America with him. Her dark sepia photograph was in our family album, smiling and beautiful, flat and unchanging, but she herself, soft and warm, who had kissed my uncle, was still there, in Australia.

Even as a primary school child, struggling to learn the geography of the housing project I lived in with my parents, and then, as my circles widened, the geography of the neighborhood and the geography of Cleveland, I can remember my father talking to me about events that were happening in the world. Telling me they mattered. Places that were only words to me as a girl – Nuremberg and Korea and Taiwan and Berlin – were a part of our kitchen conversation, had an entitlement on our lives. The family conversations were reinforced at school by the *Weekly Reader*, which included stories about Egypt, the Suez Canal, Israel, India, and Pakistan, as if those places were our backyard and the politics of those countries a matter which even we children should think about. That sense of our lives being played out across the globe, the whole world, set a context for my response to Vietnam and the U.S. presence in Vietnam decades later, a context shared by many of our generation.

The war influenced us more directly as well. It changed our family living patterns in small ways and large. As the war went on, for example, my family answered the call to grow a victory garden by expanding the plot already laid out in the very back of my grandmother's property, giving up flowers in favor of food production. One of my earliest memories is the planting of that larger garden – I suppose it must have been in the spring of 1945, the second spring after I was born – with Uncle Joe breaking the sod and my grandmother and Aunt Mary and Mother laying it out with words: peas here and beans here and tomatoes against the fence. And myself getting under everyone's feet, clutching dirt in my fist and letting it fall between my fingers, and being shooed out of the way and told not to get dirty. One of their earliest memories of me is from those victory garden times, probably the next year when I had more words and dimly remembered the routine, when they tell me I asked in my squeaky little voice, "And where will you plant the meat?" Ever since those days, in my mind, in my family's minds, vegetable gardens have had some quality of the victory garden, some primary association with a desire for triumph and with the creation of good things for the self and for the group, creation from seeds so small that it feels *ex nihilo*. I still feel it each spring as I turn the earth and lay out the rows, and each summer and fall as I give the bounty away to neighbors and students and anyone who is willing to accept a zucchini.

The victory gardens I can remember, those small ridges in the flow of childhood time, but the seismic quakes happened without my ever being conscious of them and without any memory of the slippage. The war radically altered expectations among the working classes of Cleveland, and I grew up – we all grew up — on the other side of a tectonic shift. Even though women have always worked in my family — as women always do in preindustrial cultures, in peasant cultures, in farming cultures, in poor cultures — a middle-class American ideal had seeped into their consciousnesses in the 1930s, the ideal of women being supported by their husbands and staying home like ladies to keep the house and kids. That's what the young women of my family were earnestly heading toward, but during the war they learned the pleasures of paid work, pleasures never abandoned afterward.

It happened because the men were at war. Rosie the Riveter has become a sort of national icon, especially in the women's movement, but we forget people like my mother, Annie the Pharmacist's Helper. One day Grandma came home with news from the clinic where she had been and later was again a charwoman, having given up that job for a better-paid position on the munitions assembly lines during the war. One of the doctors had approached her to say, "I need your eldest daughter to come work for me. My pharmacist has been drafted, they're taking every able-bodied man. I need someone to count out the pills and give the people the medicines they need. She's a smart girl and she doesn't have any children to take care of. We need her." Aunt Mary talked it over with her husband, but they came to the conclusion that she shouldn't go to work — he was man enough to support her, and it would be more patriotic for her to continue volunteer war work than take a paid position that someone else might need. But my 19-year-old mother said, "I want to do it."

So Mother became the acting pharmacist and never looked back. She worked her whole life in the medical profession, finally taking exams to become certified as a physician's assistant in the 1970s (along with a lot of Vietnam War vets), and work became one of the most satisfying parts of her life. Many of us have mothers who during the war took over for men at some sort of work, running their husbands' businesses, or driving buses, or working in factories, or being union stewards, like my father's mother. When we were infants, before our conscious memories, we grew up seeing women in the world, at work, managing civilian life. And those women who did so in our own families entered into a sense of self-possession, a sense of entitlement, that lies there at the threshold of our awareness. This public presence of women at work faded out gradually during our childhoods, especially during the 1950s when there was a campaign to get women back in the kitchen, but I'll never forget how much I liked it when the bus driver was a woman and how much I missed those women drivers as they were gradually replaced by men.

Another tectonic shift also predates my conscious memories or my conscious understanding of the order of things, the class shift that happened after the war to working families such as my own as a result of the GI Bill. Many if not most of the members of the Harvard-Radcliffe Class of 1965 have a long family tradition of higher education, some for generations at Harvard itself. For a few of us, however, the entitlement to higher education can be traced directly to the GI Bill, and women who come from such backgrounds, like myself, may be conscious of being the first women of their families to have a college education.

My family's educational expectations shifted radically because of the war. The men who returned from the war all went to college on the GI Bill. They were the direct beneficiaries of that amazing democratization of education that happened in the United States in the late 1940s, that opened up the lives of people who didn't grow up with privilege, and that shifted their careers and class irrevocably. Uncle Jack, the marine, became a civil engineer. Uncle Paul became a math teacher. My father headed himself toward teaching history. And their influence spread to the younger members of the family as well. My mother's twin siblings, too young to be in the war, were sent to college when the time came, and they too became teachers. College and university educations opened people up in all sorts of other ways as well, and, as a consequence of the war and its aftermath, my cousins and siblings and I inhabit a much larger world than did our parents and grandparents.

I can remember my father being in college. His oak desk and typewriter had pride of place in our small public-housing living room. His books were everywhere. He bought a gooseneck lamp and a set of Britannicas, on time payments, no doubt. Sometimes when he was writing a paper, I'd wake up at night to the pleasant, steady sound of the typewriter keys striking paper, an even rhythm, like a train over railroad tracks, that sent me back to sleep again. He worked that way in the middle of the night when everyone else was asleep, and he slept in the morning, and then we had to be very quiet. And if I got up in the night to go to the bathroom, there he'd be, a young man, 25 years old, dark-haired, under a cone of light from his desk lamp, hunched just a little as he typed, with the full ashtray by his left wrist, bluegray smoke hazing the scene. He worked, too, and my mother also worked to help put him through school. I was seven-and-a-half when he graduated and by then his education had become a kind of family enterprise. We knew his classmates from picnics, where many of the students were veterans, many his age or even considerably older, many with children. Working-class war babies have such memories of our fathers educating themselves, emigrating from their class as their parents and grandparents had emigrated from their native lands. My own trajectory through Harvard and through a Ph.D. has always seemed simple by contrast.

My father turned out to love reading and studying, learning and thinking. And when he graduated from college, with all that learning fresh in his mind, he practiced it on me. One time when I was enrolled in a summer school course at Western Reserve University, a course designed to teach French to very small children, I came across my father at the tennis court near my classroom building during recess. What a revelation to realize that he might have sat in the very room where I was taking French lessons. He watched my education, thought about what I was being taught, and became part of the process. I remember when I was learning about Thomas Jefferson and he asked me, "What does it mean, 'all men are created equal'?" And then the stream of Socratic questions: "Do they all have the same color hair and eyes and skin? Are they all the same size? Are they all equally smart? So, what does it mean?" I think I was eight at the time. Thus it went through the years, setting a foundation for my own love of learning and my own teaching career. But that was later, after the war.

For those of us born in the war, the time during World War II itself gave many of us a rather different psychosexual foundation from those of our older or younger siblings and, indeed, an orientation different from the standard presumed in Western culture and Western psychology. When our fathers went off to war, many of our mothers moved back into their own mothers' homes, bringing their young children along, even giving birth to new children in those homes.

Maria Fleming Tymoczko with her mother, grandmother, and the twins, Uncle Johnny and Aunt Emily, in the summer of 1944.

As a result, we the children grew up in multigenerational families. In some cases more than one daughter came home, so the family grouping was extended and complex. Sometimes the head of the clan was a grandfather, beloved or tyrannical or both, but often these complex families had female heads of household. This is what happened to me.

My parents were living in Rhode Island when I was born, so I started life in a conventional nuclear family. When I was three months old, my father enlisted in the army and my mother packed up and took me on the train from Providence back to her family in Cleveland. My grandmother had decided this was what should be done and she paid for the train ticket.

My grandmother lived in the central part of Cleveland in a Slovak-Italian ethnic neighborhood on a tiny property that had two houses on it. The "big" house had four small rooms and an unheated attic where the young people slept. Mother and I lived there with Grandma, the young twins Emily and John, and Aunt Bessie, who was just a little older than Mother. There was no central heating, just a kerosene stove in the living room and another stove in the kitchen. The running water in the bathroom was cold, unless you lit the tiny gas heater mounted on the wall. In the little house on the property (three rooms, located four feet behind Grandma's house on the same lot) lived Aunt Mary and Uncle Joe.

Grandma gave up her bedroom so that my mother and I had a place to live. Aunt Emily says she can't remember her mother lying down to sleep for a long time during those years: she'd just rest on the couch. We ate most suppers together, all pell-mell around my grandmother's wooden kitchen table. When I was big enough to graduate from a high chair, I sat squeezed in on the bench behind the table with my teenage Auntie Emily and Uncle Johnny, and sometimes with my mother as well. Everyone was in charge of me, everyone took turns taking care of me, especially while my mother was sick. (She was quite ill with a thyroid problem that kept her bedridden for weeks after we arrived in Cleveland, a problem that ultimately required surgery and then more bed rest.) I felt loved by everyone, even my young aunt and uncle who were themselves displaced as the babies of the family by me. We were all crowded together under the rule of my matriarchal grandmother, whom everyone but me called "Mama," living as one household complete with cats and African violets in a space that probably was little bigger than the dining room of my present house.

In many ways it was a very difficult time for us all, with my mother sick, and difficulty getting various kinds of food and other commodities, and anxiety about the safety of the young men of the family who were soldiers. From 1942, when Uncle Paul was shipped to the Pacific theater, he was not seen again until after the war, and for nine of those months he was missing in action, separated from his battalion, hiding behind enemy lines in the jungles of Luzon. So there was constant worry.

And yet, in other ways the war created a wonderful environment for a baby's first two years, in many ways better than the isolated nuclear-family environments of the suburbs that babies born in the 1950s grew up in. It was an environment more typical of an earlier era, when extended families lived together in villages or on multigenerational farms. My family lived in a real neighborhood, where people knew each other and visited together, where people from "the old country" gathered together, speaking their native languages, even as the young were becoming American. I became the baby of more than just a family, recognized and indulged by various friends and neighbors as well. Like many others born in the war, because of my nuclear family's displacement, I was raised by a village, so to speak, in our case a village within a city. For my own life, this was infinitely better and more stable than a childhood spent alone with two teenage parents. Those years when Mother was 18 to 20 and I grew from infant to two-and-a-half-year-old toddler were critical for us. Many years later my mother acknowledged that, by taking us in during the war, Grandma had "saved both our lives."

I trace many of my personal strengths to that formative period of living with my extended family, full of loving caretakers and multiple role models. My earliest memories took shape with Mother working and me being watched part of most days by someone else – Auntie Mary, or Grandma, or the twins, Johnny and Emily. There was almost always someone to meet my needs willingly, something interesting going on to watch and listen to, and someone to keep me in line. There was a surfeit of love and words – stories, debates, arguments, quarrels, reading aloud, praying, or singing – in at least three languages, the English and Slovak spoken in our house and the Italian I could hear spoken by our noisy, voluble neighbors, the Costellis, just 15 feet away.

It was an anomalous period when our domestic world – almost devoid of men – was utterly ruled by a hierarchy of women: first Grandma, then Aunt Mary as oldest married sister, then Mother as the one with the child, then Aunt Bessie, then Aunt Emily as the dominant twin. Although any of them could lose her temper and shout and although my grandmother was strict and straitlaced and uncompromising, I don't ever remember being frightened or terrorized in those early years. I was safe in my grandmother's house. And when my father came back from the war and I began to live for the first time in my remembered life with my parents alone, I was desolate. I felt I had been torn from my real family and sent away for fosterage, away from most of my mothers. Over the years I've wondered whether my feminism – and perhaps the feminism of other women my age – is anchored in the experiences of those formative and preconscious years, when our psyches were being shaped in a woman's world, where women's love enveloped us, where women worked and ruled, where women felt good about themselves, where women held power by right, where women's ways and bodies were the norm.

One of the darkest sides of being born in the war was that reunion with the men who straggled back from the fighting in '45 and '46 and '47 to shatter our

Maria Fleming Tymoczko with her father
and Aunt Mary, spring 1945.

civilian peace. So many of those young soldiers came home damaged, some physically, but more mentally. They came home strangers to their children, strangers to their wives and parents, and strangers to themselves. This was the insight most striking to my women's political group and to others I've talked with who were born in the war: how aware our generation is that many of our own men were damaged in one way or another by the Vietnam War – either by being soldiers in the war or by not being soldiers in it – and how the damage done to the men of our own generation was preceded by the damage done to our fathers and uncles and family friends during World War II. What is different in the two cases, however, is that our own generation can talk about the trauma of the Vietnam War, setting the personal in the context of a political analysis, admitting doubts about war itself. Perhaps we learned to speak from the silence of our fathers, who so often could talk of nothing about the war, could only hold it in, repress the experiences, as they tried to protect their women and children, and themselves.

As I look at these things from the vantage point of 50 years gone, it seems to me that the only man in my family who came through World War II psychically whole was, paradoxically, Uncle Jack, the marine who was raked by a machine gunner in a clearing of a tropical jungle on a Pacific island. Jack was lucky to live – lucky to have been pulled away, lucky to have survived the bullets that slashed through his legs. He was flown by stages to a military hospital in Chicago, where many skin grafts and many months later he was declared healed and released. Thirty years later his grafts were peeling off and his immune system turning against him, yet of all of the men who had been soldiers in my family, he was the one most whole, and he is the only one still alive.

The others came back war-wounded in their minds and hearts, full of rage and guilt and death, volatile and violent, erratic and dangerous. Uncle Paul in some ways never recovered from the nine months lost in the jungle. When he was found by American troops he was desperately ill with jungle rot, gangrene, and malaria, traumatized from being left for dead by the enemy troops who had pinned him to the ground with bayonets through his arms. The Americans rescued him in the nick of time, cured his wounds, and put him back to work, but he returned to us in 1946 wild and terrified and terrifying. He had nightmares, shouting and screaming in the dark. The family was told never to try to wake him at such moments or he might turn on the person who touched him. In contrast to Paul, it was perhaps the visibility of Jack's wounds and his heroism, known to all, able to be talked about, that helped him recover, where the invisiblity of the others' psychic wounds left them isolated, alienated, and silent.

My father never fulfilled that early promise of being a history teacher. He had a breakdown in his early thirties and was permanently disabled. In 1961 I was one of two students at Radcliffe College on a full scholarship, one of four National Merit Scholars that year to list for father's occupation "unemployed." How the ghosts and skeletons of World War II figured in his breakdown I don't know, but I do know that there was guilt and shame at his own cowardice and fear while he was a soldier, fear strong enough to make him inhale talcum powder so as to damage his lungs, rather than face the possibility of combat duty. Throughout the rest of his 49 short years of life, he never breathed right and he never slept right again.

Looking back, I see our fathers caught in silence. They had won the war. They were heroes. Yet their own experience of themselves was so often one of failure, of having feelings that heroes should not speak about in our culture: terror, cowardice, shirking, disgust, disillusionment, indifference, loathing, nausea, torment. Between the women and the men a terrible gulf grew, the gulf of the unspoken war. I can hear my mother's voice even now, impatient, when my father spoke of the army, spoke of the hardships of being in the army. "It's over, Bob," she seems to repeat in my memory, "the war is done." I can still hear the contempt in her voice when she told me years later how he confessed to her about the talcum powder. Those nightmares of war and the alienation from civilian life that they spawned were in some cases named and acknowledged for the first time when the fiftieth anniversaries of World War II brought the experiences alive again. Even those men who did not serve in the military fared scarcely better than the soldiers. Old enough to serve, but kept at home for industry, they often remained curiously embryonic, failing to realize their manhood. Although many, perhaps most, of the women of my world came out of World War II stronger, going from strength to strength later in their lives, the men came out battered, further widening that gulf between the sexes in the 1950s. It's hardly a wonder that those of us born in the war – who as "terrible twos" met and first lived with our alienated fathers at the war's end – were not at all happy to find our own generation called to a battlefield that did not even seem just or worthy of sacrifice.

The changes of the United States in the last 50 years are the changes of my family writ large. It is in part from the evolution of countless lower-class families such as my own that we write the palimpsest of the history of America in the last half century. And it is experiences such as those that formed me that separate our younger siblings, the Baby Boomers, from those of us who were born in the war.

Allied forces, Luzon campaign, 1945.

Parable

" ... a simple story illustrating a moral or ... lesson ... "

from Greek parabolē, *'juxtaposition, comparison'*

Dr. Charles W. Styron, Sr., holds his son and namesake,
Charles Styron, Jr., in South Carolina, spring 1945.

PARABLE

These essays are stories of World War II as remembered by its children. All of them bear witness, with some carrying morals or lessons as well.

Anthony Graham-White, older than the rest of the group, describes Coventry during the Blitz. The details offer a glimpse into the difference that only two or three years can make in what a child is able to remember, yet he also vividly captures a child's tendency to register islands of fact devoid of content, stripped of context.

For Ursula Oppens, writing for this volume generates for the first time conversations about what happened to her family during the war. She and her parents and her relatives begin to talk to each other across vast distances – from the United States to Hungary to Israel – about the Nazi deportation of grandparents, aunts, uncles, and cousins to the concentration camps. The raw quality of her writing bespeaks the undigested newness of the information this family finally begins to share.

In the centerpiece of the book, Christine Tanz explains how her astonishing father successfully hid himself, his new wife, and his teenage brother-in-law during the six years of the Nazi occupation of Poland, a success crowned with the miracle of her own birth before the end of the war. Written as her father lay dying, this especially beautiful essay is not only a powerful eulogy for him and for her mother, but a sobering testament to the element of luck that contributed to their wartime survival.

Francis Zebot's mother escaped the vicious guerilla fighting in Yugoslavia on her bicycle, carrying her toddler son along in the bicycle basket. Or did she? Along with Anthony Graham-White, Francis Zebot raises the question of a child's difficulty in discerning what is remembered from what has been heard and talked about in the family, but he also brings into question the adults' memories. His immigrant parents, like Eva Griepp's, provide hospitality and housing for innumerable relatives, friends, and distant acquaintances from the home country. The dense detail, reminiscent of Eva Griepp's, here seems not so much a memorial to those without graves as a memorial to an intense internecine struggle and terrible losses in a small country whose wartime history is not well known to the world at large. It is a memorial to those who lost the struggle.

Peter Katzlberger, a German national born to Christian parents, makes do as a little boy with his mother and grandparents in a country village south of Stuttgart, while they wait for news of his father, who is missing in action. The news never comes. Like Anthony Graham-White, Peter Katzlberger comments wryly on the ways in which scarce commodities were recycled; both capture the circumscribed geography of a child's world of home and neighborhood, even as history unrolls around them on a global scale.

Postwar Germany looks very different from the contrasting perspective of Mathea Falco, the daughter of an American officer whose job during the postwar occupation of Germany comes to include the emergency reconstruction of Tempelhof Airport during the Berlin airlift. Far from home, her family also makes do in Germany, but without the familial and communal networks of support that sustain a child. Her father's agony as he remembered these events on his deathbed matches the postwar nightmares and wrenching war memories that visited other essayists' fathers late in life.

John Dundas's father, a British naval officer, evacuates his wife and children to the Scottish countryside to escape the Blitz, but his own health is ruined by chronic stress during the years of the war at sea. John Dundas's cheerful confidence about the foundation of his optimistic personality, with four women – his mother and his three older sisters – all competing to love him most, contrasts with his postwar conflict with his father and his own later preoccupation with war.

Kazuko Iwasawa Ihara and Peter Katzlberger are the two sole representatives in this collection from the Axis powers. The simplicity of a childhood voice seeps through her writing, as it does his. From opposite sides of the world, both remember food shortages and the terrors of bombing. But both also capture the vitality, curiosity, and joy of small children, expressed even in adversity. Like some of the other women writers, Kazuko Ihara allows us to hear her mother's voice, preserving it for posterity. She identifies with her mother, yet offers a nuanced view of the past, distinguishing her own experience as a child from the realities faced by the adults who protected her.

Margaret deBeers Brown admires a father who sticks by his pacifist convictions and becomes a conscientious objector, doing alternative service in the United States during the war. His Quaker principles have important repercussions for his own career and the life of his family, but they make him a hero for his daughter long after World War II is over. The spare nature of her writing reflects perhaps her identification with the Quakerly ideal of "plain speech."

Hugh Field's father may have been an American spy. His uncle almost certainly was. The disappearance of both into the political prisons of postwar communist Europe is evocative of a Le Carré novel. The Cold War tensions and fears of another war in Europe affect the families of Christine Tanz, Matthew Stolper, Peter Katzlberger, and Mathea Falco, but none so profoundly as they do Hugh Field's family, waiting in England, hoping for years for his father's release. Even more than he allows himself to explore, readers may wonder how the mysteries about his father's activities, the absence of his father for five years, and the strain on his mother contributed to the marked difference he describes between the curious little boy he was originally and the adult he became.

Max Gitter provides the book's most extreme example of the way war tosses people about like flotsam and jetsam in a violent and capricious political sea.

In 1939, when the Nazis invaded Poland from the west and the Soviets from the east, his very young and uneducated parents were deported to work camps in Siberia. Freed by the Soviets as an incidental consequence of treaties with the Allies, his parents arrived at last in Uzbekistan, where they met and married and where Max Gitter was born. After the war they made their way across Europe, spending arduous postwar years in displaced persons camps in Germany, until immigration to the United States was possible.

Goh Cheng Teik, the son of ethnic Chinese parents, tells of surviving the years of Japanese occupation in Malaya, the long-term racial and political consequences of that occupation, and his own resolve to address such wrongs through his career in the independent nation of Malaysia.

The German Jewish family of Howard Gardner devoted enough group effort to escaping the tightening noose of the Nuremberg Laws to ensure that most of his relatives escaped the Nazis, landing in places all over the world. In contrast to the earlier essay of Nancy Blackmun who, although neither a Jew nor a refugee, becomes obsessed with the Holocaust, Howard Gardner deliberately shields himself from it, pursuing a career that explores the mind, but retreating from feelings connected with violence and death, protecting himself from the trauma.

It has been said that war is like nothing else, compelling beyond ordinary experience. William McConahey provides a glimpse into the addictive aspects of war, not just for a father who was a battalion surgeon during the landings in Normandy and the Allied march across Europe, but for his children and his grandchildren as well. Caught up in patriotism and his father's primary experiences during war, William McConahey gives little voice to other complexities of his own life and feelings.

The section concludes with the contribution of Charles Styron, speaking for all proud sons of military fathers, as he tells his father's favorite war stories, literal parables, each illustrating a moral that has been taken into the son's own life. His deep admiration for his father, a combat physician in the Pacific theater, and his identification with his father, contrast markedly with the mixed feelings toward parents in some of the other essays. As the book's only Southerner, after more than a century since the Civil War in the United States, Charles Styron, like Peter Katzlberger and Kazuko Ihara, also makes us mindful of the vanquished.

Coventry Cathedral ruins after the bombing of 14 November, 1940.

BOMBS AND BRAMBLES

Anthony Graham-White

> Born: January 8, 1940
> Tolworth, Surrey, England

I came to the United States in 1961. Sometime in the late 1970s my stomach stopped making a belly dive every time I heard a factory siren. I spent the war in Coventry, England, a city where the motor-car factories had switched to making armaments and planes, a city ringed by railway lines that outlined the target for bombers, a city so heavily bombed that Churchill tried to introduce the verb *to coventrate*, meaning 'to devastate a city by bombing.'

My parents had been engaged to marry for a number of years before the war. My father had the old-fashioned idea that he should not marry until he could support a wife, which was likely to be a long way off for an apprentice at a furniture store earning £1.50 a month. It was clear, however, that a war was coming, and my mother pushed him into marriage. I was born January 8, 1940, in Croydon, a suburb of London. In the following months my mother found it hard to bear my father's late arrivals home on trains that were constantly delayed. A friend got my father a job in Coventry and my parents moved there.

My mother also got my father to resign from the Royal Honourable Artillery Company, in which he was, I suppose, a reservist. Nevertheless, with the outbreak of war my father rushed to its headquarters, only to be told that every member had already been forwarded as officers to different units and that the headquarters was closing down. Trying to enlist in the army, he was rejected on medical grounds. He spent his nights throughout the war as an air-raid warden – no sinecure. Of that I remember only the stiffness of his uniform and the heaviness of his boots.

We lived toward the edge of town. There were two semi-detached houses on the corner of a street that was otherwise undeveloped. After each air raid we would go out onto the wasteland next to our house and pull out of the bramble bushes strips of tin foil that the German bombers had dropped to confuse the radar. I remember my pride as a drawer in my father's desk filled up. He would then take the tin foil somewhere for Allied bombers to drop over German cities, where little boys would collect it ...

Nightly bombing sent us hurrying into our backyard bomb shelter. Our neighbors, all five of them, were killed when a bomb fell directly on their shelter. I remember nothing of that. An incendiary bomb burnt itself out in our garden. Of that I remember that my father used its burnt-out shell for years to prop the front gate open.

My mother used to have to go downtown and queue for cod liver oil for her baby, me. I remember seeing rubble in the streets and looking up at rooms open to the sky because the fronts of the buildings had been neatly sliced away, as though some mad designer was putting on exhibition the dreariness of people's wallpaper and furniture choices. I think I remember smoke coming up from bombed buildings, but I could be transporting that smoke from newsreels to the images from my personal life.

That wasteland next to us was a boon. My father raised chickens and geese on it. Passers-by would run to our door to tell my mother that her baby was being attacked by 15 geese – protected, more likely. I remember the awful day I watched my father kill, with a hand-chop to the back of the neck, one of the rabbits we kept in the garden. He turned so white that I have always wondered who killed the geese at Christmas time. I am sure it was not him. The chickens remained – I remember plucked feathers falling into a big hip bath in the kitchen – but the geese and rabbits were not replaced.

By D-Day I was reading. I remember the excitement of the newspaper every day, of seeing the arrows of different thicknesses and lengths that diagrammed the progress of the war. I would replay yesterday's events with my toy soldiers, on the carpet in winter, among the blackcurrant bushes in summer. My miniature war was much tidier than the breakout from Normandy, which killed two of my uncles (missing in action forever), or the action at Arnhem in Holland, as distant to me as Arnhem Land in Australia. From the Arnhem disaster in September 1944 I retain the odd and unexplained image of my godfather, returned thence, lying full-length on our dining-room table, his paratrooper's beret folded under his head, staring at the ceiling. I remember the bonfires and fireworks of V-J Day, but no celebration of the end of the fighting in Europe.

Surrenders and treaties end wars, but *wartime* in a child's memory is not so easily stopped. The German prisoners of war I saw neatly marching down the road – to work in the fields, I think – as I had so often seen British platoons march before, were they during or after the war? I remember a car trip to somewhere, made as difficult for us as it was meant to be for the Germans by the removal of all signposts. Was that during or after the war? Another trip was to Dover just after the war. The beaches had concrete blocks with sharp iron stakes facing France and coils of barbed wire between them. On the cliffs were papier-mâché or plaster guns under camouflage netting. Some of these decoys were crumbling, whether from cross-Channel shelling or from the lack of the need to maintain them I do not know. Dover was an odd choice for a holiday at that time; perhaps there was a sentimental reason why my parents chose it. From just after the war, too, I remember Churchill driving in an open car through Coventry during the election campaign. My first political memory is of seeing grammar-school students running out across the road to surround and boo him.

War's end was associated with food. One day my mother saw a queue outside a shop, ran to join it without knowing what it was for, and brought home oranges, one for each of us. My first banana was also an event. Most wondrous, however, was a strawberry sundae, on that trip to Dover. In some ways wartime did not end until rationing ceased in 1952.

Just as I had read about the war in the newspapers, after it was over I read about it in picture histories that, I suppose, had been rushed into print. I remember lying on the lawn, singing out the captions below the pictures in a triumphal mood. When I trumpeted, "soldiers marching to Dunkirk," my mother called me into the kitchen and gave me a graphic description of the evacuation from Dunkirk in 1940. She must have felt that there was something indecent in my calling out the name so happily. If not before, from that moment I was a pacifist. I would later work with the Campaign for Nuclear Disarmament and, after coming to the United States, with the New England Committee for Nonviolent Action and with college peace groups.

My experiences from World War II, even those from the first years of my life, remain vivid. I remember the oddity of hearing it discussed as an event in past history in a college course. (Now I teach at a university and my students would probably place it in the eighteenth – meaning nineteenth – century.) Am I shorter than others in my family because of wartime food shortages? Am I a very light sleeper because of those nights when we ran to the air-raid shelter? During the fiftieth-anniversary celebrations of D-Day in 1994, I often awoke when, in my nightmares, I heard bombers. I can hear sirens now without an instant physiological reaction, but the occasional searchlights that new stores rent to attract people to their openings suggest no celebration to me.

My father died during the Gulf War, after many months in a nursing home with both Parkinson's and Alzheimer's.

> Thin as a ghost
> this ghost of a man
> down the corridor
> shuffles and stumbles,
> tells the doctor
> he's reporting for duty
> if he will tell him
> what in this war
> his duty is.

May putting all this down on paper help to put such hauntings behind me.

But that time is not yet, it seems. After writing that sentence, I had a nightmare in which I was the only survivor of a massacre of the inhabitants of a small island, carried out by storm troopers. The island was not, of course, Britain. It was off the coast of Bosnia.

Bombed building in East Berlin, January 1961.

LIFE GOES ON

Klaus Peter Katzlberger

> Born: November 11, 1942
> Lorch, Württemberg, Germany

My wartime memories are shaped by family and place. They conjure up for me images of age-old village life in Lorch, Germany, when life was static and the village was the only real world there was. It is almost incredible now to think of my life in these terms. Yet the feeling runs true. And on reflection, it makes sense.

Peter Katzlberger on the remains of a war-damaged building in 1949.

In Germany life before the war was still very much bound up in traditional ways, especially in small towns. For a few more years, the war and its aftermath forced a return to basics. In those difficult times the family was the best means of survival and the best way to achieve recovery. The town or village provided social and economic support. Besides, it was nearly impossible to go anyplace, and there was little reason to travel in any case. The ingredients were in place for a return to village life. An extended family existed in the town and surrounding villages. The town itself had traditionally played an important role, real and symbolic.

Lorch and its surrounding villages and farms had a population of about 3,500. It filled the needs of the community, and it had a history. The town was the current manifestation of human habitation which went back, visibly, at least 2,000 years. The *Rathaus*, the town hall, was built on top of a Roman encampment, and children still played in the ruins of Roman watchtowers. The medieval Hohenstauffen rulers of Bavaria originated in this part of the country, and some were buried in the local monastery.

My childhood world had a radius of about 15 miles. For the most part it was much less than that, and only very rarely did it go beyond. Life's activities – family, work, school, play – took place within a very small geographic area. The most impressive place in that world was the larger town of Schwäbisch Gmünd, some six miles away. It had a population of about 25,000. Whatever our small town did not have, could be had in Schwäbisch Gmünd. The size of my world was determined by walking distances and mindset. Walking was the way of getting around, even after the railroad was finally repaired.

The local church was one of the biggest buildings in town, maybe the biggest after the school. The church tower was certainly the tallest structure. The clocks in each of its four walls and the bells calling every quarter hour regulated life's pace. Walking out of sight of the church tower put a journey in the long category and brought on a feeling of straying from home. Even the trip to our apple orchard a few miles out of town took on aspects of an adventure. Seeing the church tower for the first time on returning from a trip brought on a sense of relief. The limits of my world in those years have become evident to me in visits I have made in recent years, when I have seen for the first time places that were but minutes away by car. After a moment's consideration, I have started a car and driven to places that would, in the old days, have been considered outlandishly far away.

The most intriguing place outside of my own village world was America. The occupying Americans, called *Amis* in colloquial German, were a presence and subjects of curiosity. They were different. They exuded well-being. They looked well fed and well clothed, and they smelled positively clean. They had trucks and equipment in abundance, and they chewed gum and handed out Hershey bars. Visits to the garrison and to the apartment of the American family for whom my aunt worked gave glimpses of life in America. It seemed a wondrous place. The mystery of the country was magnified by fantasies of the Wild West and Indians.

Whereas the war initially shrank my world, it would later expand it. In 1958 my mother and I emigrated to the United States. The war had been traumatic for my mother. She was caught up in situations out of her control and suffered greatly as a result. The prospect of further war after 1945 seemed very real in the saber rattling of the United States and the Soviet Union during the Cold War. It was a given that the conflict between the East and West would be acted out on German soil. My mother wanted to avoid repeating the experience of war, especially for me.

One of my most impressive memories on arriving in America was the sense of immense distances. All of a sudden a few hundred miles seemed the same as a dozen did in the old country. I remember a sociology class in college. The instructor was from California. He told the most fanciful stories about how far people would drive for the most ordinary purposes.

My mother was the oldest of five children. Her father had died from wounds inflicted during World War I. Her mother remarried. My step-grandfather was a traditional German head of household, authoritarian and rather distant. Grandfather was the caretaker of the local schoolhouse. The family lived on the third floor. This living arrangement had its peculiarities. Because I frequently stayed with my grandparents, I went to school by going downstairs. It also meant living in a semi-public building.

My mother graduated from teacher's college in 1939, trained to teach home economics and physical education. The school system assigned teaching positions, and she was sent to teach in southern Germany. Already the war had begun, and male teachers had been drafted into the army. The school system stayed in touch with absent teachers by designating contact teachers in their former schools. Often other teachers, mostly women, would add personal notes to be included along with the correspondence sent by the contact teacher.

This is how Mutti met the man who would become her husband, my father, a history teacher. He was in the infantry, stationed on occupation duty in France. He wrote back to her and visited on his next leave. This was in 1940. They stayed in touch through letters when my mother was transferred closer to her family's home. In the fall of 1941, my father received a three-month leave in order to teach and prepare for a master's examination. He was able to find a position near my mother's work. My parents married in December 1941. After his three-month leave, in early 1942, my father was ordered to the Russian front. He was held up in Poland for a time. This period allowed him to invite his wife for a visit. She stayed with him for two weeks. This is where my life began. After returning from Poland, my mother started to work in Lorch because she was pregnant and that was a reason to be able to live near her parents. She taught home economics in the new school in Lorch.

After Poland, my father was sent to the Russian front and saw action in numerous places including Kiev and the battlefields near Moscow. He was wounded in early 1944 and allowed to come home on leave, for the only time since he had been in Poland. A few weeks later he returned to the eastern front. The army was in retreat, pushed westward, back toward Germany, by the Russians. My mother received his last letter on her birthday in January 1945. It was mailed from somewhere near Warsaw in the final days before the German army evacuated that city and the Russians took it over. This was the last my mother heard of my father.

The Nazi Party was extremely effective in insinuating itself into everyday German life in the 1930s. My mother remembers the party takeover at the grass-

Peter Katzlberger and his father, October 1943.

roots level. A party organization was established in each community, including Lorch. Party leaders, now that they held power in government, had the leverage to make sure that community activities conformed to party directives. It was not surprising that big shots, men who already held power in the community, jumped on the Nazi bandwagon. The party set up *Sturmabteilung* groups, the SA, the Brownshirts. Young men especially were pressured to join these storm troopers. Most of them did. The party used fear and bullying to get people to join and otherwise to support party programs. The implied threat was that if you didn't go along, your family might be harmed economically, socially, or even physically.

Apparently many people in town joined the party, otherwise nonmembership would not have been such a stigma. My grandfather did not join. As caretaker of the school, he was something of a public figure in his small town. It must have been important for the local party officials to see him in the fold. To ridicule and humiliate him into joining, he was put on the hood of a car and paraded around town. A schoolmate who had become a big shot in the party may have saved him from going to prison. My grandfather's reluctance to join the Nazi Party may also have had something to do with his being drafted and sent to Norway. Men of his age were not drafted into service until later in the war. During his absence, my grandmother took over his job of maintaining the schoolhouse, a job that, as a practical matter, they had shared in the past.

The party coerced the local population into support. Families had to house and feed SA men visiting from out of town. A fundraising scheme called for every family to cook a simple dinner of leftovers once a month and to donate to the party the money saved by not preparing a more elaborate meal. My grandmother would not go along with the meal idea, but she felt pressured to give the SA a few marks.

My mother belonged to the Bund deutscher Mädel (the 'League of German Girls'), the BdM, during her school years in the 1930s. All girls belonged. It was part of school and it was mandatory. On Saturdays, instead of going to school, she went to the BdM. The meetings involved two hours of brainwashing and two hours of sports. Indoctrination consisted of instruction on the goodness of Hitler, the importance of supporting Hitler, and the superiority of the Aryan race. My mother does not remember extensive discussion of Jews, but remembers being told not to frequent Jewish stores. She does not recall Jews living in Lorch, but there were several Jewish-owned stores in Schwäbisch Gmünd. Everybody liked playing sports, so the BdM became a matter of taking the bad with the good. The principal of my mother's school asked her to inform on her parents regarding any antigovernment comments. He promised free university schooling. But she could not tell him anything.

After the war there were no Nazis to be found. Many burned their uniforms and went on with civilian life. Many of the Nazi big shots transformed themselves and became big shots in the postwar order. This was possible because in the small town the social order of those who ran things and ordinary people remained intact.

Rationing was already in place when Mutti started her first job teaching home economics, which required food and materials as teaching supplies. They were hard to come by and often of inferior quality. As the war progressed, the civilian population encountered increasingly hard times. People living in rural areas were better off than city dwellers, because many were able to keep gardens and supplement their allotted food rations. Around 1944, the civilian food ration might consist of one egg per month per person, 400 grams of meat (including bone), 500 grams of margarine, 250 grams of sugar, and some flour each month, with milk only for children. Each family was allotted about a hundred pounds of coal a month. It had to be picked up at the train station and people waited hours for it. To make the coal last longer, it was wrapped in wet newspaper before burning.

Everything was blacked out at night. Completely dark. My mother remembers more and more airplanes flying over. Probably bombers. Almost nightly the family would have to gather up and head for the air-raid shelter. My mother spent a lot of time at my grandmother's. The old schoolhouse had a very deep and well-built cellar. In time the air raids occurred in daylight. When the alarm was sounded, the teachers had to lead their classes into the basement. Because there were no able-bodied men in town, the women had to dig a tunnel for a bomb shelter. They heard the bombers going to targets in bigger cities. The

Peter Katzlberger and his parents together for the last time, summer 1944.

largest city in the area was Stuttgart, which was being heavily bombed because of the airplane factories there. My mother could see the flares released over Stuttgart and could feel the reverberation of the bombing, some 25 miles away.

Letters from the front hinted at food shortages and inadequate clothing in the extreme cold. The food situation was desperate, but the army gave the soldiers alcohol before they went into battle. My mother's youngest brother was 16 when he was drafted with his classmates to man antiaircraft guns in Stuttgart. My mother and her sisters occasionally were able to save some food and take it to him. They could take the train only part way and then had to walk. When the Americans advanced, his unit was moved. Many of the unit were killed when a bridge near Ulm was bombed with these young soldiers on it.

Air raids included dive bombers. My mother recalled an attack by a dive bomber when she and her mother were working in the garden. She threw me in a ditch and jumped in on top of me. A similar incident occurred when they were tending their apple trees in another part of town. Refugees from eastern Germany arrived in Lorch near the end of the war, mostly fleeing from the Russian troops in the east. Many pulled hand-drawn carts or had wagons pulled by oxen. Camps were set up for some. Others were quartered with families in the town. Near the end of the war, Lorch was bombed and six houses destroyed. As conditions became more chaotic, school was suspended, and the schoolhouse was occupied by German troops.

Finally American tanks arrived and took up positions in front of the schoolhouse. My family now became even more directly involved with the events of war. They and German soldiers were hiding in the cellar. An American soldier called down to come out, or else they would throw grenades in the cellar. They all came out and the German soldiers surrendered. The Americans took valuables from the German soldiers, threw the rest of their equipment out of the windows, and established their own quarters in the schoolhouse. They took whatever household goods they wanted, including parts of the piano and curtains, which they used to clean rifles. Mutti pleaded to be allowed to keep my father's violin.

My grandparents had to move out of the schoolhouse. This experience was repeated periodically for over a year. One contingent of American GIs would vacate the building, and my grandparents could move back in. When another unit needed quarters, they would reoccupy the schoolhouse for a time. Each time my grandparents had to move out. Usually they stayed with my mother. Although evicted, the family still had chores to do at the schoolhouse. My grandmother needed to take care of some parts of the building, and a garden behind the building needed tending. This work could not be done unsupervised. An armed soldier would watch as gardening or other maintenance work was done.

This contact with the Americans was not without its benefits. My mother would often take me along to the schoolhouse and her small child apparently evoked some sympathy. American soldiers would occasionally give food rations and candy to the family. Americans used the home-economics classroom kitchen as their own. They would throw their coffee grounds down the drain. The plumbing system delivered the grounds to a sink on the outside of the building. From there the local citizens, struggling with food shortages, would recycle the grounds through their own coffee pots.

The war ended, but it was not finished for my mother. She had no word about what had become of her husband. This was a time of anguish for her. Life around her was in shambles, existence was a chore, and her future was uncertain. The silence surrounding the fate of soldiers lost in the retreat from Russia was total. She was not alone in her plight. But whereas the town or village provided comfort in everyday life, it provided little in the way of emotional support.

Whether a soldier is dead or declared a prisoner of war, certainty provides a point of departure for repairing the loss and emotional damage of his family. It allows for grieving, accepting, going on. Uncertainty suspends the ability to deal with the matter, puts the future in limbo, and raises hopes which may be dashed. Often again and again. Emotions are on a rollercoaster. He could come home tomorrow. Other soldiers do. But he never does. Being "lost" is worse than dead. My father simply disappeared, as an artifact might vanish. No place or time provides a context for when or where or how. No context for his emotions at the time. There is no dignity in simply being "lost."

My mother tried to find out the fate of her husband. Clearinghouses had been established to trace the whereabouts or fate of soldiers. Soon after the war radio programs began reciting the names and units of prisoners and of soldiers killed, as they became known through aid agencies or from returning prisoners. This became an ongoing hope-raising, hope-dashing ritual on Sunday nights. Occasionally the announcement of a returning soldier would prompt contacts to determine if more could be found out about his unit.

Finally, in 1948, my mother made contact with a man who had known my father in the war. He told her that their army unit had been surrounded by Russians and only six soldiers survived the battle. So my father was probably killed. But it is not certain. Many soldiers who surrendered were deported to prisoner-of-war camps in Russia without a word of their fate. Mutti wrote many letters to find out what had happened to her husband. She even wrote the Pope. At some point, as a political gesture, the Russians let large numbers of prisoners go. Prisoners returning from Russian camps were normally transported to processing centers. Families were then informed. Returning soldiers would arrive by train and their families would meet them at the station. My mother would regularly go to the train station in the vain hope that her husband would arrive unannounced. The walk back home must have been difficult, especially when she saw other wives' prayers fulfilled.

This was a period of isolation, loneliness, and hopelessness. It was a time of struggle from day to day. People wanted to get on with their lives. They focused on themselves and their families. As the oldest child in her family, my mother had added responsibilities for her siblings. She had to give support, rather than receive it. Everyone had to do their part, as the social order had expected all along. Most profoundly, Mutti lost a husband with whom she was just beginning to undertake life's journey. The village could not help with this loss. It was good at helping with the mechanics of life, but could not deal with the pain of the soul.

When he returned from the war, my grandfather resumed his schoolhouse maintenance duties. Because he had contacts with farmers in the surrounding countryside, he was able to get some food. Occasionally when a farmer butchered a pig, my grandfather would return with a few pounds of meat. The whole family would then sit around the kitchen table and cut up strips of fat, to be rendered into lard. The bacon-like leftovers were a tasty treat. This ordinary event is one of the vivid vignettes I remember of the everyday struggle to make do. Days in the garden turning the soil and planting vegetables became memorable. Hiking in the woods in search of berries or mushrooms evoked mixed feelings of hardship and pleasure.

Without a yardstick, for me life simply was. Without a reference, I could not judge my degree of deprivation or satisfaction. The family nurtured me and loved me. Walking to local farms with Grandfather may have been a difficult journey for him, but for me it was an adventure. Making toys out of clay or tree bark was an opportunity for creativity and pleasure, not an indication of poverty or want. It was a pleasure to find the best clay or the thickest bark that made the best carved boat.

My mother's struggle to come to terms with the unknown fate of my father was apparent to me. This uncertainty set her apart from people who had all the pieces of the puzzle and were in the process of putting them back together. It allowed for a special and closer relationship between the two of us. In part she was acting out her husband's admonition: "You can lose everything, but take care of my son."

Americans, the "Amis," occupied our part of Germany. Schwäbisch Gmünd was a garrison town and the Amis were ubiquitous. Their military convoys were long, and slowly snaked down the steep road into the valley of the Rems River where our town was located, making an incredible racket, both because of their numbers and the backfiring occasioned by the steep downgrade. My aunt who worked for an American family at the garrison in Schwäbisch Gmünd was a seamstress and she also did some housework. This gave her access to some food and transportation. I remember a few visits to this American home. It was exotic in its smell and furnishings. Peanut butter was unlike anything I had ever eaten before.

As occupying troops, the Amis were well mannered, although it seemed they had a superior bearing. This had its advantages in that the soldiers would condescendingly toss chewing gum and chocolate bars at the kids. At one time

I was the proud owner not just of a candy bar, but of a whole box of Hershey bars. It was a dilemma. Like a mint set of coins or stamps, the box seemed worth more unopened and whole. As time passed, the Amis were helpful in that they contributed to improvement projects and participated in public events. We invited American soldiers to our Christmas celebrations.

As the Cold War took shape, there was a fear that a new war was not far away. We were afraid of being pawns in the global confrontation between the East and West, between free countries and controlled countries, between democracies and communism. The specter of atomic warfare was real and the images graphic. The local Communist Party maintained a display board on a wall near the local train station. I passed it every day once I was old enough to start going to the Gymnasium in nearby Schwäbisch Gmünd. On it were pasted pages from the communist newspaper. A prominent feature was the places where "wars of liberation" were taking place, including Korea and Vietnam when it was still a French-Vietnamese fight. I have clear recollections of the long struggle before Dien Bien Phu was captured by the communists. The confrontation over Berlin, the East German uprising, and other conflicts made the possibility of a new war real. Hungary in 1956 was a particularly dramatic event. It had a powerful impact in part because of the extensive news coverage. It was such a fearsome event that it contributed to my mother's decision to emigrate to the United States, in order to get herself and, especially, me away from another awful war. She was keenly aware that before long I would be of an age to be drafted into the army.

The sanctuary of the new country did not come without a price. Where before Mutti was an experienced and respected teacher, now she would have to start over again to establish herself, often doing work below her qualifications. In order to teach, she had to earn credentials which she had already earned years ago and "acquire" skills which she had practiced for years. The emotional price for having left Lorch was equally high. The village had not fully served her in the old country, but it had given her a context within which to cope. The new country was foreign in so many respects. The separation from the old country was great. We made the journey by ship. Unlike today with its rapid air travel, the distance then meant that the old town was gone, out of reach. There were no markers or bearings to guide the new experience. Everyday living skills had to be learned for the first time.

I encountered silence about the experiences of the war years. My mother was also not forthcoming about the difficulties of coping with life in the new country. I think the reason lies in the difficulty of conveying feelings. How can words express the pain and alienation felt? Words paint a stickfigure picture. If you have not shared the same experiences and felt the same anguish, how can you understand how it was?

I have asked my mother how it was possible to be, to live, in those days. How do you put the war years in a place that allows you still to function, and how do you deal with a life that still seems to be interrupted by the loss of a husband whose fate will never be known? I think she has strong feelings, but the easiest answer is that life goes on.

Peter Katzlberger and his mother in 1952 on the steps of the school in Lorch, where his grandparents were caretakers.

The mouth of death: entrance to Auschwitz – Birkenau, 1993.

SILENCE

Ursula Oppens

>Born: February 2, 1944
>New York City, New York, U.S.A.

Working on this essay finally gave me the obligation and the opportunity to ask questions that I had avoided for more than 50 years. Although I was more or less aware of some of the facts about my relatives' deaths and the Holocaust in general, my knowledge was enveloped in vagueness. My parents' strongest concern during my childhood was to shield me from the horror that they knew about. Only once, about 15 years ago, did I directly ask my father to tell me what he knew about his own father's death at Auschwitz, but he begged me not to continue, saying it was too painful for him.

My parents came to the United States in 1938. I never met any of my grandparents. When my father was 11, his mother committed suicide, and his father was later killed in Auschwitz. My mother's father died of natural causes at home in Kluges, the small town where he lived near Budapest, during the war. Her mother, however, was deported to Auschwitz when 400,000 Hungarian Jews were sent to be exterminated in the concentration camps in a six-week period in 1944.

Through the great generosity of my mother's uncle, who sponsored them, my parents obtained a visa to emigrate to the United States in 1938. Throughout his life this uncle continued to help all the relatives who had survived the Holocaust and wanted to leave Eastern Europe after the war. This uncle and his family in New York were almost our only relatives who lived in the United States. Despite his generosity, and despite the tiny number of family members who survived the war, my mother developed a truly nonsensical hatred of her uncle's wife. My father also had a sister in America, but her family was also dismissed during my youth. So I grew up with even less family than Hitler and history had allowed us. My father frequently explained such irrational behavior on my mother's part as being the result of "survivor guilt." To that extent, even though we almost never talked directly about what had happened to the rest of our family, the events were never far away.

On both sides of the family, my American cousins and I have chosen to become friends despite our parents' distance. Now even my mother is finally becoming closer to her relatives. I am also very grateful to be friends with my only cousin on my father's side, the child of his sister whose family had also been rejected.

I have realized as I worked on this essay that my own lifelong hesitation – in fact, inability – to talk about very personal matters is probably the direct result of growing up in an environment where the most important family events could not be discussed. I know very little about my grandparents, for example, because one could not talk about them without thinking of their end.

I have thought deeply about this question of silence in our family during this last year. I was able to ask newly met Israeli cousins and friends about it. They answered that silence is not a problem in Israel. There is an official national Holocaust Remembrance Day, but Israelis say that they can also talk openly about the Holocaust more generally. It is not a taboo subject at home or in public life. I imagine this is because Israelis feel they are building a new future and fighting anti-Semitism, not running away from it.

In the winter of 1997 I asked my mother to tell me what she knew or remembered of her family. The conversation came about somewhat by chance. I made longhand notes, but I did not write them up fully immediately. A few months later my parents and I went to Hungary together to celebrate the eighty-fifth birthday of my mother's sister Ella. Ella had been in Auschwitz with my grandmother. I realized that my mother and her sister had never talked about their mother's fate before our visit to Hungary, when my mother said, "They threw her alive into the fire," and Ella countered, "No, no, they gassed her first." This was apparently the first time she could ask her sister what had happened in the camp.

After we returned, I asked my mother again to talk to me about her family. This time I was prepared with a tape recorder. My mother's account of my grandmother's death was different from what it had been the previous winter. To my surprise my mother was glad to talk, finally wanting very much for me to know my history. This is what my mother, Edith Oppens, said. I am transcribing her words as she spoke, to let her voice be heard directly after so much silence:

> The beginning is that I know it from my sister [Ella]. That our mother, your grandmother, was deported from Budapest in 1944 with her sister Steffi, both to Auschwitz. My mother was totally paralyzed. She was taken right away to the gas chambers. Her sister Steffi had blood poisoning, gangrene in her legs. She was begging they should cut off her legs because she was in terrible pain, but they didn't. When my sister Ella, who is a doctor, wanted to visit [Steffi] the next morning, [she found that Steffi] was taken away to the gas chambers.
>
> The two children of Ella were taken away right away from her when she arrived and [they] were taken to the gas chambers. All my relatives which were taken there were taken to the gas chambers. Cousins were shot. My sister's husband, a doctor who would normally have been kept alive to help out, was shot because he was in an uprising against the horrible conditions of the prisoners.
>
> My sister [Ella] came home after the Russians liberated her. She came

home partly on foot, partly on wagons. She came home to Budapest and she finished her medical studies and became also a surgeon. She was a pediatrician, but she also studied surgery.

My two uncles were "saved." They died in bed before Auschwitz. My father died before Auschwitz, before my mother was taken away. The other sister of my mother, who was a physician, and her husband, [who] was also a physician, tried to commit suicide. Twice they woke up, but the third time they succeeded. There were 52 cousins of which 19 remained.

Two uncles could escape to Switzerland with the Wallenberg mission. My uncle Hillel was taken to Buchenwald because he was a communist leader. He survived and died in Romania in 1972. And all my other cousins, my aunts, my father's sister, my father's brother, were taken to Auschwitz and shot. This was all in Kluges. They were deported right away.

My family escaped much too late. I came with [your father] Kurt to Trieste in 1938 and to America. And Ella had no visa for America.

Your father's father was deported from Hamburg. His second wife, [a gentile], denounced him to the Gestapo, telling them that he was Jewish, although he didn't wear the yellow star. He was also taken to Auschwitz. He had almost starved to death – they found him trying to salvage the liver from a corpse – but then he was gassed. He had been a *Reichsfinanzrat*.

Your father's grandmother, the mother of his mother, was taken to Theresienstadt, and she died in Theresienstadt. On the other hand, the brother of his mother joined the Nazis in Spain. There were so many mixed things. Some Jews were declared non-Jews, so [your father's] uncle joined the Nazis.

My mother's sister Ella, who had been in Auschwitz and lost her children, her husband, her mother, her Aunt Steffi, and most of the rest of her family, spent the rest of her life as a doctor in charge of a home for foster children. Having seen so much death, she became responsible for the well-being of hundreds of unwanted little children. She has an adopted family of her own and is much loved. There was a truly grand celebration of her eighty-fifth birthday. She is, as far as I can tell, the sanest person I know.

The thoughts and conversations on these subjects during this past year have changed my life.

Interior of a prisoners' barracks,
Auschwitz-Birkenau, 1993.

HIDING IN THE OPEN

Christine Tanz
(born Krystyna Maria Szwienczicka)

> Born: September 27, 1944
> Warsaw, Poland

My parents' story

CRACOW

My parents were born in Cracow, my father, Henryk Tanz, in 1911, my mother, Regina Wiernicka, in 1913. Cracow was a large and cosmopolitan city. While Jews lived mostly in their own district, Kazymiersz, named after the king who had opened Poland's doors to them in 1492, there was a degree of integration between Jews and non-Jews, at least in comparison with other pockets of Eastern Europe. And although there were Jewish quotas at the university, my father was able to attend the law school there. His older brother Cesiek, who wanted to study medicine, was excluded by the quota and had to go to school in Prague instead.

At the university there was a seasonal ritual. Every spring members of the right-wing fraternity would assault members of the Jewish fraternity and battles would break out between them. The Jewish fraternity would dispatch someone to enlist help from the socialist fraternity and the socialists would join in the fray.

On September 1, 1939, when Hitler invaded Poland, my father went west to join his army regiment, moving against a tide of people streaming east, away from the front. When he got there, he discovered the regiment had been disbanded. He turned around to go home, this time traveling *with* the human tide. On the way home he came to a conclusion: under the circumstances there was only one thing to do and that was to get married. Now or maybe never.

The idea had struck many other people as well. There was an epidemic of couples wanting to get married right away. The marriage license office was mobbed and half the personnel were missing. Complete administrative chaos. My father sat down at a typewriter and filled out a form for himself and my mother and then stayed at his post to do the same for the lines of people waiting. On September 4 they were married. This was the first time. By the time the war was over, they would have been married four times (and never divorced).

Why am I telling about this minor scene of bureaucratic mayhem? I ask myself. This is how the war was presented to me. This is what I knew about it as a child growing up.

Three months later, the decrees against Jews began. When I assumed power of attorney for my father several years ago, I found some handwritten notes among his records. In December 1939 Jews were required to wear an arm band with a star and they were ordered to register for work. Gold and silver were confiscated. Beginning in January 1940 Jews were not allowed to change their residence or ride on trains.

Sometime in 1940 my parents were required to move to the ghetto. They were given no choice, but initially it was also presented as a privilege. My mother and father and my mother's sister Gustawa were sent to the ghetto. They were all of working age. My mother's parents and her youngest brother Jozef, who was only 16, were sent to a suburb.

THE GHETTO

Eventually, all the Jews of Cracow were herded into the one ghetto. My mother's parents and her brother had to come in from the suburbs. My father's father joined them too. For a brief period they were all together – all those remaining. (Of my mother's two other brothers, one had already been killed and one had fled to the U.S.S.R. My father's brother Cesiek was still in Prague.)

At first the ghetto seemed to be a safe haven, relatively speaking. To be caught outside without proper authorization, such as a work permit, was to be subject to immediate arrest and deportation, or to be shot in the street. But gradually it began to appear that the security of the ghetto was an illusion. Although my mother was a warm and loving woman, she was not self-revealing and never talked about what happened during the war. Except once. I don't remember when she told me this, or what prompted it, but she remembered looking out the window of their ghetto apartment and seeing an old woman shot, her brain and eye spattering against the brick wall of the adjacent house.

Sometime after this my parents took the first of many steps that preserved their lives. They decided to leave the ghetto.

There were a number of factors in their background that made it conceivable for them to venture such a risky move. The first was their appearance. My father was blond and had blue eyes. My mother, although she had dark hair, did not look obviously Jewish. In that milieu, long before the war, all parties had antennae for Jewish identity. Jews recognized Jews, and Poles recognized Jews. (Somehow this awareness was transmitted to me, and to this day, although I know that it is neither adaptive nor politically correct, I find myself registering whether or not a person is Jewish.) Another factor was language. My parents spoke both Yiddish and Polish. But having grown up in the city, in relatively assimilated circles, they spoke a Polish that was free of Yiddish inflections. Without these two preconditions, it is unlikely that they would have taken the chance of leaving. With them there was at least a possibility that they would not be detected right away.

My father also had the advantage of speaking German. During World War I his family fled Cracow and took refuge in Vienna. He started school there and became fluent in German. As a result he could understand the enemy. It is one of the many ironies of his life that this first experience of flight and dislocation in his early childhood helped prepare him in such a straightforward and pragmatic way to survive the next one 25 years later.

There was also the matter of age. My father was 28 at the outbreak of war, my mother 26. They had perhaps the ideal combination of youth and maturity to be able to make their way. They were adults; they were healthy and strong; they were unencumbered by children. My father also happened to be a man of imposing physical strength. Although that in itself was not of much use against the encroaching perils, I think it helped confer on him a level of confidence which *was* enormously useful.

My father managed to forge false I.D. papers. Actually he prepared some for every member of the family. I don't know exactly how he accomplished this except that there was an underground network that helped supply materials and information for such documents. New identities couldn't just be fabricated. They had to have corroborating records of birth on file with municipalities. The best documents used the name of someone who had been born about the same time as the pretender to the identity, but had died young.

My father became Jan Wojtas. My mother remained Regina Wiernicka. That name was sufficiently Polish (i.e., not Jewish) to be usable. They got married again in order to have a wedding certificate that matched their current identities.

With their appearance, their language, and their documents in place, the question was where to go? They couldn't stay in Cracow. Too many people knew them. They would have been too easy to spot. Even before the war Warsaw was the largest population center. Now, swollen with the influx of displaced people from all over Poland, it might be able to absorb them without too much notice.

So they took the train to Warsaw. They sat in the same railroad car, but didn't sit together. In fact they sat at opposite ends. They maintained this stratagem for the duration of the war. They never walked together. They reasoned that each one of them individually could pass as a non-Jew. But the data of their two physiognomies combined, along with subtle impressions about how they communicated, might yield too many clues. They would be more likely to fall under suspicion.

WARSAW

In Warsaw they rented a room. They tried to make a living and they tried to stay alive. At first they survived on a small sum of money they brought with them. Even when he wasn't working, my father would leave home at a regular hour in the morning – to make it appear *as though* he were going to work. How did work go on under conditions of war? This is something I wonder about now. I have no idea. I never asked.

Eventually their money dwindled. My father came up with a scheme to sell paper supplies. He was familiar with the paper industry in Cracow, but couldn't go there in person to transact any business. Fortunately my mother's brother Jozef, now 18 years old, had escaped the ghetto and joined my parents in Warsaw. So my father sent Jozef, who was just a kid and not known in the Cracow community, to various manufacturers to buy cigarette paper, writing paper, postcards, greeting cards. Jozef was supposed to say he'd been sent by an old classmate of theirs, a certain "Szwienczicki" (who was of course not Jewish). They would sometimes ask why Szwienczicki didn't come down himself. The reply was that he was too busy. Usually Jozef was able to come back with the merchandise, and he and my father would sell it to shops in Warsaw. Their biggest sellers were saints' day cards. People celebrated on the day of the saint they were named after rather than on their birthday. And even in wartime there was a brisk business in the cards. To this day my Uncle Jozef remembers the dates of all three of the saints' days associated with their three sets of false names.

The danger of being discovered was constant. It came from the Gestapo, from the Polish police, and from civilian informers. Once a man stopped my father on the street. "I know you," he said. "You're a Jew." My father drew back his fist and punched him, knocking him to the ground. A crowd gathered. My father, "irate," told them, with disgust, "He said I was a Jew!" and walked away.

This was my father's archetypal story. He told it to my brother and me many times. I have told it to my son Philippe. Once when he was in third grade and his class was reading *Number the Stars*, a book about the resistance in Denmark by Lois Lowry, I went to school to tell them about his grandparents' experiences. I began the story about the encounter on the street. One of the kids piped up and finished it for me! Philippe had told the story to his friends. My son turned 8 the year my father turned 80. He knew my father mostly as a frail and confused old man. So I was overjoyed to discover that he had absorbed this heroic tale about his grandfather and made it his own.

Another time in Warsaw my mother was at the train station, waiting for her brother to arrive. Suddenly several men materialized and surrounded her. My father was there too, at his usual distance of 50 feet. In this case their stratagem gave him a chance to observe first. He approached the knot of people, offered a bribe, and whisked her away.

My father said there were always informers and denouncers. Some were motivated by hatred, but others were just trying to make a profit. A bribe could sometimes get rid of the latter. But you never knew if they would come back later. Every time my parents had a threatening encounter, they would move again. They never allowed themselves to rest in the mere hope of being secure.

My comprehension of their tenacity in holding on to life continues to unfold even now. I had mute testimony to their determination and shrewdness a few years ago when I was sorting through a drawer and found a small box containing my mother's jewelry. Inside I found her wedding ring. I set it on my

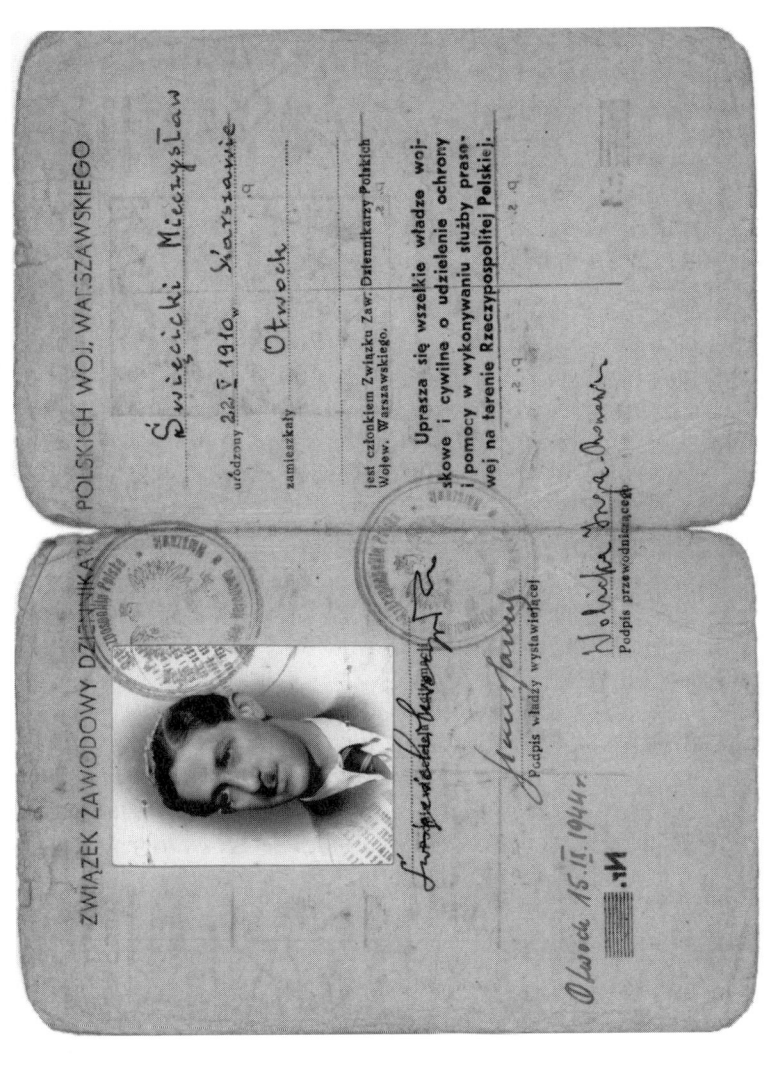

Forged identity papers of Christine Tanz's father, showing his last assumed name.

finger next to my own and when I showed it to my son, he, then a sharp-eyed 12-year-old, exclaimed, "There's writing in it! M ... L ... 24 V 41. Twenty-four versus forty-one." Of course it was not 24 *versus* 41, as he thought, but rather a date: 24 May 1941. As for the initials, *M.L.*, they were a mystery. I wondered if the ring initially belonged to someone else. But when I inspected it more carefully, I realized that the delicately engraved *L* was not an *L*, but an *S*, written in a European cursive style my son was not familiar with. *M.S.* were the initials of my father's final pseudonym: Mieczysław Szwienczicki. My parents had had the ring engraved to corroborate their new identities. How strange to discover this so long after the fact and after my mother was gone, and to contemplate anew the care with which they staged their deception, their attention to detail matching their bravado. Later it occurred to me to inspect the inside of my father's ring. There I found the same date and the name Urzsula, my mother's last false name.

When my parents moved to Warsaw, their families stayed behind in Cracow. There were their three parents, my mother's sister, and Jozef, her one remaining brother. My father had prepared false documents for them too, and they agonized about trying to make the move. But for the older people, the immediate dangers of leaving seemed too enormous, and so they lingered.

Their apartment overlooked an entrance to the ghetto. My Uncle Jozef tells me how one night at 2 a.m. they heard the tramp of marching boots. Peering through the window they could make out the preparations for an *Aktion*, a brutal roundup of Jews for arrest and deportation. My uncle had built a false ceiling under the roof, a place where they could hide. There they kept water and bread and pillows. His parents and sister retreated into the hiding place. But he, a fleet 18-year-old, accustomed to leaving the ghetto "officially" for a job at the post office outside and even to sneaking out through barbed wire and broken glass to see a movie, managed to slip away. When he came back to reconnoiter in the afternoon of the same day, he was elated. Usually an *Aktion* lasted for several days, but this time the Germans were already gone. He rushed eagerly to the apartment. There was nobody there. He never saw them again. My mother and father had never told me this story. Just recently, only two years ago, my uncle told me, "They took my parents 28 October 1942." I had no idea that anyone knew the date.

I had been reading Leni Yahil's *The Holocaust: The Fate of European Jewry*, a wrenching book that talks about the millions killed with great particularity – 998 people, to be exact, on one transport, 532 on another, and so forth. The book proceeds, month by month, community by community, sweeping across the whole of Europe, trying in some sense to cover everything. I searched for information about what happened in Cracow on October 28, 1942, and learned that 6,000 people were taken away that day and sent to Bełzec. The final *Aktion* in the ghetto, the liquidation, now familiar from scenes in *Schindler's List*, took place five months later, on March 13, 1943.

Christine Tanz and her mother in 1946.

It was a shock to be sitting alone in my house in Tucson, Arizona, 50 years later and suddenly to get this small shard of knowledge about what became of them. In a sense it was learning nothing. Somehow I had never even heard of Bełzec, one of the six death camps of the Third Reich, along with Auschwitz, Sobibor, Treblinka, Majdanek, and Chelmno, all of them in Poland. And I knew no more than I did before about how they were killed or what they underwent on the way. But pinning their disappearance to a time and place was electrifying.

I didn't tell my father about my discovery. Over his last 10 years, he slowly lost his mental capacities, and I didn't talk about these things with him. I didn't tell my uncle, either. Once I heard him say in a trembling voice that he hoped they were taken to Auschwitz, which was very close to Cracow, where they would have died quickly. I didn't want to disabuse him of that hope. And in fact, although Bełzec began as a labor camp, by 1942 it had become a death camp, so maybe their deaths came quickly anyway.

After a short interval, my Uncle Jozef fled to Warsaw, joined my parents, and remained with them for the rest of the war.

Sometime during my parents' time in Warsaw, they were able to establish contact with my father's older brother, Cesiek, who had had to go to Prague for medical school and was arrested there and sent to Sobibor. This is still a great mystery to me. How could a message from outside find its way to an inmate? How could an inmate get a message out? I think the communication system turned on payments to people in the surrounding countryside, a promise of a bicycle or some other commodity. But even if that mystery is solved, an even greater one remains. How did they discover where to send their messages? How did my father know that Cesiek was in that camp? Or if the first message went in the other direction, how did Cesiek know where to find my father under his false identity in Warsaw? Somehow, inexplicably, the connection was made, and my father urged his brother to get out of the camp in any way possible and join them.

My Uncle Cesiek was a man of great personal charm. The story goes that one of the camp commanders at Sobibor was a Ukrainian who had with him an entourage of relatives. One of them, his sister, fell in love with Cesiek. The officer was in the practice of holding seances to communicate with spirits and this gave Cesiek an opportunity. He entered into a conspiracy with the officer's sister. They plotted that during an upcoming seance she would see a vision of her dead mother (also the officer's mother), who would decree that her son must let my uncle go. The mother "appeared," the officer complied, and Cesiek was released.

He was able to make his way to Warsaw and find my parents, who took him in and hid him, expanding their little group to four. They were of course in hiding themselves, but they hid themselves out in the open. They hid Cesiek more drastically, not allowing him to be seen or heard until he could strip himself of any tell-tale markers that might arouse suspicion. Although he was fluent in Polish, his years in medical school in Czechoslovakia had contaminated his speech. Little, heedless interjections such as the "yes, yes" that marks assent as one follows a conversation, were coming out in Czech rather than Polish. "*Ano, ano,*" he would say, instead of "*tak, tak.*" Only after he managed to rid himself of these expressions did they all agree that he could surface.

My parents must have been in Warsaw during the Ghetto Uprising in April 1943, but they never talked about it. When I asked my Uncle Jozef more recently about those events, he recalled passing the ghetto on a trolley, seeing columns of smoke rising everywhere and a woman on the balcony of a burning building dropping two children over the railing. Someone on the trolley remarked, "It's good to see so many lice get burned up." The fact that my parents never talked about the Ghetto Uprising is consistent with how they reported their war experiences in general. They didn't tell us stories about what happened to other people, and the stories they told about themselves, with perhaps one exception, were stories of triumphant escape. It is too late for me to find out whether that was a deliberate decision for the sake of my brother and me, or whether it was my father's spontaneous way of constructing the narrative of his life.

In retrospect it seems that there was a tacit conspiracy among all of us. My parents protected my brother and me by telling us fragments and nothing more, and my brother and I protected our parents – and ourselves – by not asking for additional information. We never talked about the people who had disappeared, or sorrow or loss or thwarted ambitions or bitterness. In a way, we grew up in a setting that served as a paradigm of love, an encompassing love, without communication.

But the reasons for silence may not all have been tied to family dynamics. The wider culture promoted silence too. Nowadays, Holocaust survivors almost have celebrity status, but it wasn't always so. One of my parents' widowed friends always turned me down when I offered to bring her to commemorative activities in recent years. She harbored so much anger about the years after they arrived in the U.S., when no one wanted to hear what had happened to them.

One evening in Warsaw six Polish police officers appeared at the door of my parents' apartment. They said they were looking for a Jew. They'd been told there was one living there. My father told them he was not a Jew. "Not *only* am I not a Jew," he said, "I am with the underground army." "I am an officer," he continued, returning their threat. They asked for his documents. "Why do you want to see my documents? Anybody can have fake documents! Just take a look inside my pants."

In Poland, at that time, every Jew was circumcised, and no non-Jew. Neither a false I.D., nor Aryan looks, nor standard Polish, nor all three combined could counter the evidence of circumcision, so the bluff seems totally reckless, except for an astonishing truth. Sometime during the war, my father had had a surgical procedure performed, an operation to disguise the fact that he was circumcised. My father once told me a little about his operation. He described waiting in a room, alert but calm. The surgeon who came in the door was someone he recognized. At the university this man had been among the worst of the hooligans, a perennial instigator of attacks against the Jewish fraternity.

After the incident with the Polish officers, my parents felt they could no longer remain in their apartment. They didn't feel safe staying in Warsaw. They announced to their landlady that with the weather so unbearably hot, they would be going on a short vacation in the country. They acted as though they were leaving for just a while and would be back soon. They made their way across the Vistula to Otwock, on the east side of the river, and rented a room from a peasant.

Christine Tanz with her father (seated), Uncle Jozef, and her mother, 1946.

While they were on "vacation" the Warsaw insurrection erupted in August 1944, this time the revolt of the Polish resistance against the German army. Living as a Pole with a Polish I.D. had ceased to be protection. There were Nazi roundups and shipments of Poles. Hundreds of thousands of them were deported and killed. Warsaw was leveled. From their safe vantage in Otwock across the river, my parents could see the smoke rising. The visit by the six police officers had turned out to be a blessing in disguise.

When I saw *Schindler's List*, my first reaction was that it was an odd choice for a Holocaust narrative, a story with the most improbable turns of events, a story with a "happy ending." The women were sent to Auschwitz by mistake! They were released after already having been "processed." They were saved from the very jaws of death. But then I realized that *everyone* who survived must have experienced these impossible twists of fate.

It is estimated that about 300,000 Polish Jews survived the war out of a prewar total of 3,300,000. Three million (90 percent) perished. I've now read many memoirs of survivors, but few analyses of who survived. In *Survivors of the Holocaust in Poland*, Lucjan Dobroszycki divides the survivors into three basic groups: people who survived in Poland "on the Aryan side," either living "openly" with false identification or in hiding, including children who were hidden by Christians; people who survived the concentration camps or labor camps; and people who survived in the "depths of the U.S.S.R." The survivors were skewed in age. There were very few elderly people and very few children. The book brought this home to me in a startling way when it proceeded, its brief generalizations complete, to *itemize* the children who survived, giving the name of each one known, the date and place of their birth, the names of their parents if known, and their last known address. My parents matched the age profile of survivors, but they were exceptions to the generalization that most survivors were single. They were among the very few who managed to survive together. Not only that, but they managed to add one to the postwar Jewish population.

ŚRÓDBORÓW (IN-THE-WOODS)

My mother had already been pregnant twice during the war, but survival seemed impossible with a baby. Both times she had an abortion. Then she became pregnant again, this time with me. My parents liked to tell me that right away they began deliberating about what to do. They listened to a contraband radio and took out contraband maps. They drew the positions of the fronts and tracked the advancing Russian army. My uncle recalls that my father declared, "This baby will be born in freedom." He was not entirely right, but remarkably close. The war wasn't over, but they had managed to get outside the zone of German occupation.

When my mother went into labor, my parents set out for help. They were on foot, stumbling through potato fields in the no man's land between

German-occupied Warsaw and the Russian lines on the east side of the river outside the city. Shells were flying overhead. The Russian army stayed put throughout the insurrection to let the Germans and the Poles fight it out, reducing the numbers of both the German Wehrmacht and the Polish resistance with whom they would have to contend later.

Christine Tanz with her parents, free and safe in Gdansk,
January 1946.

My parents met a man with a horse and buggy. He agreed to give them a ride to a little hospital, a TB sanatorium in the tiny hamlet of Śródborów, 'In-the-Woods,' that had been converted into a Russian field hospital. A military doctor delivered me without incident. My skin was very dark when I was born. My parents used to tell me that the nurses all came in to admire my coloring. But it wouldn't have been the right complexion for a Polish baby. The date was September 27, 1944. The doctor asked my parents if they knew what day it was. They didn't. He told them it was Yom Kippur. In addition to the relief of a safe birth, there was the extraordinary sensation of having been recognized without an immediate threat implied. The doctor was a Russian Jew.

In *Children of the Holocaust*, Helen Epstein writes that children of survivors always have a story to their name. Never selected merely because it is pleasant sounding, it is usually the name of someone who was murdered. The name my parents gave me was Krystyna Maria Szwienczicka. *Krystyna* was the most Christian of given names. *Maria* was the name of both of my grandmothers, but of course it was also the name of Jesus's mother. *Szwienczicka*, the feminine form of their last false identity, is a name derived from the word *saint*.

GDANSK

When the war ended, my parents made their way to Gdansk. My father had the prospect of becoming the representative of a pen factory there and of working for the government to begin the reconstruction of industry in the northern sector of Poland. In the meantime he took over an old flour mill and began to use it to produce varnish. My parents prospered. My first memories are set in Gdansk. We had a house on a hill. We had a goat. I had a buggy and a sled. My brother Mark was born. We have photographs from those years, taken with a newly acquired camera, recording the beginnings of the new life. Images of the old life had of course all disappeared. In the photographs we look radiant.

Even so, there was continuing insecurity. My parents were budding entrepreneurs with a communist regime consolidating itself around them. They were in an environment that was still hostile to Jews. In 1946 there was a pogrom in the Polish city of Kielce. Although the war was over, my father and uncle were still Szwienczicki and Sczigielski. But my parents didn't want my brother and me to grow up not knowing we were Jews and absorbing the ambient anti-Semitism only to discover later that we were. And then, in the jostling of political forces as Soviet control of Poland was consolidated, my father began to experience pressures to be an informer. Informing was something he was unwilling to do. The feeling crystallized that they would have to leave again, and along with it the sense that if they didn't leave soon, it would be too late. In fact by the time they decided, normal channels of emigration had closed. But a friend from university days, Josef Cyrankiewicz, a man who used to rally the socialist fraternity to come to the aid of the Jewish fraternity when the fascist fraternity attacked, was now the prime minister. My father went to him for authorization, and that was how we were able, in 1948, in the nick of time, to slip through the Iron Curtain and leave Poland behind. It was not until this final moment, when they were arranging the documents for their departure, that they dropped their false names and reclaimed their true identities.

FRANCE
From Gdansk we went to France, settling first in Paris, and then Enghiens-les-Bains, a suburb known for its gambling casino. We lived on money my parents brought from Poland in the upholstery of a chair. It was very fortunate for us that that crate of furniture arrived. The money gave my father some time to learn French, but even after he could speak passably, he had a hard time finding a job. It was easier to learn French than to get a French work permit. Although he was not by temperament a gambler, he began occasionally to go to the casino and somehow managed to extract an income from it that allowed us to get by a little longer.

Jozef came to France with my parents and Cesiek joined them later, but as the Korean War intensified, my father thought that the Soviet Union might invade Western Europe and began to cast about for yet another refuge. My parents wanted to come to the United States, but in their status as "refugees of Polish origin under the administrative protection of the International Refugee Organization," they were unable to get visas. Australia, however, was willing to take us, and Australia was certainly far enough away from the travails of Europe. But my parents were reluctant to go all the way to "the other side of the world," worrying that such a huge distance might preclude their ever returning. Since no alternative presented itself, however, they decided to go ahead. They packed our belongings in crates and shipped them to Australia and prepared to follow. Somehow, at the last minute, visas to the U.S. came through and the move to Australia was canceled. We were never reunited with our crates, and one of the puzzles of my childhood, carrying with it intimations of yet another alternative life, was to wonder who was drinking out of our teacups. In October 1951 we boarded a ship called the *Liberté* and set out for New York.

The Soviet invasion never came. This was the only time I am aware of that my parents' precautionary flight turned out to be unwarranted – the single false positive. There were, of course, no false negatives. Although Cesiek lived on until the early 1970s, he and my father never saw each other again. My father's estimation of the feasibility of returning to Europe turned out to be wrong too.

Cesiek and his wife remained in France for the rest of their lives, living in Paris, on the edge of poverty, but relishing their Bohemian existence. They had a motorcycle, and, when time allowed, they would hop on it and head for the south of France. When I visited them for the first time, I was able to witness the spectacle of this man in his late fifties carrying his motorcycle up a flight of stairs to keep it safe. Cesiek died a few years later during my second visit, suddenly collapsing in front of me, leaving only the motorcycle and a long manuscript, now in my hands, about his life during the war.

NEW YORK
I actually remember arriving in New York at the age of seven in 1951, looking through a porthole at the gray November sky and sea, and seeing the Statue of Liberty (also gray). At immigration an official asked my father, or so he thought, whether he was a truck driver. He said yes with alacrity, thinking that if the U.S. government wanted him to drive a truck, he would be happy to oblige. Actually the man was asking an entirely different question, the then-obligatory, "Are you now or have you ever been a communist?" with which new arrivals were greeted. Filtering this through his imperfect French and his almost nonexistent English, my father took it to be, "Are you a camion-iste?" (*camion* meaning 'truck' in French). Somehow the error got sorted out and there were no dire consequences. This was the one story of all the stories about the war and immigration that was pure comic relief.

New York was a struggle for all of us. My father found a job for one dollar an hour and had to commute an hour each way. For me New York was walls – the walls of the buildings and the walls of incomprehension that surrounded me at school.

Not long after our arrival, at the advanced age of four years, my brother was circumcised. It was part of my family's reclaiming of our identity as Jews. I was seven years old. My parents didn't change my name.

Lured by better job prospects, after less than a year we moved to Chicago. We were happy to discover that it felt almost rural compared with Manhattan, and we stayed.

MY STORY
Usually, when I have had occasion to tell my story as a child of the war, I have told my parents' story – a string of heroic episodes, each one polished by many retellings – our own private epic. In that rendition "my story" ends with my birth. When I try to come to grips with how my life has actually been shaped by this history, I find myself with a more inchoate narrative. To begin with, it was not a subject of discussion. I didn't talk about it with my parents or my contemporaries. Probably kids don't talk about those kinds of things anyway, but beyond that, I never knew anyone my age with the same background.

All of my parents' close friends were Polish Jews who had survived the war. They had the bonds of their youth in Poland, their war experience, their adaptation as immigrants, their language. Holocaust survivors recognized each other and flocked together. But all of *their* children were younger than me. Some of my parents' friends had had children before the war, but those children had died. All of the living children of this small circle of people were born after the war and were several years younger than me. Now, of course, we would have many things to say to each other, but the community is scattered.

Back then the gap of three or four years precluded the discovery of what we had in common.

Unlike their parents, children of the Holocaust have no way to recognize each other. It was startling to discover at my college reunion 30 years later that there had been so many of us in my college Class. As a participant in a panel discussion on the subject of being born during the war, I sat there dumbfounded as I realized that although I knew every single one of the people on the panel whose story was a Holocaust story, I had not known in any of the cases that we had this background in common. The lack of opportunity to reflect on this experience with others who shared it and the failure to recognize the opportunity when it did exist have made it harder for me to develop a perspective on how it shaped my life.

Probably the most profound effect is that my family was always extraordinarily close, extraordinarily devoted to each other. We seldom had company at home and my parents never went anywhere without my brother and me. We spent our time together. When I went off to college, I took the bus all the way from Chicago to Cambridge, Massachusetts. My family took me to the Greyhound station. Everyone came – my mother, my father, my brother, and even our boarder, that year a student from Pakistan. Then the car followed me to Indiana, with all of us, them and me, waving and crying.

I never went through the compulsory rebellion of an American coming-of-age. And I remember suffering some sneers from college friends for the degree of my attachment to my parents. The literature on children of the Holocaust notes this as one of the outcomes. In my case it derived partly from my admiration for my parents. I was never subject to the feeling that afflicts (and liberates) American adolescents, that I knew more than my parents did in any fundamental way. They had been right over and over again. They managed to survive, they managed to make a new life, they managed to keep our lives from being shadowed by bitterness and terror. I also felt a great deal of protectiveness towards my parents. How could I add to the pain they had suffered? And I think I was influenced by the extended experience of being an intermediary between my parents and their new world. I learned English before they did and in the beginning there were many occasions when I would translate for them. Later I would be their connection to the world of work. When I went to college, my mother took her first and only job – teaching at a preschool run by my best friend's mother.

I participated, whether passively or actively, in my father's getting his first and his last jobs after we left Poland. In France, as our money dwindled and his continuing efforts to get a work permit yielded no results, in desperation he came up with a scheme. He took me with him – I must have been five or six years old – and went to the Ministry of Labor. There he announced, displaying me as evidence, that he was the father of two children, that he was unable to go on without a way to earn a living, and that if they did not give him a work permit, he would celebrate the upcoming two-thousandth anniversary of the founding of Paris by jumping off the Eiffel Tower. He got the work permit.

In the U.S., following the route of so many Jewish immigrants, my father found work in the garment industry. Coming from Paris, he billed himself as a "couturier" and got a job as a dress-cutter. Apart from some brief forays outside it, for example when he sold Electrolux vacuum cleaners door-to-door, he remained in the garment industry for the rest of his working life, moving through a series of cutting jobs and eventually doing white-collar work for a manufacturer of children's clothing. When that company was sold and liquidated, he found himself, in his late fifties, out of work again. Then he got his last job, this time in the men's clothing department of a catalogue distributor, through the family of a college friend of mine. Being a party to these vicissitudes influenced the nature of my relationship with my parents, putting the emphasis more on our common fate and less on the polarity of generations.

In Chicago my father commuted to work by bus. The bus stop was right below our apartment window. Every day, when the time approached for him to come home, my mother would station herself by the window. I can still see her, elbows resting on the sill, chin resting on her hands, forehead pressed against the pane. If he was a few minutes late, she would begin to get nervous. I took it for granted that all wives and mothers would react this way. As more minutes passed, her anxiety would grow – and seep into me. I remember afternoons in Chicago when I was nine or ten and I would retreat to the bathroom to negotiate with God, promising to be good (forever), if only he would let my father come back.

Here I saw the fears of the war crystallized, although I didn't realize then that that was what I was seeing. It seemed entirely normal to agonize over a few minutes of tardiness, even though the hazard my father was facing was merely heavy traffic on Lake Shore Drive. Anxiety at separation was the one great fear of my childhood. Apart from that I think I was as venturesome as other kids.

The deaths of my grandparents and aunts and uncles before I was born had a paradoxical effect on me, which I recognized only when my mother died in 1989. These wartime murders of my relatives insulated me from death. My mother's death was my first. Her grave is the first of our burial places whose location we know.

Until her death when I was 45, I had never been close to anyone who was dying. The fabric of generations had been torn and I was cut off from exposure to the basic cycles of life. I never experienced a grandmother or grandfather getting old and dying. I never saw my parents mourn. I never experienced an older cousin growing up, getting married, having a baby. I think it contributed to an illusion of being suspended in time and frozen in the primordial role of child to my parents. We were one mother, one father, one daughter, and one son, a symmetrical crystalline form, moving through space and time.

The parents of Christine Tanz in their Gdansk living room, 1947.

A later effect of our relative isolation has been a longing for extended family ties that I don't always feel, but that regularly surfaces under special circumstances. When I came to Tucson as a professor in the psychology department, I didn't know anyone. During the first week, at a lunch for new faculty members, the person next to me looked at my name tag and said, "Oh, you must be related to Dr. Tanz." I promptly looked him up in the phonebook. We met, and I was overjoyed to discover, through links to various people and places, that we were almost certainly relatives. I'm not a superstitious or credulous person, and know that a coincidence is just a coincidence, but it gave me a shiver to learn that he had a daughter my age and a son my brother's age, that his daughter, like me, was a professor, and his son, like my brother, a doctor, whose name was identical to my father's. (And as it turned out, the son had even gone to the same distant college as I!) The serendipitous parallels magnified the precious feeling of relatedness. Even recently I found myself writing to a woman with the same last name, whom I came across as the illustrator of a children's book about the desert. I suppose I should learn that it's an odd and maybe even a suspect thing to do from the fact that she didn't bother to answer me, even though I offered the title of my own children's book by way of credentials. But the impulse is very strong. My brother has always spontaneously pursued the same quest, going out of his way to track down any Tanz who has come across his path.

My husband shares with me certain aspects of my background. Jean-Paul was born and raised in Belgium, and grew up speaking French. He has memories of the war that are more direct than mine, being old enough to have experienced the Nazi occupation, the deportation of his Jewish pediatrician, food shortages, and the bombing of a neighbor's home. He came to the United States after finishing medical school in Brussels and working as a doctor for three years in Africa.

I sometimes wonder how much of my experience and my orientation to life is the result of my family's particular Holocaust history, how much simply the effect of being an immigrant, and how much might have been as it is anyway. But trying to make sense of my own life with the added burden of being trained as a social scientist, I find myself looking for a control group. Because he's there, my hapless husband is unwittingly cast in that role. He is a European immigrant, but not Jewish and not a refugee.

The world *is* getting smaller and we are able to visit Jean-Paul's family in Brussels almost every year. Until his mother died, we would always stay in the house where he was born. On our visits he would go get a sentimental haircut from his father's barber and now he takes our son there for a yearly haircut, too. It strikes me with great force whenever we are in Belgium that despite the rupture caused by his emigration, there is still such an enormous amount of continuity in his life.

EFFECTS ON MY CAREER

I have sometimes wished I had had contact with more adults as a child and adolescent for the sake of being able to imagine a greater range of adult lives for myself. The only future I could happily picture was a continuation of my life in school and this certainly propelled me toward an academic career. School was infinitely preferable to my father's tedious jobs and my mother's solitary life at home waiting for us to return at the end of each day. Although the beginning of school was painful because I couldn't speak or understand, that obstacle was quickly overcome and I loved every one of my five very nondescript elementary schools. When it came time for high school, I wanted to go to the local public school, but my father wanted me to go to the private high school at the neighboring University of Chicago. He orchestrated that outcome from two directions, taking me for walks on campus to convince me that it was a wonderful place and convincing the school to give me a scholarship. And in fact I am one of the very few people I know who will admit to having loved high school. After college I went back "home" to the University of Chicago for a Ph.D. Exposure to people who do all kinds of work and live all kinds of lives has been one of the things I've consciously tried to provide for our son. We have a stream of interesting people coming through our house, but (the best laid plans of mice and moms!) our son has no interest in them.

My wandering childhood probably had a role in my career direction within the academic framework. Polish was my first language, but I started school in France without speaking any French. At the age of seven, I went into second grade in New York without speaking any English. Continuing through high school, college, and even into graduate school, I didn't have a clear idea of what I wanted to do, other than stay "in school," but the field that finally captured my imagination was the study of how children learn to talk. I got my Ph.D. in psychology, specializing in developmental psycholinguistics, and went on to teach and do research in that subject.

NATURE

Nature was a constant companion in our life as a family, perhaps taking the place of other people. We always went for drives out to the "country" and for walks. One of my earliest memories is of my father crouching down to my level and pointing out to me the shadow of a wintry, leafless tree on a wall. He opened up my eyes. He was tireless (and sometimes even tiresome) in drawing our attention to the scenery as we passed. Sometimes I've wondered if he turned to the landscape for escape from society and for solace from the losses in his life, but on the other hand maybe he would have loved the sky, the lake, the mountains anyway. Maybe that was just his nature, and not the stamp of the war upon him. And maybe it is another injustice of the war that we are tempted to let it usurp all causality and construe it as the prime mover in every aspect of people's lives forever after.

RETURN TO POLAND

My parents never did return to Europe. Although they didn't reject the idea of going, time and money simply didn't allow. In 1966, a year after graduating from college, I went back for the first time. It was the proverbial "Grand Tour" (writ small), hopping through half a dozen countries in the company of a college friend. But I wanted to visit Poland, too, drawn by curiosity and an undefined sense of affinity. My parents had never transmitted to me a general hatred of Poland. My friend and I parted company, and I went alone. Stepping off the train in Warsaw, I had a sudden epiphany – a vision of the world divided into

Christine Tanz with her mother and brother, Paris, 1948-49.

two sets of people, those who were at that very moment in the place of their birth and those who were not.

People were very welcoming to me everywhere in Poland. As a young woman coming from America and traveling alone, I seemed to elicit interest and sympathy everywhere. Of course Poland wasn't overrun with American tourists like Western Europe. Nevertheless I was surprised that strangers invited me to their homes. In Cracow, over my objections, a woman insisted on giving me a little "piece of Poland," a salt carving from the mines at Wieliczka that she extracted from her small son. In Gdansk a young man escorted me to the university to help me find a room. He couldn't get over the fact that I could still speak Polish or that I knew some old Polish songs. He wanted to show me around the city and to introduce me to his circle of friends. All these offers were abruptly withdrawn when he found out I was Jewish. After that I never saw him again. So in my brief visit, I discovered that Polish hospitality and Polish anti-Semitism were both still intact.

On one of my excursions through the countryside, my train stopped at a quiet little station where the railroad sign read "Oświęcim." It was only later on the trip that it dawned on me that was where Auschwitz was, that that in fact *was* "Auschwitz" in Polish, a place that had been just a small rural village before its name was engraved on the world's consciousness in its German form, and that was a small village once again. It had not yet become a place of pilgrimage. I was bewildered that I had passed through ignorantly, without awareness.

LIVING IN THE UNITED STATES

I have always been profoundly moved by the way cultures rub shoulders in the United States. My son has attended public magnet schools in Tucson, where we live. In our school system the "magnets" are instruments of desegregation. In sixth grade Philippe's class participated in a program called History Alive. Kids chose an event or person in history and over a period of two months prepared elaborate reports or dramatic presentations on them. There were reports on the Holocaust and some were by Hispanic kids. And there were reports on Cesar Chavez by kids who weren't Hispanic. One of my son's classmates, a boy who was learning how to play the bagpipe, composed a song for bagpipe commemorating the victims of the Holocaust. It was very touching to see these 11-year-olds imaginatively engaged in the sufferings and triumphs of people not their own.

In 1995, as part of the fiftieth-anniversary commemorations of the end of the war that swept the country, there was a traveling exhibit from the Anne Frank Center in Amsterdam at our Jewish Community Center. I volunteered to be a docent. Kids came on school field trips from every strand of Tucson life – from the Mormon community of St. David, from the army base in Sierra Vista, from the Tohono O'odham (formerly Papago) Reservation. That same summer I visited the Holocaust Museum in Washington for the first time. At the end of the day, I was walking out the door feeling drained and full of sorrow, but my heart lifted when I saw a large group of Amish families and reflected on how they had ventured out of their insular community to learn about the fate of another beleaguered people. Nothing stirs me like these melting-pot experiences. Though it's evident that this country has severe racial and ethnic schisms, I still find so much cause for hope in these pervasive efforts of mainstream institutions to overcome them.

My family's history has given me a peculiar slant on mobility in American life. It first occurred to me when I was in graduate school back in Chicago, looking at a map of the world on the wall, and pinning my college friends on it in my mind. One was in India, one in England, others almost as far away – for all practical purposes – in New York and California. It dawned on me then that in the United States wealth and the abundance of opportunities bring about conditions that used to be brought about by war and other catastrophes. Everyone had scattered.

A series of voluntary exiles replaced imposed exiles in my life, starting with going away a thousand miles to college. Returning to Chicago for graduate school only confirmed that you can't go home again; after four years all of my close high school friends were gone. My first academic job took me to Champaign, Illinois, where I didn't know anybody, and my second one to Tucson, where the same was true. The experience of being new in so many places has left a lasting impact. Tucson has been home to me longer than any other place I've lived, 23 years, but I still feel like a newcomer, and it seems likely that I always will. I now see college in its American incarnation as preparation for leaving people behind as much as for anything else, especially the elite colleges that draw students from everywhere across the country.

THE END OF MY FATHER'S STORY

My father died in 1998 after a long, slow mental decline of more than 10 years' duration. I was the person in charge of his affairs, making the big decisions and helping with the minute decisions, grieving as I watched his capacities progressively diminish and marveling at what remained. I sometimes thought of this sad process as my continuing education in survival. It offered me another glimpse at ways of being that probably helped my father stay alive when he was young.

For a long time he managed to hide his memory loss from anyone who didn't know him well. His ancient mastery of the bluff now stood him in good stead again. Whenever he had to greet someone, he would look them up and down and then pronounce, "So, you have grown!" This little joke, applicable to anybody, always got a chuckle while it covered up the fact that he had no idea whom he was talking to. During these years he never tired of living and never showed signs of wanting to let go. Perhaps his last act of initiative was to sign up with the dating service at the Jewish Community Center, a gesture that led to his meeting a wonderful 80-year-old woman who became his companion for five years. But eventually almost all initiative was beyond this man of dazzling initiative. I would ask him if he wanted tea or coffee. It was hard for him to decide. "What is more healthy?" he would ask me. The criterion was still to preserve life. He actually enunciated that to me more than once as a principle: "My memory is not good you know and my muscles are not strong anymore. It is not pleasant to register this. But it's better than to die early. So let's hope."

One day, at this stage of measuring out his life in teaspoons, he came out of his room to tell me he was cold. I brought him a cup of tea. He warmed his hands on the cup and then stopped to wonder if it was safe. "It can be dangerous to warm suddenly a body," he told me, in a parody of his once finely tuned sense of danger.

Yet even then there were still flashes of wry humor. "So," he would greet me, "what's new with me?" And there was still a demonstrative tenderness. Even though he wasn't always sure who I was – his granddaughter? (he didn't have any) – his wife? – he would always tell me that he loved me. I thought, observing these qualities in him, that they made the current crisis more bearable, and I imagine that they must also have helped my parents bear the crisis of the war.

The war made itself felt again in my father's last days. In the series of emergencies that preceded his death, when the paramedics would come to take him to the hospital, we learned to ask them to approach quietly, to subdue the boisterous manner of their muscular young manhood, and to remove the trappings that were suggestive of uniforms. Otherwise, drifting back into the past, he would try to fight them off.

After my father died, my brother and I had to answer some routine questions from the funeral home. "How old was he?" the woman on the phone asked. My brother and I both found ourselves hesitating. In this context was it better to use his official birth date or his *real* one? Did it matter? We settled on the real date which made him one year younger than the official date. I'm not sure when in his life the discrepancy arose, under what circumstances it was practical for him to be one year older. "What was his father's name?" the woman continued. Again there was silence at both my end and my brother's end of the phone. Neither one of us was immediately sure. Trying to spare us embarrassment the woman hastened to assure us that it was OK to put "unknown." In fact neither the name nor the identity were unknown to us, but we were confronted again with the fact that what we had was a very remote kind of knowledge. It brought to mind the time my father remarked ruefully that once he knew the names of his wife, his children, and his grandchildren "by heart." My brother's memory is still intact and so (relatively) is mine, but we don't know our grandparents' names by heart.

All his life our father was concerned about the safety of his identification documents. On our annual vacation when my brother and I were little and my family would stay in a rented cabin on a quiet lake somewhere in Wisconsin, my father would carefully hide his wallet under the mattress every night before going to sleep. I vaguely remember that he may have done that at home, too. In the last year and a half, while he lived in an adult care home, his possessions shrinking to his clothes, some framed photographs, and a new recliner, he still gave anxious attention to his "portfolio," as he called the little folder that served as his wallet. When we buried him we included that too, so now he has his driver's license, his credit card, his insurance I.D., and his Golden Age Passport for all eternity.

MY STORY, AGAIN

When I came to college, I was only 16 years old, a few days shy of 17, and the war was 15 years behind. It felt so distant, not a part of my own lifetime. I focused entirely on the fact that it was over and that we were far away from where it had taken place. Now that I am in my fifties and more conscious of the war's ramifications in my life and in the world, it feels so much closer to me. Around me the survivors are dying. The people I know whose identities came to be defined by survival are yielding to death. Their disappearance advances me in the ranks. I feel myself becoming a survivor.

Everybody wants to make a coherent story of their lives. At least the desire is latent and the ritual of college reunions does a lot to activate it. When I think about my story in a detached way, purely as a narrative, it seems to call for an extraordinary resolution, more extraordinary than what I have provided with the text of my real life. And when I consider my good fortune in having been spared and warmly nurtured, then I feel I should be doing more good in the world. Through these questions and doubts, part of me guards the awareness that what I have is not anticlimactic, but the great prize: the privilege of being able to live an ordinary life.

Francis Zebot with his mother and paternal grandparents in Ljubljana, Slovenia, in June 1944. His grandfather, temporarily between internments, died of typhus at Dachau in April 1945.

OUT OF SLOVENIA

Francis L. Zebot

>Born: October 11, 1943
>Ljubljana, Slovenia, Yugoslavia (now Slovenia)

One of the first things about my wartime infancy that I remember learning from my mother was that in April 1945 she pedaled me, barely 18 months old, in the basket of her bicycle, some 50 miles from Ljubljana to Trieste on the Adriatic coast, through a Yugoslavia squeezed between the Nazi German occupation and the communist partisan guerrilla activity led by Tito. Throughout my life I have always found that episode oddly comforting, as if it explains a certain measure of insecurity that has remained with me.

Slovenia is roughly the size of Massachusetts, with a population of about two million homogeneous Southern Slavs, predominantly Roman Catholic since the ninth century. Slovenia has a language similar to Serbo-Croatian. It is blessedly spared the presence of a significant ethnic or religious minority at variance with the majority in a part of the world where that formula has been sanguinary. "Slovenija, the Sunny Side of the Alps," trumpets a T-shirt my kids, Julian and Dinah, have occasionally worn. Its provenance is the solid American Slovenian enclave in Cleveland, Ohio. Julian has said that if he were more entrepreneurially inclined, he would set up a good T-shirt shop at Bled. Bled is the jewel of Slovene tourism, a small blue-green mountain lake where a medieval castle overhangs a tiny islet featuring an ancient church. That Julian is not more entrepreneurially inclined may have something to do with my father's being a professor of economics, the sort who has little practical sense about making money and who is content to pass along the gene. On the other hand, my mother has always seemed able to make the economies that have allowed her to pull money out of a hat, both before and after my father's death.

In her middle seventies, my mother, Ivana Korun Zebot, is a matriarch of the Sloveno-Western world. In her modest widow's home in Washington, D. C., she has provided free lodging to Slovenes visiting the United States from all around the world. The visitors have ranged from old friends scattered by the winds of World War II to political types and the Pope's former travel agent, a Slovenian family friend who moved to Italy after the war and married well. This hospitality she has provided in part because of the reputation of my father, Cyril Zebot, an anticommunist exile who wrote eloquently, early, and often about an independent Slovenia, writing not just in English but mainly in his native tongue, in publications blackmarketed out of Austria into Slovenia in an attempt to influence events. Sadly, he missed seeing the prize, dying painfully of lung cancer about two years before the Soviet collapse and Slovenian independence amid the breakup of Yugoslavia. These were events he deserved to see and savor, even though he certainly would have regretted the ethnic and religious bloodshed in Bosnia and other parts of the former Yugoslavia.

On March 25, 1941, under pressure from Hitler, Yugoslavia signed the Tripartite Pact, giving the Führer his objective: a transportation corridor through Yugoslavia that would assist the Italians in their campaign in Greece and secure Germany's southern flank before its invasion of the Soviet Union. When opposition to the pact led to a putsch by the Serbian military in Belgrade, the capital of Yugoslavia, Hitler responded within two days. On April 6, 1941, without first declaring war, Hitler moved German, Italian, and Hungarian military units into Yugoslavia and had Belgrade bombed by the Luftwaffe. My father was working in Belgrade with the National Bank and narrowly escaped injury or death from the bombing. He was supposed to be evacuated with the Yugoslav government to England on a British submarine, a submarine that never arrived. Hitchhiking and traveling by foot, first along the coast and later inland, he returned after a few weeks to Ljubljana, the capital of Slovenia, where he had attended university.

Meanwhile, his father, Franjo Zebot, a career politician, was the deputy and acting mayor of Maribor, a city in northeastern Slovenia near the Austrian border. Slovenia was divided into German, Italian, and Hungarian occupation zones. The German military took over the city administration in April 1941, and the Gestapo arrested my grandfather, inquiring specifically about my missing father and confiscating some of his personal effects. As part of a general "Germanization" of this corridor to the Adriatic, my grandfather, along with priests, other government officials, and members of the intelligentsia, was shipped to the concentration camp at Dachau, where he languished. He was eventually released, through the intervention of Pope Pius XII, but after a couple of months was rearrested and returned to Dachau, where he died of typhus in April 1945, just before the liberation of that camp by the Allies. The rest of my father's family in Maribor left for Ljubljana, which was in the less repressive Italian occupation zone in the southern part of Slovenia. Only one of my father's sisters remained behind. This was Anka, whose robust tongue cost her a temporary detention in Serbia.

My father arrived back in Ljubljana from Belgrade at the end of April 1941 and was appointed lecturer in economics at the University of Ljubljana. Because the position was unpaid, he also became a consultant to a Slovenian economic board which played a vital role in maintaining agriculture and providing food to the province of Ljubljana. Later he also aided Slovenian refugees flooding into Ljubljana from German-controlled portions of Slovenia. In September 1942, after they had debated the vagaries of war, my father married my mother, a Ljubljana native, whom he had known at university. It was a small ceremony in a bishop's chapel. A nun prepared a lovely meal. I was born in October 1943 in Ljubljana, in my mother's family's house, on the edge of a woods but not far from the center of the city. About the time of my birth, after the fall of Mussolini, Germany moved to take over the Italian occupation zone in southern Slovenia, including Ljubljana. As a student political leader, my father had reason to be concerned about his fate at the hands of the Germans, so within days of my birth he left for Rome, leaving my mother and me behind. When the Germans took Rome, he made arrangements through a highly placed and influential Slovenian Jesuit to take sanctuary in the Vatican.

Being forced into exile was a godsend for a native of a country occupied by Nazi Germans and terrorized by ruthless communist partisans whose eyes were squarely on the future. Those Slovenes whom the Germans perceived to be subversive were sent off, usually not to concentration camps but to forced-labor camps. Hiding behind the label of "Liberation Front," the partisan leadership did its best to conceal its communist intentions. A prime recruiting strategy was killing the occasional German to provoke reprisals that took the form of disproportionate killings of any convenient (usually noncommunist) Slovenes at hand.

In the countryside, early partisan acts of banditry escalated to house burning, torturing (gouging out eyes, cutting off noses, and so forth), and slaughtering teachers, priests, farmers, and others who were perceived as being unsympathetic to communist aims. In the cities, with their greater German presence, the partisans sent out more selective execution squads to murder anticommunist Slovenian leaders. One such was Professor Lambert Ehrlich, a Catholic priest who had organized a strong anticommunist student group at the University of Ljubljana. My father was one of his protégés and regularly served as altar boy for Ehrlich's early daily mass. Fortunately my father slept late the morning of May 26, 1942, when Ehrlich and the altar boy substituting for my father were shot to death outside the church. In his memory I was given "Lambert" as my middle name.

In response to the partisans, some Slovenes formed the Vaske Straze (Village Guards) in the countryside to defend against the marauding. Later, as communist partisan terror increased, a more organized opposition formed as the Domobranci (Home Guards). The Germans embraced them as a sort of native military police and provided them weapons and uniforms. The thrust of the Home Guards was defense against terrorism. They acted as a local police force, but also formed four assault battalions for preemptive purposes. No doubt to most Western observers, the Home Guards appeared to be pro-German, whereas in their own eyes their concerns were local: they happened to share a common enemy, one not of their own making, with the Germans.

By April 1945 my mother had taken me in the bicycle basket with her to Trieste, having had no word of my father, but hoping to meet up with him. The timing was not great. Tito's partisans were about to fight their way into control of the city. Before that happened, fortunately, my father rescued us both. He had finagled himself into a position as interpreter of the French, German, and English languages, working for a Polish colonel who was attached to the British army in Italy. While in the Vatican, my father had befriended a priest from the South Tyrol in the Italian Alps. As a result he located a place where my mother and I could live in a small mountain village, St. Laurencen, with a farm family that had extra space. My mother and I went there, and family photos of myself – little Ferko, as I was called – in St. Laurencen show me in lederhosen in fields with rough-hewn fences, cows, and mountainside shrines. I am told I had run-ins with a cow that gave me a worrisome headbutt and with a large dog that I urged to bite me "later."

When Tito began marching towards Ljubljana in May 1945, just before V-E Day, my parents' families were among a large group of people, many thousands strong, who fled north through the Ljubelj Pass to avoid his destructive path. Working for the Polish colonel meant that my father had access to an automobile. Thus, he was able to travel and track his family down in refugee camps in Austria and Italy. His two sisters, Anka and Dora, and his mother ended up in England. My maternal grandmother and great-grandmother were in separate camps and ended up with my mother and me in St. Laurencen. My great-grandmother managed this by illegally crossing the mountains with a paid guide. She had to try it twice – she was caught the first time and sent back to the refugee camp, but the second time she was successful.

This was a perilous time for Slovenes. The Slovenian refugees in southern Austria and northeastern Italy met troops from the British Eighth Army. The

Francis Zebot in May 1947, with his father and little sister in St. Laurencen in the South Tyrol, just before his family's immigration to the U.S.

British were faced not only with the problem of thousands of Yugoslav refugees, but also with military incursions by partisan units into Austria, where Slovene speakers in the Carinthia region offered a pretext for a larger land grab. The British at this time betrayed between 10,000 and 20,000 Home Guards, together with their women and children, people who had surrendered to the British and were being held at Viktring. By written British Army order, the Home Guards were told that they were being transported to Italy, but in fact they were sent back by train to Slovenia, where they were slaughtered en masse by Tito's partisans in Kocevski rog, Teharje, and the abandoned mines of Trbovlje near Celje.

In Rome, after the end of the war, my father met an American priest from Duquesne University in Pittsburgh, Pennsylvania. Because the GI Bill brought an influx of veterans to American universities, Duquesne, like other schools, was looking for professors. My father left Rome in August 1947 and began teaching economics at Duquesne that fall. In February 1948 my mother, my sister Meta, who had been born in South Tyrol, and I came by boat to New York, where my father met us. Perhaps my earliest memories are associated with that ocean liner: a blur of a flying fish and the vague jab of a vaccination.

Our habitation in Pittsburgh was modest indeed. The four of us were crammed into a single room in another family's house. Apartments were hard to come by after the war. Struggling with English and having to prepare his classes, my father was frazzled at the prospect of our living in that one room. He borrowed some money and sent us off to Long Beach, California, to be with our immigration sponsor, Esther Walton. For four months we shared her bungalow, and some of my earliest memories include the boardwalk, sand, and sailors with tattoos. Eventually my father secured a larger apartment for us in Pittsburgh. My grandmother and great-grandmother came in the summer of 1949 to live with us there. Things only looked up from that point on, including the happy additions of my American-born siblings, Cy and Mana.

My father's career specialization in communist economic systems and his avocation of pursuing Slovenian independence within a Yugoslav framework were both clearly shaped by World War II. He went on to become a professor at Georgetown University in Washington, D. C., where he benefited from being close to the political pulse of the nation and its center of foreign policy.

I'm reluctant to speculate that the war scarred my beginnings, even though my father was much absent and my mother doubtless passed on some of her apprehensions to her infant son. It is easier for me to see that a more formative influence on my reserve and insecurities may lie in my teenage years. My family moved from Pittsburgh to Washington, D. C., just as I was sent off to a posh boarding school, where I was anxious to preserve my full scholarship and had difficulty relating to what I perceived to be spoiled East Coast rich kids. I am not sure, however, that my father would have pushed me into that path but for his own dashed political aspirations in Slovenia, aspirations swept aside by the war. Most of all, however, I think I am impressed with how my parents were not embittered by the wrenching events surrounding the war. That steadfast perseverance remains my legacy.

Nevertheless, the story of my early bicycle trip to Trieste became for me a durable symbol of the complexities of my character. Its importance was so great that I was profoundly shaken to learn more than 50 years after the event, while pressing my mother for details, that her recollection of this seminal event was less than vivid. Recently, while I was visiting my mother in Washington, she told me that she had talked with Ernest Fruman, a Slovenian friend who saw us off when we left Ljubljana for Trieste in April 1945. He told her that he distinctly remembers me waving to him at the train station as we were leaving Ljubljana. Wait a minute. What happened to the bicycle? Fruman usually has a reliable memory, my mother says. But she knows she had the bicycle with her. She knows she used it. She's sure she biked to Postojna, a good way to Trieste. She thinks she took the train from Postojna to Trieste. Maybe she had to take the train briefly to get out of the city, but she does not remember that. Franc Fasun, who accompanied her on the trip and might know for sure, lives in Argentina. But she doesn't have his address.

And if there was no bike, what then? Any retrospective by one born in the war must be as much about the imagination as reality. In the process, what role does memory play and how stable are its concrete details? I think it is important for the human race to try to learn the lessons of Nazism and Communism and to strive mightily to acknowledge the mass atrocities of which it is capable on both sides of the political spectrum. One person, such as my mother, might over time misremember or imagine a detail of an event, especially when caught up in the turmoil of an earthshaking upheaval. That detail may, by chance, develop a life and significance of its own. To the world at large, the presence or absence of the bike is indifferent, but to me it is talismanic. If there was no bike, perhaps there is no excuse for my feeling so insecure.

THE WORM IN THE APPLE

John Dundas

>Born: June 30, 1942
>Perth, Perthshire, Scotland

I was a "war baby." I haven't thought of that phrase for 35 or 40 years. When the term was in current use, in my childhood, I didn't like it. I wasn't a baby anymore and I didn't like being called a baby. But from my earliest awareness I was interested in the war because my father had been in it and, as I now reflect, it is brought home to me that I was and am invested in having been a war baby.

My father was John George Lawrence Dundas, Vice Admiral, Royal Navy, CB, OBE. Jack. Daddy. In 1906 his parents enrolled him at the age of 13 in the Royal Navy College at Dartmouth. He won a prize for reciting Thomas Macaulay's *Lays of Ancient Rome* from memory. He bowled for the school's cricket team. In Riga in 1928 he met my mother, niece of the American minister to the Baltic States. She says that he was funny, thoughtful, and very bright, and that he had an enormous and fond acquaintance through his family and the navy. "Everyone loved Jack," she says. My three older sisters – seven, eight, and thirteen years older than I – still shimmer with love when they remember our father from before the war.

From 1938 to 1940 he was a staff officer in the Admiralty and War Office in a department which planned for future wars. "The easiest job in the navy," his friends in and out of the navy said when he was assigned there. "There's not going to be any war." He had a frantic conviction otherwise. My mother says that from the mid 1930s he knew that war with Hitler was coming, that he was frantic with worry about Britain's unpreparedness, and that he stayed frantic to win the war until it was over. Immediately after the war began, he moved his wife and children from England to rural Scotland to protect us from the Luftwaffe. In the planning office he helped administer the evacuation of the defeated British army – 350,000 men – from Dunkirk back to Britain and thus helped save them so they could fight another day. After that he commanded HMS *Nigeria*, which headed a flotilla and escorted American convoys across the Norwegian and Barents Seas to Murmansk. The *Nigeria* was a new light cruiser, a fast, powerful, state-of-the-art war machine. If they gave him the *Nigeria*, he must have been good. Happily, from the family's point of view, the *Nigeria* was in dry dock for repairs during the battle with the *Bismarck*. My father was frantic to be there. By 1942, when I was born, he was chief of staff to the commander in chief of the Allied naval forces in the Mediterranean. In 1944 he was appointed Admiral of the Western Approaches, in charge of all shipping to and from America. I've always thought this was a cool title. He was considered a potential First Sea Lord. England is strong in the cool title department.

This is what I've been told. It's my mother's story of his career. I have not found my father's name cited in any of the books I have read about the war, but I've never doubted the truth of this account. He was smart, capable, energetic, and dedicated. He was a good guy. He was one among many who fought and won the war. When it was over, that same war gave me my father as I knew him.

In early 1945 his blood pressure was found to be 240/140. Normal is around 120/80. A blood pressure of 250/150 is usually lethal within hours. I have always understood that the frenzy of the war was a proximate cause of his hypertension. There were no antihypertensive medicines in 1945. Instead, he had the treatment of choice for that era, a bilateral spinal sympathectomy. A surgeon entered every intervertebral space on both sides up and down his spine, and snipped the efferent sympathetic nerve in each space. This surgery prolonged his life for several years, but he never recovered from it. When I knew him, he was a tired, weak, rather aimless, well-dressed person, given to irritability and increasingly frequent periods of confusion. We moved to America in 1949 – my mother's U.S. citizenship gave us the option to do so and both my parents saw far more opportunity for their children in the States. After two or three years of heart attacks and strokes, my father died in the Veterans Administration Hospital in Roanoke, Virginia. I was nine years old when he died.

When I was born, the family was living in Perthshire. Seven months before I was born, the United States entered the war. When I was four months old the British routed the Nazi army under Rommel in North Africa at El Alamein – it was the Allies' first outright land victory. A few months later the Russians destroyed a Nazi army at Stalingrad, killing around 200,000 Germans and losing at least as many lives of their own. These events guaranteed that Hitler and the Nazis would not invade Britain, raping and murdering us all, as had been feared. This happy change in perspective allowed my mother and sisters to relax a bit, to have hope for the future, and to dote on me. Our house was in the country. There were no near neighbors, no social life, no car (petrol was virtually unobtainable), no TV, few movies. They had only housework, schoolwork, books, radio, and wee Johnnie to occupy their attention. I had four mothers, who in varying degrees and with varying perspectives, competed with each other to love me the most. All babies should have this experience. My personality is built upon a base of good-humored and generous assurance that has served me very well all my life. The superstructure of my personality may leave something to be desired, but the foundation is solid. The first effect of the war on me was to give me a wonderful babyhood.

When my father came home, I was two years old. I liked attention, I was used to getting it, and I was perhaps used to being the autocrat of the nursery. He was Ulysses, the hero home from the war, and he was sick. He wanted the attention, he didn't want competition, and he was used to having people follow his orders. I was certainly his son and he was never abusive, but I think that in his heart he saw me rather more as one of the suitors than as Telemachus. The idyll was over and the home front had to adjust to the impact of the war. He was not the man he had been, the person he had become was disagreeable, and he was dying.

John Dundas and his father, home on leave from the British Navy in 1943.

To make matters worse for me, another baby, my younger sister, was born in 1946. Dandling a baby prompts delight in the dandler. Because of the war my father did not know me as a baby. When he met me, I was not into being dandled. I was into enthusiastic rushing about and making a lot of noise. My baby sister was pretty, agreeable, and monstrously receptive to being dandled. He adored her. I was an irritant, she was the happy favorite, and he was dying. It was ugly. She and I established our current warm relationship only in recent years, coming to understand long after the fact that neither one of us was the worm in the apple we had previously believed. The worm in the apple was his illness. The worm in the apple was the war.

I seem to remember that Plato said, "Only the dead have seen the end of war." Machiavelli wrote, "A prince should have no other object or thought, nor regard anything as so much his business, as the art of war and its institutions and discipline." Churchill said, "War is the normal occupation of man ... war and gardening." Despite the damage that World War II did to my father and my family, I have never doubted the rightness of my father's participation. Consider what he saved us from. He had to fight World War II. He and his millions of colleagues will always be heroes to me, heroes standing beside the Spartans at Thermopylae, and Joan of Arc, and the defenders of the Alamo.

A major indirect consequence of World War II was to create in me a lifelong armchair interest in war. War is an intensely interesting phenomenon. Look at the thing. Gangs of testosterone-addled young men organized by their seniors to kill people. Horrible. Who would do it? Who would sign up? Who would go? Well, most of us, given convincing circumstances. Most of us in the United States would have gone to war in 1861-1865 or in 1941-1945. Many of us would have gone in 1775 or in 1917-1918. When it came to 1962-1975, however, the circumstances mostly did not convince. Vietnam compelled Kennedy, Johnson, Nixon, and many others for understandable reasons, but, like others of our generation, it did not compel me. I didn't go to war in Vietnam not because I thought it was wrong, nor because I foresaw defeat, nor because I feared terror, mutilation, or death, although I will avoid these when I can. I didn't go because it did not convince me. And because it was so easy to stay. Given that I had options, I compared Vietnam to my father's war, and I didn't buy it. It did not create in me a call to war, the will to war.

One other event in my life may have had its roots in World War II. Some time ago I read somewhere that after World War II most if not all children suffered from "nuclear anxiety." I thought about it and could not recall ever worrying about The Bomb, either by myself or with my friends. But then I remembered that when I was six, I had been panicked by a friend's remark, a remark which in retrospect may well have been inspired by Hiroshima and Nagasaki. Four of us were standing on the street in front of our houses in London. Two blocks down the street a block was missing. It was just rubble. It had been hit by a V-2. The sky was magnificent. Two or three different layers of broken clouds, each moving at different speeds in different directions, were underlit by the late afternoon sun, creating an intense vision of shifting whites and grays with tinges of color. We were all struck by how it looked, and we stopped playing and stood still, admiring it. Guy, who was seven and therefore an opinion leader, said something like the following, perhaps echoing words he had heard in August 1945: "Out of skies like that come thunderbolts which can destroy a whole city." The tone of the moment turned brutally sour. I was afraid and I ran indoors to be safe from the sky.

The United States has fought 11 major wars in 220 years, six of them in the last hundred years. Despite my full consciousness of this history and of the wars currently in progress around the world, I live my life as though there will be no more war. I live like my father's friends. I suspect most of us do. It is a good way to live. But of course there will be more war. Even today there are people, like my father in the 1930s, who are frantic about the next war. Inevitably most of their predictions will prove to be wrong. Inevitably some of them will be right. I can only hope that the next war will be necessary and that the right side will win it. In the event that war happens once more in our lifetime, I expect that I will again feel like a child under a thunderbolt sky.

Margaret deBeers Brown and her mother, 1944.

REFLECTIONS ON A QUAKER FATHER

Margaret deBeers Brown

>Born: September 24, 1943
>Washington, D.C., U.S.A.

In 1943 my father, John deBeers, received his draft notice. Believing that disputes should never be resolved by violent means, he had been a pacifist for several years. If everyone resisted war and refused to fight, he felt, wars would end. All pacifists, therefore, had a moral duty to act on these beliefs and refuse to fight. When he met my Quaker mother, he learned about the Society of Friends (Quakers) and felt drawn to the Quaker philosophy and beliefs. He married my mother in 1939 and joined the two Friends' Meetings that my mother and grandmother belonged to in Maryland and Washington, D.C.

Dad had completed course work for a Ph.D. in economics, but had not yet written a thesis. He worked as a Treasury Department economist, studying financial relations between Latin America and the United States. He had moved to the Treasury Department because he felt that his work in an earlier position at the Tariff Commission studying commodities – where they could be obtained and how much of a stockpile existed in the United States – contributed to supporting the war effort.

Some pacifists draw a distinction between World War II and other wars. They believe that pacifism is usually the best moral choice, but that the unprovoked aggressions of Germany and Japan could only be stopped by fighting. Those who knew or suspected the true extent of the Holocaust were reinforced in such beliefs. This distinction was particularly drawn during the Vietnam War, when many who claimed conscientious objector (C.O.) status admitted that they would have fought in World War II. However, my father was uncompromising in his belief that pacifism was always the best choice.

In response to his draft notice, he submitted a form declaring that he was a C.O. A hearing before his draft board was scheduled. A Quaker friend counseled him on what to expect. At the hearing, right before my birth, there were four or five men seated at a table facing him. He explained his pacifist philosophy and beliefs, and stated that he was a Quaker. He was given permission to do alternative service as a C.O., passed his physical, and was assigned to a camp near Gatlinburg, Tennessee. My parents sublet their apartment and moved in with my mother's parents.

My father was able to enjoy a week or two with his newborn daughter (me) before traveling to Gatlinburg in October 1943. The camp, run by the Central Committee of Conscientious Objectors, had formerly been a Civilian Conservation Corps camp. It housed about 150 conscientious objectors from a variety of religious backgrounds – a few Quakers, but also Jews, Methodists,

Presbyterians, Catholics, and others. The men maintained the trails and roads, and did other work in the Great Smoky Mountains National Park.

Dad had a variety of jobs at the camp – blasting rocks from the hillside, crushing them for use on the roads, and planting pine seedlings on park lands. In March 1944 he became the cook at a smaller camp. He was given a cookbook but no special training. The men liked his hand-cranked ice cream, but not his more exotic dishes (such as eggplant). He made a large kitchen knife, which he still uses, by attaching a handle to an old saw blade and grinding the blade on a grindstone. In May or June 1944 he was called back to the main camp to be the bread baker. When the dietitian left, he was assigned that job and was sent to Washington, D. C., to learn about nutrition and to get some sample menus.

Meanwhile, there was constant turnover in the camp. Men left for other forms of alternative service – for example, to participate in medical experiments or to be attendants at mental health facilities. My father had been a dairyman in college, so he applied to be a dairy-herd tester in the area around New Haven, Connecticut, where the prior tester had been drafted. He was accepted and given two days' training. Borrowing a car, he drove to New Haven in the summer of 1944, and my mother and I joined him in October. We lived in the home of a Czech woman, in two rooms with kitchen privileges. Later we moved to an attic apartment.

Dad worked for the Dairy Herd Improvement Association, which was supported by fees paid by the farmers. His job was to travel from farm to farm, testing the dairy herds. He weighed the milk from each cow, tested it for butterfat content, and recorded the results. Accurate records for each cow were particularly important when the cow was sold. If there were more than 30 cows in a herd, he got credit for a two-day job and was given room and board at the farm. After he learned the routine and used his math skills to estimate the records for the two-month gap between his arrival and the departure of the former tester, dairy testing was fairly easy work. He found that he could do the assigned 27 days of work per month in about 21 days. On one occasion, however, the job was not so simple. He noticed that one cow's milk production and butterfat numbers had markedly improved from the prior month. He discovered that her identification picture didn't match the cow in front of him – the farmer had switched cows.

In 1946 my father was discharged and returned to the Treasury Department. My parents bought a house in Bethesda, and Dad began working at night on his thesis, after he had built an addition to the house to write it in. He received his Ph.D. in 1951. But his trials as a C.O. were not over. In the early 1950s his name appeared on one of Senator McCarthy's lists of communists in the federal government. Dad learned that he was placed on the list because (1) he had belonged to a communist-infiltrated book club in the 1930s, (2) he was a Quaker, and (3) he had been a conscientious objector. Our family lawyer was outraged and was able to keep him from being fired, but Dad found that he couldn't do any meaningful work because his security clearance had been revoked and all the documents he needed to read were classified. After a period of frustration during which he tried to change these policies, he left the Treasury Department in 1955.

In the years that followed, the principles he had declared and had lived by during the war continued to be put to the test. Our neighborhood in Bethesda in the 1950s was racially restricted, a common situation at the time. Our property consisted of two lots. When we sold the empty lot, my father removed the restrictive covenant. A Jewish family bought the lot and built a house, causing a neighborhood controversy, but my parents stood firm and the family settled in peacefully. My sister and I played with the family's sons. Our play included constant pretend gun battles. It must have pained my Quaker parents to see us girls shouting "Bang! bang! You're dead!" with such enthusiasm.

Quakers believe – with a rare sincerity and commitment – in the equality and dignity of all people. As I was taught in First Day School, "There is something of God in every man." When my father ran into a dead end at the Treasury Department, he took a job as an economist working for the government of Puerto Rico, where we lived from 1955 to 1958. In 1958, when we returned to Maryland from Puerto Rico, Dad was moved by the plight of members of minority racial groups, including many diplomats and professionals from Latin America, who were unable to find decent, integrated housing in the segregated Washington, D.C., area. He began what eventually became a second "job" promoting integrated housing. He invested in several all-white apartment complexes and rented apartments in them to members of minority groups. He was also active in fair-housing groups of various kinds in the area. He and I marched with many thousands of others, black and white, in the March on Washington led by Martin Luther King in August 1963. It seemed important to be there with the busloads of people coming from all over the country. We ignored advice to stay home and avoid possible riots.

Many people have told me that they think it took great courage to be a C.O. during World War II and that my father must have been subjected to hostility and criticism. That's probably true, but I never heard him complain of such treatment. I have no memory of those times – I wasn't even three when he was discharged from his alternative service in 1946. He did what seemed right to him and I expect that most people respected him for it. I don't recall wondering why other children's fathers had fought in the war and mine had not. I knew he had been a conscientious objector because Quakers didn't believe in fighting. That was fine with me. As my younger sister and I grew up in Bethesda, we didn't have family discussions about these matters, and our parents didn't lecture to us about pacifism or civil rights. I realize now that both of my parents were rather reserved and not prone to talk about themselves, which was perhaps part of their Quakerly ethos. Because of their reticence, I didn't learn until years later about the accusation that my father was a communist and about his frustrations at the Treasury Department.

Rather than lecturing to us, my parents taught by example – the example of their scrupulous honesty in all things, their courtesy toward everyone they came in contact with (including our teenage friends), their belief in the importance of education, including education for women as well as men. In high school and college, I began to value my parents more and more. I became more aware that the racism in the Washington, D.C., area went beyond the "Colored" and "White" drinking fountains that I saw as a child. I began to see the importance of what Dad was doing to enable members of minority groups to live in the Maryland and Virginia suburbs and to join country clubs. I attended a Quaker camp whose theme was international peace and understanding, and I worked as a volunteer for the Friends Committee on National Legislation. Far from opposing me when I wanted to ride a Freedom Bus on spring vaction or when I wanted to demonstrate for the nuclear test ban treaty in front of the Kennedy White House, my parents were proud of my actions. They even fed and housed a large group of my fellow demonstrators. Some of my friends expressed surprise that my parents were willing to do these things. To me it was a foreign concept that other people's parents would *not* welcome a bunch of peace demonstrators.

As I reflect on my father's service as a C.O. during World War II and on my parents' lives as Quakers, I reach two conclusions. First, for me personally their examples were powerful models of moral behavior. After my college years I no longer joined sit-ins and protests, but I continued to work for change in other ways. Although I have traveled a somewhat different path from that of my parents, becoming a Presbyterian elder and deacon rather than a Quaker and being active in different forms of community service, I believe that I am following their examples.

Second, as I look back at the turbulent 1960s and 1970s and at the protests against racial inequality and the Vietnam War, I see my father and mother and others like them as representing examples of morality in a broader sense to people outside their immediate families. Those who protested the war in Vietnam were supported by the fact that there had been pacifists in earlier wars. Those who staged sit-ins, marches, and other civil rights demonstrations were supported by the thousands who refused to accept racism and who took what steps they could to end it. If the students and others who protested had not known, either personally or by report, a few honest, committed, and respectful humanitarians, would they have been inspired to protest and march and sit in? Societies in the midst of change need inspiring leaders – Martin Luther King and Nelson Mandela come to mind – but they also need ordinary citizens like my father who are peacefully working for change and living according to their religious beliefs. I thank my father for setting me such a good example.

OF OUR LIFE IN JAPAN DURING THE WAR

Kazuko Iwasawa Ihara

>Born: October 23, 1942
>Kamakura, Kanagawa, Japan

Kamakura, a city about 50 kilometers southwest of Tokyo, was the place where I was born in October 1942 and where my family and I mostly lived during and after World War II. My mother's parents had owned a summer house there, and my parents were asked to live in that house after their marriage in March 1941, since in those days vacant houses had to be handed over to the government. This turned out to be a great blessing for us, because Kamakura, an ancient capital of Japan, escaped being bombed during the war. For this we are thankful to those American scholars who pleaded with the U.S. military command not to bomb old cities like Kyoto and Kamakura, stressing their historical value and at the same time showing their lack of strategic importance.

We were blessed in other ways also. My father, for reasons of health, did not have to go into the army to fight. We also had my father's parents in Kiryu to help us out. So ours is not a typical case, but through my vague, fragmentary memories and the more concrete ones of my mother who is still alive, I will try to recapture some aspects of our life during the war.

In Kamakura the house we lived in was located about a 10- or 15-minute walk from the beach, opposite a small temple and next to a little bakery. By Japanese standards it had a fairly spacious yard with flowering trees and shrubs. Between the front gate and the house, there was a bomb shelter, as was quite commonly found in many houses. Ours was a semi-cylindrical concrete covering over a shallow dugout in the ground. I have a vague memory of taking shelter there once with my family, but actually it seems that we hardly used it.

Although Kamakura ultimately escaped bombing, there were always sirens announcing the approach of enemy planes, particularly after the beginning of 1945, when Allied bombing raids on Japan became almost incessant. I vaguely remember the sound of those sirens. Then mother would hurriedly put out the already dim light in the room – already dim because the light was covered by a long, dark cloth that hung down almost to the table beneath. This was the practice in all houses, in accordance with the strictly enforced regulation, called the "control of lights," to prevent the light from leaking out and indicating the location of the houses to the enemies. Mother remembers that once, as she was making a fire in the furnace to heat water for the bath, she heard the stern voice of the next-door neighbor saying, "Iwasawa-san, put out the fire quickly! The smoke will be seen by the enemies!"

Aside from the fear of being bombed, the greatest concern in those days was the shortage of food. Because most manpower went into the military, there were not enough workers left to engage in the necessary farming and fishing. Added to this difficulty was the fact that Japan was not self-sufficient in food production, so when shipping was interrupted toward the end of the war, the country faced starvation. It could not produce enough food locally for its population.

Mother remembers the empty shelves in the stores. Nothing was being sold there, everything was rationed by the government. The most important rationing affected rice, but as the war continued and the supply of rice ran low, wheat or sweet potatoes were substituted. It often happened, moreover, that a ration – for example, a week's supply of rice – would be announced for a certain date. Then it would be announced that there would be a "delay of the ration," then another "delay," and in the end, no ration would arrive at all. When the rations did arrive for each neighborhood group, the person on duty, usually a housewife, would go around the houses crying out, "The ration has come!" Then people would gather at her house, each with a pot or a pan in hand to obtain a share. Mother recalls what a hard task it was for the person on duty to divide the ration equally among the 10 or 12 families that constituted the neighborhood group, for sometimes the ration consisted only of two medium-sized fish.

Since the rations were so undependable and insufficient, many women went to the farmers in the countryside, traveling either on foot or on crowded trains. They took with them fine garments, such as a silk kimono or obi, to exchange for rice or whatever vegetables or food might be available. Mother was no exception, but she was lucky that she did not have to do this very often. My father's parents were engaged in a small domestic textile industry in Kiryu, about 100 kilometers north of Tokyo, and they helped us out by sending us rice from time to time. So that the rice would not be seized, it would arrive in a sturdy wooden box used for storing textiles, and it would be labeled as "books," which have about the same weight per volume as rice.

My own memories connected with the food shortage concern an occasion on which I accompanied Mother to the seashore to scoop up sea water. It was Mother's idea to get salt by evaporating the sea water, since even salt was rationed. To her great disappointment, however, it did not work out, as too much sand and too many impurities were mixed in with the salt at the end of the process.

To escape the bombing, people were evacuated from the cities to live with their relatives in the country whenever possible. Although we mostly stayed in Kamakura, we went to Kiryu, my father's hometown, in the spring of 1945 for my mother to give birth to my brother. Mother recalls the overcrowded trains, such as she had never seen before or after, with people on the platforms, on the steps, even clinging to the locomotives. It was a marvel that she was able to get to Kiryu safely, taking me along with her.

My sister was born at home in Kamakura after the war, in August 1947. By that time the food situation had become much better for us. Although the bomb shelter still remained, my mother's parents had the yard cultivated, and, together with a young girl sent by my father's parents to help her, Mother planted beans, potatoes, corn, and other vegetables.

In 1950 my father was invited to speak at the International Congress of Mathematicians held in Cambridge, Massachusetts, and then to spend two years at the Institute for Advanced Study in Princeton, New Jersey. After the two years, he decided to join the faculty of MIT and brought his family over to the United States. He obtained a permanent resident visa for all of us, but he probably did not dream at the time that he and Mother would end up staying in the United States for over 30 years.

Mother says that the war did not have any effect on my father's decision to leave Japan and live in the United States. Perhaps so, but it cannot be denied that life *was* very hard in Japan after the war. And Father must have thought that in the United States he would be able to concentrate much more on mathematics, which he loved. My father's decision to stay in the United States had a decisive influence on the lives of his children and a great role in shaping my character. So, in a certain sense it may be said that I, too, was affected by the war.

Kazuko Iwasawa Ihara with her mother (on left), her younger brother and sister, and her mother's helper in the countryside, August 1950.

For me, Kamakura brings back memories of those relatively peaceful days after the war and memories of my early, happy school years. But I think I understand more now why my mother never seemed to feel as much nostalgia for the life in Kamakura as I did. I think that for her it was too closely connected with the hardships she had endured during the war.

I will close this essay with my mother's words: "And this war – it was the Japanese army who started it – to think how many ordinary people suffered! We were the more fortunate, but how much sadness it caused to so many people ... "

Seven-year-old Kazuko Iwasawa Ihara (far right) on a school excursion with classmates from Kamakura, November 1949.

CHILDHOOD MEMORIES OF POSTWAR GERMANY

Mathea Falco

> Born: October 15, 1944
> Montgomery, Alabama, U.S.A.

During the many celebrations of the fiftieth anniversary of the Marshall Plan in 1997, Americans remembered the extraordinary role the United States played after World War II when the nation pledged its resources to the reconstruction of war-ravaged Europe. The celebrations honored the valor and vision of leaders who were willing to invest in a new future for defeated enemies, a future that would bind nations together through common interests and the love of freedom. The U.S. Secretary of State, Madeleine Albright, herself a war refugee from Czechoslovakia, reminded graduating college seniors of the sacrifices that people must still be willing to make to promote fundamental human rights around the world.

I remember the period after the war not from the perspective of a student of history but through the eyes of a very little girl. My mother and I arrived in Germany in October 1946, just after my second birthday. My father, a U.S. Air Force colonel, had gone over to Germany almost a year earlier, as part of the Allied occupying forces. A civil engineer with extensive experience, he was responsible for rebuilding troop facilities, airports, and basic infrastructure. My father, a naturalized citizen from Cuba, was intensely patriotic. He had been one of the first Army Air Force fliers in World War I, and he believed in America with unquestioning faith.

Getting to Germany was not easy. My mother and I traveled in the first civilian transport, a converted troopship where we were packed four to a cabin with only the most basic necessities. Toilets and sinks were communal and showers a rare luxury. The first week at sea, one of the engines broke down, considerably slowing our headway through the stormy North Atlantic. Another ship was sent to push us along, and we finally arrived a month later in Bremerhaven. By that time, most of the children were seriously ill with flu, isolated from the adults in sick bays. The mothers were worn to exhaustion.

My father, splendid in uniform, was on the dock to meet us. He had been looking forward to this moment for months, to seeing his rapidly growing baby girl and to having us reunited at last. I no longer recognized him and immediately began shrieking when he tried to hug me. This scene was repeated all along the dock, as fathers were furiously rejected as strangers by their children. Although she was recovering from a broken back from a fall down the stairs, my mother picked me up and carried me to the army truck waiting to take us to the train station. My father carried the bags and our life in Germany began.

From Bremerhaven, we made our way to Wiesbaden in southern Germany, the headquarters for the U.S. Air Force. Along with other officers' families, we were quartered in what once had been an affluent residential neighborhood of huge homes and manicured gardens. General Curtis LeMay lived down the street. His legendary temper was often on display as he raced from his front door into waiting military vehicles, much to the delight and terror of my small friends.

We were assigned to an enormous house, previously occupied by a Nazi general. The rooms were of Wagnerian proportions, lined with massive built-in furniture and lit by elaborate crystal chandeliers. But light bulbs were scarce – the chandeliers remained largely ornamental. It must once have been a splendid place, said to have been owned by a wealthy schnitzel manufacturer whose

Mathea Falco in her father's air force flier's jacket with her mother in Germany, 1947.

property was confiscated early in the war. By the time we arrived, the house had lost any charm it might formerly have had.

My parents, grateful to have a real home when many families were placed in temporary quarters, set off to explore the many rooms. My mother was as determinedly cheerful then as she is now, five decades later. She began explaining how a few curtains here and there would make all the difference. She later discovered that there was no fabric to be had. Undaunted, she cut up bedspreads from our household goods and managed to cover the windows in considerable style.

To my childish eye this new home was not the haven it seemed to my parents. The cavernous rooms were full of menace, spirited by ghosts and monsters. They still appear in my dreams, where I am forever a tiny girl, trying to find my way through the gloomy corridors out into the sunlight.

To help reduce local unemployment, we were required to hire at least three servants, and we soon acquired several more. Two were assigned to care for me, while the others cleaned and cooked. None of them spoke English and we spoke no German, which made communication a daily challenge. One of the women, Frau Hilda, spent an hour each morning vigorously brushing the tangles from my waist-length hair and braiding it into tight coils around my head, in a hairdo that unbeknownst to us was the traditional style for girls in the Bund deutscher Mädel during the Nazi era. In family pictures of that period, I look like a stereotypical German child, except that I am decidedly better fed than most of my contemporaries, who faced serious food shortages.

Hilda and Helen, her assistant, lectured me constantly in German. Somehow I never behaved well enough to suit these stern custodians. I realize now how bitter they were, but at the time they seemed like impossible adults, as oppressive and inescapable as the house. My parents frequently traveled without me, so I was left in the care of Hilda and Helen for days on end. Gradually I began to understand German, which made them somewhat less impatient with me. But their voices stay with me. Even after many trips to Germany as an adult, German remains for me the language of reprimand and correction.

Everything was scarce in Germany after the war, especially food and fuel. People came often to the kitchen door for handouts – extra bread, outgrown clothing, old shoes. Nothing was wasted. The occupying military families also faced shortages, since the entire country lay in ruins. A spool of thread was a handsome gift, a yard of ribbon seemed a wild extravagance. My mother's ingenuity was limitless. She managed to get a dozen discarded parachutes and used the silk to fashion underwear, shirts, pajamas. Some she dyed bright colors and transformed into scarves which she gave to her friends. But she could do nothing about the cold. In the winter of 1949, the Rhine froze for the first time in 50 years. Because most of the roads and train lines had been destroyed during the war, this shut down virtually all transport of goods and fuel within Germany. Suffering was intense. Many people died from starvation and exposure. Military personnel were given weekly allotments of coal, but these were usually inadequate to heat our cavernous quarters. When the temperature dropped to just above freezing, my mother and I got into bed and

Mathea Falco in overalls made by her mother, with her father in uniform, Wiesbaden, Germany, 1949.

stayed there. I developed pneumonia. My father, beside himself with fear and rage, began chopping up the huge built-in wooden armoires to burn in the furnace. Somehow, the situation resolved itself. We obtained more coal, I recovered, spring came.

During these years I was often sick with tonsillitis, so sick that I had to be hospitalized again and again for weeks at a time. The military hospitals were clean, efficient places, with large wards policed by crisp, starched nurses. The only treatment at the time seemed to be penicillin, which the nurses injected into my bottom at regular intervals. My parents were allowed to visit half an hour every afternoon. The military rules prohibited anything more, even for the very youngest patients. My terror as I watched my parents leave, their backs receding down the long white corridors, still makes my heart contract. The sense of utter helplessness, my endless tears, the struggle to convert my custodians into friends became the building blocks that shaped my life.

My father never talked much about his German experience. He still grimaced years later whenever I asked about this period. When he arrived in 1945, one of his first tasks was visiting the recently liberated concentration camps to determine what use, if any, could be made of them as troop facilities. In the course of these trips, he talked with Germans who had worked in and near the camps, heard their stories, saw with his own eyes the crematoria, the gas chambers, the mountains of small personal possessions left behind by the victims. When my mother arrived, he took her with him, flying his own military plane to crisscross the country. Once they took me, too, but they found it too painful to try to explain what we were seeing, so next time they left me at home with Hilda and Helen.

Our biggest crisis occurred when the Soviet Union cut off Allied access to Berlin, which in the Yalta Agreement had been declared an open city under quadripartite rule. Russian troops occupied the thin corridor that connected Berlin to West Germany. The only way to sustain the beleaguered city was by air. The existing airport – Tempelhof – was totally inadequate, its runways largely destroyed by Allied bombing during the war. My father was immediately sent to Berlin to oversee construction of new runways, which had to be completed virtually overnight. For more than a year, the U.S. flew supplies into Berlin 24 hours a day. Keeping the runways open was critical to the success of the operation.

Fifteen years later, when I was studying modern European history in college, my father tried to describe this experience for me, to give the textbook accounts reality. Instead, he cried, something I had rarely seen him do. Shaking his head, he said, "They had been our deadly enemies, these Germans. They had done terrible things. Here they were, defeated, working on the runways to keep Berlin open. But they didn't look like enemies. They were women and children, working all day, clearing the runways by hand in the bitter cold, just for a bowl of soup and a piece of bread." Thirty years after the war's end,

Mathea Falco and her mother
at the site of a concentration camp in Germany, 1948.

when he lay dying of cancer, he returned to this experience, recounting every painful detail. Haunted by their faces, he lived with those Germans until the very end of his life.

During this period, when the Soviet invasion of Germany seemed imminent, most military dependents were sent back to the States. My mother, however, decided to stay in Wiesbaden. In the early months, the military arranged regular evacuation drills for the remaining families. A very loud siren would go off, usually in the middle of the night. She and I would jump in the car and begin driving toward the Swiss border until the emergency radio network notified us that we could return home. The trunk of the car was stocked with food rations, bedding, flashlights, and extra clothing. After the first few drills, when we realized that the Soviets might not be invading, these forays came to seem perfectly normal, and sometimes even rather fun.

Childhood tends to assert itself even in difficult circumstances. I had wonderful moments, running through the garden hedge to play with the four American girls who lived next door, going to the army nursery school, singing Christmas carols around the family tree, making presents out of bits and pieces. We lived in a war-torn country, but we were the victors. My mother and father loved me and they loved each other. Although I was often frightened and they were sometimes distressed, the threats seemed largely external.

We returned to the United States when I entered first grade. After some adjustment, I became a typical American girl. I stopped speaking German and I no longer marveled at the sight of white bread. I wanted to fit in completely, so that no one would ever guess I had lived in such a strange war-ravaged world. By the time I was a teenager, I had blended in perfectly. When I traveled through Europe during college summers, people would stop me on the streets of Paris and London and ask me if I were related to friends of theirs in Ohio, Indiana, Michigan. I looked like the quintessential Midwesterner.

But the dissonance remains. Fifty years later, I still see starving Germans, begging for bread at our kitchen door, their faces pinched and angry. I still feel them watching us, the privileged children of the occupying armies, as we played in large front yards that once belonged to them. I still hear my parents arguing about whether my mother and I should be evacuated back to the safety of the United States even if it meant another long separation.

I am nostalgic for another kind of childhood, one without defeated but still dangerous enemies, where life is simple, if a little monotonous, and no sirens sound in the night.

Hugh Field at 19 months, January 1945.

TROLLING ALONG AT THE BOTTOM

Hugh Field

>Born: June 16, 1943
>New York City, New York, U.S.A.

The time is 1948, the place postwar suburban Cleveland. On a shady street in a green-and-white house live a couple in their thirties with their two boys, age five and three. The father is an architect, working on plans for a downtown campus for Western Reserve University. The mother, English-born, is a housewife. The boys are ... two little American boys.

Cleveland Heights was our new home and it looked like a permanent one. No longer were we in a city apartment building, isolated. I was attending the nearby kindergarten and I was curious about everything. Although I was quite content with being five, I would think about how very long it would take to pass through 12 whole grades of school. Some time after that, I would get myself a fine job like my father. But that was so far away.

I had been born in Manhattan, where my parents were living in a fourth-floor walk-up on Second Avenue. My father, of Quaker background, had a job designing army camps, ironically enough. He had already seen World War II firsthand. With war raging overseas, it must have been a subdued time, and I consider myself part of a rather subdued, gentle, and reserved pre Baby-Boom age group. We were the last young children without television and its musical soulmate, rock music. There is a subtle discontinuity between us and the Baby Boomers.

By nature I was more pensive than sociable. My parents had found a modern pediatrician for me named Benjamin Spock, who was working on a book. In an anonymous article he wrote for a diaper magazine (free with the weekly diapers), he contrasted me at six months, not yet crawling, with another baby: "Hugh looks contentedly on the world and finds it good."

Far from her own mother in England, my mother was a bit nervous with me, her first child. Then my colicky brother came along. Early in life I learned not to bother her with my needs. Instead I used to ask questions about everything – my father fondly called me "Mr. Why." Trying to figure out why became my "winning formula" in dealing with life. This and my other practice of not bothering people both tended to isolate me. My father remembers watching me trudging home after kindergarten, zigzagging up the street alone, oh-so-slowly building and pushing a giant snowball.

My parents had first met in 1938 in England, at the summer school of the Left Book Club, a left-wing political organization. My father, an American born in Switzerland, had returned there for his architectural degree and had watched with horror the rise of Hitler next door in Germany. When my parents met, my father was working as an architect in England, and my mother was assisting refugees from Czechoslovakia. The two became lovers. When Hitler seized all of Czechoslovakia, she suggested that he go to Poland to help Czech refugees there get to England. And so it was that on September 1, 1939, my father awoke in Cracow to the sound of German aerial bombing. He quickly gathered together about 700 refugees and they set off in a desperate rush for the Russian lines. Most were cut off by the German armored advance, and my father narrowly escaped death himself when his hotel in Lublin was bombed. Abandoning the goal of reaching Russia and veering south instead, he and a few others finally made it to Romania, which was still neutral. From there he flew to Yugoslavia and then made his way back to England.

Back with my mother in England, my father wanted to return to America. They got married and took one of the last liners out of Europe to New York. So there we all were in 1948, five years after my birth, with our own home in Cleveland, and World War II over. I was a boy with a lot of curiosity. I wanted to be important like my father. But my social skills were weak; still, there was time for them to improve.

The next year, 1949, my parents decided that we would take a summer vacation in England to visit my grandparents, while my father attended an architectural conference in Italy, intending as well to take an architectural tour of Poland. This family voyage was an exciting prospect for a young boy. I still have the diary that I, a week short of six years old, kept on the voyage. My father flew on from London to the Continent. I got a postcard from him showing the great fountain in Geneva. Then, suddenly, he vanished.

I remember my mother, my brother, and me leaving my great-grandmother's house in a taxi. My mother was sobbing uncontrollably. But very quickly she and her parents began to handle things with English reserve, so as not to upset us boys. She told us that we would soon return to Cleveland to wait for my father, who would probably show up soon. I remember drawing a picture of our Cleveland home. Too young to react fully, I waited, too.

The events behind my father's disappearance are still murky. It seems that nobody had heard from his brother Noel for several months, having lost touch when Noel was in Prague, where he had claimed he was seeking a teaching job. Like my father, Noel had worked with political refugees and later, as the war wound down, helped with resettlement. Meanwhile, because of dangerous omens of the new Cold War, my father had decided against visiting Eastern Europe. But while visiting Noel's wife in Geneva, he gave in to her entreaties and agreed to go to Prague to look for his brother. At the end of a brief visit to Poland, he was seen off by friends at the Warsaw airport, but when the plane landed in Prague, he was not on it. My mother contacted the American Embassy. The State Department queried the Polish and Czech governments, but each said that it knew nothing of his whereabouts. From that point on, my mother bravely made it her major task to keep the issue alive in the hope that he

Hugh Field with his father and brother in 1947.

would be located and released. This continued for more than five years.

She soon realized that she would be better off staying with her parents than taking us back to Cleveland. So she took the plunge and enrolled us in a local private school. Because it was a coed progressive school, it was not the shock to me that it might have been, and my shyness matched British temperament. But I still had to learn new ways. Within a year I had become "English." I remember an American boy enrolling in the school – he seemed exotic and lanky compared to my porridge-fed peers. But I was not quite on the same wavelength as the rest, either (not imbued with the English idea that the adjective that goes with "boy" is "naughty," for example). Though I had friends in my new English school, they were not close, and I did not grow out of my social disconnection. I sank more deeply into isolation.

After three years my mother moved me to a more rigorous, traditional boys' private school. There I got to wear a striped uniform with gray shirt and shorts (even in winter). I was taught to touch my cap when I passed a mistress (a woman teacher). Although most of the teachers were kind, the school was intimidating. It had given up caning as punishment only the year before. I learned to fear those in authority. In this unfamiliar setting I started trying to make connections all over again. Increasingly vulnerable and lonely, I escaped into my schoolwork with considerable success. In fourth form (fourth grade) I was first in Latin and did almost as well when we started Greek and algebra the following year. In geography class I learned how England's prosperity came from "invisible exports" (investments); in English class we memorized poems weekly. Schoolwork was not a game but a responsibility and I remain grateful today for its quality and rigor. In a way I felt older at that time than I ever have since. I remained a serious child. Although not athletic, I did enjoy the exuberance of rugby football, where I could tackle other players. My main outside interest was London buses and I spent hours "bus-spotting," usually alone. This is a very English pastime, where interest is invested in machines, not people. And I learned not to think of the future. It was all so uncertain.

With my mother anxious and preoccupied, my grandparents were like second parents, periodically taking us all on trips to places like Hampton Court and St. Albans. My grandmother even brought me with her to the stands in Piccadilly on Coronation Day in 1953 to watch the new young Queen Elizabeth ride by in her amazing golden coach.

Meanwhile, in Hungary and Czechoslovakia, spy trials were announced at which communist officials and others were charged with being agents of "the American spy, Noel Field." My father was also implicated. Hundreds of people were locked up, many made false confessions under torture, and dozens who had been helped by my uncle or father were executed. My family felt the charges could not possibly be true because my father was vaguely leftist and my uncle perhaps even a communist. Yet Stalin did get rid of European communists who had been in the West. Throughout it all neither my father nor uncle was produced, nor were their whereabouts acknowledged.

Suddenly, in September 1954, a former Polish official who had slipped over to the West announced that my father was imprisoned in Poland. In fact he said that he was the very man who had arrested my father. A month later the Polish government announced my father's release. A month after that my uncle was also released in Hungary, where he elected to stay.

My parents were finally reunited in Switzerland, and during the Christmas holidays my brother and I joined them. The family was together at last after a separation of five and a half years. My father looked a bit more worn than his picture on my mother's bedroom wall. We hid from the press in a remote Swiss village. My brother and I listened enthralled while he told us about his prison guards and his other experiences. He did not talk about his year in solitary, his hunger strikes, or the mock execution he endured. He taught us how to ski. Finally, in February 1955, my parents returned to London and my father held his first press conference. (I wanted to hold one, too.) Our pictures were on the front page of the newspapers.

We were a family again. I was happy. My father had been absent almost half my life. It had to seem a long hiatus, but I found it bridgeable. He was warmer and more casual than the adults I was used to in England. He was more American, and I loved it. I was intrigued by how he pronounced "new" *noo* and called the lavatory "the john." Never stern, he showed great interest in us boys. We had a great year together, especially on holidays in the Cotswolds and Cornwall. For my twelfth birthday party, he organized a great treasure hunt for my school chums and me. He took me to concerts at the Royal Festival Hall on the bicentenary of Mozart's birth, and he discussed Monet with me and my art teacher at school. But strangely, at school my grades dropped. I couldn't concentrate.

Not having had my father during my boyhood, I idolized him like the six-year-old I was when he disappeared. To some degree I still do. In my mind he was someone I, an English boy, could never match, much as I might want to. For his part my father noticed that I lacked enthusiasm, that I had no really close friends, that I didn't even know what a friend was. He thought that I was, if anything, even more disconnected than when he had disappeared.

After all this time I still cannot fully understand these events or the impact of my parents' lives on myself. So I am left with memories of my own experience and with questions that came to me. Was my father clever or naive? Was he a victim or a spy? Who was to blame for tearing our family apart? Was it part of Stalin's purges or the result of some American plot to stir up Eastern Europe to revolt? What I know is that my father returned intact, going on to have a fine career as an architect and professor. With his cellmate in prison, he also coauthored two novels, one of which became in 1985 the basis of a German movie, *Angry Harvest*, that received an Oscar nomination for best foreign film. Approaching 90, my father remains an amazing man, still traveling to

186   *Born into a World at War*

international conferences.

For me, on the other hand, life has been a long story of hope and struggle, isolation and attempts to connect. Without connection it is hard to make something of oneself. We returned to America, settling in Boston rather than the more appealing (to me) Midwest. While my father immersed himself in his own

Hermann Field, accompanied by his wife and sons,
Hugh, 11, and Alan, 9, meets with the press outside the London home of his
parents-in-law, following his release from prison in Poland, February 1955.

interests, I started over yet again as a day student at a local prep school. I made myself an American again and did well in school despite my loneliness. I then made the mistake of choosing to go to Harvard, which did not match my real needs at all. Depressed, I dropped out of college after a year. Someone found me a job in a machine shop of all places, where I was nicknamed "the zombie." I left lathes and cranes and other machines for another failed attempt at Harvard. At 20, I was devastated when President Kennedy was shot; he was another ideal figure for me and in the aftermath of the assassination I learned more about killing and cover-up. Obsessed with conspiracies, I was still "Mr. Why." Much later I joined offbeat groups. One failure followed another. As Bob Dylan said, "When you've got nothing, you've got nothing to lose."

Following a stint as a file clerk, I eventually finished college at the University of Massachusetts in Boston with a major in psychology. Associating education with loneliness and pain, I have never gone back for more. I became a case worker for the state welfare department, working with people at the bottom of life, a comfortable role because that was where I had been trolling along for years.

I married a local girl I had met when we were both file clerks. At last I was connecting! Unfortunately, this meant disconnecting from my more cultured background. My wife's father was a Pentecostal minister, my wife "spoke in tongues." I came to feel that I could no longer be myself without giving offense. Nonetheless I enjoyed the warmth and security of my wife's family, and for years I was happy as a married man raising two children, until finally financial and religious pressures brought an end to the marriage. When I divorced, I was still at the welfare department, working with computers and writing reports.

How much of who we are is due to events in our lives? I feel, without altogether understanding how, that this history of mine is somehow connected to those events of my early childhood, but the connections themselves are missing. When a child loses a parent as I did, it can leave a hole in the person's life forever. How much did my mother's remoteness mean that I did not learn how to express love and be a friend? Was I paralyzed by my father's absence from my key boyhood years and paralyzed by his return as well? How does one grow up whole when one's family is caught in a web of mystery, when the ground keeps shifting, when there is no certainty to be found anywhere about major childhood events? How many times can one adjust? At night my dreams are of struggling to get somewhere among lots of people and being totally out of sync with all of them.

But things are finally looking up for me. Perhaps my trolling days are over and I will dare to do new things with my life. I am in a steady relationship where I can be myself. I have parachuted and bungee-jumped, to counter a main truth about myself, that I am very fearful. Maybe now I can confront my greatest fear – that of my unused potential. Then I will be ready at last to revisit Cleveland Heights and to connect in spirit with that pensive, curious little boy of long ago who had such great hopes for the future.

Max Gitter (arrow) being fed with other children in a displaced persons camp near Lechfield, Bavaria, in 1947.

BORN IN SAMARKAND

Max Gitter
(born Manes Giter)

>Born: November 17 or 18, 1943
>Samarkand, Uzbek, U.S.S.R. (now Uzbekistan)

I was born in 1943 (on November 17 or 18, my parents don't remember which) in a most fascinating place, Samarkand – the ancient capital of the Mongol empire, the key metropolis of the Silk Road, and the fabled city of Matthew Arnold's romantic poem *Sohrab and Rustum*. The story of how I came to be born there is not romantic at all. It is, instead, part of a grim, little-known chapter of the Holocaust in which the immediate villains responsible for the deaths of untold thousands of Jews were not the Nazis but the Soviets. At the same time, it was an unintended consequence of that chapter (certainly unintended by the Soviets) that many other thousands of Jews – including Israel's former prime minister, Menachem Begin; the great Yiddish writer, Chaim Grade; and my parents – survived the Holocaust. Let me explain.

On the eve of World War II, Germany and the Soviet Union entered into the Ribbentrop-Molotov Pact, by which the two powers divided Poland and parts of the Baltic region. On September 1, 1939, Germany invaded western Poland and immediately thereafter, pursuant to the pact, the Soviet Union annexed and occupied the eastern regions: Wilno (now Vilnius, Lithuania), parts of Byelorussia (e.g., Pinsk), and eastern Galicia. The territory ultimately annexed by the Soviets, including the three Baltic republics and Bessarabia, was home to two million Jews, bringing the total Jewish population of the Soviet Union up to five million.

My mother, one of eight brothers and sisters, came from a small Polish city, Międzyrzec ("Mezrich" in phoneticized Yiddish), that was famous in the eighteenth and nineteenth centuries as the seat of a great rabbi. Mezrich, just east of Warsaw, was in the Nazi sphere of Poland. Upon the Nazi invasion, with the help of a small sum of money provided by her mother and a brother-in-law, my mother, then 21, managed to flee east to Brest Litovsk in the Soviet sphere.

The huge populations annexed by the Soviet Union posed severe problems, imagined and real, for the Soviet government. The new citizens were not yet properly sovietized, and they included such "undesirables" as free-thinkers, radicals, Zionists, and hundreds of thousands of homeless, unemployed refugees. There were waves of arrests – political arrests, as in the case of Zionists like Begin, and arrests of refugees who had "illegally" escaped to the Soviet zone from the Nazi zone, as in the case of my mother, who was jailed in Brest Litovsk for several months in early 1940.

But the chief method by which the Soviets dealt with the "undesirables" – one that goes back to czarist times – was deportation to the "interior." The "interior" usually meant Siberia, site of numerous slave-labor camps. From her prison in Brest Litovsk, my mother was deported to Siberia and wound up in a labor camp at which hundreds of single women worked as seamstresses manufacturing underwear for the Red Army.

My father was from a tiny, impoverished *shtetl* in eastern Galicia, 25 kilometers west of Lvov (now part of Ukraine), which was in the Soviet sphere. The waves of deportations to Siberia in 1939 and 1940 culminated in a massive deportation in June 1940 that included my father (then 23), his parents, and his older brother. They were packed in rail cars for three weeks and taken to a timber-cutting camp in Novosibirsk Province. Nearly 60 years later my father is still haunted by memories of the clang-clang-clang of that rail journey. Since neither my father nor his family were political activists or refugees from the Nazi zone, it is unclear why they were exiled from their shtetl to Siberia. So far as I can determine, they merely happened to be in the wrong place at the wrong time – or, in light of the later mass extermination by the Nazis of the eastern Polish Jews who were not exiled to the Soviet interior, perhaps they were in the right place at the right time.

In Siberia my father's brother and father, like many thousands of other deportees, perished from the hard labor, cold, and hunger. His brother suffered a particularly painful death from exposure and gangrene. My father and his mother were able to survive only because, after a full day in the snows cutting down trees, my father spent his nights repairing shoes (a skill he acquired in Siberia) in exchange for extra food.

On June 22, 1941, Germany invaded the Soviet Union, bringing an end to the Ribbentrop-Molotov Pact. Sometime later the Soviet Union concluded an agreement with the Polish government in exile, whereby Polish nationals detained in Soviet jails and labor camps were granted amnesty and freed. Once released, each of my parents was sent to separate cotton-producing collective farms near Samarkand in the former Soviet Socialist Republic – now the full-fledged country – of Uzbekistan. Uzbekistan, which for centuries has been home to an indigenous population of "Bokharan" Jews, proved to be a relatively safe haven for Ashkenazic Jewish refugees from Eastern Europe like my parents.

My parents met in Samarkand proper in 1942, when each came to the city on one of their periodic trips to pick up relief food packages sent by the Allies through the Polish government in exile. They were married in a traditional Jewish wedding on August 6, 1942, and set up house in a village that is part of greater Samarkand. I was born 15 months later.

My family's sojourn in Samarkand was hard. Food was scarce, living conditions were appalling. My father's mother died there three weeks after I was born. My mother contracted typhus when I was nine months old and she gave me over to the care of another family for about six months while she was hospitalized. Although my father visited me daily, my mother obviously could not. I'm told that I was unable to recognize her when she finally came to take me home and, as I did with any stranger, I begged her for food upon meeting her.

I had been told about my mother's illness and our long separation by the time I was an adolescent. Yet I somehow transformed that story in my mind: even as an adult I believed that I had been given over to the care of a family of gypsies who refused to give me up when my mother recovered, and that my parents therefore had been forced to steal me back just before they left Samarkand. For decades I clung to that false memory and did not fully exorcise it until I discussed the events again with my parents while preparing this memoir.

After the war ended in 1945, my parents, with me in tow, traveled by train to the Polish frontier, and from the frontier through Poland, often by foot, to search for surviving relatives. In my father's case there were none – none of his five sisters and half sisters, not an uncle or aunt, not even a distant cousin. To this day I have never known a relative of any kind on my father's side. Indeed, no one he knew before the war survived.

My mother was luckier. Although the Nazis killed both her parents and five of her siblings, two of her sisters survived. One, my Aunt Itka, who had married before the war, survived with her husband much as my mother had done – first in Brest Litovsk, then in Siberia, and then somewhere in Soviet Asia (she can no longer remember where). My other aunt, Cela, who was interned at various concentration camps, was alive in a displaced persons camp maintained by the Allies in Germany.

My family and my Aunt Itka's family were able to meet up in mid 1946 near the Polish-German border, and we all traveled (by truck and foot) to Germany, where we found my Aunt Cela. She had married immediately after liberation – at the outskirts of the very concentration camp at which she and Uncle Jack had been imprisoned. Their joyous celebration was attended by thousands of camp inmates and others from all over Eastern Europe.

My brother Marty was born at a D.P. camp in Germany in November 1946, and we spent the next three years at still another camp, near the Bavarian town of Lechveld. Most of my memories of that period are of hardships: of my brother's illnesses (he was a very sickly child); of my father's scavenging for food, including the time he brought home a live chicken on his bicycle. One of my few pleasant memories of our life in the D.P. camps was my fourth or fifth birthday party, when I was truly excited to receive my first present – a bar of soap.

Thanks (as I learned much later) to the Displaced Persons Act of 1948, which opened the American borders to thousands of immigrants per year for four years, my family was able to emigrate to the U.S. in June 1950. My aunts' families were also fortunate in obtaining immigration slots. I remember vividly

Max Gitter with his parents and new baby brother
in a German town in early spring 1947.

the voyage from Bremerhaven, Germany, and our arrival in New York on June 15. The former troopship was crammed to the gunwales with refugees and everyone was seasick, all the time. At the immigration station in New York, my father, accustomed to surviving by paying bribes to border officials and other functionaries, had me wearing two Swiss watches hidden on my upper arms by my sleeves. My father was afraid that unless they were hidden, the precious watches would have to be paid over. I was terrified that my smuggling would be discovered and I would be punished, or that our few valuables would be confiscated.

With food and housing allowances provided by Jewish relief organizations, we secured a small apartment in the Bronx and made do until my father found a job. Two and a half months after our arrival, still bewildered by my new surroundings, I had to continue my schooling, having had a year or two of Jewish kindergarten – *cheder* – at the displaced persons camp at Lechveld. I was sent to a yeshiva not far from our home in the Bronx. The mornings at the yeshiva were devoted to religious studies in Yiddish and the afternoons to secular studies in English. Although fluent in Yiddish and German and still having some Russian, I spoke no English. But, like all young children who are immersed in a new language, I learned it very quickly.

Through the 1950s my father worked as a laborer in various shoe factories in lower Manhattan. My mother was an occasional seamstress. We were very poor. Like many immigrant children, by the age of 11 or 12, I was obliged to start working during the summers, taking shoes and slippers made by my father and selling them door-to-door in the Catskills. And because I was the first in my family to learn English, I was also obliged to shepherd my parents through the New York City subway system and through their evening language and citizenship classes.

Until everyone in my family became a naturalized citizen in the late 1950s, I filled out numerous forms from the government and other organizations for my family. Often the forms contained a question about the country of citizenship, for which our required response was "stateless." That term, which evoked a sense of not belonging, disturbed me as a young boy and still evokes a little of the anxiety of rootlessness.

I excelled in the yeshiva, and my teachers and parents pressed me to continue my studies in the traditional way at Yeshiva University High School in upper Manhattan. Nevertheless, in 1957, after passing the entrance exam, I insisted on attending the Bronx High School of Science. For tolerating my rebellious act, my parents earned the wrath of the head of the yeshiva, Rabbi Savitz, who pronounced upon them a terrible curse – that I would some day leave the Jewish fold – as I stood there watching in terror. Superstition-bound by the shtetl culture from which they came, my parents were deeply affected by the curse, so much so that 12 years later, when they met my future wife, they peppered her with questions to test whether she was really Jewish.

I excelled at Bronx Science also and was admitted to Harvard College in April 1961 with a full scholarship. Neither of my parents had completed grade school. In September 1961, again over the protests of my parents, who were still under the spell of Rabbi Savitz's curse and who implored me to live at home and attend Columbia, I enrolled as a freshman at Harvard.

Although something of an outsider at the yeshiva and at Bronx Science because I was an immigrant, I nevertheless felt at home in both schools and developed warm attachments to teachers and many of my classmates. At Harvard, however, I always felt an awkward outsider, never finding a comfortable niche either socially or academically. My clothes seemed wrong, my manners unpolished. When my freshman roommate, a graduate of St. Paul's School, donned formal wear for the opening of the opera season in Boston, I could not have felt more out of place: I had never actually seen a live person in tails. Another freshman, from the Iowa farmlands, who obviously had never met a Jew, confided to me on the way to lunch one day that he felt sorry for our Jewish classmates because they had to date such ugly girls. Mortified, I said nothing in response. While ultimately I made a fair number of friends, I formed almost no lasting relationships. Academically I earned good grades only because I read voraciously on my own, cutting most of my classes. I never had a feeling of belonging. In a sense I was a displaced person again.

The journey of a young boy – then named Manes Giter – from Samarkand to Ellis Island, official entrance to the New World, was long and difficult. In some ways the journey of a poor immigrant teenager from the Bronx to a new world in Cambridge was just as long and difficult. Since graduating from Harvard in 1965, I have been extraordinarily fortunate in my career and in my family. But even at the age of 55, I don't believe I've yet fully come to terms with either of those journeys. Achieving citizenship does not necessarily erase all vestiges of statelessness.

A BABY OF THE JAPANESE OCCUPATION

Goh Cheng Teik

>Born: October 16, 1943
>Bagan Dalam, Straits Settlement of Penang (now Malaysia)

The world war came to Malaysia, then a territorial possession of the British Empire, at the same time as it did to America. While some Japanese warplanes were flying eastward on December 8, 1941, to bomb Pearl Harbor, Hawaii, others were heading southward to attack Kota Bahru, Kelantan. In fact, the landing at Kota Bahru was made an hour and 20 minutes before the air attack on Pearl Harbor. Two days later, the *Prince of Wales* and the *Repulse*, Britain's prize warships, were sunk by Japanese planes off Kuantan. Within a matter of nine weeks, Japanese troops overran the entire Malay Peninsula, capturing Singapore on February 15, 1942, and taking General A. E. Percival and his men prisoners. Thus began three and a half years of a reign of terror and deprivation for my parents.

I was – literally – a baby of the Japanese occupation. By the time I arrived on October 16, 1943, in the village of Bagan Dalam (The Inner Landing-Place) on the outskirts of the city of Butterworth, Japanese troops had occupied the Straits Settlement of Penang for 22 months. Father, the son of an immigrant from Fujian Province, China, was then struggling to keep up a small sundries shop. Mother, the youngest daughter of a boatman, assisted him in the business. Her parents were Straits Chinese who had been settled in the Straits of Malacca area for several generations.

The Japanese occupation forces had entered Butterworth from the north on bicycles. Retreating British troops had bombed bridges in order to delay the enemy's advance. Bicycles were handy because they could be placed in the sampans and rowed across rivers. The Japanese met no resistance in Butterworth because the British troops had already retreated to the south prior to their arrival.

Father and Mother recall that the Japanese were utterly cruel. The commander of the garrison who had stationed himself at the Sungai Nyior Dockyard in Bagan Dalam was nicknamed Tiger Head by the locals because of his notorious savagry. Any annoyance, however slight, would result in verbal abuse, slapping, punching, or kicking by the men of this Tiger Head. Those who were alleged to be opponents of the Japanese regime were beaten, tortured, and beheaded. Ethnic Chinese, domiciled in the former British colony of Penang, like my parents, were singled out because, by and large, they had little love for the Japanese, particularly after Japan invaded China in 1937. The Japanese were reported to have committed atrocities in China, and the Rape of Nanking was widely reported in the local Chinese and English newspapers in Malaysia.

Those ethnic Chinese who had raised funds for or contributed money to the China Relief Fund, set up by Singapore's Tan Kah Kee and others to collect money in support of China's war effort, were rounded up and interrogated. Father remembers that at least four residents of Bagan Dalam, a village of fewer than a thousand inhabitants, were executed. This figure does not include others from elsewhere who were killed in the village. Usually the victim would be tied up and forced to kneel down. Then the executioner would chop off his head with a sword. The executions took place at night. The public were not allowed to view the executions and the corpses were buried by the authorities themselves. Father believes that the number of executions was substantial.

Women were harassed, molested, and raped, particularly when the occupation forces first arrived in Butterworth. Mother and other young women lived in constant fear of the Japanese. To try to escape notice, they hid themselves from public view as much as they could. They kept their hair short and wore men's clothes in order to disguise their gender. Some of the women who were unlucky enough to be seen and taken away never returned.

Father and Mother also recall that the occupation caused great suffering to the common people. Food was extremely scarce. Rice, sugar, salt, cooking oil, and other essential food provisions were rationed. As a result there was a black market in almost everything. The famous banana notes printed by the occupation regime were in circulation, but so many were printed they became practically valueless.

Since Father's shop sold food provisions, I was supposedly luckier than other war babies, but even so I had no milk to drink. I had to be fed on rice porridge until the Japanese surrender in August 1945. Moreover, there were times when there was no food in stock, and the family had to go hungry for days.

Although I was not yet two years old, I remember the end of this reign of terror. I can still picture in my mind gangs of ragged Japanese soldiers hastily on the move. They carried rifles but appeared frightened and bewildered. I can also remember the arrival of British forces. Standing in front of my grandpa's house, I watched truckload after truckload of British soldiers enter New Ferry Road, cheered on by onlookers.

The terrible tales of the Japanese occupation, which I had heard not only from my parents but also from uncles and aunties, had a deep effect on me during my teenage years. When I was at school at St. Xavier's Institution, Penang, I read and reread *Ma-rai-ee*, a novel about the war years, in which Chin Kee Onn, a local author, narrated the exploits of local youths who fled into the thick tropical jungles of Malaya to organize armed resistance against the Japanese invaders. I remember how I hero-worshipped those brave youths in the novel. I also remember watching the film *The Bridge on the River Kwai*. My feelings were entirely for the British prisoners of war. Colonel Nicholson's dignified defiance of the Japanese commander's authority filled my heart with pride and anger.

The events of the war also contributed, albeit indirectly, to my going to Harvard. By treating the native Malays better than the Chinese, the Japanese had caused these two core races of Malaya to suspect each other. When Chinese resistance fighters summarily executed some Malay "collaborators" at the end of the war, the Malays retaliated by sacking Chinese houses in some parts of the country. The outbreak of rebellion against the British government led by these same anti-Japanese resistance fighters in 1948 further exacerbated race relations. Tunku Abdul Rahman, the first prime minister of independent Malaya, managed to bring moderate Chinese, Malays, and Indians together, to win independence from Britain and to govern the country for the benefit of all races. For some years, there was racial harmony, but by 1959 race relations were again in crisis. Although still a student, I was determined by 1960-61 to embark on a political career and to work for interracial peace and harmony. When the time came for me to apply to university, my choice was clear. I applied to Harvard (the alma mater of John Kennedy, who was elected president in 1960), Brandeis, and other American universities. In my application, I made no bones about the fact that I wanted to study government and that I also wanted to play my part in preserving the fragile interracial peace of my newly independent country. Brandeis immediately offered me admission and a scholarship, but I had to turn down its offer when – to my pleasant surprise – Harvard also offered me admission with advanced standing status and a full scholarship.

When I entered college in the autumn of 1962, I spent my spare hours in the stacks of the library devouring every bit of information I could get on the Japanese occupation of Malaysia. I read the reports in the *London Times* dispatched by its war correspondents describing in great detail the humiliating retreat of British forces from the Malay Peninsula. I studied the big debate in Britain ignited by the defeat in the Malay Peninsula. I became so interested in research on the Japanese occupation and its aftermath that I wrote my senior thesis on the turbulent postwar politics of my country. In my thesis I argued that the insurgents who took up arms against the British government in 1948 were not Marxist ideologues acting on instructions from Moscow. They were disillusioned anti-Japanese resistance fighters. Had their wartime ally, the British government, handled them appropriately (for example, by offering them land to farm and settle down on), they would probably not have returned to the jungle.

After college and two years of graduate work at Leiden University in the Netherlands, where I learned Malay and Indonesian, studied the history of Islam in the Malay Archipelago, and sought in every way possible to deepen my knowledge about the peoples of Malay and Indonesian stock, I returned to my home country. I was – and still am – determined to fulfill the pledge I made to my classmates as the 1965 Harvard Commencement English orator, namely, to overcome the sense of alienation from my people that years abroad had caused, to slowly regain the trust and acceptance of my countryfolk, and to utilize the knowledge I gained in the West to serve my country and my people.

I was not able to enter politics at once, but seven years of teaching at the local university were valuable preparatory years for me. I watched politics as it was played out from the sidelines, but from time to time I did manage, thanks to the support of my mentor, Tun Dr. Lim Chong Eu, to participate indirectly. I helped Tun Lim's party, the Gerakan, which I subsequently joined, to campaign in the 1969 general elections and to capture the state government of my home state, Penang.

The violent race riots that broke out in Kuala Lumpur on May 13, 1969, a few days after the general elections, reinforced my conviction that the problem of race relations had to be urgently addressed. I felt that Western-educated intellectuals had a duty to stay and help out, whereas migration to the West was tantamount to running away at a time when the country needed us most. I remember an offer from a diplomat friend in a Commonwealth embassy to assist me in emigrating. He was pessimistic about the future of the ethnic Chinese in Malaysia. I said to him politely that I would leave my country only as an exile or refugee, never as a willing migrant.

Books on the May Thirteenth riots traced this racial conflict to the damage in race relations caused by the authorities of the Japanese occupation and the eruption of interracial violence in certain parts of the Malay Peninsula in the intervening weeks between the Japanese surrender and the return of British forces. For Tun Abdul Razak, who succeeded Tunku Abdul Rahman as prime minister in September 1970, and others who were helping him to bind up the wounds of conflict and to restore peace and harmony, however, it was academic to blame the Japanese. They had surrendered and left the Malay Peninsula more than a decade previously. Tun Abdul Razak believed it was up to present-day Malays, Chinese, Indians, and others to get along with each other and to look ahead to the future.

Tun Lim Chong Eu, who became chief minister of Penang after his party won the 1969 elections, responded positively to Tun Razak's call to put partisan politics aside. He brought the Gerakan into an enlarged coalition, the National Front, that Tun Razak had initiated. At the subsequent general elections in 1974, Tun Lim invited me to run for Parliament on a Gerakan-National Front ticket. I won my election and, on Tun Lim's recommendation, was appointed by Tun Razak as one of his parliamentary secretaries. Thus I began the political career that college had prepared me for.

I am aware that some observers from the West do not view the political process in Malaysia with full favor. To them it appears that the Malaysian government is totally Malay-dominated. The non-Malays in it are merely wallflowers. The prime minister, who is invariably a Malay, is perceived to be overly powerful. Also the rights of non-Malays are perceived to be trampled upon.

As a member of the government for the past quarter-century, I can say with a clear conscience that the picture as seen from the inside is not so clearcut. Malays comprise a majority of the voting population. Election after election, most of them vote without fail for the Malay party (the United Malay National Organisation). At the same time, they also vote without fail for UMNO's non-Malay coalition partners. Since Malay MPs outnumber non-Malay MPs, it is not illogical for the government to be Malay-led. Moreover, Malay leadership of the government has not resulted in Malay tyranny over the rest of the population. Within the cabinet, where Malay ministers also outnumber non-Malay ministers, issues are not decided by voting. By convention, the prime minister

In the 1980s, on behalf of the Malaysian Government, Dr. Goh proposes a toast to the health of the Emperor of Japan on the occasion of his birthday; looking on is the Japanese ambassador to Malaysia.

is allowed to formulate the cabinet decision after listening to arguments from all sides. Cabinet friends tell me that there are numerous occasions on which the Malay prime minister overrules his Malay ministers in favor of the non-Malays. Foreigners find it hard to understand, but this is why many non-Malays view our present prime minister, Dr. Mahathir Mohamad, as a protector, not a represser, of minority rights.

For all its imperfections, the National Front Government's way of tackling the racial problem has produced results. Just compare the different ways in which Indonesians and Malaysians are reacting to the current Asian economic crisis. In Indonesia the populace loot and destroy business premises owned by ethnic Chinese who are Indonesian citizens and rape their womenfolk, blaming this ethnic minority for their economic woes. In Malaysia the different races, whether Malay, Chinese, Indian, Iban, or Kadazan, accept the government's explanation that a recession is a fact of economic life and that all races ought to work together to end it speedily.

As a student and in my adult years, I have grappled with my personal feelings vis-à-vis the Japanese. I have asked myself whether present-day Japanese people are as ruthless and cruel as those who ill-treated my family in Bagan Dalam during the war. I have made numerous visits to Japan and have found no streaks of cruelty in the Japanese I have met. On the contrary, I have found them to be courteous and very civil to foreigners.

While my aging parents may still harbor residual distrust of the Japanese, I have long ago given the Japanese the benefit of the doubt. This applies particularly to those who had nothing to do with the war effort. They are blameless. The atrocities committed in the occupied territories of East Asia were the work of the wartime generation. Guilt is not biologically transmitted. Yet I must confess that misgivings return to haunt me each time I read about Japanese people who do not believe that Japanese soldiers committed atrocities during the Pacific war and each time I hear about Japanese politicians who visit the Yasukuni Shrine to pay respects to officers and soldiers of the Japanese Imperial Army who died during the war. At such times I cannot help but feel that although World War II is historically over, it still lingers on within me.

DISSOLVING REPRESSION
A HALF-CENTURY REPORT

Howard Gardner

> Born: July 11, 1943
> Scranton, Pennsylvania, U.S.A.

At Harvard College in the early 1960s, friends and roommates were surprised when they met my parents. Ralph and Hilde Gardner had strong German accents. My person had given no clue about this parental trait: I looked like a reasonably nondescript American, had no accent myself, had attended a small private school in northeastern Pennsylvania, and – perhaps most important – bore a name that suggested an Anglo-Saxon background. Little did my friends know that my parents had been "Gärtner" in Nuremberg, Germany, their birthplace, which they fled a scant 10 days before the infamous Kristallnacht, November 9-10, 1938. My parents moved briefly to New York City before settling in Scranton, Pennsylvania, where I grew up.

While it did not come up in ordinary conversation, I made no effort to hide my identity as a German Jew. Indeed, my German Jewish ancestry was certainly a central fact in my identity, as my college tutor, psychoanalyst Erik Erikson, would surely have reminded me. Ours was a close-knit family, and everyone in the older generation continued to converse in German, despite the fact that English was the primary language of the homes. I had attended temple as a child and become bar mitzvah, though I slowly abandoned ties to the formal religion. Actually, though I have no memory of it, I apparently spoke English with a German accent when I began school. How could one avoid such a marker when all the adults around rolled their *r*'s in the same way?

But other aspects of my background had been hidden from me. Throughout my early childhood, my parents remained silent about the two most important facts in their lives – their narrow escape from the Holocaust and the accidental death of their only child, my older brother Eric, in a sledding accident in January 1943, when my mother was three months pregnant with me.

This silence was, as they say, overdetermined. In general, members of the European bourgeoisie of that time did not discuss such serious matters with children. Germans were especially reserved about personal matters. Add to this the fact that my extended family is also relatively "uptight" in this respect. I am sure, however, that the major reason for the silences was that these topics were simply too painful to talk about. More than 50 years later, my father still finds it difficult to talk about Eric's death. Moreover, the family was silent about the trauma of the Holocaust. Some family members and many friends lost their lives in concentration camps. I remember my own shock – and the ensuing nightmares – when, at the age of 11 or 12, I learned that my aunt and uncle had been thrown out of their Nuremberg home on Kristallnacht, and my uncle had been trampled to death. Aunt Emily survived, but her face remained disfigured until her death at age 97. Around the same time I learned that before their marriages to my uncles, my Aunt Gretl had been in several concentration camps and my Aunt Elsbeth had been in Auschwitz and had in fact been experimented upon by Dr. Mengele. Both had been liberated as skeletons, and both had been very sick for years thereafter, though they eventually recovered their health. Elsbeth retained the inmate number branded on her arm for many years.

When confronted with painful information, one can attempt to deal directly with it, or one can repress it. Just about all the Gardners, Weilheimers, and Seidenbergers chose the route of silence for themselves and for their children. Relatives who had been in hiding for years in France and Holland never breathed a word about their ordeals to their children. Slowly, some of us were able to confront the facts of the Holocaust directly, but many – including myself – were not. In general, I eschewed any photographs or films related to the Holocaust. I just could not take it. I did read books and, ultimately, I visited Holocaust museums here and abroad; but in the latter cases, unlike that of cinematic portrayals, I could control the amount of exposure and "drop out" entirely. To this day, when it comes to a discussion of Nazi cruelty, I skim or shut the book entirely. I can well understand why the ambitious politician Madeleine Albright simply refused to confront the possibility that she was Jewish. She probably did not want to have to deal with the resultant psychic trauma.

My reluctance to read or view accounts of Nazi atrocities has extended to a range of other topics. Even more than other squeamish individuals, I am unable to read about or watch depictions of violence, sadism, or other kinds of physical abuse. I skip those sections in books. I avoid or walk out of movies that contain depictions or simulations of violence. When I hear members of the audience laugh or snicker as blood oozes out, I become angry and distraught. Truth to tell, I also distance myself from the interpersonal conflicts of others and, more than I should, my own conflicts. Metaphors of "charged experiences" that have been banished to an inaccessible region of the mind, or of psychic scabs too painful to remove, are uncomfortably apt.

Only within the last year did I become conscious of a fundamental part of my family's heritage. I have always known that my extended family is close, getting together and celebrating almost every conceivable event. I have welcomed that intimacy – in most respects! It is fun to let down your hair with individuals who have known you – and whom you have known – since birth. These celebrations are perhaps compensations or substitutes for pains that are too difficult to confront overtly. It is natural, as well as educational, to monitor life's passages in those to whom you are closest. Strangely enough, it was only within the last year that I came to appreciate a principal reason for this familial intimacy. My eight-year-old nephew Daniel Eric was interviewing family members for a school project. As happens nowadays, all this was videotaped. He asked my parents and one of my uncles to talk about the "olden days" (his actual term). And when I heard their responses, I realized that they had spent the first years of their adulthood on an extended project to preserve what they could of our family.

Once it had become clear in the middle 1930s that Hitler was out to act upon his vicious threats, the chief goal for the extended family was to make sure that all members could escape the Nazi clutches. Each healthy member of the family took it as a priority to explore ways of escape and to make sure that no stone was left unturned in securing safe passage somewhere, anywhere. All things considered, they were amazingly successful in this endeavor. Nearly all our close relatives had left Germany by 1939 – and the success of their mission thereby sealed the closeness of the survivors for the next half-century. Like many other German Jewish refugee families, I have relatives throughout the United States, Canada, England, France, Argentina, Israel, and South Africa. Like the overseas Chinese or Indians, we have become a global community of expatriates. We relate easily to people from other cultures, and I myself feel at least as European (if not global) as I do American.

I came to welcome the more overt aspects of my German Jewish background. I eventually became a social scientist – specifically a psychologist – thus entering a field that was filled with people from a similar background. A surprisingly large number of the scholars whom I worked with and admired – scholars like Erik Erikson, political theorist Stanley Hoffmann, art historian Ernst Gombrich, and psychologist of art Rudolf Arnheim – shared my heritage. I knew that some of my friends came from the same background, and an ever-increasing number of friends – and classmates – turn out to have been German or Austrian or Eastern European Jews whose families narrowly escaped incarceration or death. My wife's father was born in Prague and escaped to the West to attend Harvard College in the late 1930s, while members of his immediate family died in concentration camps.

Why does one become a social scientist? As the proverbial Jewish boy who hated the sight of blood, I was originally headed toward law school. I certainly can see myself as a lawyer, though legal practice would have bored me, and I would probably have ended up as a teacher of the law. I was attracted to work in psychology and other social sciences, however, and once I determined that one could make a living as a scholar, I readily pursued that route. (I doubt that, as an ambitious youth, I would make the same career decision today, yet in spurning the academy I would have been the loser.)

In retrospect, I see another reason for my career choice. As a social scientist, one can examine aspects of human life and experience from a distance that is not possible for the artist, the writer, or even the medical practitioner. Topics dealing with human feelings, especially those tinged with sadness or cruelty, were very difficult for me to confront directly. If I donned the lenses of the cultural anthropologist or the social psychologist, at least I could confront these issues in a more protected way. Even so, I was cautious. As I reflect on the topics that I studied, became fascinated with, and wrote about, I note that they permitted me to retain the studied distance of the scholar. When I examined "the mind," I focused on intelligence and not emotions. When I studied the arts, I was oriented toward the more contained forms, such as abstract art or traditional classical music, rather than dramatic tragedy or grand opera. And when I investigated pathology, I looked at the cognitive results of brain damage, rather than, say, the phenomenology of manic-depressive disease or paranoia. I note these preferences because they are unusual. Most people attracted to psychology want to deal with charged affective matters. And most people are attracted to books or movies that deal with raw emotional content. In such cases, I run in the opposite direction.

So I have found myself in a quandary. I have until now spent much of my life avoiding, spurning, running away from the Holocaust – arguably the central event of twentieth-century Western history, and clearly the central event in the immediate past history of my entire family. To be sure, I have admired those who can write about these topics, who can confront the awfulness of what has happened, who somehow managed to survive – but I have not been able to emulate them.

However – and here I explicate the title of this essay – I have recently begun to feel differently about these matters. Whatever silence there may have been across the land (indeed the Western world) about the Holocaust has vanished. In this time of the grandchildren of victims and survivors, the Holocaust is so widely discussed that even I have been somewhat desensitized. After half a century, members of my own family have also become more willing to talk about what happened – perhaps because they know that if they do not share these remembrances with the younger generation, their memories will perish forever.

In 1996, thanks to the generosity of my Harvard roommate, Tom Lee, I was given the opportunity to collaborate with an organization that I much admire: Facing History and Ourselves (FHAO). With headquarters in Brookline, Massachusetts, FHAO has for 20 years been developing historical and literary curricular materials for teachers and students, primarily in secondary school. Initially the work centered on the Holocaust, but in recent years, FHAO has treated an ensemble of issues having to do with racism, intergroup relations, group conflict, eugenics, and other hot-button topics.

Much of my own work as a psychological researcher over the past decade has been devoted to school reform. I advocate the teaching of important but difficult topics, with a focus on how to convey such material to students in ways that are accessible to them. Once the opportunity arose to work with FHAO, I realized that the Holocaust was exactly the area for me to investigate, with knowledgeable and sympathetic colleagues. And so, after a half a century of avoidance, if not repression, I feel prepared to confront an epochal event that also constitutes a crucial but hitherto unexplored area of my own past. Of course, I am still approaching these issues as a scholar, a social scientist, an educational reformer. These distancing lenses help me. But I hope that they will help me not only to avoid feeling unmanageable pain but also to probe more deeply than before into the awfulness of our time and the evils (and, at least occasionally, the altruism) of which human beings are capable.

The only good achieved by the Nazis is of a perverse sort. Hitler and his henchmen shattered illusions. Any notion we had that a highly civilized society, one that thought of itself as the apogee of civilization, was immune from the most horrific deeds has been forever dispelled. One can go from Goethe to Goebbels in a century, from Weimar to Auschwitz in a generation. And lest one think that the Holocaust was unique, one need only think about Rwanda or Bosnia – and the West's silences in the wake of these contemporary holocausts – to affirm that genocidal impulses have not been stilled.

These reflections have stimulated an ambitious project on which my colleagues in FHAO and I have recently embarked. In search of "humane creativity" we ask the following question: Is it possible to have a society in which people can do original, creative, cutting-edge work, on the one hand, but also embody an active and enduring sense of responsibility for the implications of that work, on the other? We are carrying out this study by interviewing people who work in several domains (the media, science, the professions) and searching for replicable patterns in those individuals who seem to embody humane creativity – as did, for example, Pablo Casals or Niels Bohr or Rachel Carson earlier in this century. We hope to discover the ways in which certain, all-too-rare persons have been able to lead lives in which they have blended creativity with an ethical orientation toward their work. Once our study has been concluded, we would like to develop programs that will help young professionals carry out cutting-edge work in a responsible way. Indeed, we hope that we can help students to see this amalgam in a new way: not as a "zero-sum" situation, where creativity and ethics pull in opposite directions, but rather as an exciting challenge, where one is even more creative when one can pursue one's work in a responsible manner.

Our project in "humane creativity" was not framed with particular reference to the Holocaust, though it is clear that people like the Nazi doctors raise the issue in the starkest terms. I would suggest, however, that not only individuals face the choice of humane versus inhumane creativity – this choice is faced as well by groups and even whole societies. In times of stress, not all people act the same way – witness the courage of Oskar Schindler or Raoul Wallenberg during World War II. Nor, indeed, do nations – the reactions of the Danes and the Dutch to the Third Reich were quite different from the reactions of the Austrians or the French or, as we have recently learned, the Swiss.

Need I insist that these issues matter? In a way that was not true when war babies like us were born, the world can now destroy itself. It is up to us and our children to make sure that such destruction is never realized. By the same token, awesome discoveries – such as those of the human genome project – can be used constructively (to treat abnormalities) or destructively (to deny insurance to a person). Again, the choice is ours. I am reminded of Margaret Mead's trenchant observation: "Never deprecate a small group of people who come together to discuss new ideas. Nothing important in the world has ever begun in any other way."

Repression is not wholly bad. No less an authority than Freud asserted that civilization depended on it, and he was merely echoing Schopenhauer. Yet Freud also showed us that repression is not healthy in the long run. It is important to confront our most painful experiences directly, else they will ultimately, if insidiously, undermine us in other spheres. I do not hold it against my parents that they modeled repression. They needed to repress in order to survive and to raise their children as best they could. I have tried to be a more open role model for my children, though it has not come naturally. As I confront the finitude of my years with increasing clarity, I am relieved that I can now at last begin to confront, more directly, those events that undergirded my own personal history. I will be grateful if through my work I can help to dissolve the taint of the phrase "humane creativity," untangling the oxymoron implicit in it.

MY FATHER, BATTALION SURGEON

William M. McConahey III

> Born: April 27, 1943
> Philadelphia, Pennsylvania, U.S.A.

"And when we came out in the morning, we discovered that our 'safe' refuge could have gone up like a fireworks factory at any time during the night with that munitions truck parked right outside!" At that both men laughed, slapped their thighs, and carried on in a manner most uncharacteristic of at least one of them, my father, who was usually quite reserved and very much in his role as a distinguished Mayo Clinic physician. I was a spellbound 10-year-old boy listening to my father and his former jeep driver, Peter Wedl, recount their war adventures. My mother, sister, and baby brother were off with the jeep driver's wife and daughter, and I was alone with the men. This was a summer ritual that changed little each year. The two families would get together for a picnic, either in Rochester, Minnesota, where my father practiced medicine, or in St. Paul, where the Wedls lived. We would go to a park, eat a picnic meal, and then while the others entertained themselves elsewhere, I would listen to stories and get a glimpse of a father I never saw otherwise. I knew he was a twice-decorated medical officer who had been in the thick of battle for most of the war from the Normandy invasion on, but it took me a while to understand what that meant.

I grew up in the Midwest far from the war. I learned a little about World War II in school. When "I like Ike" was a campaign slogan, I knew that "Ike" was a famous general who had been in "my dad's army." Our family had never experienced persecution, nor had any of our friends. It took me several visits to the scenes of my father's involvement in this war to comprehend the evil that caused millions to be murdered just for who they were, their properties taken, and all traces of them obliterated. It took time to realize that with enough commitment and personal sacrifice, such as that exemplified by my father, even such a great evil could be defeated. The human costs involved are still incalculable, but I learned that such evil can, should, and must be fought and overcome. How could I understand that as a child? How well do I truly comprehend it now with no firsthand experience? The memories shared and values imparted over the years by my father have helped me come to terms with the world's good and evil, even if at first vicariously. But back then, as a small boy, I was mostly just enthralled by my father's tales.

I heard about that apparently safe aid station my father and his jeep driver had set up after dark in a bombed-out school, only to find it an explosive deathtrap by daylight. I marveled at their luck when, behind enemy lines, they rounded a corner and found themselves looking down the large-bore weapon of a very surprised German antitank crew. Only the surprise, the red crosses on the jeep, and a very quick reverse by the driver saved them. I shared Dad's fright as a bomb whistled down from a German plane toward him as he lay helplessly on the ground under a tiny tree, only to have it land a few feet away with a dull thud – a harmless dud. I was enchanted by the rescue of the two young Luxembourg girls and their mother, who had been hiding in a back room of a house occupied by German soldiers until the Germans were driven out. They were hungry, dirty, and scared, covered with sores and lice. And they liked chocolate. Years later I met them and their families. I also heard about the Flossenberg concentration camp in Germany. My father was the first medical officer to enter it after it was liberated. I suffered as he recalled that without many more assistants and supplies, there was nothing he could do for most of the barely living survivors. I exalted in the exploits of General George "Blood and Guts" Patton, as they were told and retold. I soared above enemy lines with my father as he went with one of the reconnaissance pilots in a small plane to see if the downed pilot of the other plane could be helped. Those picnics were

Dr. McConahey, battalion surgeon, in front of the house in Tarchamps, Luxembourg, where he rescued two little girls and their mother, January 1945.

my introduction to my father's part in World War II, something that would become a family focus in the years ahead. Through my father's reminiscences I learned about the war, the kind of world in which it could happen, and the capacities for good and evil that we all share. I also learned about my father and perhaps had the seeds planted that would eventually come to fruition as I, too, pursued a career in medicine.

Initially, as the oldest child, I was the only family member interested in my father's tales, but later my sister and my brother became absorbed as well. My mother was not at all interested in any of this for many years, and even later not to the degree that I was. My father's belief is that she had an anxious, uncertain time during the war. She was glad it was over and relieved he had survived, and she wanted to hear nothing further about it. For my father, on the other hand, reliving those experiences was therapeutic. His other therapeutic outlet came from writing a book about his experiences while on occupation duty after the war.

The next war experiences I was to have were pure delight to a young boy – souvenirs! Some of them even worked. Many times I enthralled my friends after school by showing them the boxes filled with Nazi flags, bayonets, daggers, and real guns. Our family had uniform patches, belt buckles, propaganda leaflets, maps, shrapnel, spent shells, even a flare parachute and a Nazi helmet to fire our imaginations. On a handful of occasions, I got to shoot the Mauser rifle and the Walther pistol that Dad had brought home, but only under his supervision. There was one occasion, however, while my parents were away, when I convinced a gullible baby-sitter that it was all right for me to take souvenirs to school for show-and-tell. There I was at school in the fourth or fifth grade with a German dress sword, a German ceremonial dagger, and both American and German bayonets. No one was hurt, nothing untoward happened, and I was a vicarious hero for the day. I think it was many years later that my father found out about that escapade.

My father's wartime job was that of a front-line doctor or battalion surgeon. This was to be the last war in which physicians were actually at the front, because helicopters later made that practice obsolete. I had been born near the end of his internship. Following that year, he trained in Colorado and staged in England. In June 1944, as part of the 90th Infantry Division, he went into combat at Utah Beach on D-Day-Plus-Two. He was in Patton's Third Army from then through the Battle of the Bulge, the invasion of Germany, and the advance into Czechoslovakia at the war's end. He was on occupation duty in Germany for a year after that and while there wrote his self-described "worm's-eye" view of the war entitled *Battalion Surgeon*.

Reading that book in manuscript as an adolescent provided my next intensive experience with the war. By then I was seriously considering a career in medicine. The book may have influenced me as much as did my father's daily example as a practicing physician. For him, writing the book was a healing experience. He remembered, processed, and relived it all during his stint of occupation duty in the first year after the war, while things were still fresh in his mind. He was able to ask others who had been through the same horrible and memory-searing events to corroborate his impressions and validate his emotions. And then he was able to leave it alone, except for certain occasions, occasions that occurred largely by choice. He was not one to be awakened often by nightmares or to suffer posttraumatic stress.

My father and many other veterans are of the opinion that no one who has not been in combat can have any inkling about what it is really like. Although my father has had a rich life and a distinguished career, for him, as for many soldiers who have been in combat, the war was a defining event, perhaps the most intense and compelling of his life, the action forcefully etched in his mind. It became a focus for issues of right and wrong, good and evil, life and death, serving as a measure for later experiences. World War II gradually came to serve similar purposes for my entire family.

In 1960, when I was in high school, my family made the first of a series of pilgrimages of intentional remembrance, visiting the scenes of my father's war service. We went to Europe for the summer. I was the oldest child and at 17 still the family member most interested in Dad's wartime deeds. Handicapped by inadequate maps and the lack of a translator, we had some trouble finding the places that had been important to him. In Germany, however, we located the area where Dad's jeep swerved to miss a crater in the muddy road and almost overturned into the pitch-black Moselle River at night. We met the girls he had rescued in Luxembourg, now grown and married with families of their own. They all welcomed us royally and entertained us lavishly. The husband of one of the girls later went on to become the chief justice of the supreme court of Luxembourg.

In France we had an unsettling experience when we visited a little-known concentration camp as tourists. Our ancestry is mostly Scottish and we are all light-skinned, fair-haired, and blue-eyed. We were driving a Mercedes sedan with German plates and looked the part of German tourists. The camp itself was depressing and appalling, and we returned to our car in a somber mood. The nonverbal communication directed at us by the other tourists as we climbed into our car and drove away was frightening. They clearly thought that we or some of our predecessors had been responsible for the camp and its atrocities. We had a difficult time even believing what had occurred at the camp or understanding why the events had happened. We felt that we ourselves were in no way able to murder and enslave others, yet we are all human, and what had been done at that camp had been done by other human beings.

Eleven years later we took another trip to Normandy, one better prepared and better guided. Following in my father's footsteps, I had finished medical school and rewarded myself in 1971 with a three-month trip to Europe with my wife. My father flew over and joined us for the Normandy segment of the trip.

By this time he had some French friends and acquaintances and had gotten better maps. One of his friends had even fought early in the war in the French cavalry – on horseback against Hitler's panzers. The man took a week off to drive us around Normandy. With him we found many of the towns, intersections, and, in some cases, the very buildings where Dad had established aid stations in the early days of the Allied landing in Normandy. It was exciting and moving to locate a barn he had used 25 years beforehand, to share that information with the farmer who owned it, and to be invited in for reminiscences and celebration over a glass of the best of whatever the farmer had in the house. Like Dad the local citizens had not forgotten the rescue brought by the Allied invasion. Their gratitude was still tangible. Things like that happened several times during our week's trip. We discovered several burned out and rusted hulks – all that remained of warring tanks – still poised aiming at each other across fields and behind hedgerows. Even then, a quarter-century after the fighting, there were shell casings and lumps of lead to be picked up with ease from the earth. In the Normandy cemeteries we stood in silence and contemplated rows and rows of grave markers, each topped by a star or a cross. It seemed impossible that so many had died fighting and inconceivable that so many more had been killed in the camps. Dad's presence confirmed for us, however, that it had all been real.

Up until this point my mother had not shown any interest in revisiting the scenes of Dad's struggles. Then in 1981, when my brother and sister expressed an interest in seeing them, she finally came around. It had taken her 35 years to decide that this era of her life needed to be actively remembered rather than intentionally forgotten. Dad again toured the old battlefields, but this time he did it with Mother, who had shared that time with him from afar and whose own life during the war had been so different. My parents also took my sister, my younger brother, and their spouses on that trip. Not only did they "reinvade" Normandy, they went on to "refight" the Battle of the Bulge, memorializing the action in the freezing forests of the Ardennes.

The interest in World War II and our family history relating to it extended to the next generation when my children reached the age where they became aware of the war and wanted to know more about their grandfather's part in it. In 1990 my wife and I took our children, then age 18 and 15, on a long summer vacation to Europe. We naturally included visits to the sites of the Normandy invasion and the Battle of the Bulge. The family circle interested in World War II spread even wider as Aunt Florence, my father's sister, was included for the first time that year. Just as some degree of health and growth seemed to come to us from sharing this process as a family, so the world was by then actively remembering and learning from World War II as the fiftieth anniversaries associated with the war were beginning to be celebrated. On this trip more shrines, museums, and other memorials to the soldiers who had fought in the war were in evidence. Compared to earlier trips, there was even more cross-cultural sharing for us as we lodged and dined in the homes of private citizens who had lived in the areas we were visiting or had fought there during the war. We again visited the Normandy beaches and the huge cemeteries and my father's very first aid station, an ancient stone barn, still in use and still shell- and bullet-marked from the fierce battle that had erupted right outside it that night. We climbed around the rusted hulks remaining from a ferocious tank battle and saw the spot where Dad had found a young American officer, binoculars still around his neck, slain by a sniper's bullet through his helmeted head. My children became nearly as interested in their grandfather's stories and memories as I had been at their age and as I still remain.

In 1994, the fiftieth anniversary of the Normandy landings, Dad returned to both Luxembourg and Normandy, with my mother along as a willing participant in the remembrances. We later saw their souvenirs, including citations, medals, and newspaper articles written about local heroes, one of whom was Dad. We came even more to appreciate how much a part of Dad's life World War II had been and still remained.

It seemed amazing that 50 years later the soldiers of the war were still heroes. Small wonder so many of my generation had posttraumatic stress disorder trying to adjust to the aftermath of our war. The Vietnam veterans were often seen as villains rather than heroes, as imperialist invaders rather than selfless liberators. They were welcomed neither at home nor abroad. Only now are they coming to be seen more as victims than victimizers. But in the eyes of the world they are not yet heroes, as the veterans of World War II are.

When the veterans returned home after World War II, they returned to a nation that had wholeheartedly supported the war, a country that celebrated victory with them and honored them for their sacrifices. They also returned slowly by troopship amid continuing celebration. When the United States entered the war, my father and many others felt that fighting was the right thing to do. This feeling was enhanced when they joined with other allies in England prior to the Normandy invasion. The gratitude of the liberated populations of the Western European countries made them feel that they should be there. So did freeing soldiers from nations conquered by Germany who had been impressed into the German army and slave laborers imprisoned by and forced to work for the Germans. When they liberated the concentration camps, they knew they had to be there. They were heroes and saviors then and remain so today in the eyes of the people they freed and their descendants.

My father set a path for me to follow in many ways. I went to college where he had gone to medical school, majoring in English but already planning a career in medicine. After graduating from medical school, I specialized in internal medicine, as he had done, training at the very institution where he was chairman of a division and professor of medicine. Though I shared with my contemporaries many misgivings about the Vietnam War, I would have gone if called. I did not seek military deferment during my medical training, but remained draftable. During my internship I was called up for a preinduction physical, but fortunately for me, the war ended before I was drafted. In mid career as a physician, after practicing as an internist for 15 years, I switched to emergency medicine. Some have suggested that part of the motivation for that switch may have been to get closer to the type of action my father found on the battlefield. I do not personally believe that emergency medicine in the United States is much like medical care on a battlefield, and I don't think that following my father's example has much to do with my motivation, but it is an interesting theory.

My father has often said that he does not worry much about what might happen because he has already been through worse. Though I have not faced anything nearly so horrific as a world war, I have learned, in part through his example, to harbor few regrets about the past and to entertain few worries about the future.

The children of my brother and sister are now in their teens, and Dad is contemplating a trip to show them around his battlefields just as he has already done for me, my siblings, and my children. He will share his memories along the way and as always will impart values shaped by the war to his listening family. They will learn about the bravery of the liberating soldiers, the fortitude of the conquered civilians, and the suffering of those persecuted in the camps. And they will learn about the evil that was Hitler and his SS troops, the evil that caused all the rest. They will understand that we all must always resist tyranny however we can, wherever it exists. I hope he does make that trip. If he does, I may go with him yet again. Each time I do, I learn more about my father and my heritage. I learn more also about humanity's defining event of good and evil in the twentieth century. It is more than worth the trip.

Three generations of McConaheys and some French friends with a World War II jeep in Normandy in June 1999.

Lt. Commander Charles Woodrow Styron, M.D., in 1944.

WAR STORIES, PAST AND PRESENT
A TRIBUTE TO LIEUTENANT COMMANDER CHARLES WOODROW STYRON, M. D.

Charles Woodrow Styron, Jr.

>Born: October 29, 1943
>Raleigh, North Carolina, U.S.A.

"The war" in my grandmother's generation usually meant the Civil War, and I probably heard more about that particular conflict from my elders than I ever heard about World War II from my parents' generation. There were a number of stories about my family's experience in "The War between the States." As a Southerner I still feel a modicum of pride remembering that one of my forebears was reputed to have been the youngest colonel in the Confederacy. A measure of roguish haughtiness arises when I recall the story of Yankee soldiers vainly thrusting their bayonets into the sandy waters of the creek at Devereux Meadow, looking for silver which my forebears, the Devereux women, had secreted there. Haa! The bastards never found it.

In a monograph celebrating the stately Victorian mansion in which she was born, my mother wrote about the shadow that the Civil War had cast over her life.

> The aura of the former glory of plantation days lived on in the Hinsdale house ... but subtly the climate in the South had changed. Marriageable men after the Civil War were in the minority and many had come back wounded from the war. The women assumed a protective attitude toward them, relieving them of many duties the men had previously performed.
>
> Like Scarlett's mother in *Gone with the Wind*, the wives had had to assume the reins of the plantation, the discipline of the children, the religious instruction, the management of the servants, and the nurture and care of all. Quietly the pattern of the Southern matriarch had been established.

When my father married my mother, he entered into the sphere of the second strong matriarchy in his life. I have always thought that the powerful presence of women in his early years had something to do with his bearing of reserve – a reserve that he even took to war and that appeared to have gentled his spirit.

The fact that I was conceived and born during the war never really held great significance for me. No one in my immediate family was killed and, although my father and an uncle both received Purple Hearts, no one in the family suffered serious injury. My father did not talk very much about the war's impact on him, even though my mother was convinced that it was the seminal experience of his life. Whether seminal or not, however, like other soldiers he brought home stories about the experience. Also, like many Southerners, he had a great fondness for good stories as well as a talent for telling them. As forms of communication, stories are always more than they seem to be. They are often compressed experience. They communicate partly through their form, in the same way that parade dress communicates decorum in the military. My father's stories of World War II have always constituted my principal connection to the war and some of them carry a personal lesson for me. The following selection is a small sample from his repertoire (and mine), beginning with one of his (and my mother's) about my birth and ending with a couple of mine about his death.

The parents of Charles Styron early in 1942.

Strong connections can begin slowly
My father read about my birth in the morning newspaper while sitting on the front porch of my Grandmother Joslin's house. He had just come home on leave, knowing that I was about to be born, and he had arrived in Raleigh, North Carolina, very early in the morning. It was late in October 1943, and he did not enter my Grandmother Joslin's house, waiting patiently instead for a couple of hours until everyone got up. My mother was still at the hospital. When she later asked him why he had not gone into the house, he said, "I didn't want to awaken Mrs. J." In mid morning my father briefly visited my mother and me at the hospital before going fishing with one of his mentors. My mother did not appreciate this particular fishing expedition very much, but I later learned (the hard way) that fishing was a form of meditation for him. The fact that he brought his catch back to the hospital in the evening to show my mother still makes me laugh. This very gradual introduction to each other set the tone of my relationship to my father because, while serving in the Pacific, he later missed the entire first year of my life. As the present father of a two-year-old daughter, I find it difficult to contemplate such a separation. For him that was simply the way it was.

Arrogance and ignorance are a dangerous combination
All of my father's close friends accepted his easy braggadocio with regard to things at which he truly excelled. These same people also knew that he hated arrogance when it was coupled with ignorance and they often witnessed his anger about it. He was unwilling even to pretend to tolerate it and for this reason used to tell the following story with particular venom. My father served as a navy physician attached to the U.S. Marines. Toward the end of the war, he served in the Pacific, where he was stationed on a battleship. Even 40 years after the war, his pupils would dilate when he described the power of its 16-inch guns. When the batteries fired at night, one could see the red-hot shells disappear over the horizon and feel the entire ship shift in the water. He was among the forces that landed with the marines on both Saipan and Tinian. On one of those two occasions, he was in a large fleet of amphibious craft that were about a mile offshore when the large guns of the armada set off an ammunition dump near the island's shoreline. The explosion was massive and created a tidal wave that headed in the direction of the fleet.

There were between 30 and 50 men in each craft. The captain of each turned the bow into the wave and rode over it without serious incident. The captain of my father's vessel decided to take the wave broadside, however, angrily resisting my father's suggestions to the contrary as the wave approached. My father, fearing the worst, positioned himself next to the gunwale nearest to the approaching wave and held onto the rail. As the craft rode up the steep crest of the wave, the bottom rotated up past vertical, dumping all of the men and their gear into the sea. My father, who held tight to the rail, said that his feet dangled out over the water before the heavy motors on the underside of the craft righted it again with the passing of the wave. He was flung violently against the gunwale. When he reoriented himself and looked around, he discovered that only he and the captain, who had held onto the helm, were still aboard. Both of them began frantically hauling the men out of the water, and those first recovered also joined in the effort. The last men to be saved were unconscious and cold, heads down in the water, and they had to be revived. Miraculously, no one drowned. The captain, however, never openly admitted that he had made a serious mistake. My father never forgave him for his silence.

A little bravado goes a long way
My father was an inveterate gamesman, who loved the excitement of seizing the moment. There was a bully in his company of marines who used to get drunk periodically and become uncontrollably violent. As with most bullies, there was a predictable pattern to his behavior. After he had sobered up on the day following a rampage, he would apologize to all concerned and say that he didn't know what had happened. Because my father was one of the corps's physicians, he often took care of the bully's victims. On one occasion after delivering an unusually brutal beating, the bully came to my father's medical tent to apologize personally to him. A very diminutive colleague of my father's also happened to be present at the time. The bully was full of remorse, made an emotional apology, and promised never to harm anyone again. He seemed to think that he had made a good show of it, but neither my father nor his colleague made any response to his peroration. Finally, thinking that he had performed adequately, the bully turned to walk out, but just as he was lifting up the flap of the tent, my father shouted, "Wait just a minute you son-of-a-bitch! ... Let me tell you something!" Pointing to a hammer hanging on the tent wall, he shouted, "You see that hammer over there? ... If you ever so much as lay a hand on me, I'm going to take it and beat your f------ brains out .... Do you understand me?" The fellow was shocked and taken aback. He stood transfixed in the doorway, not knowing quite what to do. My father let his message sink in thoroughly and then added with emphasis, "Now get the hell outta here!" As the bully turned to leave, my father's diminutive colleague pulled himself up to full height and chimed in, "And that goes for me, too!"

We find our true compass in the heat of battle
My father often sounded tough. He liked it that way, but deep inside he was actually a rather gentle man. On a very dark night shortly after landing on Tinian, the marines in my father's company were sitting in their foxholes, listening to episodic rifle fire as it blazed in the distance. Japanese forces were scattered about, and everyone squatted quietly at the ready, gazing into the darkness. Without perceptible warning, a Japanese scout materialized at

about two o'clock with respect to my father, anxiously scanning in the dark. The scout was standing almost close enough to touch. My father's rifle was poised at his waist and aimed at the scout, but he did not fire. He waited for several seconds, at which point someone else shot the scout through the heart. When I asked him why he had hesitated, he said that his entire mission during the war had been that of a physician ministering to the wounded and that, despite his complete belief in the military effort, he did not really wish to kill anyone himself. He was prepared to do so if necessary and would have, but he also knew that many others around him had no qualms about killing. He chose to let them do the shooting. He was later decorated for bravery with both the Silver and Bronze Stars for ministering to the wounded while under heavy enemy fire. Yet he also remained content that he had never fired his own rifle at an enemy soldier.

The enemy is also a teacher
Although he was horrified by the war and hated "the enemy" in the abstract, my father never spoke disrespectfully about the Japanese people themselves. He appeared to regard them with considerable interest and I think that he learned some valuable lessons from them. After the capture of the island of Saipan, my father had the opportunity to explore a deserted Japanese village. He went into a number of houses and was amazed at how tidy and beautiful they were. Telling about his impressions later, he said, "Everything was so simple and well made, and everything was in its place. It made me realize how much Americans had and how careless we were about it." He admired the order of the Japanese, not so much for its own sake, but because of the cultural discipline that it demonstrated. Throughout his long career as an internist, he kept on the bookshelf behind his desk a small stainless-steel Japanese medical kit that he had found on the battlefield. The implements were impeccably arranged inside the case, each nicely made and each secured in its place. He showed it to me on several occasions and I now have it myself on a shelf of my own. I believe the kit reminded him that there were doctors in the Japanese forces, too. The kit belonged to one of them who had perhaps been killed in battle and, thus, it reminded him of both his connection to humanity and his own mortality.

The meaning is often in the form
I saw my dad alive for the last time in the early afternoon of July 27, 1992. He was in the hospital because of a myocardial infarction and congestive heart failure. He had been in the hospital several times during the year and he was probably more aware than anyone else that his time was short. My wife, Nancy, and I were visiting my family in Raleigh. It was our last day in town. I had been to the hospital in the morning to see him privately and we had communicated many heartfelt things to each other. I had told him, for example, how proud I was to have had him for a father, which brought tears to his eyes. Over and

over again he also said how proud he was of me. When we met again in the afternoon, his second wife, Helen, and my wife were present with us. I was wearing a navy blue suit, a white shirt, and a blue Hermes tie – a civilian's dress uniform, perhaps. It was my conscious intent to look my best. Nancy and I gave my father a couple of cards and some jelly beans, which he always loved, and we shared some brief, polite conversation together. We were both aware that we might be seeing each other for the last time. When the moment came to depart for the airport, we said our good-byes and hugged each other. Before turning to leave the room, I drew myself up to attention, looked straight at my father, and entreated, "Captain, permission requested to disembark." He smiled knowingly before replying and said, "Permission granted." We saluted each other for the last time, and Nancy and I walked out of the room.

A true officer never hesitates to command
For me one of my father's most enduring and straightforward lessons has been that one must always personally implement one's own fundamental intentions. He believed and often demonstrated that it was necessary to take initiative in this regard. He lived this belief to the last. After being at home for a couple of weeks, late in the afternoon about a month after I saw him for the last time, my father was again taken to the hospital, this time for uncontrolled angina. By evening he was stabilized medically and appeared to be in fairly good shape, but early the next morning he awoke with breathing problems that were probably due to congestive heart failure. It had been his articulated wish not to be resuscitated or kept alive by extraordinary means. He had made this wish known to his wife and to his doctors. Nonetheless, he heard his physicians discussing potential extraordinary measures. Although he was very weak and barely able to attend, by shaking his head and hand, he signaled emphatically that he did not want such measures. Medical treatment was withheld and shortly thereafter he died.

Mt. Fuji, as seen from the USS *South Dakota*,
Tokyo Bay, August 1945.

Christine Tanz with her mother and brother on board the *Liberté*, leaving France to immigrate to the United States on October 24, 1951. The large *E* behind them is part of the ship's name.

Parallax

"...an apparent change in the direction of an object, caused by a change in observational position that provides a new line of sight..."

from Greek parallaxis, *'change of position'*

Lunebach, Germany, 1945.

PARALLAX

The unfamiliar word *parallax*, the title of this final grouping, comes from astronomy and optics. It refers to the way that objects look different when seen from different positions. In this section writers approach their subject matter from more than one significant viewpoint, suggesting alternate interpretations and alternate possibilities of understanding.

The first two stories, those of Marina Sulzberger Berry and Steven Kilston, are the book's most irrepressibly ebullient. The families of both writers endured more than enough wartime trauma to leave deep scars, yet both have a striking optimism. Is this optimism a sign of human resilience? Is it the influence of character on mood? Or is it perhaps denial? Whatever the reasons for their sunshine, in an examination of the impact of war on children and families, these two writers bring a welcome perspective.

Most often in this volume, it is the father who is featured. In recounting her parents' wartime romance, however, Marina Berry casts her mother in the starring role. Like Ursula Oppens earlier, she goes to special lengths to preserve her mother's speech. But the sunshine of the essay also has a dark side, as Marina Berry includes a piercing story about her mother's work in a daycare center in Athens where, when food rations are cut in half, the staff must decide which children will live and which will die. It is a story that cuts uncomfortably close to the *Selektions* in the concentration camps.

Steven Kilston's pride in the Allied victory of the "good guys" and his joy in wartime movies and songs, particularly the ones that make fun of Hitler and "ac-cent-tchu-ate the positive," are part and parcel of the postwar era's enormous burst of energy, fueling his own productive life. Most pointedly of those who here address the relationship of the Vietnam War to World War II, however, he also goes straight to the heart of the antiwar fervor of the 1960s when the war-baby generation reached draft age, recounting how he took his draft deferment exam wearing a sign with the slogan "Score High or Die."

Betty Chang Sun's family survived the Rape of Nanking and the reign of terror in China during the Japanese occupation, only to leave in 1949, fleeing the Chinese civil war. When they arrived in California, they encountered the still-rampant prejudice against and hatred of the Japanese that Robert Sakai describes in the first section, sentiments strong enough to make a mob even of first-graders. Betty Sun reflects on racism and ethnic identity from perspectives that span her entire lifetime.

Laurel Strange Hayler begins with estrangement from her returning soldier father, who didn't know her as a baby and toddler and never made up for lost time during her youth. Yet she ends during her father's old age, almost a mother to him. She comes to see in him not just a clumsy parent, but also a lost and haunted child. With tenderness and compassion, she connects with that child in her father, helping him through his final years.

Over several decades and from several standpoints, including both avoidance and immersion, Andrew Cohen, an American Jew, wrestles with his diffuse sense of Jewishness. In the end, finding no center of gravity, he can only envy his wife's coherent sense of ethnic identity as a daughter of concentration camp survivors.

Helena Worthen's keen sense of disparities makes her acutely aware of social hypocrisy and injustice, as well as of the contrasting values of prewar and postwar life, as the two eras, represented by two generations, grind against each other. She is left mired in such rage at her father that she finds it difficult, even when he is on his deathbed, to let go of her anger at him. After his death, however, reading his wartime letters to her mother written from the South Pacific, she finds another father who idealistically writes of his hopes and plans, even as he makes beautiful jewelry out of seashells for his young wife. Ironically, the objects speak to his daughter in a way that he himself never could.

Like Laurel Strange Hayler's father, the father of Sarah Niles Kafatou had a difficult childhood, and for him the military became more of a home than home. She writes a poem about this distant father, the third poem in this collection revolving around difficult issues in the lives of parents. Closing with the now-familiar theme of the Vietnam War, she portrays a new element of unity between parent and child, literally arm-in-arm at a peace rally.

The collection ends with Kevin Lewis's thoughtful piece, from which we have taken the title of the book, *Born into a World at War*. He addresses deep spiritual questions generated by the war and the demoralized state of its survivors in Europe. Thus, a book that begins with Julie Coryell's essay, which looks straight into the face of the atom bomb, comes full circle with Kevin Lewis looking "steadily into the gas chambers for a fuller understanding of the human heart."

World War II was one of the most destructive events in human history. During the six-year period from 1939 to 1945, war casualties numbered 40 to 50 million worldwide, with more deaths in the West than in the East, and more in Eastern Europe than Western Europe. Among the military, Soviet deaths numbered 11.5 million in battle, 3 million as German POWs, and another million as other POWs. Of every five Soviet POWs, four died. There were 3 million Wehrmacht deaths and 1.5 million deaths in the Japanese army. The U.S. military deaths numbered 300,000; the British, 250,000; and the French, 200,000. Civilian deaths in the U.S.S.R. were more than 7 million; in China estimates run to many millions. In Germany 600,000 deaths were attributed to bombings; 500,000 in Japan; 60,000 in Britain. In 1945 alone, 2 million civilians died in expulsion and flight from Eastern Europe, many of them on forced marches from the concentration camps. Countries which suffered death rates in excess of 10 percent are the U.S.S.R. (with more than 20 million), Poland, and Yugoslavia, the latter chiefly during the prolonged severe guerilla fighting, which killed a million people. Poland's losses were the most severe of any single country, with 18 percent of the prewar population killed. Of the 6 million Polish dead, almost half were Jews. Poland's prewar Jewish population of more than 3 million was almost completely wiped out. The concentration camp murders numbered 6 million European Jews and more than 3 million others: political prisoners (especially communists), gypsies, homosexuals, and "defectives," but the majority Polish civilians.

As the volume ends, these staggering numbers make it impossible not to remember Christine Tanz's feeling that things for her, compared with the intense drama of her parents' lives, have been an anticlimax. We join her in recognizing that a major legacy of World War II was to leave most of its children with "the great prize: the privilege of being able to live an ordinary life."

Mathea Falco and her mother in front of Kronenburg Castle,
used as an officers' hotel by the occupying American forces after the war.

A formal portrait of the Sulzberger family in their Paris home, 1958.

HOME IS ABROAD

Marina Sulzberger Berry

>Born: September 11, 1944
>Cairo, Egypt

In 1934, when he left college, my father was certain of only one thing, that he "would never enter the grubby newspaper business in which [he] had family connections." Having failed to obtain a job as a forest ranger in Arizona, however, he decided to try publishing. He was told to spend a year on an out-of-town newspaper, learning to copyread and edit. Despite his vow at graduation, he remained a journalist all his working life.

After making some money from *Sit-Down with John L. Lewis* – which he called later "perhaps the worst book ever printed" – my father sailed for London in 1937, adding to his economies by playing poker with the ship's doctor and two fellow passengers, one the male half of an American dancing team and the other an English jockey returning with the savings of a lifetime on Havana tracks. He wrote in his memoirs, "I won a great deal of money and, in fact, had to make a small present to the jockey to help him complete his journey."

Because my father did not have a regular newspaper job when he arrived in London, he freelanced and was eventually taken on by Lord Beaverbrook's *London Evening Standard*. In 1938 he set off for Vienna and Prague to see fascism for himself. He had been given a letter of introduction to Eduard Beneš, the president of Czechoslovakia, and sought Beneš's advice on what to do should war come. "Go to the Balkans, Cyrus," said the president. "There is nobody in the Balkans. That will be the most interesting place. The other side of the Axis – the West knows little about it."

My father followed this advice and traveled all around the Balkans (his diaries from this period read like something out of *Boys' Own Paper*). Eventually he was persuaded by the *New York Times* to become bureau manager for all the Balkans, with an option to terminate the contract two weeks after an armistice. He was to undertake a special survey of Balkan communications that would be available in case of war. "By the time World War II ended," he wrote, "I headed the *Times*' entire foreign service so I never exercised my two-week option to get out."

When Greece defeated Italy in Albania, the Germans arrived to sort matters out. As a result, Greece was occupied by the Italians in the west and in the islands, and by the Germans in the main strategic cities of Athens and Salonika, as well as on the Turkish frontier. The Bulgarians occupied western Macedonia, rekindling hatred from the Balkan Wars 30 years before. The Italian occupation was relatively humane, but the Germans used their well-known tactics of repression, reprisals, and deportations. The Allies blockaded all the

Greek ports, so that Greece, which imported a lot of its food, particularly grain, was starved. So great was the misery that the Greek government in exile even appealed to the Allies to lift the blockade during the winter of 1941-42.

My Greek mother was the niece of Shan Sedgwick, the bureau chief of the *New York Times* in Athens, who had married my grandmother's sister. My parents met each other at the Sedgwicks' in 1940 and, just before the Germans marched into Athens, my father proposed. In an account of that period that my mother wrote much later for my brother and me, she said, "He did not seem frightfully enthusiastic so I said no I wouldn't [marry him] until the war was over, [a decision] which he promptly accepted and turned his attention to the menu, ordering bisque de hommard, which I have not been able to touch since." She spent a night of "tears and deep gloom" and he left the next day "in a funny little boat." She wrote in her own charming English, with spelling and punctuation peculiar to her, and I quote her here exactly:

> For months after that I had no idea if he had arrived anywhere safely, or had gone down like so many others under the bombs of the Germans .... All this time I had no news of your father and was preparing myself for a dismal Old Maidhood .... Those first months of occupation were dreadful. We were very hungry, very very indignant, and a bit bewildered and lost. Occupation, like everything else in life, has to be organized, and it took us quite some time to realise that it really was true, that we had nothing to eat, that we could at any moment be shot as hostages or deported as labourers. Little by little though, we learned how to make bread from broom seeds and sugar from carobs, and how to eat cat and donkey, and how to fight the enemy quietly.

One haunting story she told us was about the *crêche* where she worked. The crêche was a day nursery where mothers could leave their young children, knowing that the little ones would be fed and cared for while the mothers worked and tried to find food. A terrible day arrived when the staff learned that the food allocation for the crêche was to be halved. My mother went around the wards with the doctor as he decided which children he would be able to keep and which ones would have to be rejected. It surprised her that he selected the strongest to remain. She realized later that in his predicament he was obliged to give the hope of survival to those who had the greatest chance. The staff then drew lots to decide who would have to tell some of the mothers that they should not bring their children back to the crêche the next morning. My mother pulled the short straw. All her life she was tormented by the memory of the mothers whose children were more or less condemned to starve.

After my father's escape from Greece in the "funny little boat," my mother heard nothing more of him. News was very hard to obtain and the BBC could only be listened to clandestinely. A German officer was billeted in her family's house, making it even more difficult to turn on the radio. One night, however, an opportunity arose. As my mother wrote,

> There was an air raid and we all woke up very excited at the sound of sirens and bombs. When it was all over it was just a little before one in the morning and we thought that being so late we would be safe to turn on our radio and hear some news from the BBC. Immagine my state of mind when while fiddling with the buttons to find the right station I heard your father's voice saying. This is Cy Sulzberger calling the *New York Times* from Ankara. In one second I had learned out of the air *si j'ose dire* not only that he was alive and well, but that he was next door so to speak. We were all tremendously excited, as you can imagine, and my mother in a moment of exuberance called to our beloved, faithful cook Yiannoula to use up the last drops of coffee in the house and "make good strong coffee for everybody and whatever isn't left over we wont drink."

With the uncertain communications of the war, journalists rented time on the radio to broadcast their pieces. The newspapers would receive the transmissions and print them. The more difficult or ambiguous words were spelled out, *m* for *mother*, *d* for *daddy*, etc. In his broadcast my father had said *m* for *Marina* (my mother's name) and *d* for *Dora* (my grandmother's name). There could be no mistake that he was still thinking of her and her family. My mother's reaction was immediate:

> Well, from that day on, my one idea was how to get out and join him. But as he had so easily accepted my refusal to marry him, I was no longer sure that he wanted to be followed around the world in war time by a wife. So I got a good idea. An American friend of mine from the Embassy, was leaving those days for Persia, and I asked him if he would take a letter for me and post it on his way. He very kindly obliged, and so I sat down and wrote the most complicated letter of my life. I explained to your father that I was listening to his broadcast, and asked him to use a code by which to let me know if he still wanted me to try and join him to marry him. I gave him every way of escape by putting into the code all kinds of possibilities: such as *E* for *Edgar* meaning I love you very much but don't think it is a good idea that you should come just now, *E* for *Ernest* [meaning] I don't care for you anymore. *A* for *Alexander* was the key word which would mean I adore you try and come at once.

After a long period of waiting and hoping, *a* for *Alexander* came over the air. With a great friend who spoke German, my mother went to the German authorities, wearing her best dress and her last drop of perfume. She told the Stadt Commandant that she wanted to go to Turkey to marry a carpet dealer and later wrote, "Well either the commandant had just been promoted or had just had a new born son or something wonderful had happened to him, or else he was one of those rare things, a nice German. Whatever it was I was lucky because in five minutes he had said certainly I could leave and wished me the best of luck and given me a paper authorising me to leave the country any time I wished."

Travel at that time was extremely complicated and difficult. Eventually my mother was able to bribe her way onto a German plane leaving for Sofia, Bulgaria. An episode of the sort found in movies ensued. Athens is a small city and everyone knows everyone else's secrets almost immediately. My mother wrote,

> The day before I left I got a strange telephonne call from an unknown man who said it was urgent for him to see me. It was all very thrilling and Hollywoodish and I met this man in a small caffe where he explained to me that he had heard I was going and it was important for me to take out some vital information and give it to the British as soon as I got to Turkey. He handed me a paper on which were all kinds of extremely secret information about the arrival of submarines in the Mediterranean, pipe lines being put down on the side of the Corinth Canal, for oil transportation in case the canal was blown up, airoplane repair factories etc etc. I felt frightfully important and left with the precious paper in my pocket which I was supposed to learn by heart and destroy immediately.

She memorized all this information, kissed her family and friends, and left. With two girlfriends also planning to marry foreigners, she flew to Bulgaria and then took the train to Istanbul. When she finally arrived in Istanbul, she found that my father had been sent the day before to Moscow. To her horror she also found the famous paper she had worked so hard to memorize and thought she had then destroyed as instructed. It was tucked in the folds of her honeymoon nightie. As she wrote, "The very next day I took this little paper to the British military attaché and, when I told him the story, he was angrier than I care to remember, and assured me even though he thanked me for my trouble, that if I had any idea of embarking on a spy career I might as well give it up there and then."

The parents finally met up in Jerusalem. They were married by an American Protestant air force chaplain on January 21, 1942, in Beirut, as neither the Jewish rabbis nor the Greek Orthodox priests in Jerusalem were prepared to sanction a mixed marriage or to shoulder the responsibility for their union. My father remembered the chaplain's charming prayer: "Dear God. I know I am departing from custom and, as it were, stepping out of my bailiwick today as I join these two young people in wedlock. But you are undoubtedly aware of all the trouble that exists nowadays on earth. I can only assure you that their two hearts beat as one." This ceremony was never recognized by the Greek Orthodox Church, which was not separated from the Greek state until the 1980s under Papandreou's government. As a result, at my mother's death my brother and I were considered illegitimate in Greece. The American government seems to have been less perturbed.

My parents eventually settled in Cairo, the home base from which my father traveled. My mother worked for British Intelligence (as a translator, not a spy) until pregnancy made her too ill to work and she was obliged to stay in bed. I was the result of this pregnancy. Two years later, in 1946, my brother was born in Athens.

This very long introduction is necessary in order to explain my unusual upbringing. My father became head of the foreign service of the *New York Times* and we settled in Paris. We spoke English at home and French at school, and we picked up a little Greek during the summer holidays when my mother took us back to visit her mother in Athens. We were not rootless. Rather, we had more roots than most people, being in our own minds half American, half Greek, and half French. Our heroes were Joan of Arc and Napoleon, as well as George Washington and Abraham Lincoln, and Hercules and Jason and his Argonauts.

The Paris I remember is not the freezing, disrupted, postwar city I later learned about. It was school and homework and memorizing the summaries at the end of each chapter of history to recite by rote the next day in class. It was our American convertible filled to the brim with children and dogs. It was going for picnics in the enchanted forests just out of town. It was picking

On an expedition in the convertible with children and dogs.
Marina Sulzberger Berry and her brother (left),
with her mother (far right), a friend, and nannies in June 1951.

daffodils and lilies of the valley which we would bring back in glorious bunches to fill the house. The friends we made were mostly French. Some, like us, had an English nanny and were, like us, totally bilingual. There were others with whom we felt slightly ill at ease when we were asked to lunch. At home we did not use knife rests and it took a few surreptitious glances to know what to do with the little block by the side of the plate. And yet this did not make any difference to our friendships, and I remember still the tremendous games of marbles or cops and robbers. We fitted right in with the rest and, like all children, it was our age which determined who our friends would be. My closest friend to this day is French. We met when we were three, and she too married an Englishman and settled in London.

It was not until I was 10 or so that I realized what an amazingly privileged life I led. We lived in a large ramshackle house behind the Invalides, with a butler and a cook and Nursie to look after us when the parents were on their constant travels. We ourselves traveled more than most children, going to America by boat every three years when the paper gave my father home leave, and going to Greece to see my grandmother every three years. The year when we "couldn't afford to go anywhere," as my mother put it, we would go to the seaside in Spain, Normandy, or the Pays Basque. In my memory there seem to be many more summers than winters, and I remember them in a splendid, sunny haze. I was blessed with a wonderful mother who made everything we did together seem different and special, and I had one of the happiest childhoods I know.

My father made one attempt to Americanize his two hybrid children by sending us for a short period to the American Community School in Paris. He found that the English spoken at home, despite my mother's wonderful fluency and Nursie's impeccable language, seemed to owe a lot to French. When he found himself writing "the question does not pose itself" in the paper, echoing the French "la question ne se pose pas," he decided to take steps. His solution was not a success. We felt lost among the American children whose parents were in Paris on brief postings, mostly military, and they found us strange. Eventually we were sent to boarding school in England, which was closer to home than the States, and from there we went across the Atlantic to college in America.

Even in college I felt more European than American, although I knew intellectually that I had returned to my own country, the land where my passport came from. One episode sticks in my mind. At college in the days when there was not much mixing of colors in America, a black American girl whose father worked in Geneva for the U.N. became a good friend of mine. We found we were only at ease together when we spoke French. In English all the prejudices we never met at home in Europe rose up to complicate our relationship. Skin color was not a barrier in Europe. Religion, nationality, and class separated people, but this was the first time I had encountered prejudice against blacks.

Speaking French and slipping back into our European skins, neither of us was self-conscious about race.

Shortly after college I married my English husband. Having lived in London for the past 30 years, I now have dual nationality and one more set of roots. Perhaps because I am too old to develop new heroes, I don't seem to have added English ones to my Pantheon, and I still support Joan of Arc and Napoleon against the British. And when I stroll in Paris and meet a particularly haunting smell – a bakery or rain falling on a dusty street – I suddenly feel again like a small child. I suppose that the final result of my being a war baby is that I am now half American, half Greek, half French, and half English.

The parents of Steven Kilston, Los Angeles, early 1944.

GLORY REMEMBERED IS HOPE PRESERVED

Steven Kilston

> Born: September 3, 1944
> Hollywood, California, U.S.A.

This afternoon I was doing what my grandfather would have called noodling away on my viola, perhaps echoing some klezmer forefather, when a melodic fragment popped up and triggered memories complex and emotion-laden, as bittersweet in their sentimentality as those conjured up by Proust's madeleine. I recognized the musical source as a piece I loved as a child, the *Warsaw Concerto* by Richard Addinsell. Most people today no longer know that piece, once very widely heard, or the 1941 British motion picture it comes from. The film is *Dangerous Moonlight* (*Suicide Squadron* in the U.S.), where a Polish pianist becomes a pilot in the Royal Air Force. Deep in my heart I feel resonances with sounds and images from similar movies, produced in a decade that created

The parents of Steven Kilston in 1943.

intensities of experience and meaning rarely matched in the decades I've seen since. The overwhelming sense of evil danger, sacrifice, and ultimate triumph by noble humanity was captured in many such sentimental films of the 1940s.

I learned about Warsaw and Poland because of my Polish Jewish maternal grandmother and early in life came to know that World War II began with the blitzkrieg there. I learned that her many relatives in Poland were killed by the Nazis. Gloom wasn't the pervasive mood in our Los Angeles household, however, because all of us felt joy in the very recent triumph of the Allies, a joy amplified by the victors' selfless sacrifices and the enemies' unmitigated evil. Those messages were all around – in my family, in the classroom, and in the war-related films on the screens of the movie theaters near our home. The use of the word *corny* was suspended when dealing with the depths of feeling expressed in films like *Casablanca* and songs like "I'll Be Seeing You" that still have their power over me. I think such feelings were ubiquitous in wartime America and were probably strongest among those who were refugees from the evil. Cynicism had no place when the challenges were so real.

My mother, an only child, was born a dark-complexioned Jew in Berlin in 1921. Forced out of secondary school after the Nazis came to power in 1933, she suffered many indignities and fears. My grandfather's small limp – developed during his time as a soldier in World War I, when he served as a doctor's assistant in Vienna – grew into a lifelong impediment. His left foot usually dragged, often tripping him, after he suffered a complete nervous breakdown in 1935, the result of the Nazis confiscating his business license (taking away his livelihood) and his citizenship papers (making him stateless and creating immense anxiety while he made his many attempts to get his small family out of Germany). In November 1938, when my mother might have started college had she not been Jewish, she and her parents cowered behind closed drapes in their apartment while the street below was filled with yelling and the screaming of obscenities and the crashing noises of Kristallnacht. The family's good friends, the Jewish people from the bookstore on the ground floor, never reappeared after that night. Finally, in response to a personal plea my grandfather mailed directly to President Roosevelt, the small family was granted visas to the United States. They crossed the Atlantic in August 1939, on the penultimate ship to leave Germany before the war began.

My father was born in Los Angeles in 1914 to Ukrainian Jewish immigrants. Escaping the pogroms and the czar's troops was a definite factor in their immigration to the U.S., as my paternal grandmother came to America soon after her brother had died from injuries inflicted in the 1905 *Potemkin* rebellion, ridden down by Cossacks on the Odessa steps. My paternal grandfather likewise sought safety and opportunity across the sea, and soon brought over his parents and his 16 younger siblings. My father's parents met in New York, where his mother was working in a typical sweatshop in the garment district and his father worked odd jobs in factories and peddled produce. Seeking better luck, they got married, pushed on to Los Angeles, and opened a small shoe-repair shop, with lodgings in the back where my father was born. When he was 10 years old, they scraped together funds to allow him to start violin lessons. His training earned him a music scholarship to UCLA as concertmaster of its orchestra. My father eventually became a handsome solo violinist, gracing the screen in *Strike Up the Band*. The Nazis' rise first affected him when a flood of refugee musicians made it hard for him to continue earning a decent living with his fiddle in Hollywood. Subsequent prewar employment at Lockheed Aircraft, riveting warplane components, caused him

The father of Steven Kilston as a professional violinist in Hollywood.

significant hearing loss that made it hard for him to play the violin at all. Finally, he met my refugee mother, married her three months later in June 1942, and enlisted in the Army Air Corps in December 1942.

Conceived at an Army Air Corps camp in Marana, Arizona, near Tucson, I was born in Hollywood (maybe that's why I discuss several movies here) in September 1944. This was nine days after the liberation of Paris, a time when both the German and Japanese forces were finally headed toward destruction. Exhilaration was growing in a United States that was succeeding in its "mighty mission" to overcome what many considered the greatest threat in our country's history. I think my parents felt a personal as well as a national pride in our victory. After all, my mother escaped the fate Hitler intended for her, a fate suffered by most of her relatives, and my father helped in the effort to punish her oppressor's forces, while soothing the nervous feathers of the delicate *Flüchtling*, the girl who had to flee. I suppose my parents also felt particular joy in my birth, an only child who might easily never have existed. Continuing the ancient Jewish experience, from Pharaoh and Inquisitor to Czar and Führer, some of our people managed to escape, to find a promised land and a path to the future. (Of course, far too many others did not. On the very day I was lucky enough to be born, Anne Frank was put on the last train to leave the Netherlands for Auschwitz.)

I think World War II was America's finest hour. The dangers were great and clear, and our nation banded together in common cause as never before or

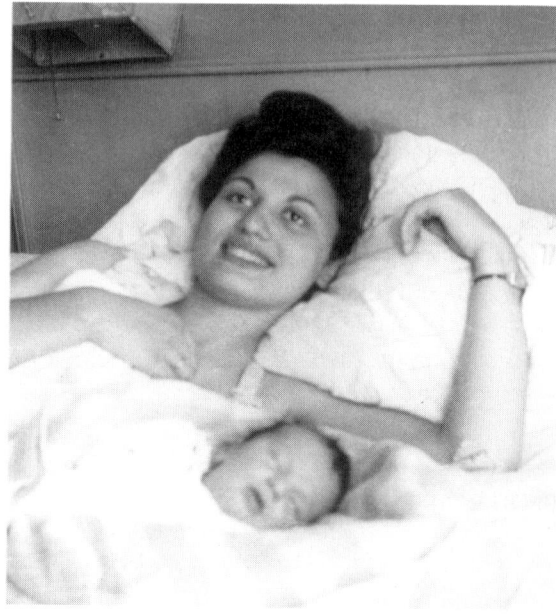

Ellen Kilston, a radiant mother, with Steven, her new baby, 1944.

since. My first memories are from the extremely happy era of the late 1940s, a time of sweet victory in America and, briefly, a time free of most dissent, certainly as seen from a child's eyes. All my grandparents were alive and near my home in Los Angeles. The songs I heard were joyful, from "Swinging on a Star" and "Ac-cent-tchu-ate the Positive" to "I'm Looking Over a Four-Leaf Clover," "June Is Busting Out All Over," and "Zip-a-dee-doo-dah." My father could buy a house by using a loan fund reserved for veterans. To their surprise many other soldiers could afford college, thanks to the GI Bill. Jackie Robinson symbolized growing tolerance and some reduction of racial and class discord. And we had the charity and good sense to assist nations that were victims of the war, even if they had been our enemies. It was a glorious time to grow up, building a very positive view of life and of one's country.

My two earliest memories have strong war connections. One is of my father mixing food coloring to make white margarine look more like butter (a consequence of food rationing and anticompetition rules influenced by the dairy industry). The other is of our family frolicking at the ocean shores at Venice Beach on a moistened GI canvas mattress cover inflated with sea air and perfect to float and bounce on. That happy association with army paraphernalia also helped me have a generally favorable attitude toward the military, so that later I avidly studied the ranks and insignia in my father's U.S. Army manual (*The Ordnance Soldier's Guide*) and learned self-defense techniques from the *Get Tough!* handbook he had been issued.

Unlike my grandparents' or my mother's experiences, it was very easy being Jewish where I grew up. I was completely unaware of any prejudice. Part of that must have come from the large proportion of Jews in my schools, usually close to 90 percent of the students, but I wonder how much the absence of discrimination was aided by the adults' consciousness of the horrors seen in Europe. Until my college days I never knew that words like *kike* existed. Even today I can say that I've never been addressed personally with such words. My grandfather took me to small storefront synagogues from my earliest walking years, and I identified with nice friendly aspects of Jewish culture: rich Yiddish expressions, enjoyable holiday traditions, and special foods. My mother took pains to tell me about famous and respected Jews, I'm sure in reaction to the negative messages she had grown up hearing in Berlin.

Much of my information about World War II came directly from my mother, who, starting when I was the age of seven or so, told me of her Berlin days and of relatives who perished in the camps. (Recently she has contributed her videotaped memoirs to Steven Spielberg's project on Holocaust history.) My parents' main friends were other German Jewish refugees, four married couples without children. The 10 adults spent a great deal of time together and called themselves the *Kränzchen*, or 'little circle.' I think those years as the sole child in their midst strongly Europeanized me and made me more interested in adult activities and perspectives than most children I knew. Without their need to escape Hitler, the intellectuals who migrated to Los Angeles wouldn't have been there to enrich the cultural environment I grew up in. I wouldn't have met composers and artists, or have gained as much respect for both elegance and bittersweet irony.

As I grew older, a book in my mother's parents' house opened a new window for me. It was *The New Order* by Arthur Szyk, full of scathing cartoon caricatures of the Nazi and Italian fascists, ridiculing their many pretensions so perfectly that I was a delighted 12-year-old sharing in the joy of tweaking the bully's nose. (Szyk's works so infuriated Hitler that they led to his personal order condemning Szyk's mother to death.)

The power of humor to deflate tyrants made a very strong impression on me. I believe it to be an important factor in the victory of the righteous in World War II. Charlie Chaplin in *The Great Dictator* (1940) and Jack Benny in *To Be or Not to Be* (1942) provided images of exaggerated fascist pomposity that made the triumph of the meek seem much more possible than before. (Twenty years later, Chaplin explained how different his values were from those of a fascist: "I remain just one thing and one thing only – and that is a clown. It places me on a far higher plane than any politician.") These poignant but fabulous comedies helped through ridicule to topple Hitler by giving courage to his victims. They showed that the Nazis, who took themselves so solemnly, could be beaten in life by people who refused to accept their perspective, provoking so much hilarity with a film-Hitler's "Heil myself" that his very real threat to human existence appeared conquerable. For those who wanted a view of the enemy tinged with even more slapstick, Spike Jones and Donald Duck obliged with the song and animated cartoon *Der Führer's Face*. All such mockeries helped me to resist inheriting the fears that my mother and her parents couldn't completely erase from their minds.

Many people of our generation love the biggest and most lasting wartime film hit, *Casablanca*. Even today its combination of sentimentality, threat, and heroism can give people a sense of the spirit and camaraderie evoked by memories of the war years. To my child's eyes, the country was very close – all Americans seemed to realize what they stood to lose and were pulling together to win the war. Perhaps most important of all, very few people remained confused about the difference between right and wrong. This positive view of the American spirit has remained with me my whole life.

But the repercussions of the Nazis and the war turned out to reach further into my life as well. My mother has suffered severe claustrophobia and ulcerative colitis throughout her adult life, probably a form of posttraumatic stress disorder resulting from her experiences in Germany. And many times I saw my grandfather react with great fear to the approach of dogs, undoubtedly from similar causes. Each time I took him home to his apartment in his later years, I had to check the closets to reassure him that no one was lurking in wait there. His anxiety had roots reaching back to threats long past.

Steven Kilston in 1946 with his mother and her father,
both refugees from Germany.

The war's realignment of world power produced growing tensions with the other main victor, the Soviet Union, the country that suffered the most and that we helped the least. This conflict in turn produced domestic strains, as the McCarthy era and the nuclear arms race weighed heavily on our minds. In junior high school, as a fan of the *Perry Mason* television show, I wanted to be a lawyer. During my first science course in eighth grade, however, the Soviets launched *Sputnik*, and I was instead strongly counseled to go into science to help the United States recover the balance of power we feared had been upset by Soviet missile power. My father showed me all the classified ads for engineers.

Meanwhile the germ of social consciousness was growing in me. I think my distaste for the arbitrary use of power was a legacy of an early understanding of the war against fascism, as well as of an exposure to the love for the underdog that remains a popular thread in American culture. I was also very sensitive to the many horrors of war, best crystallized for me in the 1948 movie about war orphans, *The Boy with the Green Hair*. At 16 I attended a rally for a Republican congressional candidate, a rally that included a screening of the House Un-American Activities Committee's propaganda film, *Operation Abolition*, depicting the government's problems with – and overreactions to – protesters asking for more protections of civil liberties. I drew the conclusion common to many who saw the film: fascism was still possible in our own country and danger was more likely to come from the right wing than from the left. I became sympathetic to the poor and oppressed of America, and I began tutoring in ghettos and participating in civil rights meetings and demonstrations. Eventually I was involved in protesting the Vietnam War, mocking the first student draft deferment examination by taking it while wearing a sign on my back reading "Score High or Die."

Although I demonstrated many times against the war of my generation, I did maintain a draft deferment during the Vietnam War years as a graduate student in astrophysics. After teaching for a while, I began a career in aerospace systems engineering, which included considerable involvement in Ronald Reagan's ill-conceived and unworkable "Star Wars" programs. Awareness of technology's amplifications of the machinery of war led me to host a weekly radio talk show on science and technology. Moreover, in 1982 at UCLA, I taught perhaps the first American university course on the science of nuclear war.

Probably my most profound experiences of World War II have occurred in Europe, where the war remains far more in evidence than in America. In 1970, during my first travels in Europe, I was deeply touched by the display in Prague showing the yellow Stars of David that the children in the Terezin concentration camp had made for their dolls to wear, concluding that if their own Jewishness must be identified, so must that of their dolls. In 1971 the government of West Berlin began a program of sponsoring fully paid, week-long return visits by Jews who had managed to flee and survive the Nazi era, beginning with the oldest survivors. My mother's father asked me to accompany him in my grandmother's place, for she had died eight years earlier. We landed at Tempelhof Airport, where the planeload of mostly ancient Jews was greeted by a German brass band and, soon after, welcomed by the mayor at a reception at the Rathaus, the town hall. The irony of the situation was obvious, but the sincerity of the efforts to make amends seemed real, even though no gesture could come close to adequate compensation for those who had lived there through many of the Nazi years. Still, this introduction to Germany helped me begin to see that the present reality did indeed differ from the horrible events barely a quarter century earlier. It also helped me communicate more easily with the German friends I made later.

In the summer of 1994, my mother finally showed her old Berlin haunts to her two grandchildren, who saw both legacies of the war and some signs of improvement: a jackbooted skinhead beating up a middle-aged man, student volunteers of many backgrounds and from many countries cleaning and beautifying the Jewish cemetery where my great-grandparents are buried, a machine-gun-toting policeman on guard against racist vandalism at the synagogue where my mother had been an elementary school student long ago, and a lot of graffiti condemning the neofascists. Afterward my family visited Prague together with thousands of other international delegates from Sokol, a Czech gymnastics and cultural association that first the Nazis and then the communists had banned for 52 years. During the Sokol parade through town, the huge throngs of spectators included countless joyfully crying older women, many of them probably World War II war widows. There were thousands of shouts in

Czech of "Long live Sokol!" I myself must have shaken hands with about a thousand people. All the cheering amazed us and made us feel that the war and its aftermath were only then just ending in the Czech Republic and that we were a welcome army helping to complete the job of liberation at last!

In conclusion, I would like to emphasize that my main inheritance from World War II is an ingrained, highly optimistic attitude: a belief that good will ultimately triumph over evil, truth over falsehood, and the righteous over the powerful. My mother was lucky to escape the Nazis, I was lucky to be born, and we experienced the euphoria of victory and identification with the just and noble side of the struggle. Today we are encountering an era where people are longing for connections, searching for meaning. The memories and lessons of World War II should provide us with inspiration and strength. They prove to us that there are times when entire nations can be heroic.

Betty Chang Sun and her family in autumn 1945.

CHINESE GIRLS DON'T WEAR HATS

Betty Chang Sun
(born Chang Zung Wei)

>Born: December 22, 1943
>Shanghai, China

When I was first asked to participate in this project on the impact of the war, I declined. I believed that World War II had a very limited direct effect on my life and that of my family. I was born in Shanghai at the end of 1943 and lived in China through my preschool years, until my family emigrated to the United States in 1949. For me, the effects of World War II were completely eclipsed by the subsequent Chinese civil war between the Nationalists and the communists. It was the civil war that resulted in the communist takeover of the mainland and, thus, in my family's exodus to the United States.

 My image of those who could justifiably claim to have been directly affected by World War II was of people who had suffered grave physical injury or mental stress, or people whose loved ones were victims of the war's atrocities. Beyond being deeply appreciative that the Allied victory assured my life and liberties as a new American, I felt little direct connection to the war's events. Moreover, having immigrated to the U.S. at the age of five, I retained few memories of life in China. My view and understanding of World War II were primarily shaped by an American education that focused predominantly on the European war. I recall both junior and senior high school social studies classes that typically spent seven or eight months on events in Europe and two weeks on corresponding events in Asia.

 In spite of my initial skepticism that the war had a significant effect on my life, I gave the topic deeper thought. I researched the war's influence on my past by questioning numerous relatives and Asian friends of my parents' generation, and I was astonished to discover that my life and that of my family had been far more influenced by World War II than I realized. The war was a major factor in creating the chain of events that resulted in my becoming a Chinese American. Perhaps even more importantly, it left a legacy of attitudes that I am only now beginning to understand.

 Although I had always been aware that World War II set the stage for the civil war in China, I was surprised to learn the extent to which Japan's role in the war both precipitated and insured the communist conquest of mainland China. The Japanese occupied much of China for the eight years spanning from 1937 to 1945, but their occupation of the country actually lasted 14 years, for it began with their conquest of Manchuria in 1931. The Japanese occupation had a direct impact on the outcome of China's subsequent civil war by creating chaos and weakening the government, thus facilitating the communist conquest. The war against Japan also provided the communists with an unparalleled opportunity for political and military expansion. With the Nationalist forces engaged in the struggle against Japan, the communists gained control

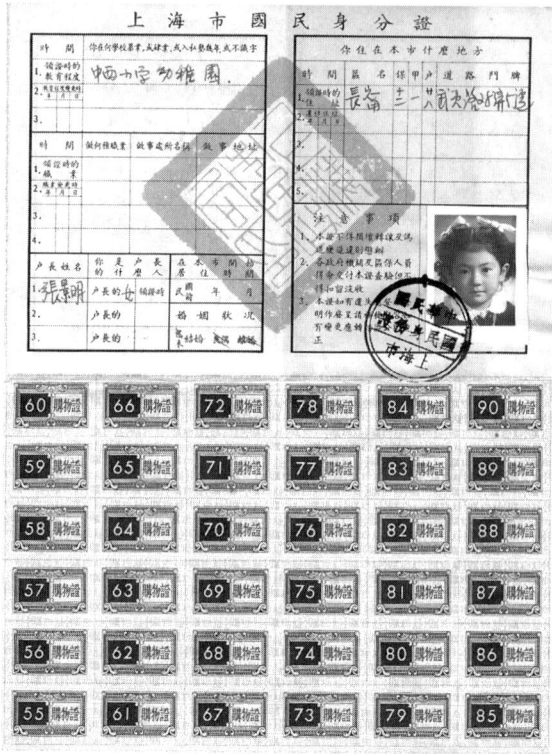

City of Shanghai ration card for Betty Chang Sun, 1947-48.

over vast areas in northern China that the Japanese had conquered but lacked the manpower to defend. In addition, the communists greatly enlarged their army by recruiting peasants from the countryside as soldiers and by organizing rural citizens to provide them with food and shelter. They also won popular support by advocating social revolution and by redistributing land to local peasants in communist-controlled areas.

When China's war against Japan ended in August 1945, the communists held areas in the north with a population of 100 million people and their army had grown to over 900,000 soldiers. In direct contrast, the war against Japan drained Nationalist resources and caused severe inflation, further weakening popular Nationalist support. In the civil war that ensued, the superior military tactics of the communist forces, peasant support for a social revolution begun during World War II, and Soviet military and economic aid together turned the tide against the Nationalists and insured a communist victory.

Sadly for the Nationalists, at the conclusion of World War II, the Soviet Union claimed the vast inventory of Japanese armaments stored in Manchuria. By supplying extensive state-of-the-art Japanese weapons to the communist Chinese in exchange for subsequent Soviet influence in China, the Soviets insured a relatively rapid conquest of China by the communist forces, who quickly and decisively defeated the poorly equipped and ill-funded Nationalist forces. On October 1, 1949, Mao Zedong proclaimed the establishment of the People's Republic of China. By December 1949 Chiang Kai-shek's Nationalist forces had retreated to Taiwan, marking the conclusion of a civil war whose outcome had been largely determined by the events of World War II.

In addition to its influence on the country's political direction, World War II also had a profound effect on my personal life. From the moment of my birth in Shanghai, war conditions threatened my survival. Because of the dangers of venturing outside the house, my mother chose to give birth to me at home instead of going to the hospital. I arrived in the middle of an air raid, when houses had to be darkened to limit their likelihood of becoming targets. Lights were dimmed and the windows were covered with heavy fabric. Although there was a physician in attendance, I was a difficult delivery, a blue baby, and almost died at birth. Resuscitation maneuvers were especially difficult given the dim lighting necessitated by the air raid. Luckily for me, the raid ended and the physician was able to coax me to life.

The war also had a significant effect on my family's living conditions. There were daily curfews, frequent air raids, a shortage of supplies including food and oil, and, as a result, extensive rationing. Still, my family was relatively fortunate. There were shortages, but no real material hardships.

The true hardships and physical dangers of that time related to the menacing presence of the Japanese occupation. What was much harder to deal with than shortages of supplies was the brutality and oppression of the occupation, as well as its extended duration. In 1931 the Japanese occupied Manchuria. In

1937 Japan invaded Nanking, then the capital of China, in a bloody massacre of civilians. Japan fully intended to build a dynasty within China's borders. The Japanese went on to conquer Shanghai and other major cities, which they occupied until 1945. Thus, beginning with the conquest of Manchuria, the Japanese occupation of China spanned 14 long years.

I was surprised to find a uniformly intense dislike of the Japanese among numerous relatives and family friends in my parents' generation, despite the passage of five decades since the occupation. I discovered that their intense reactions were the result of Japan's overt policy of brutality, a policy which encouraged inhumane and oppressive acts. In direct contrast to the Germans, who committed outrageous atrocities while denying their occurrence, the Japanese officially sanctioned widespread atrocities and then broadly publicized their occurrence in order to intimidate and control China's enormous population. Japan's policy was a concerted effort to scare their captives into submission.

Japanese rule in China was both absolute and arbitrary. My relatives talk about indiscriminate massacres of men, women, and children. Pregnant women were used for sport, with soldiers betting on the gender of the unborn child and then splitting the expectant mother open to determine which soldier had won the bet. Huge numbers of people were beheaded. Rape and plunder were rampant. Females were kidnapped and forced to become "comfort girls" for Japanese soldiers, with each woman made to provide sex for a multitude of soldiers. Many of the horrifying stories that I heard from family friends and relatives have been confirmed and widely discussed in the media.

During the Japanese occupation of China, homes could be searched without warning. Houses were arbitrarily appropriated by Japanese officers or simply burned at whim. Often atrocities were committed with greater license in rural areas, but fear of the Japanese was just as intense in the cities. In many cities Chinese citizens who saw a Japanese soldier on the street were required to bow from the waist in submission or risk being beaten or shot for not showing proper respect. One of my uncles was arrested for owning a firearm, even though it was merely a collector's piece. He was jailed for two months before being released one day without explanation. He was one of the lucky ones.

Initially, my immediate family was somewhat sheltered from the worst Japanese atrocities because we lived in the French concession in Shanghai. Following the Opium Wars that began in 1839, many areas of Shanghai were divided into "concessions" controlled by different foreign powers. Living in these areas in the earlier part of World War II provided greater protection from Japanese harassment. One of my aunts moved from southern Shanghai to the international settlement specifically because the location provided greater safety. Theoretically, Japanese forces were not permitted in the international concessions in Shanghai. In reality, however, the Japanese often committed aggressive acts there as well, for example, disguising vehicles as public buses

The parents of Betty Chang Sun during the war.

in order to kidnap civilians by the busload when they exited the cinemas in the concessions. Men would be killed or enslaved, and women were sent to work in comfort houses. Later in the war, following the Japanese attack on Pearl Harbor, residents of Shanghai's international community were openly rounded up and interned.

It was a scary time, a time when thoughts of survival were paramount. Many of my parents' friends said they felt their lives were in constant danger. Fear was perpetual and life was precarious, too often dependent on whimsy and luck. If a Japanese soldier felt like stopping you on the street to interrogate or shoot you, he could, and if you were unlucky enough to be passing by a soldier who had a sudden fit of anger or rage, then you became his victim.

War exaggerated the impact of chance occurrences on life's circumstances and on life itself, as can be seen in an incident related by my husband, Pershing. In 1941 his father was a brigadier general in the Nationalist communication corps. When war broke out between Japan and the Western Allies, Pershing's father attempted to move his family back to northern Guangdong Province, a part of China as yet unoccupied by the Japanese, from Hong Kong, because the Japanese had taken control of that city. My future father-in-law returned to Hong Kong to accompany his family. They all traveled as civilians along with an entourage of 50 other civilians. At the time Pershing was not yet born, and his family consisted of his parents and their three young sons. The two younger boys – an infant and a toddler – were carried by his father's bodyguard in two baskets hung from a shoulder harness. Fluent in Chinese, English, Italian, and Japanese, his father feared that he would be drafted to aid the Japanese as a translator if his presence were discovered. Thus, his military insignia and official papers were all hidden under his infant son. His decision to hide his identity would have put all their lives in jeopardy if the papers had been discovered. Leaving Hong Kong, the entourage had to walk through a checkpoint where they were accosted by Japanese guards. The guards were brusque and unpleasant and demanded that everything be emptied for inspection, including the baby's and the toddler's baskets. When no one moved to comply with their orders, one guard, intent on searching the baskets, grabbed the baby to lift him out. As Providence would have it, the baby's timing could not have been more opportune. He soiled his diaper so profoundly at that very moment that the guard abruptly changed his mind, dropped the baby back into his basket with disgust, and impatiently waved the whole group through.

So it was that a commonplace event saved dozens of lives, including those of my husband's entire family. While the elements of luck and chance are always factors in our lives, war magnifies the importance of such occurrences because it raises the stakes to life-and-death proportions. War intensifies the effects of even ordinary events because it gives them inordinate consequences.

I believe that the legacy of World War II and China's subsequent civil war lies to a great extent in how these large historical events shaped the attitudes and behaviors of succeeding generations. The pragmatic attitudes fostered by fear and economic uncertainty combined with cultural attitudes and behavioral patterns to become part of the legacy of World War II for China. Most noticeably, the uncertainty and economic deprivation engendered by war have led to a tendency on the part of many Chinese and Chinese Americans to work assiduously towards providing for a secure future. Fear of uncertain economic conditions has been a primary motivation for my parents' generation and has led to a tendency to build and save for tomorrow. Their generation is characteristically frugal, hard-working, and highly supportive of education – especially in fields that emphasize practical, professional skills judged to be dependably marketable, such as engineering and medicine. The heightened fear and sense of danger brought on by war have also reinforced for many Chinese of my parents' generation the importance of invisibility, of blending in and not making waves. Thus, their generation is also largely conservative and apolitical. While World War II is clearly only one factor in the development of these attitudes, it was a major contributor to attitudes which are to this day still highly characteristic of many Chinese and Chinese Americans.

When my parents emigrated to the States, they gave up everything familiar – their homeland, close relatives and friends, wealth and material comforts, and my father's successful career – to save my brother and me from living – or perhaps dying – under a communist regime. My dad was a botanist turned businessman. He had established a successful import-export company. My mom grew up in a vastly privileged and prosperous household that was decorated with museum-quality jades, porcelains, and antique Chinese bronzes. Her home contained both an opera theater and a ballroom among its numerous courtyards. My maternal grandfather had been the Undersecretary of Finance for China and president of the Bank of Peking. He had been educated in the West at a time when few Chinese went abroad. Although my mother's family fortunes declined somewhat following her father's early death from cancer, the family wealth was well-managed by my maternal grandmother, who despite the lack of any formal education (women of her generation were not schooled) was nevertheless a savvy financier. Thus, when my parents decided to emigrate to America, they relinquished financial security as well as strong family and community networks in order to insure the safety of their children.

My dad was already in the United States on a business trip in late 1949 when, fearful for our lives with the rapid communist advance, he and my mom decided that she would bring our family out of China to join him in the States. Time was of the essence. Unable to liquidate family assets without drawing attention to her intended departure, my parents chose to leave their assets behind. Visas were hard to obtain and there was much uncertainty. Packing lightly, Mom took two small children out of Shanghai against her family's vehement objections, spending a month in Hong Kong to obtain the necessary visas. She took only a small amount of cash and no valuables, for fear of being

Betty Chang Sun's maternal grandfather, a finance minister, and her capable grandmother, the family financier.

searched and detained, yet she packed lots of clothing for my brother and me because we were her priority. And so it was that my parents emigrated to the United States and an uncertain future with barely a few thousand dollars.

In America my parents took odd jobs, fought discrimination, and over the years bought a small restaurant. Opportunities for Asians were very limited in those years. They managed gradually to build the restaurant into a considerable financial success, working seven days a week over two decades. Yet even in the toughest times, my parents made sure that my mom was always there when my brother and I came home for lunch or returned after school. She would then return to work, often walking a mile in the rain to save the bus fare. In our early years in the U.S., money was tight and there was great uncertainty because my parents essentially had to start from scratch. Yet my brother and I never felt deprived because we never wanted for anything, especially our parents' love.

Because my parents worked so hard, however, there was a premium on time that left little room for introspection or discussion of political or social issues. Many issues and behaviors were simply not discussed. That Chinese Americans do not get involved in politics, for example, was a given, taught matter-of-factly to the next generation. It required no explanation.

Nor were explanations required for attitudes and dress codes. As a small child, I was enthralled with hats, especially Easter bonnets. I let my mother know that I was eager to be the owner of such a lovely piece of apparel. My mom's very kindly but emphatic response was, "Chinese people don't wear hats, dear." It was so definite, so absolute, delivered like a natural law. Thus the authority of her statement went unchallenged for close to a decade, when in my teens I finally thought to ask, "Why not?" But the response could have been predicted: "They just don't." And so it was that I learned that Chinese girls don't wear hats and they don't get involved in politics, either.

World War II reinforced the apolitical attitudes of my parents' generation. They learned early and well that it is dangerous to be political, to be an activist, to take controversial positions. The art of maintaining one's invisibility in a crowd was tied to issues of safety and of avoiding recrimination. Even moderate or conservative political positions were dangerous, given the general instability in China's political arena. Thus, it was best to take no position.

I recall with great affection advice that my dad once gave me during my years as a graduate student at Columbia University. It was in 1968, during the time of student demonstrations, and the student sit-ins at Columbia were well publicized in the media. Following TV coverage at the height of the Columbia sit-ins, my dad telephoned to ask if I was involved. I told him I was not, but fearing that in my college years I had learned to think for myself and had adopted new ideas, grave parental concern led him to give me some enigmatic but well-intentioned advice: "Don't get involved in the sit-ins – but if you do, make sure you sit in the middle!" The idea of pushing myself into the center of a sit-in for student rights ("Excuse me, but my dad said I have to sit in the middle") so that I would be less vulnerable to physical harm would no doubt not have gone over well with other demonstrators. But his advice was given out of love, and I will always cherish it.

Like most Chinese parents, mine taught my brother and me as children not only to be apolitical, but to be nondisruptive and nonconfrontational as well, and with good reason. As Chinese children in a predominantly Caucasian society, we already stood out. My parents' attitude was partly the result of their cultural heritage, but it also grew from their awareness of the need for caution, not just in a China occupied by the Japanese but also in their adopted homeland, the United States, where they were a visible minority. Their caution was rooted in firsthand knowledge of the dangers of prejudice and fear, in America as well as in Shanghai.

In the U.S. we lived first in California, where in late 1949 Asians were numerous and the prejudice against Japanese people, even Japanese Americans, was still rampant. Anti-Japanese sentiment often generalized to other Asians, especially among young children, who for the most part had little appreciation of cultural diversity. Sadly, many adults also had difficulty separating other Asians from the atrocities committed against American soldiers by Japan. As a small child, I frequently heard stories of Chinese homes in the U.S.

Betty Chang Sun and her brother Jim play ringtoss on board the *SS General Gordon* en route to the United States, autumn 1949.

being burned and Chinese families being assaulted because they were mistaken for Japanese.

Largely as a result of the war and the anti-Japanese sentiment still prevalent in California in the fall of 1949, I had my first experience as a victim of prejudice. As an Asian who spoke no English, I was an easy target. Although I had been told that we were moving to America, as a five-year-old I had no inkling what being in a different country would mean and was ill-prepared for my first day in an American school. We arrived in San Francisco shortly after the school year had begun and my mother promptly enrolled my brother and me in the local elementary school. At recess on that first day, I was suddenly surrounded by a group of two dozen or more American children who joined hands and formed a menacing, moving circle around me, shouting taunts and chanting ridicule. Despite my lack of English, their message was not lost on me. I was terrified, but beyond fright – humiliated and bewildered. Thankfully, my sobs and the mob frenzy that encircled me were, in time, both ended by the kindly intervention of the teacher on duty. I never forgot the incident, but never truly understood it until years later. Unfortunately, it was not to be the only incident of prejudice that I encountered. I also remember having to run home after school on several occasions because I was being chased by children who didn't like Asians. It didn't happen frequently or with any regularity, but the fact that it had happened at all made the possibility of it happening again a realistic fear.

These personal encounters made stories that circulated in the Chinese community about the prejudices and outrages committed against its members as a result of their ethnicity all the more real. And so my parents' advice to be a model citizen, to do my best, and not to make waves seemed reasonable advice, even though I did not at the time realize how much I and other Chinese American children of my generation internalized such teachings.

Unfortunately, these encounters and the stories of anti-Asian prejudice that I heard had another result, which was to feed my own developing prejudices about Japan. Even at a very young age I used to think that Japan must be pretty terrible for so many Chinese and American people to hate it so much. On a personal level, I had no awareness of conscious prejudice against the Japanese, although I recognized the deep feelings held by the Chinese of my parents' generation and understood the factual basis for their sentiment. Yet I realize now that throughout my childhood, the thought of Japan immediately brought to mind vivid stereotypes of cruel Japanese soldiers, crazed kamikaze pilots, or lovely, subservient geishas, images absorbed from American cinema and literature. Thus, I too played a role in perpetuating those stereotypes. In retrospect World War II and its after-effects taught me about prejudice as its promoter as well as its victim. War promotes and justifies prejudices because it is natural to bear animosity toward those who do harm to oneself or one's loved ones. War also instills fear, and fear breeds animosity against both the oppressors and the oppressed.

It occurs to me that one of the reasons that prejudice is so difficult to eliminate is because the experience of it is entirely different for the perpetrator and the victim. Perhaps we need to experience prejudice from both perspectives before we can fully comprehend its devastation. As experienced by the perpetrator, it can often be an impersonal process. It can be casual, thoughtless, even unintentional – deed done, thought completed, followed through with action or not – it is readily dismissed or forgotten. Prejudice from the victim's view, however, is never impersonal and it is rarely fleeting. Even minor incidents of discrimination have the potential to leave lasting impressions.

The number of times I was personally the victim of racial discrimination is relatively small. More often than not, my ethnicity has served as an asset. Yet I can vividly recall every discriminatory incident, even the insignificant ones, and I can attest to the impact of those incidents. At college I was once riding on the subway to visit a psychiatric ward as part of a social science course. I was accosted by a bulking man who tried to pick me up because I was Asian and then cursed me profusely when I ignored his overtures. I changed my seat several times, and each time he and his racial epithets pursued me. Luckily, while I was mentally planning an escape route, we arrived at his stop before mine, and he exited my life forever. It is perhaps one of the least typical and least consequential incidents of my years in college, and yet it is one of the experiences I recall most vividly.

I believe it is the attitudinal legacies of World War II that have the potential to be the war's most pervasive legacy, particularly because of the ease with which prejudicial attitudes can be unintentionally passed on. I first realized this when my daughter, who at four found goodness in everyone and everything (with the exception of bugs and bean sprouts), proclaimed emphatically, "Mommy, I don't like the Japanese. They're mean!" I was mortified and immediately tried to discover the source of her statement. Several weeks before her proclamation, she had overheard that two of my mother's close friends – both very kindly and thoughtful Chinese ladies of my mother's generation – did not like each other because the father of one had spied for the Japanese during the Japanese occupation of China in order to advance his own career. My daughter had asked why Mrs. X didn't like Mrs. Y, and what was an occupation. I had simply explained what I took as simple fact: that Japan had taken charge of China during the war, and that Mrs. X didn't like Mrs. Y because Mrs. Y's father had helped the Japanese who had been cruel to the Chinese when they ruled China during the war. It had not been a lengthy conversation. I relate this incident simply to point out how easily young children can unwittingly adopt prejudicial attitudes, even when the lesson is unintended. Most alarmingly, we may not even be aware that they have internalized such impressions unless they happen to tell us. In addition, it is often the seemingly insignificant, unintentional prejudices that are the most damaging. Because they escape detection, they remain unchallenged and can easily infect others.

By nature, children tend not to focus on racial differences until they are taught to do so. I think their natural tendency is to view differences in race and ethnicity much the same as differences in hair color or height. My daughter's nursery school friend once said to her with great innocence and charm, "Jennie, you're Chinese, Chris is blond, Andy is Jewish, and I'm tall." I also recall a humorous and totally unexpected comment made several years later by one of our son's fourth-grade classmates. The boys had been friends since second grade. One day, my son's friend, Jason, came over to play and happened to notice a photograph of Michael with some other classmates. He said with genuine surprise, "Hey, Mike, isn't that funny. You look Chinese in this picture!" In three years of friendship, Jason had never taken note of my son's racial identity, yet he could see it in a photograph. It is not that young children do not recognize ethnic and racial differences. It is more that they do not assign importance to these differences unless they have been taught to do so by the example or teachings of others. More significantly, young children tend not to assign positive and negative values to these differences even when their existence is recognized.

Ironically, our ability to treat members of minority groups as individuals – which is how it should be – and not as representatives of their groups allows us to perpetuate our prejudices and negative stereotypes more comfortably. One of my uncles, for example, married a Japanese girl during his college days in Japan and brought her back to China where she became a much loved member of the family. Loving my aunt, who happened to be Japanese, was not viewed as a contradiction to the family's disdain for Japan the nation. We consciously strive to avoid labeling those we like or know well as members of minority groups. We are conscious that part of the identity of these individuals rests in their ethnic, racial, or religious identity, but familiarity often leads us to minimize the importance of their group identity. Paradoxically, then, we are less likely to incorporate our positive perceptions of these individuals into our perceptions of their minority groups. The ability to separate individuals from their ethnic and racial groupings is, surprisingly, the very mechanism that allows us to maintain our prejudices against any given group or nationality over time. We think we are not prejudiced when we treat a person as an individual, but every time we treat the exception to a negative stereotype in isolation, as a special case, we eliminate the need to readjust our perception of that stereotype.

World War II has left a multitude of legacies – social, political, economic, and attitudinal, some affecting us uniformly as war babies and others in ways highly specific to our particular life circumstances. The war played a major role in shaping my life because it began a chain of events that resulted in my becoming a Chinese American and because it left a broad attitudinal legacy that also taught me much about the nature of prejudice. Perhaps it is the war's attitudinal legacy and teachings that will have the greatest impact on future generations. I believe that fortunately we have the power to continuously shape that legacy in a positive direction.

Because the events surrounding World War II ultimately resulted in my move to the United States, my children have been blessed with the benefits of both Chinese and American culture. Now in their twenties, they have a strong sense of self and family, and yet they are independent thinkers with strong social consciences. And they own many hats – which I encourage them to wear whenever they choose to do so.

WARTIME SEPARATION OR WHY IT TOOK MY FATHER FIFTY YEARS TO GET USED TO ME

Laurel Strange Hayler

> Born: March 10, 1943
> Los Angeles, California, U.S.A.

My story doesn't have a vast global sweep. For me, the effects of World War II occurred on an intimate scale, right inside my family. Since my mother is dead and my father's memory is failing, I will focus on myself and the almost mythical family stories I grew up with – stories of separation and the profound effect it had on us all.

Dad enlisted in the Army Air Force in 1942 to avoid the draft. Separation came gradually for my parents. For almost a year they lived together on Balboa Island, a California resort area, while Dad "bought rides" to the base. He taught aircraft recognition to pilots, bombardiers, and navigators to keep us from "shooting down too many of our own planes." As a teacher in peacetime, this was the perfect assignment for him. His memories are mostly positive. He broadened his horizons, made some good friends, and accumulated stories about teaching Alan Ladd and the son of Claire Chenault. He even got to fly the Goodyear blimp.

Just before my birth in 1943, Mom moved in with her family in Los Angeles to be near her doctor. When I was born, Dad went AWOL from Santa Ana Army Air Base and hitchhiked to the hospital to see me. The story of him catching a ride with a sergeant from the base, hitching on a vegetable truck, and walking miles from the market district to the hospital is told annually on my birthday. Writing this story made me cry, thinking of women giving birth, without husbands or families, in short-staffed hospitals. The desire to counter war with life was very strong.

Of course there was another side to this easy stateside picture. Dad met my mother when she was 16. Anxious to settle down and have a family, he married his "child bride" when she was 18. Because of a terrible childhood that included divorce and an abusive stepfather, being a responsible father was very important to him. Any separation was painful, leaving him feeling guilty and inadequate. To describe the Balboa Island period, Dad says, "I had to leave my wife on a sand bar, pregnant, with no car."

My dad was far from alone in missing his family. The absence of women and children in the army affected all the soldiers, sometimes in strange ways. One of his stories provides an example. When his cadets had latrine duty, they preferred to clean the ladies' restrooms so they could buy sanitary napkins from

Laurel Strange Hayler and her father, 1943.

the dispenser. They argued that these purchases were perfectly rational because "sanitary napkins are good for polishing shoes."

For my parents, greater separation came after my birth. Dad was moved around California from Santa Ana Army Air Base to Merced Field to Stockton Field. Then he went out of state to Roswell, New Mexico ("We all knew what was going on in Los Alamos"), and, finally, to Orlando, Florida.

While Dad was moving around the country, Mother began raising her daughter. She came from a tradition of independent women and she blossomed. Luckily, she also knew how to ask for help. When she had to move, she "picked up" another mother with five-year-old twins one day at the beach. Together they moved all of our belongings in the twins' little red wagon. She then enlisted the help of our landlords, "Aunt" Harriet and "Uncle" Ray, in bringing me up. One of her stories was of how she and Aunt Harriet saved up all their ironing for New Year's Eve so that they could celebrate by ironing together and listening to the radio broadcast from Times Square. Despite the fact that I was still only a baby, she fought isolation by taking me to all of the local P.T.A. meetings.

In late 1944 my sister Vicki was born, and Mom moved to Glendora, California, to live in her in-laws' farmhouse. Their huge house even had a walk-in closet with a window, a closet big enough for Vicki's crib. Mother and I had twin beds and our own bathroom. We became our own little family of three, sharing the house with Dad's parents.

At last it was my dad's time to come home. We must both have been uncomfortable and even frightened by this change. I have often heard the story of how I walked into the room where my parents were sharing a bed and asked, "Is he going to live here?" Dad was traumatized by this reaction and the experience played right into his insecurities about marriage and parenting. I have heard this story so often that my stomach contracts when it is told. My father's version of his homecoming, with a little help from Sigmund Freud, was that he kicked me out of Mama's bed and I never forgave him. When I first heard this explanation, I was furious that he could blame a three-year-old for "rejecting" him.

Vicki was too young to say awkward things and Dad became much more comfortable with her. My early memories are of my cute, blond little sister sitting on my father's lap, laughing and sharing a closeness that he and I did not have. Naturally my sibling rivalry with my sister was horrible and I was very mean to her. I convinced her that I was an adopted princess and that she was an adopted tramp. We fought regularly and fiercely.

Later I wondered whether this favoritism was as bad as I remembered. I was both gratified and shocked to learn that my mother and Vicki shared my view that Dad was much more comfortable with Vicki and favored her. Mother tried to soften this experience by explaining that the homecoming fiasco made Dad "afraid" of me. This explanation helped a bit, but I still wished I, too, could be special to my father.

I tried to hide my hurt and so I focused on school to win him over. This was a good strategy with him, a self-described "culture vulture" who loved college, reading, and plays. I took school very seriously. My first-grade teacher wrote on my report card that having me as a student was "like having another adult in the classroom." When I was 11, Dad had a talk with me and promised to pay for a master's degree so I could have an interesting career and support myself if necessary. Although Dad respected my achievements, they didn't really help make him more comfortable with me. As a teacher he acknowledged that he preferred his "dumb bunnies." Unlike my first-grade teacher, he was clearly threatened by the very smart students who asked too many questions.

When I approached the time to go to college, I had another opportunity to gain Dad's affection. He was fascinated by colleges and described himself as "a college snob." He even collected college catalogues for fun. Although no one from my high school in Fullerton, California, had ever gone to Harvard or Radcliffe, I dared to apply. I felt like I hit the jackpot when I was admitted. Dad was tremendously pleased, although he partially spoiled it by saying he wished I had picked Smith or Vassar, like some of his favorite authors.

I went off to college, having been told that there was enough money for one year and that I would have to do well and get a scholarship, or return to the nearby junior college or UCLA. There was not even enough money for me to return home for Christmas vacation during my first year. I had to beg a college dean for financial aid, even though my freshman grades were poor. My father never asked how I managed to stay in college. A year later my sister left for college without this burden.

In view of the popular concept of the proper role for women in the 1950s, this emphasis on school did not help me feel confident as a woman. Fortunately there were compensations. When mothers and daughters talked about "the ratio" at colleges, we all knew this meant the ratio of men to women. At my college the ratio was an outstanding 6:1 and I hoped to make up for lost time. Helped by those wonderful odds, I married and stayed on the East Coast for 16 years. After my first son was born, my husband and I moved back to California. Even then, at the age of 33, I was afraid of returning, afraid that I would magically become an insecure teenager again.

My mother died a few years after my return to the West Coast, which gave me a series of opportunities to build a closer relationship with my father. First I helped him move into a retirement community. Later he developed a chronic illness and paradoxically this gave us another chance to heal. He needed help understanding the tests, the slow process of arriving at a diagnosis, and the implications of his condition. He needed home care and lost some precious independence. To his relief, I took on the complexities of managing his care. Finally there was something I could do for him.

In the course of his illness, Dad became very anxious and depressed. I talked him into psychotherapy and used my professional contacts to match him with an excellent therapist. In addition to dealing with his illness, he used this opportunity to work on his feelings about his abusive stepfather. At age 87, he stopped having daily nightmares about his stepfather. It was inspiring to see the changes he made.

I believe that he asked for my help because he wanted the chance to be closer to me. Dissatisfaction with our distant relationship may even have helped keep him alive, as he did not want to die before we became closer. We now talk regularly and he thanks me often. Dad sent me a huge bouquet of flowers for Mother's Day this year. I was tremendously touched, because he had never sent flowers to anyone before in his life. We are both thankful that life gives us repeated chances to heal.

XXOO

Helena Worthen

> Born: October 22, 1943
> Cleveland, Ohio, U.S.A.

In 1943, during the war, my mother was teaching piano at a girls' private school in Cleveland. When she informed her headmistress that she was pregnant (with me) and asked to go on leave, the headmistress was outraged. She declared, "Some of us *knew* what we wanted to do!" Women who wanted to work – not working-class women, but women who could choose to work or not – were expected to claim their work as a vocation, defend it against the temptation of "family." To exercise both options, work and family, was to betray those who had sacrificed to be able to work. My mother left that school and never went back, but the headmistress was still there when I began as a student some 12 years later.

My parents lived at a boys' school where my father taught, some 20 miles south of Cleveland. The boys' prep school and the girls' prep school were unofficially sibling institutions. When my mother was eight months pregnant, my father was told by one of the other "masters" that her presence in the school dining hall, where faculty and faculty wives took their meals with the boys, had become "inappropriate." She was made "obscene" in the original sense of the Greek word: 'off stage.'

My father's job was a 24-hour, seven-day-a-week job. Like the other masters, he had a room in a dormitory, in addition to the apartment where he and my mother lived. Masters were expected to occupy their dormitory rooms on nights when they had dorm duty. During the first month after my birth, my father was assigned to dorm duty every night but one. The boys' school was no more tolerant of an employee's personal life than the girls'.

In both schools there was a hierarchy of people who had to be served. The wealthy parents of pupils came first; the alumni, second; and the sons and daughters of the first two sets of people, third. The status of the teachers was full of contradictions. At my father's school the teachers were called "masters" and boys were expected to rise to their feet when a master entered the room. Yet in relation to the headmaster, the teachers were at-will employees who could be asked to do nearly anything and fired at a moment's notice.

Teachers at these places looked like members of the upper classes. Their speech, clothing, personal habits, and cultural preferences proclaimed them as such. They inhabited an elite, hierarchical world, which was part palace, part prison, but in that hierarchy they were dependent and anxious. The world I am describing is a small one, but it was designed to replicate itself with a vengeance and to resist change. Events in the outside shaped this small world as little and as late as they could be made to.

A striking feature of this period as it emerges in the letters and diaries of my parents is confidence in the future. In 1942, although the war in Europe had been blazing for three years, there is no hint that they had second thoughts about having children. The immediate future held hardship and danger. The appropriate and expected response was faith and courage. My mother learned to roll bandages at the Red Cross. My father, who already knew celestial navigation and the use of a sextant from teaching sailing at a boys' summer camp in Maine, practiced semaphore and Morse code. Rationing was in place. Even in Cleveland's exclusive suburb of Shaker Heights, a hundred people lined up to buy coffee. Gas, sugar, and rubber for tires were scarce. My grandmother could not buy tin dishpans. Yet there is no complaining in my mother's diary. My mother and father voted the Democratic ticket, for Roosevelt. They attended lectures ("Life under the Nazis" by a Dutch refugee; "Horse Trainers and Prussian Education"; "The Future of Aviation"). They saw plays (*In the Zone* by Eugene O'Neill). There was no question about where the center lay and what was at the edges. My mother reported a performance in which a blind man played the xylophone and a blind girl read Braille with gloves on. Human wonders! The planetarium presented the sky at Christmas 2000 years earlier, a representation of change that managed to celebrate both modern science and the stability of tradition simultaneously. Even after my father, age 32, had received a notice from his draft board and had gone to navy and coast guard interviews, he and my mother continued trying to get pregnant. They seem to have shared in the general confidence that "our side" would win. "Our side" meant their world, the world before Dachau, before Hiroshima.

It is hard to know where to look for this world today. It is not the world of the low-wage workplace, although that is also severely gender-segregated. It is not today's upper-middle-class world where feminism has shifted the anchors of many social relationships. As a feminist, activist, and labor educator, I can find no direct path between the present I inhabit and the domain of my parents' past. If the turning years since World War II unraveled the fabric of the world my parents knew, they also knit together, out of the same events and landscapes, the world I live in now.

Many of my friends are people who during the 1960s and 1970s decided that the world would have to change significantly before they could risk being parents in it. For them change was a necessary precondition of parenthood. For my mother and father, the promised absence of change made parenthood possible.

Confidence that the future was real, that good things lay ahead, that normal arrangements would resume when "we" won, is reflected in the way my parents' life proceeded while the war ground forward. After my father joined the navy, he was assigned first to Washington, then to the West Coast, so my mother and I went to live with her parents. There the principles of gender roles were the same, but the particular circumstances flowed from my mother's status as daughter, not wife, and especially not the wife of a teacher, who though called a master was in fact an at-will employee. Her family revolved around the scholarly work of my grandfather, a tenured professor and chair of the English department at a small liberal arts college near Philadelphia. His income supported at least four people comfortably, even through the Depression. My mother's diary records dresses she wore ("long pink," "yellow"), books she read (*War and Peace*; *Wind, Sand and Stars*; *The Life of Paderewski*). The books that my grandfather read out loud after dinner (Jung on education; *Passage to India*) get the same mention as war news. The women oversaw the vegetable garden, cooked, played tennis, picked flowers, produced oil paintings, went to concerts, played chamber music, visited with friends, went on picnics, and supervised local "girls" who came in to "help." *Help*, not *serve*, is the exact word – the "girls" worked side by side with, although under the direction of, the women of the family.

"Great excitement over German surrender ... Then heard 'twas fake," wrote my mother on April 28, 1945. The symphony was playing lots of Russian music in honor of the Allies. Then on August 13: "Japan still slow at surrendering." She noted Kaethe Kollwitz lithographs at the museum, a nationwide railroad strike.

Meanwhile my father had begun the experience that would change him irrevocably. Just as for other people for whom the war was finally an experience of success, my father's horizons expanded dramatically because of what he encountered. He had started out as a bright, good-looking New Hampshire country boy without a penny to his name. At college he supported himself and his widowed mother by teaching cram courses to rich boys who didn't like to study. After college he got jobs in the world of prep schools and private summer camps. He traveled as a courier for a wealthy family making a Grand Tour of Europe. His horizons were defined by the cultural, recreational, and educational territories of the rich and their children.

The war offered an opportunity to change that. Because he had a college degree, he entered the navy as an officer. In the navy every possible circumstance dramatized the difference between officers and enlisted men. As an officer he went to California on a train, first class in a Pullman compartment, but in his letters he described enlisted men packed into coach cars or sleeping on the platforms in the little towns through which they passed. In Los Angeles he and other officers were wined and dined at nightclubs where they saw movie stars: "Judy Garland is such a wisp of a mite and not even pretty .... Bob Hope nearly ruined the show with his ad libs ...." He lived in a house in the hills above the navy base, not on a ship or in barracks.

His first assignment took him out of this elite world and broadened his horizons considerably. He was to write job descriptions of enlisted men on naval transport ships. The result was a book-length report on 95 different jobs

Helena Worthen's father as a young naval officer, circa 1942;
photo found in his wife's wallet after her death in 1999.

("billets"), describing them in terms of training requirements, special job knowledge, health and accident hazards, and duties under battle, emergency, and routine conditions. He gathered this information by observing and interviewing the men who did the work. For example, in August 1944 he wrote about a Water Tender Third Class named Marvin Totsch (all these details are in the report):

> The incumbent is stationed at all times below the water line, works in congested areas, and is subject to temperatures in the room that often rise to over 100 degrees F. All work is done under artificial lighting and forced ventilation. In case of enemy submarine action, a torpedo hit would be extremely hazardous in this location .... It is necessary to take salt tablets regularly as prescribed. Also when making repairs or when operating valves on the steam lines, exposed arms often touch the lines which cause painful deep burns ... (Worthen, 95)

Once, checking on stored equipment deep in the hull of a ship, he came across the brig, a windowless cell next to the perpetual thunder of the engine. In it lay a lone sailor whose crime had been to vomit on the deck instead of over the side. This sailor had opted to vomit on the deck after being warned that the safety chains were weak and that men who fell overboard would be left to die at sea. My father saw the miseries of the enlisted men and came to dislike what he called "this big ship Navy – feudalism at its worst." Slowly he learned to hate the navy and the war.

He was lucky. He both escaped danger and learned from it. Although he served on board the *Clay* at the battles of Saipan and Guam and on the *Morrison* at Truk and Okinawa, he was never injured. He left the *Morrison* two weeks before it was sunk by a kamikaze. Then he was given the job of writing to the families of all the men who had died, men whom he remembered personally. When he was assigned to navigate the empty tanker *Androscoggin* on a return trip from Okinawa to Ulithi Atoll, his shipmates picked up the signal of a Japanese submarine on their sonar and outran it. Safely back on Guam, he learned that the cruiser *Indianapolis* had been sunk at that very spot with the loss of 1,100 lives.

His letters from the last months of the war are V-mail – photos of letters – sometimes with black stripes where the censor had been at work. His signatures are always followed by *XXOO*, meaning hugs and kisses. More than two X's or O's were prohibited by the censor because they might be code, so *XXOO* is both a signal and a symbol of a barrier to communication.

"If you have been reading the papers, you know where we are," he wrote. He was on the *St. Paul*, part of Admiral "Bull" Halsey's fleet, some 10 miles off the coast of Honshu, the main island of the Japanese homeland. This was part of the preparation for the invasion of Japan. "The great raids on Japan have just begun, and when they reach their zenith, hell itself shall have been matched," he wrote. The fleet steamed west toward Honshu. Planes took off, dropped their bombs, and circled back to their ships, which had reversed direction and were steaming east, away from Japan. Many planes ran out of fuel and couldn't catch up with the ships. My father had heard officers promise the pilots that the fleet would wait, but he saw the planes drop into the sea to be left behind.

The atomic bomb fell. He knew then that he would never have to be part of an invasion of Japan. "Somehow the future seems to begin now," he wrote.

His world was bigger by this time, but his view of it bitter. "One of the causes of the next war will be the Hearst and McCormick publications," he exclaimed. "You citizens know nothing of the real thing .... If people really knew the cost of all this!" Then: "I have no illusions of permanent peace or permanent harmony on earth .... The thing uppermost is to make money with war inventions, with war skills, with war booty."

He received a command on Guam, overseeing demobilization efforts. His months on Guam he called "the richest single experience I have ever had." He set up re-entry job training for returning soldiers and began to create a public school and civilian higher education system.

For those Americans who survived physically, whose marriages and friendships and families were intact, who had homes to return to and even jobs, the experience of the final months of the war and its immediate aftermath was like living in a giant jigsaw puzzle in which the pieces were fitting into place. The picture represented by this puzzle would not hold for long, but at least for the time being it presented a plausible future. Atomic power was not yet fearsome. The Russians were our allies – "God bless the Russians!" my father wrote. Managing the world in peacetime would be hard, but not as hard as war. There was a place for him in this expanded future. "We" had won. He wrote: "We must keep the peace of the world, even if we have to keep it single handed." On August 8, 1945, two days after the bomb was dropped on Hiroshima: "How grand to have our little girl alive in such a brave new world."

His letters are full of plans. He would use the GI Bill to get a master's degree. With a master's degree he could quit his job and start his own prep school, maybe in California or Florida. He and my mother could live in a Quonset hut. Quonset huts were cheap. They were a solution to the acute housing shortage in the States. He drew picture after picture in his letters to her, showing her where the piano would go, where my grandparents would live, how big the living room could be. He would buy a boat, surplus navy war matériel, fix it up, operate it as a floating camp for boys. It didn't occur to him to leave the world of private preparatory schools.

But he had come to understand and deeply hate the machinery of state that drew us into wars. On dark days he was someone for whom all men and boys were potentially soldiers, all women potentially widows, all children potentially orphans. For six months after his return, he was severely depressed. Yet he took up his old job. The war had given him the opportunity to develop into a man comfortable with the role of command. After the war, perhaps because his plans to create situations in which he could continue to play this role did not materialize, he found an outlet for it in his classroom and in his family. He made a lot of small compromises that added up to big ones.

Now I have to shift to the more personal story of my relationship with this man as a father. When he finally came home, I greeted him as a stranger and an enemy. I was about three. The person I had emotionally come to know as my father was my grandfather, the white-haired scholar who, in retirement, seemed to me to have nothing else to do but take me on walks and write funny poems for me to read. I neither recognized nor trusted this new person who dressed up in his navy uniform to drill me and eventually my little brother around the kitchen table. What did his presence in our house mean? What were his rights? I knew my father as a loud, unpredictable, abrupt, intractable man, quick to disagree with me and quick to condemn me or anyone I summoned to my defense, swift with the use of vivid language that stuck in the mind long after words were uttered.

I think of the years that I knew my father – the 50 years between our meeting after World War II and his death in 1995 – as a bridge from past to present. To have been born before the end of World War II means having bridged two worlds. I see myself and my father face to face, struggling on that bridge. We are struggling over what things mean.

At the beginning of the bridge between the two worlds I am talking about, all the details of life fit into a consistent whole. The cruelest contradictions in this first world, from the point of view of someone protected by it, could be adequately sorted out and resolved in terms of the narratives and dramas of the Western literary canon. The picture begins to come apart as time passes. There was the news of the concentration camps. The Russians became "our" enemies, not "our" allies. Atomic power became fearsome, not something to celebrate. Television reached everyone, but not with great literature. My parents were horrified by McCarthy, but also horrified that Carl Van Doren cheated on *The $64,000 Question*. The civil rights movement revealed the shakiness of the foundations of the culture some people thought was ordained in heaven. The Vietnam War tore the country apart. Birth control – the pill – became available. The women's movement enabled people like me to say things they had been thinking but had not known how to understand.

Our quarrels often seemed to be about art or culture – for example, whether the sound of harmonica music is as pleasing as violin music, or whether a film can be considered art if it shows depravity. But these were all disguises for the central theme which was about men and women. Much of the struggle had to do with what girls or women should and could do and not do. The work on gender equity that had taken place on the home front during the war did not affect my father or my mother. The women's movement, once it took off in the 1960s, was a critical support to me, but it never reached him.

When I agreed to write this essay, I expected that it would be a quick report of events that I could understand because, having lived them, I was the authority on them. Instead, when I sat down with a box of my father's letters to my mother, written between January 1944 and the final months of 1946, I found myself meeting a person I felt I had never known. His optimism, his plans, above all his conviction that beyond the war lay a secure peace in which the powers dedicated to war would be redeployed to create a good world and that he would have a significant role in this new world, were a surprise to me. I was even more jolted when I read my mother's diaries of the same years. The story in them is not one that I lived. I am not the authority on it after all.

I had begun to have such an intimation while he was dying and he started to tell stories about the war. It was 1995 and memories of the war, already wakened by parades and other anniversary commemorations, broke through into the present. Agitated, almost gasping, my father retold his experience at Saipan: wading through shallow waves amid chopped-up floating bodies of other men – the "boys," he called them, men who were hardly older than the generations of boys he had taught at prep school. Without pausing, he described treating the wounded aboard ship, no fans to move the steamy air below decks, no fresh water, no medicines or painkillers.

Two years after my father died I sat at the dining-room table reading his letters. On the tape deck was Brahms that my mother used to play on the piano. I felt torn out of the present and heaved into the past as if struck by a tidal wave. I read how he made necklaces for my mother out of shells that he found on the beaches of the islands of the South Pacific. Necklaces? The next time I went to see my mother, I asked her to look for them.

When she brought the necklaces out, I saw that they were much finer than I had expected them to be. There were two. They were still wrapped in the paper in which my father had shipped them. After 50 years the polished shells still gleamed. The shells were matched, graduated in size like pearls, and strung on thread in a complicated criss-cross pattern, almost like macramé, to make a two-dimensional design.

The war took my father to many islands. Sometimes he fitted out a sailboat and sailed off by himself or with a friend, exploring a whole atoll. In his letters, my father describes how he was taught by another man to look for shells on the beaches. After finding the shells came polishing them. He did this on the ship, sitting on his bunk, while talk, music, gambling, letter writing went on around him. Cleaning them, buffing them, choosing among them, drilling holes, stringing them helped him concentrate. Sometimes the right shell would be missing and he would make a note of it and plan to look for it the next chance he got. He focused on how to design the net of threads, how to knot them, how to pack them, how she would wear them, how he would feel when he saw her wear them. It was a way of making the future concrete.

Looking for shells is a meditative, solitary activity, something one thinks of doing on an empty beach where the only sounds are the waves and the rustle of wind in the fronds of palm trees. At such a moment even a war might seem like a distant form of weather, a hurricane that cuts a swathe of destruction and moves on. Perhaps at such a moment a man can imagine that all the emblems that link him to war have been carried away on the storm – the medals and insignias of rank, the gun. They belong to the war – they disappear with the war. Perhaps other kinds of power, power that distorts relationships, also blow away. Then the person who reaches down to pick up seashells is nothing but a person – not a soldier, not a master, not a father. And the person who receives the shells a generation later is also nothing but a person.

If mine were the only story of the last 50-odd years, I would worry. Luckily, at every turn, other stories have intersected with mine, presenting alternatives. And objects bear a kind of witness where words fail.

Andrew Cohen and his father, 1945.

THE HOLOCAUST BY MARRIAGE

Andrew D. Cohen

> Born: March 14, 1944
> Washington, D.C., U.S.A.

This essay is about the zigzag way I lost my sense of religious identity and ethnicity and then refound them as a consequence of events at the time of World War II and after. It's the story of one person's development when his own life and inclinations run against the grain of the experiences and history of his family and ethnic group.

I did not grow up with any keen sense of the plight of Jews in the Holocaust, yet being Jewish shaped my early life. My dad made a decision in June 1944 to go on leave from his prestigious job as a lawyer for the Federal Communications Commission in Washington, joining the navy in order to serve his country. His stint in the navy, however, was cut short to 11 months, both because my mother was hospitalized in August 1944 with a paralyzing attack of rheumatoid arthritis and because V-E Day came in May of the following year. During the months that my dad was in the navy, I was looked after by relatives and friends. My mom had been a promising lawyer herself, aiming at being a judge, but she never recovered sufficiently from her arthritis to resume her career. She was, nonetheless, able to do volunteer work, and she chose to dedicate much of her energy to the cause of the United Jewish Appeal (UJA).

When the state of Israel came into existence in 1948, it became a special safe haven for Jews from around the world. Most importantly, it was a haven for many Holocaust survivors who chose to live in a nation that was committed to the survival of the Jewish people and to being a state that would not betray Jews in time of need. My mother was motivated to take an active role in the UJA by an enormous concern for the many Jewish victims of the Holocaust who had become refugees in Europe, in North and South America, and in other parts of the world, and, as a consequence of her concern for Holocaust survivors, she herself took an interest in Israel and its crucial role in the relocation of Jewish refugees. She could not have anticipated that among those survivors helped by one of the UJA agencies would be the parents of her future daughter-in-law.

Despite my parents' experiences, I did not grow up with a very strong sense of ethnicity or of being Jewish. My family belonged to a Reform Jewish synagogue, we observed the major Jewish holidays, and I occasionally went to Friday night services, especially while I was preparing for my bar mitzvah. But at the same time, we were very assimilated to mainline American culture. We were minimally observant and religion was not a large part of our lives. I grew up in a comfortable, affluent, secure, loving environment. We lived in a suburb that had a high concentration of Jewish families and many of our family friends were Jewish. After my freshman year at the local high school, my parents and I selected a very WASP Eastern prep school, Andover, so that I could have a more productive learning environment for the remainder of high school studies. Only one out of ten students there was Jewish. I avoided Hillel in college.

In fact my youth and my family background made me want to have nothing to do with Jewishness or Israel. Not only did I have no desire to travel to Israel or to learn modern Hebrew, I was even reluctant to donate my dollars to plant trees there. My dad's legacy of having to contend with anti-Semitism in a Christian world was passed on to me as an oppressive feeling about being Jewish, a feeling that continued strong throughout college. I felt that the Christian world was holding me personally responsible for the death of Jesus.

After I graduated from college, I went directly into the Peace Corps. I worked in rural community development, living with the Aymara Indians on the high plains of Bolivia for two years. My grandmother wanted to know what a nice Jewish boy was doing risking his life by living with some primitive Indian tribe at 13,000 feet in a deserted wilderness with no running water, toilets, electricity, paved roads, telephones, or other amenities common to the developed world. I never shared my grandmother's attitudes toward what I was doing. I felt that every person on the planet was as important as any other and that it was not my mission to serve only Jewish people. All the same, during my time in the Peace Corps, I regained my commitment to Judaism, perhaps partly because I was so removed from anti-Semitism. I had also learned the importance of belonging to an ethnic group.

While Mother's many years of devoted service to the UJA contributed to my rejection of Israel, perhaps because of jealousy that I had to compete with it for her attention, what did get me to go to Israel was a major upheaval in my thinking and behavior. This upheaval began with a renewal of interest in being Jewish, triggered by my grandmother's comments. It was also stimulated by reading Max Dimont's *Jews, God, and History* while I was in the Peace Corps. What made a major impact on me in Dimont's book was how many Jews went to their deaths because they insisted on maintaining their Jewish identity, while I was being so reticent about my own. The book prompted me to be more proactive about my Jewishness.

When I returned to the States and began a doctoral program in California, I made a beeline for the Friday night services at Hillel House. There I met Sabina, who became my wife. As destiny would have it, she was the daughter of concentration camp survivors. Sabina had grown up in Brooklyn along with her younger brother – the two shining lights in a family swamped by horrors and darkness. She wanted to please her parents so much, in a way to compensate them in some small part for all that they had lost. At the same time she was plagued by a desire to find a truly meaningful experience for herself and her own family. She had recurring dreams of opening a closet and seeing it filled with the heads of her relatives, all crying out to her, "Save me!" All of the suffering in her family dwarfed any experiences of anti-Semitism that I had had in my life. Both being the daughter of Holocaust survivors and spending a summer on a kibbutz in Israel just after the Six Day War pulled Sabina irresistibly to Israel.

Strangely, my own ethnicity was also fortified by the experience of working with the Mexican-American minority community in California. While at Stanford, I became internal evaluator for a bilingual education program. I got so caught up in encouraging Mexican-American children to maintain their language of origin, Spanish, and to preserve their ethnic roots, that I became poignantly aware that I had no sense of my own Jewish identity and could not speak Hebrew. I felt a sense of hypocrisy and became ashamed of abandoning my own ethnicity.

A few years after our marriage, Sabina and I began talking about moving to Israel. We came to this decision for different reasons. For me it was an outgrowth of wanting to feel proud of my Jewish heritage and ethnicity. For Sabina it was mostly her sense that only the Jewish state would be there to protect Jews in need and her deep regret that, at the time when her parents were suffering so indescribably at the hands of the Nazis, there was no Jewish state to come to their rescue. Her excitement about Israel was infectious. Before long she had me swept up in the same enthusiasm to see what Israel could offer us as "returnees" (which is the way all Jews are referred to in Israel, regardless of whether they have ever been there). Part of what attracted me to Sabina in the first place was her clarity about her Jewish identity and the prospect of creating a family together which would have a sense of ethnic belonging, perhaps even in a Jewish homeland. From the beginning of our marriage, there was a commitment to making a Jewish life together. We lit *Shabbat* candles on Friday evening and looked for ways to make Jewish holiday celebrations special.

Despite Sabina's enthusiasm our departure for Israel in 1975 also found her full of trepidation. We went with the understanding between us that we would come back to the U.S. if the situation became too scary for her to deal with. Given the horrors of war that her parents had suffered, she did not want to go through anything similar in Israel. She did not want to be trapped there at a time of war, as her parents had been trapped in Poland.

When we left the States for Israel with our two-year-old daughter Judy in tow, we were determined to make it our home. For the next 16 years, we hardly looked back. When we returned to the States on sabbatical in 1980, I assisted Sabina's dad in writing down his story of the Holocaust. The experience opened my eyes to what he had actually gone through. Parts of his story, entitled *A Spark of Life*, make the film *Schindler's List* seem tame. Many years later, in 1996, I assisted Sabina's mother in recording her own war experiences for the sake of family history.

During the years in Israel, our careers took second place to the desire to

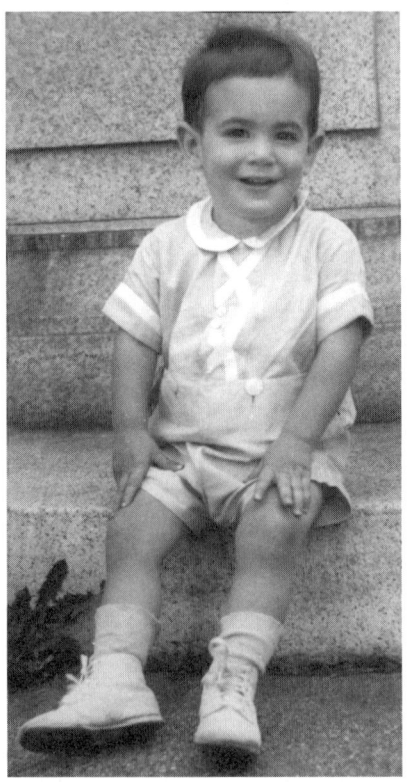

Andrew Cohen at the age of two.

be in the country of our choice, a homeland for our people. So it was until Saddam Hussein invaded Kuwait in August 1990. At this point the real paradox emerged. Sabina's indisputable ethnic heritage began to tear her in two directions – to stay in Israel, her one real home, or to fly from danger and entrapment, an imperative lesson she had learned from her roots, a lesson that could not be ignored. Sabina found that after Iraq's invasion of Kuwait, she could no longer sleep at night. Her terror was so extreme that in early November 1990 she took our 12-year-old son Daniel and went to Atlanta to stay with her brother and his family, while our then 16-year-old daughter Judy remained behind to finish up her senior year of high school. Sabina's flight was in part a reaction to a madman intent on changing the course of history, but also in part a response to having her "war button" pushed – a button connected to the experience her parents had had of being trapped in Europe and almost annihilated by the Nazis.

As it turned out, there was no war yet. After a month Sabina decided to return to Israel with Daniel. She was in a heart-wrenching dilemma. She loved Israel, but she also needed to be out of danger. At that time I was not the most understanding husband. I was annoyed that she had left Israel in its hour of need. But she was in agony. Making *aliyah* (going to live in Israel, literally 'going up') and then *yerida* (leaving Israel, literally 'going down') are not actions taken lightly. For Jews, living in Israel constitutes a statement about what is important. It constitutes a choice that is highly emotionally charged.

Sabina considered Israel her one and only home. For me Israel represented a roller-coaster of ups and downs, marked by enormous financial sacrifice, humbling professional experiences, and more satisfaction from the land, the holidays, the people, and the foods than from anything associated with the workplace. I was happy to stay in Israel, but because of Sabina's turmoil, I decided to look for a job in America. In response to my applications, I got three favorable replies and set off to the United States for job interviews. Unfortunately the interviews started five days before the date President Bush delivered his ultimatum warning Saddam Hussein to pull out of Kuwait.

Although I phoned Sabina and asked her to stay put in Jerusalem with the kids until I returned, she was unable to do that. During the week that followed, all international carriers except El Al ceased fights to Israel. This terrified her. The very thought of being trapped inside Israel – just the way her parents had first been trapped in Poland during the war and then been trapped in concentration camps during the Holocaust – was intolerable to her. And all around her our Israeli neighbors were assuring her that "it wouldn't happen here," that no missiles would fall on Israel – just the way that Jews in Poland had been unable to believe that anyone would attempt to annihilate them. She was haunted by family memories.

When the Israeli people were all issued gas masks and given lessons in how to use them, Sabina was seized by panic. Israelis were shown how to inject themselves with an antidote against mustard-gas poisoning – just what every teenager or protective mother does not want to know about! Beside herself with fear and exhausted from sleepless nights, Sabina packed up the kids and grabbed one of the last flights out of Israel, ironically on Lufthansa. Not only was Germany the means of escape this time, it was a further irony that German corporations were responsible for supplying Iraq with the gas that they were using to tip their missiles. It was these gas-tipped missiles that had Sabina most terrified. And irony indeed that this ancestral memory ultimately drove Sabina from Israel.

This was hard for me to understand, because I did not have this particular piece of Jewish heritage in my gut. I promised our kids that we would be back on a plane to Israel as soon as my interviews were over, in order to finish out the school year, but that was not what fate had in store for us. The evening before our flight back to Tel Aviv in January 1991, Saddam Hussein launched the first of his many missile attacks on Israel. Relatives contacted me immediately to let me know that I would be insane to attempt to return to Israel at that point, thus endangering the lives of our children. So we became refugees, first in Los Angeles with my parents and then in Minneapolis, waiting for my new job to come through at the University of Minnesota.

In order for me to leave Israel definitively, I needed to justify to myself that the move was the appropriate thing to do. What I could not hear with open ears was all the hurt, all the despair, all the ambivalence that my wife was going through in abandoning Israel. Sabina did not feel anger at Israel. Rather she felt more than ever that Israel was where she wanted to be. Yet her fears set a trajectory from that environment into a safer one, just as her parents had moved from a war zone to a safer environment many years before.

Now, writing from Minnesota where Sabina and I are living, I find myself asking, "What is ethnicity?" I've tried to share here some of the paradoxes that have beset me in my own dance toward and away from being Jewish during much of my lifetime. How can I compare a form of engaged or committed ethnicity like Sabina's with an assimilated or sublimated or vicarious ethnicity like my own? Sabina's ethnicity is experiential, mine cerebral. The Holocaust lives inside Sabina. For me it is primarily a matter of acquired knowledge. Finally, can any of us take up an historical event as vast as the Holocaust by choice, even through the choice of marriage? I've learned that I couldn't do it, not even by being Jewish, not even by making *aliyah* to Israel.

MY FLIER

Sarah Niles Kafatou

>Born: April 24, 1943
>New York City, New York, U.S.A.

On Pearl Harbor Day, December 7, 1941, the United States entered World War II. My father immediately volunteered for the U.S. Navy. Later the same day he phoned my mother and asked her to marry him. Her answer, "Why didn't you ask me last weekend?" meant yes. She was delighted that her hopes for just such a call were fulfilled, and her fear for him now made marriage mean more. "He might have been going away to be killed," she recalled to me 55 years later. "I couldn't say no."

Indeed, on the day I was born, the headline news was that my father's ship had been sunk, leaving no survivors. Days later this was found not to be true and in six months' time the news of my birth reached him at sea. I grew into toddlerhood, was issued a ration book, and still hardly knew him. Like so many other people's fathers, he remained away, except for brief visits, until the end of the war. He rose to the rank of lieutenant commander in the Naval Air Force, serving on two aircraft carriers, the *Ranger* and the *Ticonderoga*. At first active in convoy escort across the North Atlantic (one such convoy carried Churchill to a secret meeting with Roosevelt), he later asked to be transferred to the Pacific theater, where he saw combat in the Philippines and off the coast of Japan.

My father, who was an orphan from early childhood and retained no strong ties to the relatives who had raised him, became attached to the navy and thought of his ship as home. To him at the time, as he later told me, spending a leave with my mother and me was a matter of visiting "those people," after which he could return to "my ship." The transition from military to civilian and family life at the end of the war was not completely easy for him. Nor was it for me. When my father returned and my brother was born, I abruptly lost my exclusive relationship with my mother. Did many people born during the war feel shock and disorientation, as I believe I did, in the quick shift to the nuclear family and the Baby Boom?

About 10 years ago I wrote the poem entitled "A Flier." Set in the 1950s, it moves back in time to World War II and then reaches back even further to World War I. What moved me most was to imagine my father as a child with his brother, playing with model planes, just as my brother and I used to do. In the poem, and in life, he is a caring parent. He is also a boy whose hopes for life have been shaken and disappointed. Perhaps, as the poem suggests, the trauma of war and homecoming taught us tenderness.

A Flier

for my father

My brother and I watched pigeons on warm evenings
tip like paper boats, dipping a wing,
then right themselves on the bumpy air, soaring
out over the arc of the Atlantic.
At the window, on rainy days,
waiting for you to get home through traffic,
we heard their perishing cries.
Sometimes we'd spread out the morning paper
and with a tube of airplane glue and bits of molded plastic
would make our models: MIG-15, Canberra, Messerschmidt.
On clear days the dark heavens opened up
into a glory of early morning
scavenging gulls rode crisscross, cawing
for garbage, spillage, the wind's paper playthings,
and you would walk for miles with field glasses
and a bird book, looking for nested eggs, or follow
the long-drawn-out, looping flights of the full-fledged.
The tidewater flashed in the low distance
like the wet floating runway shuddering forward
where you'd shivered and waited for daybreak.
Some friends had not recovered
and little that was promised was fulfilled
except the coming home. Home to two kids!
Dozing in the back seat on the way home
from beach trips, we dreamed of danger;
you glimpsed our bodies in the rear-view mirror
and hugged the highway closer.
Where was the time when, standing in the grass
in knee-patched knickers, shoulder to shoulder with your brother,
you held up high your paper biplane, ready to run
out on the wind, going to save the nations?

My father died in the fall of 1996 and we arranged a memorial gathering at my brother's house in Berkeley. Most of those present spoke and my brother's words brought the memories clustered in this essay closer to many of us. During the Vietnam War my brother was a conscientious objector, doing alternative service. Our father, though he treasured his own military experience and was more reluctant than we were to mistrust our national policy on that issue, was consistently supportive of my brother. In time my father also became opposed to the Vietnam War. Of all the moments of our life which my brother might have chosen to remember our father by, he chose this: the two of them, not shoulder to shoulder but arm in arm, walking down Market Street in San Francisco together as participants in one of the great marches against the war.

Allied troops enter Germany, 1945.

INNOCENCE AND EXPERIENCE

Kevin Lewis

>Born: July 13, 1943
>Asheville, North Carolina, U.S.A.

My sister, my mother, my grandparents, a dog – all inhabit my earliest memories. But my father is not there.

To me our earliest childhood memories seem like fleeting glimpses of a mythic past, an original and static time before our own chronological time began. We strain with dreamlike scraps of earliest memory to grasp the world of that primal past, a golden age, which our selective, fragmentary recall provides so tantalizing and yet so inadequate a means of knowing. A child falls into the conflicts and ambiguities of history from a once-upon-a-time world, a sort of dream time. And those first memories, in contrast to the stories told of that time by parents and grandparents, hold the crux of our origins as conscious beings. They seem the truer link, somehow, to the first grounding of the self, to the persons we travel the subsequent years to become – in my case, son, brother, husband, and father.

My father did subsequently enter my life. Memories of him as a vital pillar of the family, as a hard-working professional, as a bookish, map-loving intellectual and community servant, are clear and strong. Indeed from my early years he marked me in some ways that have been easy to trace and in others that I am still working to understand. In my youth the shape of his undoubted love for me, like mine for him, was elusive. That reciprocal love was strong, but neither well scripted nor spontaneous. Undemonstrative as we were together, our love was difficult to express and, thus, to clarify and cherish. Like other sons, I am occupied in later life by a need to fathom and to honor that love.

What is the connection, if there is one, between the absence of my father from my earliest memories and the quality of our relationship in the later years of my youth and young manhood? I have been worrying this project for half my lifetime in my father's absence. He has been dead for 30 years. Soon after I graduated from college, my father died in a hospital bed, at the age of 54, from system shock at the amputation of a foot, necessitated by the diabetes he developed as an adult. It was an illness that perhaps, or so I believe the doctors said, he might have fought more conscientiously than he did over many years, preoccupied as he was by the pastoral work into which he threw himself with gusto as a Presbyterian minister with a progressive vision of social change.

Father sailed for France in May 1945 when I was 22 months old. He returned after a stint of service with a French Protestant refugee relief organization in June 1946, in time for my third birthday that July, or so I am told. My older sister's fifth birthday would come later that summer. My younger sister was six months old. Soon after his return my father left for another year, to raise money around the country for the World Council of Churches' fund to rebuild churches in Europe destroyed during the war. I have no retrievable memory of my father until after I turned four.

As often as we revisit our earliest memories, they are never sufficient. Always we are haunted by the thought of what more we might see if our own gaze into the dream time would clear. We want to know what else happened then and what mattered that matters still. Retrieve what it will and refuse what it won't, selective memory holds clues to the people we became and are becoming. I borrow this belief from psychologists. And we work the collective family memory and the historical record over against the mystery of personal memory, back and forth, to sound the waters of the self. In my case, I work to recover a father who was not there at first and whose work consumed him when he was.

In 1945 Father resigned a church pastorate in Glendale, a suburb of Cincinnati, in order to put into practice on an international scale the social gospel he had earlier learned at McCormick Seminary in Chicago. As a clergyman deferred from the draft, he had not served in the armed forces. But he felt an obligation to his generation. And, as later when he passed it on to his children, he was prompted by his own family's interest in global affairs – at Princeton he had thought he was headed for a career as a diplomat. With my mother's concurrence, he had decided he was called to a France in crisis after the war. He was 32 years old. He left my 30-year-old mother, pregnant with her third child, to find shelter with myself and my older sister in the home of my welcoming maternal grandparents in Asheville, North Carolina.

Father, for whom French was a second language, together with a Belgian-born minister-colleague, were the first two representatives of the Presbyterian Church (U.S.A.) to be sent to Europe to work with CIMADE (Comité Inter-Mouvements auprès des Evacués, or the Inter-Movement Committee Serving Evacuees). This was a Protestant interdenominational organization founded in 1939, in conscious memory of the courageous Huguenot resistance to tyranny and persecution. Its purpose at first was to save Nazi victims during the war and then later, following the cease-fire, to provide humanitarian aid to victims and refugees in France. Its religious purpose was to aid in the reconstruction of the morale necessary to rebuild civic culture and to restore sociopolitical order amid the wreckage in Europe.

At two and three years old, I was passively aware that I had no father to go with my mother – "passively," meaning I had no way of knowing someone was missing. Though I am certain I was told where he was – indeed I was probably reminded constantly – I have no memory of knowing who or where he was at the age when consciousness establishes the fixed members of the immediate family circle.

Phebe Ann Lewis with Kevin and his two sisters, summer 1946.

I have long since passed the age of 32 at which he left the family briefly and have even passed 54, the age when he died. At his death I was 24, too young to respond sufficiently to him and his experience, to have crossed that divide of reticence between father and son. What makes this particularly poignant is to come upon the postcards he addressed to me from France in 1945-46. My mother saved them, along with his letters to her, his postcards to my sister, and his photos of coworkers, bombed-out towns, and CIMADE chalet retreat houses, as well as newspaper and church magazine articles describing the organization's initiatives.

I do not remember seeing this material Mother saved until two years ago when, deciding it was time to pass it on to her children, she made copies of everything for each of us. "Dear little boy" or "Dear little son," he addresses me, some of the cards typed, some written in a consistent, decisive hand. "When I can't see you, it gives me great joy to write to you." On the back of a *carte postale* featuring a sepia photo of an interior of a country dwelling, labeled *chambre de paysans*, he writes, "Here is what a little boy grows up in in this part of the world. It is quite different from what you have at Grandmother's and Grandfather's, isn't it? And do you know, they heat their rooms with a stove that stands right in the middle of this room! Every day now I see little boys helping their fathers gather wood on the mountain side for the long cold winter, which they will burn in their stoves."

Father's home base was St. Dié, a market town on the river Meurthe in Lorraine. The Nazis had devastated it in 1944. The letters he wrote my mother tell of doing anything and everything relief workers could to help bring hope and the most basic of services back to that city. He preached in French at services of worship. He counseled, he married, he baptized. Through an interpreter he conducted occasional services for German prisoners of war quartered in French army barracks outside St. Dié. And everywhere he found, as he put it, "the sickness of Europe, the corrosion of the moral fibre." In March 1946 he saw it "everywhere like a great suffocating wave." More damaging than the earlier bombs and fires and loss of lives was the numbed spirit of the inhabitants. It was this demoralization in a landscape following war that he was most driven to fight against by his American idealism and his Christian belief, and his strong physical constitution made the fight possible.

His work took him temporarily to Le Chambon sur Lignon, the old Huguenot village in the highlands south of Lyons, where Calvin's Protestants had withstood the royalist persecutions of the seventeenth century, where the Camisards had fought for religious liberty in the nearby Cevennes. During the war the entire village of Le Chambon had shared the risk of giving sanctuary to Jews and others fleeing the Nazis. (This unique place was the subject of Bill Moyers's film, *Weapons of the Spirit*.) Father was asked to aid the resettlement of the older, more fragile refugees still remaining in the village.

Coincidentally, Albert Camus, a year younger than my father, had spent several months during the winter of 1942-43 in seclusion at Panelier near Le Chambon. Fighting the tuberculosis which would recur a decade later, Camus was writing for the Resistance paper *Combat* and working out the plan of his allegory of war, *The Plague*, a novel I teach regularly to my undergraduates. In the spring before my father arrived at Le Chambon, Camus glanced at the "sickness of Europe" and commented in his notebooks (99-103): "Utter disgust for all society. Temptation to flee and to accept the decadence of one's era ... But disgust, nauseating disgust for such dispersion in others ... "; he writes, "Meaning of my work: So many men are deprived of grace. How can one live without grace? One has to try it and to do what Christianity never did: be concerned with the damned." These and other entries connect me to the father who – unknown to me at the time, bound as I was in the chrysalis of dawning self-consciousness – was working to be an example, confronting the paralyzing corruptions and compromises of Europe's defeated spirit, Camus's "decadence." As he understood it, my father was going about the business of restoring once more the hope of living with grace, by concerning himself daily with "the damned" of Europe.

But Father found French colleagues who were not to be counted among the damned. Again and again his letters recount working side by side with men and women who, though they had suffered during the Occupation, had behaved not only well but with extreme courage. These were a rare few who, when civic values had collapsed on all sides, had proved and were proving capable of what Father termed "sacrificial witness" and of acts of heroism born of a special "purity and intensity of spirituality." Father writes of finding these "saints of the earth" wherever CIMADE assigned him: Paris, Le Chambon, Boulogne, Calais, Dunkirk, and St. Dié.

He attended a meeting of the city fathers to hear Le Corbusier present a plan for rebuilding the rubble of St. Dié into "the first completely modern city in the world." Noting, realistically, that the "French peasant and small landholder" found it difficult to envision this, Father added, "You can see how deeply I am interested in the result from the fact that we are trying to bring the Gospel to bear in the architectural as in other areas of reconstruction." His was a hopeful, liberal religious vision of collaborative transformation in all the connected parts of the ailing body of Europe. A consistent note, deeply religious, deeply humane, is sounded in each of the letters from that year, all retyped by my mother. This record makes me more proud of him with each rereading. He voluntarily suffered privations, he adapted to awful conditions, he worked side by side with local city governments, churches, and various other aid organizations without tiring and without losing his idealism. And he voiced his special interest and hope in "the youth of France, and I suppose it is general all over Europe, [who] are alone going to save it."

My father, Burt, had a younger brother. Uncle Archie was to come gradually into my life years later, outliving my father by 23 years and serving as a father figure to me after my father's death. Following service during the war as a first lieutenant and captain in intelligence assigned to an artillery unit from 1942 to 1946, my uncle held appointments as a medieval historian at the University of South Carolina (where I have taught for 20-odd years), at the University of Texas at Austin, and then at the University of Massachusetts at Amherst. By temperament a peace-maker, he chaired the history departments at both the latter universities. His career as an academic seemed as exuberant as it was peripatetic. As children we relished occasional visits from this vibrant, jolly man, who told stories of frequent travel to archives in exotic European and Japanese cities. He was neither as solemn nor as religious as my father.

After Father's death, as my own academic career was slowly getting off the ground, Uncle Archie took a welcome fatherly interest. His touch was always light. His advice – publish soon and often, don't worry about getting it perfect – was helpful. His example inspired me. He was one of the first Fulbrighters in Egypt, and, by encouragement, partly responsible for my taking a Fulbright in Poland 10 years ago. And he was affected by the war.

In 1989, a year before my uncle died, he published a memoir, written in the 1940s, of his experiences trekking with the American First Army from Omaha Beach through St. Lô in pursuit of the retreating Germans, through the same northern French landscape Father was to travel a year later in 1945. Uncle Archie took part in the bitter campaign in the Hürtgen Forest of the Ardennes in the fall of 1944, as 12 American divisions struggled to take the Roer Dams and then to cross the Rhine at Remagen. His memoir takes him on the dash across Germany to Leipzig and then to Pilsen and the celebrated meeting with the Red Army. But what he does not include – I had to discover this by asking him directly – is an account of his participation in the liberation of Buchenwald.

The absence of that portion of his wartime experience from the record he left is as striking and as important to me as the detailed, wry, and avowedly pessimistic descriptions of the people and places he encountered elsewhere during his wartime service. In his introduction to the memoir, written in 1989, my uncle remembers everywhere noting evidence of the "brooding evil of Nazi occupation," as he witnessed the end-game of the war in Europe playing itself out around him. When, near the end of his life, I asked him finally what he had done and what he had seen at Buchenwald, he replied that he could not tell me. But – and this is the only religious statement I can ever remember him making, either before or after – he said with uncharacteristic gravity that what he had seen made him believe in Calvin's doctrine of original sin.

How did the war affect my family? For me the question shades invariably into the personal question of identity. Raising the one leads to addressing the other. My older sister and I were born into a world at war. On the day in July 1943 when I came into the world, the 200 Jews of Michniów, Poland,

Kevin Lewis with his sisters, summer 1946.

reportedly departed it, massacred by an *Einsatzgruppen* unit, a "special duty group" clearing the "eastern territories" for settlement by Aryan stock. (Perhaps because it is too small, or perhaps because it no longer exists, I am unable to find that rural village on a map.) My younger sister joined the family in a world straining to recover from war and its considerable effects. Ours became a close and happy family, as families go, and lucky. I have never wished things other than they were.

Only later, much later, did growth of mind compel attempts to imagine and to grasp as well as I could the conditions of Europe under Nazi terror. Only later, as an academic, did my evolving mix of personal and professional concerns begin to include fascination with the same grim reality that my father had struggled briefly to heal before returning to the responsibilities of marriage and fatherhood, as well as fascination with the most awful feature of that same reality, the death camps, of which my uncle chose not to speak. And only later, in middle age, have I begun to see how deeply influenced I have been all along by the interests and values that set in motion those two brothers, Burt and Archie. Their personalities and career choices differed. But they are linked by the common encounter with the effects of that disorienting terror that fell over Europe, and by their respective efforts to record and to interpret.

It is not as simple as this: personal identity descried through some sort of triangulation between influence of father and uncle, respectively. Obviously I have left out the influence of my mother, who was far more affected by the war than my sisters or I. Her strength in mothering under adversity, like her profound devotion to her husband in life and in death, remains a living inspiration for her children, whom she continues in her eighties to nurture. I have left out my grandfather, my sisters, and my younger brother, who was born in the early 1950s. I have left out teachers, not the least of whom was the existentialist Paul Tillich during my first two years at Harvard, followed by the Anglican churchman Stephen Sykes and the philosopher of religion John Hick, when I spent two years at the other Cambridge. I have left out a failed marriage followed by the miraculous emotional nurture and intellectual support of Becky, my wife of 21 years. It was she who leaped at the opportunity in the 1980s to spend a year with me in Durham, England, and then a more challenging year in Cracow, Poland – where the physical and political effects of war had lingered on for 40 years. It was in Poland in 1988-89 that I came closest to the "sickness of Europe" that my father had left the family in 1945 to challenge.

In Poland I certainly came closer to the Holocaust. By 1988 I had been teaching about it for 15 years in South Carolina. I had read the accounts of deportations and concentration camps, I had seen the films. I had taught Miklos Nyiszli's *Auschwitz: A Doctor's Eyewitness Account* and Tadeusz Borowski's *This Way for the Gas, Ladies and Gentlemen* again and again. I had screened Alain Renais's *Night and Fog* in so many classes I knew it by heart, frame by frame. In Cracow we were 35 miles from Auschwitz-Birkenau, and I visited it on five separate occasions that year, wanting to see deeper into the riddle of its evil, deeper into the source of Primo Levi's recurring dream after "liberation." From teaching American literature and culture that year to young Poles, most of whom really wanted only facility in spoken and written English sufficient to make it in the West, I returned a more knowing interpreter. I wrote a piece on Auschwitz for the liberal weekly *Christian Century*, then found in the republished autobiographical memoirs of Rudolf Höss, the Auschwitz camp commandant, tantalizing insight into the formation of his particular Nazi heart of darkness.

I have been immersed in Holocaust materials all this while, I realize, with the enabling support of a particular religious inheritance. I am not sure I understand it fully. In one hand I carry my father's intellectual, liberal Calvinism. He loved Calvin, and I recall his mentoring conversations with me about the great reformer's attempts as an intellectual system-builder to balance human freedom with the absolute sovereignty of God. (Camus [104 ff.] in a notebook entry, hoping against long odds to reconcile liberty and justice, seems driven to a similar, perhaps the same, pass.) In the other hand I carry the immensely liberating precept of Montaigne: *Homo sum, humani nihil alienum a me puto* ("I am a man, and nothing human can be alien to me"). Why did this refusal of all parochialisms, this permission granted by traditional humanism to search any and every dark corner of experience for the truth it will yield, fall upon such fertile soil in me? I do not know, unless it was somehow because of my father's passionate contextualizing of his Calvinist conviction of original sin. It was he who must have initially prepared me to look steadily into the gas chambers for a fuller understanding of the human heart. When much later I read in Simone Weil the assertion that it does not matter what path toward a truth one takes, for all paths lead eventually to the Truth, I recognized myself instantly.

When I reread Borowski's much-anthologized work of short fiction "Silence," I see my uncle in the idealistic American officer who arrives at the door of the newly liberated camp barracks to urge the inmates to forgive their tormentors and look to the future. I see him in that officer who then leaves, hoping for the best, while the freed prisoners proceed to trample their kapo to death in revenge. But I see in my father, carrying his reasoned Calvinism into the world, a toughness of spirit and a worldly survivor realism. The pastoral social vision I have grown to admire in him seems better armed and provisioned than alternative visions of progressive social change upon which we are asked to pin our hopes. A flexible toughness of spirit sustained him in France and returned home with him to his short career in the Presbyterian ministry. A firmly grounded visionary fervor shored up his native idealism, enabling him to face down the cycle of revenge which perpetuates evil. Father was not "deprived of grace."

Seeping down to me from the remembered war experience of the previous generation, through the works of my father and uncle in particular, seems to have come permission to embrace a self-critical doubleness of mind. In another life, I might possibly have found my way to a similar formal philosophical dualism. Twenty years ago, writing initially on this topic as an academic subject, as I did, I would have claimed to have worked it through without benefit of any family intellectual or spiritual heritage whatsoever. This strategic doubleness – "metaphysical schizophrenia" seemed then an appropriate label – has proven for me a life-giving instrument for the balancing of useful but irreconcilable claims upon the modern mind. Ralph Waldo Emerson's old saw in "Self-Reliance," "A foolish consistency is the hobgoblin of little minds," need not be a trivial observation. I find it a liberating appraisal, but one to be earned, when earned, by the blood, sweat, and tears of hard experience and responding reflection.

War teaches it. War especially, but other evils, too, teach a survivor doubleness of mind, enabling some to discover evil, maintain belief in good, and go on, as the religious would say, in grace. But while some learn doubleness for good, others learn it for evil. Doubleness carries risk. It has a pathology. Joseph Mengele, at the work of "selection" on the arrival platform at Auschwitz, thrived notoriously between conflicting value systems. Robert Jay Lifton (337-83) has aptly described in Mengele a functional "doubling" of personalities. In their different ways, by precept and example, my uncle and my father prepared me to negotiate the pervading cognitive dissonance and ambiguity of our era. In my father's Calvin, who taught that the mind is a continuous idol-making factory, I have found a postmodern prophet before his time, but certainly a prophet for mine.

The only formal academic lecture I ever heard my uncle deliver was a sparkling celebration of the medieval cult of romantic love, a medieval legacy for our age. In my teaching, like him, I find myself recommending romantic love. And like my father, who was always interesting in the pulpit, I find myself wrestling with the demands and opportunities of the freely offered love propounded in the religious tradition. To affirm that mind is effectively a balance of more minds than one is for me both a reasoned conclusion and an appreciable inheritance.

Cremation ovens at the Ravensbruck concentration camp for women, 1993.

Holding Dad's army gun: Steven Kilston and his father, 1947.

Epilogue

Nancy Chodorow (right) and a girlfriend, 1948.

INDIVIDUALS IN HISTORY AND HISTORY THROUGH INDIVIDUALS

Nancy J. Chodorow

>Born: January 20, 1944
>New York City, New York, U.S.A.

My double title suggests the dilemma: should I begin with my own experiences – history through my individual senses – or with theoretical reflections on individuals in history? Both are equally relevant, neither taking precedence over the other. How is the major cataclysmic and tragic event of the twentieth century to be held in mind in all its compelling and sweeping wholeness and impact while we also hold in mind the specific uniqueness of individuals, especially when just such obliteration of the recognition of each individual's humanity contributed to the development of World War II? The varied accounts found in this remarkable book help to solve the dilemma, each so palpably experiencing that war then and now, its precedents and aftermath, each so relentlessly conveying the particular experience of the contributor. The volume's contribution does not lie in its providing a new generalized investigation or new documentation of the war, a new historical inquiry into its causes or into the general behavior of populations and leaders. Rather, it lies in the illumination of specificity and pattern: the varied life stories, with their commonalities and differences, that this particular group of writers describes.

From the initial moment of the panel offered during the thirtieth reunion of the Harvard-Radcliffe Class of 1965, I was enthralled, both by the accounts of Class members themselves and by the tumble of associations that occurred to me as I listened. The stories of classmates were enlivened by my own personal creations of affect and story. I was born in January 1944, so I was six months old on D-Day and a year and a half on V-E Day. During a trip to France in the early 1990s, I revisited Omaha and Utah Beaches with French friends. From a childhood visit I remembered vividly the concrete bunkers and gun emplacements left by the Germans, so bizarre to find on a beach. But on this visit I also noticed for the first time various monuments with inscriptions like "In Memory of the 248th Engineering Division of the U.S. Army, landed June 5, 1944" or "In Honor of the Men of the 126th Division of the United States Marines, landed June 4, 1944," listing all the men who had died during that invasion. I began to cry and could not stop weeping. Since before memory I have been mesmerized by footage of the D-Day landings, those men with weapons and vehicles rising out of the waters onto the beach. This is perhaps my fantasy image of this landing. I am to this day not sure if this is how the real footage goes. I was obviously too young to have seen such footage in contemporary newsreels, and my father did not go away to war. A physicist, he was involved in developing microwave radar tubes used in tracking and searching for ships, planes, and other objects.

Nancy Chodorow, a passionate cowgirl, at age four.

During the analysis undertaken as part of my psychoanalytic training, one dream was most vivid. It became central and I returned to it again and again. In my dream I am standing up in my crib. My mother and my analyst's mother, both dressed in unmistakably 1940s suits and hats, are going off to Times Square to celebrate V-E Day. Here World War II again enters my unconscious via cultural images, but accurately pinpointed at the right time in my life when babies stand up in their cribs, to be picked up, or, as in this case, to be left behind. The dream portrays loss and abandonment, as well as the exciting images of those V-E Day celebrations, neither part of my actual experience of the war. My mother, in her mid thirties when I was born, was glad to give up her career as a social worker and become my full-time caretaker. She did not, she says, go into New York City from Long Island to celebrate V-E Day. But loss and being left behind, as I describe below, are prominent among the affective themes that this war seems to have evoked in my agemates. Events that happened in World War II have not simply entered my fantasy life in dreams and day images. These fantasies, as in the case of my dream, place me at the right age within historical events.

In addition there is the actuality of the effects of that war on my life. My father's coworkers during the war were for the most part non-Jewish scientists and electrical engineers from the American West who had been colleagues and students at Stanford. After the war they went back to Stanford and, a couple of years later, arranged for my father to join the Stanford Physics Department. So in 1947 my father, born in Buffalo and the son of poor Jewish immigrants from Ukraine, and my mother, born in New York City and the daughter of successful Lithuanian Jewish immigrants, and I traveled across the country. We went by train, so it felt long and far. My mother was leaving all her sisters and brothers, I my cousins, for what felt like the other end of the universe. Because of World War II, I grew up in California instead of in New York, where of course the daughters of emphatically nonreligious Jewish intellectuals should grow up. As a preschooler I wanted passionately to be a cowgirl (or cowboy). In my high school class of 300, I was one of five Jewish children and the only Jewish girl. As a child I puzzled over why all my friends seemed to think that World War II took place in the Pacific and was against Japan. In our outdoor rough-and-tumble play (the advantage of growing up in a still undeveloped and rural California), playing games like "King of the Mountain," we would yell, "Bombs over Tokyo!" I had no idea what it meant.

I introduce these memories to make several related points. First, I want to document the individuality of historical experience while also documenting the inevitable consequences of belonging to a particular generation or age cohort. Second, I want to suggest that history, when it matters, always matters emotionally and unconsciously to individuals, as well as registering in their consciousness and cognition. Both of these points are made again and again in the work of Erik Erikson, who provides a felicitous and complex theoretical underpinning to this volume.

We can find a historical convergence in turning to Erikson here. My own interests in matters of culture and psyche, interests I have pursued through many related fields – anthropology, sociology, feminism, and psychoanalysis – was itself shaped by reading *Childhood and Society* during the summer after my freshman year in college. More significantly, the very cohort that has written this book was influenced by Erikson and was the subject of Erikson's own work. Ours was the Harvard-Radcliffe generation that attended *en masse* Erikson's hugely popular course on identity and the life cycle. My own memory is of articles in the college newspaper with headlines concerning the identity crises and identity moratoria of people our age (and it seems probable that just as we learned to think of our identity crises from Erikson, he refined his concepts by teaching and studying us). It is probably no accident that a volume of writings by people of our particular college Class can be best theorized by Erikson, who himself affected so many of us culturally, personally, and intellectually. Just as being born *during* the war – not being Baby Boomers – is "our" cohort experience, so Erikson is, I believe, "our" psychosocial theorist. Erik Erikson's concern with the setting of psyche in a particular cultural-historical cohort and generation constitutes a great contribution to twentieth-century thought.

I begin with the personalization and individualization of history. Social scientists have theorized age-related social groups like cohorts and generations, people born during a particular era whose common experiences lead to common ways of knowing and perceiving. In his study "The Problem of Generations," the sociologist of knowledge, Karl Mannheim, claims that a generation requires more than chronology: "individuals of the same age are united as an actual generation in so far as they participate in the characteristic social and intellectual currents of the society and period, and in so far as they have an active or passive experience of the interactions of forces which made up the new situation" (304). To the point of this volume, he argues that by virtue of living in the same "historico-social space" or "historical life community," generations will share perspectives on life.

This conception of generations became a popular cultural trope as a result of one generation in particular – those known as the "Baby Boomers." More recently it has been picked up in the characterization of "Generation X." But it seems that dividing people into generations has been a prevalent American practice throughout this century, beginning with the "Roaring Twenties" and the flappers. It is my impression that those who get playfully and colloquially named tend to be noticed for their culture and lifestyle, not for being affected in serious and irrevocable ways by political or economic events. Thus, although we know – and find documented in this volume many times over – that the military experience and return of the GIs after World War II made a cohort, these men do not have a generational nickname. They are not recognized as a cohort, even though the GI Bill, which radically affected education, housing patterns, and the economy in many ways, was created for their benefit. Similarly, much American social policy was created for those who suffered during the Great Depression, but we don't think of the Depression generation in playful or colloquial cultural terms, either.

I think the generation or cohort of writers in this volume is similar: we need to name ourselves as those born into a world at war, and this does not have a cheerful ring. A couple of the contributors remind us that we were "war babies," but this name has not stuck as a label for our generation. Hugh Field's aside, "There is a subtle discontinuity between us and the Baby Boomers," struck me very much. We are not Baby Boomers. We do not have the buoyant optimism of Baby Boomers and their sense of limitless possibility. From what we know of our generation, some of the contributors may have participated in the cultural politics of "never trust anyone over 30." But we see equally in these accounts, perhaps especially from the children of immigrants, a great sense of orientation toward parents: trying to do what parents want and to support and protect them. We certainly were part of the generation that initiated student protest against the war in Vietnam. We certainly can imagine that our deep conscious and unconscious immersion from birth in a war where right and wrong were absolutely clear, where humanity itself was threatened, and where parents were forever affected, played some part in the questions asked by those who challenged the Vietnam War as well as in the urgency of those men who felt that participation and fighting were the right things to do. Maria Tymoczko speaks for the antiwar side when she notes that she learned from World War II that war doesn't simply make men, it can also break them.

As a generation we were very much born into history – into the biggest historical event of the twentieth century – and we seem self-aware about this historical location. That this volume was written and that so many wanted to write for it attest to this sense of self in history. We were not born during postwar prosperity to united families with optimistic parents. In all cases we were born to families in which parents were directly or indirectly affected by war, in which fathers were often far away and mothers – often far from home themselves – were worried and overwhelmed, in the most tragic cases to families torn apart and destroyed. When our families moved, it was not only part of a general pattern of American mobility or a function of economically determined job transfers in a booming economy, it was more often because of dislocation and war. For many of us there was a general cultural atmosphere of anxiety and fear about the present and future. Before we could speak, these were the affective messages communicated by our parents along with their love and concern.

We definitely have here a group: contributors to this volume are all men and women who were at the same university in the same town during the first half of the 1960s. We also have an extremely fine-tuned birth cohort: the list of birthdates shows that, with only a few exceptions, no one was born before

1943, no one after 1944. Such a group could be said to already occupy elite status in virtue of their education. Yet, equally remarkably, there is no common pathway that led them to this university, no sense, as was probably the case in previous Harvard and Radcliffe generations, of coming from similar class or ethnic backgrounds, from the same kind of family, from the same region. We find over and over in these accounts descriptions of displacement: people came from all over the world, taking varied paths to arrive at this safe haven at age 17 or 18, and many have lengthy stories of migration from here to there. We were brought together in the same classrooms and dormitories from the most far-flung places and backgrounds.

As readers, our sense of the effect of being born during the war is also decentered by these accounts. We find here those who most stand for the great destruction and genocide wrought by the Nazis – the children of German Jewish and East European Jewish survivors – but in the accounts of Betty Chang Sun and Goh Cheng Teik we are also reminded of the great brutality experienced by those from countries invaded by the Japanese. Robert Sakai's narrative calls our attention to the American internment of U.S. citizens and immigrants of Japanese origin, even as members of these same interned families were serving in crucial roles in the U.S. armed forces. Francis Zebot and Hugh Field document how closely the experiences of the generation born during World War II could be tied to the Cold War that followed so immediately. Peter Katzlberger gives us insight into the consequences of Germany's policies for some ordinary German citizens. Anthony Graham-White filters a childhood in war not through the experience of an American child, but of an English child in a bombed-out city with food shortages. Many others experience the effect of war because of mobility or because of the absence or loss of fathers.

As I have suggested earlier, among cultural thinkers Erik Erikson most clearly theorizes the intertwining of individual and cultural-historical experience – the individualized and personalized filtering of history – that this book documents so well. Erikson argues that history, society, and culture become inextricably involved in the fundamental organization and experience of self and psyche, animating fantasies, identity, and conflicts. He shows how World War I, World War II, and immigration are drawn into unconscious fantasy life and meet his patients' inner worlds and identities. Reciprocally, history as a cultural force is created in individual minds: *Childhood and Society* (1950) has case examples drawn particularly from children born during World War II and from war experiences. He discusses the little boy, "Son of a Bombadier," left at home with his mother and female relatives while his father became a war hero and was then killed, and the marine who froze as he was supposed to fire a gun and subsequently developed a severe war neurosis. For Erikson ego identity – sameness and continuity in one's own and the other's view – is the foundation of psychic health. Identity depends not simply upon identifying with others but upon being confirmed and recognized by others as a particular individual in a particular universe. Speaking directly and indirectly to the experiences of many contributors to this volume in "Identity and Uprootedness in Our Time," Erikson investigates the special psychologies of refugees, immigrants, and migrants. He explores the consequence of losing your place in historical and generational continuity, of losing your native language and your country, as well as – especially relevant in the case of World War II – of losing so many family members and the very physical space of your home and community. Thus, he shows that an uprooted people faces the very difficult challenge of preserving identity in the face of radical historical change. For the immigrant, he says, history does not meet the person with a continuity of generations and tradition. Uprooted people have a "basic hope for recognition and [a] basic horror of its failure: the dead, the still-born identity" (1964, 95).

In a claim that could serve as an epigraph for this volume, Erikson says, in *Identity and the Life Cycle*: "Men who share an ethnic area, a historical era, or an economic pursuit are guided by common images of good and evil. Infinitely varied, these images reflect the elusive nature of historical change; yet in the form of contemporary social models, of compelling prototypes of good and evil, they assume a decisive concreteness in every individual's ego development" (1959, 18). Erikson is not being a cultural or historical determinist here. He is describing individualized usages of historical and cultural contributions to identity that are deeply implicated in selfhood, personalized through identifications with parents, and related in complex ways to life goals and goals that are shunned. They are tied up with affects like shame, guilt, and fear.

Finally, we take from Erikson the psychoanalytic admonition to attend to childhood. While calling upon psychoanalysts to theorize how history assumes decisive concreteness in the individual psyche, he makes a complementary demand upon historians and social scientists: "Students of history continue to ignore the simple fact that all individuals are born by mothers; that everybody was once a child; that people and peoples begin in their nurseries; and that society consists of individuals in the process of developing from children into parents" (1959, 18).

In this volume World War II assumes decisive concreteness in each life, but it is a different war for each contributor. Events like World War II, the Holocaust, the Japanese invasion of China, affect everyone involved. But this volume documents that, although we can elucidate various psychic and narrative themes that will characterize many people's experiences of these events, we can never predict their exact effect or outcome, even when it comes to how a family will react to losing members in the concentration camps. In each account in this collection, we can see how the war is folded into identity, feeling, family, and history, but we also see, graphically documented, how the "same" event or experience – Kristallnacht, being the child of Holocaust survivors, being a survivor – can be experienced and handled very differently. Among the children of survivors, we find everything from ebullient optimism and a claim that all is right with the world, to simple relief at having survived, to emotional frozenness and painful depression. In the families of Ursula Oppens and Eva Botstein Griepp, there is silence and occlusion of a loss too painful to acknowledge. Steven Kilston's family, by contrast, celebrated its survival and made cheerful, positive thinking a goal, rather than mourning its losses. Matthew Stolper's father's half-brother was killed in Auschwitz, and his Swiss and German Jewish parents endured between 1933 and 1943 five years of separation, a hemophiliac first child, and the loss of family in the Holocaust, but Matthew calls these the "happiest 10 years" in his parents' lives and claims that they had a "charmed existence." People bring personal interpretations to parental fantasies and identity and to unconsciously as well as consciously transmitted cultural and historical circumstances. In each individual case such personal interpretations help generate identity – who someone is or becomes.

Childhood does not determine the rest of life, but in childhood we are forming our individual selves. The personal filtering of history, through our parents especially, is likely to be as nonverbal as it is verbal. It is therefore less able to be weighed and thought than later learning or learning from less emotionally important sources. The stories in this volume attest to the psychic weight of early childhood, the deep affective resonances of experience that cannot at the time, and can only sometimes afterward, be named. Nancy Blackmun discovers in mid adulthood some of the origins of her obsession with the Holocaust and the death camps as these resonate with her own personal, two-year-old's holocaust of losing mother and father at the same time, while the radio played World War II news and music. Hugh Field describes another frightening, inexplicable disappearance, such that, even when his father reappeared in his life, something of his childhood intensity and curiosity was forever lost. Howard Gardner, one of our country's most eminent psychologists, acknowledges

Two cowgirls: Nancy Chodorow (right) and a friend, 1948.

with great candor how he manages early feelings of terror and loss: he cannot sit through violence in movies, skips sections on violence in books, and has shied away from or avoided entirely the study of affects in his professional work. Steven Kilston, as he describes playing the *Warsaw Concerto*, refers to early childhood resonances of sounds and images "produced in a decade that created intensities of experience and meaning rarely matched in the decades I've seen since." We can have no independent corroboration of Nancy Blackmun's or Steven Kilston's very early musical memories, but both are certain that this is the music that they heard. We come upon affect through another medium than language, through the evocative and resonant power of music.

When we begin from and refer to childhood, we are very much in the modality of all the senses, not just in the mode of intellectual reflection that might otherwise come so naturally to these Harvard-Radcliffe products. Anthony Graham-White is a bit older than the rest, so he has more actual memory of the war years, but what is striking in his account is how he remembers the most basic elements of daily life, those that matter to children. He describes the physical surround – rubble in the street and rooms open to the sky. For him, "war's end was associated with food": you could get oranges and bananas. He ties current life experience to this childhood time, wondering whether he is a light sleeper because of an early childhood spent in one of the most bombed cities in England, and he contrasts *the* war with *his* war. *His* war was food shortages, two uncles missing in action, and German prisoners of war marched up the streets. As he puts it, "*wartime* in a child's memory is not so easily stopped." Peter Katzlberger also describes basics – "the everyday struggle to make do" and find enough to eat.

I have suggested that a major contribution of this volume is its insistent documentation of the infinite ways in which history assumes decisive concreteness in the individual. But we can also trace significant themes that run through many of the contributions, salient patterns of subjectivity, common affective and familial stories, that in no case characterize all the contributions, but that often characterize several. What are some of the themes we find within these accounts? What can we trace in the thinking and feeling of this generation and this group born into a world at war?

What I first noticed was a pervasive emotional tonality to many contributions. Members of our generation (or at least those who chose to write for this volume) often experience the world through what we might consider, loosely, a depressive lens. Not everyone is sad, and no one is sad all the time, but a reader (this reader) feels this generalized affective tonality. This kind of sadness and depressive tone, and in some cases a sense of emptiness and hopelessness, can come from loss and mourning. Of course, we begin here with the experience of the children of survivors, and not only Jewish Holocaust survivors, but also Betty Chang Sun, whose family came from China, and Francis Zebot, whose family fled Slovenia. Memories are of loss and puzzlement.

Especially for very young children, not knowing why things happen can lead to a sense of futility. This sadness has different sources in different cases. In the case of the contributors whose parents were originally European, like Christine Tanz, Eva Botstein Griepp, Ursula Oppens, Howard Gardner, and others (all of whom are enormously successful professionals with richly creative and personally fulfilling lives), there was probably a terrible sadness, disorientation, fear, and mourning in parents as they were taking care of these children born before the war was over. Such affects would be sustained or would deepen as, in their children's early years, the parents learned more and more about their personal losses as well as about the scale of the devastation.

Unlike these contributors, whose sadness, mourning, and coping are described directly, Matthew Stolper seems to cope with sadness in a more indirect way. Despite his repeated insistence on his parents' "happiest 10 years," extraordinary fortune, and "privileged and lucky" lives, and on their having no mourning, no longing for the lost land, and a "muted sense of the atrocities" of the war, his own puzzled and painful conclusion about trying to make sense of the relation between inner and outer worlds, his mention in passing of "holes in the family," and his astute understanding of how his brother's hemophilia took over the traumatic core of his family all speak to a devastating sense of loss. Like his parents, Matthew Stolper seems to cope with sadness through displacement, keeping losses and separations disconnected, so that it becomes difficult to piece together the several grandparental marriages and the fates of various paternal siblings and step-siblings. I believe with Erikson that the generalized sense of loss also results from displacement. We can see this as it ranges from my own more benign experience of living with a mother separated from her family of origin, to those who, along with their parents, lost native language, homeland, and familiar culture.

In addition to themes of loss filtered through parents, there is the direct experience of loss and separation reported especially by the children of soldiers, including Peter Katzlberger, Mathea Falco, Robert Sakai, John Dundas, Sarah Niles Kafatou, Laurel Strange Hayler, Francis Zebot, and Deborah Lucas Schneider. As a child, Deborah Schneider's fantasy is that German fathers, unlike American fathers, don't leave, a fantasy that sends her around the globe after college to create a German familial and professional identity. She didn't at the time know Peter Katzlberger, whose German father went to war and never returned. Nancy Blackmun experienced the temporary loss of her mother, and Hugh Field's father was there in infancy, only to disappear a few years later. My own dream about V-E Day, whatever its manifold roots, is also about loss and separation. Contributing, finally, to this tonality of sadness is the general anxiety and fear that, I believe, simply hung over the world during the infancy of this group.

Another more specific theme, though not as widespread, is a sense of coping with horror: holocausts in the generic sense as well as the specific Holocaust.

Crashing, explosions, and massacres reappear: Julie Coryell's father worked on the Manhattan Project and she wishes she could be a "daughter of deuterium." Somehow, but Julie is not certain exactly how, since secrecy surrounded his work, her father was involved with the largest explosion of all time, which her mother captured in poetry. Her father had manic psychological explosions himself, and her mother, tragically, ended her own life. Betty Chang Sun learned, first implicitly and then through explicit teaching, of the Rape of Nanking, the rageful devastation and torture that took place there, and Goh Cheng Teik learned similarly of the Japanese invasion of Malaysia. The shattered glass of Kristallnacht, along with the murder of relatives, is evoked by Howard Gardner and Steven Kilston and resonates for the reader with other Jewish accounts.

At the other end of the spectrum from explosions and shattering glass are silences. Here, especially, we see wide variation in how Holocaust survivor parents and other relatives talked or did not talk about their experience or about what happened to family members. But Peter Katzlberger, born in Germany to non-Jewish parents, also describes his mother's silences about the years in which she lost her husband, he his father, and life was a shambles. Holocaust-survivor parents found their memories and experiences, and what they knew had been the experiences of relatives and friends, much too painful to talk about. Psychoanalysts who work with Holocaust survivors describe an internal deadness that can take over parts of the psyche: not talking was probably not only a conscious choice to spare children, but also a way of surviving psychically. One has the impression that Christine Tanz always knew what happened to her parents – their story of courage and survival, of triumphant escape. But she did not know, until reading it in a book, about what had happened to those family members who did not survive: "We never talked about the people who had disappeared, or sorrow or loss or thwarted ambitions or bitterness." Howard Gardner's parents also followed what he calls "the route of silence." Finally, we find that the great musician of our Class, Ursula Oppens, titles her contribution itself "Silence." In her family, "the most important family events could not be discussed," but I would like to imagine that the subtleties and communicative modalities of different silences also contributed to Ursula's attunement to the nuances and powers of sounds.

What about parents, not as they are filtered through emotional tone, but as we find them directly in mind? Fathers and mothers appear differently. Fathers figure large in many of the accounts in this book – Charles Styron's, Sarah Niles Kafatou's, and Kevin Lewis's contributions, for example, are exclusively and explicitly stories about their fathers – and we can find some general themes. Several accounts, and these seem to be especially the accounts of sons, idealize soldier fathers and their brave exploits (for example, John Dundas, William McConahey, and Charles Styron). For other children of soldier fathers (and in some cases for the same person from another vantage point – John Dundas, for example), father-absence is more significant. Psychological preoccupation with father-absence developed in the 1940s and 1950s, just when the fathers of these contributors were themselves absent. Mothers also helped to idealize these soldier fathers and protected them from the rambunctious demands of children. Several contributors describe father-absence and the inability to connect emotionally with fathers until late in life, or talk wistfully about watching fathers who had already formed attachments with older siblings or who were able to form closer attachments to younger siblings born after the war, when the father had returned full-time to the family and civilian life. Laurel Strange Hayler titles her contribution "Wartime Separation, or Why It Took My Father Fifty Years to Get Used to Me." Kevin Lewis echoes her thought: "My sister, my mother, my grandparents, a dog – all inhabit my earliest memories. But my father is not there."

For some, the loss of fathers was more absolute, either temporarily or permanently. In these cases father-absence could not be filtered by a mother who was worried, but who knew, more or less, where her soldier husband was. Hugh Field describes the wrenching experience of having his father simply disappear for five years, getting on a plane in Warsaw and not debarking in Prague. Peter Katzlberger's father, in the German army for most of his son's babyhood, sent his last letter in January 1945 and was presumably killed shortly thereafter, but no confirmation ever arrived. As Peter Katzlberger puts it, "Being 'lost' is worse than dead." Francis Zebot's father disappeared for several months. The fathers of Nancy Blackmun and Deborah Lucas Schneider disappeared into their work. John Dundas's much older father, a war hero, was incapacitated and needy for much of his son's childhood, not knowing how to relate to a demanding toddler and energetic boy; he died when John Dundas was nine. Mathea Falco's father was part of the occupation forces in Germany for a year before she and her mother followed, and she screamed in fear when they first met again.

In contrast to fathers, mothers in these accounts appear in more varied guises, but they are never a central focus in the way that fathers are for some. Sometimes they are subsumed, especially by survivor children, into the parental couple. Sometimes they are described in passing, as when someone writes about what he or she and mother did, or where they went. When they are described as depressed or absent, longing for their presence is more implied than stated. Even when described positively, mothers do not seem to be, like fathers, so much the objects of curiosity or wonder. Some are described as having energy and enthusiasm: Maria Fleming Tymoczko focuses on the varying work roles played by her mother and other female relatives; Mathea Falco describes her mother's determined cheerfulness and resilience as a soldier's wife in postwar Germany; and Marina Sulzberger Berry, relying on her mother's autobiography, portrays a feisty, energetic woman who communicated with her future husband in code. Several mothers had jobs or careers before, during, and after the war, and several accounts describe three-generation war households, where mothers returned to live with their own parents while birthing and raising their war babies. Other accounts present mothers who are depressed, distracted, claustrophobic, or simply finding it difficult to cope. Julie Coryell, Deborah Lucas Schneider, Steven Kilston, and Nancy Blackmun, for example, all describe mothers who are themselves suffering, either in the absence of their husbands or as a reaction to their separations and family losses. Peter Katzlberger tells with sympathy of his mother's plight as a war widow who is not sure of her widowhood, and he describes her life as a confused immigrant to the United States.

As a product of this same psychocultural cohort that I am describing, and perhaps partly as an occupational hazard of being a psychoanalyst, I may have noticed too much the silences, the shatterings, the explosions, the sadness, and the loss. But the reader of these accounts is also struck by the many different forms of creativity and survivorship found in each of these families: the many ways that parents, in spite of tremendous losses, danger, fears, and dislocation, conveyed strength, love, generosity, and a sense that even the worst adversity can be suffered and personally surmounted. All contributors are active with work and family, all seem to have remained deeply attached to their parents and forebears – no small feat in our mobile, leave-your-roots-behind age. In their youth, these people born into a world at war seem to have trusted people over 30 – parents and teachers, some political leaders – and they now seem to trust people over 80, as well as to have positive memories of parents no longer alive. Family stories, even from the most traumatized families, include accounts of resilience and the capacity to move forward. Steven Kilston tells on the one hand of his family's experience of Kristallnacht and on the other of his great joy in the *Warsaw Concerto* and "Zip-a-dee-doo-dah." Many describe parental teaching about how to protect yourself from upheavals: Eva Botstein Griepp and her siblings were taught to create portable careers; Christine Tanz, whose parents were multilingual and who was, with them, a postwar immigrant, focuses her professional energies on how children learn languages; Julie Coryell is taught to hold the world together, even if it may blow up. In one of the most memorable parental admonitions in this book, Betty Chang Sun's immigrant Chinese father, worried greatly about the consequences of her political activity, tells her, "Don't get involved in the sit-ins – but if you do, make sure you sit in the middle."

History assumes decisive concreteness in the identity, experience, and emotional life of each individual. During the summer of 1998, just as I was reading the essays in this volume and thinking about my contribution, I happened to attend a showing of two films at the San Francisco Jewish Film Festival, both circling around World War II. This war certainly assumed very different forms of decisive concreteness in the individual lives portrayed in the films. One film, *A Letter without Words*, based on the home movies of a German Jewish woman who had been at the very, very top of the German class hierarchy, begins before the war. Starting approximately with World War I, the film portrays the opulent life of her family, its mansions, horseback riding, parties and balls, and the rise of Nazism – swastika banners in full color on the streets of Berlin. The film then traces the family's trip to the United States, the first viewing of the Statue of Liberty, and the eventual home on Long Island. A second film, *17 Rue Saint Fiacre*, describes how two Jewish French children from a small town were saved and protected by a working-class Catholic woman after their parents were deported. Like most members of my generation, I am riveted by such accounts and horrified by the larger event of which they are a part. These two portrayals took place in Europe, one continent and two generations removed from my own family experience. But in the course of the second film, which I was watching with great interest, I was startled by the narrator's voice saying: "On January 20th, 1944, Charles Malmed [age five] was deported to Auschwitz. In his convoy, number sixty-six, there were one thousand, one hundred, and fifteen Jews. Two hundred and six were children. None of the children survived." That was the day on which I was born into a world at war.

Christine Tanz with her mother,
Gdansk, 1946.

Hugh Field watching the trains arrive, waiting for his father, 1946.

NOTES ON CONTRIBUTORS

Marina Sulzberger Berry lives in London, England. Married to Adrian Michael Berry, a writer and former science correspondent for the London *Daily Telegraph*, she is the mother of two grown children and the grandmother of one. She enjoys travel, returning to Greece once or twice a year and going to France as often as possible, where she has a house in the Midi. She comes to America at least twice a year; although she has family and many friends in America, she is now resigned to being European.

Nancy Blackmun is a clinical psychologist and psychoanalyst in Framingham, Massachusetts. She earned an Ed.M. in counseling from Harvard and worked for several years in public and private schools. While her two children were small, she returned to school for a doctorate from the Massachusetts School of Professional Psychology. In celebration of her fiftieth birthday, she began psychoanalytic training and traveled to Poland.

Margaret deBeers Brown grew up in Montgomery County, Maryland, except for her junior high school years, which were spent in Santurce, Puerto Rico. After graduating from college, she began law school at Harvard, completing her degree at the University of California, Berkeley, in 1968. Since then she has practiced law in small and large law firms and has also worked as an in-house lawyer for Pacific Bell and Pacific Gas & Electric Company. As a volunteer she has served many organizations, including the California Committee of Bar Examiners. She is an elder and deacon of Calvary Presbyterian Church in San Francisco. Married to a real-estate lawyer, Timothy Nils Brown, she has two grown children who work on various aspects of the Internet. The family stays in touch by e-mail.

Nancy J. Chodorow is a psychoanalyst in private practice, a faculty member of the San Francisco Psychoanalytic Institute, and Professor of Sociology and Clinical Professor of Psychology at the University of California, Berkeley. She is an unreconstructed product of the Harvard Department of Social Relations and its vision of an integrated, humanistic, sociocultural-psychoanalytic social science: after teaching and writing in the areas of feminism, social theory, and psychoanalysis for 20 years, she began her psychoanalytic training and career in 1984. She is author of *The Reproduction of Mothering* (1978), *Feminism and Psychoanalytic Theory* (1989), *Femininities, Masculinities, Sexualities: Freud and Beyond* (1994), and *The Power of Feelings: Personal Meaning in Psychoanalysis, Gender, and Culture* (1999). Mother of a daughter in college and a son in high school, she enjoys yoga, skiing, opera, and occasional work in her garden.

Andrew D. Cohen holds an M.A. in linguistics and a Ph.D. in education from Stanford University. Currently chair of the Department of English as a Second Language at the University of Minnesota, where he also directs the National Language Resource Center, he has also taught in the ESL Section of the English Department at UCLA and at the School of Education at Hebrew University, Jerusalem. He recently served as secretary general of the International Association of Applied Linguistics. Author of several books on bilingual education, language-learning strategies, and language testing, including *Assessing Language Ability in the Classroom* (1994) and *Strategies in Learning and Using a Second Language* (1998), he has also published articles on language teaching, learning, testing, and research methods.

Julie E. Coryell concentrated in Chinese at Radcliffe College and completed an M.A. in Chinese Regional Studies at Harvard. She married Seelye Martin, an oceanographer, and moved with him to Seattle. At the University of Washington, she was cofounder of the Program for Women Studies. In 1990, after travel to Japan, she began to study Japanese and to serve as a guide for the Japanese Garden in Washington Park, Seattle. Her lifelong interests include handwork, music, t'ai chi, and centering prayer. She is the mother of two grown children.

John Dundas attended Groton School and concentrated in English at Harvard. He earned an M.D. from Boston University in 1971 and is currently a psychiatrist practicing in the Boston area. Father of four grown children and two grown stepchildren, he has many loves, including hiking, canoeing, fishing, and skiing, both cross-country and downhill. He exercises regularly to enable him to pursue his many loves and to avoid his father's terminal experience.

Mathea Falco holds a J.D. from Yale Law School. She has served as Chief Counsel and Staff Director of the United States Senate Judiciary Committee Juvenile Delinquency Subcommittee, Assistant Secretary of State for International Narcotics Matters, and Director of Health Policy for the Department of Public Health of the Cornell University Medical College in New York City. Author of *The Making of a Drug-Free America: Programs That Work* (1994), she is president of Drug Strategies, a nonprofit research institute that identifies effective approaches to substance abuse. She has been a member of the Board of Overseers of Harvard University, a trustee of Radcliffe College, and a member of many national boards. She lives in San Francisco with her husband, Peter Tarnoff, and their son.

Hugh Field is a data analyst involved with case sample selection for the Massachusetts Department of Transitional Assistance (formerly the Massachusetts Department of Public Welfare). A resident of Norwood, Massachusetts, he enjoys writing essays about world politics, frequently contributing letters to the editors of newspapers.

Howard Gardner has lived in Cambridge, Massachusetts, since his freshman year in college. He has been involved with Harvard as an undergraduate, a graduate student in psychology, a postdoctoral fellow in neurology, a researcher at Project Zero, and a professor at the Graduate School of Education. He has conducted research on intelligence, learning, and creativity, with a special focus on the arts. Recently he has also been involved in American educational reform efforts. He has written many books, including *The Shattered Mind* (1975), *Frames of Mind* (1983), *Creating Minds* (1993), *Leading Minds* (1995), *The Disciplined Mind* (1999), and *Intelligence Reframed* (1999).

Max Gitter, a graduate of Yale Law School, is a senior litigation partner in New York at the international law firm Cleary, Gottlieb, Steen & Hamilton. He has taught at Yale Law School and the University of Chicago Law School, and has written for a variety of publications, most recently the *New Republic*. He was appointed by Mayor Koch to investigate the office of the Chief Medical Examiner of New York City. He is vice-chairman of the board of YIVO Institute for Jewish Research. He is married to the former Elisabeth Karla Gesmer, a professor of English at John Jay College of the City University of New York. They have two grown children.

Goh Cheng Teik studied at Assumption School, Butterworth, and St. Xavier's Institution, Penang. He concentrated in government at Harvard and delivered the Undergraduate English Address at the 1965 Harvard Commencement. He earned a doctorate in political science at the University of Leiden, specializing in Indonesian politics, followed by research in South-East Asian international relations at the Centre for International Studies at Cambridge University. Before entering politics he taught at the University of Malaya. Since 1974 he has served his country in various capacities – as a backbencher in parliament, a state executive councilor in Penang, and a deputy minister in the Malaysian government. Married to Ng Yoon Lin, he is the father of three grown children.

Anthony Graham-White pursued training as an actor in England before entering college in the United States at the age of 21, beginning at Dartmouth and then transferring to Harvard College. He earned a Ph.D. in dramatic literature from Stanford. After teaching at Southern Methodist University, he joined the faculty at the University of Illinois at Chicago, where he was head of the Department of Communication and Theatre for 10 years. He is presently director of graduate studies in the Department of Performing Arts. Author of *The Drama of Black Africa* (1974) and *Punctuation and Its Dramatic Value in Shakespearean Drama* (1985), he is currently writing on traditional drama from around the world. He and his wife have one son, a Prairie School house, a garden in which an informal British style and prairie plants mix, and two golden retrievers.

Eva Botstein Griepp immigrated to the United States in 1949. She grew up in New York City and attended the Bronx High School of Science. At Radcliffe College she concentrated in history and literature. After graduation from New York University School of Medicine in 1969, she was subsequently certified in pediatrics and pediatric cardiology. She is a Clinical Associate Professor of Pediatrics at NYU School of Medicine and is a member of the graduate faculty of Sarah Lawrence College. She has written articles on subjects ranging from developmental biology to the impact of cardiac surgery on the brain. She lives with her husband and son in New York City.

Laurel Strange Hayler holds advanced degrees in social work and public health. She has been a psychotherapist and agency administrator, building a small program into an ongoing United Way agency and directing a unique new public/private collaboration to improve public health in Silicon Valley. She is currently an independent consultant for nonprofit and governmental organizations, specializing in health and human services program development and strategic planning. Mother of two grown sons, she lives in Palo Alto, California, with her husband Don.

Kazuko Iwasawa Ihara came to the United States in 1952 and lived in Belmont, Massachusetts, through her college years. After graduating from Radcliffe College, having concentrated in French language and literature, she returned to Japan. Her parents and siblings remained in the United States. Married to Yasutaka Ihara, a mathematician, she is the mother of three grown children. Except for one year each in California and in Germany, she has lived principally in Tokyo, acting for many years as an interpreter for non-Japanese defendants in the district court. Since 1990 she has resided in Kyoto. She enjoys swimming and gardening, and together with her husband she sings in a choral group that performs classical Western music. She has recently taken up calligraphy.

Sarah Niles Kafatou acquired a second nationality and culture – Greek – through marriage. She lives part of each year in Cambridge, Massachusetts; in Heidelberg, Germany; and on the island of Crete. She has taught literature at several universities and has published a book entitled *Capitalism and Periphery: A History of Underdevelopment in Latin America* (1981), as well as many articles on political and cultural subjects. She is a poet and painter. She and her husband, a biologist, have two grown children.

Peter Katzlberger immigrated to the United States in 1958. After undergraduate studies in architectural sciences at Harvard, he received an M.A. in city and regional planning from the University of California, Berkeley. He has worked in planning positions for the city of San Mateo, California, and was planning director for the city of Santa Cruz, California, until 1995. He currently works as a planning consultant. He is married and lives in Felton, California.

Steven Kilston wrote his Harvard College thesis, "A Search for Intelligent Life on Earth," under Carl Sagan. His UCLA doctoral dissertation proved that stars manufacture the chemical elements in our bodies. He has discovered a comet, taught many subjects to students of all ages, hosted a science radio program, and chaired an AAAS symposium on astronomy and philosophy. At Hughes Aircraft and Lockheed he studied optics and stars, and showed that tides trigger certain California earthquakes. His optical designs created IKONOS, the first commercial, high-resolution, earth-observing satellite. He now lives in Boulder, Colorado, and does research at Ball Aerospace on extra-solar planet detection and interstellar spaceship concepts. With his wife and colleague, Vera, he has raised five children. They pursue philosophy, music, and gymnastics, and grow trees in Oregon.

Kevin Lewis has taught since 1973 in the Religious Studies Department of the University of South Carolina, Columbia, where he developed the specialty field "Arts, Literature, and Religion" for both undergraduate and graduate students. He has published on a variety of topics including Southern religion, confessional poetry, Muggletonianism, William Blake, and the Holocaust. He has been a visiting fellow of Trevelyan College, University of Durham, England, and of Wolfson College, Cambridge, England, and a Fulbright Lecturer in American Studies in Cracow, Poland, and at the Islamic University of Gaza. He holds graduate degrees from St. John's College, Cambridge University, and the University of Chicago.

William M. McConahey III grew up in Rochester, Minnesota, where he attended public school. After graduating from Harvard, he earned an M.D. from the University of Minnesota, followed by an internship at the Geisinger Medical Center in Danville, Pennsylvania, and a residency at the Mayo Clinic. He practiced internal medicine in South Boston, Virginia, for 14 years before switching to emergency medicine in Danville, Virginia. He also serves as ship's physician for Holland America Line and Windstar Cruises. He and his wife, Ora Linda Schneider McConahey, have two adult children.

Ursula Oppens studied piano with her mother, Edith Oppens, as well as with Leonard Shure and Guido Agosti, and received her master's degree at the Juilliard School of Music, where she studied with Felix Galimir and Rosina

Lhevinne. As an undergraduate at Radcliffe College, she studied English literature and economics. She has won equal international renown as a pianist of the established repertoire and a champion of contemporary music, performing with many of the world's leading orchestras, including those of Boston, Chicago, Cleveland, St. Louis, San Francisco, and London. A native New Yorker, she made her debut under the auspices of Young Concert Artists in 1969, the year she also won first prize in the Busoni International Piano Competition. She was appointed John Evans Distinguished Professor of Music at Northwestern University in 1994.

Robert G. Sakai joined VISTA after graduating from Harvard and worked on community development on the Navajo Reservation in New Mexico. Two years later, demonstrating how far the third-generation Sakais had assimilated into American culture, he seriously considered going to Canada as an alternative to the draft. Instead he joined the navy, where he participated in the recovery of the *Apollo 11* capsule carrying the first astronauts to land on the moon. After the navy he attended graduate school at the University of Hawaii, the University of Tokyo, and the University of California, Berkeley. He did not complete his dissertation on the social and psychological adaptation of Koreans in Japan from Berkeley, but did receive a master's degree in city planning from Berkeley. Currently he directs the international trade and technology development program for Alameda County, California.

Deborah Lucas Schneider holds a Ph.D. in Germanic languages and literatures from Harvard. For many years she taught English as a foreign language at the University of Erlangen-Nuremberg and the Friebel Institute for Translators and Interpreters in Erlangen, Germany. She has translated 10 books and numerous scholarly articles from German into English and is a contributing editor of *Harvard Magazine*. A widow with two grown children, she lives in Massachusetts and travels frequently to Germany.

Matthew W. Stolper concentrated in architectural sciences as an undergraduate at Harvard and holds graduate degrees from the University of Michigan in Near Eastern studies, specializing in Assyriology and ancient Near Eastern history. He has participated in archaeological excavations in Iran and Libya. Following an initial position in the Department of Near Eastern Studies at the University of Michigan, he has been on the faculty of the Department of Near Eastern Languages and Civilizations and the Oriental Institute at the University of Chicago since 1980. He is the author of 85 articles and five books, including *Entrepreneurs and Empire* (1985), *Texts from Tall-i Malyan* (1984), and *Elam* (1985).

Charles Styron is a clinical psychologist, married to Nancy Frumer Styron, who is also a clinical psychologist and an attorney. They have a young daughter, born in 1995. After graduation from college he served in the Peace Corps in Nepal, returning in the late 1960s to study architecture at MIT. After two decades in architecture, he changed his career to psychology, finishing the transition in 1991. His interests include Buddhist practice and study, the landscape of the West, collage, classical piano, computers, opera, and NASCAR (another genre of opera).

Betty Chang Sun immigrated to the United States with her family in 1949. After graduating from Harvard-Radcliffe, she worked as a research psychologist, obtaining an Ed.M. in developmental psychology from Harvard and a Ph.D. in social psychology from Columbia. As a proponent for the gifted, she coauthored *Resources for Children* (1982). She served as an educational consultant and curriculum specialist from 1982 to 1993 and was curriculum chair for the Lawrence Central Council, Lawrence School District, Nassau County, New York. She was an active member of the admissions and scholarship committees for the Harvard-Radcliffe Club of Long Island and has served as a member of its board. She is currently a board member of the Lawrence Educational Foundation and a business consultant to Salex Corporation. She is married to Pershing Sun and has two children.

Christine Tanz was born to Jewish parents in Poland in 1944. Her family left Poland in 1948 and after three years in France came to the United States in 1951. She holds a B.A. in history and literature from Radcliffe College and a Ph.D. in psychology from the University of Chicago. Her progressive westward migration has ended in Tucson, Arizona, where she taught psychology at the University of Arizona. She has written articles and a book about the language of children, and she is also the author of several books for young children. At present she is a public artist, putting down roots in the local soil in the form of site-specific monuments. She is married to Jean-Paul Bierny, a physician born in Belgium. Their son is a native Tucsonian who has lived in the same house for all of his 16 years.

Maria Fleming Tymoczko is Professor of Comparative Literature at the University of Massachusetts Amherst. She writes about cultural interface in diverse domains, from oral tradition to literary development in multilingual societies to translation theory and practice. President of the Celtic Studies Association of North America, she is the author of a book on James Joyce's use of early Irish literature, entitled *The Irish "Ulysses"* (1994). Her translations of early Irish literature were published as *Two Death Tales from the Ulster Cycle* (1981), and her theoretical studies of translation appear in *Translation in a Postcolonial Context* (1999). Mother of three grown children, she lives in Northampton,

Massachusetts, where she is actively engaged in politics and holds elected office.

Helena Worthen is a novelist (*Perimeters*, 1980; *Damages*, 1986) and playwright. She taught for many years in the California community college system and served as an elected officer and staff member for the California Federation of Teachers AFL-CIO. After receiving a doctorate in education from the University of California, Berkeley, she became director of education and political action for a small Philadelphia union of garment and men's clothing workers. Currently she is Assistant Professor of Education at the University of Illinois at Chicago. Mother of two children, she is married to Joe Berry, also a labor educator.

Francis L. Zebot immigrated to the United States in 1948. He attended secondary school at Portsmouth Priory in Rhode Island. At Harvard he concentrated in classics, and he took an M.A. in classics at Ohio State University. After attending law school at the University of Chicago, he spent a year studying French civil law at the University of Aix-Marseilles. His legal career has been wide-ranging, from a brief stint at Sherman & Sterling on Wall Street, then the world's largest law firm, to defending convicted criminals on appeal for the State Appellate Defender Office for the State of Michigan, to a year as a visiting professor at the University of Detroit (Mercy) law school. Currently he is Assistant United States Attorney in Detroit. Married to Nancy Wiggers, he is the father of two children.

ACKNOWLEDGMENTS

There are many people to whom we owe thanks. In their enthusiasm over our thirtieth-reunion symposium on the impact of World War II on our parents and ourselves, it was our classmates who proposed this book. Their interest and encouragement has kept us going through the long process of pulling together so much material. All but one of the original symposium presenters wrote for this collection, joined by two dozen others. All generously agreed to open their lives in response to our requests to write about their family stories and to reconsider those stories as a slice of social history. They were responsive to our suggestions, willing to rewrite, to go ever deeper, and remarkably patient and good-humored with an editorial process that extended over a period of three years. Many parents, aunts, uncles, and siblings helped by providing information and by being willing to delve into their own memories of more than 50 years ago.

We are grateful to the Harvard-Radcliffe Class of 1965 for paying for the copyediting to prepare the manuscript for publication. Alice Davies, the Class treasurer, deserves a special note of thanks for facilitating the financial aspects of this edition. On short notice Jean Martin, our able copyeditor, devoted a massive number of hours to the manuscript; her sensitivity, discretion, and discernment have improved the manuscript immeasurably and have saved us from many errors. Mona Baker and Ken Baker of St. Jerome Publishing have been committed to the project, maintaining their high standards despite the narrow window available to publish the book in time for the thirty-fifth reunion of the Class of 1965.

It was Max Gitter who proposed an article on the book to *Harvard Magazine*. John Rosenberg, its editor, and Jean Martin, senior editor, responded with enthusiasm, drawing attention to our project by publishing Maria Tymoczko's essay in its entirety in the issue for September-October 1999.

Howard Gardner and Nancy Chodorow encouraged us at every step of the way. Howard's cogent and timely advice began with the planning for the original symposium and continued throughout. Howard also arranged for the funds from Harvard University that enabled us to get off the ground. Nancy came forward after the symposium to urge that the materials be published and agreed to write a commentary on the essays. She also read, responded to, and brought her excellent judgment to bear on the entire manuscript as it approached its final form, making numerous helpful editorial suggestions.

In addition to their more general sustenance and support, the following deserve special commendation. Joseph Donohue's sustained interest in the project extended to reading many essays, and he became the textual arbiter par excellence, the final authority on grammar; he also played a central role in editing the photographs for publication. With discernment about their central importance and focus, Julianna Tymoczko also read many essays and provided some crucial insights. Alexei Tymoczko shared his historical expertise, particularly his knowledge of World War II, illuminating our understanding of the context for the essays. Steven Kilston actively encouraged us throughout the process, and he was indefatigable about running down information about things that puzzled us; Steve also contributed substantially to the glossary. Deborah Schneider provided technical advice on a number of points; she and James Cathey also gave advice about elements of German language and culture in the text. Molly Donohue researched the British Navy and made possible the verification of essential material. Frieda Ployer consulted on Yiddish and read a number of the essays, penetrating to the heart of them. Clark Miller and Jack Anderson, World War II history buffs from childhood, offered critical help on the historical context. Theodore Nadelson drew our attention to the repetitive, compulsive, addictive nature of war. George Herbster and David Hannon provided legal counsel. David arranged for the Class of 1965 to distribute the books at the thirty-fifth reunion, and he offered other support as well. Framingham Psychiatric Counseling Associates set no limits on its provision of xeroxing and FAXing.

We also wish to acknowledge *Ploughshares* for permission to reprint the poem "A Flier," by Sarah Niles Kafatou. We are grateful for the photographs of World War II on pages 9, 34, 69, 76, 100, 221, 224, and 284, which have been reprinted from publications of the government of the United States of America, notably the comprehensive collection *United States Army in World War II: Pictorial Record,* as well as the more recent *War and Conflict,* edited by Jonathan Heller. The photograph of Coventry Cathedral on the cover and p. 106 is by permission of Coventry Central Library. The staff of Photographic Services at the University of Massachusetts Amherst has our special gratitude for their meticulous and expert work preparing all the photographs for publication.

The book is understated about its debt to psychology and, particularly, to psychoanalysis. Nancy Blackmun wishes to include in her acknowledgments those who were a formative influence on her training in these fields. Erik Erikson, on the Harvard faculty during our college years, pursued a career "outside the box" in his devotion to looking at lives in the context of history. The very titles of his books convey the concepts that have shaped this volume: *Childhood and Society*, *Identity and the Life Cycle*, and *Insight and Responsibility*. Another seminal influence was Robert W. White, who was at the forefront of studying lives and the varied forces that shape them, exemplified in his book *Lives in Progress*, another title relevant to the essence of this work. Psychoanalyst teachers who nurtured her curiosity and her effort to understand the interior life and the development of human beings, one individual at a time, include Padraic Burns, James Dalsimer, Ralph Engle, Ramon Greenberg, Judith Huizenga, Edward R. Shapiro, Judith Teicholz, Lora Hiems Tessman, Louis Vachon, and Peter Wohlauer. Lora Tessman, who celebrated her tenth birthday on the boat taking her refugee family away from Nazi Germany, backed this project unequivocally and offered significant specific insights. Most important of all, Edward R. Shapiro provided the crucible within which it became possible to grasp the deeply interior ways that World War II infiltrated the very being of its children. Without his ability to accompany – Virgil to a Dante struggling in the Inferno – there would perhaps have been no book.

There were also many friends and family members whose interest, time, and loving support have made important contributions. These include Erwin Arias, Douglas Bernon, Nicholas and Kristen Coniaris, Mathea Falco, Ann McNeal, Jörg Meyer-Piton, Zofia Michniak and her family, Esther Miller, Victoria Fleming Natco, Marta Niewiadomska and her family, Malgorzata Olszewska Nierzewska, Monika Wojciech Phuah and her mother Barbara Szymanowicz-Wojciech, Rozalia and Arkady G. Pansovoy, the family of Walther and Regina Reichling, particularly their daughter Leonora, Robert Reid, Emily Ringenberg, Mary Schoun, Virginia Tay, Dmitri Tymoczko, Lyuba Vartikovski, Robert Wald, and John Winslow.

Maria Tymoczko
Nancy Blackmun

GLOSSARY

Anschluss: The German word for 'annexation,' this term is often used to refer to the first international test case of Nazi expansionist aims. Under the false pretext of a call for German help from the Austrians (a telegram actually sent by a German agent in Vienna), Hitler invaded Austria on March 12, 1938. The ensuing Austrian enthusiasm allowed Hitler to annex Austria outright the next day.

Auschwitz: Auschwitz-Birkenau was the largest and most notorious Nazi concentration and death camp, located 37 miles west of Cracow, Poland. Established in 1940 as a concentration camp for Polish political prisoners, by 1942 it included a killing center at Birkenau. Also part of the huge camp complex was I. G. Farben's slave-labor manufacturing camp, known as Buna-Monowitz. Auschwitz was liberated on January 27, 1945, by the Soviets.

Bataan Death March: After the evacuation of General Douglas MacArthur to Australia on March 11, 1942, and the surrender of U.S. troops under the command of General Jonathan Wainwright on Bataan on April 9, 1942, the Japanese forced about 70,000 U.S. and Filipino prisoners of war to march 85 miles by foot to a prison camp. The march occurred between April 11 and May 5, 1942, and was conducted with extreme sadism, in part because the Japanese viewed soldiers who surrendered as unworthy of food or humane treatment. The prisoners were already starving and ill from the long siege on Bataan and Corregidor; the casualties on the march were very high.

Bełzec: One of the four camps in Poland devoted exclusively to extermination of deportees upon their arrival. It is in a small Polish town in the southeast of the district of Lublin, 45 miles northeast of Przemysl, close to the current Ukrainian border. The camp area included a railroad siding with room for 20 freight cars. There were two huts for the arrivals – one for undressing and the other for storing clothes and baggage. At the end of February 1942 the installations for mass extermination were completed. Operations at this camp, where an estimated 600,000 Jews were killed, were completed by June 1943.

Bergen-Belsen: A Nazi holding center in northern Germany, operating from July 1943 to April 1945, Bergen-Belsen was transformed from a prisoner-exchange camp to a concentration camp in March 1944. Thousands died there from planned starvation and epidemics, due to lack of food, heat, medicine, and elementary sanitary conditions. Currently it is only a graveyard.

Bismarck: Launched in 1939, the *Bismarck* was Germany's most powerful battleship. On May 24, 1941, the *Bismarck* sank the *Hood*, a British cruiser, at the cost of 1,500 lives, but was itself disabled by the Royal Air Force and sunk by British ships in the Atlantic Ocean about 600 miles off the coast of France on May 27, 1941, taking with it more than 2,000 men.

blitzkrieg: From the German word for 'lightning war,' a very rapid air and land attack designed to create psychological shock and disorganization in an enemy. It was used by the German air force and artillery against Poland to begin World War II on September 1, 1939, and also used later in the invasions of Belgium, the Netherlands, and France.

Bronze Star: The award given since 1944 by the United States military for heroism or achievement in military operations other than those involving aerial flights.

Bund deutscher Mädel (BdM): The 'League of German Girls,' the female branch of the Hitler Youth, was designed to indoctrinate girls with National Socialist views. It trained them to be physically fit future mothers and home-makers, to bear Aryan children, and to take care of the household rather than seek employment or higher education. In parades members wore navy blue skirts, white blouses, and brown jackets and had their hair arranged in braids. By 1936, when it was becoming mandatory, more than 2 million girls were members of the Bund deutscher Mädel.

Civilian Conservation Corps: Funded by the United States Congress in 1933 as part of the effort to relieve unemployment during the Depression, the Civilian Conservation Corps employed more than 2.5 million young men in conservation and reforestation projects.

Displaced Persons Act: On December 22, 1945, President Harry Truman signed measures to admit 42,000 war refugees to the United States. On June 25, 1948, the act was extended to admit an additional 205,000 displaced persons from Europe, and the numbers were increased again on June 16, 1950, to allow entry of an additional 341,000 people by the next year.

Dunkirk: A seaport in northern France, 10 miles from the Belgian border on the Strait of Dover. During May and June 1940, almost 400,000 British and other Allied troops were surrounded and cut off by the Germans at Dunkirk. Supported by R.A.F. defense against the Luftwaffe, most of the forces were evacuated from Dunkirk by hundreds of civilian vessels as well as naval boats. Only 40,000 were taken prisoner. It was a humiliating but heroic escape.

Einsatzgruppen: A German term meaning 'task forces,' these special units within the SS were created by Heinrich Himmler. They were placed under the command of Reinhard Heydrich in September 1939. The Einsatzgruppen became mobile killing units charged with liquidating all political enemies of the Third Reich over a wide area of Eastern Europe, just behind the advancing German troops. They eliminated "undesirables" and "political criminals," but their main task was to murder Jews. The victims were often transported to a wooded area or a ravine, stripped, shot, and buried. The Einsatzgruppen were responsible for killing about a third of the six million Jews murdered in the Holocaust.

El Alamein: Located west of Alexandria, El Alamein was the site of two major battles between British and Axis forces in 1942. In July 1942 German Field Marshall Erwin Rommel's North African campaign was stopped at El Alamein, preventing the capture of the Suez Canal; the November 4, 1942, defeat of Rommel at El Alamein turned the tide in North Africa, with Rommel in full retreat thereafter.

Executive Order 9066: Designed to prevent domestic sabotage after Pearl Harbor, Executive Order 9066 was issued on February 19, 1942, by U.S. President Franklin D. Roosevelt. The order authorized the military to detain all persons of possible danger to the United States. On February 20 Lieutenant General John DeWitt was appointed to carry out the order. While E. O. 9066 was construed as applying primarily to enemy aliens (i.e., citizens of Germany, Italy, and Japan), in practice it was applied almost exclusively to Japanese Americans, particularly those living on the West Coast. Because of a 1924 ban on the naturalization of Asians, Roosevelt's order affected one-third of Japanese Americans immediately, but the order was applied to native-born Japanese Americans as well. Unlike Germans and Italians, who were released fairly soon, Japanese Americans were interned in "relocation camps," a euphemism for what were essentially concentration camps. Approximately 110,000 persons living in Arizona, California, Oregon, and Washington were transported to relocation camps in California, Arizona, Utah, Idaho, Wyoming, and Arkansas. Some qualified for release, but most remained imprisoned, with consequent loss of homes, property, and jobs, until January 2, 1945, when the order was rescinded. On June 30, 1952, over President Harry S. Truman's veto, the U.S. Congress passed the McCarran-Walter Immigration and Naturalization Act ending the 1924 ban on Asian immigration and the racially based ban on naturalization that had prevented Japanese Americans born in Japan from becoming citizens of the United States.

Final Solution: *Endlösung* in German, this is the euphemistic phrase devised by the Nazis in 1941 to refer to the plan to kill all of Europe's Jews, an idea apparently generated by the prospect of invading the U.S.S.R., which had a huge Jewish population. As early as 1925 in *Mein Kampf*, Hitler had clearly stated his intent to rid Germany of what he viewed as the polluting influence of Jews on the racial and cultural purity of Aryans. Despite the persecution of Jews in the 1930s and the Nuremberg Laws disenfranchising Jews, earlier plans to force large numbers of Jews to emigrate and to remove the remainder to Madagascar had not worked out. The Final Solution, a formal directive to the government officials who would be responsible for its execution, was presented at the Wannsee Conference on January 20, 1942, by Gestapo chief Reinhard Heydrich. It laid out plans to transport all Jews from Germany and countries controlled by Germany to labor camps "in the east," where it was expected most would be worked to death. The rest, viewed as a core group of especially resilient persons who could in the future regenerate, breed, and cause difficulties, would be "dealt with," i.e. exterminated.

GI Bill: On June 22, 1944, President Franklin D. Roosevelt signed the GI Bill, providing up to four years of tuition, fees, and student living expenses for higher education, as well as low-interest mortgages and other benefits, to veterans returning from World War II. The GI Bill democratized higher education in America and transformed the society in many other socioeconomic and demographic ways as well, supplying the burgeoning postwar industries with trained personnel and launching both the suburban real-estate boom and the Baby Boom.

Gymnasium: The German term for an academic high school, originally with a classical curriculum, that prepares students for the university.

Holocaust Remembrance Day: *Yom Ha-Shoah* in Hebrew, Holocaust Remembrance Day is observed on the 27th day of Nisan, the first month of spring in the Hebrew calendar, 13 days after Passover. In many countries it is observed on April 19 or 20.

Hoover Mission: Immediately after the end of World War II, at the request of President Harry Truman, former President Herbert Hoover traveled to various parts of the world to evaluate food supplies. Hoover had gained experience in postwar relief work after World War I; the Hoover Mission was intended to yield recommendations on how to prevent a repeat of that earlier catastrophe.

International Refugee Organization (IRO): The IRO was established by the United Nations in 1946 to aid war refugees and displaced persons, of whom there were an estimated 30 million worldwide. It was opposed by the U.S.S.R., which viewed the IRO as encouraging refugees to flee the Soviet bloc countries.

Kapo: The German version of the Italian word *capo*, 'head, chief,' the term used to refer to a prisoner in a concentration camp who, under the supervision of the SS, cooperated with the Nazis in controlling the other prisoners, usually in expectation of privileges and freedoms for himself or herself. The kapos "encouraged" prisoners to do their jobs through the use of bull whips, rubber clubs, rods, iron bars, and so forth. In urban ghettos kapos were officers of the Jewish policing force, meting out punishment under Nazi orders.

Kristallnacht: Kristallnacht ('the night of broken glass') occurred on November 9-10, 1938. Organized by Nazi propaganda minister Joseph Goebbels to strike terror into Germany's Jews, it was ostensibly explained as retribution for the killing of a German diplomat in Paris by a Jew whose parents had been deported, along with 15,000 other Jews, to their Polish homeland. A week of government-sanctioned actions against Jews, in which synagogues were burned and Jewish businesses ransacked, was climaxed by a night of widespread violence in cities and villages throughout Germany. Some 7,500 Jewish businesses were gutted and had their storefront glass shattered (sounding like broken crystal, *Kristall* in German). Jews were attacked in the streets, dragged from their homes, and assaulted; approximately 100 died and 35,000 others were shipped to concentration camps.

Luftwaffe: The term used for the German air force during the Third Reich.

Majdanek: An extermination camp in the city of Lublin, set up in 1940 and closed in July 1944. Although estimates vary, probably about 840,000 people, mostly Jews, were murdered at Majdanek. Today, one-fifth of the camp is intact, including the gas chambers and crematoria.

Marshall Plan: A relief program, first called the European Recovery Program, was proposed by U.S. Secretary of State George C. Marshall on June 5, 1947, in a commencement address at Harvard University. Funded by the United States with comprehensive planning provided by the Europeans, it was designed to rehabilitate the economies of western and southern European nations after World War II in order to create stable conditions that would aid the survival of democratic institutions. Refusing involvement, the U.S.S.R. branded it an imperialist plot to enslave Europe. The Marshall Plan was adopted by Congress on April 2, 1948; it distributed about $12 billion in economic aid over four years, with great success in achieving its goals.

McCarthy Hearings: Joseph McCarthy, an undistinguished senator from Wisconsin, capitalized during the postwar period on the growing paranoia in the United States associated with the buildup of the Cold War. As chair of the permanent subcommittee on investigations of the Senate Government Operations Committee, he held a series of hearings that electrified the nation with damaging accusations pertaining to communist spying and membership in communist organizations leveled at particular individuals and groups. Government officials, the military, professors, writers, members of the entertainment industry, industrial workers, and others were accused of being "soft on communism." The uncontrolled nature of his investigations eventually resulted in his being himself investigated and discredited in the Army-McCarthy Hearings, televised in 1954. Censure in the Senate followed.

Military Government: The government imposed on Germany by the four major Allied occupying powers (the U.S., the U.S.S.R., Britain, and France) after the end of World War II. Military Government superseded all civil authority and supplied law and judiciary until Germany's own civil government was reestablished. Agreements pertaining to the organization of the Military Government were reached by the Allies at Yalta in February 1945.

Nuremberg Laws: A group of anti-Jewish laws adopted unanimously by the Reichstag on September 15, 1935, on the occasion of the annual congress of the Nazi Party in Nuremberg. These laws defined a Jew as someone with one Jewish grandparent. This biological definition increased the number of Jews in Germany from the half million who self-identified to some two million. The laws also formally deprived Jews, as "persons of non-German blood," of citizenship, denied them civil rights, and forbade marriage and sexual relations between Jews and Aryans. The Nuremberg Laws were preceded by earlier discrimination against Jews in Germany. When Hitler became chancellor in 1933, Jews were excluded from the civil service, public office, the media, entertainment, teaching, and the stock exchange. Publicity about Nazi abuses against the Jews had resulted in a threatened boycott of German products, in response to which the Nazis accelerated attacks on Jews, dismissing judges, excluding physicians from hospitals, and expelling students from universities. By 1937 Jews were forbidden to practice law and medicine, and they were not permitted to shop at most stores. There followed exclusion from cinemas, public transportation, and primary and secondary schools. Jews were forbidden to own businesses or real estate and they were subject to an 8 p.m. curfew. Ultimately they were required to wear a yellow Star of David identifying them as Jews and to reside only in ghettos, thus preparing the way for the Final Solution.

Purple Heart: Established by George Washington in 1782 but awarded only three times before 1932, it has since been given to members of the United States military who are wounded in combat.

Referendariat: A two-year provisional period for teachers and lawyers in Germany, when work must be done under the supervision of a fully qualified member of the profession. Similar to an internship, the Referendariat falls between two required examinations.

Glossary

Reichstag: The lower house of the German parliament during the period 1871-1945.

Ribbentrop-Molotov Pact: The German-Soviet Treaty of Nonaggression, signed secretly by the German foreign minister, Joachim von Ribbentrop, and the Soviet prime minister, Vyacheslav Molotov, on August 23, 1939. It cleared the way for Hitler's attack on Poland on September 1, 1939, the beginning of World War II.

Rosie the Riveter: Rose Will Monroe, born in Kentucky in 1922, worked as a riveter at the Willow Run Aircraft Factory in Ypsilanti, Michigan, building B-29 and B-24 bombers for the U.S. Air Force during World War II. She starred in a promotional film about the war effort at home and was also featured in a poster campaign, becoming known as "Rosie the Riveter," perhaps the most widely recognized icon of the war era. The films and posters she appeared in were used by the U.S. government to encourage women to go to work in support of the war effort. After the war, American women were encouraged to return to their kitchens to make room in the factories for the men returning from Europe and the South Pacific. Unlike many, Rose Will Monroe didn't stop working after the war: she held jobs as a taxi driver and a beauty salon operator, and she formed her own construction company in Indiana.

SA: The German abbreviation for *Sturmabteilung*, literally 'storm division' in German. Civilian units of a special armed branch of the Nazi Party, a paramilitary organization that played a major role in the rise of the party in the early 1930s. Known as the Brownshirts after their uniforms, they were storm troopers infamous for brawling and violence, particularly during elections when they attacked and even murdered opponents of the Nazi Party. By 1933 they numbered over 2 million men, but in 1934 there was a purge and many SA leaders were executed at Hitler's orders, thus strengthening his control over the Nazi Party. Thereafter the SA played a minor role in the Third Reich.

Selektion: The term used for the division of prisoners into those who would live and die. At concentration camps, for example, prisoners arriving were divided into two groups: those who could work and would live were sent to the left; those who would die were sent to the right. Within the camps selections also occurred at roll call: prisoners were forced to stand outside at all seasons, sometimes naked, often for hours at a time, while doctors and SS men examined them to determine who would live and who would die.

Silver Star: The citation awarded by the United States Army for conspicuous gallantry in action.

SS: The German abbreviation for the *Schutzstaffel*, literally 'protection squad,' the Blackshirts of the Third Reich. The SS was formed initially in 1925 as Hitler's personal bodyguard and later built by Heinrich Himmler into a giant organization which ultimately became the terror of Germany and German-occupied Europe, the most powerful armed group in Germany after the armed forces. The SS had four branches under its command: the Gestapo (the secret police), Hitler's bodyguards, the guards of the concentration camps, and military troops under the name Waffen SS, who were distributed throughout the Third Reich and by the end of World War II consisted of 35 divisions, the most powerful rival to the army. From 1931 to 1934 the SS was nominally under the jurisdiction of the SA, but thereafter the SS had the ascendancy and assumed more and more executive functions.

strategic bombing: Directed against industrial targets and military installations, strategic bombing is intended to reduce the enemy's ability to wage war in a general sense. In Europe during World War II, the primary targets in order of importance were submarine yards and all aspects of the aircraft, transportation, and oil industries. American attacks emphasized daylight raids on industrial installations, but the British air command preferred night raids on workers' housing, thus blurring the line between strategic attacks on industrial capacity and generalized attacks on cities and civilians. Germany's industry, under the exceptionally able direction of Albert Speer, proved more resilient and resistant to destruction than the Allies anticipated, actually increasing production toward the end of the war despite widespread destruction. The attacks on the oil industry, however, left the military without fuel. Strategic bombing against Japan in 1945 involved primarily night raids, when the inadequate Japanese night defenses permitted low-altitude precision bombing of cities with highly flammable, largely wooden buildings. The result was tremendous damage, bringing the country to the point of starvation by the time the two atomic bombs were dropped on Hiroshima and Nagasaki.

Strategic Bombing Survey: The United States Strategic Bombing Survey was established in November 1944 to assess the effectiveness of strategic bombing. Members of the survey team made a close examination of several hundred German sites and interviewed thousands of Germans, amassing volumes of statistical material and setting a standard for future survey research methods. After V-J Day Japan was also surveyed. *The United States Strategic Bombing Survey: Summary Report (European War)* was issued September 30, 1945, one of many resulting publications. The Survey was abolished in 1947.

Theresienstadt: The German name for the Czech town of Terezín. A concentration camp for Jewish "prominents" or VIPs was established in the walled town of Theresienstadt and used during the war as a facade for international inspections, particularly those of the International Red Cross. Set up as a bogus spa, the camp included art, music, performances, and other activities intended to suggest that the detention of the Jews in such camps was beneficent. Although not a death camp like Auschwitz, after the adoption of the Final Solution, it served as a way station to the ghettos in Nazi-occupied Eastern Europe and to the death camps. Of the nearly 140,000 people deported to Theresienstadt, 34,000 died there. From 1942 to 1944 transports carried 87,000 people from Theresienstadt eastward, of whom 83,000 perished.

Tripartite Pact: The signing of the Tripartite Pact on September 27, 1940, created a formal alliance among Italy, Germany, and Japan, uniting the fascist powers and creating the Berlin-Rome-Tokyo Axis. In joining the Axis, Japan pledged to create a new order in Greater East Asia.

United Nations Relief and Rehabilitation Administration (UNRRA): On November 9, 1943, in order to provide aid for populations in Europe and the Far East that had been devastated by war and occupation and that were liberated by the Allies, 44 nations signed an agreement establishing the United Nations Relief and Rehabilitation Administration. UNRRA discontinued most of its operations in 1947 and its functions were transferred to various U.N. agencies.

Wallenberg mission: Raoul Wallenberg (1912-47?) was a Swedish businessman who persuaded his government to send him to Budapest in July 1944 on a mission to rescue Jews. Although this was just after the Nazi roundup and deportation of some 400,000 of Hungary's Jews to the death camps in Poland, Wallenberg managed to find and to shelter several thousand in safe houses under the flags of neutral countries, including Sweden. In November, when the Nazis began sending Jews on death marches toward the border with Austria, Wallenberg followed with trucks full of food and clothing for the prisoners, despite threats from Adolf Eichmann. He also saved thousands more by providing passports and papers to anyone with even the remotest connection to Sweden. As the Nazis prepared to abandon Budapest in December, the officer ordered to murder the 90,000 Jews remaining in the ghetto was persuaded by Wallenberg to back down. Wallenberg is credited with saving more than 100,000 people, contributing significantly to preserving the largest Jewish community in Europe to survive the Nazis. In the confusion of the final months of the war, Wallenberg was arrested for espionage by the Soviets, who were suspicious of his dubious diplomatic status and his large sums of money supplied by the U.S. Refugee Board and the American Jewish Joint Distribution Committee. He disappeared into the Soviet prison system, reportedly dying of a heart attack in 1947.

Warsaw Ghetto Uprising: The Warsaw ghetto was sealed in November 1940. As part of the Final Solution, it was designed to be the collection site from which half a million Jews would be deported to the death camps and exterminated. By July 1942 the first deportations had begun, with almost 70,000 people sent to Treblinka and gassed. In January 1943 the residents of the ghetto responded to mass deportations and SS murders in the ghetto with street fighting, forcing the SS temporarily to abandon further deportations. In April 1943 the Nazis reentered the ghetto with tank support to resume final deportations, but, in what became known as the Warsaw Ghetto Uprising, they were driven out by organized Jewish resistance, which was sustained from April 19 to May 8, 1943. The Nazi forces then returned, burning the ghetto systematically house by house and murdering its inhabitants. More than 56,000 Jews were killed or deported, but about 15,000 escaped to "Aryan" areas of Warsaw, mainly by way of the sewers.

Warsaw Uprising: On August 1, 1944, General Tadeusz Bor-Komorowski of the Polish Home Army attacked the German occupation forces in Warsaw with a force of 35,000 to 50,000 partisans. Joined in the fight by the city's Polish population, they had taken control of most of the city by August 4. The Germans sent reinforcements from the Wehrmacht, then retreating before the advancing Soviet army. As the Germans razed the heart of the city, the Polish forces became fragmented and were pursued into all refuges, including sewers. By October 2 virtually all the Polish resistance forces had perished. During the 63 days of fighting, the Soviet army, encamped on the east bank of the Vistula within sight of the fighting, never offered the Polish partisans assistance, but waited for resistance and Nazi forces to destroy each other. This strategy facilitated both the capture of Warsaw and communist ascendancy after the war. When hostilities ceased, most of Warsaw was destroyed, the Polish Home Army annihilated, and much of the remaining population had been deported. By the time the Germans were eventually defeated, there were no forces left in Warsaw to oppose Soviet political domination in Poland.

Wehrmacht: Literally 'defense force,' the term for the regular German armed forces during World War II. The Wehrmacht consisted of the army, the navy, and the air force (Luftwaffe), as opposed to the police and the military organizations within the SA and the SS.

Yad Vashem: The Holocaust Martyrs' and Heroes' Remembrance Authority which serves as Israel's national institution of Holocaust commemoration. Located in Jerusalem, its name comes from Isaiah 56:5, " ... a monument and a name." Yad Vashem houses exhibits and monuments, including the Children's Monument and the Monument to the Lost Communities of Europe, as well as archives of material pertaining to Jews who died in the Holocaust and non-Jews who put themselves at risk to help Jews. It hosts seminars and conducts other activities related to the Holocaust.

Yalta Agreement: This declaration was signed at Yalta in the Crimea on February 11, 1945, by the three principal leaders of the Allies: President Franklin D. Roosevelt of the United States, Prime Minister Winston Churchill of Great Britain, and Premier Joseph Stalin of the U.S.S.R. The agreement was formalized at a conference held February 4-11, 1945, during the final months of World War II, to discuss strategies for the invasion and final defeat of Nazi Germany and the terms of settlement. The three powers agreed to demand Germany's unconditional surrender and planned to divide Germany into four zones of occupation, with France being the fourth occupying power. The Soviet Union promised to enter the war against Japan after the German surrender. The conference discussed Poland's postwar boundaries and pledged to help liberated European nations settle political and economic problems by democratic means and postwar elections (a specific reference to Poland under Soviet occupation). It also established the dates for the meeting in San Francisco to draft the Charter of the United Nations and determined that only two Soviet republics would be allowed full representation at the United Nations, where veto powers would be vested in the three big powers, the U.S., Britain, and the U.S.S.R.

NOTES

Page

TYMOCZKO & BLACKMUN, RECORDED ON THE BODY, ETCHED ON THE HEART

27 **a multiple consciousness**: The terminology here is suggested by W.E.B. Du Bois's concept of the "double consciousness" of African Americans.

PARADOX

33 **paradox**: Definitions and etymologies are taken from the *American Heritage Dictionary*.

CORYELL, LEGACIES OF THE MANHATTAN PROJECT

37 **The Manhattan Project**: Thanks to Lawrence E. Glendenin (codiscoverer with Jack Marinsky of promethium) and to Ethel Glendenin for reading a preliminary draft of my essay.

37 **the United States Army**: The Manhattan Project was directed by General Leslie Groves.

42 **"no secrets are hid ... "**: From "Collect for Purity," *Book of Common Prayer* (355).

GRIEPP, GROWING UP IN THE SHADOW OF THE HOLOCAUST

46 **the Red Cross**: Principally Hans Zellweger, whose daughter, Helen Judith Zellweger, was also a member of the Harvard-Radcliffe Class of 1965.

48 *tzores*: 'Troubles, problems, worries.'

49 *Luftmensch*: Literally, 'an air-person.'

SCHNEIDER, SHAPE UP, KID

53 **Hildy**: The study was published as Werner F. Leopold, *Speech Development of a Bilingual Child*.

BLACKMUN, FALLING THROUGH A WRINKLE IN TIME

57 **a law school classmate of my father's**: Telford Taylor, chief prosecutor of the Nuremberg Trials.

57 **William Styron's Sophie**: The title character in Styron's *Sophie's Choice*.

60 **a blow upon a bruise**: The phrase is inspired by Waugh (167).

61 **a famous portrait by Vermeer**: Vermeer's *Head of a Young Girl* in the Mauritshuis, The Hague.

61 **All of this I heard**: For information on the liberation of the concentration camps, I am indebted to Chamberlain and Feldman, esp. intro., ch. 3, ch. 5. Murrow's broadcast was "April 15, 1945."

61 **its German words**: The words are from Heinrich Heine, "Die Lorelei"; the English translation is my own.

62 **their lines echo in my memory**: The lines are taken respectively from "Where the Blue of the Night (Meets the Gold of the Day)," by Roy Turk, Bing Crosby, and Fred E. Ahlert; "Always," by Irving Berlin; "What'll I Do," by Irving Berlin; "I'll Be Seeing You," by Sammy Fain and Irving Kahal; "Till We Meet Again," by Raymond B. Egan and Richard A. Whiting; and "Now is the Hour" ("Maori Farewell Song"), by Maewa Kaihan, Dorothy Stewart, and Clement Scott.

62 *The World at War*: Produced by Thames Television (1973).

63 **a wrinkle in time**: The metaphor comes from Madeleine L'Engle, *A Wrinkle in Time*.

SAKAI, FROM POSTON TO PALAU

67 **own property**: Prior to the McCarran-Walter Immigration and Naturalization Act of 1952, immigrant Japanese Americans could not be naturalized; thus, they could not vote and they were also not permitted to own property. This presented problems when my grandfather tried to purchase land. He solved the problem by providing the money for the land and asking a Caucasian neighbor to hold title for him. The Sakai family was fortunate that this neighbor was willing to turn the land over when my father's older brother turned 18. My uncle could own the land once he became an adult, because he was an American citizen by virtue of his birth in California.

Although my grandparents and other *issei*, first-generation Japanese Americans, were as loyal and committed to the United States as if they were citizens, technically they were not stripped of their citizenship during World War II, because until 1952 they had been denied citizenship. My father and the nisei, on the other hand, were American citizens, and did have their rights taken away from them.

74 **the Japanese government**: This award symbolizes a consistent theme in his life – that of bringing about better understanding between the two cultures. He did fight against Japan, but he fought against a military government that has largely been repudiated by the Japanese people in the postwar period. Even on the battlefield he made it clear that he held the Japanese people in high esteem. Before, during, and after the war he has worked hard to bring about better understanding among Americans, Japanese, and Japanese Americans.

STOLPER, THEIR HAPPIEST TEN YEARS

81 **my grandfather opposed it**: I refer to the exhaustion of the victors (taking it for granted that the vanquished were worse than exhausted). At the end of World War II, Britain, France, and Russia were terribly impoverished. Food and money were scarce, infrastructure wrecked; while the Iron Curtain was descending and the Greek civil war was being fought, there were serious political struggles in France and Italy. Post World War I history had shown how futile and disastrous it would be to try to rebuild the European

victors on the backs of the vanquished and to crush the "economic engine" of Germany, especially while the U.S. was booming at the possible expense of recovery in Europe. At least it seemed clear to people of my grandfather's persuasion and to the drafters and supporters of the Marshall Plan, but not to Morgenthau or to the people who needed to fight the war to an absolute conclusion. The policy of unconditional surrender was certainly not a foregone conclusion, since negotiated terms could have served a lot of political and economic interests. The policy of reconstructing Germany as part of reconstructing Europe was even less of a foregone conclusion – in fact, it was outright anathema – while the war was being fought.

GRAHAM-WHITE, BOMBS AND BRAMBLES

108 **the Arnhem disaster**: On September 17, 1944, British airborne forces landed in Holland at Arnhem and Eindhoven. They encountered a surprisingly strong German defense and were defeated at Arnhem. Failing to outflank the German defense of the West Wall (Siegfried Line) and gain a bridgehold on the Rhine, they were withdrawn after heavy casualties.

108 **boo him**: The Labour Party won the national election held in Britain on July 26, 1945. Churchill was booed in Coventry, an industrial town, as leader of the Conservative Party.

OPPENS, SILENCE

123 **a six-week period in 1944**: Between April 16 and May 23, 1944, Adolf Eichmann, chief of the SS Gestapo, with only 50 SS officers directing local militia, attempted to round up the 800,000 Hungarian and Transylvanian Jews, many of whom went into hiding with Christian families. Approximately 400,000 Jews were deported to Auschwitz; most were gassed immediately upon arrival.

125 **Reichsfinanzrat**: Counsel to the treasury department of the German Reich.

TANZ, HIDING IN THE OPEN

135 **so many lice**: In Nazi propaganda Jews were frequently referred to as lice.

137 **the children who survived**: I am not one of the children enumerated, so there must be others overlooked, which isn't surprising.

ZEBOT, OUT OF SLOVENIA

153 **Julian**: Named in part after the Julian Alps.

154 **the Tripartite Pact**: The Tripartite Pact was signed by Germany, Italy, and Japan on September 27, 1940, to formally establish the coalition of Axis powers. Hitler tried to force other nations in his orbit to adhere to the pact. In the case of Yugoslavia, he was prepared to accept limited adherence to the Axis, pledging not to march through Yugoslavia, but only to use its roads and railways for military supplies in the event of operations against Greece. See Churchill, 159.

154 **the center of the city**: When I visited the house where I was born years later, it had been appropriated by the communist regime, except for a small flat left to my maternal grandfather, whom I visited. Ironically, it was only a stone's throw from one of the many palatial compounds of Tito. My mother recently arranged dual Slovenian-American citizenship for me in the event that after her death there should ever be reparations available for the seizure of the homestead.

155 **its communist intentions**: This occurred after Hitler attacked the Soviet Union in June 1941.

155 **Slovenes at hand**: After the Allies opened a new European front in southern Italy, they withdrew their support of Draza Mihajlovic (the royalist war minister of the Yugoslav government in exile) and his Chetnik ('trooper') underground in favor of the partisans. The Chetniks were Yugoslav army guerrillas organized in Serbia to resist the German occupation; they soon came into conflict with the partisans. The Allies withdrew their support largely because Mihajlovic was unwilling to increase guerrilla activity that he knew would provoke dreadful German reprisals on an unprotected native population.

155 **outside the church**: Though there was no hard proof of a partisan death threat against my father, he had reason to be fearful. From 1941 through 1943 he never ventured outdoors in Ljubljana without a personal bodyguard.

155 **with the Germans**: As noted by a British observer, the Home Guards "never accepted German leadership, and if sometimes compelled by the civil war to fight on the same side against Tito, they had been at most [the Germans'] co-belligerents, never their allies" and they "hoped for an Anglo-American victory in the war" (Nicolson, 115).

157 **near Celje**: Captain Nigel Nicolson, a British intelligence officer with the British fifth Corps, which had custody of the Home Guards as well as refugee Slovenian civilians such as my parents's families, testified that the Corps considered the turnover to Tito "one of the most disgraceful operations that British troops have ever been ordered to undertake" (Nicolson, 130). During the fiftieth anniversary of the end of the war, my family and I accompanied my mother on a commemorative tour that included some of these significant sites in Slovenia.

DUNDAS, THE WORM IN THE APPLE

159 **Royal Navy College at Dartmouth**: The Britannia Royal Navy College is located at Dartmouth in Devon, England. The U.S. equivalent is Annapolis.

159 **American minister to the Baltic States**: The U. S. did not consider Latvia, Lithuania, and Estonia big enough then to merit an ambassador, so a "minister" was appointed instead.

159 **Dunkirk**: On May 24, 1940, exactly two weeks after Hitler began his attack on Holland, Belgium, and France, the German army had an Allied army –

which consisted largely of the British Expeditionary Force – trapped on the French/Belgian coast around the port of Dunkirk. From May 24 to June 4, supported by the R.A.F., the Royal Navy evacuated almost the whole army – with no small thanks due to hundreds of civilian craft and the French units that defended the perimeter.

159 **Bismarck**: The *Bismarck* was the fastest and most powerful warship in the world and represented a potentially decisive threat to England's survival, based on the possible ability of the *Bismarck* to sink supply convoys from America. It was sunk by the Royal Navy in May 1941 in a three-day battle, during which some 3,500 men died.

160 **First Sea Lord**: The English equivalent of the U.S. Navy Chief of Staff.

160 **200,000 Germans**: Sources vary in their estimates of the casualties in this battle. The figure here is taken from Parrish, 600.

161 **Machiavelli wrote**: See *The Prince*, ch. 14, "In Respect of Military Afairs."

161 **Churchill said**: Quoted in Manchester, 581.

162 **it did not convince me**: In retrospect, I would say that I experienced the activists on both sides of the Vietnam War as representations of my father at his worst – demanding, hostile, dismissive, dangerous, confused, and unconvincing.

BROWN, REFLECTIONS ON A QUAKER FATHER

165 **they would have fought in World War II**: For this and other reasons, including the large number of applicants, it may well have been more difficult to become a C.O. during the Vietnam War. One friend of mine was investigated so thoroughly that two FBI agents interviewed me about him, for about an hour, in 1966.

165 **alternative service as a C.O.**: Men who weren't Quakers sometimes had much more difficulty obtaining C.O. status.

166 **on park lands**: The lands were formerly owned by local farmers, who were not happy to see their fields turned back into forest.

IHARA, OF OUR LIFE IN JAPAN DURING THE WAR

169 **50 kilometers**: About 30 miles.

170 **100 kilometers**: About 60 miles.

FALCO, CHILDHOOD MEMORIES OF POSTWAR GERMANY

175 **the Nazi era**: The women must have gotten grim satisfaction out of making their small American charge, daughter of the occupiers, look like the perfect little Nazi girl.

177 **access to Berlin**: The U.S.S.R. imposed its blockade on all land traffic beween Berlin and West Germany on June 24, 1948. The Western powers immediately organized the Berlin Airlift to supply the 2 million residents of West Berlin with food and other provisions.

FIELD, TROLLING ALONG AT THE BOTTOM

181 **a diaper magazine**: See *Baby Talk*, January 1944.

182 **refugees from Czechoslovakia**: My mother worked with the Czech Refugee Trust; among those supported by this organization was the family of Madeleine Albright, then a small child.

182 **Romania, which was still neutral**: In 1939 Poland bordered Romania.

185 **stir up Eastern Europe to revolt**: In 1974 in *Operation Splinter Factor*, Stewart Steven alleged that it was not Stalin but Allen Dulles who had sought to have my father and uncle arrested, in the hope that spy trials would bring on an anticommunist revolt. After much general reading I have come to believe that my father and uncle were probably victims of British strategic policy to build up the Cold War in order to make the U.S. and the U.S.S.R. mortal enemies, destroying their economies and reinstating Britain as the world's top economic power.

185 **two novels**: See Field and Mierzenski, *Angry Harvest* (1958); *Duck Lane* (1961). In order to obtain writing materials to compose these books, my father went on hunger strikes. His longest – 27 days – was an attempt to gain release. A full account of the events of those years can be found in Field and Field, *Trapped in the Cold War*.

GOH, A BABY OF THE JAPANESE OCCUPATION

195 **December 8, 1941**: The U.S. date for the bombing is December 7, because the Japanese bombers crossed the international date line on their way eastward.

195 **daughter of a boatman**: My grandfather's seven sampans were commandeered by the Japanese invaders.

196 **banana notes**: The currency in circulation during the Japanese occupation featured bananas and, hence, became known as banana notes.

196 *Ma-rai-ee*: "Maraiee" was the name given to Malaya by the Japanese during the occupation.

197 **independent Malaya**: Penang and Malacca, the two former Straits Settlements, together with the Malay sultanates of Perlis, Kedah, Perak, Selangor, Negeri Sembilan, Johore, Pahang, Trengganu, and Kelantan, became the Federation of Malaya in 1948. This Federation of Malaya obtained independence in 1957. Malaya became Malaysia in 1963 with the entry of Singapore, Sarawak, and Sabah into the federation. Singapore left Malaysia two years later, in 1965.

197 **returned to the jungle**: John Davies, a Force 136 agent, once told me a story. One day Chin Peng, the secretary-general of the Malayan Communist Party and head of the Malayan People's Anti-Japanese Army, asked him to help his father obtain a business license. This took place after the war, when the British Military Administration was in control. "I tried to move heaven and earth," he told me, "but the BMA was so bloody corrupt." This story illustrates the attitude of British Military Administration officials toward their wartime allies – they could not be bothered about them. Even the intervention of a British official did not yield a business license for the father

of a former chief of the Malayan People's Anti-Japanese Army.
198 **one of his parliamentary secretaries**: A minister in Malaysia is usually assisted by – in order of rank – a deputy minister and a parliamentary secretary.

GARDNER, DISSOLVING REPRESSION: A HALF-CENTURY REPORT
204 **I was given the opportunity**: Thanks to the generosity of a college classmate, Tom Lee.

STYRON, WAR STORIES, PAST AND PRESENT
215 **a monograph**: Nell Devereux Joslin Styron, *Fall of the House of Hinsdale*.

PARALLAX
226 **war casualties**: These figures come from Keegan (92-93, 204-205); see also Williams (597). Some representative figures for the rates of those killed in the military versus those wounded are 250,000 British dead and 277,000 wounded; 300,000 U.S. members of the armed forces dead and 614,000 wounded; 3 million Germans dead and a million wounded.

BERRY, HOME IS ABROAD
229 **family connections**: C. Sulzberger 1969, 6.
229 **the worst book ever printed**: C. Sulzberger 1969, 20.
229 **complete his journey**: C. Sulzberger 1969, 20.
229 **the West knows little about it**: C. Sulzberger 1969, 33.
229 **my two-week option to get out**: C. Sulzberger 1969, 73.
230 **fight the enemy quietly**: All quotations from my mother are taken from M. Sulzberger, 12-15.
232 **two hearts beat as one**: C. Sulzberger 1969, 191.
232 **Papandreou's government**: Andreas Papandreou, the first socialist prime minister of Greece, was elected in 1981, shortly after Greece became the tenth member of the European Economic Community. In his election campaign Papandreou promised change, including the withdrawal of Greece from NATO and the closing of U.S. military bases in Greece. Papandreou died in 1996, after a scandal-filled tenure in office.

Until Papandreou's election there was no separation of church and state in Greece, and in order to be considered married under Greek law, it was necessary to have been married by the Greek Orthodox Church. A marriage certificate from another authority was not recognized. Consequently, when my mother died in 1976, my brother and I were not considered legitimate by the Greek state. We are rather amused by our "bar sinister" and feel like medieval knights.

KILSTON, GLORY REMEMBERED IS HOPE PRESERVED
237 **Glory Remembered Is Hope Preserved**: "Land of Hope and Glory" is the

title of Britain's second most popular patriotic song, written in 1902 and set to the melody of Sir Edward Elgar's *Pomp and Circumstance March No. 1* (played at many high school graduation ceremonies, including my own). It inspired the title of the splendid motion picture made in 1987, *Hope and Glory*, which portrayed the strength and spirit of the British people after their cities were bombed in World War II. The film gave me my title.

238 **on the Odessa steps**: Eisenstein's 1925 film, *Battleship Potemkin*, immortalizes the 1905 rebellion of Russian and Ukrainian citizens and sailors against the oppressive practices of the czarist regime. Its most memorable scene portrays Cossack soldiers at the top of the hundreds of steps leading to the Odessa harbor below, shooting women, children, and scores of other defenseless people as a baby in its carriage rolls down and down the steps.

241 *Get Tough!*: See Fairbairn 1942.

242 **any politician**: Quoted in "Sayings of the Week," *The Observer*, June 17, 1960. Also see the description of the making of *The Great Dictator* in Chaplin's *My Autobiography*. Chaplin writes (387) that he knew very early on that "Hitler must be laughed at."

    I have been a fan of Chaplin's since going, at age six, to his Hollywood studios to see showings of some of his silent films. It is remarkable that he was born just four days before Hitler in 1889 and that they both had (when Chaplin was in his "Little Tramp" guise) famous, nearly identical mustaches. Otherwise they differed mightily, in that one provided joy, the other only pain. One exalted the underdog, the other was for killing underdogs.

242 **Heil myself**: This perfect phrase occurs near the end of Mel Brooks's 1983 remake of the Jack Benny version of *To Be or Not to Be*. The Hitler impersonator (played by Brooks) is responding to the real SS guards on his way out of the theater lobby.

SUN, CHINESE GIRLS DON'T WEAR HATS

247 **December 22, 1943**: My birth date here is the day that has always appeared on documents and that I have always celebrated, but it was calculated according to the Chinese lunar calendar; the date according to the Western solar calendar is actually January 17, 1944.

250 **a bloody massacre of civilians**: Outrageous atrocities were committed by Japanese soldiers. As many as a thousand women and children were raped nightly. Children as well as adults had their eyes gouged out. Others were beheaded, dismembered, or torched. More civilians were brutally slaughtered by the Japanese military in the city of Nanking alone than were killed in the combined atomic bombings of Hiroshima and Nagasaki (as reported in "The John Rabe Diaries: The Good Nazi," *Nightline*, ABC, December 11, 1997).

250 **widely discussed in the media**: For example, "The Tortuous Life of Japanese Comfort Women during World War II," reported by CNN World, as taped by Shanghai TV. This video report, aired in 1997, noted that more than 200,000 Chinese females were kidnapped, starved, and held in captiv-

ity as sex slaves, and that 75 percent of these victims died in captivity.
252 **brigadier general in the Nationalist communication corps**: Because he was a grandnephew of Sun Yat Sen, founder and first president of the Chinese Republic, it was preordained that Pershing's father, Edward Kin Sun, would pursue a military career. His family heritage and his personal celebrity as a former Asian Olympics gold and silver medalist for volleyball and basketball made him especially vulnerable to personal harm or ransom demands if he were captured.

COHEN, THE HOLOCAUST BY MARRIAGE

276 **dollars to plant trees there**: As in other cases, it was common practice at my synagogue's Saturday school to encourage pupils to support the state of Israel by regularly contributing one or more dollars to purchase saplings for planting in Israel, thus producing forests where there had been only barren land.

277 **the Six Day War**: Opposed to the existence of a Jewish state, President Nasser of Egypt called for the destruction of Israel. Egyptian forces packed the Sinai Peninsula, and then Nasser closed the Straits of Tiran, an important trading link between Israel and other countries. Israel considered the closure an act of war and reacted with full force. On June 5, 1967, the Israeli air force destroyed Egyptian air power and then moved in ground forces to Sinai to complete the attack. When Jordanian troops attacked the Israeli half of Jerusalem, Israeli troops seized all of the city and pushed the Jordanian forces back to their side of the Jordan River. In response to intense shelling by Syrian forces in the Golan Heights, Israeli troops also gained complete control over the Golan Heights. In six days the small nation of Israel had defeated the armies of three Arab nations intent on its destruction.

279 *A Spark of Life*: A copy of his account is preserved in the Holocaust museums in Jerusalem and Washington, D.C.

KAFATOU, MY FLIER

282 *A Flier*: This poem was first published in *Ploughshares* 15 (1989):1.72-73.

LEWIS, INNOCENCE AND EXPERIENCE

285 **son, brother, husband, and father**: I romanticize. But I like the words of the great writer on comparative mythology, Mircea Eliade, his oft-cited description and theory in *Cosmos and History* of common cultural and religious myths of origin as an analogy for the feel and function of earliest childhood memory. In Eliade I detect an emotional truth similar to my experience of grappling with memory fragments for the personal meanings that might connect and organize those sightings of my personal dream time – always incomplete, sheared off, broken like the archetypal plots of old ballads, stripped by the parings of oral transmission, and cut adrift from the plausibility structures of history.

286 **Inter-Movement Committee Serving Evacuees**: CIMADE was an interdenominational, evangelical organization founded in 1939; it was comprised of five French Protestant youth movements including the Christian Student Youth Movement, the YMCA, the YWCA, the Boy Scouts, and the Girl Scouts.

290 **His memoir**: Archibald R. Lewis, *A War in the West*.

292 **on a map**: After writing this essay, I did in fact finally locate the village. Michniów appears only on the most detailed maps of present-day Poland. It is a few kilometers south of Skarzysko-Kamiena (north of Kielce), a little to the east of Route E77, on rolling, forested farmland. It sits on the edge of the Sieradowicki national park preserve, named for the nearby Monastery of the Holy Cross.

292 *Auschwitz: A Doctor's Eyewitness Account*: A vivid, disturbing work. Nyiszli's text has been published with Bruno Bettelheim's controversial preface scolding the Hungarian doctor for not taking his own life rather than participating in Joseph Mengele's genetic experiments at the camp clinic.

293 **Primo Levi's recurring dream**: Levi (378 ff.) tells of a dream full of horror that recurred again and again for years after his release from Auschwitz. Each recurrence of the dream asserted that the normal life to which he had returned was in fact a deception – *normal* life was the dream and nothing was true outside the camp to which the recurring dream returned him cruelly, inexorably, destroying the illusion of recovered home, family, and peace.

293 **a piece on Auschwitz**: See K. Lewis 1991.

293 **Simone Weil**: Her views are discussed, for example, in *Waiting for God*.

293 **"Silence"**: The story is translated in Borowski 1976, 161-63.

294 **writing initially on this topic**: See K. Lewis 1981, presented initially at the annual meetings of the Southern Humanities Conference in Charleston, South Carolina.

CHODOROW, INDIVIDUALS IN HISTORY AND HISTORY THROUGH INDIVIDUALS

304 **As I have suggested earlier**: What follows draws upon Chodorow, *The Power of Feelings*.

311 *A Letter without Words*: The film is directed by Lisa Lowenz, granddaughter of the woman whose footage is used in the film. Her grandmother had some of the earliest color home footage in Germany.

312 *17 Rue Saint Fiacre*: Directed by Daniel Meyers.

GLOSSARY

327 **GLOSSARY**: The primary source for historical material in this volume is Neville Williams and Philip Waller, *The Modern World 1763-1992*. Material has also been taken from Asimov, Axelrod and Phillips, Dawidowicz, Dupuy and Dupuy, Gilbert, Goldhagen, Grun, Keegan, Langer, Morris and Morris, Parrish, Shirer, P. Smith, Snyder (1960, 1976), and Urdang.

SOURCES AND WORKS CITED

American Heritage Dictionary of the English Language. Ed. William Morris. Boston: American Heritage Publishing, 1969.

Asimov, Isaac. *Asimov's Chronology of the World*. New York: Harper Collins, 1991.

Axelrod, Alan, and Charles Phillips. *What Everyone Should Know about the Twentieth Century*. Holbrook, MA: Adams Media Corporation, 1998.

Blakely, Mary Kay. *American Mom: Motherhood, Politics, and Humble Pie*. Chapel Hill, NC: Algonquin Books, 1994.

The Book of Common Prayer. [Greenwich, CT]: Seabury Press, 1979.

Borowski, Tadeusz. *This Way for the Gas, Ladies and Gentlemen*. Trans. Barbara Vedder. New York: Penguin, 1976.

Camus, Albert. *Notebooks: 1942-1951*. Trans. Justin O'Brien. New York: Knopf, 1965.

Chamberlain, Brewster, and Marcia Feldman, eds. *The Liberation of the Nazi Concentration Camps 1945: Eyewitness Accounts of the Liberators*. U.S. Government Printing Office for the U.S. Holocaust Memorial Council: Washington, D.C., 1987.

Chaplin, Charlie. *My Autobiography*. 1964. Rpt. New York: Plume, 1992.

Chodorow, Nancy J. *The Power of Feelings: Personal Meaning in Psychoanalysis, Gender, and Culture*. New Haven: Yale University Press, 1999.

Churchill, Winston. *The Grand Alliance*. Boston: Houghton Mifflin, 1950.

Dawidowicz, Lucy S. *The War against the Jews: 1933-45*. New York: Holt, Rinehart, and Winston, 1975.

Dimont, Max. *Jews, God, and History*. New York: Simon and Schuster, 1962.

Dobroszycki, Lucjan. *Survivors of the Holocaust in Poland: A Portrait Based on Jewish Community Records, 1944-1947*. Armonk, NY: M.E. Sharpe, 1994.

Dupuy, R. Ernest, and Trevor N. Dupuy. *The Encyclopedia of Military History: From 3500 B.C. to the Present*. Rev. ed. New York: Harper and Row, 1977.

Eliade, Mircea. *Cosmos and History: The Myth of the Eternal Return*. Trans. Willard R. Trask. New York: Harper, 1959.

Epstein, Helen. *Children of the Holocaust: Conversations with Sons and Daughters of Survivors*. New York: Putnam, 1979.

Erikson, Erik. *Childhood and Society*. New York: W.W. Norton, 1950.

------ *Identity and the Life Cycle: Selected Papers*. New York: International Universities Press, 1959.

------ "Identity and Uprootedness in Our Time." In *Insight and Responsibility: Lectures on the Ethical Implications of Psychoanalytic Insight*. New York: W.W. Norton, 1964. Pp. 81-107.

Fairbairn, William E. *Get Tough!* New York: D. Appleton-Century, 1942.

Faulkner, William. *Absalom, Absalom!* 1986. New York: Vintage, 1990.

Fermi, Rachel, and Esther Samra. *Picturing the Bomb: Photographs from the Secret World of the Manhattan Project*. New York: Harry N. Abrams, 1995.

Field, Hermann, and Kate Field. *Trapped in the Cold War: The Ordeal of an*

American Family. Stanford: Stanford Univercity Press, 2000.
Field, Hermann H., and Stanislaw Mierzenski. *Angry Harvest.* New York: Crowell, 1958.
------ *Duck Lane.* New York: Thomas Y. Crowell, 1961.
Gilbert, Martin. *The Macmillan Atlas of the Holocaust.* New York: Da Capo Press, 1982.
Goldhagen, Daniel. *Hitler's Willing Executioners.* New York: Vintage, 1997.
Grun, Bernard. *The Timetables of History.* New York: Simon and Schuster, 1991.
Heller, Jonathan, ed. *War and Conflict: Selected Images from the National Archives: 1765-1970.* Washington, D.C.: National Archives and Records Administration, 1990.
Höss, Rudolf. *Death Dealer: The Memoirs of the SS Kommandant at Auschwitz.* Ed. Steven Paskuly. Trans. Andrew Pollinger. Buffalo, NY: Prometheus Books, 1992.
Kafatou, Sarah Niles. "A Flier." *Ploughshares* 15 (1989):1.72-73.
Keegan, John. *The Times Atlas of the Second World War.* New York: Harper and Row, 1989.
Langer, William L. *An Encyclopedia of World History: Ancient, Medieval, and Modern, Chronologically Arranged.* 5th ed. Boston: Houghton Mifflin, 1973.
L'Engle, Madeleine. *A Wrinkle in Time.* New York: Farrar, Straus, and Giroux, 1962.
Leopold, Werner F. *Speech Development of a Bilingual Child.* 4 vols. Evanston: Northwestern University Press, 1939-49.
Levi, Primo. *If This Is a Man and The Truce.* Trans. Stuart Woolf. London: Abacus, 1987.
Lewis, Archibald R. *A War in the West.* Worcester: Heffernan Press, 1989.
Lewis, Kevin. "Anybody Who Isn't Schizophrenic These Days Just Isn't Thinking Clearly." In *The Humanities: Philosophical Designs and Practical Visions.* Ed. C. Edward Kaylor. Charleston: Medical School Press of MUSC, 1981. 26-31.
------ "The Clash of Memories at Auschwitz." *The Christian Century* 108 (January 23, 1991), 3.75-77.
Lifton, Robert Jay. *The Nazi Doctors: Medical Killing and the Psychology of Genocide.* New York: Basic Books, 1986.
Lowry, Lois. *Number the Stars.* New York: Yearling/Dell, 1989.
Maclean, Norman. *A River Runs through It and Other Stories.* Chicago: University of Chicago Press, 1976.
Manchester, William. *The Last Lion: Winston Spencer Churchill.* Boston: Little, Brown, 1983.
Mannheim, Karl. "The Problem of Generations." 1928. Rpt. in Mannheim, *From Karl Mannheim: Essays on the Sociology of Knowledge.* Ed. Paul Kecskemeti. London: Routledge & Kegan Paul, 1952. 276-322.
McConahey, William M. *Battalion Surgeon.* Rochester, MN: privately published, 1966.
Millett, Kate. *Sexual Politics.* New York: Doubleday, 1970.
Morris, Jeffrey, and Richard Morris. *Encyclopedia of American History.* New York: Harper Collins, 1996.

Nicolson, Nigel. *Long Life*. New York: G.P. Putnam's Sons, 1998.

Nyiszli, Miklos. *Auschwitz: A Doctor's Eyewitness Account*. Trans. Tibere Kremer and Richard Seaver. With a foreword by Bruno Bettelheim. New York: F. Fell, 1960.

The Ordnance Soldier's Guide: U.S. Army Ordnance Replacement Training Center, Aberdeen Proving Ground. Aberdeen, MD: U.S. Army, 1942.

Parrish, Thomas, ed. *The Simon and Schuster Encyclopedia of World War II*. New York: Simon and Schuster, 1978.

Rabe, John. *The Good Man of Nanking: The Diaries of John Rabe*. Ed. Erwin Wickert. Trans. John E. Woods. New York: A.A. Knopf, 1998.

Rhodes, Richard. *The Making of the Atomic Bomb*. New York: Simon and Schuster, 1986.

Shirer, William L. *The Rise and Fall of the Third Reich: A History of Nazi Germany*. Greenwich, CT: Fawcett, 1960.

Smith, Alice Kimball. *A Peril and A Hope: The Scientists' Movement in America 1945-47*. Chicago: University of Chicago Press, 1965.

Smith, Page. *Democracy on Trial: The Japanese American Evacuation and Relocation in World War II*. New York: Simon and Schuster, 1995.

Snyder, Louis L. *Encyclopedia of the Third Reich*. New York: Marlow and Co., 1976.

------ *The War: A Concise History 1939-1945*. New York: Julian Messner, 1960.

Spiegelman, Art. *Maus: A Survivor's Tale*. New York: Pantheon, 1986.

Steven, Stewart. *Operation Splinter Factor*. Philadelphia: Lippincott, 1974.

Stolper, Gustav. *German Economy, 1870-1940: Issues and Trends*. New York: Reynal and Hitchcock, 1940.

Styron, Nell Devereux Joslin. *Fall of the House of Hinsdale*. Raleigh, NC: privately published, 1986.

Styron, William. *Sophie's Choice*. New York: Random House, 1979.

Sulzberger, C.L. *A Long Row of Candles: Memoirs and Diaries, 1934-1954*. New York: Macmillan, 1969.

------ *Sit-Down with John L. Lewis*. New York: Random House, [ca. 1938].

Sulzberger, Marina. *Marina: Letters and Diaries of Marina Sulzberger*. Ed. C.L. Sulzberger. New York: Crown Publishers, 1978.

Szyk, Arthur. *The New Order*. New York: G.P. Putnam's Sons, 1941.

United States Army in World War II: Pictorial Record: The War Against Germany: Europe and Adjacent Areas. Washington, D.C.: Department of the Army, 1951.

United States Army in World War II: Pictorial Record: The War Against Japan. Washington, C.C. Department of the Army, 1952.

United States Strategic Bombing Survey: Summary Report (European War) September 30, 1945. [Washington, D.C.: U.S.G.P.O.], 1945.

Urdang, Laurence. *The Timetables of American History*. New York: Simon and Schuster, 1996.

Waugh, Evelyn. *Brideshead Revisited*. Boston: Little, Brown, 1975.

Weil, Simone. *Waiting for God*. Trans. Emma Cruafurd. With an introduction by Leslie A. Fiedler. New York: Putnam, 1951.

White, Robert W. *Lives in Progress: A Study of the Natural Growth of Personality*. New York: Holt, Rinehart, and Winston, 1952.

Williams, Neville, and Philip Waller. *The Modern World: 1763-1992*. New York: Simon and Schuster, 1994.

Worthen, Eugene Mark. *Billet Analysis Schedules for APA Enlisted Billets*. Seattle: Bureau of Navy Personnel, APA Pre-Commissioning School, October 1944.

Yahil, Leni. *The Holocaust: The Fate of European Jewry*. New York: Oxford University Press, 1990.

automatic transmission fundamentals

william I. husselbee
santa ana college,
santa ana, california

reston publishing company, inc.
a prentice-hall company
reston, virginia

Library of Congress Cataloging in Publication Data

Husselbee, William L
  Automatic transmission fundamentals.

  1. Automobiles—Transmission devices, Automatic.
I. Title.
TL263.H87 1980   629.2'446   80-10398
ISBN 0-8359-0257-9

© 1980
by Reston Publishing Company, Inc.
A Prentice-Hall Company
Reston, Virginia 22090

All rights reserved. No part of this book may be reproduced in any way, or by any means, without permission in writing from the publisher.

10 9 8 7 6 5 4 3 2 1

Printed in the United States of America

contents

preface ix
chapter one—introduction to automatic transmissions 1
   automatic transmission functions 2
   the engine needs help 2
   torque varies with the engine's operating mode 4
   automatic transmission ratios 6
   ratios provided by other power train components 7
   gear ratios also are torque ratios 8
   advantages of using automatic transmissions 9
   summary 9
   check-up questions 10
chapter two—gear construction and design 12
   torque multiplication of gears 13
   planetary gear train 18
   ratios achieved by simple planetary gearsets 19
   compound planetary gear trains 23
   Simpson gear train 28
   ratios of a Simpson gear train 31
   summary 34
   check-up questions 36
chapter three—automatic transmission fluids 40
   fluid functions 40
   fluid structure 43
   fluid types and usage 45
   fluid cooling 47
   fluid energy 50
   fluid force and pressure 51
   summary 53
   check-up questions 53

chapter four—torque converters 56
- need for a coupling device 56
- fluid coupling design 58
- fluid motions produced by the impeller 61
- coupling operation 64
- converter as a torque multiplier 66
- stator operation—torque increase 67
- stator operation—coupling phase 69
- lock-up converters 70
- lock-up converter design 71
- lock-up converter operation 73
- advantages provided by torque converters 74
- converter size and torque capacity 74
- combination low and high capacity converters 75
- advantages of using variable pitch stators 76
- converter installation 77
- other converter functions 78
- summary 79
- check-up questions 81

chapter five—clutches used in automatic transmissions 85
- function of the clutch 85
- disc clutch design 86
- primary clutch operation 90
- secondary clutch design and operation 92
- stationary clutch design 92
- stationary clutch operation 94
- mechanical overrunning clutches 95
- roller clutch design 96
- roller clutch operation (stator mounted) 96
- sprag clutch design 97
- sprag clutch operation (carrier mounted) 97
- summary 98
- check-up questions 99

chapter six—bands and servos 102
- band function 102
- band design 104
- band operation 107
- function of servos 109
- servo design and operation 109
- band adjustments 112
- summary 114
- check-up questions 115

chapter seven—hydraulic fundamentals 118
- hydrostatics 119

hydraulic levers 120
force 120
pressure 121
pressure on a confined fluid 121
force multiplication 122
piston travel 123
basic hydraulic system 124
system operation 125
summary 127
check-up questions 128

chapter eight—automatic transmission hydraulic pumps-function 131
rotary pump theory 132
gear pump design 134
gear pump operation 136
rotor pump design 137
rotor pump operation 138
pump displacement 138
pump capacity 138
pump efficiency 139
multiple pump systems 139
benefits of multiple pump systems 140
pump reservoir, filters, and vent 141
summary 142
check-up questions 143

chapter nine—hydraulic pressure control system-function 146
relief valve design 147
relief valve operation 147
pressure-regulating valve function 149
spool valve design 150
spool valve operation 151
pressure regulator design 152
pressure regulator valve operation—noncompensated 153
pressure regulator valve operation—compensated 155
summary 156
check-up questions 157

chapter ten—hydraulic relay valves 160
function of the valve 160
manual valve function and design 161
manual valve operation 163
shift valve function 167
shift valve train design 168
shift valve operation 171
other flow control valves—ball check valve 174
orifice 176

vi CONTENTS

    accumulator function and design 177
    accumulator operation 178
    summary 179
    check-up questions 180

chapter eleven—hydraulic signal devices..183
    governor function..183
    single-stage governor design 185
    single-stage governor operation 186
    two-stage governor design 186
    two-stage governor operation 188
    throttle valve function 189
    throttle valve design—mechanically activated 190
    throttle valve operation 190
    design of vacuum-controlled throttle valve trains 192
    operation of vacuum-controlled throttle valves 194
    kickdown valve function and design 196
    kickdown valve operation 197
    design of an electrically-operated kickdown valve....................................197
    electrically-controlled kickdown valve operation 200
    timing valves found in the hydraulic system 200
    summary 201
    check-up questions 203

chapter twelve—hydraulic system sealing devices—their function.......206
    leakage control—a large task 206
    static sealing devices—gaskets 209
    lathe-cut seals 211
    o-ring seals..212
    dynamic sealing devices 213
    dynamic lathe-cut seals..214
    dynamic o-ring seals 215
    dynamic lip seals...216
    metal-clad lip seals...217
    metal sealing rings 222
    teflon seals 223
    summary 223
    check-up questions 224

chapter thirteen—hydraulic system diagrams—their function 227
    symbols used on diagrams 229
    circuit codes 231
    valve definitions 233
    interpreting the diagrams 234
    trouble-shooting malfunctions using hydraulic diagrams 238
    summary 240
    check-up questions 241

chapter fourteen—operation of the transmission 243
    description of a T-300 transmission 243
    converter 244
    planetary gear train 245
    forward clutch 245
    low band 246
    reverse clutch 246
    function of hydraulic system components 246
    neutral or park—hydraulic operation 250
    neutral or park—powerflow 250
    drive, low-range—hydraulic operation 251
    drive, low-range—powerflow 253
    drive, direct—drive hydraulic operation 253
    drive, direct—powerflow 255
    reverse ratio—hydraulic operation 255
    reverse ratio—powerflow 257
    description of the torqueflite transmission 257
    converter 258
    planetary gear train 258
    clutches 259
    bands 260
    function of hydraulic system components 261
    neutral and park—hydraulic operation 264
    neutral and park—powerflow 265
    drive, breakaway—hydraulic operation 266
    drive, breakaway—powerflow 267
    drive, second—hydraulic operation 268
    drive, second—powerflow 269
    drive, third—hydraulic operation 270
    drive, third—powerflow 271
    reverse—hydraulic operation 272
    reverse—powerflow 273
    summary 274
    check-up questions 276
appendix 280
index 288

The goal of this text is to cover in a clear and detailed manner the basic fundamentals of automatic transmission construction and operation. Once a person masters these fundamentals, he can apply them to any type of automatic transmission because they all operate in much the same manner. In other words, the material covered in this book applies to all types of modern automatic transmissions.

This book covers automatic transmission theory; it is not a service manual. But when utilized with the Shop workbook *Automatic Transmission Service,* **the two books will provide the student in a vocational high school, trade school, or community college with the knowledge and skills necessary for entrance into the specialized field of automatic transmission service and repair.**

A thorough knowledge of automatic transmission theory is very important to a person desiring to become a transmission technician for several reasons. First, an understanding of how the automatic transmission operates is necessary before the mechanic can successfully diagnose malfunctions in the various types of units. If a person does not know what the various components of the transmission do or how they interact with other parts to make the unit operate, it will be extremely hard for him to locate and correct different kinds of problems which occur within the various units.

Second, by understanding the construction and operation of the many transmission components, the mechanic will have less difficulty in grasping the service requirements of the various types of automatic transmissions. For instance, by knowing the construction of a typical multiple-disc clutch assembly and its operation, the technician will better understand the reasons behind the need for installing new seals, soaking new clutch discs, and checking clutch disc clearance when overhauling the transmission. Also, since most all of these clutch assemblies have similar construction, operation, and service requirements, it will be easy for the repairman to apply this knowledge when rebuilding units he is not familiar with.

In order to provide the reader with a clear explanation of how the automatic transmission operates, this text describes the function, design, and operation of each of the major transmission components. It explains how these components interact with one another in order to make the whole unit operational. The last section of the text explains in detail the mechanical and hydraulic operation of a two- and a three-speed automatic transmission; here the knowledge of component design, function, and operation will be put to good use.

The mechanical components covered in this book are the planetary gear train and the overrunning clutch. Chapter 2 reviews gear design and how the gear uses the principle of the lever to control both torque and speed. Then it describes the design, function, and ratios achieved by a simple planetary gearset, in addition to the compound and Simpson planetary gear trains.

Chapter 3 is an important description of automatic transmission fluids. The chapter describes the purpose, types, and structure of the fluid. Also, it provides information on the two types of factory systems, along with several kinds of after-market devices utilized to cool the fluid.

Chapter 4 is devoted to torque converters and deals with the construction, purpose, and operation of these units. It describes all the converter components and how they function. This explanation also points out how the impeller produces Vortex and Rotary fluid flows within the converter. Finally, the chapter explains the operation of the standard, lock-up, and variable-pitch torque converters.

Two types of overrunning clutches are covered in Chapter 5, the roller and the sprag. This description points out the purpose and design of both of these units. And it explains the operation of a stator-mounted, overrunning clutch and a carrier-mounted, sprag clutch.

In Chapters 5 and 6 the reader will find a thorough description of the different types of friction clutches and servo-operated brake bands. These explanations contain the design, function, and operation of these units and relate how these units control planetary gear train operation.

Chapters 7–13 deal with the subject of hydraulics. Without the effects of hydraulics, the transmission could not function. Therefore, the subject matter contained in these chapters is very important to understanding automatic transmission operation. The reader should study them very carefully.

Hydraulic fundamentals are dealt with in Chapter 7, including hydraulic levers, force, and pressure in addition to "Pascal's Law." Further, the chapter describes the basic components of a simple hydraulic system and then explains how these parts operate together to make a simple hydraulic system transmit pressure and motion.

Chapter 8 begins the explanation of the actual hydraulic components of the transmission by describing the various types and designs of hydraulic pumps and how they operate. Chapter 9 covers relief valves and pressure-regulating valve circuits. Chapter 10 explains the design, function, and operation of manual, shift, and check valves. There are descriptions in Chapter 11 of the three types of hydraulic signaling devices, the governor, throttle, and kickdown valves.

Hydraulic system sealing devices are covered in Chapter 12. Various problems encountered in attempting to seal the hydraulic system against excessive fluid leakage are described. The chapter also covers the different types of sealing devices utilized in an automatic transmission, in addition to how the mechanic should install certain types and why the manufacturers use certain seal designs in a given location.

Chapter 13 covers circuit or system diagrams. This chapter describes the special symbols and codes utilized on the schematics, and it also explains how to interpret these charts and utilize them in trouble-shooting transmission malfunctions.

And finally, Chapter 14 explains the operation of two transmissions, the T-300 and the Torqueflite. This description includes the major hydraulic and mechanical components of each transmission. Also, it covers the hydraulic operation and mechanical powerflow of both units in the Drive and Reverse ranges.

1

introduction to automatic transmissions

Since 1940, the automotive industry has designed and manufactured many types of fully automatic transmissions. The differences that exist among them lie in component structure, size and some variations in hydraulic system operation. As for their basic operation, they all operate in much the same manner. Therefore, the person who understands the operation of one automatic transmission can apply this knowledge to other transmission types. Before studying the actual construction and operation of an automatic transmission, the reader should understand a few basic facts. This chapter covers the functions of an automatic transmission, characteristics of piston engines that make a transmission necessary, speed and torque ratios, and advantages of an automatic transmission over the manual shift type.

Located between the engine and drive wheels, the automatic transmission is a component of the power train. The power train has the task of carrying the rotary motion developed in the engine to the drive wheels (Fig. 1–1). The number and type of components needed by the power train depend on the type of transmission used, the location of the drive wheels, and the location of the engine. For example, the power train of a vehicle with a standard (manual-shift) transmission will consist of a friction clutch, transmission, drive shaft, differential, and the rear axles. On the other hand, vehicles with automatic transmission use, as part of the above-mentioned power train, a torque

2 INTRODUCTION TO AUTOMATIC TRANSMISSIONS

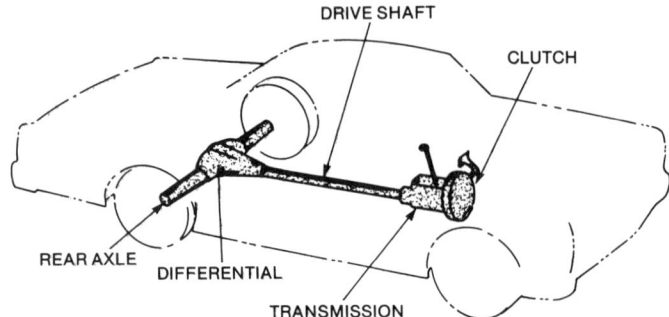

fig. 1-1 Typical power train on an automobile with a conventional transmission.

converter instead of the foot-operated clutch. Finally, motor vehicles that use either front-wheel drive or rear-mounted engines do not require drive shafts to complete their power trains.

automatic transmission functions

The automatic transmission is a torque transferring and multiplying device that can also change the direction of the drive wheels and act as a braking device. *Torque* is a twisting effort produced by the engine. If the engine is operating and the driver places the shift level into a forward or reverse driving range, torque will pass through the automatic transmission. Furthermore, if the engine becomes overloaded during acceleration or from pulling a vehicle up an incline, the transmission will multiply torque without the operator moving the gear selector into a lower driving range. But some automatic transmission designs also give the driver partial to full manual control of all driving ranges. Also, the automatic transmission provides a means to reverse the direction of the drive wheels so that the vehicle can go backwards. Most automatic transmissions provide a lower gear range that, when activated under certain conditions, will force the engine to act like a brake to slow the vehicle down. This braking action of the engine is especially useful when the vehicle is moving down a long mountain grade to prevent the brakes from overheating.

the engine needs help

As previously mentioned, the function of the engine is to produce torque that rotates the drive wheels in order to set the vehicle in motion and to maintain certain road speeds. But engine torque is not sufficient to propel the vehicle under all driving conditions because of certain engine operating characteristics (Fig. 1-2). First, if an engine is under a load and operating at low speeds, torque output is low but reaches a maximum value at about 50 to 60 percent of the engine speed giving maximum horsepower. Above this 50 to 60 percent range, torque begins to taper off. Second, if an engine is operating with no load applied, torque output will be lower than that of a loaded engine operating at the

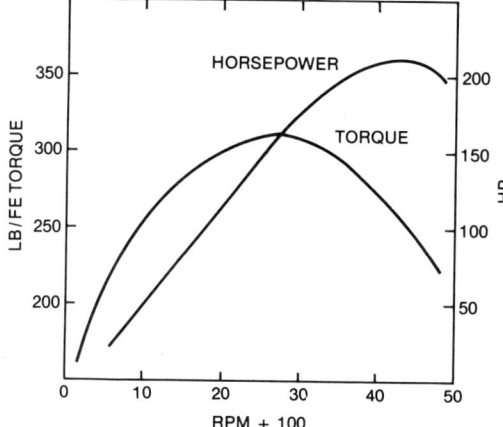

fig. 1-2 Torque and horsepower output curves of a typical piston engine.

same speed. Third, the engine will not produce any additional torque than is necessary to rotate the drive wheels. Finally, the engine will not operate under an excessive load condition.

In order to clarify the reasons for these engine characteristics, a description of torque production by an operating engine is necessary. For simplicity, the discussion will focus on the operation of a single cylinder engine. Just keep in mind that final engine torque output will be the result of the total number of cylinders the engine has all working together.

Torque is the tendency of a force, a pushing or pulling effort, to produce rotation of an object on its axis; the unit of measurement for torque is pound-feet. In the case of the gasoline-piston engine, the force will be the pressure caused by the burning air-fuel mixture pressing downward on the piston head. Since the connecting rod attaches the piston to the crankshaft, the downward piston movement forces the crankshaft (the object) to rotate (Fig. 1–3).

The factors that determine the extent of the force produced by a piston on the crankshaft are the bore of the cylinder, the stroke of the piston, the compression ratio, and the quantity of air-fuel mixture admitted into the cylinder and combustion chamber. The *bore* is the diameter of the cylinder; the *stroke* is the distance the piston travels from the top to the bottom of the cylinder or from the bottom to the top; *compression ratio* is the volume of the cylinder and combustion chamber when the piston is at the bottom divided by the volume when the piston is at the top. These factors are design dimensions of the engine. In order to change these dimensions, a complete reworking of the engine is necessary.

On the other hand, the quantity of the air-fuel mixture entering the cylinder varies with throttle valve position. The throttle valve of the carburetor operates by mechanical linkage connected to the gas pedal, and opens to allow additional air-fuel mixture into the cylinder as the driver presses down on the gas pedal. When the driver releases foot pressure on the gas pedal, the throttle valve closes and restricts the amount of air-fuel

4 INTRODUCTION TO AUTOMATIC TRANSMISSIONS

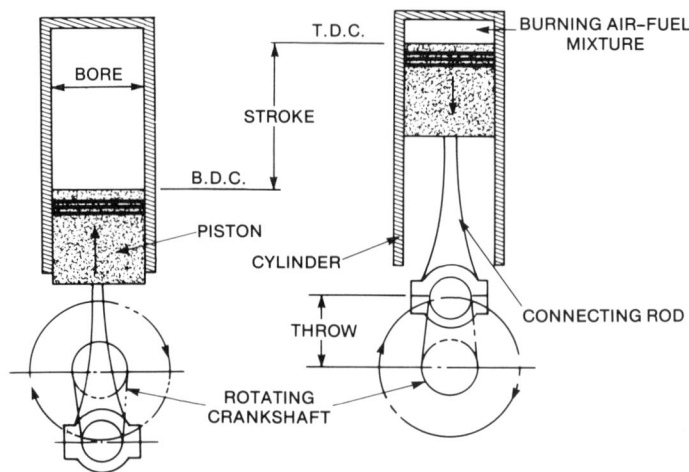

fig. 1-3 Torque production with the piston engine.

entering the cylinder (Fig. 1-4). It should now be apparent that the main factor used to raise or lower torque output of an operating engine is the amount of air-fuel mixture allowed to enter the cylinder.

torque varies with the engine's operating mode

The amount of torque produced by a loaded engine varies with speed. For example, when the engine is operating at idle speed, measured in revolutions per minute (rpm), with the automatic transmission in gear, the throttle valve allows a relatively small air-fuel charge to enter the cylinders. Engine vacuum at this time will be relatively high. Since the quantity of the air-fuel charge determines the force applied to the pistons, total engine torque output at this time will be too low to set the vehicle in motion. As the driver opens the throttle valve to accelerate the vehicle, vacuum drops and additional air-fuel

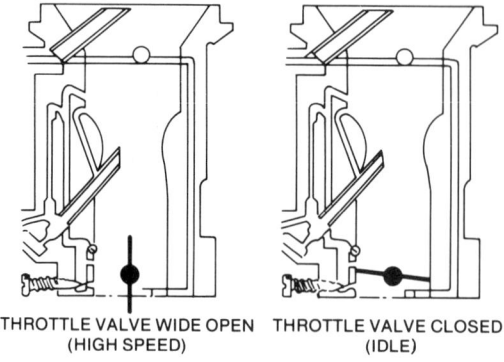

THROTTLE VALVE WIDE OPEN (HIGH SPEED)   THROTTLE VALVE CLOSED (IDLE)

fig. 1-4 The carburetor throttle valve controls engine speed and torque by regulating the amount of air-fuel mixture entering the engine.

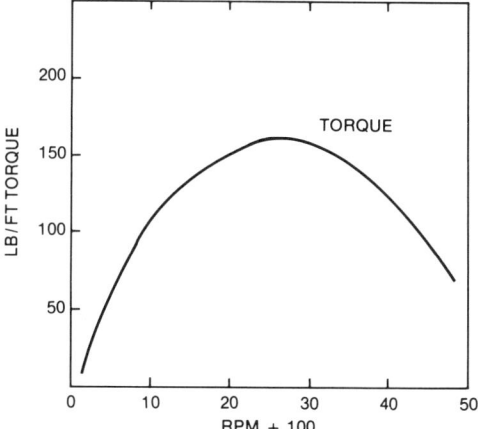

fig. 1-5 Torque curve of a loaded piston engine.

mixture enters the cylinders; consequently, torque will rapidly increase until torque reaches a maximum near the midpoint in the engine's operating range (Fig. 1-5). To assist the engine, the automatic transmission and torque converter multiply engine torque from the moment the driver releases the brakes until the engine reaches sufficient torque to propel the vehicle.

An unloaded engine operating at the same rpms as a loaded engine of the same size produces less torque than the loaded engine. This engine characteristic is also the result of throttle valve action. To accelerate both engines to a given rpm, the unloaded engine will require a smaller throttle valve opening than the loaded engine; consequently, a smaller opening results in a higher engine vacuum and a smaller quantity of air-fuel mixture entering the cylinders of the unloaded engine. This reduced charge, when ignited, produces less push on each of the piston heads with the result of a decrease in torque output.

Since the action of the throttle valve and the rate of air-fuel flow controls torque output, the engine never produces any additional torque than is necessary. For example, to maintain a given vehicle's road speed, an engine must develop a torque of 150 pounds-foot. The driver depresses the gas pedal until the vehicle reaches the desired road speed. The opening of the throttle valve allows enough air-fuel charge to enter the cylinders to produce the 150 pounds-foot of engine torque—and no more. In other words, the engine produces just enough torque to bring the vehicle up to a certain speed.

The engine will not operate if overloaded. An engine of a certain bore, stroke, and compression ratio will produce, with a sufficient charge of air-fuel mixture, an output of torque that is sufficient to rotate the drive wheels of most moving vehicles on a level road. If, at any time, the torque needed to rotate the drive wheels exceeds the maximum torque production of the engine, the transmission or some other torque multiplying device must increase the torque coming from the engine, or the engine will stall. Even if the engine is operating at a point of maximum torque output and the amount of torque was high enough to set the vehicle in motion, the acceleration would be slow, noisy, and

6 INTRODUCTION TO AUTOMATIC TRANSMISSIONS

sometimes uncomfortable for the occupants of the vehicle. Furthermore, the engine speed would be too high, placing a strain on the engine as well as the other power train components of the vehicle. With the knowledge of the engine's torque characteristics in mind, it should be apparent why the automatic transmission and other power train components are necessary to multiply torque and control engine speed.

automatic transmission ratios

As previously mentioned, the automatic transmission provides the vehicle with various driving ranges or ratios that control engine speed. The component within the automatic transmission that produces these ratios is the planetary gear set. The actual ratio is the relative speed of the transmission's input shaft that brings torque into the transmission to the speed of the transmission's output shaft that delivers torque to the drive shaft or directly to the ring and pinion (Fig. 1–6). The transmission manufacturers express gear ratios in numeral form. For example, a certain planetary gear set provides a ratio of 2.50:1. A 2.50:1 ratio means that the input shaft is making two and a half revolutions to each complete revolution of the output shaft.

If the engine were to drive the input shaft, the engine also would be rotating two and a half times faster than the transmission's output shaft.

Planetary gear trains provide two or more forward ratios and a reverse. A lower gear ratio, such as the 2.50:1 mentioned above, allows the engine to operate at a higher speed while the drive wheels turn at a lower speed. A high-gear ratio, on the other hand, permits the input and output transmission shafts to revolve at the same speed, 1:1 or one to one. In the case of the 1:1 ratio the engine will still be operating faster than the drive wheels because of the gear ratio provided by the ring and pinion. An overdrive ratio, approximately 1:1.50, permits the engine and input shaft to revolve slower than the transmission's output shaft. Finally, the reverse gear ratio not only provides a speed differential between the input and output shafts but also a change of direction.

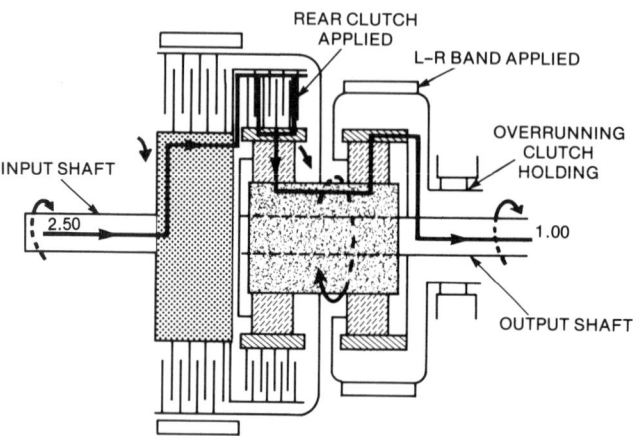

fig. 1–6 Gear ratio between the automatic transmission's input and output shafts.

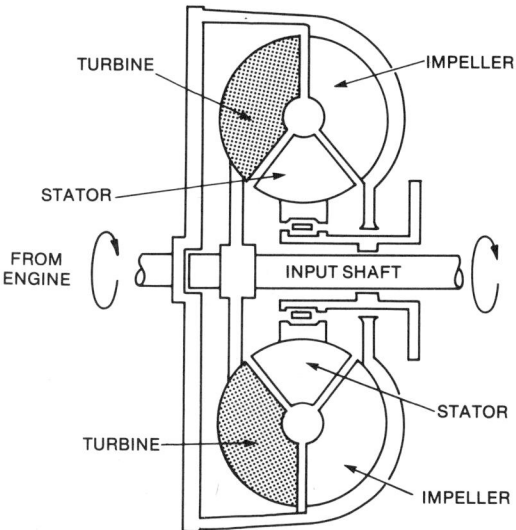

fig. 1-7 The impeller and the turbine of the torque converter.

ratios provided by other power train components

The torque converter which replaced the foot-operated clutch produces an unlimited number of speed ratios. The torque converter is a device that uses the impact energy of moving fluid to transmit torque from the engine's crankshaft to the automatic transmission's input shaft. To transmit torque, the converter has two main moving parts: the *impeller* and the *turbine* (Fig. 1-7). The impeller and turbine operate within a sealed housing that is full of fluid.

The speed ratio of the torque converter is the number of revolutions the impeller rotates compared to a single rotation of the turbine and input shaft. For example, with a stationary vehicle, with the engine operating at idle and the transmission in gear, the impeller rotates at engine speed but the turbine is stationary. The speed ratio is zero, the converter producing zero percent efficiency. The engine will be rotating the impeller at about 600 rpm, but the turbine is still. On the other hand, if the impeller is turning at 1,000 rpm and the turbine at 900 rpm, the converter efficiency now is about 90 percent. Between zero speed ratio and a ratio of about 1:9, the converter produces a wide range of constantly changing speed ratios.

The ring and pinion gears that are part of the drive axle assembly produce a fixed gear ratio between the transmission's output shaft and the drive axles (Fig. 1-8). This gear ratio which varies between 3:1 and 5:1 for passenger car applications serves to control engine rpm and engine torque output during all phases of vehicle operation. For instance, when the automatic transmission is operating in a low gear, the transmission's ratio is multiplied by the ring and pinion ratio to produce the total speed ratio between the input shaft and the drive axles. If the transmission is operating in low gear that has a 2.5:1 ratio and the ring and pinion ratio is 5:1, the total speed ratio is 12.5:1. The converter ratios are effective during this time, but since these ratios are changing very

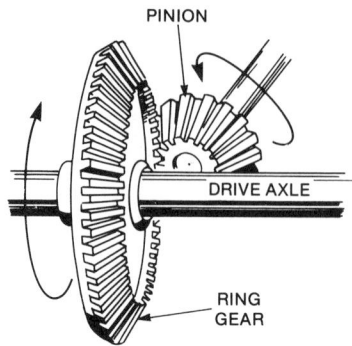

fig. 1-8 The ring and pinion gears of the drive axle assembly provide a fixed gear ratio between the transmission's output shaft and the drive axles.

rapidly, it is difficult to figure them into the total speed reduction between the engine and drive wheels. Also, when the automatic transmission upshifts to high gear, the ring and pinion ratio remains effective in controlling engine rpm. At vehicle cruising speed, the engine should be nearly producing maximum torque, but the ring and pinion ratio also have the effect on the vehicle of reducing engine load by increasing torque. By allowing the engine to operate the vehicle with less torque output, the engine has some reserve torque which the driver can use to accelerate the vehicle. Therefore, the automatic transmission will not have to downshift whenever the engine receives additional demands for torque. The disadvantage in utilizing a ring and pinion ratio of more than 1:1, direct drive, is a loss of fuel economy. A 1:1 ratio is more economical because the engine would be operating at a more efficient speed, but when additional engine torque is necessary to accelerate the vehicle, the transmission would have to downshift into a ratio that provided the necessary torque increase.

gear ratios also are torque ratios

Whenever a set of gears provide a speed reduction between two objects, the gears also multiply torque or produce a torque increase ratio between the two. For example, the low gear of an automatic transmission has a gear ratio of 2.5:1 between the input and output shafts. The torque increase ratio would be 1:2.5. Now, if the input shaft's torque is 100 pounds-foot, the output shaft's would be 100 pounds-foot times 2.5 or 250 pounds-foot. The same rule applies for the ring and pinion gear ratio except the torque increase would be between the transmission's output shaft and the drive wheels. As in the case of speed ratios, the total vehicle torque ratio is equal to the transmission's ratio multiplied by the ring and pinion ratio. The important idea to remember is that speed reduction also means torque increase, and the speed reductions allow the engine to operate at a more efficient torque producing rpm while the gears themselves are increasing torque.

The torque converter also has the ability to multiply as well as transmit torque. In order to accomplish a torque increase, the converter requires a third component called a stator. The stator fits between the impeller and turbine and begins to multiply torque whenever there is an impeller to turbine speed ratio greater than about 1:9. Since the speed ratios of the torque converter vary, the torque ratios do also. The maximum torque ratio of most automotive converters is about 1:2.25 and vary during acceleration until it reaches 1:1 which is zero torque increase, direct coupling.

advantages of using automatic transmissions

In any type of motor vehicle, the automatic transmission offers several advantages over the manual-shift transmission. The automatic transmission provides the vehicle with a smooth start, proper upshift pattern, and the best possible gear ratios for all driving conditions. The automatic transmission also responds to the will of the driver as well as to the requirements of the various highway and vehicle speed conditions. An automatic transmission makes a motor vehicle more comfortable and easier to drive because this transmission requires no foot-operated clutch to set the vehicle in motion or to shift gears; consequently, the driving of the vehicle in heavy traffic or up a steep, twisting mountain road requires little driver effort. Finally, the automatic transmission, with its simple-to-operate controls, requires little skill on the part of the driver to start the vehicle in motion, or to select the proper gear ratio at the correct time.

summary

1. The automatic transmission is a member of the power train team.
2. The automatic transmission is a torque transferring and multiplying device that can also change the direction of the drive wheels and act as a braking device.
3. Under certain driving conditions the engine will not produce enough torque to propel a vehicle.
4. High gas pressure, caused by a burning air-fuel charge, forces the piston and rod to rotate the crankshaft.
5. In an operating engine, the quantity of air-fuel mixture admitted to each cylinder determines torque output.
6. At engine idle, torque output is low; but engine torque reaches a maximum around the midpoint in the engine's operating range.
7. Engines will not produce any more torque than needed and will not operate under an overload condition.
8. Gear ratios control engine rpm and multiply torque.
9. The automatic transmission, torque converter, and ring and pinion gears provide speed ratios and torque multiplication.

10 INTRODUCTION TO AUTOMATIC TRANSMISSIONS

check-up questions

The questions listed below will assist you in determining how well you remember the material contained in this chapter. Read each question carefully before choosing the answer to each item. If you can't answer the question, review the section in the chapter that covers the question.

1. Torque defined is a _____.
    a. twisting effort
    b. push-pull effort
    c. up and down effort
    d. law of inertia
2. The engine, when it is operating, produces _____.
    a. inertia
    b. energy
    c. torque
    d. force
3. Engine torque output is low during _____ speeds.
    a. idle
    b. high
    c. intermediate
    d. both b and c
4. The factor that alters torque production of an operating engine is the _____.
    a. bore
    b. stroke
    c. size of the valves
    d. quantity of the air-fuel mixture
5. Automatic transmission ratios are between the _____ and the _____.
    a. output shaft, differential
    b. input shaft, output shaft
    c. engine, input shaft
    d. engine, differential
6. A ring and pinion ratio of 3:1 means that the transmission's output shaft will be rotating _____ faster than the drive wheels.
    a. one time
    b. two times
    c. three times
    d. both a and c

7. If an engine produces a torque at 100 pounds-foot and the transmission has a 3.1 gear ratio, torque increases to _____ before leaving the transmission.
   a. 50 pounds-foot
   b. 150 pounds-foot
   c. 225 pounds-foot
   d. 300 pounds-foot
8. If the torque converter is operating at 90 percent efficiency, the impeller will be turning at about 1,000 rpm but the turbine will be rotating at _____.
   a. 700 rpm
   b. 900 rpm
   c. 1,000 rpm
   d. 1,200 rpm
9. The ring and pinion ratio increases _____.
   a. torque
   b. fuel economy
   c. force
   d. energy
10. The part of the torque converter that multiplies torque is the _____.
    a. impeller
    b. turbine
    c. housing
    d. stator

For the answers to these check-up questions, turn to the Appendix located at the back of the text.

2

gear construction and design

As previously mentioned, transmission and the ring and pinion gears transfer torque and can provide the vehicle with changes in speed, torque and direction. To be able to accomplish these functions, a gear must be very strong and have certain design features. *Gears* are nothing more than wheels which have small extensions called teeth around their circumference (Fig. 2-1). In order to withstand the torque loads, gears have to be made of high-quality material such as steel alloy, nickel, and chromium which, while red hot, a machine hammers into the general shape of a gear. Then, precision machinery cuts the teeth and other precision areas. Finally, a special heat-treating process produces a smooth, hard surface on the gear teeth combining with a somewhat softer but tough gear body.

    Designed into the construction of each gear are features such as teeth clearances, circle, pitch and root diameters, in addition to gear teeth angle. When two gears are in mesh, some tip and backlash clearances which are several thousands of an inch each must exist between the mating gear teeth to allow for lubrication expansion and possible size irregularities (Fig. 2-2). Circle diameter refers to the circumference—the full distance—around the gear. On the other hand, pitch diameter is an imaginary line running through the gear teeth at a point about half way from the bottom to the tip of the teeth; pitch diameter is the true diameter utilized in calculating exact gear ratios. The

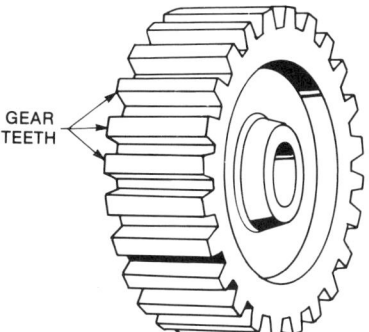

fig. 2-1 A gear is a wheel that has extensions called teeth located around its circumference.

minimum diameter of the gear is the root diameter. Finally, automatic transmission gears are not cut straight but are cut at an angle which increases the gear's strength and promotes quieter operation (Fig. 2-3).

torque multiplication of gears

To alter torque, transmission gears use the principle of the lever and the fulcrum. A *lever* is a simple machine that can serve two purposes: (1) it provides a mechanical advantage; (2) it changes the direction of applied forces. A simple lever is nothing more than a rigid bar which rotates around a fixed point called a *fulcrum* (Fig. 2-4).

By applying a small force over a greater distance, the lever can use a small input force to move a larger output force. For example, if a person cannot lift a heavy box, he could position a crowbar or lever (Fig. 2-5) and lift the box with half the effort that would normally be necessary to raise it. Suppose that in order to raise the end of the box, 200 pounds of force is necessary. By placing the lever under the box at a location 1 foot from the fulcrum and pushing downward on the opposite end of the lever at a point two feet from the fulcrum, only a 100 pounds of downward force is necessary to move the box

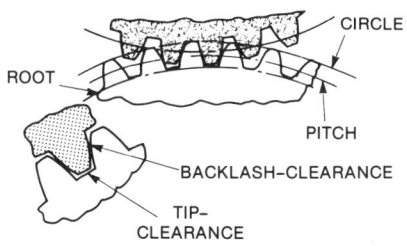

fig. 2-2 The circle, pitch, and root diameters in addition to the backlash and tip clearances of a typical gear.

14 GEAR CONSTRUCTION AND DESIGN

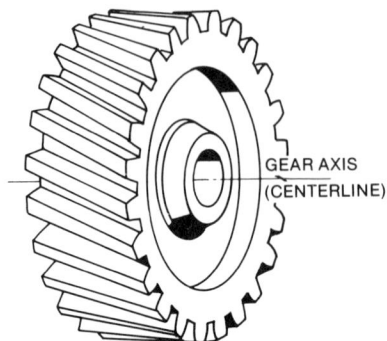

fig. 2–3 The teeth of a helical gear are at an angle to the gear's axis.

upward. Notice that in this situation the box (output force) and the downward force (input force) are moving in opposite directions.

The term given to the relationship, or ratio, between the input and output forces is *mechanical advantage.* In the example above, the ratio is between the input force of 100 pounds and the output force of 200 pounds, or 1:2. If a ratio is 1:1, the lever performs no mechanical advantage.

In gaining a mechanical advantage between the input and output forces, the distance each force travels is different. In the above example, the input force travels two inches downward to raise the output force one inch. In other words, the person lifting the box must apply the downward input force over a longer distance in order to raise the box. The ratio for the distance traveled by the input and output forces is two inches to one inch, 2:1. Whenever the lever produces a mechanical advantage, watch for an accompanying loss in distance traveled by the output force.

Gear design is such that it will provide a mechanical advantage in the same manner as a simple lever. For instance, if a clamp or other device secured a simple lever to a movable pipe or shaft and someone applied a force to one end of the lever that caused the lever to move either up or down, the shaft would rotate (Fig. 2–6). The shaft's rotation is known as *shaft torque,* and the amount of shaft torque is equal to the applied force on the lever arm multiplied by the distance the force is applied from the center of the fulcrum of the shaft. For example, a 20 pound force pushes down on the lever at a point one foot from the fulcrum point, the attached shaft will rotate with a torque or 20 pounds times one foot or 20 pounds-foot. Also, if the shaft torque is known, the output

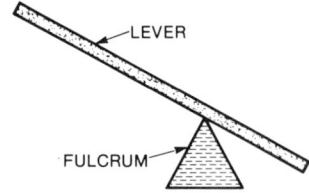

fig. 2–4 A simple lever and fulcrum.

TORQUE MULTIPLICATION OF GEARS 15

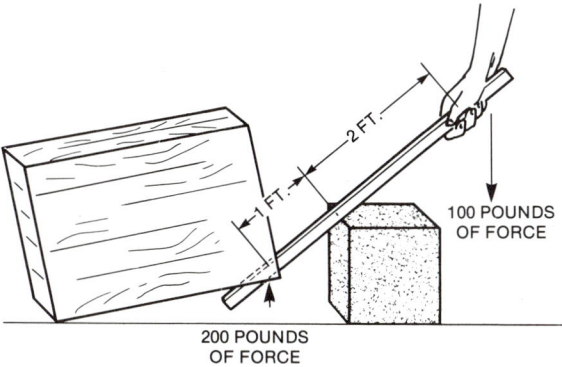

fig. 2–5 A lever utilized to lift a heavy box.

force at the ends of the lever is equal to shaft torque divided by the lever's radius. For instance, a shaft delivers 30 pounds-foot of torque to a lever arm with a radius of one foot, the output force on the ends of the lever will be 30 pounds-foot or 30 pounds (Fig. 2–7).

If the end of one simple lever contacts the end of a second lever, force can move from one lever to the other. The same situation occurs anytime two gears are in mesh. The gear teeth act as lever ends that extend all around each gear (Fig. 2–8). On the small gear, the ends of each lever (teeth) will apply a push (force) on the teeth (lever ends) of the second gear. Each gear rotates around its own center which is the fulcrum point but in opposite directions. As shown in Fig. 2–8, the small gear is the input gear in that the input shaft drives the gear at its fulcrum point. The large gear is the output gear because the shaft attached to its fulcrum point is the output shaft.

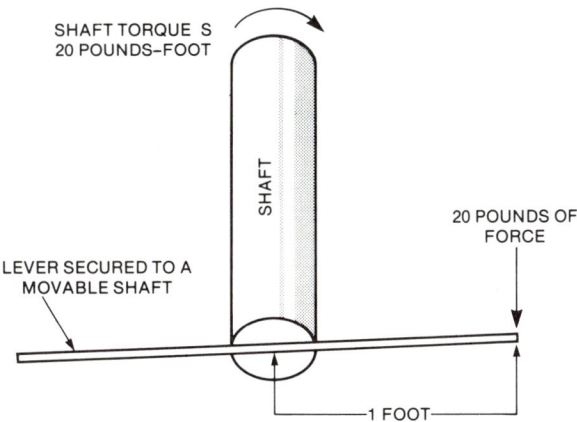

fig. 2–6 The movement of a shaft mounted lever causes the shaft to twist or torque.

16 GEAR CONSTRUCTION AND DESIGN

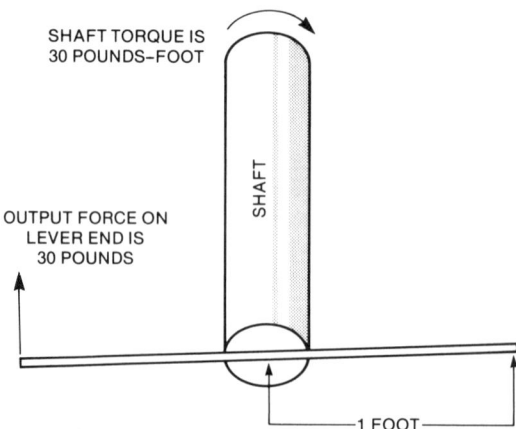

fig. 2-7 Rotation of the shaft causes the ends of the lever to move with a given amount of force.

In the above arrangement, any time the input shaft turns, torque multiplication occurs in the output shaft. To understand how this torque increase takes place, an explanation of each step in the flow of torque, which many people refer to as powerflow, between the two shafts is necessary. If the input shaft applies a torque of 150 pounds-foot to the fulcrum point of a gear which has a radius of two feet (Fig. 2-8), the gear teeth will have an output force of $\frac{150 \text{ pounds-foot}}{2 \text{ feet}}$ or 75 pounds. Since the output gear has a radius of four feet, the torque of the output shaft is 75 pounds times four feet or 300

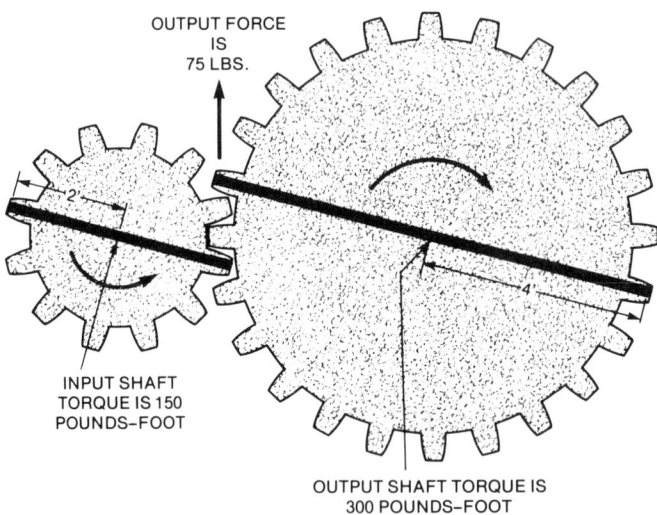

fig. 2-8 The gear teeth act as lever ends that extend all around each gear.

TORQUE MULTIPLICATION OF GEARS 17

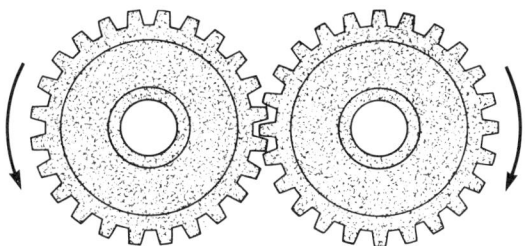

fig. 2-9 No torque multiplication occurs if two meshing gears have the same number of teeth.

pounds-foot. The mechanical advantage (torque increase) between the input and output shafts is 150 pounds-foot to 300 pounds-foot or 1:2.

An easier way to figure the torque multiplication accomplished through gearing is to count the number of teeth located on the input and output gears. For instance, Fig. 2-9 shows two gears that have the same number of teeth and have the same diameter. Each gear has 24 teeth; therefore, the torque multiplication ratio is 24 to 24—1:1. On the other hand, if an input gear has 12 teeth and the output gear has 24 teeth (Fig. 2-10) the ratio of torque increase is 12 to 24, 1:2. In both cases, the gear will always operate in opposite directions.

As previously mentioned, torque increase means a speed reduction. To figure the speed reduction gears produce, compare the number of teeth on the output gear to the number of teeth on the input gear. For example, in Fig. 2-9, both gears have the same number of teeth; consequently, the speed ratio is one to one—1:1. But Fig. 2-10 shows two gears of different sizes. The smaller gear revolves twice as fast as the larger gear because the small gear has 12 teeth and the large gear has 24 teeth. The speed ratio, with the small gear driving, is 12 to 24–2:1. Finally, just remember that the speed (gear) ratio between any two meshing gears is a comparison of the relative speeds (rpm) with which they both operate.

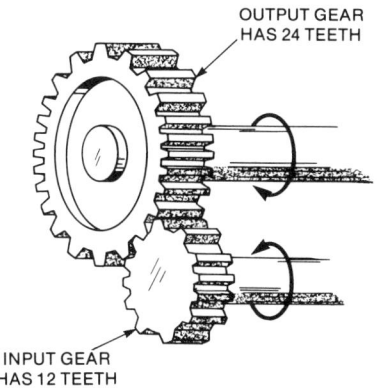

fig. 2-10 Torque multiplication can occur when two gears have different number of teeth.

planetary gear train

The *planetary gear train* is the heart of any automatic transmission (Fig. 2–11). This mechanical device is responsible for all forward driving gear ratios and reverse. The complete gear train may consist of one or more simple planetary gearsets, a compound planetary gear train, or two simple planetary gearsets connected by a common sun gear.

A simple planetary gearset consists of a sun gear, a carrier with three or more planet pinions, plus an internal gear also called the ring or annulus gear. The gear, located in the center of the unit, is the *sun gear.* The sun gear's teeth are in constant mesh with the teeth of the planet pinions. The *carrier* supports the pinion gears on rigid pins, and each gear is free to rotate on these support pins. The *planet pinions* are in mesh with the internal gear which has teeth cut into its inside circumference. Since the pinions have the ability to turn on their centers and at the same time revolve with the carrier around the sun gear, the unit's activity is similar to a planet's movement in our solar system; therefore, the unit is commonly known as a planetary.

The planetary gear train offers several advantages over the sliding gear arrangement found in manual-shift transmission. First, the device is smaller in size because all planetary gear train components revolve around a common axis, the sun gear. Second, all planetary gears are in constant mesh which eliminates the possibility of gear teeth damage from gear clashing caused by partial engagement or improper shifting techniques. Also, the constant mesh characteristic permits quick gear ratio changes without the loss of torque flow through the transmission. Third, planetary gear trains are stronger because the distribution of torque load is over more gears; consequently, more teeth are in contact to carry the torque loads. Finally, the location of the various planetary gear train components makes the task of holding or locking the components together for ratio changes relatively easy.

Planetary gearsets are very versatile because the gearset can produce a wide variety of gear ratio combinations. In all, a simple planetary gearset can produce six different gear ratio combinations and a direct drive. In order to achieve a reduction of either speed or torque through the gearset, one member of the gearset, either the sun

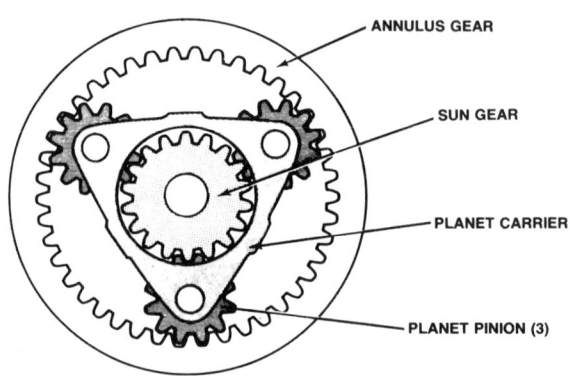

fig. 2–11 The design of a simple planetary gearset. (Courtesy Chrysler Corp.)

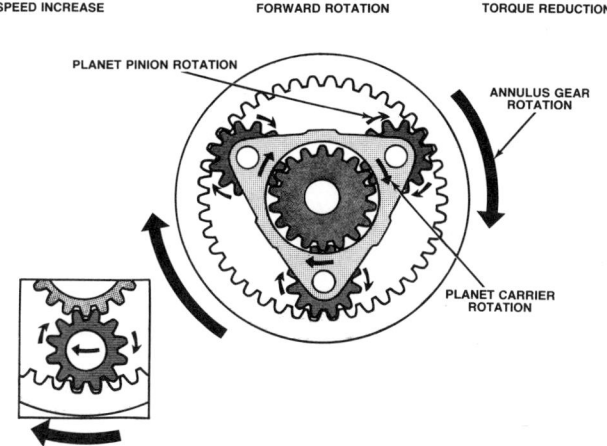

fig. 2-12 A simple planetary gearset operating in ratio number 1 (Courtesy Chrysler Corp.)

gear, carrier, or the ring gear, is stationary or locked to the transmission case; and the input shaft drives a second member. The third remaining member is output, and transmits torque to the output shaft. On the other hand, to achieve direct drive, high gear, the planetary gearset must have two of its three members driven at the same speed which will lock the gearset up. As a result, the input shaft's speed is the same as that of the output shaft.

Before studying some of the actual gear ratios produced by a simple planetary gearset, it is important to understand certain rules that pertain to the action of planetary gears. First, whenever the carrier is stationary with either the ring gear or the sun gear driving, the planet pinions rotate, "idle", on their pins and force the remaining unused gear to turn. Second, if either the sun gear or ring gear is stationary and the free sun or ring gear acts as the driving member, the planet pinions "walk" the carrier, output member, around the stationary gear. Finally, the sun and planet pinions gears always rotate in opposite directions; but the planet pinions and the ring gear rotate in the same direction.

ratios achieved by simple planetary gearsets

A simple planetary gearset operating in ratio number 1 produces a speed increase and a torque reduction (Fig. 2-12). The input shaft drives the planet carrier, and the ring gear is the output, driven member. As the input shaft rotates the carrier clockwise, the planet pinions "walk" around a stationary sun gear in a clockwise direction. The walking pinions also cause the ring gear to rotate in the same direction as the pinions. With this ratio, the input shaft is rotating slower than the output shaft at a ratio of .7:1. In other words, the gearset is producing an overdrive condition that reduces torque but increases output speed in comparison to input shaft speed.

20 GEAR CONSTRUCTION AND DESIGN

To calculate the actual gear ratio of a simple planetary gearset operating in gear ratio number 1, overdrive, divide the sum of the number of teeth on the sun gear (S) and the ring gear (R) into the number of teeth on the driven gear (D). For example, in Fig. 2–12, the sun gear has 18 teeth and the ring gear has 42 teeth; the sum of which is 60. Also, the driven gear is the ring gear which has 42 teeth. Since the formula states that this gear ratio is equal to $\frac{D}{S+R}$ or $\frac{42}{60}$, the input to output ratio is .7 to 1 (.7:1).

A simple planetary gearset operating in gear ratio number 2 also produces a torque reduction and speed increase (Fig. 2–13). The input shaft drives the planet carrier; the ring gear is stationary. The output member is the sun gear. As the input shaft drives the carrier clockwise, inside of the ring gear, the planet pinions turn counterclockwise. Since the pinions are in mesh with the sun gear, the sun gear has to rotate in a clockwise direction. The input to output ratio is .3:1 which is the best ratio for a forward speed increase, but the ratio also achieves a greater reduction in torque than ratio number 1.

To calculate the actual gear ratio of any simple planetary gearset operating in gear ratio number 2, overdrive, use the number 1 gear ratio formula, $\frac{D}{S+R}$ to find the answer. Since the sum of both the sun gear teeth and the number of ring gear teeth is 60 and the driven sun gear has 18 teeth (Fig. 2–13), the ratio is $\frac{18}{60}$ or .3 to 1 (.3:1).

Gear ratio number 3 provides an overdrive and a reverse relationship between the input and output shafts (Fig. 2–14). In this case, the planet carrier is the stationary member; and the input shaft drives the ring gear clockwise. The output member is the sun gear. As the ring gear rotates, it causes the planet pinions to "idle" clockwise. Because of this planet pinion rotation, the sun gear and output shaft rotate in a direction opposite to that of the input member, the ring gear. The ratio is .43:1. The output shaft is spinning faster than the input shaft but with reduced torque output.

To calculate the actual gear ratio of a planetary gearset operating in ratio number 3, divide the number of teeth on the driving gear (D1) into the number of teeth on the

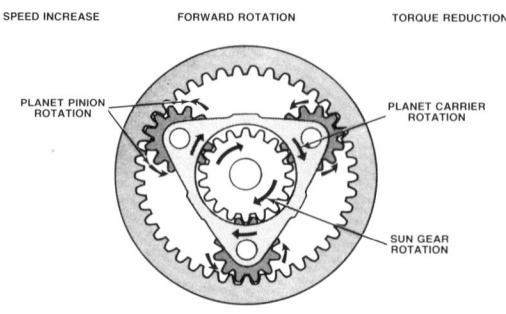

fig. 2–13 A simple planetary gearset operating in ratio number 2. (Courtesy Chrysler Corp.)

RATIOS ACHIEVED BY SIMPLE PLANETARY GEARSETS 21

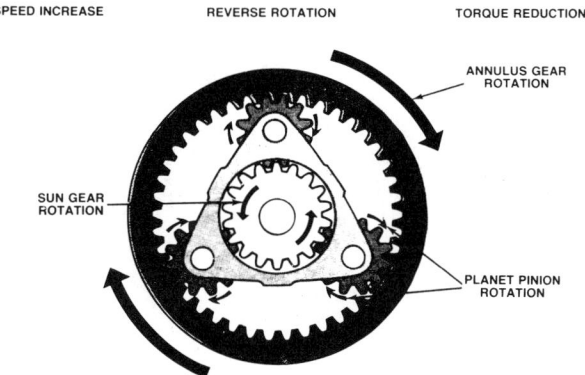

fig. 2–14 A simple planetary gearset operating in ratio number 3. (Courtesy Chrysler Corp.)

driven gear (D). In Fig. 2–14, the driven gear has 18 teeth and the driving gear has 42 teeth. The ratio is $\frac{D}{D1}$ or $\frac{18}{42}$ or a rounded off figure of .43 to 1 (.43:1).

Gear ratio number 4 provides a speed reduction and a torque increase between the input and output shafts. During this ratio, the input shaft drives the ring gear in a clockwise direction with the sun gear held stationary. The output member is the carrier. As the ring gear turns, it forces the planet pinions to rotate in a clockwise direction. The pinions "walk" the carrier around the held sun gear in a clockwise direction. The ratio between the input and output shafts is 1.43:1 which indicates an increase in torque and a reduction in speed (Fig. 2–15).

To determine the actual gear ratio of any simple planetary gearset functioning in ratio 4, divide the number of teeth on the driving gear (D1) into the sum of the teeth on both the sun and ring gears. In Fig. 2–15, the driving member, ring gear, has 42 teeth.

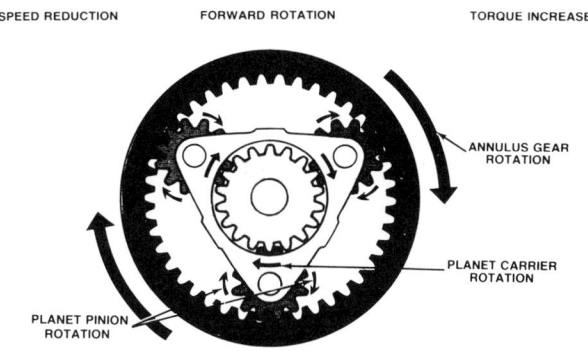

fig. 2–15 A simple planetary gearset operating in ratio number 4. (Courtesy Chrysler Corp.)

22 GEAR CONSTRUCTION AND DESIGN

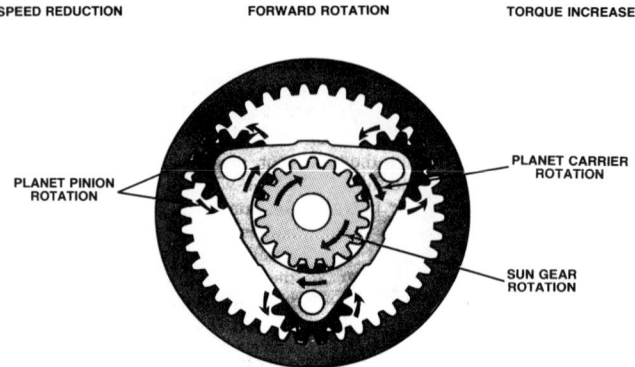

fig. 2-16 A simple planetary gearset operating in ratio number 5. (Courtesy Chrysler Corp.)

The sun gear (18 teeth) and the ring gear (42 teeth) combined have 60 teeth. Therefore, the gear ratio is equal to $\frac{S+R}{D1}$ or $\frac{60}{42}$ or 1.43:1.

Simple planetary gear ratio number 5 also produces a speed reduction and a torque increase between the input and output shafts (Fig. 2-16). The ring gear is stationary while the input shaft drives the sun gear. The output member, in this case, is the planet carrier. With the sun gear rotating clockwise, the planet pinions "walk" the carrier around the inside of the held ring gear. The gear ratio between the input and output shafts is 3.33 to 1 (3.33:1).

The same formula that calculated the gear ratio of a simple planetary gearset operating in condition 4 will also determine the ratio for condition 5. Since the driving gear is now the sun gear which has 18 teeth and the sum of the sun gear and ring gear teeth is 60, the gear ratio is equal to $\frac{S+R}{D1}$ or $\frac{60}{18}$ or 3.33 to 1 (3.33:1).

Gear ratio number 6 is the most common method of providing the automatic transmission with a reverse gear ratio that has a speed reduction and torque increase

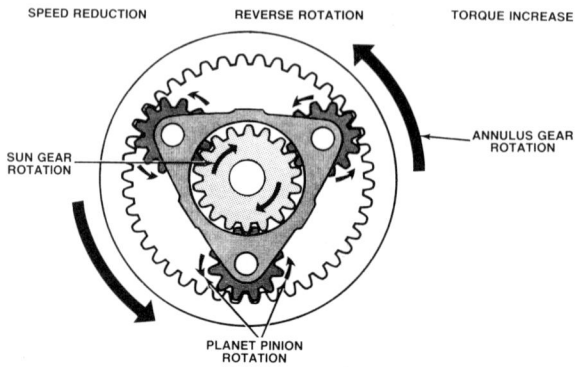

fig. 2-17 A simple planetary gearset operating in ratio number 6. (Courtesy Chrysler Corp.)

COMPOUND PLANETARY GEAR TRAINS

(Fig. 2-17). During this ratio, the sun gear is the input, driving member; and the output member is the ring gear. The carrier is the held stationary member. As the sun gear turns in a clockwise direction, the planet pinions "idle" in a counterclockwise direction. The idling pinions force the ring gear to turn the output shaft backwards. The input to output ratio is 2.33 to 1 (2.33:1).

To calculate the actual gear ratio of any planetary gearset functioning in ratio 6, divide the number of teeth on the driving gear ($D1$) into the number of teeth on the driven gear (D). In Fig. 2-17, the driven ring gear has 42 teeth and the driving sun gear has 18 teeth. The ratio is equal to $\frac{D}{D1}$ or $\frac{42}{18}$ or 2.33 to 1 (2.33:1).

A simple planetary gearset that is operating alone in an automatic transmission will only produce a limited number of the above mentioned gear ratios. As previously stated, a simple planetary can function in six different ways to produce a speed reduction, an overdrive, or a reverse. Also, by driving two members at the same speed, the gearset will operate in direct drive. But whenever the manufacturer permanently fastens one member to the output shaft, this action limits the number of ratios to either two forward or to one forward and a reverse. Consequently, in order to provide a vehicle with additional forward ratios, an automatic transmission must have several simple planetary gearsets, a compound planetary gearset, or two simple planetary gearsets connected together by a common sun gear.

compound planetary gear trains

The design of a compound, Ravigneau, planetary is such that the unit can produce two- or three-forward ratios plus a reverse. The two-speed unit (Fig. 2-18) consists of an input sun gear and input shaft, a set of long planet pinions that are in mesh with the input sun

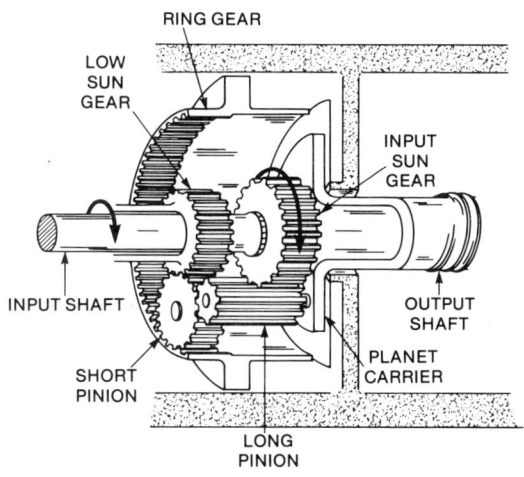

fig. 2-18 The design of a two-speed compound planetary gear train.

24 GEAR CONSTRUCTION AND DESIGN

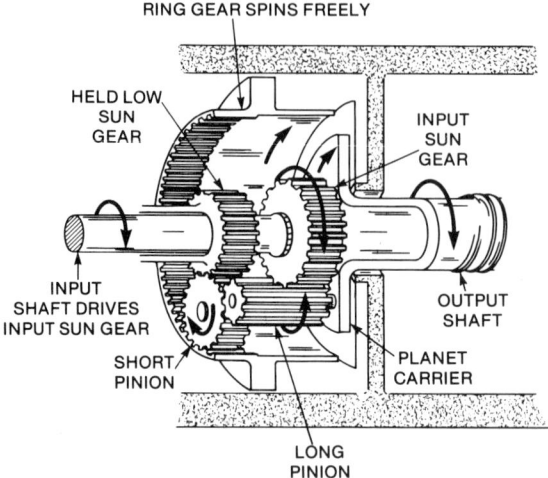

fig. 2-19 A two-speed compound planetary gear train operating in low ratio. A friction device (not shown) holds the low sun gear.

gear, and a set of short planet pinions which mesh with the long planet pinions but not the input sun gear. In addition, the short pinions mesh with a low sun gear that the input shaft drives during one ratio, and a braking device locks to the case during another ratio. All planet pinions mount on a single planet carrier which is the output member. And finally, a single ring gear meshes with the short planet pinions. This two-speed design can produce a low, high, and reverse gear ratio.

In low ratio, the input shaft drives the input sun gear clockwise (Fig. 2-19); a braking device prevents the low sun gear from rotating. Since the input sun gear turns clockwise, the long planet pinions spin counterclockwise. The long planet pinions also force the short planet pinions to rotate clockwise. The short pinions then "walk" the planet carrier and output shaft around the low sun gear in a clockwise direction but at a slower speed than the input sun gear is turning.

When this planetary gear train upshifts to high, direct drive (Fig. 2-20) the input shaft drives both the input and low sun gears in a clockwise direction. A frictional unit connects the low sun gear to the input shaft during this ratio. By observing the rotation of both sets of planet pinions in low ratio and again in direct drive, the reason why the unit rotates at a 1:1 ratio will be obvious.

During low ratio, the long pinions rotated counterclockwise and the short pinions turned clockwise. Now in high ratio, the input sun gear still causes the long pinions to rotate counterclockwise, but the low sun gear also now drives the short pinions counterclockwise. Remember that both the long and short pinions are in mesh and must rotate in opposite directions. Since the sun gears attempt to spin the long and short pinions in the same direction, the pinions lock up and the entire gear train rotates as a solid unit. In other words, the input and output shafts rotate at the same speeds.

During a reverse gear ratio, the input shaft drives the input sun gear clockwise; the ring gear is the stationary member. The carrier serves as the output member. The long

COMPOUND PLANETARY GEAR TRAINS

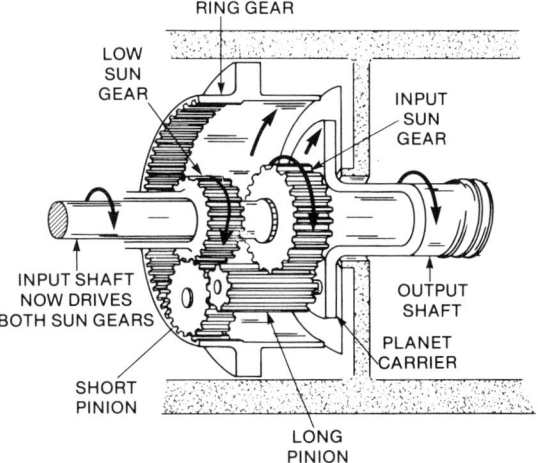

fig. 2-20 A two-speed compound planetary gear train operating in high (direct) ratio. A friction device (now shown) connects the low sun gear in the input shaft.

pinions will turn counterclockwise, and the short pinions will rotate clockwise. Since the ring gear is stationary, the short pinions "walk" around inside the ring gear pulling the planet carrier with them. This action imparts a reverse motion to the output shaft and a reduction in speed between the input and output shafts (Fig. 2-21).

A compound planetary gear train can develop three forward ratios by arranging the members in a slightly different manner than they were in the two-speed unit (Fig. 2-22). The center, inside gear of this unit is the primary sun gear which the primary sun gear shaft drives. In mesh with the primary sun gear are three short primary planet pinions. These planet pinions rotate in an opposite direction to the primary sun gear. Meshed

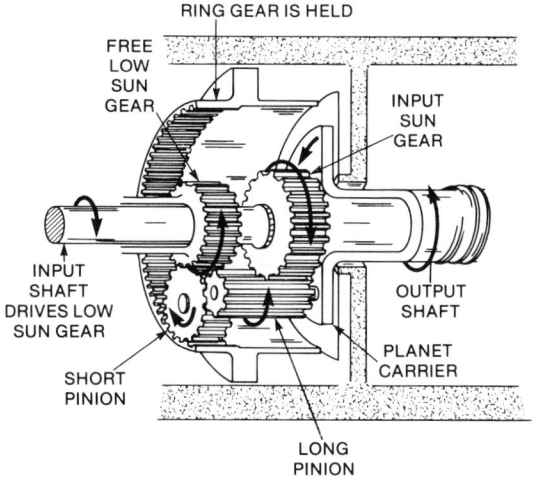

fig. 2-21 A two-speed compound planetary gear train operating in reverse ratio.

26 GEAR CONSTRUCTION AND DESIGN

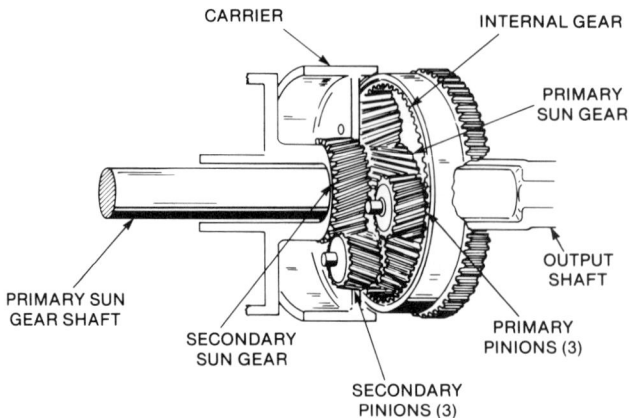

fig. 2-22 The design of a three-speed compound planetary gear train.

with the primary pinions and also the secondary sun gear are three long secondary planet pinions. These secondary planet pinions rotate in a direction opposite to the primary pinions and mesh with the internal (ring) gear which attaches to the output shaft. In addition, both the primary and secondary pinions mount on a common carrier which can serve as a driving member or a stationary member. With this gear train arrangement, this unit can produce first, second, third, and reverse ratios.

With this compound planetary in first ratio, the turbine (input) shaft drives the primary sun gear shaft which in turn drives the primary sun gear clockwise; the planet carrier is the stationary member (Fig. 2-23). The clockwise direction of the primary sun gear forces the primary pinions to rotate counterclockwise. Since the primary pinions are in mesh with the secondary pinions, the secondary pinions will rotate clockwise. The carrier is stationary; therefore, the secondary pinions "idle" and cause the internal gear and output shaft to rotate in a clockwise direction but at a slower speed than the turbine

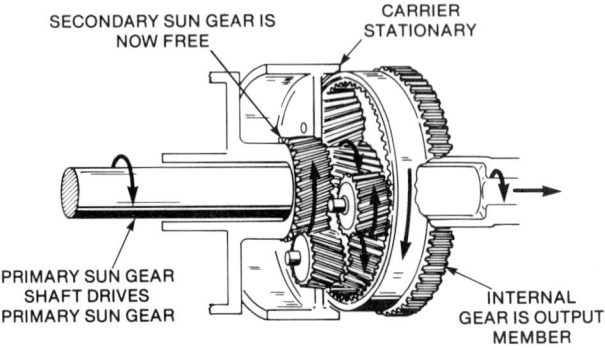

fig. 2-23 The three-speed compound planetary gear train operating in first ratio. The turbine shaft (not shown) turns the primary sun-gear shaft.

COMPOUND PLANETARY GEAR TRAINS 27

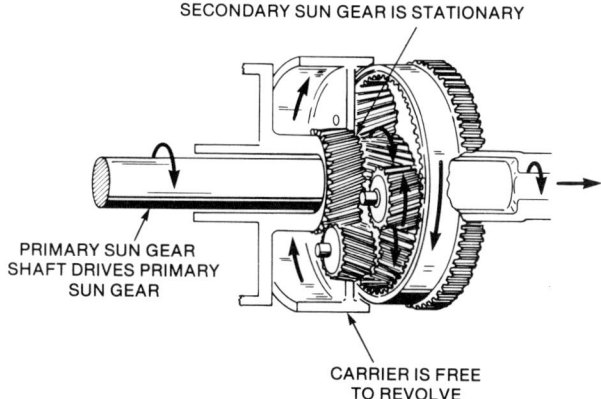

fig. 2-24 The three-speed compound planetary gear train operating in second ratio. The turbine shaft (not shown) turns the primary sun-gear shaft.

(input) shaft. During this gear ratio, the secondary sun gear turns freely in a reverse direction and has no effect on the gear train.

To obtain a second ratio, the turbine shaft again drives the primary sun gear shaft which, in turn, drives the primary sun gear clockwise; the secondary sun gear is the stationary member (Fig. 2-24). The primary pinions are rotating counterclockwise and drive the secondary pinions clockwise; the secondary planet pinions "walk" the planet carrier around the held secondary sun gear. At the same time as the secondary planet pinions "walk" the carrier, they drive the internal gear in a clockwise direction but at a slower rate than the primary sun gear.

In third gear ratio, direct drive, the turbine shaft drives both the primary and secondary sun gears in a clockwise direction (Fig. 2-25). The primary sun gear attempts to

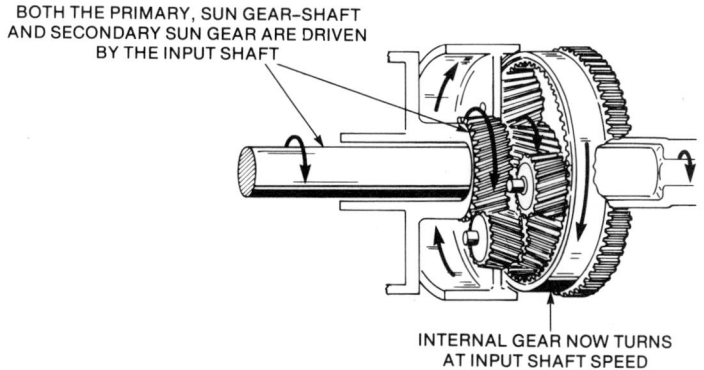

fig. 2-25 The three-speed compound planetary gear train operating in third ratio. The turbine (input) shaft (now shown) drives both the secondary sun gear and the primary sun-gear shaft.

28 GEAR CONSTRUCTION AND DESIGN

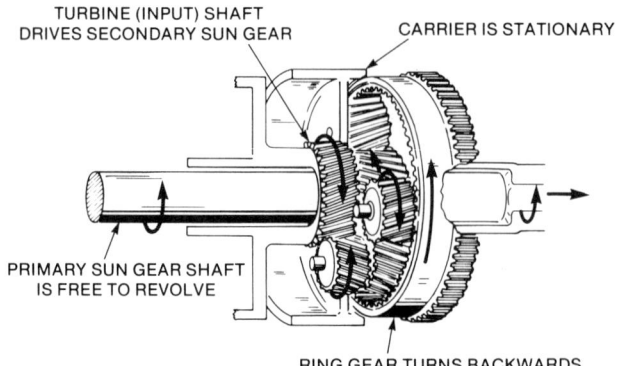

fig. 2-26 The three-speed compound planetary gear train operating in reverse ratio. The turbine shaft (not shown) drives the secondary sun gear.

drive the primary pinions counterclockwise, and the secondary sun gear attempts to turn the secondary planet pinions counterclockwise. The primary and secondary planet pinions are in mesh with each other and must rotate in opposite directions; therefore, the planet pinions cannot turn and the entire planetary gear train revolves as a unit. In other words, the output shaft spins at the same speed as the turbine (input) shaft.

To produce reverse, the turbine shaft drives the secondary sun gear clockwise, and the planet carrier is the stationary member (Fig. 2-26). Since the secondary sun gear is turning clockwise, the secondary pinions are rotating counterclockwise. The planet carrier is stationary; consequently, the secondary pinions "idle" and rotate the internal gear in a reverse direction. In this situation, the internal gear (output member) spins slower than the secondary sun gear. The primary pinions and sun gear spin freely and have no effect on the gear train.

Simpson gear train

In place of a compound planetary gear train, an alternative method used now to produce a transmission with three forward gear ratios is a Simpson gear train, invented, developed, and patented by Howard W. Simpson. This gear train system (Fig. 2-27) consists of two simple planetary gearsets, referred to in this chapter as the front and reverse units, which Simpson ingeniously connected together. The gear train has two identical ring gears, six identical planet pinions, and a single long sun gear serving both gearsets. The use of identical gears allows a minimum of tooling because only three different gears and two slightly different carriers are necessary to complete the entire gear train.

In order to make the flow of torque (powerflow) through the Simpson gear train easier for the reader to understand, a detailed examination of the build-up of this gear train, piece by piece, as it is found in an actual automatic transmission is necessary. While studying this build-up, consider the construction of each piece and its possible connection with other components.

SIMPSON GEAR TRAIN

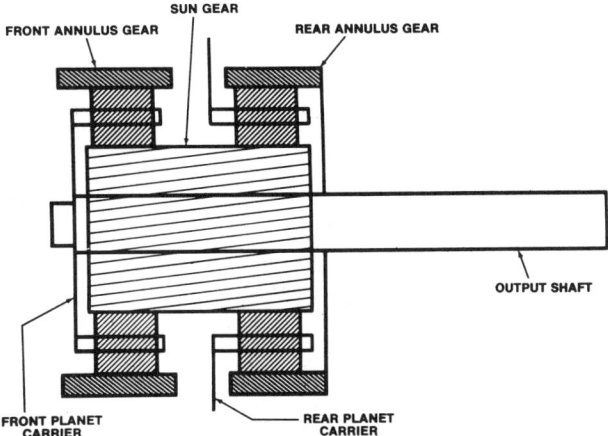

fig. 2-27 The design of a Simpson planetary gear train. (Courtesy Chrysler Corp.)

First of all, an input shaft which has splines on both ends brings torque into the gear train (Fig. 2-28). Splines are slots or grooves cut into this shaft which mate with similar splines cut into a bore located in the center of the turbine and the rear clutch cylinder. These splines insure that the turbine will drive the input shaft which in turn will drive the rear clutch cylinder and clutch assembly.

The rear clutch assembly connects and disconnects the front unit ring (annulus) gear to the input shaft. For the moment, this is all the reader need know about this unit. Further on in the text is a detailed explanation of the construction and operation of the different types of clutch assemblies.

Splined to the left end of the output shaft (Fig. 2-29) is the front unit carrier with its planet pinions. Since the front unit carrier attaches to the output shaft, it will be the output planetary member of the front unit gearset.

The long sun gear can be a driving or stationary planetary member. In order to accomplish this task, the sun gear attaches to a driving shell by means of splines (Fig. 2-30). The driving shell has a series of large teeth which mate between teeth machined into the front clutch cylinder. The front cylinder (drum) and clutch assembly, when activated, connects the driving shell and sun gear to the input shaft. On the other hand, if the front clutch cylinder is stationary, the driving shell and sun gear will not rotate.

fig. 2-28 The input shaft, rear clutch cylinder (drum), and clutch assembly.

30 GEAR CONSTRUCTION AND DESIGN

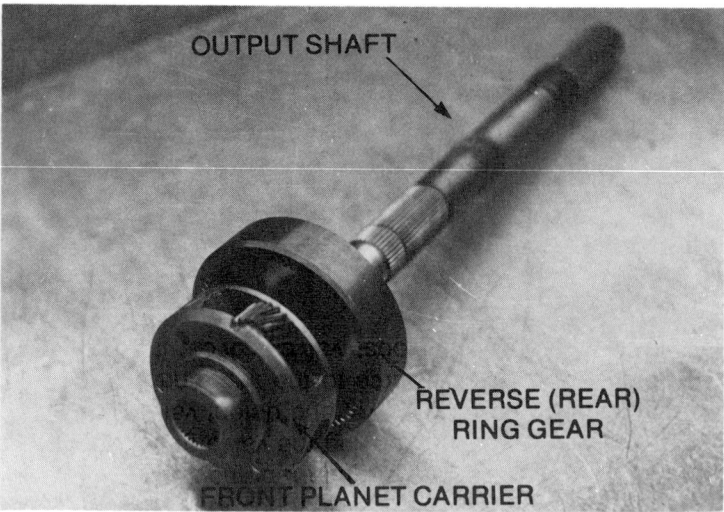

fig. 2–29 Splined to the output shaft are the front planet carrier and the rear ring (annulus) gear.

If the sun gear is rotating, it will deliver torque to the reverse unit pinions. These pinions are part of the reverse unit carrier which will be the rear unit's stationary member. The reverse unit carrier has a series of large machined teeth that mate between teeth cut into the low and reverse drum. By holding the low and reverse drum stationary, the reverse unit carrier will not rotate; and the planet pinions will "idle" on their support pins. Therefore, torque moves from the sun gear, to the pinions which "idle", and finally to the reverse unit ring (annulus) gear.

Splined to a flange is the reverse unit ring gear. The flange has internal splines which mate with external splines machined into the output shaft. The reverse unit ring gear serves as the output member for the reverse unit gearset.

fig. 2–30 Driving shell and sun gear, front clutch cylinder and clutch assembly, plus the brake band.

In summation, the two driving planetary members of the Simpson gear train are the front unit ring gear and the long sun gear. Also, the holding members are the long sun gear and the reverse unit carrier. Finally, the output members are the front unit carrier along with the reverse unit ring (annulus) gear. By utilizing both the front and reverse units or each unit by itself, the Simpson gear train can produce three forward ratios and reverse.

ratios of a Simpson gear train

In first ratio, low gear, the front unit ring gear is the driving member for both gearsets; the reverse unit carrier is the stationary member for both gearsets (Fig. 2–31). Engine torque flows through the converter and drives the input shaft in a clockwise direction. Since the input shaft drives the now activated rear clutch assembly, the front unit ring gear turns in a clockwise direction; a one-way clutch or brake band holds the carrier stationary.

The front unit ring gear also rotates the front planet pinions in a clockwise direction. The planet carrier, splined to the output shaft, has the weight of the vehicle imposed on it; consequently, the carrier has a tendency to remain stationary. This action causes the front planet pinions to temporarily "idle" on their support pins and rotate the long sun gear counterclockwise.

Counterclockwise rotation of the long sun gear causes clockwise rotation of the reverse unit planet pinions. Since the reverse unit carrier is the permanently held, stationary member, the pinions "idle" and drive the reverse unit ring gear and output shaft in a clockwise direction but at a slower speed than the input shaft.

This output shaft rotation forces the front unit carrier to turn at the same speed and in the same direction as the output shaft. Consequently, the front unit ring gear and planet carrier are both rotating clockwise, but the front unit carrier is rotating at a slower speed than the ring gear. The actual gear ratio, in this case, between the input and output shafts is the result of a combination of the ratios provided by the front and reverse unit planet assemblies.

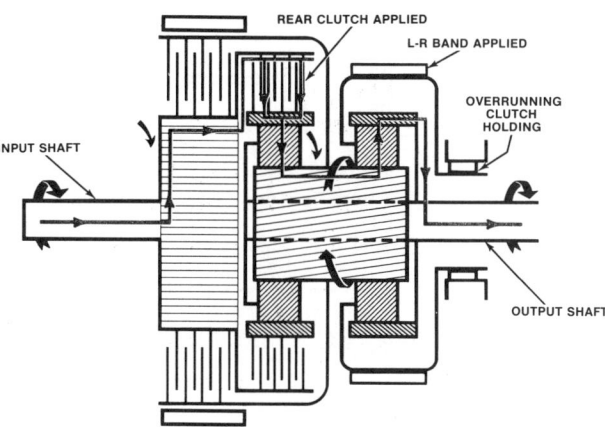

fig. 2–31 The Simpson gear train operating in first ratio. (Courtesy Chrysler Corp.)

32 GEAR CONSTRUCTION AND DESIGN

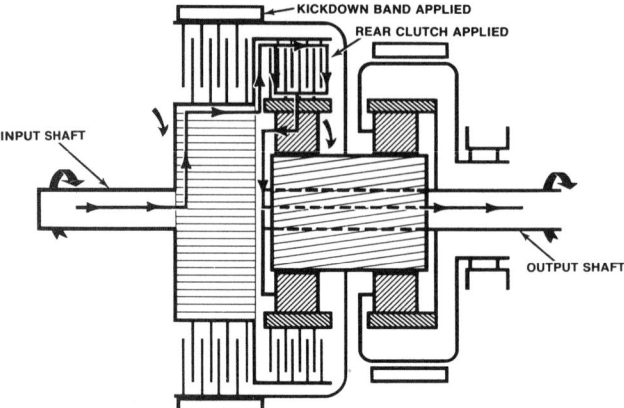

fig. 2–32 The Simpson gear train operating in second ratio. (Courtesy Chrysler Corp.)

When this planetary gear train is in second ratio, the front unit gearset alone produces the speed reduction and torque increase. The front unit ring (annulus) gear is the driving member. The long sun gear is the stationary member; the front unit carrier is the output member (Fig. 2–32).

Engine torque passes from the torque converter turbine to the input shaft, to the rear clutch cylinder, through the activated clutch, and to the front unit ring gear. The front unit ring gear rotates clockwise which also forces the front unit planet pinions to rotate clockwise. Since the long sun gear is stationary, the rotating front unit planet pinions "walk" the front unit carrier and output shaft around the held sun gear at a speed which is slower than the driving front unit ring gear.

During this particular gear ratio, the device which actually prevents rotation of the sun gear is a brake band. A complete description of these devices and their activating servos will come later in the text. For the moment, the main thing to remember about a band is that it holds planetary members stationary. In the gear train under discussion,

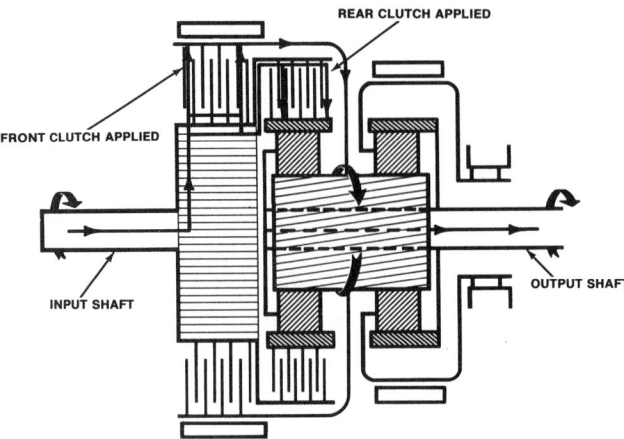

fig. 2–33 The Simpson gear train operating in third ratio. (Courtesy Chrysler Corp.)

the band tightens around the front clutch cylinder. This action stops the rotation of this cylinder along with the driving shell and sun gear.

The gear action in second ratio of a Simpson gear train is the same as any simple planetary gearset operating in gear ratio 4 presented earlier in this chapter. The ring gear is the driving member; the sun gear is stationary; the output member is the carrier.

During the third gear ratio, direct drive, the front unit ring gear and the long sun gear are the driving members. The front clutch connects the long sun gear to the input shaft. Also, the rear clutch connects the front unit ring gear to the input shaft (Fig. 2–33). During direct drive, the front unit gearset again is responsible for providing the ratio.

Engine torque flows through the torque converter to the transmission's input shaft, through the rear clutch assembly, and to the front unit annulus gear. Therefore, the front unit ring gear rotates clockwise at input shaft speed. At the same time, input shaft torque passes through the front clutch and turns the driving shell and the sun gear in a clockwise direction at input shaft speed. Since the front unit ring gear and the sun gear rotate at the same speed and in the same direction, all gear rotation in the gearset stops; and the gearset revolves as one piece.

This lock-up condition results from the inability of the front unit planet pinions to rotate in two directions at the same time. For instance, the front unit ring gear rotates clockwise which should turn the front unit planet pinions clockwise. But at the same time, the long sun gear which also is turning clockwise attempts to drive these same pinions counterclockwise. The front unit planet pinions cannot rotate in two directions at the same time; as a result, the entire planetary gear train locks up and the output shaft and input shaft spin at the same speed. Although the front unit gearset started the process, the reverse unit must, due to its interaction with the front unit, lock up also.

In reverse ratio, the long sun gear is the driving member; the reverse unit carrier is the stationary member; the output member is the reverse unit ring gear. Moreover, since none of the front unit gearset members are held, the reverse unit gearset has total responsibility for this ratio (Fig. 2–34). This simple gearset arrangement is the same as condition 6, previously mentioned in this chapter, and is the most common way to achieve a reverse ratio.

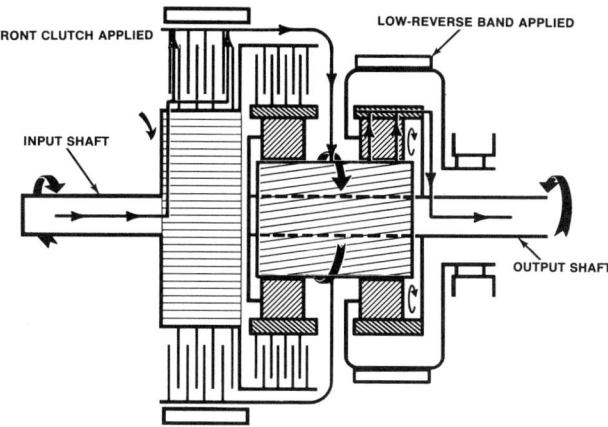

fig. 2–34 The Simpson gear train operating in reverse ratio. (Courtesy Chrysler Corp.)

Engine torque flows through the torque converter to the input shaft, to the rear clutch assembly and stops, across the front clutch assembly which is now operational, and to the driving shell and sun gear. This action causes the sun gear to turn clockwise at input shaft speed. The sun gear rotates the reverse unit planet pinions in a counterclockwise direction which, in turn, turns the reverse unit ring gear and output shaft in a direction opposite to the sun gear.

This reversal of the ring gear's direction occurs because the reverse unit planet carrier is stationary; therefore, the planet pinions "idle" and drive the ring gear backwards. The low and reverse band which wraps around the low reverse drum holds the reverse drum and carrier stationary in low and reverse ratios.

In neutral, the input shaft drives none of the planetary gear train members; and the brake bands hold no members stationary. Engine torque will pass through the converter and drive the input shaft clockwise. The input shaft drives the rear clutch cylinder clockwise, but at this point, torque flows stop.

When Simpson gear trains appear in different makes of automatic transmissions, the names given to the various components may be different from those chosen for use in this chapter. Also, the size and position of components may be slightly different in each brand of transmission. But all of these gear trains operate in much the same manner and produce three forward gear ratios and a reverse.

summary

1. To be able to carry the torque loads, gears must be very strong.
2. Designed into the construction of each gear are features such as teeth clearance, circle, pitch, and root diameters, in addition to gear teeth angle.
3. To alter torque, transmission gears use the principle of the lever and the fulcrum.
4. By applying a small force over a greater distance, the lever can use a small input force to move a larger output force.
5. The term given to the relationship between the input and output forces is mechanical advantage.
6. In gaining a mechanical advantage between the input and output forces, the distance each force travels is different.
7. Shaft torque is equal to the force on the gear teeth times the gear's radius.
8. Gear teeth force is equal to shaft torque divided by the gear's radius.
9. If the end of one simple lever contacts the end of a second lever, force can move from one lever to the other; the same situation occurs anytime two gears are in mesh.
10. An easy way to figure the torque multiplication accomplished through gearing is to count the number of teeth located on the input and output gears.
11. Torque multiplication results in a speed reduction.
12. The planetary gear train is the heart of an automatic transmission.

13. A planetary gear train offers several advantages over the sliding gear arrangement found in manual-shift transmissions.
14. A simple planetary gearset consists of a sun gear, a carrier with three or more planet pinions, and an internal (ring) gear.
15. Simple planetary gearsets can produce six different gear ratio combinations plus direct drive.
16. During gear ratio 1, the input shaft drives the carrier; the sun gear is stationary; the ring gear is the output member.
17. During ratio 2, the input shaft drives the planet carrier; the ring gear is stationary; the output member is the sun gear.
18. During gear ratio 3, the input shaft drives the ring gear; the carrier is the stationary member; the sun gear is the output member.
19. During gear ratio 4, the input shaft drives the ring gear; the sun gear is stationary; the output member is the carrier.
20. During gear ratio 5, the input shaft drives the sun gear; the ring gear is stationary; the carrier is the output member.
21. In gear ratio 6, the input shaft drives the sun gear; the carrier is stationary; the ring gear is the output member.
22. During direct drive, two planetary members are driven by the input shaft.
23. A simple planetary gearset that is operating alone in an automatic transmission will produce a limited number of gear ratios.
24. A compound planetary gear train can produce either two or three forward gear ratios and a reverse.
25. When the two-speed compound planetary gear train is in a forward reduction, the input sun gear is the driving member; the low sun gear is stationary; the carrier is the output member.
26. When the two-speed compound planetary gear train is in direct drive, both the sun gears are driving members.
27. When the two-speed compound planetary is in reverse, the input shaft drives the input sun gear; the ring gear is stationary; the carrier is the output member.
28. A compound planetary gear train can develop three forward gear ratios by arranging the members in a slightly different manner than they were in the two-speed units.
29. With a three-speed compound planetary gear train in first ratio, the primary sun gear is the driving member; the carrier is the stationary member; the ring gear is the output member.
30. With a three-speed compound planetary gear train in second ratio, the primary sun gear is the driving member; the secondary sun gear is the stationary member; the ring gear is the output member.
31. With a three-speed compound planetary gear train in direct drive, both the primary and secondary sun gears are the driving members.

36 GEAR CONSTRUCTION AND DESIGN

32. With a three-speed compound planetary gear train in reverse, the secondary sun gear is the driving member; the carrier is the stationary member; the ring gear is output.
33. In place of a compound planetary, an alternate method, now extensively used to produce three-speed automatic transmissions, is the Simpson gear train.
34. The Simpson gear train consists of two simple planetary gearsets connected together by a common sun gear.
35. The two driving members of the Simpson gear train are the front unit ring gear and the long sun gear.
36. The holding members of the Simpson gear train are the long sun gear and the reverse unit carrier.
37. The output members are the front unit carrier and the reverse unit annulus gear.
38. When a Simpson gear train is operating in first ratio, the front unit ring gear is the driving member; the reverse unit carrier is the stationary member; the front unit carrier and the reverse unit ring are the output members.
39. When a Simpson gear train is operating in second ratio, the front unit ring gear is driving; the long sun gear is stationary; the front unit carrier is the output member.
40. When a Simpson gear train is operating in direct drive, the front unit ring gear and the long sun gear are the driving members.
41. When the Simpson gear train is operating in reverse, the long sun gear is the driving member; the reverse unit carrier is the stationary member; the reverse unit ring gear is the output member.

check-up questions

The questions listed below will assist you in determining how well you remember the material contained in this chapter. Read each question carefully before choosing the one or more answers to each item. If you cannot answer the question, review the material in the section of the chapter that covers the question.

1. The portion of the gear which acts like a lever end is the _____.
    a. root
    b. center
    c. teeth
    d. clearance
2. The term given to the relationship between the input and output forces is _____.
    a. mechanical advantage
    b. mechanical advance
    c. work
    d. inertia

3. If the shaft torque is 100 pounds-foot and the gear's radius is two feet, the output force of the teeth is _____.
   a. 50 pounds-foot
   b. 200 pounds-foot
   c. 100 pounds-foot
   d. 150 pounds-foot
4. The torque multiplication ratio of two gears in mesh which have 12 teeth and 36 teeth is _____.
   a. 1:2
   b. 1:3
   c. 1:4
   d. 1:5
5. What is the speed ratio of the gear train in the above question if the smaller gear is driving?
   a. .5:1
   b. 1:1
   c. 2:1
   d. 3:1
6. The mechanical heart of the automatic transmission is the _____.
   a. planetary gear train
   b. clutches
   c. bands
   d. torque converter
7. The outer gear of a simple planetary gearset is the _____.
   a. sun gear
   b. pinions
   c. ring gear
   d. carrier
8. The two planetary gears which always rotate in opposite directions are the _____.
   a. sun and ring gears
   b. sun and planet pinion gears
   c. planet pinions and ring gear
   d. carrier and ring gear
9. If the sun gear rotates clockwise, with the carrier held, the ring gear will _____.
   a. not turn
   b. turn counterclockwise

38 GEAR CONSTRUCTION AND DESIGN

   c. turn clockwise
   d. lock up
10. A simple planetary can produce, excluding direct drive, how many ratios?
    a. six
    b. five
    c. four
    d. three
11. When installed in an automatic transmission, a simple planetary will produce a maximum of _____ forward ratios.
    a. five
    b. four
    c. three
    d. two
12. The compound planetary gear train has several single members. They are the _____ and the _____.
    a. pinions   sun gear
    b. carrier   pinions
    c. carrier   ring gear
    d. ring   sun gear
13. A compound planetary that has the ring gear as the output member can produce _____ forward speeds.
    a. four
    b. three
    c. two
    d. one
14. The planetary gear train which has two simple planetary gearsets hooked together by a long sun gear is the _____.
    a. Simpson
    b. compound
    c. Ravigneau
    d. complex
15. When a planetary gear train is in direct drive,
    a. one member is driving and one is stationary.
    b. two members are stationary.
    c. no members are stationary or are driving.
    d. two members are driving.

16. In order for a planetary gear train to be in a speed or torque reduction,
    a. one member is driving and one is stationary.
    b. two members are stationary.
    c. no members are stationary or are driving.
    d. two members are driving.
17. The gearset that produces second ratio in a transmission using a Simpson gear train is the _____.
    a. forward unit
    b. rear unit
    c. front unit
    d. reverse unit
18. If the carrier is stationary and the sun gear rotates, the planet pinions are said to _____.
    a. walk
    b. idle
    c. slide
    d. run
19. The unit that normally drives the transmission's input shaft is the _____.
    a. impeller
    b. stator
    c. turbine
    d. clutch
20. The component which the pinions always "walk" is the _____.
    a. carrier
    b. ring gear
    c. sun gear
    d. planet pinions

For the answers to these check-up questions, turn to the Appendix located at the back of the text.

3

automatic transmission fluids

Up to this point, this text has briefly covered the functions of the torque converter, clutches, and bands, in addition to the construction and operation of various planetary gear trains. These parts by themselves will not produce an automatic transmission which is operational. The automatic transmission, like any other hydraulic device, must have fluid to make it function. *Automatic transmission fluid (ATF)* is therefore of utmost importance to the operation of the unit and plays an important role in the life of the transmission as well.

The name given to the special liquid used in automatic transmissions and other hydraulic devices is fluid. Over the years, fluid producers have used the term "fluid" along with a special red dye to prevent confusion of this substance with other lubrication oils. Also, since engine oil and ATF have different colors, the bright red color of ATF assists the mechanic in determining the location of leaks from either unit. Finally, ATF has to be superior over other lubricating oils because ATF has to perform more functions than regular lubricating oil.

fluid functions

The first function of ATF is to transmit torque from the engine crankshaft to the transmission's input shaft. To accomplish this task, the fluid circulates in a sealed torque converter (Fig. 3–1). As previously mentioned, the converter has an impeller which delivers

FLUID FUNCTIONS 41

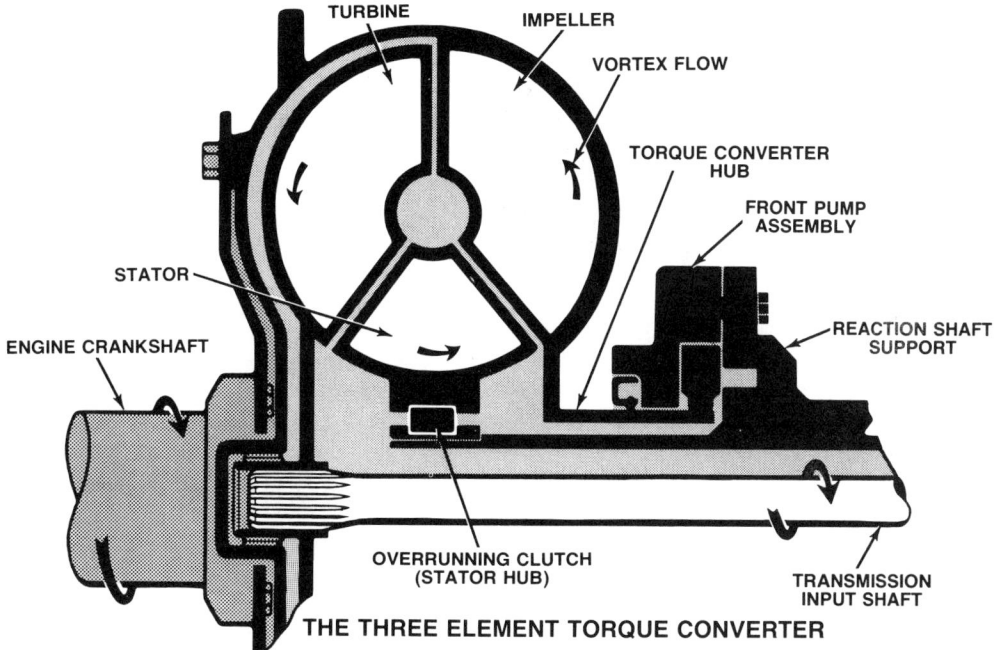

fig. 3-1 The impeller and turbine of the torque converter. (Courtesy Chrysler Corp.)

quantities of fluid, moving at high speeds, into the turbine that connects to the transmission's input shaft. When the impact energy of the moving fluid is great enough to overcome the load on the turbine and input shaft, torque will transfer from the crankshaft to the input shaft.

The second function of ATF is to transmit hydraulic pressure in an operating transmission. The fluid under pressure is the medium used to operate the clutches and bands. If you remember, the clutches connect and disconnect various planetary gear train member(s) to the input shaft. Bands, on the other hand, just hold members stationary.

Fluid, under pressure, also serves as hydraulic signals. These fluid signals are responsible for altering hydraulic pressure and determining upshift patterns. In order for the automatic transmission to function smoothly, hydraulic system pressure and shift points must relate to engine load and vehicle speed.

The third function of ATF is to carry the heat that is built up in an operating transmission to a cooling device. During the operation of the automatic transmission, the torque converter generates a great deal of heat. Also, during an upshift, the clutches or bands produce excessive temperatures. This heat passes directly into the fluid. The fluid acts as a medium to carry the heat to a cooling device. This device may be either an air-cooled or water-cooled transmission cooler. In either case, the device lowers the temperature of the fluid, thereby preventing the otherwise excessive temperatures from ruining the fluid and transmission components.

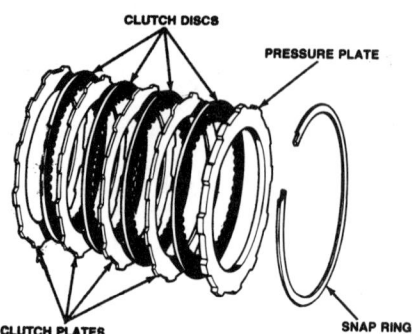

fig. 3–2 Fluid prevents dry friction between the clutch plates and clutch discs. (Courtesy Chrysler Corp.)

The fourth function of ATF is to lubricate, clean, and seal all the moving parts of an automatic transmission. As a lubricant, fluid reduces friction, heat, and wear when introduced as a film between moving parts. If the fluid does not maintain this lubricating cushion between the moving parts, friction will cause premature failure of the moving parts. Fluid also has the task of carrying the dislodged clutch or band materials as well as any metal particles down into the fluid reservoir, the pan. At this point, the foreign matter will either sink to the bottom of the pan or, as the particles attempt to move through the filter, the filter element traps and holds them. Furthermore, many grades of ATF contain additives which reduce the build-up of varnish and sludge. Finally, it is the natural characteristic of fluid to act as an agent which seals off excessive hydraulic pressure leakage around valves, rotating shafts, in addition to servo and clutch pistons.

The final function of ATF is to act as an agent to control the amount of friction between clutch plates or between a band and drum. *Friction* is the resistance to motion between two objects in contact with each other. In the automatic transmission, friction would normally be thought to exist between the clutch plates or between the band and the drum (Fig. 3–2). But this is not entirely the case because if dry friction did exist between these units, the shifts would be very harsh and the units would wear out very rapidly. To avoid this problem, automatic transmissions use lubricated "wet" clutches and bands to change ratios.

By using a constant supply of fluid between the clutch plates or between the band and drum, friction occurs not between dry units but between a number of fluid layers and between the fluid layers and components themselves.

This type of friction is known as *viscous friction.* The fluid layers cling to each of the components, and when the units are not necessary for transmission operation, the fluid layers act as a wedge to keep the components separated. At this time, the fluid layers lubricate, separate, the clutch plates, band, and drum; and little or no friction exists between them.

When a clutch assembly or band activates, the fluid continues to form a wedge between the units to prevent actual contact until the majority of the fluid "squeezes" out from between the components. During this time, the friction between fluid layers will either increase or decrease due to fluid structure. When the clutch plates or band and drum do come together, a film of fluid still remains on these parts. This remaining fluid, under pressure resulting from the force applied to it by the clutch or servo piston, forms a "liquid lock" that helps to control slippage between the contacting components.

fluid structure

In order to meet the above demands, ATF has a mineral oil base and certain additives. These additives improve the fluid's performance under abnormal conditions and extends its life. The performance qualities which the additives give the fluid are oxidation stability, antifoam suppression, viscosity improver, compatibility, wear resistance and certain friction characteristics.

Additives are necessary to stabilize oxidation because of the relatively high temperatures which the automatic transmission may encounter while operating. *Oxidation* is the union of oxygen with the fluid under high temperature conditions. For instance, when a vehicle is pulling a trailer or operating under conditions encountered in hot weather or in congested city traffic, the temperature within the automatic transmission may exceed 300 degrees F. Furthermore, during an upshift, local temperatures at the clutches or bands may reach as high as 600 degrees F. These temperatures, along with the introduction of air through normal transmission breathing, results in severe oxidation which changes the normal fluid characteristics.

Fluid oxidation can produce six abnormal effects on automatic transmission operation. First, oxidation can alter friction characteristics of the fluid which will result in excessive clutch and band slippage. Excessive slippage produces high clutch or band temperatures which, in turn, make oxidizing conditions more severe. Second, acids or peroxides, formed in fluid oxidation, may corrode bushing and thrust washer materials, damage seals, and harm the composition clutch plates. Third, oxidation increases viscosity (rate of flow) great enough to lower effective automatic transmission operation. Fourth, oxidation produces a sludge which can plug fluid passages and hydraulic controls. Fifth, oxidation forms a brown substance, varnish, which can lead to control valve or governor sticking and ultimate failure of the automatic transmission. Finally, by-products of oxidation reduce the effectiveness of antifoam additives.

The suppression, by the use of additives, of the foaming tendency of fluid in an automatic transmission is essential to the proper operation of the unit. *Foam* is a light, frothy mass of fine bubbles formed in or on the surface of the fluid by the action of the internal transmission components violently agitating the fluid. Foaming of the transmission fluid can produce erratic pump, torque converter, and hydraulic system operation. And finally, foaming can result in the loss of fluid through the breather or filler tube.

Using additives to improve fluid viscosity has improved the torque converter's and the automatic transmission's efficiency under all types of temperature conditions. *Viscosity* is the resistance to flow exhibited by the fluid, and heat has a definite influence on viscosity. High temperatures will normally thin the fluid and allow it to flow easier. A fluid viscosity that is lower than normal can cause internal leakage in pumps, valves and

44 AUTOMATIC TRANSMISSION FLUIDS

servos which will reduce hydraulic pressure. On the other hand, cold weather will make fluid heavier and flow much slower. High viscosity fluid produces sluggish transmission performance, improper shift patterns, in addition to possible bushing and clutch plate failures from lack of lubrication. To reduce the above-mentioned problems, manufacturers add viscosity improvers to their fluids to stabilize the fluid's viscosity to a nearly constant level during changes in temperature.

Automatic transmission fluid contains corrosion inhibitors and other additives to assure protection of various transmission components. The inhibitors in the fluid will protect the components from chemical and moisture corrosion. The additives will make the fluid compatible with the various materials used in the transmission. The additives protect the metals, seals or friction materials from chemical activities that would deteriorate them.

Modern automatic transmission fluid also contains additives which reduce wear and scoring or rubbing surfaces. *Scoring* is a scratching or grooving effect caused by foreign materials caught between two rubbing surfaces. Scoring, for example, can take place on the surface of a drum where a band rides.

Modern ATF contains additive substances that alter the friction characteristics of the fluid. As previously mentioned, these friction characteristics are important in automatic transmissions that use lubricated clutches and bands to change ratios. No single fluid satisfies the best friction requirements of all transmission types now in service; consequently, some modification of mineral oil fluid's friction level is possible by the use of additive substances. This modification of the basic fluid is responsible for the two main fluid types now in service—Type F and Dexron.

ATF *Type F* has a friction level which increases as the sliding speed between drive and driven clutch plates or between the band and the drum decreases (Fig. 3–3). Sliding speed, in feet per minute, refers to the difference in speeds between the drive and driven clutch plates or between the band and drum. At the start of application of these units, the speed difference is great; but as the clutch or band applies, the speed of the drive and

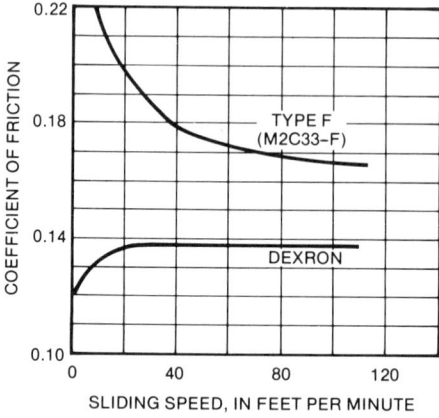

fig. 3–3 The coefficient or amount of friction between sliding components varies with the type of fluid utilized.

fig. 3–4 Type A Suffix A fluid.

driven members reduces as the clutch assembly or band picks up the load. With Type F fluid, the friction level increases as sliding speeds equalize. This action gives the transmission a firm, aggressive shift.

On the other hand, *Dexron* fluid provides a lower friction level as the sliding speeds equalize. This provides a transmission with a soft, smooth shift. Finally, the mating of the fluid's friction level with the transmission's clutch and band material is necessary to obtain the designed transmission shift characteristics and prevent premature failure of the clutch plates and bands.

fluid types and usage

Since 1951, the Ford Motor Company has used several types of fluid in its automatic transmissions. From 1951 to 1961, all Ford automatic transmissions used Type A Suffix A fluid. This fluid was, at this time, the only one utilized by vehicle manufacturers for automatic transmissions. Several approved fluid suppliers marketed this product after receiving approval for their product from the Armour Research Foundation, Illinois Institute of Technology, I.I.T. Research Institute. If a fluid met all the specifications of Type A Suffix A fluid, it received an AQ (Armour Qualification) number (Fig. 3–4).

In 1961, Ford vehicles equipped with automatic transmissions came from the factory filled with a new fluid, Type F. Ford Motor Company developed this fluid and gave it a Ford Specification M-2C33D. By 1964, Ford recommended this fluid for all their automatic transmissions; the pre-1961 units could use either Type F or Type A Suffix A fluids. In 1968, Ford upgraded Type F Fluid, Specification M-2C33F. This fluid replaced the old Type F (M-2C33D) (Fig. 3–5) for use in all Ford automatic transmissions but one.

fig. 3–5 Type F fluid.

46 AUTOMATIC TRANSMISSION FLUIDS

fig. 3-6 Dexron fluid.

In 1976, Ford redesigned its C-6 automatic transmission for the 1977 model year; and this and later C-6 transmissions use a new fluid, referred to as the C-J fluid, Ford Specification M-2C138-CJ. The C-J fluid is red with an orange tint and is only available at Ford Service Centers. Finally, because C-J fluid is quite similar to Dexron II, Ford announced in 1978 that Dexron II be a suitable alternate to C-J fluid for use in 1977 and later C-6 and other Ford transmissions which use C-J fluid.

Many petroleum suppliers market Type F fluid. If the Ford specification number is not on the can, do not use it because the product may not meet Ford's standard for ATF. Finally, now that Ford automatic transmissions can use either Type F, C-J, or the alternate for C-J—Dexron II—*be sure to check the owners or the Ford service manual before adding or changing the fluid in a Ford automatic transmission for the correct type to use.*

Over the years, American Motors, Chrysler, and General Motors have used two types of fluid in their automatic transmissions. Before 1968, they all used Type A Suffix A fluid in all their units. In 1968, General Motors developed a new fluid—Dexron (Fig. 3-6) for all its automatic transmissions. This fluid has a qualification number, B-XXXXX, on its container. The X's represented the five-digit number which each fluid manufacturer assigned to the fluid. This new fluid functioned better than Type A fluid at low temperatures; it resisted fluid oxidation more efficiently; and it contained properties needed for smooth shifting that Type A Suffix A fluid did not have. Lastly, American Motors and Chrysler adopted Dexron for their units and followed the same policy as General Motors of using either Dexron or Type A Suffix A for all their pre-1968 transmissions.

Since 1968, General Motors has changed its formula for Dexron. For example, in 1973, GM introduced Dexron II with a C-XXXXX on its container. This new formula has a higher resistance to oxidation and higher frictional stability than Dexron-B, but it corroded the transmission-cooler, inlet fitting on some model vehicles. In 1976, GM developed Dexron II with a D-XXXXX number. This new fluid passed the same tests as Dexron II-C but did not cause cooler, inlet-fitting corrosion.

FLUID COOLING 47

The Dexron II-D fluid now replaces both Dexron-B and Dexron II-C fluids in all General Motors, American Motors, and Chrysler automatic transmissions. Consequently, *before adding Dexron-B or Dexron II-C to any GM, AMC, or Chrysler automatic transmission, check the service manual for the correct type to use.* Furthermore, never use a product if it does not have the trademark on the can of "Dexron" followed by the proper number or letter designation.

fluid cooling

The purpose behind providing a cooling system for ATF is to prolong the fluid's useful life and thereby directly affect the life of the transmission. As previously mentioned, the constant action of the recirculating fluid in the torque converter and the application of the clutch or band will increase the fluid's temperature a great deal. This system does not "cool" the fluid but attempts to keep the fluid at a normal operating temperature of around 175 degrees F. At this temperature, the fluid has the potential of lasting 100,000 miles.

Vehicle manufacturers have used two different systems, the water-cooled and the air-cooled, to reduce the operating temperature of ATF. The *water-cooled system* consists of a water-tight cooler, located in the radiator's lower or side tank, two lines which carry the fluid to and from the transmission, and valving to control fluid pressure and flow (Fig. 3–7).

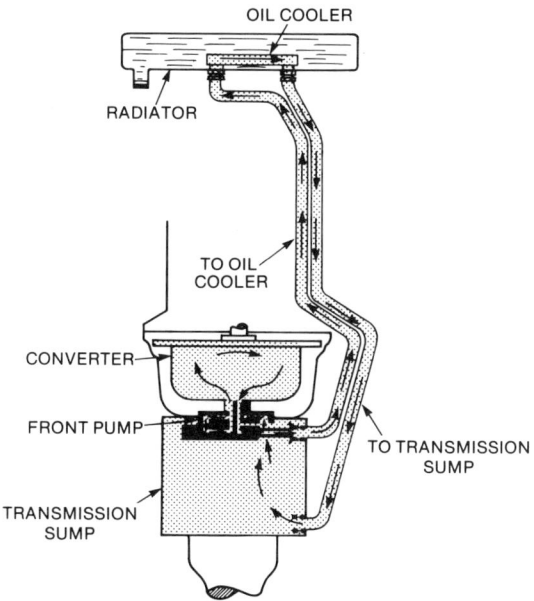

fig. 3–7 A typical water-cooled, fluid cooling system.

48 AUTOMATIC TRANSMISSION FLUIDS

When the transmission is operating, fluid under pressure flows from the transmission to the radiator cooler and returns to the transmission pan or to the transmission's lubricating system. As the fluid passes through the cooler, the excess heat in the fluid passes into the engine's coolant which surrounds the transmission cooler.

Engine coolant can cool or heat the fluid. If the engine coolant has a lower temperature than the fluid, the fluid temperature will go down. But if the engine coolant's temperature is much hotter than the temperature of the fluid, the fluid will warm up as it passes through the cooler. This action helps to warm up the fluid in extremely cold climates.

The *air-cooled system* consists of a torque converter which has a series of fins around its outer circumference, an inlet baffle or cooling shroud that is fixed to the converter's housing and directs the incoming air over the entire converter, and an outlet duct (Fig. 3–8).

As the torque converter rotates, it acts like a centrifugal air pump. A low-pressure area, formed between the air inlet and the pockets between the converter's air fins, pulls in outside air. This air flow passes over the converter, removes excess heat from the fluid contained inside the converter, and expels the heated air by centrifugal force through the outlet duct into the atmosphere.

Even in the cooling systems mentioned above, certain driving conditions can cause the fluid to overheat. For instance, if a vehicle becomes stuck in sand or mud and the driver rocks the vehicle back and forth, the fluid temperature will increase faster than the normal system can cool it. Also, when a vehicle pulls excessive loads such as a trailer or camper or operates with a restricted or blocked fluid flow to the external cooler, the transmission fluid will overheat to a point that its useful life is cut short.

The fluid's life is less because fluid temperatures above normal cause rapid oxidation. Oxidation, remember, is the union of fluid with oxygen in the presence of high temperature and results in failure of the fluid to properly lubricate. The rate of oxidation

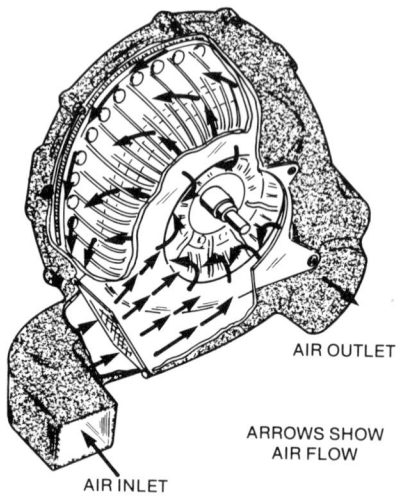

fig. 3–8 A typical air-cooled, fluid cooling system.

FLUID COOLING 49

> Temperature above normal — Rate of oxidation to double for each temperature increase of 20 degrees above normal. As oxidation rate doubles, useful life is cut in half.
>
> Now;
>
> at 175 degrees F, life is 100,000 miles
> at 195 degrees F, life is 50,000 miles
> at 212 degrees F, life is 25,000 miles
> at 235 degrees F, life is 12,000 miles
> at 255 degrees F, life is   6,250 miles
> at 275 degrees F, life is   3,000 miles (approx.)
> at 295 degrees F, life is   1,500 miles
> at 315 degrees F, life is   750 miles

fig. 3–9 The rate of fluid oxidation at a given temperature above normal.

doubles for each temperature increase of 20 degrees F. above normal, which is 175 degrees F. Furthermore, as oxidation rate doubles, useful life is cut in half (Fig. 3–9). To assist the normal transmission cooling system in maintaining a reasonable fluid temperature, several aftermarket devices are available which assist in reducing fluid temperatures and oxidation build-up.

The first device is an auxiliary cooler mounted in front of the radiator or any place where air can pass through it. This auxiliary device includes a tube or series of tubes which run the full length of the cooler and layers of air-fins surround the tubes (Fig. 3–10). If the auxiliary cooler is to handle all the fluid cooling, both the transmission cooling lines connect to the auxiliary cooler. This type of installation is sufficient for normal cooling demands where no other type of cooler is available or for assisting the factory installed air-cooled system in reducing fluid temperatures.

When the auxiliary cooler is to assist the water-cooled system, the auxiliary cooler lines connect in series with the transmission cooler return line. This second installation allows all the fluid leaving the radiator cooler to pass through the auxiliary cooler; consequently, the auxiliary cooler reduces the temperature even more before the fluid returns to the transmission (Fig. 3–11).

With either type of installation, the auxiliary cooler reduces the fluid temperature in the same way. As the fluid passes through the cooler's tubes, it gives off heat to the

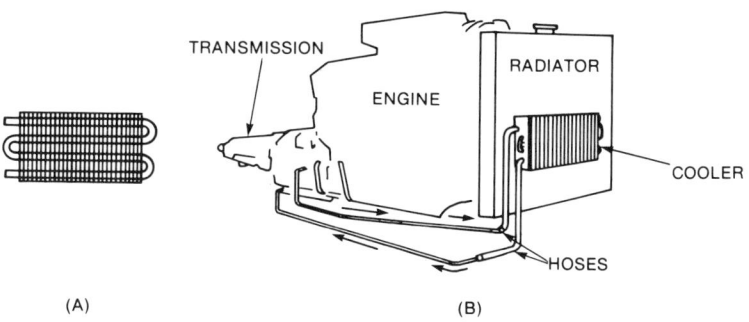

fig. 3–10 Auxiliary cooler shown at A. B shows the cooler connected directly to the transmission's cooler lines.

50 AUTOMATIC TRANSMISSION FLUIDS

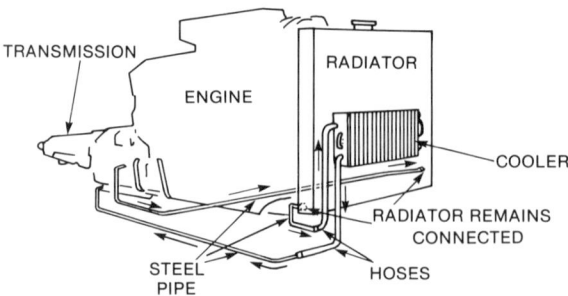

fig. 3–11 An auxiliary cooler connected in series with radiator cooler in order to provide extra fluid cooling.

tubes. The tubes, in turn, give off their heat, via the air-fins, to the air passing around the tubes. The engine cooling fan or the forward movement of the vehicle assures adequate air-flow through the auxiliary cooler.

The second aftermarket device is a specially designed transmission pan. This pan has about a one-quart larger capacity than the standard pan, and running the length of the pan are a series of air-fins (Fig. 3–12).

Fluid in the transmission will normally give off heat to the pan, and the air passing over the base of the pan removes some of this heat. With the new type of pan, the fins provide additional radiating surface for heat transfer and, at the same time, direct the cooling air over the base of the pan. In addition, the extra quart of fluid tends to reduce the overall temperature of the fluid in the transmission.

fluid energy

A moving fluid is said to possess kinetic energy. Water flowing down a mountain can turn a water wheel because of this form of energy. *Kinetic energy* is the stored capacity for performing work possessed by the moving fluid by virtue of its momentum. *Fluid*

fig. 3–12 Special air-cooled fluid pan with additional capacity for fluid storage.

momentum is the effect that the moving fluid has on other objects which determine the length of time required to bring the moving fluid to rest when the fluid is under the action of a constant force. In other words, kinetic fluid energy represents the work necessary to bring the fluid from its actual velocity (rate of flow) to a state of rest. This energy can drive the converter turbine.

The engine supplies the needed constant rotary force (torque) necessary to drive the impeller which is part of the torque converter. In turn, the impeller blades set the fluid in motion. As engine speed increases, fluid velocity increases along with kinetic energy.

The device which attempts to slow or stop the moving fluid is the turbine blades. The turbine which is also part of the torque converter attaches to the transmission's input shaft, and if the transmission is in gear, the input shaft and turbine will have the vehicle's load imposed on it (Fig. 3–13).

As the fluid flows through the turbine, the fluid decelerates or slows down. During this process, the kinetic energy originally possessed by the moving fluid on entering the turbine expends itself against the turbine blades. If sufficient kinetic energy is available in the fluid, the turbine will rotate and the vehicle will move. In other words, the moving fluid performs work.

fluid force and pressure

In studying the laws of fluids and other liquids, the reader must understand the difference between "force" and "pressure". *Force* means to push or pull an object. The unit of measurement for force is pounds. *Pressure*, on the other hand, is the result of a force applied to a fluid trapped in a sealed container system. The fluid is not compressible; therefore, fluid pressure is the end result. The fluid pressure measuring unit is pounds per square inch (psi).

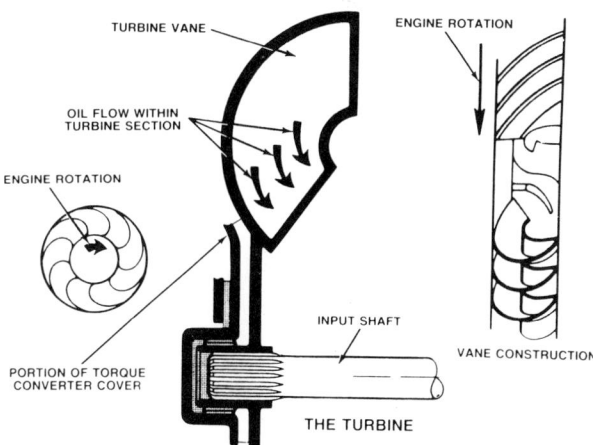

fig. 3–13 The turbine blades (vanes) attempt to slow or stop the moving fluid. (Courtesy Chrysler Corp.)

52 AUTOMATIC TRANSMISSION FLUIDS

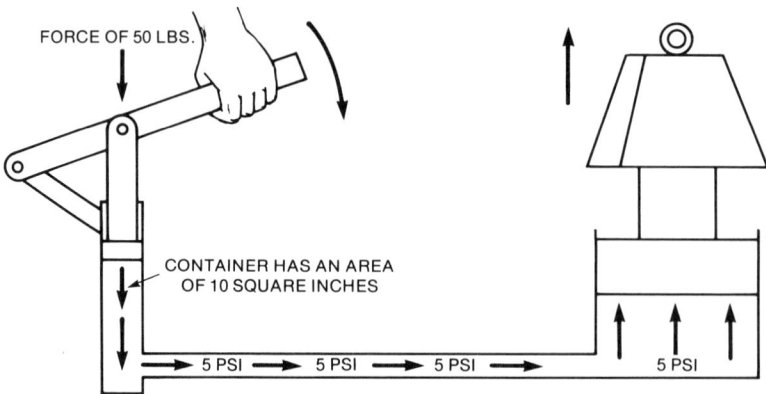

fig. 3–14 Force is a push or pull measured in pounds; pressure is the result of force applied to a fluid in a sealed system.

To determine the amount of pressure in the system shown in Fig. 3–14, divide the area of the container into the force applied to the fluid. The area of the container is 10 square inches and the force is 50 pounds. The fluid pressure is $\frac{50 \text{ pounds}}{10 \text{ square inches}}$ or 5 pounds per square inch, 5 psi. Figuring out the actual pressure in an automatic transmission is much more difficult because a rotating pump supplies a varying force to the fluid, and the actual system area changes due to many factors. These factors will be covered later in the text.

Fluid pressure can apply a force to an output piston. An output piston, placed in a hydraulic system, will have an output force equal to the area of the piston multiplied by the pressure of the system. In Fig. 3–15, the output piston has an area of 20 square inches and the system pressure is 5 psi. The output force is 20 square inches times 5 psi or 100 pounds. In automatic transmission hydraulic systems, the output pistons apply the clutches or bands.

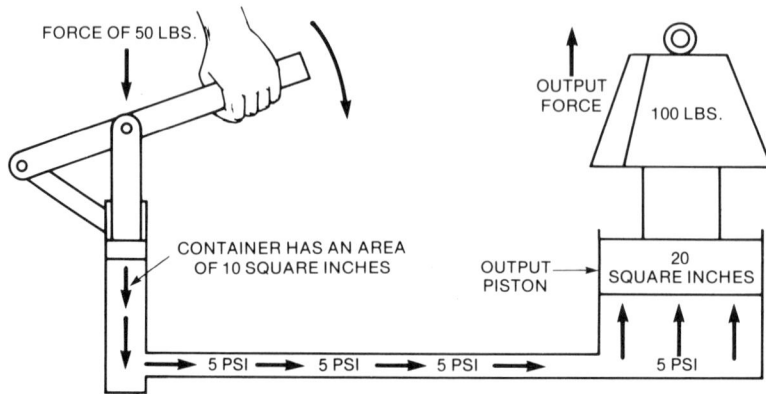

fig. 3–15 Fluid pressure can apply a force to an output piston.

summary

1. Automatic transmissions will not function without ATF.
2. Fluid is the name given to the substance used in automatic transmissions.
3. Fluid transmits torque between the engine and the transmission.
4. Fluid transmits pressure in an operating transmission.
5. Fluid carries heat to the transmission cooling system.
6. Fluid lubricates, cleans and seals moving transmission parts.
7. Fluid acts as a frictional agent.
8. Fluid has a mineral oil base and several types of additives.
9. Fluid additives retard oxidation.
10. Fluid additives reduce the foaming tendency of fluid.
11. Fluid additives stabilize viscosity.
12. Fluid contains corrosion inhibitors.
13. Fluid additives reduce wear and scoring.
14. Additives alter the fluid's friction characteristics.
15. Type F fluid has a high friction level as sliding speed equalizes.
16. Dexron provides a lower friction level as sliding speed equalizes.
17. Ford automatic transmissions now use Type F or C-J fluids.
18. American Motors, Chrysler, and General Motors all use a form of Dexron fluid in all their automatic transmissions.
19. A fluid cooling system prolongs the useful life of the fluid.
20. The two fluid cooling systems are the water-cooled and air-cooled types.
21. Two aftermarket devices, the auxiliary cooler and a specially designed pan, can assist the regular fluid cooling system in reducing high fluid temperatures.
22. Moving fluid possesses kinetic energy.
23. Kinetic fluid energy drives the turbine.
24. Force is a push or pull.
25. Pressure is the result of a force applied to a confined liquid.
26. Pressure can supply the force needed to apply a clutch or a band.

check-up questions

The questions listed below will assist you in determining how well you remember the material contained in this chapter. Read each question carefully before choosing the answer to each item. If you cannot answer the question, review the appropriate section of the chapter.

54 AUTOMATIC TRANSMISSION FLUIDS

1. What is the term used to designate the substance which lubricates an automatic transmission?
    a. oil
    b. lubricant
    c. fluid
    d. Type A
2. Fluid acts in the _____ to transmit torque between the engine and transmission.
    a. torque converter
    b. clutch
    c. band
    d. pump
3. What type of friction exists in an automatic transmission clutch?
    a. dry
    b. greasy
    c. viscous
    d. kinetic
4. Fluid has a _____ oil base.
    a. caster
    b. mineral
    c. synthetic
    d. fish
5. Oxidation of the fluid occurs in the presence of _____ and _____.
    a. additives, oxygen
    b. cold, additives
    c. cold, oxygen
    d. heat, oxygen
6. What is a frothy mass of fine bubbles called?
    a. oxidation
    b. viscosity
    c. foam
    d. compatibility
7. What is the main cause of varnish?
    a. viscosity
    b. oxidation
    c. foam
    d. compatibility

8. Which fluid has a high friction level as sliding speeds equalize?
   a. Type F
   b. Dexron
   c. Type A
   d. C-J
9. Chrysler automatic transmissions use _____ fluid.
   a. Type F
   b. C-J
   c. Dexron
   d. Type A or C-J
10. Normal operating fluid temperature should be around _____ degrees F.
    a. 300
    b. 250
    c. 200
    d. 175
11. Which fluid cooling system uses a converter with fins?
    a. air-cooled
    b. water-cooled
    c. aftermarket
    d. both a and c
12. If a vehicle is pulling a trailer, fluid temperatures may reach an average temperature of _____ degrees F.
    a. 175
    b. 225
    c. 300
    d. 500

For the answers to these check-up questions, turn to the Appendix located at the back of the text.

4

torque converters

need for a coupling device

All motor vehicles require some method of disconnecting the engine from the load imposed on the drive train so that the driver can start the engine. As stated in Chapter One, the engine produces zero torque at zero rpm; consequently, the engine will not start if placed under a load of any size. The two methods of overcoming this problem are the use of a coupling device, clutch, or the driver placing the transmission in neutral or in the case of an automatic transmission in neutral or park.

In addition, for stationary operation, such as when the engine is operating with the transmission in gear, a coupling must break the load from the engine (Fig. 4–1). Remember, the engine also produces very little torque at idle; and the vehicle's load, at this time, will exceed the engine's ability to produce torque. If not disconnected, the load will cause the engine to stall.

Finally, a coupling is necessary to gradually connect engine torque to the drive train. If the coupling is overeffective in connecting the load to an engine operating at too slow a speed, the engine may stall. If on the other hand, the coupling is overeffective and the engine is operating very fast, the drive wheels will spin; the driver may lose control of the vehicle; or damage may occur to the engine, power train components and the tires.

NEED FOR A COUPLING DEVICE 57

fig. 4–1 The types of coupling devices, the friction clutch and torque converter, utilized to connect the vehicle's load to the engine.

The type of coupling used with a manual-shift transmission is the foot-operated, friction clutch. In addition to the above-mentioned tasks, the clutch is necessary to change gear ratios. In transmissions with slide-type gear arrangements, torque flow must stop between the engine and transmission in order to change gear ratios.

When the automatic transmission replaces the manual-shift type, the torque converter replaces the foot-operated clutch. Since the use of planetary gear trains in automatic transmissions permit gear ratio changes without breaking the flow of torque, the torque converter need only disconnect the load from the engine for starting of the engine and stationary operation. In addition, the torque converter controls engine rpm and provides a gradual, smooth connection between the engine and the load. Finally, when conditions exist which call for torque multiplication, the converter will multiply engine torque to improve vehicle performance.

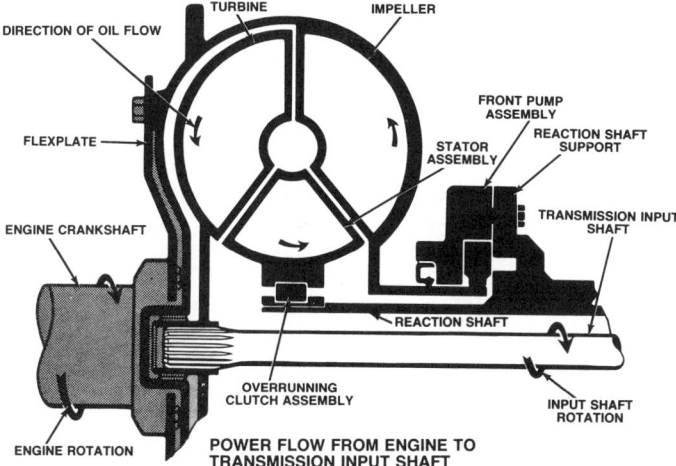

fig. 4–2 Torque converter components: the coupling members are the impeller and turbine; the torque multiplying device is the stator. (Courtesy Chrysler Corp.)

58 TORQUE CONVERTERS

To make it easy for the reader to understand torque converter theory, this chapter divides the unit into two areas of study: the converter as a coupling device which uses fluid as the medium that connects the engine to the load, and the converter as a torque multiplyng device that increases engine torque by controlling the direction of fluid flow (Fig. 4–2).

fluid coupling design

To illustrate the fluid coupling principle, contemplate the action of two electric fans, facing each other, one with the power connected and the other without power (Fig. 4–3). As the speed of the power-driven fan increases, the flow of air transmits torque to the motionless fan, and it begins to turn. The free-operating fan gains speed until it is rotating almost as rapidly as the power-driven fan. This same action takes place in the fluid coupling mechanism found in a torque converter except that fluid instead of air transmits the torque.

As in the simple example of the fans, a fluid coupling mechanism also consists of two main rotating members (Fig. 4–4). The *impeller* is the driving member which corresponds to the power-driven fan. The *turbine* is the driven member that corresponds to the fan without power. Both components are inside a stamped steel housing connected to the engine through a flexible drive plate. The housing is full of fluid constantly supplied by the transmission's hydraulic system.

Both the impeller and turbine also have a different construction than the electric fans. Both units have a shape similar to a side view of a doughnut which is cut in half. Inside the impeller, starting at the center and terminating at the rim, are a series of blades that cause circulation of fluid within the converter (Fig. 4–5). These blades have curvature in a backward direction. This curvature design gives acceleration and energy to the fluid before it leaves the impeller's rim and enters the turbine. Moreover, an inner ring, called the split quide ring, reinforces the blades and prevents fluid turbulence at the

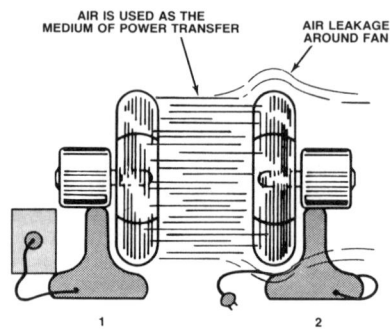

fig. 4–3 Two electric fans illustrate the coupling principle. (Courtesy Chrysler Corp.)

FLUID COUPLING DESIGN 59

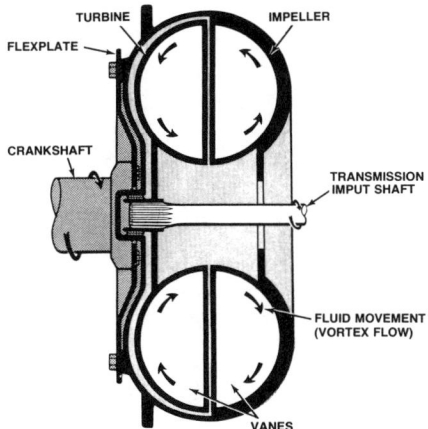

fig. 4-4 The impeller and turbine of a fluid coupling. (Courtesy Chrysler Corp.)

impeller's center by channeling the flow of fluid in a circular pattern. A series of welds holds the impeller inside the converter housing; consequently, whenever the engine is running, the impeller revolves with the housing and induces fluid flow which eventually causes the turbine to turn.

The turbine, due to its design, absorbs the kinetic energy from the moving fluid and converts it to rotary motion (Fig. 4-6). Except for the following differences, the turbine resembles the impeller. First, the turbine is free to rotate in close proximity to the impeller, and a set of splines connect the turbine to the transmission's input shaft. Second, the turbine has several more blades than the impeller does; these additional

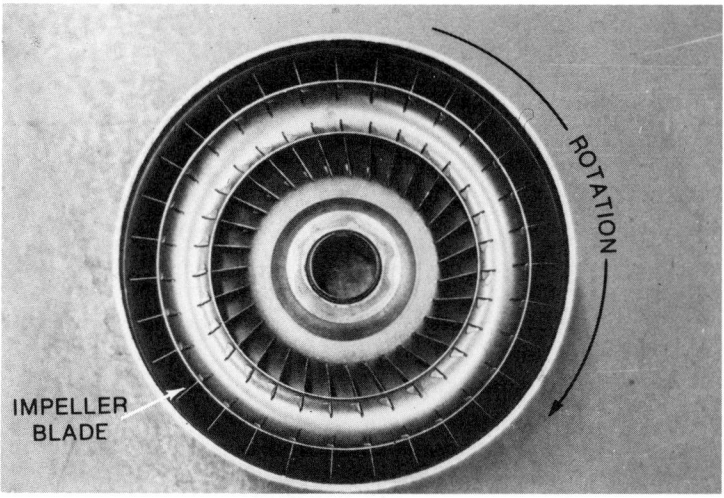

fig. 4-5 The impeller blades have a slight backwards curvature to the normal clockwise rotation of the impeller.

60 TORQUE CONVERTERS

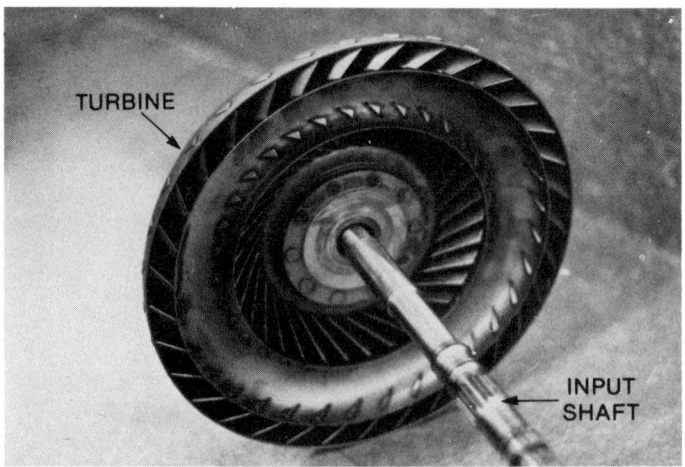

fig. 4–6 The turbine splines to the input shaft.

blades increase turbine efficiency. Finally, the turbine blade curvature is such that it reduces the shock losses due to sudden changes in fluid direction between the impeller and turbine. But at the same time, the curvature must allow the blades to absorb as much energy as possible from the fluid as it flows through the turbine (Fig. 4–7).

The curvature of the leading edge of each turbine blade prevents shock losses as the fast moving fluid begins its travel through the turbine. If the blade were straight, some of the incoming fluid would strike and bounce off the flat surface. This breakup in the otherwise smooth fluid flow would result in a loss of fluid energy (Fig. 4–8). With a curved inlet, the entering fluid now gradually changes direction as it moves along the blade.

fig. 4–7 Turbine blade curvature is such that it reduces shock losses and absorbs energy from the moving fluid.

FLUID MOTIONS PRODUCED BY THE IMPELLER 61

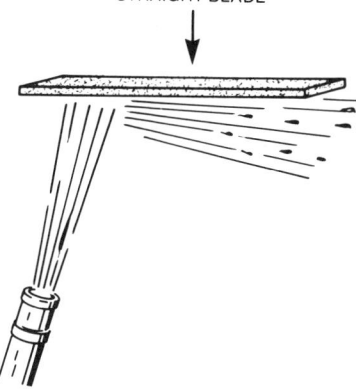

fig. 4–8 Moving fluid, if it strikes a straight blade, does not impart much of its energy to the blade.

By curving the tailing half of each turbine blade in a direction opposite to impeller rotation, the blades absorb more fluid energy because this curvature changes the direction of fluid flow (Fig. 4–9). As previously mentioned, kinetic energy is a measurement of the amount of work required to slow or stop a moving object, the fluid. By completely changing the fluid's direction, the curved blade decelerates the fluid's velocity and, therefore, receives more force from the moving fluid than it would if the blade were straight.

fluid motions produced by the impeller

As the impeller rotates at engine speed, it produces two fluid motions. The first fluid motion is *rotary,* produced by the impeller blaces pushing on the trapped fluid. The blades force the fluid to follow the clockwise direction of the impeller as it spins. This action creates a vertical, spinning mass of fluid, a vertical fluid whirlpool (Fig. 4–10).

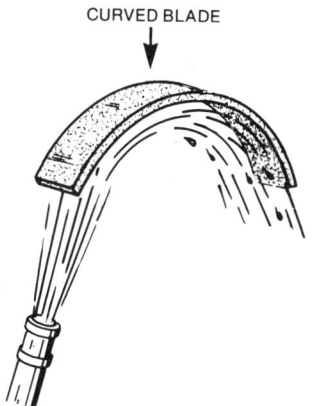

fig. 4–9 A curved blade absorbs a great deal of the energy from the moving fluid.

62 TORQUE CONVERTERS

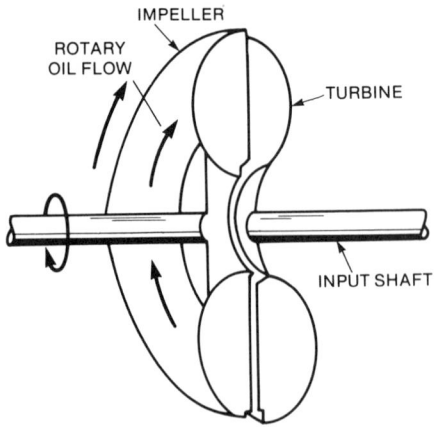

fig. 4–10 Fluid trapped between the spinning impeller blades causes a rotary fluid flow.

The second fluid motion is *vortex*, produced by centrifugal force acting upon the fluid trapped between the blades of the impeller. Centrifugal force is a force that tends to impel the fluid outward from the center of rotation. In this case, the fluid moves from the center of the impeller toward the rim. The exact same thing happens to a marble placed at the center of a spinning phonograph turntable. But since the rim of the impeller has curvature, the fluid leaves the rim at a right angle to the spinning fluid mass produced by rotary motion (Fig. 4–11). This vortex flow is responsible for driving the turbine and the transmission's input shaft.

The relative strengths of the two fluid motions determine the actual exit angle of the vortex flow as it leaves the impeller's rim and enters the turbine (Fig. 4–12). As previously mentioned, vortex flow operates at right angles to that of rotary flow. But rotary

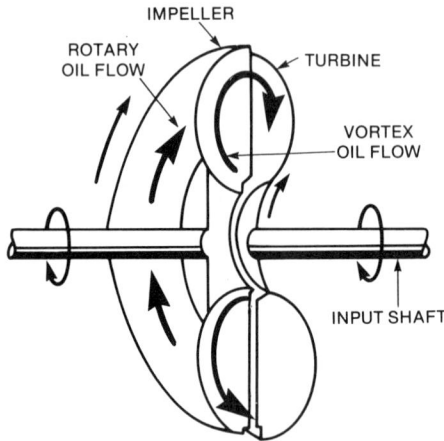

fig. 4–11 Centrifugal force, acting on the fluid trapped between the rotating impeller blades, produces vortex flow.

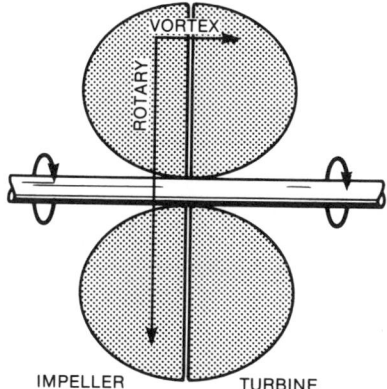

fig. 4–12 The normal vortex flow is at a right angle to that of rotary flow.

flow deflects the vortex flow from the perpendicular to form the actual exit angle.

If rotary and vortex flows are weak, due to slow impeller speed, the combined motions produce an exit angle which causes the fluid to strike the turbine blades with only a glancing blow (Fig. 4–12). This condition occurs within the converter when the engine is idling. During this time, the turbine blades do not absorb much energy from the moving fluid; consequently, the vehicle will not move.

As the engine speed increases, the turbine will begin to turn, and the fluid's exit angle from the impeller gradually changes until it reaches its maximum deflection as the turbine approaches impeller speed. With high impeller speed and low turbine speed, rotary and vortex flows are high; and the exit angle they produce is as shown in Fig. 4–13. But as the turbine starts to accelerate, the impeller's vortex flow begins to slow down and the exit angle also changes. This action is the result of the counterpumping action of the turbine; the turbine itself begins to produce rotary and vortex flows. This

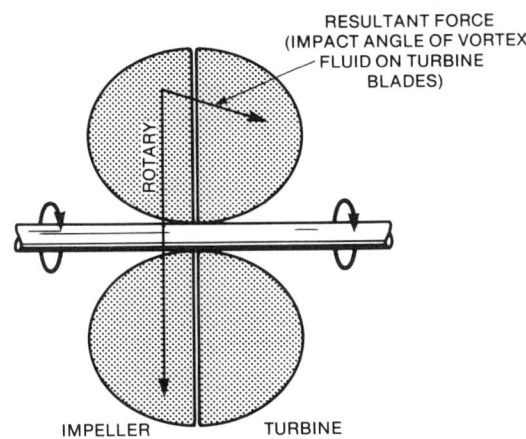

fig. 4–13 The normal vortex exit angle changes as the turbine accelerates.

64 TORQUE CONVERTERS

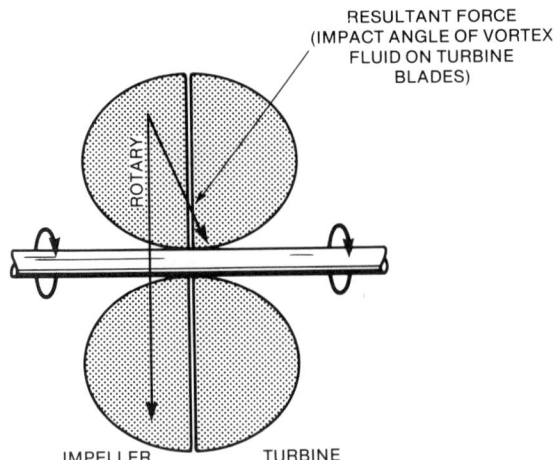

fig. 4-14 The vortex exit angle is very effective during the coupling phase of converter operation.

condition causes the impeller's fluid exit angle to change even more from the perpendicular and form a more effective impact angle on the turbine blades. This action continues until the turbine approaches the speed of the impeller. At this point, the fluid leaving the impeller has the best exit angle, and the fluid now impacts on the turbine in a more direct manner (Fig. 4-14). Consequently, torque transfer, at this time, is very efficient.

coupling operation

As previously stated, in order to start the engine, a break in torque must exist between the engine and the load. Automatic transmissions have safety switches which prevent a vehicle's starter from operating unless the transmission's selective lever is in the neutral or park position. By being in neutral or park, the turbine has no load imposed on it and is free to turn. During engine start-up, a small amount of fluid does flow between the coupling members, but even if the turbine starts to rotate, the neutral or park ranges provide a break in torque.

With the engine idling and the transmission in gear, torque still does not transfer between the engine and transmission. This 100 percent slippage is the result of two factors: (1) the combined fluid motions produce a poor exit angle for impeller fluid entering the turbine; (2) the impeller is slowly rotating; therefore, the fluid velocity produced is insufficient to overcome the load on the turbine imposed by the vehicle's weight on the transmission's input shaft. The fluid from the impeller just circulates through the turbine and returns to the center of the impeller for recycling (Fig. 4-15). This impeller and turbine slippage provides the vehicle with the necessary break in torque which is mandatory for stationary vehicle operation.

As the driver accelerates the engine, torque begins to transfer between the impeller and turbine and the vehicle begins to move. The impeller has now produced enough

COUPLING OPERATION 65

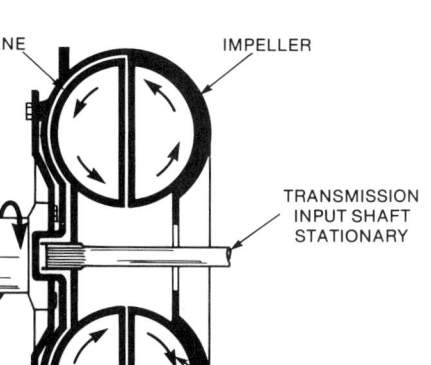

fig. 4–15 Fluid circulation within the coupling during stationary operation.

fluid velocity to overcome the vehicle's load. The fluid, once it has contacted the turbine blades, follows the contour of the blades and leaves the center of the turbine in a counterclockwise direction. Next, the fluid re-enters the center of the impeller (Fig.4–16).

But since the fluid which is leaving the turbine is moving in a counterclockwise direction, it enters the impeller and attempts to slow it and the engine down. This action reduces the efficiency of the engine in producing torque; consequently, the vehicle accelerates very slowly. It is for this reason that the fluid coupling portion of a torque converter by itself is very inefficient whenever a large difference in speed exists between the impeller and turbine.

From the time the turbine begins to rotate and until it approaches impeller speed, the exit angle of the impeller's vortex flow is constantly changing. Remember that this action results from the counterpumping action of the turbine. The fluid leaving the

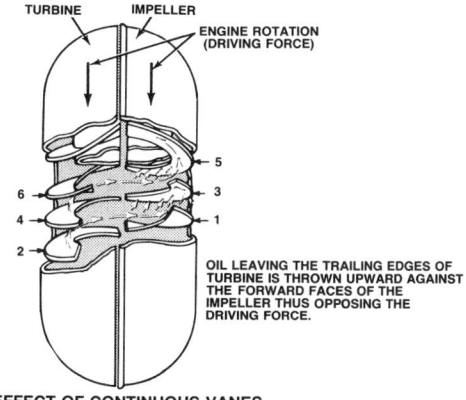

fig. 4–16 Fluid returning from the turbine to the impeller attempts to slow the impeller and engine down. (Courtesy Chrysler Corp.)

66 TORQUE CONVERTERS

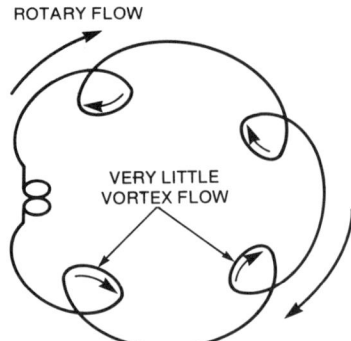

fig. 4-17 Vortex flow between the impeller and turbine is low during the coupling phase.

impeller begins to impact on the turbine blades at a constantly changing angle until the turbine approaches impeller speed. Then, the fluid leaving the impeller reaches its most effective angle as the turbine nears impeller speed.

As the turbine reaches the approximate speed of the impeller, the fluid coupling enters its most effective period known as the coupling phase. At this time, about 10 percent slippage exists between the impeller and the turbine. The impeller's vortex flow now is low because both members pump fluid toward their outer diameters (Fig. 4-17). Therefore, each member produces a pressurized wall of fluid which resists any shearing action.

In all instances, when the fluid coupling is transferring torque, one member must turn faster than the other. The faster rotating member maintains the circulation of fluid necessary to keep all the bladed areas of both members full of fluid and maintain some effect of fluid impacting on blades. If both members rotate at the same speed, fluid circulation will stop and so will the transfer of torque between the two members.

If the driver reduces engine speed so that the vehicle begins to drive the engine through the fluid coupling, the engine will exert a braking effect on the vehicle. Under these conditions, the turbine acts as the impeller or pump creating flow within the coupling. Fluid will pass from the turbine to the impeller, impose a push on its blades, and return to the turbine. This condition will exist until the impeller once again overspeeds the turbine.

converter as a torque multiplier

By installing a third member, the *stator*, between the turbine and impeller, the fluid coupling becomes a torque converter which can multiply torque (Fig. 4-18). The stator has a series of curved blades designed to change the direction of the fluid leaving the center of the turbine. This action causes the fluid to flow back into the impeller in the same direction that it is turning. As mentioned earlier, the fluid coupling is inefficient whenever a large difference in speed exists between the turbine and impeller because the returning turbine fluid attempts to "buck" or slow down the engine. But the stator redirects the fluid to a helping direction which overcomes this design deficiency. Finally,

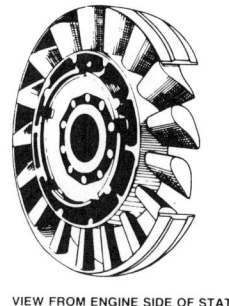

VIEW FROM ENGINE SIDE OF STATOR
SHOWING VANE CURVATURE

fig. 4-18 The location of the stator assembly is between the turbine and impeller. (Courtesy Chrysler Corp.)

the torque converter does not require the stator's action during all its phases of operation.

In order to get the stator out of the way when its job is over, the stator has an overrunning clutch (Fig. 4–19). The overrunning clutch allows the stator to free wheel in a clockwise direction, but it prevents the stator from turning counterclockwise. In addition, the inner race of the stator supports the whole assembly; this race has a series of internal splines which mate with external splines located on the stationary stator support. The stator support is part of the front pump assembly and does not turn (Fig. 4–20). A portion of the next chapter covers the construction and operation of overrunning clutches in more detail. For now just remember that the overrunning clutch allows the stator to rotate clockwise; but the clutch locks the stator to the case, via the stator support, if the stator attempts to turn counterclockwise.

stator operation-torque increase

Whenever the impeller overspeeds the turbine any appreciable amount, the stator is stationary, and the torque converter multiplies torque. During these periods, the fluid leaving the center of the turbine still has some kinetic energy remaining. This relatively

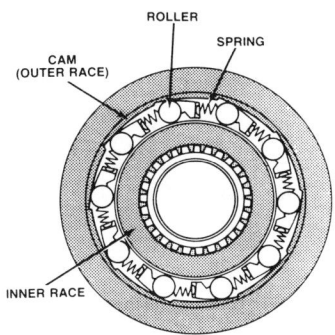

fig. 4-19 The stator's overrunning clutch. (Courtesy Chrysler Corp.)

68 TORQUE CONVERTERS

fig. 4–20 The stationary stator support is part of the front pump assembly.

fast moving fluid strikes the front face of the stator blades and attempts to turn them counterclockwise; but the overrunning clutch locks the stator to the case. Then, the curved stator blades change the direction of the fluid to a helping direction before the fluid re-enters the impeller (Fig. 4–21). Next, this fluid and the fluid accelerated by the impeller both move back into the turbine. The recirculating fluid adds even more push to the turbine blades. During this stationary operation, the stator serves the same function as the fulcrum serves in a lever system. But in this case, since the stator is stationary, locked to the transmission case, the case receives the force required to change the fluid's direction and not the impeller blades.

The continuous flow of fluid, from the impeller into the turbine, back to the impeller where its remaining energy adds to the fluid being accelerated by the engine, and then back into the turbine again, is the basis for torque multiplication within the torque converter. Each time the total vortex flow passes from the impeller to the turbine, the moving fluid imparts a push to the turbine blades. The fluid will still have some kinetic energy remaining as it leaves the turbine on its way back to the impeller; and the stator reverses its direction before the fluid re-enters the impeller. When the same fluid comes into the turbine again, its remaining energy provides additional push on the turbine. Repeated applications of this push, caused by the fluid which received its initial kinetic energy from

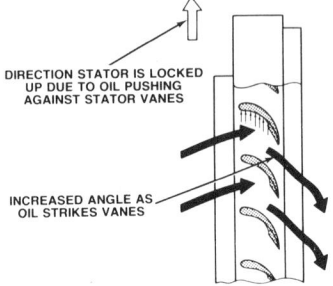

fig. 4–21 The stator's operation during the torque multiplication phase of the converter. (Courtesy Chrysler Corp.)

STATOR OPERATION-COUPLING PHASE 69

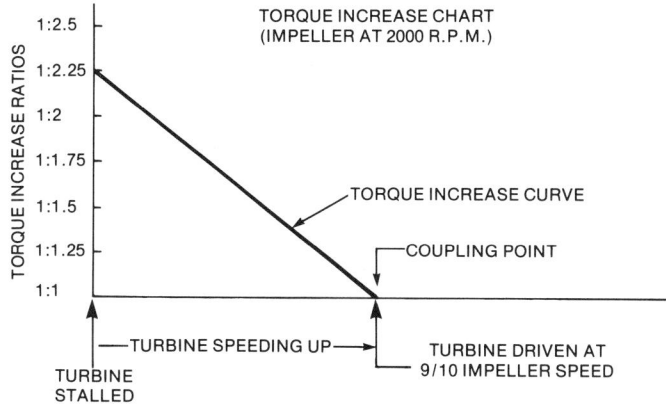

fig. 4-22 Chart of a typical converter torque multiplication curve.

the engine driven impeller, increases the total turbine torque. Total turbine torque, in other words, is always equal to energy remaining in the returning turbine fluid plus the energy in the fluid accelerated by the impeller. Consequently, when the turbine is rotating at very slow speeds with the impeller revolving at high speeds, the torque on the input shaft, attached to the turbine, may be several times the torque of the engine.

Most torque converters provide a maximum torque increase in passenger car applications of between 1:2 to about 1:2.5 at stall speeds (Fig. 4-22). Converter stall speed is a condition where the impeller rotates as fast as the engine will drive it at wide open throttle, but the turbine is stationary. At this point, the converter has absorbed a given amount of torque or reached its torque capacity; the rpm of the engine stabilizes, and the converter just slips.

stator operation-coupling phase

As the torque converter approaches the coupling point, turbine approaches impeller speed, the stator is no longer necessary because turbine torque multiplication has smoothly and gradually decreased. At this point in converter operation, rotary flow of the impeller's fluid is high, but vortex is low. The fluid leaving the center of the turbine has been constantly changing since the turbine began to rotate. By the time the converter reaches the coupling point, the returning turbine fluid strikes the back faces of the stator blades, and the stator begins to turn in a clockwise direction carried along by the rotating fluid mass produced by both the turbine and impeller (Fig. 4-23). If the stator does not rotate, its blades will interfere with the normal fluid flow and create a drag within the converter which slows everything down.

The stator's overrunning action occurs at about 90 percent turbine and impeller speed ratio or when the turbine is about 9/10 of impeller speed (Fig. 4-22). If the turbine again rotates at less than this 90 percent of impeller speed, the stator will slow and stop; and torque multiplication will again occur within the converter. Finally, if the coupling

70 TORQUE CONVERTERS

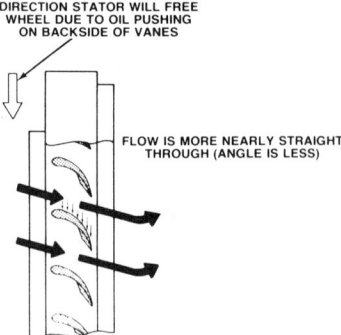

fig. 4–23 The stator's operation during the coupling phase of the converter. (Courtesy Chrysler Corp.)

mechanism forces the engine to act as a braking device, the stator also overruns and the turbine pumps fluid into the impeller.

lock-up converters

The *lock-up torque converter* is not new to the field of transportation. This device has been used for a number of years in truck and other industrial applications. But due to the fact that this converter costs more to produce, it has not until recently been used in passenger cars. However, with the rise in the cost of gasoline and the increased problems in obtaining good fuel economy, the lock-up converter pays for itself in a short period of time.

The lock-up converter (Fig. 4–24) has a turbine that operates at impeller speed when the converter is in the coupling phase and because of this feature, this converter provides three benefits over the conventional converter. First, with a lock-up converter, the vehicle does achieve better fuel economy because, during the coupling phase, the turbine revolves at impeller speed. Remember, that with the conventional converter, about 10 percent slippage must exist between the turbine and impeller, during the coupling phase, in order for torque to transfer between these two units. This 10 percent slippage reduces the fuel economy of the vehicle.

Second, the lock-up converter lowers the transmission's operating temperature during the coupling phase. In the standard converter, fluid must continue to circulate during this time in order to maintain torque transfer, and fluid circulation within the converter always increases its temperature. With the lock-up converter, the turbine locks up to the converter housing by means of a clutch; therefore, fluid circulation is no longer necessary during the coupling phase to transfer torque. As a result, the converter's fluid temperature goes down.

Finally, the lock-up converter reduces engine speed during cruising speeds. Not only does the lower engine rpm save fuel, it allows the engine to operate somewhat

LOCK-UP CONVERTER DESIGN **71**

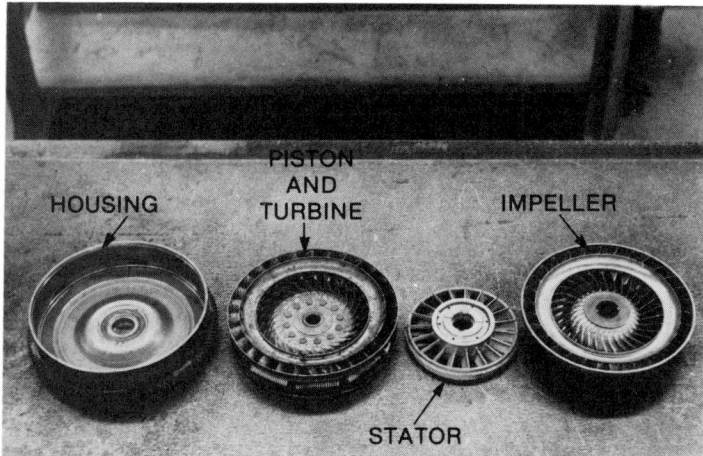

fig. 4–24 A lock-up converter consists of a housing, movable piston and turbine, stator, and the impeller.

more quietly and, at the same time, extends engine life. Although these benefits may seem small, in the long run they account for a significant savings for the owner of the vehicle.

lock-up converter design

In order for a standard three-member converter to have this lock-up feature, three additional components are necessary. The first component required is a movable piston (Fig. 4–25). One side of this piston is in contact with the turbine through a series of tabs machined into the piston's outer circumference. The tabs ride between cushion springs

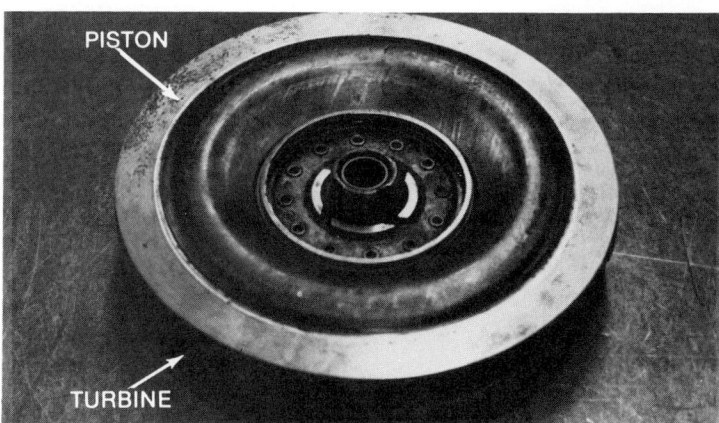

fig. 4–25 The movable piston and turbine of a lock-up converter.

72 TORQUE CONVERTERS

fig. 4-26 The converter housing has a friction lining bonded inside it.

mounted on the turbine. The opposite side of the piston has a machined surface that during lock-up, bears against a friction material.

This friction material is the second component (Fig. 4-26). The converter manufacturer bonds a ring of friction material to the inside of the converter's front cover. When the machined surface of the piston contacts this friction lining, the piston and turbine will operate at front cover speed which will be the same as that of the impeller.

The final component necessary to have a lock-up converter is a series of damper springs (Fig. 4-27). These springs fasten to the outer circumference of the movable turbine between the piston tabs. These damper springs are necessary in the lock-up converter because during the lock-up phase of converter operation, the damping of

fig. 4-27 The damper springs are located around the outside of the turbine.

LOCK-UP CONVERTER OPERATION 73

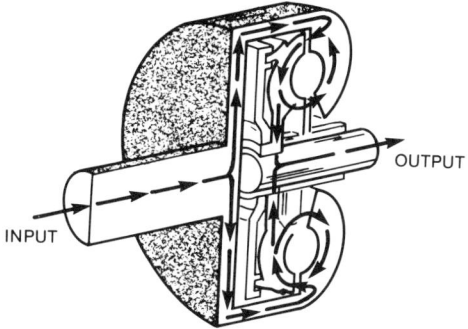

fig. 4–28 The lock-up converter operating in the torque-multiplication phase.

engine torsional vibrations by the fluid has stopped. Therefore, the damper springs now absorb any torsional vibration load transmitted by the engine.

lock-up converter operation

When a lock-up converter is operating in the torque multiplication phase, the piston keeps the turbine away from the friction lining (Fig. 4–28). During this period, the hydraulic control system sends pressurized fluid to the left side of the piston. This hydraulic pressure forces the piston and the turbine to the right away from the friction lining. The turbine, at this time, operates in the same manner as any turbine in a conventional torque converter.

But as this converter enters the coupling phase, the turbine begins to operate at housing and impeller speed. At this point, the hydraulic control system cuts off fluid pressure to the left side of the piston. Next, normal converter fluid pressure forces the turbine and piston against the friction lining which locks the turbine to the front cover and housing. This action causes the turbine to rotate at housing speed (Fig. 4–29).

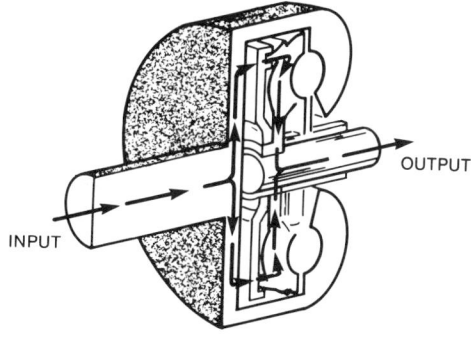

fig. 4–29 The lock-up converter operating in the coupling phase.

advantages provided by torque converters

The torque converter provides several advantages over the conventional clutch: (1) the torque converter helps to dampen out engine torsional vibrations and acts as a shock absorber during gear ratio changes which adds to shift quality; (2) the torque converter eliminates manual-clutch operation which makes the vehicle easier to operate in traffic and permits engine operation while the vehicle is stationary; (3) the torque converter provides a break in torque necessary for engine starting; (4) the torque converter acts as a fluid coupling to transfer torque from the engine to the transmission; (5) the torque converter automatically multiplies engine torque whenever there is over about a 10 percent difference in turbine and impeller speed. This action permits the converter to automatically adjust its torque output to meet the load demands placed on the turbine but only up to its design limits.

converter size and torque capacity

The overall size of the converter and stator blade angles are design features which determine the capacity of the converter—its rate of torque absorption, the converter's stall speed, and its coupling point. Small converters with steep stator blade angles reduce the volume of fluid flow between the turbine and impeller, consequently, the impeller can operate at a faster rpm before its stall speed occurs. Furthermore, these low capacity converters will have a coupling point that occurs at a higher rpm and produces higher torque increase ratios than the larger converters (Fig. 4–30).

Larger converters, high capacity design, will have shallow stator blade angles. This design provides the converter with a low stall speed and coupling point. But the unit produces sufficient torque multiplication for average vehicle acceleration under moder-

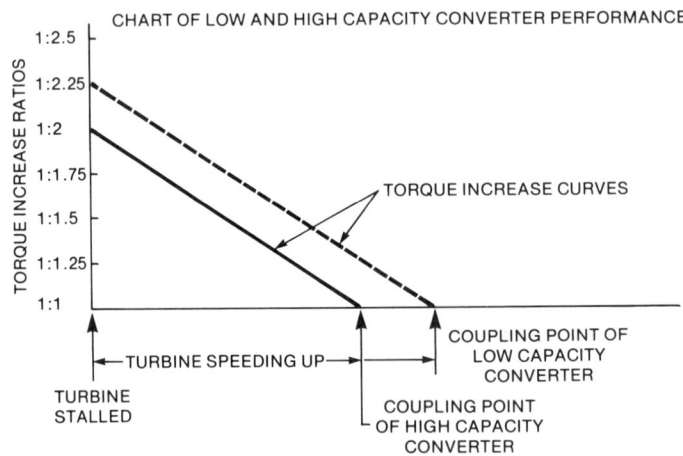

fig. 4–30 Chart of low and high capacity converter performance.

ate loads. Vehicles with small engines utilize the low capacity converters, and vehicles with large engines use large or high capacity converters.

Converter designers use either converter size or stator angle or a combination of the two to develop converters that allow minimum creep at idle and provide a stall speed about 30 percent lower than the engine rpm producing maximum engine torque. If a converter reaches its stall speed at a point where the engine reaches its maximum torque, the converter will multiply high torque values. This action can overheat the converter.

Furthermore, high stall speeds which are an inherent characteristic of low capacity converters, if not needed for vehicle performance, will make the engine burn excess fuel and be noisy. In addition, the high stall speed results in a high coupling point which allows the engine to operate at a high rpm at crusing speeds that reduces engine life. Therefore, modern converter designs are of necessity a compromise between the performance characteristics of both low and high capacity converters. Finally, stall and coupling speeds which do not mate with the size of the engine make it impossible to fully utilize the torque and speed range of the engine.

Smaller four- and six-cylinder engines usually use relatively low capacity converters. This converter permits these engine types to operate at near their maximum torque output, which is usually at a much higher rpm than large V-8 engines, before stall speed occurs. Also, this converter design permits a relatively high coupling point. Finally, a low capacity converter like this one absorbs engine torque with greater slippage; but it provides more fluid energy for torque multiplication.

Large engines utilize relatively high capacity converters. These converters provide the vehicle with a smaller overall torque multiplication curve and a low coupling point. Even under a heavy acceleration, the torque multiplication curve does not stretch itself as far as it does with the low capacity converter and coupling may occur at 45 mph.

In many cases, the vehicle manufacturer will install the same transmission in several identical automobiles with different engine sizes. To mate the converter to the engine, the manufacturer will change either the converter's size, stator blade angle or a combination of the two. Therefore, it is important that the mechanic does not alter the converter because it has the design characteristics required by the engine. If the converter malfunctions, replace it with a unit which meets all the factory specifications.

combination low and high capacity converters

A method used by manufacturers to provide a converter with the benefits of both low and high capacity converters, incorporates a variable-pitch stator (Fig. 4–31). This converter has a hydraulic piston and control system which moves the stator blades from the high to the low angle position. An electrical switch, usually connected to the throttle linkage, signals the control system when it is time to activate the piston which, in turn, changes the blade angle.

When there is a large difference in speed between the impeller and turbine, the stator blades move to a high angle (Fig. 4–32). This action produces a low capacity

76 TORQUE CONVERTERS

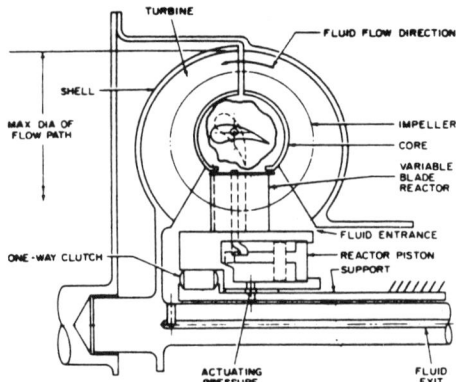

fig. 4–31 A converter with a variable-pitch stator. The reaction piston changes the stator (reaction) blade angle. (Reprinted with permission from the SAE Handbook, © 1978 Society of Automotive Engineers, Inc.)

converter with considerable fluid flow restriction. This restricting action causes the converter to have a high stall speed and torque multiplication.

When the converter approaches the coupling point, under normal acceleration, the stator blades move to a low angle position (Fig. 4–33). This action produces a high capacity converter with less fluid flow restriction. Also, to minimize creep of the vehicle at curb idle, the converter remains in the low angle position until the driver accelerates the engine.

advantages of using variable pitch stators

The following advantages are prominent in converters with variable pitch stators: (1) with the stator blades in the low angle position, high capacity condition, the converter provides little vehicle creep at curb idle and is a very efficient coupling; (2) with the stator blades in the high angle position, low capacity condition, engine speed increases for

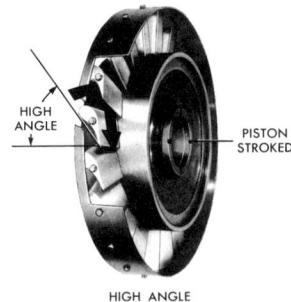

fig. 4–32 Variable stator blades in the high angle position. (Courtesy Hydro-matic Division of General Motors Corp.)

CONVERTER INSTALLATION 77

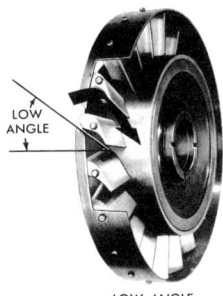

fig. 4-33 Variable stator blades in the low angle position. (Courtesy Hydro-matic Division of General Motors Corp.)

higher stall speed and torque multiplication; (3) the driver can extend the high angle position by keeping the gas pedal depressed. This action extends the torque multiplication range of the converter to higher speeds and raises the converter's coupling point which is very useful when a vehicle is pulling heavy loads.

converter installation

As previously stated, the engine drives the converter by means of a flex drive plate bolted to the crankshaft. Furthermore, manufacturers employ several methods to support and center the converter. For instance, a bushing, a special type of round bearing pressed into the front pump housing, supports and centers the hub located on the back side of the converter (Fig. 4-34).

The hub located on the front side of the converter or special studs center and support the front portion of the converter. One converter type uses the hub that fits

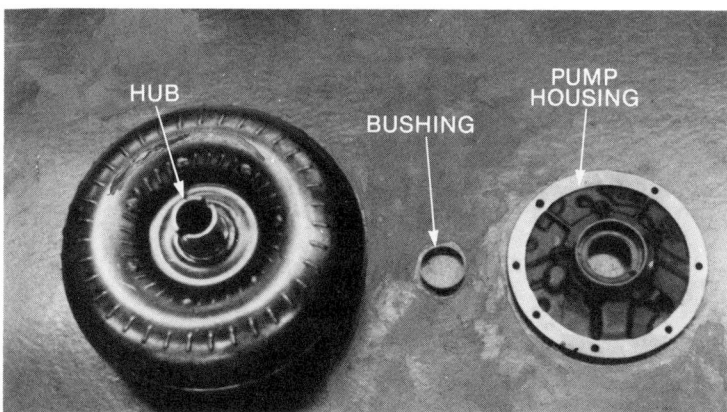

fig. 4-34 The converter's hub, its bushing, and the pump housing.

78 TORQUE CONVERTERS

fig. 4–35 The front hub on many converters is supported in a counterbore at the end of the crankshaft.

snugly into a specially machined counterbore in the back of the crankshaft (Fig. 4–35). Another converter style uses the drive studs which have specially machined shoulders that mate with precised drilled holes in the flex plate. The studs not only drive the converter but center and support it as well (Fig. 4–36).

other converter functions

The torque converter drives the front hydraulic pump and, in some cases, has the starter ring gear mounted on it. The hub located on the back side on the converter housing has either two flats or two slots machined into its end which mate with similarly machined areas located on the drive gear or rotor of the front pump (Fig. 4–37). As the converter

fig. 4–36 Converter drive studs support the front end of some converter types.

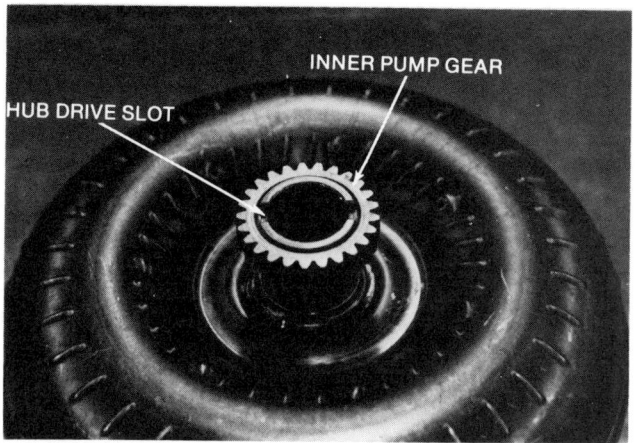

fig. 4–37 Slots in the converter's hub drive the inner, pump gear.

housing rotates with the engine, it drives the gear or rotor which, in turn, causes the pump to produce hydraulic pressure.

Some converters also have the starter ring gear welded to the converter housing (Fig. 4–38). In other installations, the ring gear fastens to the flex drive plate. In either case, the starter rotates the ring gear which, in turn, turns the engine over for starting.

fig. 4–38 A starter ring gear welded to the converter housing.

summary

1. All motor vehicles require some form of coupling device to disconnect the load from the engine so that it can be started and for stationary operation.
2. The type of coupling used with manual-shift transmission is a foot-operated friction

clutch; the type of coupling utilized with the modern automatic transmission is the torque converter.
3. The torque converter contains a fluid coupling mechanism and a torque multiplying device.
4. The fluid coupling mechanism has an impeller and a turbine.
5. The engine drives the impeller which then produces rotary and vortex flows.
6. The turbine absorbs the kinetic energy from the moving fluid and converts it to rotary motion.
7. The transmission's input shaft connects the turbine to the planetary gearset.
8. Turbine blade curvature is such that it reduces shock losses but, at the same time, absorbs as much energy as possible from the moving fluid.
9. Rotary flow is a spinning mass of fluid.
10. Vortex flow is flow due to centrifugal force.
11. Vortex flow drives the turbine.
12. The relative strengths of the two fluid motions determine the actual exit angle of the impeller's vortex flow.
13. The 100 percent slippage in the fluid coupling at idle is due to the low fluid velocity and the poor exit angle for impeller fluid entering the turbine.
14. When the turbine reaches the approximate speed of the impeller, the fluid coupling enters its most effective period known as the coupling phase.
15. If torque is to transfer between the two members of a fluid coupling, one member must be moving faster than the other.
16. By installing a third member, the stator, between the turbine and impeller, the fluid coupling becomes a torque converter which can multiply engine torque.
17. The stator redirects the returning turbine fluid to a helping direction.
18. In order to get the stator out of the way when it is no longer needed, the stator has an overrunning clutch.
19. Whenever the impeller overspeeds the turbine any appreciable amount, the stator is stationary, and the torque converter multiplies torque.
20. The total turbine torque is the result of the combination of the fluid energy remaining in the returning turbine fluid and the energy contained in the fluid accelerated by the turbine.
21. As the converter approaches the coupling point, the stator freewheels in a clockwise direction.
22. Lock-up converters have a turbine that, during the coupling phase, rotates at impeller speed.
23. Smaller engines utilize low capacity converters which have higher stall speeds, torque increase ratios and coupling points.

24. Larger engines use high capacity converters which have lower stall speeds, torque multiplication ratios and coupling points.
25. To combine the effects of both low and high capacity converters, some converters have variable pitch stator blades.
26. When these converters multiply engine torque, the stator blades move to the high angle position.
27. When these converters are in the coupling phase, the stator blades move to the low angle position.
28. Manufacturers employ several methods to center and support the torque converter.
29. The torque converter drives the front hydraulic pump and, in some cases, has the starter ring mounted on it.

check-up questions

The questions listed below will assist you in determining how well you remember the material contained in this chapter. Read each question carefully before choosing the answer to each item. If you cannot answer the question, review the appropriate section of the chapter.

1. When the automatic transmission replaces the manual-shift transmission, the _____ replaces the foot-operated clutch.
    a. clutch
    b. band
    c. turbine
    d. torque converter
2. The fluid coupling provides a break in torque necessary for _____ and _____.
    a. engine starting, stationary operation
    b. acceleration, coasting
    c. stationary operation, acceleration
    d. engine starting, acceleration
3. The member of the fluid coupling mechanism that causes fluid flow is the _____.
    a. turbine
    b. impeller
    c. stator
    d. flex plate

82 TORQUE CONVERTERS

4. The portion of the fluid coupling which absorbs the energy from the moving fluid is the _____.
   a. housing
   b. impeller
   c. turbine
   d. flex plate

5. The fluid flow caused by the blades pushing on the trapped fluid inside the converter housing is _____.
   a. vortex
   b. rotary
   c. centrifugal
   d. both *a* and *c*

6. The angle of the _____ flow changes with turbine speed.
   a. vortex
   b. rotary
   c. vertical
   d. both *b* and *c*

7. During stationary operation, the _____ is rotating and the _____ is stationary.
   a. turbine, impeller
   b. impeller, turbine
   c. housing, impeller
   d. impeller, housing

8. When the fluid coupling reaches its coupling point, the turbine and impeller speed ratio is about _____.
   a. 6:10
   b. 7:10
   c. 8:10
   d. 9:10

9. For the fluid coupling mechanism to transfer torque, both members must be _____.
   a. rotating at the same speed
   b. rotating
   c. stationary
   d. rotating at different speeds

CHECK-UP QUESTIONS 83

10. If the driver reduces speed so that the vehicle begins to drive the engine through the fluid coupling, the _____ causes fluid flow within the unit.
    a. impeller
    b. turbine
    c. stator
    d. housing

11. The component which changes the fluid coupling into a torque multiplying device is the _____.
    a. turbine
    b. impeller
    c. stator
    d. housing

12. The stator's _____ allows it to turn when the stator is not necessary for torque multiplication.
    a. overrunning clutch
    b. blades
    c. support
    d. assembly

13. When the torque converter is increasing torque, the stator is _____.
    a. moving clockwise
    b. moving counterclockwise
    c. stationary
    d. locked to impeller

14. Torque converters which are low capacity have _____ stall speeds.
    a. low
    b. high
    c. zero
    d. moderate

15. Converter capacity is a result of the unit's _____ and _____ angles.
    a. size, turbine blade
    b. size, impeller blade
    c. size, stator blade
    d. both *a* and *b*

16. Transmissions which utilize torque converters, as mentioned in this chapter, do not _____.
    a. require foot-operated clutches

84 TORQUE CONVERTERS

   b. have impellers
   c. have stators
   d. have housings
17. When a torque converter has the lock-up feature, the _____ locks to the housing during the coupling phase.
   a. impeller
   b. stator
   c. turbine
   d. overrunning clutch
18. Vehicles with larger engines use _____ capacity converters.
   a. high
   b. low
   c. moderate
   d. none of the above
19. Special drive studs can drive, _____ and _____ the torque converter.
   a. balance, support
   b. center, support
   c. balance, center
   d. center, balance
20. The _____ drives the transmission's hydraulic pump.
   a. turbine
   b. stator
   c. converter housing
   d. impeller

For the answers to these check-up questions, turn to the Appendix located at the back of the text.

5

clutches used in automatic transmissions

function of the clutch

When the average person encounters the term "clutch" he usually thinks of the foot-operated device required with a manual-shift transmission. However, an automatic transmission also has clutches which, in some applications, perform similar functions as the foot-operated unit. By their design, automatic transmission clutches are known as the multiple-disc wet type and the mechanical overrunning type.

The multiple-disc wet clutch can perform several functions even in the same automatic transmission. First, this clutch directly or indirectly connects and disconnects member(s) of the planetary gear train to the transmission's input shaft. Remember, the input shaft splines to the turbine within the torque converter; if the turbine rotates with the clutch applied (activated), torque transfers from the turbine to the planetary gear train member.

Second, a transmission manufacturer can build a gear box that uses the multiple-disc clutch to hold a member of the planetary gearset stationary. In this case, the clutch replaces the use of a band for this purpose because the clutch does not require any adjustment after prolonged usage. Furthermore, disc clutches have the ability to withstand large torque loads for their size with a minimum of slippage.

86 CLUTCHES USED IN AUTOMATIC TRANSMISSIONS

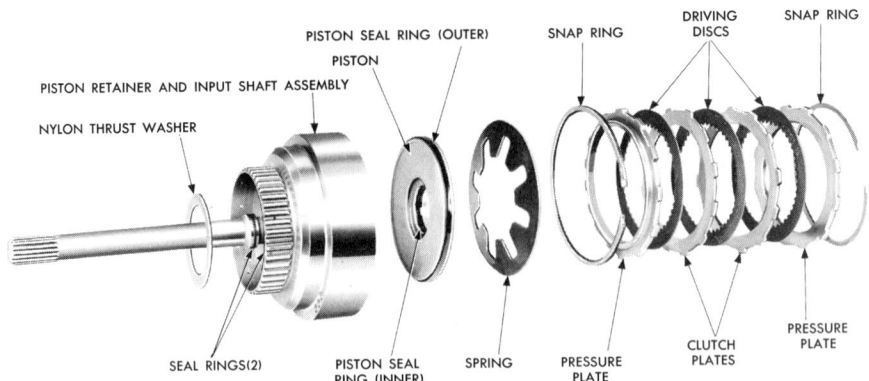

fig. 5-1 A primary clutch assembly. (Courtesy Chrysler Corp.)

disc clutch design

For the sake of simplicity in discussing the various kinds of disc clutches used in automatic transmissions, this text refers to them as primary, secondary, and stationary clutches. A *primary clutch* is one that has a drum which attaches directly to the input shaft. On the other hand, the drum of a *secondary clutch* does not. And finally, a *stationary clutch* has no drum at all because the transmission case itself houses all the clutch components.

A primary clutch assembly consists of a drum, hydraulic piston, drive and driven clutch discs, in addition to a clutch hub (Fig. 5-1). Drum manufacturers usually use a good grade of cast iron and several machine processes to form the drum or cylinder. Also, some manufacturers produce stamped steel drums as clutch housings to reduce weight and cost. In either case, the machined area inside the drum is large enough to retain the hydraulic piston, clutch discs, and the clutch hub. Finally, the clutch drum, as previously mentioned, attaches to the transmission's input shaft and rotates at input shaft speed.

Inside the drum at the very bottom is a machined area that forms the cylinder or guide for the *hydraulic piston* (Fig. 5-2). Hydraulic pressure directed to the area under the piston's base moves the piston within the machined area. In turn, the moving piston compresses all the clutch discs together.

A type of return spring is necessary to push the hydraulic piston to the base of the drum when hydraulic pressure ceases, and because the spring resists any piston movement, it cushions clutch application. Some automatic transmissions use only one large compression spring for this purpose; others use a series of small compression springs or a diaphragm spring. In any case, a *snap ring* that fits into a narrow groove, cut into the drum, secures the spring retainer and spring(s) to the drum. As a result, the force of the spring(s), when compressed, exerts against the movable piston and also the retainer, snap ring, and drum.

Also, inside a cavity located in the base of the drum or the hydraulic piston itself is a residual check ball and seat (Fig. 5-3). The residual *check ball* allows any fluid trapped

DISC CLUTCH DESIGN 87

fig. 5-2 The cylinder section of the drum forms the guide for the piston.

below the clutch piston to escape whenever there is no hydraulic pressure under the clutch piston. This check valve is mandatory if the clutch assembly is to have a long life. If the clutch did not have a check ball, high drum rotation would create sufficient centrifugal force in the residual fluid, under the piston, to cause it to partially engage the clutch discs. The partially engaged clutch discs will then overheat due to friction and prematurely wear out.

During clutch operation, hydraulic pressure under the clutch piston seats the check ball. This action seals off the area from leakage past the check ball and seat. When hydraulic pressure stops and the drum is rotating, the residual check ball opens due to centrifugal force created by the rotating drum. With the ball off its seat, any residual fluid can escape from under the piston.

A primary clutch assembly has two types of clutch discs or plates: the steel type that are the drive plates and the friction type that are the driven plates. The *steel drive plates* are usually flat and have a series of teeth machined into their outer circumference (Fig. 5-4). These teeth fit into slots or grooves cut into the inside wall of the clutch drum.

fig. 5-3 A residual check valve located in the clutch piston.

88 CLUTCHES USED IN AUTOMATIC TRANSMISSIONS

fig. 5-4 The steel plates found in a typical clutch assembly.

With the drive plates installed in the drum, any rotation of the drum will force the steel drive plates to turn.

Some clutch assemblies do have steel plates which are not flat. The clutch design shown in Fig. 5-5 has steel plates which have a coning on the inside diameter of the plate of about .010 inch. Another clutch design uses a wavy steel disc that has no external teeth to lock the plate to the drum (Fig. 5-6). The purpose of these special steel plates, when used, is to cushion the application of the clutch assembly.

The *driven friction plates,* on the other hand, have teeth cut into their inside diameter. These teeth fit between teeth machined into the clutch hub (Fig. 5-7). Also, the friction plates and hub are free to rotate inside the drum when the transmission does not use the clutch to change ratios. In addition, these plates are flat and have a friction material (lining) bonded to both mating surfaces. In most cases, the lining surface has a pattern of grooves which provide passageways which assist the normal flow of fluid from the clutch assembly as the plates come together.

Transmission manufacturers use several types of material for friction plate lining. For instance, one transmission model that has two clutch assemblies has friction plates with a bronze lining in one clutch assembly and a composition plate lining in the other.

fig. 5-5 A mechanic checking the coning of a clutch plate with a feeler gauge.

fig. 5–6 A wavy steel cushion plate.

Other transmission manufacturers use composition lining on all friction plates within their clutch assemblies. Manufacturers use bronze and certain grades of composition lining for heavy duty installations where the clutch plate may encounter large torque loads or high temperatures.

The composition lining has an asbestos fiber or paper base and, in heavy duty installations, has metal flakes embedded in the material. These metal flakes are slightly abrasive in nature and, when used in composition plates, prevent the steel plates from becoming glazed or highly polished. The plate manufacturer molds the composition material, under high pressure and temperature, into the shape of the lining and then bonds the lining to each surface of the plate. In recent years, the trend has been to use a specially compounded composition plate material which, when used with a certain fluid type, provides a given friction characteristic to the clutch.

fig. 5–7 Various designs of friction, clutch plates or discs.

fig. 5-8 A clutch hub and annulus (ring) gear.

This friction characteristic determines how harsh or soft the application of the clutch will be. If the amount of friction between the clutch components is too high during clutch application, the clutch application will be harsh and so will the change in gear ratios. On the other hand, if the friction between them is too low, excessive slippage will occur between the clutch components which soften the gear ratio changes but can lead to premature clutch plate failure. Therefore, the transmission manufacturer now coordinates the materials used on the friction plate with a certain type of fluid. This mating of the fluid to the type of plate material assures the manufacturer that his transmission will have a certain shift quality and long clutch life.

The final component of a primary clutch assembly is the *clutch hub* (Fig. 5-8). Along with the teeth which index with the teeth on the friction plates, the hub usually may have a series of drilled holes between the teeth for the purpose of lubricating the plates. In addition, the hub attaches directly to a planetary gear train member; therefore, when the clutch assembly activates, torque passes through the plates, to the hub, and finally to the planetary gear train member.

primary clutch operation

Whenever the transmission requires a primary clutch to connect a planetary member to the input shaft, hydraulic pressure enters the clutch drum below the clutch piston (Fig. 5-9). The hydraulic pressure causes the piston to move within its bore. This piston movement does two things: (1) Movement of the piston compresses the return spring(s). The springs(s) reach full compression as the piston reaches the end of its travel in the drum. (2) As the piston moves, it forces the drive and driven plates together which, in turn, causes the driven plates to operate at input shaft speed. And since the hub and a planetary member together connect to the driven plates, the planetary member rotates at input shaft speed.

The fluid within the clutch assembly cools, lubricates, and determines the harshness of the clutch application. As the clutch plate clearance begins to lessen during clutch application, the force on the fluid layers, trapped between the clutch plates, begins to increase. The temperature of the fluid begins to increase rapidly because of

PRIMARY CLUTCH OPERATION

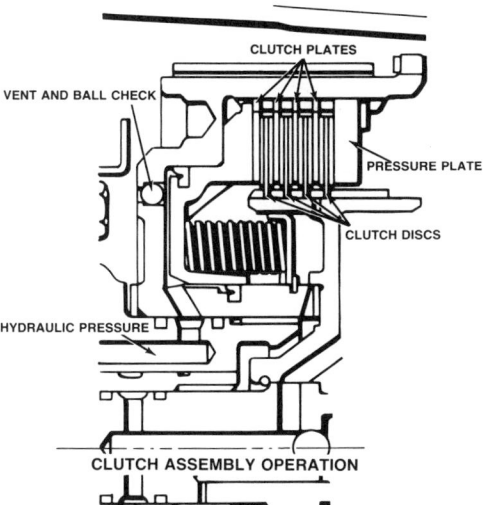

fig. 5-9 Hydraulic pressure causes the clutch, apply piston to move in its bore and lock the drive, clutch plates and the driven, clutch discs together. (Courtesy Chrysler Corp.)

the friction between the individual fluid layers and between the fluid layers and the plates themselves. The majority of the heat, generated during clutch application, leaves the clutch assembly in the fluid as the moving piston "squeezes" the excess fluid from between the plates. The heated fluid returns to the pan where it is cooled by the surrounding fluid which has had its temperature lowered by the transmission's cooling system.

The fluid between the clutch plates also reduces plate wear caused by friction. The fluid layers prevent the actual contact between the drive and driven plates as the clutch piston force "squeezes" the majority of the fluid from between the plates. Even as the plates come together, the lining material of the driven plates absorbs some of the fluid, and a thin layer of fluid also remains on the surface of the drive plate. When the plates lock together, the residual fluid on the plates allows only spot contact between the plates. Thus from the beginning of clutch application until the plates lock together, the fluid controls the amount of actual plate contact and therefore the amount of friction.

The type of fluid in the clutch determines the harshness of clutch application. At the beginning of clutch application, the drive and driven plates are rotating with a great difference in speed between the two. The measurement for plate rotation within the clutch is in feet per minute. As the clutch applies, the difference in speed reduces as the clutch assembly picks up the load, imposed on the driven plates, until the drive and driven plates rotate at the same speed. As the speeds of the drive and driven plates equalize, the amount of friction between the fluid, the steel, and friction plates increases with Type F fluid to provide a firm, aggressive clutch application. Whereas with Dexron fluid, the amount of fluid, steel, and friction plate friction decreases, which results in a smooth, soft clutch application.

To disengage the clutch assembly, the hydraulic system cuts off fluid pressure to the clutch piston. With no hydraulic pressure on the back of the piston, the return spring(s) move the piston to the bottom of its bore. Then, the residual check ball opens to allow any trapped fluid to escape. The drive and driven plates separate; and the clutch hub and planetary member ceases rotation. As the plates are separating, fluid under pressure from the transmission's lubricating system again enters the clearance area between the plates.

secondary clutch design and operation

Except for a few differences, the secondary clutch resembles a primary clutch (Fig. 5–10). For instance, the drum of a primary clutch attaches directly to the input shaft; the drum of the secondary clutch attaches to a member of the planetary gear train. The drive plates of the primary clutch are steel, but the drive plates of a secondary clutch are lined with a friction material. In addition, the primary clutch hub connects to a planetary member; the secondary clutch hub is part of the primary clutch drum (Fig. 5–11). Therefore, the secondary clutch hub turns with the primary clutch drum; it is through this design that the secondary clutch receives the driving torque from the input shaft.

When the hydraulic system activates the primary clutch piston, torque passes from the input shaft to the drum, to the drive plates, to the driven plates, to the clutch hub, and to the planetary gear train member. Within the secondary clutch, torque moves from the secondary clutch hub, driven by the primary clutch drum, to the friction drive plates, to the steel driven plates, to the secondary drum, and finally to the planetary member. In addition, inside the primary clutch, the moving piston presses against a steel drive plate; in the secondary clutch, the piston applies its force to a steel driven plate.

stationary clutch design

The design of a stationary clutch assembly is such that instead of locking a planetary member to the input shaft, it holds the member stationary or locks it to the transmission case. The stationary clutch assembly does not have a rotating drum to house its operat-

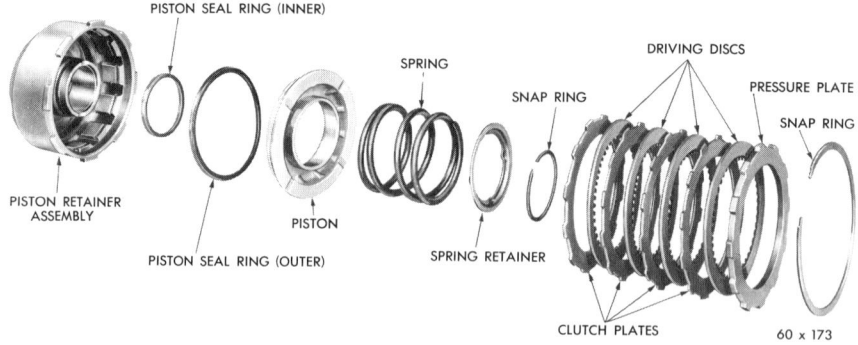

fig. 5–10 A secondary clutch assembly. (Courtesy Chrysler Corp.)

STATIONARY CLUTCH DESIGN 93

fig. 5–11 The hub of the secondary clutch assembly is part of the primary clutch drum.

ing components. Instead, the transmission case forms the housing for the clutch components; and since the housing does not turn, a residual check ball is not necessary in this installation.

But some manufacturers do install a ball-check valve in a stationary clutch piston for a reason. For example, the C-6 transmission has a check valve in its stationary, reverse-clutch piston to provide a complete clutch apply-fluid leakdown. By permitting all the fluid to leak out of this clutch, the next clutch application will require a complete refill; this softens engagement of the clutch.

Fig. 5–12 shows the location of a stationary clutch in the rear section of the transmission case. At the very back of the case is a recessed bore which accommodates the clutch piston. The piston moves back and forth in this bore but does not turn. Holding the piston at the furthest end of its travel are a series of compression springs. One end of each spring bears directly against the clutch piston; the other end fits into a retainer which a snap ring secures to the transmission case (Fig. 5–13).

fig. 5–12 The location of the stationary clutch assembly.

fig. 5-13 A stationary clutch piston, return springs, and retainer.

Furthermore, the steel plates of a stationary clutch assembly do not rotate; and most manufacturers refer to them as reaction plates. In much the same manner as their counterparts in rotating clutch assemblies, these reaction steel plates have a series of teeth located on their outer circumference. But these teeth ride in slots cut into the transmission case (Fig. 5-14).

The friction plates have teeth cut in their inside diameter. These teeth fit between the teeth machined into the clutch hub. The types of materials used to line these plates are the same as those used to line the friction plates of rotating drum assemblies.

The stationary clutch hub attaches directly to a planetary member. In Fig. 5-15, the hub shown is actually made as part of the ring gear. Therefore, when this clutch assembly applies, the ring gear stops turning, and the clutch assembly locks it to the case.

stationary clutch operation

When a stationary clutch is necessary to provide the transmission with a gear ratio, hydraulic pressure enters the area behind the piston. The piston moves within its bore, compressing the return springs. As the piston moves, it applies a force to the reaction

fig. 5-14 Reaction, steel plates and friction plates of a stationary clutch assembly.

MECHANICAL OVERRUNNING CLUTCHES 95

fig. 5-15 Stationary clutch hub and ring gear.

plates which, in turn, move against the friction plates. This plate movement continues until the fluid "squeezes" out from between the plates and all the plates become stationary. Finally, since the friction plates, splined to the hub, are stationary, the hub and planetary member also are stationary or locked to the transmission case.

When the stationary clutch is no longer necessary to operate the planetary gear train, hydraulic pressure to the piston stops. The piston return springs push the piston back in its bore, and all the plates separate as lubricating fluid returns between them. The friction plates and hub now are free to rotate inside the stationary clutch assembly.

mechanical overrunning clutches

Another method used to stop the rotation of an automatic transmission component is the use of a mechanical overrunning clutch (Fig. 5-16). As previously pointed out, the stator, within the torque converter, mounts on an overrunning clutch which prevents torque or rotation in one direction during the converter's torque multiplication phase. But this clutch allows the stator to turn freely in the other direction when the stator's action is no longer necessary to converter operation. Furthermore, some early converters used an overrunning clutch on its secondary pump so that when the secondary pump was not necessary to converter operation it could overrun the primary pump.

Because of the special properties of this type of clutch design, it has also found its way into the planetary gear train as a holding device. First, the overrunning clutch has a large torque-holding capacity for its size. Second, because this clutch is relatively small, it fits into a small area within the transmission. Finally, the overrunning clutch is completely automatic in that it requires no external control for its operation. Any counterclockwise torque applied to a component, mounted on an overrunning clutch, will cause the clutch to lock the part to the transmission case. When the reverse torque stops, the overrunning clutch very smoothly changes a holding component into an overrunning or freewheeling device that revolves in a clockwise direction.

96 CLUTCHES USED IN AUTOMATIC TRANSMISSIONS

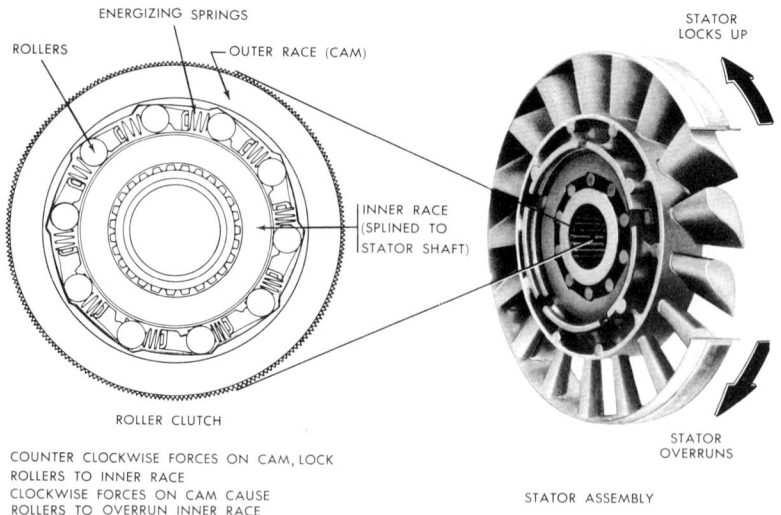

fig. 5-16 A stator-mounted, overrunning clutch. (Courtesy Hydro-matic Division of General Motors Corp.)

roller clutch design

Overrunning clutches may be of two different designs, the *cam and roller* or the *sprag*. The cam and roller design has an inner and outer race. Located on one of these races is a series of high spots or cams evenly spaced around its entire circumference. In Fig. 5-16, the cam is part of the outer race assembly which fastens to the stator assembly; the inner race splines to the stator support and is stationary.

    A number of hardened steel rollers, one for each cam, lie in the low areas between the high spots on the cam. The inner race holds these rollers in place. In addition, a roller retainer or cage simply retains the rollers in their proper relative positions; each roller usually has a spring that maintains a force on the roller in a direction of clutch engagement. In other words, the spring forces the roller in the direction which results in the roller wedging between the inner and outer race.

roller clutch operation (stator mounted)

When the returning turbine fluid strikes the front face of the stator blades, the stator assembly, outer race, and cam attempt to rotate counterclockwise. The rollers, assisted by spring force, move toward the low area of the cam. This action causes the rollers to wedge between the inner and outer races, and the stator assembly locks to the transmission case through the stator support.

    But as the returning turbine fluid strikes the back face of the stator blades, the stator assembly, outer race, and cam begin to move clockwise. The rollers now move down the ramp toward the large end of the cam compressing the springs. In this location, the rollers no longer wedge between the inner and outer races, and the stator assembly can rotate freely in a clockwise direction. If at any time the stator assembly moves toward a counterclockwise direction, the rollers will again wedge between the races, and the stator assembly will stop.

sprag clutch design

The sprag type overrunning clutch has no race-mounted cam or rollers (Fig. 5-17). Instead, the engaging unit consists of a cam-shaped segment which looks like a flattened roller spaced in a case between a smooth inner and outer race. Springs, positioned within notches cut in the sprags, hold the sprags against the races.

sprag clutch operation (carrier mounted)

In Fig. 5-17, the manufacturer has machined the sprag's outer race into the forward section of the planet carrier and the inner race into the center support, which is stationary. When the planetary gear train action is such that the carrier attempts to roll coun-

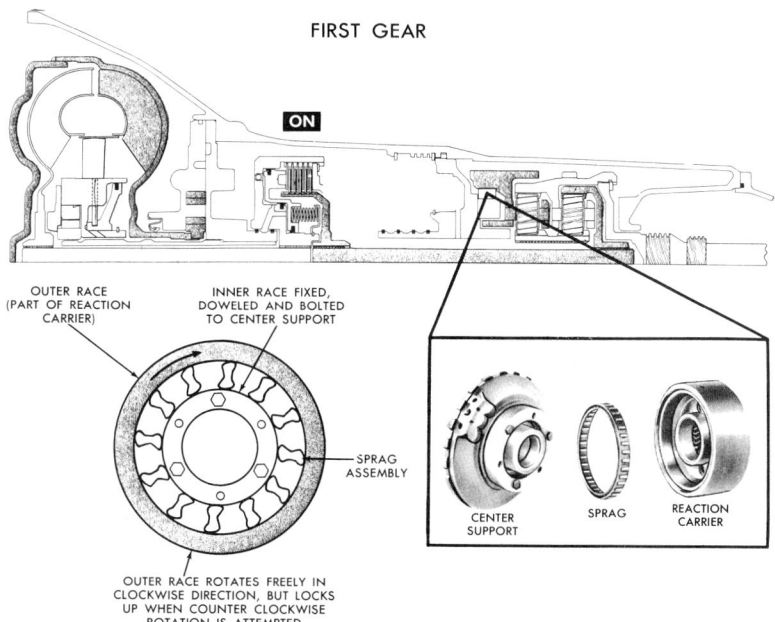

fig. 5-17 A carrier mounted, sprag clutch (Courtesy Hydro-matic Division of General Motors Corp.)

terclockwise, the sprags jam between the inner and outer races and the carrier stops. The sprag clutch locks the carrier to the center support that splines secure to the transmission case.

If the carrier moves in a clockwise direction, the sprags tip slightly. This action releases the outer race so that it and the carrier can turn freely in a clockwise direction. The inner race remains stationary with the center support.

Manufacturers use both types of overrunning clutches in torque converters and to hold planetary members in one direction, but these clutches cannot hold the planetary members during vehicle coast conditions. The reason is that during a coast condition the involved planetary member moves in a direction which releases the clutch. Consequently, along with the overrunning, clutch manufacturers usually provide the transmission with a disc clutch or band that performs the same function as the overrunning clutch, but in both directions. This disc clutch or band will activate only when the vehicle is coasting. Finally, in the majority of transmissions, the driver has control over the application of this disc clutch or band so that the engine can act as a breaking device during vehicle coast conditions. If not used, the disc clutch or band will allow the overrunning clutch to freewheel the planetary member, and torque transfer will cease between the drive wheels and the engine.

summary

1. Wet-type automatic transmission clutches can either hold a planetary member stationary or connect a member to the transmission's input shaft.
2. A primary type clutch has a drum which directly attaches to the transmission's input shaft.
3. A secondary clutch drum attaches to a planetary member.
4. A stationary clutch assembly has no drum because the transmission case itself houses the clutch components.
5. A primary clutch assembly consists of a drum, hydraulic piston, drive steel plates, driven friction plates, and a hub.
6. The primary and secondary drum forms the cylinder or guide for the hydraulic piston; in the stationary clutch, this area is part of the transmission case.
7. The hydraulic piston changes hydraulic pressure to mechanical force to apply the clutch, and return springs move the piston to the bottom of its bore when the clutch is no longer necessary to transmission operation.
8. The residual check valve allows fluid to escape from under the piston when the clutch is off.
9. Drive or driven steel plates are usually flat and have external teeth.
10. The drive or driven friction plates are flat and have internal teeth.
11. Friction plates can have a bronze or composition lining.

12. The type of lining and the fluid used with it determines the friction characteristic of the clutch.
13. The internal teeth of the friction plates mate between the teeth of the clutch hub.
14. When a clutch actuates, hydraulic pressures move the piston within its bore; piston movement forces the steel and friction plates together.
15. The fluid within the clutch assembly cools, lubricates, and determines the harshness of clutch application.
16. A primary clutch, when activated, directly connects a planetary member to the input shaft.
17. When a secondary clutch activates, it connects a planetary member to the primary clutch drum.
18. A stationary clutch assembly, when activated, holds a planetary member stationary.
19. An overrunning clutch stops the rotation of a component in one direction only.
20. The two types of overrunning clutches are the cam and roller and the sprag.
21. The roller type consists of an inner and outer race, a cam, a set of rollers, a roller retainer, and a set of springs.
22. The sprag type consists of a smooth inner and outer race, a series of sprags, and a cage.
23. When the roller clutch holds a component in one direction, its rollers are wedged in the low area between the inner and outer races.
24. If a spray clutch holds a member, the sprags jam between the inner and outer races.

check-up questions

The questions listed below will assist you in determining how well you remember the material contained in this chapter. Read each question carefully before choosing the answer to each item. If you cannot answer a question, review the material in the section of the chapter that covers the question.

1. The two types of clutches found in the automatic transmission are the multi-disc, wet type and the _____.
    a. friction
    b. liquid
    c. overrunning
    d. antifriction
2. Within a primary clutch assembly the drive plates are _____.
    a. the steel type
    b. the friction type

    c. half the steel and half the friction type
    d. none of the above
3. Which clutch type does not require a drum?
    a. secondary
    b. stationary
    c. primary
    d. both b and c
4. The valve that releases the trapped fluid from under a clutch piston is known as the _____.
    a. pressure regulating valve
    b. residual check valve
    c. by-pass valve
    d. compensating valve
5. Excessive temperatures generated during clutch application leave the clutch plates via the _____.
    a. drum
    b. hub
    c. piston
    d. escaping fluid
6. Friction plates have teeth cut into their _____.
    a. inside diameter
    b. outer circumference
    c. linings
    d. both b and c
7. Composition lining can be made up of asbestos, metal, and _____.
    a. steel
    b. copper
    c. lead
    d. paper
8. The clutch type that when activated directly connects a planetary member to the input shaft is a _____ assembly.
    a. stationary
    b. secondary
    c. primary
    d. overrunning

9. The device that applies the force to "squeeze" the clutch plates together is the _____.
   a. hub
   b. piston
   c. retainer
   d. springs
10. The clutch type which holds a planetary member in one direction only is the _____.
    a. primary
    b. secondary
    c. stationary
    d. overrunning

For the answers to these check-up questions, turn to the Appendix located at the back of the text.

6

bands and servos

band function

Along with disc and overrunning type clutches, most automatic transmissions also have one or more brake bands (Fig. 6-1). All of these devices can hold a planetary member stationary. On the one hand, a disc-type clutch and the brake band, when applied, will hold the planetary member and prevent its rotation in either direction. But the overrunning clutch holds the planetary member against rotation in one direction only.

A *band* is a device that stops or causes to stop the movement of another object by a constricting or squeezing action. In the automatic transmission, a metal band, lined with a friction material, encircles a revolving drum which, in turn, attaches to a planetary member, the object. Fig. 6-2 shows a drum, connected by tabs or large teeth, to the input shell which also splines to the sun gear. When the hydraulic system activates the band, it squeezes tightly around the drum and prevents its rotation. And because the drum holds the input shell, the sun gear will also be stationary.

As previously pointed out, for design reasons, many transmissions manufacturers prefer to use a disc or overrunning clutch instead of a band to stop the rotation of a planetary member. One reason is that the disc clutch never requires any adjustment after its initial installation, and its hydraulic operation is fairly easy to control. Also, overrunning clutch operation is completely automatic; therefore, it requires no hydraulic

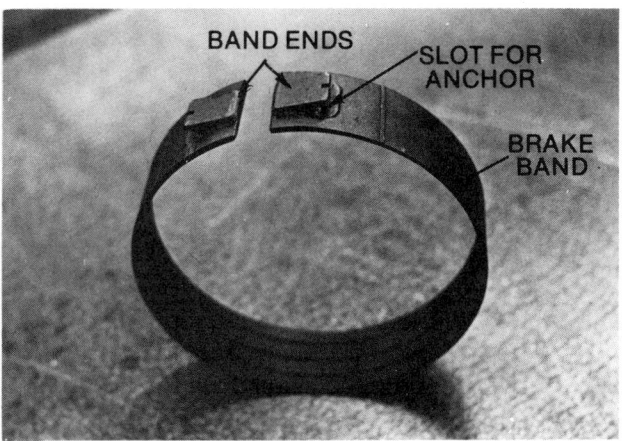

fig. 6–1 A typical brake band.

system at all to activate it. Finally, disc and overrunning clutches, for their relatively small sizes, can handle large torque loads without slipping. This feature assists the manufacturer in reducing transmission case size.

Most bands, on the other hand, do require periodic adjustment for wear during the life of the transmission. In addition, the use of a band to hold a planetary member in a forward ratio usually requires the transmission to have a somewhat more complicated hydraulic system than a unit which utilizes a disc or overrunning clutch for this purpose. The reason for the more complex system is that in order to lock the band around a drum, the band's activating piston or servo has to move much further than the piston which locks the plates of a disc clutch together. This excessive servo movement causes a

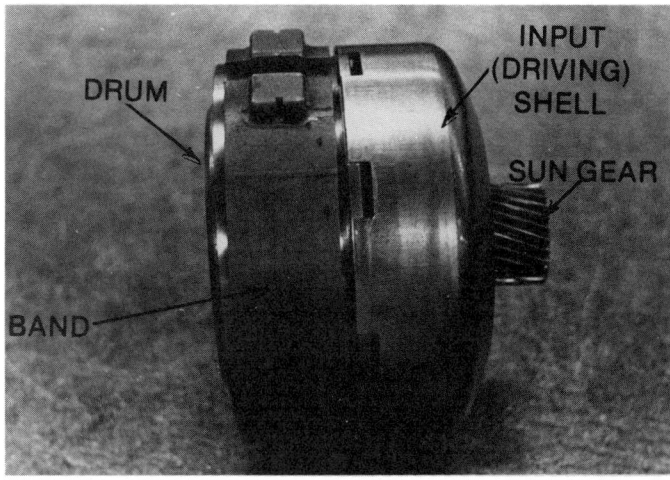

fig. 6–2 The band installed around a drum, locked to the input (driving shell) and sun gear.

timing problem on both upshift and downshift operations of the band, especially if the band application must coincide with the operation of a disc clutch.

band design

By design, there are primarily two types of brake bands, the solid and the split or dual type. The *solid type* is made in one piece from either cast iron or steel. The manufacturer forms and machines these materials in such a manner that the band is elastic. In other words, the ends of the band will spring apart after the servo has forced them together. This band elasticity maintains the band in the released, open position whenever it is not in use. Also, the inner circumference is large enough to accommodate a friction lining but, at the same time, allows sufficient free-opening clearance for the rotating drum (Fig. 6-3).

In most cases, a piece of linkage fastens to each end of the band. For example, one of these links, called an anchor, has a ball socket on one end. This ball socket mates with a ball-type pivot point within the transmission case itself (Fig. 6-4). In most cases, this pivot point also serves as the band adjuster. The opposite end of the anchor fits into a v-slot machined into the end of the band. With this anchor arrangement, the band can slightly pivot on the ball and socket, but the stationary ball prevents the band from turning inside the transmission case.

The other link or struct fits into a v-slot in the opposite end of the band from the anchor. The other end of the struct rides against the end of the servo piston rod (Fig. 6-5). Some band arrangements are such that the servo piston rod itself pushes directly against the end of the band and does not use a struct. In either case, when hydraulic pressure moves the servo piston, it moves out and forces the ends of the band together. Initial servo piston movement attempts to roll the band around inside the case; but since the anchor end of the band fastens to the case, the band just tightens up around the drum.

fig. 6-3 The band's inner circumference and lining.

BAND DESIGN

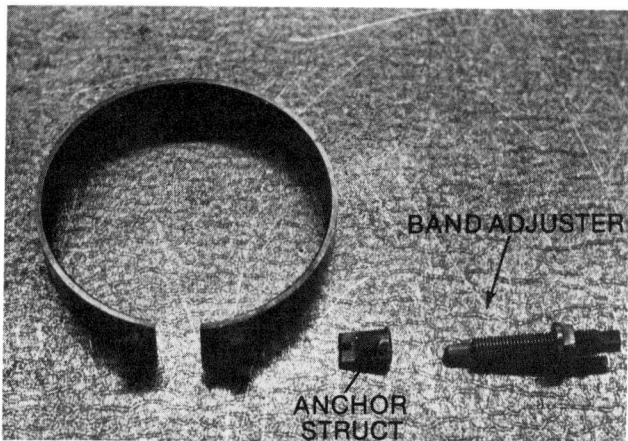

fig. 6–4 A typical band, anchor, and adjuster.

As previously mentioned, on the inside surface of the band is a friction lining. This lining material is very similar to what is found on the friction plates within the disc clutch assembly. In other words, the lining may be a composition material formed from either an asbestos or paper base and may have metal flakes embedded in it. Furthermore, this composition band lining, in later automatic transmissions, mates with a certain type of fluid to provide a certain friction characteristic to the band and drum during their application. Also, the band, in some instances, may have grooves in it which allow excess fluid to escape as the band tightens around the drum.

The width of the band and its lining is one of the determining factors as to how much torque the band can hold before allowing the drum to slip. Fig. 6–6 shows two bands that the same type of automatic transmission can use. The manufacturer installs the larger band on the right if the transmission bolts up to a V-eight engine. But if the vehicle has a six-cylinder engine, the transmission comes from the factory with the narrow band on the left. The wide band, therefore, carries the increased torque output produced by the V-eight engine.

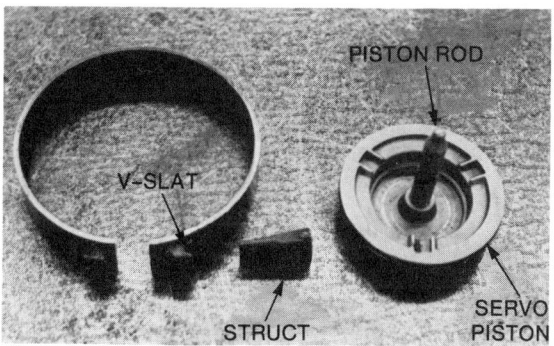

fig. 6–5 A typical band, servo struct, and servo piston.

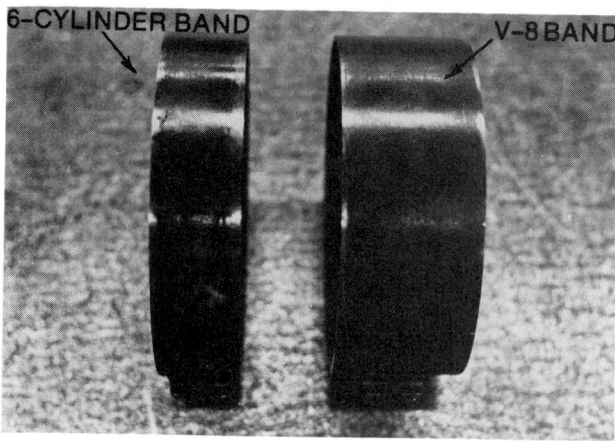

fig. 6-6 Two bands used in the same transmission design but with different widths.

Because of its special design characteristic, many transmissions use a *split or dual band* instead of the solid type. In place of the one solid piece of curved metal, the split band is a unit formed of three narrow individual band segments (Fig. 6–7). During the forming process of this type of band, the manufacturer connects the two servo ends of the two outer bands, along with one end of the center band, together with a metal strip. The free end of the center band fastens directly to the servo's apply linkage, and the two free ends of the outer bands fit into an anchor that pivots in the transmission case. Finally, the split band usually has an asbestos type lining bonded to each band segment; because of its split construction, the band lining conforms very well to the drum.

Due to its unusual design, the split band is more sensitive to the natural *self-energizing action* that occurs with any type of band forced against a rotating drum. In

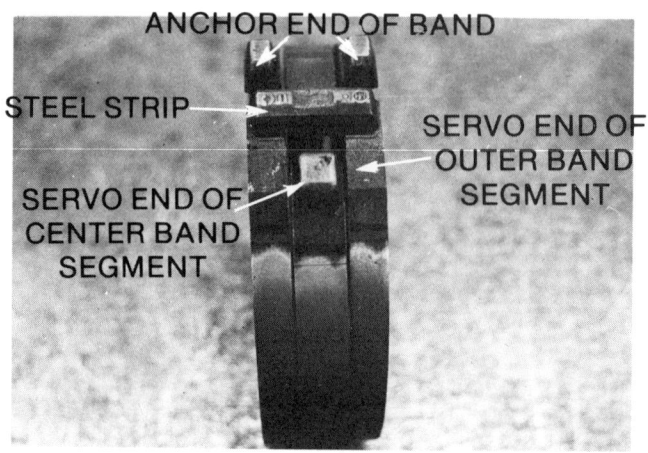

fig. 6-7 The construction of a split or dual band.

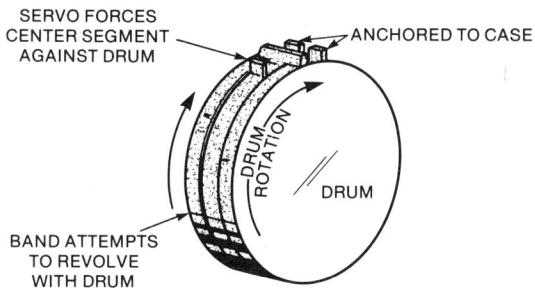

fig. 6-8 "Self-energizing action" begins as the servo piston forces the center segment against the rotating drum.

simple terms, this self-energizing action is the tendency of the band, after contacting a revolving drum, to roll with the drum. This action occurs during initial band application and only if the servo applies the band in the direction of drum rotation. Self-energizing action assists the servo's piston in applying the band and helps prevent excessive band to drum slippage. Finally, this action works well enough to permit the manufacturer to reduce the size of the split band's operating servo piston but still maintain the same tightening effect as a solid band with a larger piston.

In the case of the split band, the self-energizing action begins as the servo piston forces the center segment against the rotating drum (Fig. 6-8). This band segment attempts to revolve with the drum, and since the opposite end of the center segment fastens to the servo ends of the two outer bands, the entire unit begins to turn with the drum. But since the opposite, outer band ends also anchor to the case, the entire unit begins to wind or cinch up around the drum. This action, along with the servo's applied force, only tends to permit a minimum amount of slippage between the band and drum, because any slippage will cause the band to cinch up even more around the drum. Consequently, in installations in which the manufacturer expects high torque loads, or which, for a design reason, needs to reduce servo piston size, a split band will replace the conventional solid type.

band operation

When the band is necessary to operate the transmission, the hydraulic control system sends fluid under pressure to the servo. In turn, the servo piston begins to force the ends of the band together and self-energizing action begins (Fig. 6-9). The band's squeezing action also begins to decrease the operating clearance between the band's lining and the drum; consequently, the drum's speed begins to decrease. At this point, the band's and the drum's operating temperature begins to increase rapidly because of the increasing friction between the fluid layers, band, and drum.

As in the disc clutch, the fluid removes the excess heat and controls the amount of friction between the band's lining and the drum. The fluid between the lining and drum

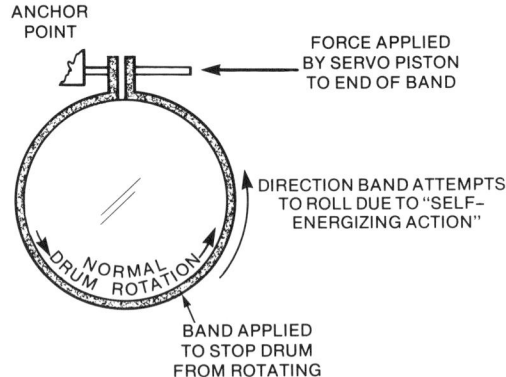

fig. 6-9 The force of the servo applies the band around the drum and stops its rotation.

absorbs a good deal of the heat and carries it away as the fluid squeezes out from between the band and drum. Then, the heated fluid returns to the fluid pan where the surrounding fluid cools it down.

Because the fluid layers between the lining and drum act as a wedge, band-to-drum friction is low. As the band tightens around the drum, the fluid layers lubricate, preventing actual contact between the two units, until the drum stops rotating. By this time, most of the excess fluid is gone from between the two units and some actual contact occurs. But the contact usually is minimal or spotty because of lining material, lining roughness, and residual fluid.

When the hydraulic control system stops sending pressurized fluid to the servo, the band begins to open (Fig. 6-10). The servo's activating piston moves back out of the way, and the band's elasticity causes it to open. Next, the drum begins to rotate within the band as soon as operating clearance appears between the two. Finally, once the operating clearance returns, fluid again fills this area and prevents any band-to-drum contact and cools the components.

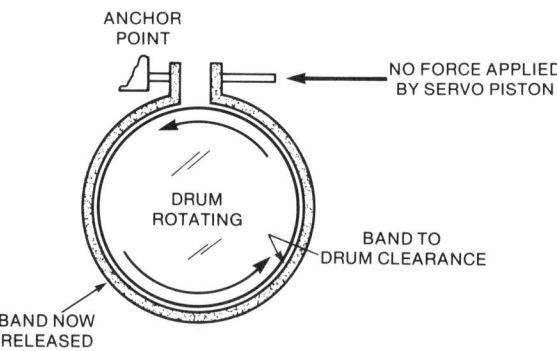

fig. 6-10 As the servo piston releases its force on the band, it springs open.

SERVO DESIGN AND OPERATION 109

fig. 6–11 A typical servo housing cast into the transmission case.

function of servos

A *servo,* simply speaking, is a device that converts hydraulic pressure to mechanical force required to apply the band. It normally consists of a servo housing, a servo piston, return spring, and piston rod or stem. The servo housing itself may be a detachable unit, or the transmission manufacturer forms it into the transmission case (Fig. 6–11). In either situation, the servo housing has a bore or cylinder which acts as the guide for the servo piston and has the apply- and sometimes release-pressure ports machined into it.

    A notable difference between servos, found in various transmission types, lies in the number of pistons needed by the unit in order for it to do its job. In this text, if the servo assembly has one piston, the servo is the standard duty type. If, on the other hand, the servo has two pistons, the servo is the controlled-load type.

servo design and operation

A *standard duty servo piston* operates within the servo housing bore (Fig. 6–12). The outer circumference of this piston has a sealing device(s) which prevents excessive fluid leakage between the piston and the housing bore. Furthermore, at the center of the piston is the piston rod or stem. As previously mentioned, this stem is in contact with one end of the band usually through a link or struct. The area of the piston multiplied by the hydraulic apply pressure (psi) determines the actual force, applied by the piston, to the band. For example, if the servo piston has an area of 2 square inches and the apply pressure is 50 psi, the force on the band is 2 inches squared times 50 psi or 100 pounds. The standard duty piston also has a relatively strong compression type return spring. This spring maintains the servo piston at the bottom of its bore when the band is open. The spring not only pushes the piston back in its bore when hydraulic pressure below the

110 BANDS AND SERVOS

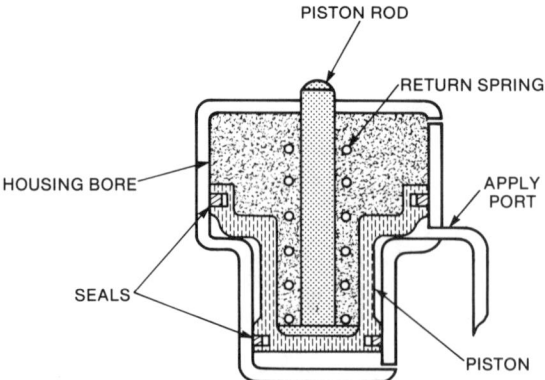

fig. 6–12 A standard-duty, two-diameter, servo piston in its housing bore.

piston stops, but during the band's apply period the spring's tension helps to cushion band application around the drum. In other words, in order for the piston to tighten the band around the drum, hydraulic force acting on the piston must first overcome spring tension.

In one design of a *controlled-load servo,* the piston has a spring-loaded piston plug located at its center; this piston plug also moves to cushion the band application (Fig. 6–13). When the band is open, a plug spring extends the piston plug in its bore in the main piston. If the control system admits hydraulic pressure to the area above the main servo piston, it and the piston plug move down, taking up all the band-to-drum operating clearance. Additional movement of the main piston causes the plug's spring to compress, and the main piston continues to move down on the piston plug until a shoulder on the plug stops the main piston's movement. The period of time from initial band movement until the main piston is down against the piston plug's shoulder represents a

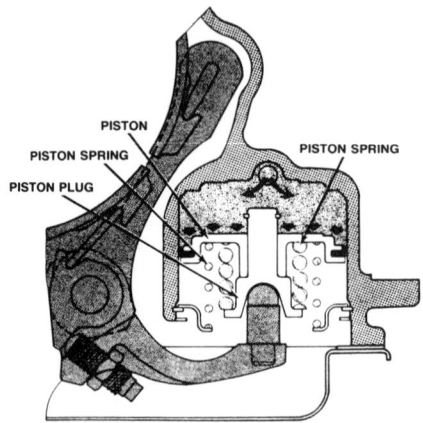

fig. 6–13 A controlled-load servo piston with its spring-loaded plug. (Courtesy Chrysler Corp.)

SERVO DESIGN AND OPERATION 111

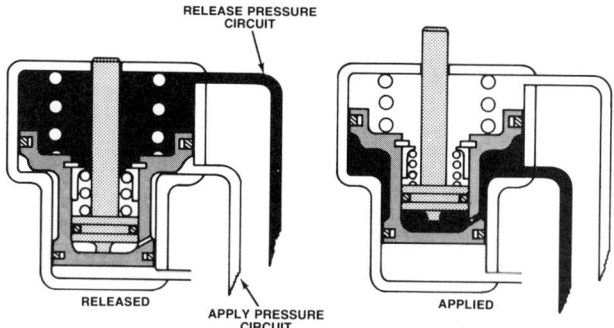

FRONT SERVO OPERATION
(CONTROLLED-LOAD)

fig. 6–14 A controlled-load servo that has two hydraulic pistons. (Courtesy Chrysler Corp.)

delay in the band tightening period. This action cushions the total band application around the drum.

Another type of controlled-load servo is shown in Fig. 6–14. This unit consists of a two-land main piston which operates in the servo housing bore, and each land of this piston has a different diameter. The lands are the machined areas of this piston style upon which the hydraulic pressure will act to move the piston against spring force. The center section of this piston also forms a guide or bore for a smaller piston and stem; but, in this servo, the smaller piston also had hydraulic pressure applied to it.

This dual piston arrangement requires two return springs. The larger spring maintains the two-land piston at the bottom of its travel when the band is open, whereas the smaller spring will attempt to keep the smaller piston at the base of its bore in the larger piston when the band is open.

To activate this servo, the hydraulic control system directs pressurized fluid to the apply side of the servo. The fluid fills the cavity between the two lands and pushes against the bottom of the large land. This action causes the main servo piston to move upwards in its bore within the servo housing. Once the band applies, the inner bore of the main piston will try to fill with fluid admitted through the orifice (the calibrated opening).

As the servo releases during a gear ratio change, the return spring moves the main piston back in its guide. The inner piston fills up with a small amount of fluid trapped between itself and the main piston. This trapped fluid prevents the small spring from pushing the inner piston all the way back in its bore within the main piston.

If and when the servo applies the band again, the fluid, trapped between the main and inner piston will act to cushion band application. In order for the inner piston to move back to the base of its bore so that the servo can fully load the band, the trapped fluid has to move out from beneath the inner piston through the orifice. The movement of fluid through the orifice controls the loading, full tightening, period of the band and therefore, cushions band application.

112 BANDS AND SERVOS

fig. 6–15 A band adjuster located at the servo-piston end of the band.

Transmission manufacturers can use several methods to return a servo piston to the base of its bore as the band opens. For example, the most common method is the use of one or more compression-type springs. In other applications, the servo piston must move faster than the spring can push it. To accomplish this, the servo piston has hydraulic pressure applied to its spring side. The hydraulic pressure supplies the extra push necessary to move the servo piston back quickly. In other words, depending on how fast the servo must release, the piston can move back from spring action alone or from a combination of spring force and hydraulic pressure.

band adjustments

When an automatic transmission consistently uses a band for its normal operating sequence, the band may require periodic adjustment, or it may no longer be able to hold the drum from revolving. The reason for this adjustment is twofold: the servo piston can only move so far before it runs out of travel, and the band-to-drum clearance may be too great due to lining wear. Therefore, band adjustment is periodically necessary during the life of the transmission and always at major overhauls to maintain the proper operating clearance. Finally, proper band clearance is also necessary to allow sufficient fluid to circulate between the band and drum for proper cooling and lubrication. For this reason, the band clearance should never be less than what the manufacturer specifies.

Some transmission models do not have a means or mechanism for band adjustment. For example, neither band in the General Motors T-400 transmission is adjustable for wear. But in this transmission, the one band provides the vehicle with reverse and manual low; the other assists on overrunning clutch in holding a planetary member in second ratio during a vehicle coast condition. In both of these instances, the transmission does not utilize these bands that often, so the band-to-drum clearance will normally not become excessive during the normal life of this transmission.

Bands which are adjustable will have an adjusting device either at the servo or anchor end of the band. Fig. 6–15 shows an adjustment screw and locknut located on

BAND ADJUSTMENTS

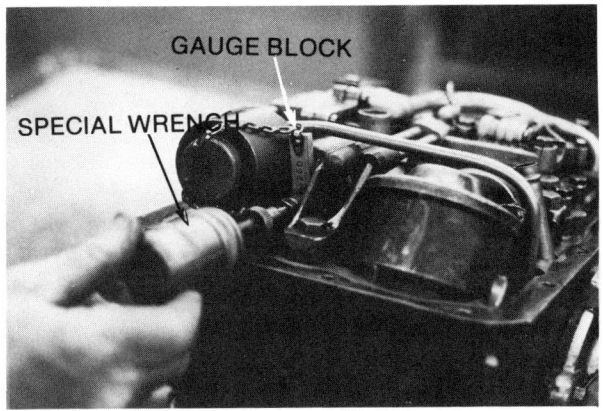

fig. 6-16 An internal band adjustment utilizing a special wrench and gauge block.

the linkage between the servo piston stem and the band. To properly adjust this type of arrangement, a special wrench and gauge are necessary.

To make the band adjustment, the mechanic must first remove the fluid pan. Then, after loosening the adjusting screw, the mechanic positions the gauge between the servo adjusting screw and piston stem. Next, he tightens the wrench until it overruns (Fig. 6-16). Finally, he backs off the adjusting screw the specified number of turns. With the locknut tightened, the procedure is complete. Now, the proper clearance exists between the band drum and the pan can be put back on.

Fig. 6-17 shows an anchor type of band adjuster located in the outside of the transmission case. This adjusting screw fits into the anchor to prevent rotation of the band within the case. By turning the adjusting screw, the band clearance will increase or decrease.

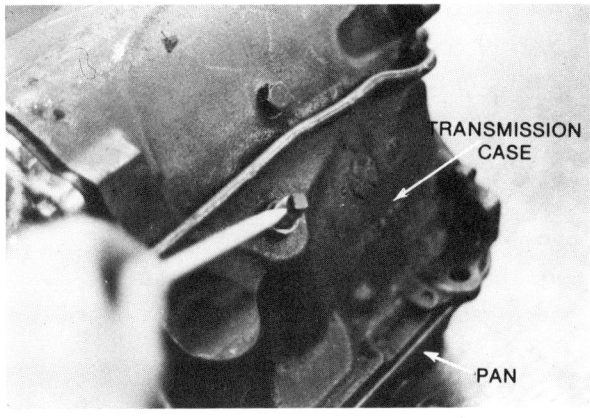

fig. 6-17 An external band adjuster located on the outside of the transmission case.

114 BANDS AND SERVOS

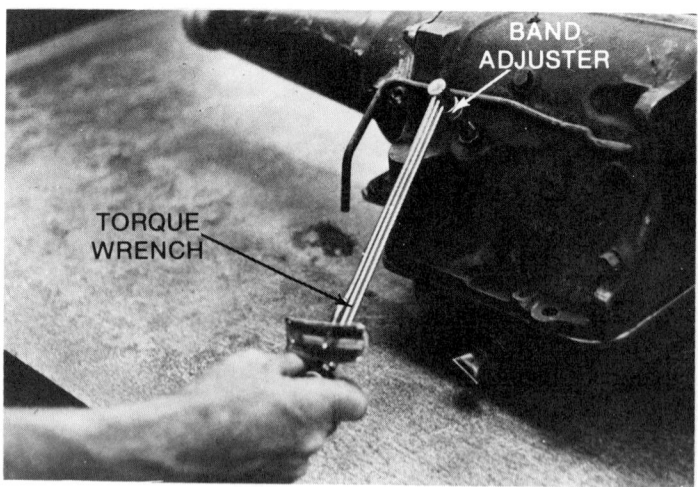

fig. 6–18 An external band adjustment using a torque wrench.

To set the band-to-drum clearance with this arrangement, the mechanic tightens the band adjuster a specified amount with a torque wrench (Fig. 6–18). This action tightens the band around the drum. Next, he backs off (loosens) the adjusting screw a specified number of turns to set the actual band-to-drum operating clearance.

summary

1. A band holds a planetary member stationary.
2. A band wraps around a drum which fastens to a planetary member.
3. Bands take longer to operate than a disc or overrunning clutch.
4. There are two types of bands, the solid and the split.
5. Bands are made out of cast iron or steel.
6. Manufacturers line the inside of the band with a composition material.
7. Some form of linkage usually secures the band to the case and to the operating servo.
8. The engine size determines the width of the band.
9. The split band consists of three segments.
10. Because of its construction, the split band is more sensitive to a self-energizing action.
11. Self-energizing action occurs when the band contacts a revolving drum.
12. The ends of a band come together due to the action of the servo.
13. Fluid between the band and drum cools and lubricates both units.
14. A servo converts hydraulic pressure to mechanical force.

15. A standard servo has one piston.
16. A controlled-load servo has two pistons.
17. Servos have one or more return springs.
18. During their operation, controlled-load servos cushion band application.
19. Depending on how fast the servo must release, the piston can move back from spring action alone or from a combination of spring force and hydraulic pressure.
20. Most bands require periodic adjustment.
21. Band adjustments set the proper operating clearance between the band and drum.
22. Band adjustments can be either on the servo or anchor end of the band.

check-up questions

The questions listed below will assist you in determining how well you remember the material contained in this chapter. Read each question carefully before choosing the answer to each item. If you cannot answer a question, review the material in the section of the chapter that covers the question.

1. A band holds a planetary member stationary in _____.
    a. one direction only
    b. two directions
    c. a clockwise direction
    d. a counterclockwise direction
2. The band wraps around a _____.
    a. drum
    b. servo
    c. piston
    d. planetary member
3. The device that operates a band is a _____.
    a. actuator
    b. adjuster
    c. spring
    d. servo
4. The band type which is most effective in holding a planetary member is the _____.
    a. plain
    b. solid
    c. split
    d. both *a* and *b*

116 BANDS AND SERVOS

5. Bond lining is usually a _____ material.
   a. lead
   b. bronze
   c. steel
   d. composition
6. The piece of linkage that connects the band to the case is the _____.
   a. anchor
   b. struct
   c. link
   d. linkage
7. Fluid flows between the band and drum to reduce their operating temperature and _____.
   a. friction
   b. wedging effect
   c. efficiency
   d. none of the above
8. The self-energizing effect on the band occurs during band _____.
   a. release
   b. application and release
   c. application
   d. loading
9. The type of servo which cushions band application is the _____.
   a. single acting
   b. dual acting
   c. standard duty
   d. controlled-load
10. The standard duty piston has _____.
    a. one piston
    b. two pistons
    c. two springs
    d. always an external housing
11. Band adjustment is necessary in many automatic transmissions because of _____.
    a. band wear
    b. servo wear

c. weak servo springs
d. insufficient servo travel

12. If the band-to-drum clearance is less than what the factory specifications calls for, the band may burn out due to a lack of _____.

   a. wear
   b. lubrication
   c. servo travel
   d. elasticity

For the answers to these questions, turn to the Appendix located at the back of the book.

7

hydraulic fundamentals

To understand the operation of and trouble-shooting procedures for an automatic transmission, a person must possess a working knowledge of hydraulics. This working knowledge is necessary for many reasons. For example, the torque converter uses one form of hydraulics to transfer torque between the engine and transmission. Furthermore, the clutches and band servos, in addition to the lubricating and cooling systems, depend on another principle of hydraulics in order for them to function. The automatic transmission also utilizes the principles of hydraulics to sense and select the correct amount of torque multiplication needed by a vehicle. And finally, to completely understand and interpret the transmission's hydraulic diagrams, a mechanic must master hydraulic fundamentals. A mechanic can diagnose about 90 percent of all automatic transmission malfunctions using hydraulic test gauges and diagrams, but these trouble-shooting tools will not be available to him if he does not have a working knowledge of hydraulics.

Hydraulics is a very exact and complicated field of science that deals with the effects of a moving liquid such as ATF, and the ability of ATF to transmit motion and pressure. This science has two general categories: hydrodynamics, the study of moving fluids; and hydrostatics, the study of fluids under pressure. Chapter Four of this text covered the principles of hydrodynamics as it applies to torque converter operation; therefore, this chapter will mainly deal with the laws of hydrostatics.

hydrostatics

The basic principle of hydrostatics is that a liquid resists compression and therefore, can transmit motion and pressure. To comprehend fully why a liquid like ATF is not compressible, the reader must be aware of a few fundamental facts relating to the physical make-up of all objects. Science classifies all substances (objects) as being either a solid, liquid, or a gas; and all of these substances have a given arrangement of molecules.

A molecule is the smallest particle, or building block, into which any substance can be divided and still retain its original physical properties. For instance, if a scientist divided a grain of salt in two and divided each subsequent grain again until he finished the division as finely as possible, the smallest particle having all the properties of salt would be a salt molecule. This molecule would be almost one millionth of an inch in diameter and need to be enlarged about 100 times before it could be seen in a microscope. Finally, the arrangement of these molecules in solid, liquid, or gas substances are somewhat different (Fig. 7–1).

A solid object, such as a piece of steel, has a rigid molecular structure. The molecules are close to each other and have a strong attraction for one another. This molecular arrangement resists any attempt to physically change the steel object's shape. For this reason, solid substances, for practical purposes, are not compressible.

In a liquid such as ATF, the molecular structure is not as rigid as it is in a solid material. The molecules, in this case, do move in relation to one another or have less attraction for each other. This property allows a liquid to conform to its container's shape. The distance between the molecules in a liquid substance remains relatively close; consequently, the liquid is also not compressible by normal means.

A gas such as steam has molecules which are far apart and move about at high speeds. These molecules can move freely in relation to one another and tend to repel each other. These factors give a gas its limited expansion quality, yet the gas substance is compressible by normal means because of the distance between the molecules.

The combination of the flexibility of a liquid, the ability of the substance to conform to its container, and the relative incompressibility of a solid are the two characteristics of ATF which permit it to transmit motion and pressure. For example, if a piston applies a

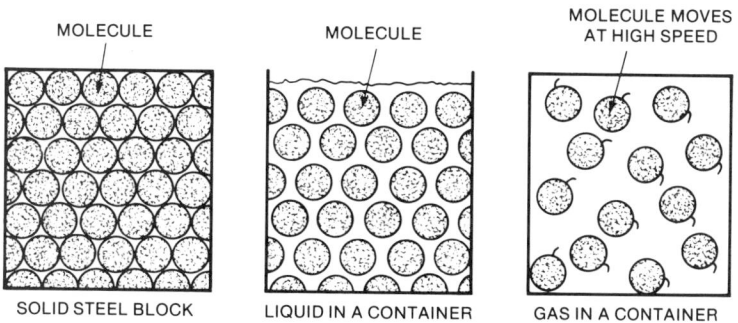

fig. 7–1 The three classifications of objects: solids, liquids, and gases.

120 HYDRAULIC FUNDAMENTALS

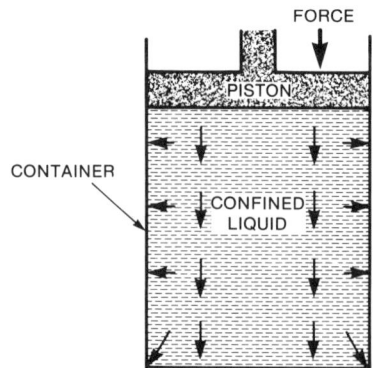

fig. 7-2 A piston applying a force to a column of fluid.

force to a column of confined liquid (Fig. 7-2), the force of the piston transmits not only straight through the liquid to the other side but also equally and undiminished in every direction. In other words, the force would be present in the fluid column in forwards, backwards, and sideway directions.

hydraulic levers

After experimenting with liquids, a French scientist, Blaise Pascal, in 1653, discovered the hydraulic lever. Through controlled laboratory experiments, Pascal proved that a confined liquid could transfer force and motion. By experimenting with weights and pistons of varying size, Pascal also found that a hydraulic system could produce a mechanical advantage or force multiplication, and that the relationships between force and distance were exactly the same as with a mechanical lever.

From the data Pascal collected in his laboratory, he formulated a law which states: "Pressure on a confined fluid is transmitted equally in all directions and acts with equal force on equal areas." This law is too complex to understand completely without some explanation. In order to simplify Pascal's Law the following sections deal with each concept separately and thoroughly.

force

Force, as mentioned earlier, is the push or pull exerted on an object; and its unit of measurement is pounds (lbs). Friction and gravity are two kinds of forces. The force of gravity is nothing more than the mass or weight of an object. For instance, if a steel block weighing 100 lbs. is sitting on the floor, it exerts a downward force of 100 lbs. on the floor (Fig. 7-3).

The force of friction is present when two objects attempt to move against each other. In the example above, if a person moved the same 100 lb. block of steel across the floor, he would encounter some resistance to its movement. This resistance to motion is the force of friction present between the block and the floor.

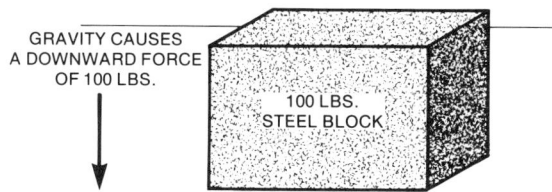

fig. 7-3 A steel block exerting 100 lbs. of force on the floor.

When dealing with hydraulic valves, a person will encounter a third type of force. This third force is that which a spring provides (Fig. 7-4). Spring force is the push or pull the spring produces when compressed or stretched. The measurement for spring force is also the pound or a division of the pound such as the ounce (oz.).

pressure

Pressure is nothing more than the applied force (lbs.) divided by the contact area (in.^{2} or ft.^{2}). In other words, pressure is force per unit area. For example, if the 100 lb. steel block (Fig. 7-3) rested on a 10-square-inch area on the floor, the pressure exerted by the block is $\frac{100 \text{ lbs.}}{10 \text{ in.}^2}$ or 10 pounds per square inch, 10 psi.

pressure on a confined fluid

A force applied to some given area in contact with a confined fluid also causes pressure to be exerted in the fluid. For instance, Fig. 7-5 shows a cylinder that is full of fluid, and the cylinder has a piston which fits closely in the cylinder's bore. If any force attempts to move the piston down, the piston force results in pressure in the fluid.

Of course, the applied force will not create pressure in the fluid if the cylinder or piston leaks at any point. The fluid would simply leak past the opening. The piston force would cause fluid flow but no pressure. In other words, there must be a resistance to flow in order to create pressure.

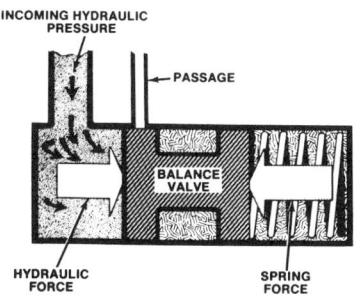

fig. 7-4 Spring tension exerted on a valve. (Courtesy Chrysler Corp.)

122 HYDRAULIC FUNDAMENTALS

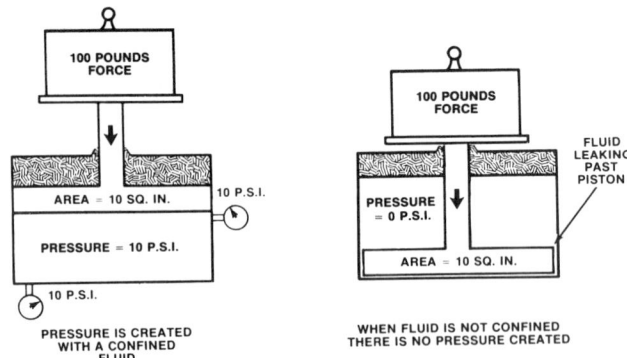

fig. 7-5 Force applied to a given area, in contact with a confined fluid, causes pressure to be exerted in the fluid. (Courtesy Chrysler Corp.)

The pressure created in the fluid is also equal to the applied force (lbs.) divided by the piston's area (in.² or ft.²). In Fig. 7-5, the force is 100 lbs. and the piston's area is 10 square inches. Therefore, the pressure created equals $\frac{100 \text{ lbs.}}{10 \text{ in.}^2}$ or 10 psi. Finally, this pressure of 10 psi exists everywhere in the cylinder.

This total pressurization of the fluid within the cylinder exemplifies another interpretation of Pascal's Law which is: "Pressure on a confined fluid is transmitted undiminished in all directions." In other words, regardless of the container's shape or size, the pressure is the same throughout as long as the container has no leaks. The pressure at the top near the piston is exactly the same as it is at the bottom of the cylinder or container, and the pressure at the sides is exactly the same as it is at the top and bottom.

force multiplication

The secret of *force multiplication* in hydraulic systems lies in the total fluid contact area employed. Looking back at Fig. 7-5 and using the 10 psi created in this illustration, an input force of 100 lbs. can move an output force of 1000 lbs. To accomplish this force multiplication, an output piston that is ten times larger than the original input piston's area is necessary (Fig. 7-6).

Since the 10 psi pressure is the same everywhere in the system, the 10 psi is also underneath the larger piston. By using another simple formula, a person can determine the output piston's force. Output force is equal to the system pressure (psi) multiplied by the area of the output piston (in.²). In the example, the pressure is 10 psi and the output piston has an area of 100 in.², Therefore, the output force is 10 psi times 100 in.² or 1000 lbs. In other words, a 100 lbs. of input force on the small piston is balancing 1000 lbs. of force on the output piston.

This concept is extremely important in the design and operation of hydraulic system components. The concept is nothing more than using a difference between two areas to create a difference in pressure in order to move an object. Designers use this

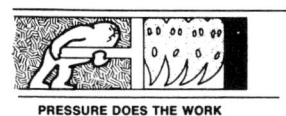

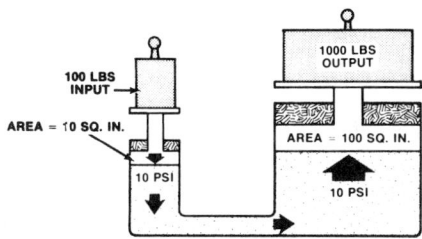

fig. 7-6 Force multiplication by a hydraulic system. (Courtesy Chrysler Corp.)

rule in determining the contact area(s) of various values found in the hydraulic control system of the transmission, in addition to the area of the servo and clutch apply pistons.

piston travel

When a hydraulic system which uses input and output pistons provides a mechanical advantage, the pistons will have different travels. Referring back to Fig. 7-6, the small piston will have to move ten times as far as the larger piston. Consequently, for every one inch the large piston moves, the small piston must move about ten inches.

A common garage floor jack is a good example of a device that uses this principle. To raise a vehicle weighing 2000 lbs., an effort of only 50 lbs. is necessary. But for every inch the vehicle moves upward, the jack handle moves many times the distance downward.

If, on the other hand, the input and output pistons are the same size, their travel will also be the same (Fig. 7-7). If the input piston moves three inches, the output piston also

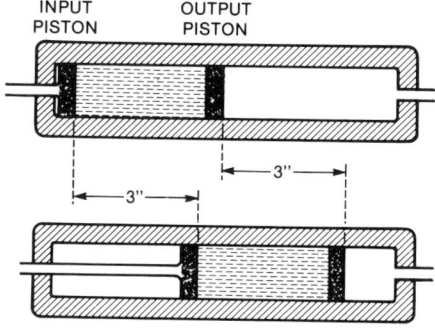

fig. 7-7 If the input and output pistons are the same size, their traveling distance will also be the same.

124 HYDRAULIC FUNDAMENTALS

travels three inches. In this case, the system does produce motion but no mechanical advantage between the two pistons. Finally, the relationship between the hydraulic and mechanical lever is the same with the exception that with a hydraulic lever it's pressure-to-area output rather than a weight-to-distance output of the mechanical lever.

basic hydraulic system

To show that pressure hydraulics is not difficult to understand, let's build a simple hydraulic jack system and see how it operates. The basic system consists of a reservoir, pump, valving, and an actuating mechanism. These components will change a small input force into hydraulic pressure, then convert the pressure to a larger output force to raise the load.

The first thing the system requires is a storehouse for the fluid until the system needs it. This storehouse is the sump or reservoir (Fig. 7–8). In other words, the reservoir acts as the fluid source for the hydraulic system.

Also, the reservoir has a vent line, suction line, and a return line. In order for the fluid pump to operate properly, the fluid must move from the reservoir to the pump. The vent line allows atmospheric pressure to enter the reservoir. As the pump operates, it creates a low pressure area from the pump down to the reservoir via the suction line. The atmospheric pressure will then push the fluid up to the pump due to a difference in pressure between the atmosphere and the pump's suction port. Finally, the return line is necessary because with a system that is constantly operating, the fluid eventually has to return to the reservoir for recirculation through the system.

The pump applies force to the fluid and creates flow (Fig. 7–9). Remember, force is necessary to create pressure in the system; but the pump's force also creates fluid flow within the system. If the flow does not meet any resistance, there is no pressure build-up in the system, just a free flow of fluid. In other words, there must be resistance to flow in

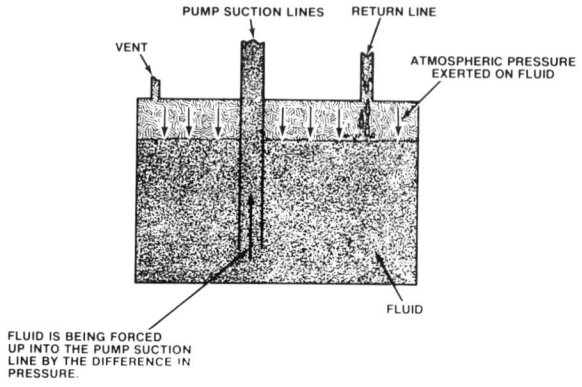

fig. 7–8 A fluid reservoir. (Courtesy Chrysler Corp.)

SYSTEM OPERATION 125

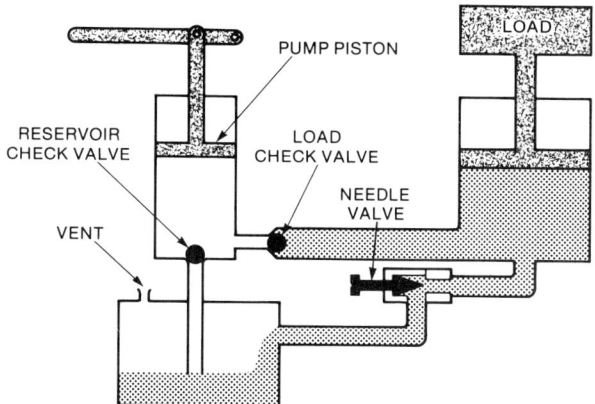

fig. 7-9 A basic, hydraulic jack system.

order to create pressure. Finally, the pump used for this basic system is a piston type which the jackhandle will operate.

When the pump begins to pump fluid, the system will need some sort of valving to control the direction of its flow. In this system, two valve types are necessary, check and needle. The check valves are nothing more than one way valves which allows fluid flow in one direction only, and they are necessary to permit repeated stroking of the pump.

In our simple system, two ball type check valves are necessary. The load check valve prevents the load from coming down on the intake stroke. The reservoir check valve prevents pressure loss to the reservoir during the pump's power stroke.

The lower the load, a needle valve is a necessary part of the system. The location of this valve is between the large output piston and the reservoir. Opening this valve allows the load on the output piston to push the fluid back to the sump.

Once the fluid has passed through the pump, valves, and lines, it will end up at the actuating mechanism. This is the place where the hydraulic pressure will move a piston, causing the piston to do some sort of mechanical work. This output piston is actually the dead end that the fluid flow encounters in the system, and this termination of flow causes the pressure to build up in the system. The pressure then works against the surface area of the piston causing a force to be applied to the load. In this case, the force lifts a vehicle (the load) upward.

system operation

As the operator moves the jack handle up on the intake stroke, the small pump piston moves up creating a low pressure area (vacuum) below it (Fig. 7-10). The reservoir check valve opens and allows fluid to flow from the reservoir to the pump. The load on the output piston tries to lower the piston, but this action creates a pressure that seats the load check valve and traps the fluid in the system.

126 HYDRAULIC FUNDAMENTALS

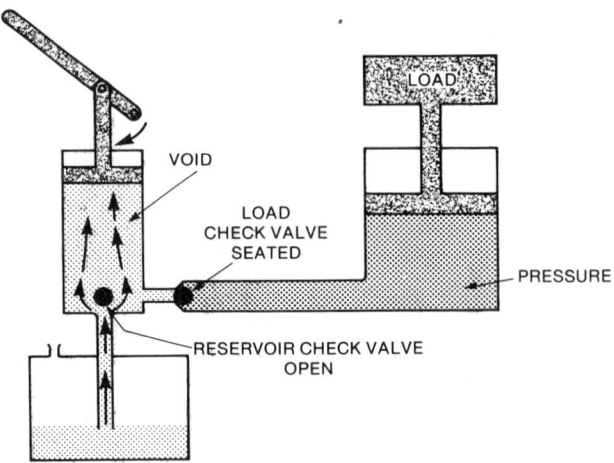

fig. 7-10 Operation of the jack system during the intake stroke of the pump.

When the operator moves the jack handle downward, the pump piston comes down and creates a pressure in the fluid below it (Fig. 7-11). The pressure seats the reservoir check valve and opens the load check valve. The pressurized fluid now flows under the large output piston. This action raises the vehicle another notch.

To lower the vehicle, the operator unscrews the needle valve slowly (Fig. 7-12). Opening this valve allows the load to push the fluid back to sump. The vehicle will lower in relation to the amount of fluid returned to the sump, and the operator has control of this flow by how much he opens the needle valve.

This simple system has an output of both force and motion. Therefore, this system uses pressure and continuous fluid flow. The pressure applies the force, and the flow creates motion.

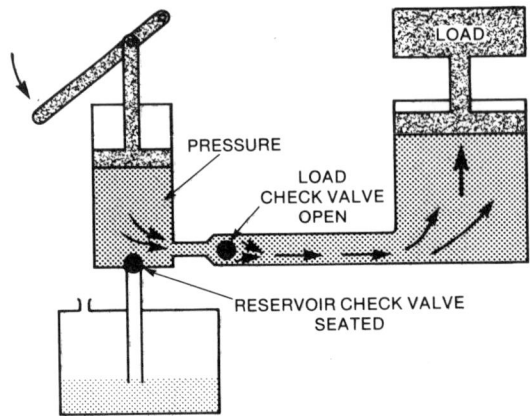

fig. 7-11 Operation of the jack system during the pump's pressure stroke.

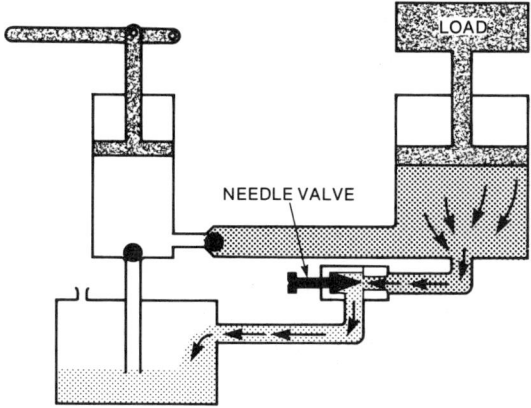

fig. 7-12 Operation of the jack system as the load is lowered.

summary

1. To understand the operation of an automatic transmission, a person needs a working knowledge of hydraulics.
2. Hydraulics is the science of liquids.
3. Hydrodynamics is the study of moving fluids.
4. Hydrostatics is the study of fluids under pressure.
5. Liquids resist compressure due to their molecular structure.
6. A molecule is the smallest particle of any substance.
7. Because ATF is not compressible, it can transmit pressure and motion.
8. Pascal discovered the hydraulic lever.
9. Pascal's Law states: "Pressure on a confined fluid is transmitted equally in all directions and acts with equal force on equal areas."
10. Force is a push or pull on an object measured in lbs.
11. Pressure is force per unit area measured in psi.
12. A small input piston can move a large output piston; this action within a hydraulic system is force multiplication.
13. When force multiplication takes place, the distance the input and output pistons travel are different.
14. A simple hydraulic system consists of a reservoir, pump, valving, and an activating mechanism.
15. The reservoir is the storehouse of fluid for the system.
16. The pump applies force to the fluid and creates flow.

17. The valves control the fluid direction.
18. The activating mechanism changes hydraulic pressure to output force to do some form of work.

check-up questions

The questions listed below will assist you in determining how well you remember the material contained in this chapter. Read each question carefully before choosing the answer to each item. If you cannot answer a question, review the material in the section of the chapter that covers the question.

1. The science that deals with the effects of moving liquids is _____.
    a. physics
    b. chemistry
    c. hydraulics
    d. pneumatics
2. The smallest particle or building block of a substance is the _____.
    a. molecule
    b. atom
    c. electron
    d. neutron
3. The property of a liquid which makes it not compressible is its _____.
    a. viscosity
    b. molecular structure
    c. fluidity
    d. flow rate
4. Pascal discovered _____.
    a. the hydraulic lever
    b. hydraulics
    c. molecules
    d. force
5. If a small input force raises a larger output force, _____ occurs.
    a. pressure
    b. force
    c. force multiplication
    d. viscosity

6. Force per unit area is _____.
   a. pressure
   b. torque
   c. force
   d. force multiplication
7. In hydraulics, one common type of force is that of a _____.
   a. spring
   b. weight
   c. ram
   d. pull
8. If a column of fluid has a force of 100 pounds applied to it by a two-square-inch piston, system pressure will be _____.
   a. 50 psi
   b. 100 psi
   c. 200 psi
   d. 250 psi
9. The output force of a hydraulic system is equal to system pressure times _____.
   a. input piston area
   b. output piston area
   c. pressure
   d. input force
10. If a hydraulic system that uses an input-output piston arrangement produces a force multiplication, the two pistons _____.
    a. move in opposite directions
    b. move the same distances
    c. move different distances
    d. do not move at all
11. The storehouse for the hydraulic system is the _____.
    a. sump or reservoir
    b. pump
    c. actuating mechanism
    d. valving
12. The device in a hydraulic system that produces force on the fluid is the _____.
    a. valving
    b. sump

    c. pump

    d. actuating mechanism

13. To control the direction of flow, a hydraulic system needs _____.

    a. valving

    b. a pump

    c. an actuating mechanism

    d. a sump

For the answers to these check-up questions, turn to the Appendix located at the back of the text.

8

automatic transmission hydraulic pumps- function

Any hydraulic system requires a pump to make the system operational. The pump applies force to the fluid which, in turn, generates system pressure and creates flow. In most cases, the system's design, pressure, or flow requirements determine the type of pump the system uses.

The simple hydraulic jack system, presented in the previous chapter, used a piston-type hydraulic pump. This pump required a strong arm or leg, as the power source, to operate it. In other words, the pump mechanism employed an external source of power or energy, in this case human strength, to apply a force to the fluid. The pump developed no power or force of its own; the pump simply transferred the energy or power from an external source to the fluid in the system.

In addition, the pressure and flow requirements of the simple jack system were not too great. Therefore, a person's strength by means of the hydraulic system could, without a great deal of effort, raise the motor vehicle. In other words, the pump converted the person's efforts on the jack handle to fluid pressure that transmitted force and motion to the activating mechanism, and this mechanism lifted the vehicle.

The pump located in the hydraulic system of an automatic transmission does exactly the same thing (Fig. 8–1). But in this case, the external power source for this pump is the engine. This *rotary hydraulic pump* converts engine torque to a force which causes system pressure and generates flow in the system. Finally, the piston pump

132 AUTOMATIC TRANSMISSION HYDRAULIC PUMPS-FUNCTION

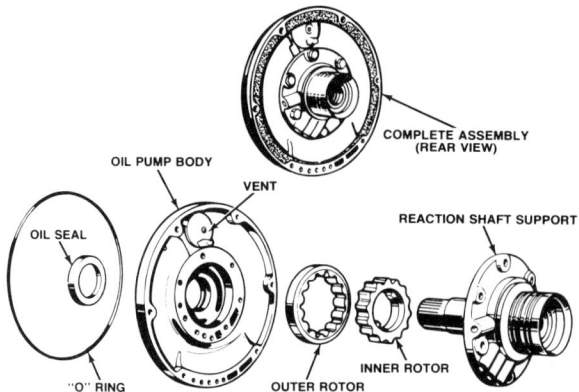

fig. 8-1 The design of a typical rotor-type hydraulic pump. (Courtesy Chrysler Corp.)

used to pressurize the hydraulic system of a hydraulic jack has a much smaller job to perform than the rotary pump used to operate the transmission's hydraulic system.

The jack's piston pump only has to produce enough pressure to cause the activating mechanism to raise the vehicle. On the other hand, the transmission's rotary hydraulic pump not only has to produce enough pressure to properly operate the activating mechanisms, the clutch and servo pistons, but has to produce enough pressure to cause fluid flow through various system restrictions, the torque converter, plus the cooling and lubricating systems of the transmission.

The piston pump of the jack only displaces (expels) enough fluid to raise the output piston a small amount with each pump stroke. The rotary pump, in contrast, must displace enough fluid that not only will transmit the motion to the clutch or bands but also will supply fluid to the converter, cooling and lubricating systems.

It should be obvious that a well-designed and constructed pump is necessary to operate the hydraulic system of an automatic transmission. If the pump malfunctions, the automatic transmission will begin to operate erratically or fail to function at all. To meet these special pressure and flow requirements of the hydraulic system, the automatic transmission utilizes one or more durable rotary pumps.

rotary pump theory

The rotary pumps usually have two round members of different sizes (Fig. 8-2). The small inner member which the converter drives inside the outer member rotates at engine speed. The small member then turns the outer member within the pump housing. Furthermore, these two members rotate on different centers so that at one point there is no clearance between them; then the clearance varies through a half revolution to a point of maximum clearance.

ROTARY PUMP THEORY   133

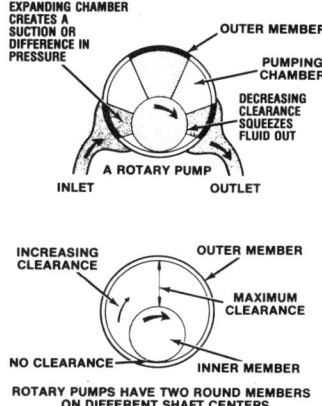

fig. 8-2 Rotary pump member design and operation. (Courtesy Chrysler Corp.)

The pumping mechanism which can be either gear teeth or rotor lobes forms sealed chambers between the two members. These chambers move around inside the pump housing carried along by the rotation of both members. Finally, these chambers which trap the fluid are constantly expanding and contracting as the two members rotate.

As any one pump chamber passes the pump's inlet, its size increases or expands, creating a void between the pump inlet and the sump. The atmospheric pressure, present over the fluid in the sump, pushes the fluid into this pumping chamber. Once the fluid fills the pumping chamber, the inlet portion of the pump's cycle for this particular chamber is complete.

As the filled pump chamber moves past the pump's inlet port, the chamber traps the fluid. For the next few degrees of pump rotation past the inlet port, the chamber's size does not change. But further rotation causes the size of the chamber to decrease, and this reduction in chamber size applies the force to the trapped fluid. Consequently, the chamber, by decreasing in size, squeezes the fluid out into the hydraulic system as the pumping chamber passes over the outlet port. Once this chamber travels completely past the outlet port, the delivery or displacement portion of the pump cycle is complete.

By having successive chambers which closely follow each other, the rotary pump produces a smooth, continuous output. In addition, these continuous chambers seal the outlet from the inlet port. Therefore, the pump's delivery is positive even against high system pressure.

The most common types of rotary pumps used today in automatic transmissions are the IX gear and rotor pumps. The term "IX" is an abbreviation for internal-external, referring to the location of the pumping chambers on the rotating members. For example, an IX gear pump has a large, outer member with internal teeth which form pumping chambers (Fig. 8-3). Also, these internal teeth mesh at one point with teeth located on the smaller member; these external teeth also form pumping chambers.

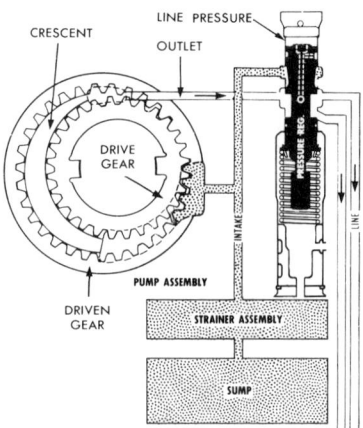

fig. 8–3 The outer and inner members of an IX gear pump. The drive gear is the inner member, and the driven gear is the outer member. (Courtesy Hydra-matic Division of General Motors Corp.)

gear pump design

An *IX gear pump* consists of a pump housing, drive, and driven gears, in addition to a stator support. The *pump housing,* as its name implies, houses or encloses the pump members (gears) and bolts to the front or converter end of the transmission case. The pump manufacturer forms this housing from a good grade of cast iron, and this component contains a counterbore or cavity, inlet and outlet ports, plus several additional fluid passages (Fig. 8–4).

The counterbore forms a guide for the driven gear as it rotates within the housing. The clearance between this gear and the wall of the counterbore is only sufficient to

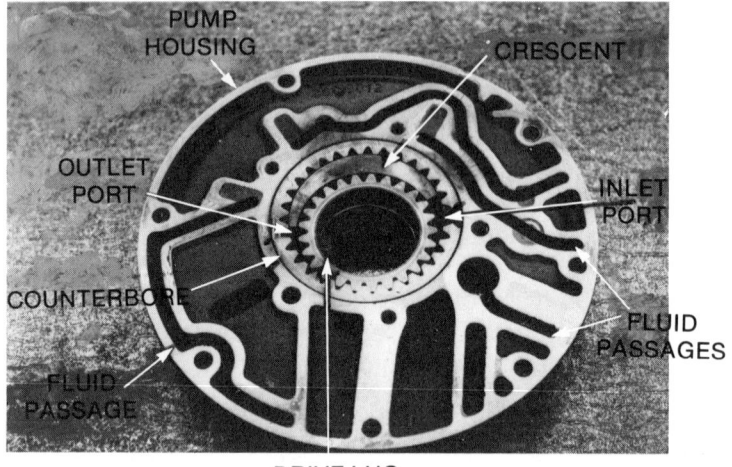

fig. 8–4 The design of a typical pump housing.

GEAR PUMP DESIGN 135

allow for lubrication. Also cast in the counterbore, in the area where the two gears separate, is a crescent shaped filler block. This crescent forms a guide for the small gear and helps to separate the pump's inlet from the outlet. At the point of greatest separation, the gears both fit closely to the crescent. The crescent and the space between the gear teeth form the chambers which trap the fluid as the gears turn past the inlet port. In other words, the crescent prevents the fluid from getting back to the inlet port.

Also found in the counterbore, in the area where the rotating drive and driven gears first separate from mesh, is the inlet port. With the pump bolted to the transmission case, this port aligns with a passageway leading to the sump. And as previously mentioned, during the inlet cycle of the pump, fluid enters this port and flows between the separating gear teeth.

Located in the area of the counterbore where the rotating drive and driven gears mesh once again is the outlet port. Because the crescent prevents the fluid from returning to the inlet port, the meshing gears force the trapped fluid into the outlet port. And since the outlet port aligns with a passageway leading into the pressure side of the hydraulic system, pressure in the system increases and fluid, when needed, flows to various components of the system.

Depending on the design of the transmission, the fluid passages, machined into the pump housing may feed several transmission components. For instance, most pump housing have the inlet and outlet passages which feed the torque converter. In addition, many transmission models use the pump housing as part of the hydraulic circuit that applies a clutch or band, and directs fluid to the cooling system and parts of the lubricating system.

The small drive gear has external spur (straight) type gear teeth. This gear also has flats or lugs cut into its inside circumference which mate with flats or slots located on the rear converter hub. Consequently, whenever the converter rotates, the drive gear will spin.

fig. 8–5 The design of a typical pump cover and stator support.

The teeth of the drive gear mesh with the teeth of the driven gear. These gears mesh only in the lower area of the counterbore opposite the crescent. But since the two gears are in mesh, any rotation of the small drive gear will force the large driven gear to turn.

The one-piece pump cover (Fig. 8–5) performs three functions. First, it covers and therefore seals the pump counterbore where the gears operate. Second, the splined, round, extended tube section, "stator shaft," supports the inner race of the stator's overrunning clutch. Consequently, when the overrunning clutch locks up, this section of the cover has to withstand the counter torque applied to the stator blades. Finally, on the opposite side of the stator shaft is a shorter, round extended section which fits into the clutch assemblies. This section not only supports the clutches but contains the fluid passages which feed the clutches with apply fluid.

gear pump operation

When the torque converter drives the small, inner gear, it causes the large, driven gear to revolve. Pump inlet occurs as the teeth of the two spinning gears separate from mesh (Fig. 8–6). The enlarging space between these separating teeth produces a low pressure area (vacuum) that fluid from the sump fills due to the action of atmospheric pressure.

Next, the revolving gears carry the fluid, between their teeth, to the crescent. The crescent divides or separates the pumping chambers formed on the inner gear from

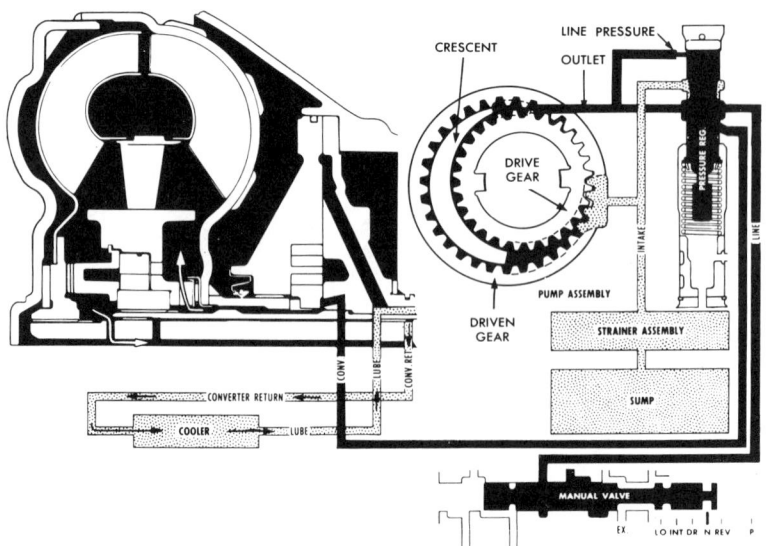

fig. 8–6 The operation of a typical gear-type hydraulic pump. (Courtesy Hydra-matic Division of General Motors Corp.)

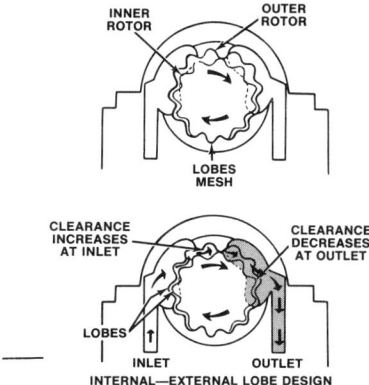

fig. 8-7 The operation of a rotor-type hydraulic pump. (Courtesy Chrysler Corp.)

those of the outer gear. And since the gear-to-crescent clearances are relatively small, this traps the fluid in the chambers so that it cannot leak out and return to the inlet port.

Further rotation of the pump gears brings the sealed pump chambers toward the output port area where the gear teeth will mesh once again. As the teeth of the two gears begin to mesh, the meshing action applies a force to the fluid; and the applied force squeezes the fluid out into the hydraulic system via the outlet port. As long as the engine operates, a continuous, pressurized fluid flow will leave the pump as successive chambers come together at the outlet port.

rotor pump design

The main difference between the IX gear and *rotor pump* lies in the pumping chamber design. In the gear pump, the area between the teeth of both gears forms the pumping chambers; in the rotor pump, the area between several rotor lobes forms the pumping chamber.

Fig. 8-1 shows a typical rotor pump that consists of an inner and outer rotor, pump body, and a stator or reaction shaft support. The inner rotor has twelve external lobes, and the converter drives it within the outer rotor but on a different center (Fig. 8-7). The outer rotor has thirteen lobes and rides in a bore within the pump body.

The lobes of both rotors are in mesh only at the bottom of the outer rotor in relation to the mounting of the pump on the transmission case. This limited lobe meshing is due to the fact that the center line of the outer rotor is above the center line of the inner rotor.

Furthermore, the two different center lines make it possible for a lobe tip on the inner rotor and a tip on the outer rotor to almost contact each other at a point about 180 degrees from where the lobes mesh. This close clearance between the two lobe tips actually separates the inlet from the outlet chambers of the pump. And when the outlet chamber delivers fluid to the outlet port, the meshing lobes on one end and the close lobe tip clearance on the other prevents outlet fluid from leaking back to the inlet side.

Finally, the pump body and reaction (stator) shaft support serve the same overall functions as the housing and cover found in a gear type pump.

rotor pump operation

As the converter turns the inner rotor, it drives the outer rotor. Because the rotors revolve on different centers, the lobes begin to separate. This lobe separation creates a low pressure area, and fluid from the sump, due to the effect of atmospheric pressure, fills the area between about four lobes via the inlet port.

At the same time, the distance between the lobes on the outlet side of the pump begins to decrease. Remember that since the rotor tip clearance at the upper center of the pump is only enough for free operation, this construction seals the two pump areas from each other. Since the trapped fluid cannot return to the inlet, the decreasing chamber size applies a force to the trapped fluid; as a result, the fluid squeezes through the outlet port and into the hydraulic system. Since as the pump revolves the various lobes form chambers that expand and contract, a continuous pressurized fluid flow leaves the pump.

pump displacement

Any hydraulic pump which has the outlet port sealed from the inlet is a positive-displacement or positive-delivery type. Positive-displacement or delivery means that as long as this pump type is revolving and fluid enters the inlet port, the pump will deliver fluid. The pump's volume or amount of flow will always be in proportion to the speed that the converter drives it.

This pump design therefore is such that the pump can deliver more fluid than the hydraulic system needs. In other words, the pump, because the engine drives it at all times, will continue to deliver fluid against system pressure regardless of how high the pressure reaches in the system. This build-up of hydraulic pressure, by the pump, could have no end. Consequently, to protect the hydraulic system against an overload that overheats the fluid and can cause failure of weak areas in the hydraulic system, a relief valve or control pressure-regulating valve is necessary in the system. The next chapter will discuss these devices in detail.

pump capacity

Pump capacity is the amount of fluid flow produced by a pump at a given pressure and pump rpm. This capacity must be large enough to provide pressure and flow at all times. It is especially critical at lower vehicle speeds with heavy acceleration because, during this time, the hydraulic system requirements are very high.

On the other hand, if pump capacity is too large, the pump will require excessive engine torque to operate it. In addition, the relief or regulating valve will not be able to handle the excess pressure, and the high pressure will damage the system. At cruising speeds the capacity of a pump found in an average automatic transmission is about 30 gallons of fluid flow per minute at a pressure up to about 250 psi.

pump efficiency

If at any time parts of the pump become worn or damaged, fluid can leak from the outlet to the inlet chamber. This leakage causes a loss of efficiency. Efficiency in this case is the actual pump output with respect to displacement or flow rate. In other words, if a given pump should produce 30 gallons per minute at cruising speeds but only delivers 15 gallons per minute, its efficiency is only 50 percent.

A loss of efficiency does not always mean a reduction in system pressure, but this of course depends on how much efficiency is lost. Pressure can still build up as long as the pump delivers fluid to the system and the fluid is not leaking off somewhere else in the hydraulic system. A loss of pump efficiency, in most cases, does cause a slow down in the application of pressure on and the movement of the actuating mechanisms.

multiple pump systems

Up until the mid-1960s, many automatic transmissions had two hydraulic pumps, a front and a rear (Fig. 8-8). The front pump, found in a multiple pump system, has a larger capacity than the rear unit. The engine drives it through the hub on the converter. The

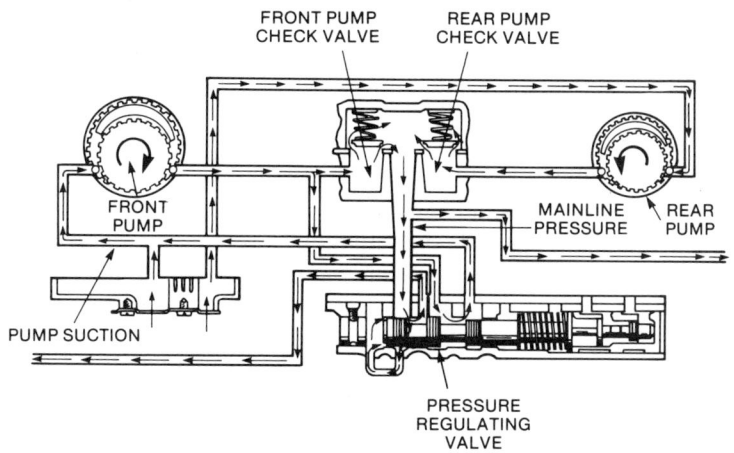

fig. 8-8 A multiple pump hydraulic circuit

transmissions output shaft rotates the rear pump that develops pressure and flow only when the vehicle is in forward motion. With this arrangement, one or both pumps will supply the pressurized fluid to the system.

With the engine running and the vehicle stationary or at very low speeds, the front pump supplies all pressurized fluid to the system. In other words, the front pump has the responsibility of supplying the pressurized fluid necessary to fill the converter, cooling and lubricating circuits in addition to activating the bands and clutches. The front pump meets all these requirements until the vehicle reaches a predetermined speed.

At this predetermined speed, the rear pump then produces sufficient pressure and flow to relieve the front pump of its system responsibilities. At this time, the front pump "idles" or recirculates its fluid output back to the sump. But if the vehicle slows down, the front pump once again takes over the main pressure and flow requirements of the system. Finally, the pressure regulating valve and two pump check valves coordinate the operation of the two pumps so that during the changeover period, the system will not lose any pressure or fluid flow.

benefits of multiple pump systems

The two-pump hydraulic system offers several advantages over the single pump design. First, by using a rear pump which the output shaft drives, the vehicle can be push started. And second, since the rear pump must rotate whenever the vehicle is in motion, this action reduces the amount of engine torque that is necessary to drive the front pump.

In a single pump system, the one-engine driven pump supplies all the pressure and flow necessary to operate the transmission at all times. If the engine cannot be started by normal means, the hydraulic system of the transmission will not have the pressure or flow necessary to apply the clutches or bands; and torque flow through the planetary system would be impossible. Consequently, the vehicle cannot be push started.

But the multiple pump system has a rear pump that operates whenever the vehicle is in motion. Therefore, by pushing a vehicle with a rear pump, the hydraulic system will have sufficient pressure and fluid flow to apply whatever frictional units necessary to activate the planetary system. Consequently, by pushing the vehicle, drive shaft torque, applied through the transmission, will turn over the engine.

As previously mentioned, a second benefit of using two hydraulic pumps is to conserve engine torque. In a hydraulic system with one pump, the engine uses up a given amount of torque at all times just to drive the pump. This expenditure of engine torque is especially high when the hydraulic system requires high pressure. But even during vehicle cruising speeds, where system pressure needs are lower, the engine still must drive the pump.

With the two-pump system, the engine only has to use some of its torque to drive the pump until the vehicle reaches a certain speed. Then, the rear pump takes over the requirements of the hydraulic system thereby reducing the load on the engine. In other words, the vehicle's momentum assists the engine not only in keeping the vehicle in motion but rotates the rear pump by means of the drive and output shafts.

Since hydraulic pump design in general has improved over the years, transmission manufacturers have discontinued the installation of rear pumps. The reason for this deletion was twofold: (1) two-pump systems produced more noise; (2) two-pump systems are more expensive to produce.

But there are two disadvantages of not having a rear pump in the automatic transmission. First, as previously mentioned, the vehicle cannot be push started. And second, the vehicle should not be towed with the rear wheels on the ground. Without a rear pump to circulate the fluid necessary for lubrication, towing a vehicle, with the rear wheels revolving, will cause severe frictional damage to the unit. Therefore, if the vehicle must be towed with the rear wheels on the ground, the engine must be operational or the drive shaft removed.

pump reservoir, filters, and vent

The pump reservoir or sump is the storehouse for the fluid (Fig. 8-9). The reservoir for the automatic transmission is the fluid pan attached to the bottom of the transmission. This metal pan, depending on the type of transmission, holds about 4 quarts of fluid. In addition, a filler tube and dipstick that extends from the pan to the engine compartment provides a convenient method of filling and checking the fluid level in the transmission. Finally, because the fluid is constantly recirculating, the fluid pan aids in the cooling of the fluid. Some of the heat contained in the fluid transfers to the outside air that passes over the bottom of the pan.

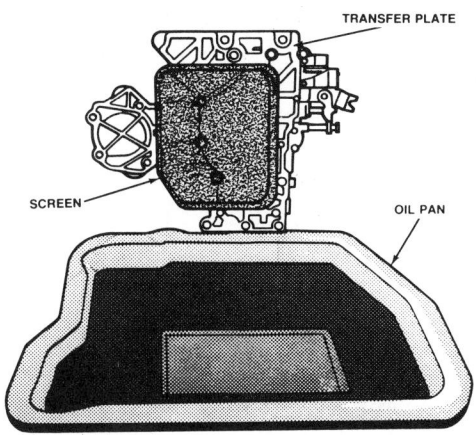

fig. 8-9 The transmission oil pan reservoir and a filter secured to the transfer plate of the valve body. (Courtesy Chrysler Corp.)

142 AUTOMATIC TRANSMISSION HYDRAULIC PUMPS-FUNCTION

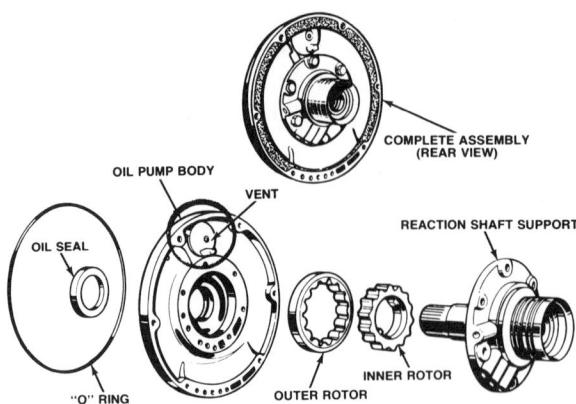

fig. 8-10 A transmission vent located in the body (housing) of the hydraulic pump. (Courtesy Chrysler Corp.)

To protect all the lubricated components of the transmission from foreign particle damage, the hydraulic system must have some form of filtering device. Manufacturers now utilize three types of material for these transmission filters, either fine wire mesh, treated paper, or a synthetic fiber called Dacron.

The location of the main filter is between reservoir and the pump's inlet part. Also, many transmissions have small screen-type filters, installed in key locations in the hydraulic system to provide extra protection to a given component or valve. Finally, the owner of the vehicle must have the main filter changed periodically. The time element between changes, of course, depends on where and how the operator drives the vehicle. But in any case, a dirty filter restricts the fluid flow to the pump which can cause pump failure and a reduction of fluid flow to hydraulic system components.

And finally the reservoir must have a vent (Fig. 8-10). Manufacturers install the vent in the main transmission case above the fluid's level or in the pump housing (body). This vent allows atmospheric pressure to enter the transmission and sump area. This pressure is necessary to push the fluid up through the filter and into the pump's inlet port. If the vent clogs, the pump's action will slow down or completely stop.

summary

1. All hydraulic systems require some form of pump to apply a force on the fluid.
2. A transmission hydraulic pump converts engine torque to mechanical force to create pressure and flow in the system.
3. The transmission hydraulic pump must produce high pressures and a great deal of fluid flow.
4. Automatic transmissions have one or more rotary pumps.

5. Rotary pumps usually have two round members of different sizes which operate on different centers.
6. The pumping mechanism which can be either gear teeth or rotor lobes form sealed chambers between the two members.
7. The most common types of rotary pumps are the IX gear and rotor pumps.
8. An IX gear pump consists of a pump housing, and drive and driven gears, in addition to a pump cover.
9. Located in the counterbore of the gear pump housing are the crescent, inlet, and outlet ports.
10. The small pump gear has external teeth, and the converter rotates it.
11. The large pump gear has internal teeth, and the small gear drives it.
12. The cover section of the pump usually performs three functions.
13. The space between the gear teeth forms the fluid chambers.
14. The separating gear teeth or rotor lobes create a vacuum at the pump inlet.
15. The gear crescent or lobe tips prevents the fluid from leaking from the outlet to the inlet parts.
16. The meshing of gear teeth or rotor lobes applies a force to the fluid; this force creates system pressure and flow.
17. A positive displacement pump, when operating and supplied with inlet fluid, will always deliver fluid to the system.
18. Pump capacity is the amount of fluid flow produced by a pump at a given pressure and pump rpm.
19. If a pump becomes worn or damaged, its efficiency goes down.
20. Some transmissions have two hydraulic pumps. The second or rear pump supplies the transmission with sufficient pressure and flow so that the vehicle can be push started and relieves the front pump of its load at vehicle cruising speeds.
21. The fluid pan, located at the bottom of the transmission, is the reservoir for the hydraulic system.
22. The main fluid filter prevents foreign particles from entering the pump's inlet.
23. An open transmission vent allows atmospheric pressure to enter the case above the level of the fluid.

check-up questions

The questions listed below will assist you in determining how well you remember the material contained in this chapter. Read each question carefully before choosing the answer to each item. If you cannot answer a question, review the material in the section of the chapter that covers the question.

144 AUTOMATIC TRANSMISSION HYDRAULIC PUMPS-FUNCTION

1. A hydraulic pump applies _____ to the fluid.
   a. pressure
   b. flow
   c. force
   d. displacement
2. The external source of power for the transmission's hydraulic pump is the _____.
   a. engine
   b. converter
   c. input shaft
   d. driven gear or rotor
3. Pump members are _____.
   a. the same size
   b. not the same size
   c. on the same operating center
   d. both b and c
4. Atmospheric pressure forces fluid into the pump during _____.
   a. the inlet cycle
   b. the delivery cycle
   c. the outlet cycle
   d. every third revolution
5. The most common types of IX pumps are the gear and the _____.
   a. tip
   b. vane
   c. lobe
   d. rotor
6. The inner pump member receives driving torque directly from the _____.
   a. drive shaft
   b. torque converter
   c. engine
   d. driven member
7. The gear teeth or lobes apply force to the fluid as they _____.
   a. come together
   b. expand
   c. repel each other
   d. turn in opposite directions

8. The crescent, inlet, and outlet parts are in the pump's _____.
   a. stator support
   b. counterbore
   c. sump area
   d. case
9. The portion of the gear pump that prevents outlet fluid from returning to the inlet is the _____.
   a. teeth
   b. lobes
   c. tips
   d. crescent
10. Transmission hydraulic pumps are the _____ type.
    a. positive-displacement
    b. efficient
    c. full-delivery
    d. semi-displacement
11. If a pump is 80 percent efficient, its _____ only is cut back.
    a. pressure
    b. flow
    c. force
    d. rpm
12. In order to successfully push start a vehicle, the transmission must have a _____.
    a. rear pump
    b. front pump
    c. drive rotor
    d. filter
13. The filter prevents foreign particles from entering the _____.
    a. pump's outlet port
    b. pump's inlet port
    c. fluid pan
    d. vent

For the answers to these check-up questions, turn to the Appendix located at the back of the text.

9

hydraulic pressure control system-function

The last chapter discussed the construction and operation of positive-displacement pumps. These pump designs produce sufficient hydraulic pressure and fluid flow to normally operate the automatic transmission at low pump speeds. Consequently, at high pump speeds, pressure and fluid flow will be high enough to cause damage to hydraulic system components. To offset this inherent characteristic of rotary pumps, manufacturers install one or more pressure-relief or regulating valves in the hydraulic system.

A pressure-relief or regulating valve is a device that bleeds off excess system pressure and flow. These safety valves route the excess pressure either back to the intake side of the pump or directly to the reservoir. By bleeding off a given amount of fluid flow and pressure, the regulating valve will maintain hydraulic system pressure to a safe operating limit.

Within the hydraulic system of an automatic transmission, two types of regulating devices are sometimes necessary: *the relief* and *the regulating*. The pressure-relief valve is a very simple device; this valve will relieve excess pressure which, in turn, maintains system pressure to a fixed amount. In other words, the system's pressure may be lower, but never higher than a given amount. And finally, since this device controls system pressure to a set amount, it usually acts in a hydraulic system as a high-pressure relief valve which protects the system against the build-up of extremely high pressures.

RELIEF VALVE OPERATION 147

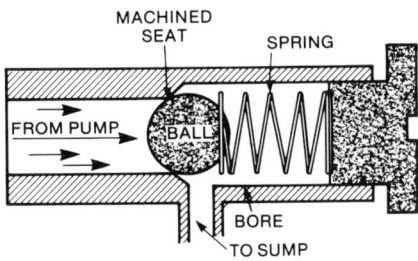

fig. 9-1 The design of a ball-type relief valve.

relief valve design

Manufacturers use two different designs for relief valves, the ball or the poppet. The *ball-type check valve* consists of a steel ball that operates in a special bore against a machined seat (Fig. 9-1). In addition, a compression-type spring holds the steel ball against its seat; hydraulic pressure pushes against the seat end of the relief ball which attempts to move the ball off of its seat.

The *spring-loaded poppet relief valve* can either have a flat or pointed reaction area (Fig. 9-2). The reaction area, in this case, is the surface of the relief valve that hydraulic pressure acts on and attempts to move the valve in its bore against the force of the spring. Furthermore, if the valve has a flat reaction area, the outer circumference of the valve covers or uncovers the sump port as the device moves in its bore. On the other hand, the pointed poppet valve has a specially machined seat that the spring holds the pointed reaction surface against to seal off the sump opening.

relief valve operation

Relief valves operate on the *balanced valve principle.* This important principle means that the valve can move in its bore, in one direction or the other, as a result of forces being applied to both of its ends. Referring to Fig. 9-3, the valve may either move to the right by hydraulic force or to the left by spring force according to which force can overcome the other. When the spring force is greater than the hydraulic force, the valve

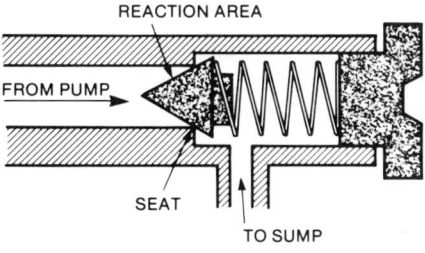

fig. 9-2 The design of a poppet-type relief valve.

148 HYDRAULIC PRESSURE CONTROL SYSTEM FUNCTION

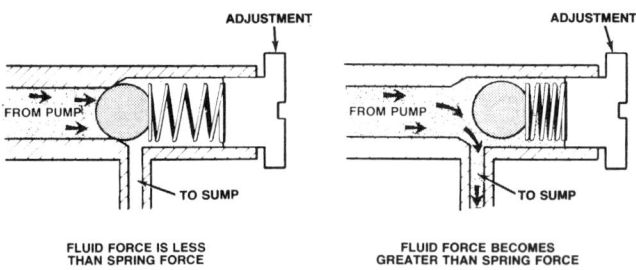

fig. 9-3 Typical relief-valve operation. (Courtesy Chrysler Corp.)

moves to the left. But if hydraulic pressure is high enough to overcome spring force, the pressure will push the valve to the right compressing the spring even more. In other words, hydraulic pressure moves the valve against the force of the spring whenever the system's pressure multiplied by the valve's reaction area is more than spring force.

The valve will continue to move to the right until spring force stops it or it reaches the end of its bore. It should be obvious that as the valve moves to the right, it compresses the spring which, in turn, will increase its force against the valve. If the spring's tension increases to a point where it offsets, or balances, the force of the hydraulic pressure on the valve's reaction area, the valve will stop moving. In other words, if the effect of the hydraulic pressure, acting on one end of the valve, is the same as the spring force on the opposite end of the valve, the forces will be in balance and the valve will not move any further in either direction.

The same principle applies in the operation of both ball and poppet relief valves. On the right side of these relief valves, a spring applies an initial force to seat the valves, and any movement of the valves to the right increases the springs' force. On the seat end of each valve which is its reaction area, system pressure will apply its force.

When system pressure is below a predetermined amount, its force will not be able to move the valves against the tension (force) of the spring. As a result, the relief valves remain seated. And none of the system's pressure and flow returns to the sump or pump inlet port.

But as pump rpm increases, system pressure increases to a point where the relief valves begin to move. Now, the pressure working against the valves' reaction area is great enough to overcome spring force. Consequently, the relief valve moves to the right. This action opens the sump port, and some pressure bleeds off to the sump or pump inlet.

If the pump is operating at a constant speed and has satisfied system demands for pressure and flow, the relief valves assume a fixed open position. Under these conditions, spring force and system pressure balance off and valve position stabilizes. The valves are far enough open to permit the excess pressure and flow to leak off to the sump which controls system pressure to a fixed amount. Finally, if the pump speed or system demands change, the forces applied to the valves again balance each other off, and the relief valves change position accordingly.

A threaded adjustment screw, located on the end of the spring, can alter the tension of the spring. By turning the screw in or out, spring force and system pressure will increase or decrease. Manufacturers of modern automatic transmissions no longer use an adjustment screw to set relief valve spring tension. Instead, they use a calibrated spring. A calibrated spring has a tension which is known, and the hydraulic force (system pressure), required to balance it is easy to figure.

pressure-regulating valve function

The pressure-regulating valve also operates on the balanced valve principle, but it has more functions to perform than the relief valve and has a more complex design (Fig. $9–4). The pressure-regulating valve, like a relief valve, controls system pressure to a predetermined amount. This valve's calibrated or adjustable spring regulates this pressure to between 50–75 psi, depending on transmission design. This regulated pressure, sometimes referred to as control pressure, is present in the hydraulic system whenever the transmission is operating in a zero or low torque output phase. These phases occur when the vehicle is stationary, and the transmission is in neutral, park, or drive, plus during vehicle cruise conditions.

But when the transmission is producing a high torque output such as in low, reverse, or any drive upshift condition, the pressure regulating valve must also raise control pressure. This higher pressure, up to around 275 psi, is necessary for two reasons. First, any time an upshift occurs, the demand for fluid flow needed to apply a clutch or band will drop the normal hydraulic pressure. Second, by raising the hydraulic pressure to compensate for the normal drop which occurs during a shift, the remaining pressure will be high enough to firmly lock up the applied friction components. In reverse and in manual low where no up-shift occurs, the increased pressure just firmly locks up the friction components to prevent slippage.

In addition to regulating pressure, this valve also directs pressurized fluid to various transmission components. For example, most regulating valves, upon initial opening, direct fluid from the pump to the torque converter, cooling, and lubrication systems. In some systems, a second regulating valve controls the pressurized fluid sent to the torque converter and cooling system.

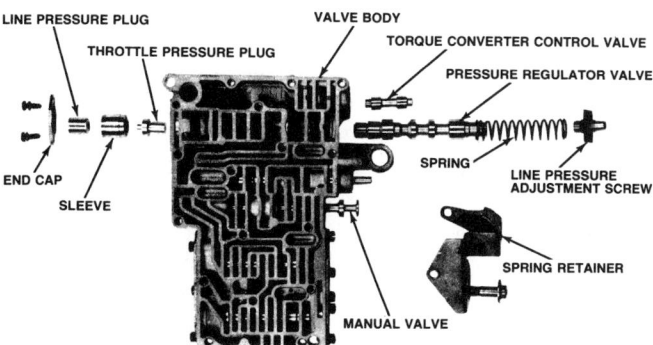

fig. 9–4 The components of the regulator-valve train. (Courtesy Chrysler Corp.)

150 HYDRAULIC PRESSURE CONTROL SYSTEM FUNCTION

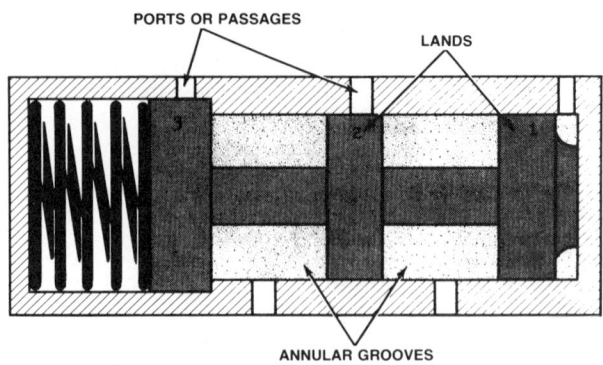

fig. 9-5 The design of a balanced, spool valve. (Courtesy Chrysler Corp.)

spool valve design

To accomplish the above-mentioned functions, the pressure-regulating valve has a more complicated construction than the simple relief valve; consequently, manufacturers use a valve with a spool design for this purpose. The spool valve, Fig. 9-5, is a cylindrical-shaped device which looks much like a thread spool. In addition, this special valve has two or more lands and annular grooves between the lands. Finally, this spool valve fits into and moves within a special bore, located in the pressure-regulating valve housing or the valve body, on a pressurized film of fluid.

The function of the valve lands is to uncover or close the ports located in the bore in which the valve rides; the annular grooves provide chambers between the lands in which fluid moves from one port to another depending on housing or valve body design. Referring back to Fig. 9-5, the number three and two lands, for example, block the center and upper-left ports while the upper-right and lower ports remain open. Pressurized fluid can, at this time, enter the grooves located between lands numbers one and two and two and three but will travel no further. Fluid also can enter the upper-right-hand port and fill the small area on the right-hand end of valve-land number one.

If the fluid pressure working against the end of the number one land, its primary reaction area, forces the spool valve to the left, fluid moves from the lower ports to the upper ports (Fig. 9-6). Since land two has cleared the center-upper port, fluid moves from the lower-right port through the annular groove, and out the center-upper port. Also, land three has cleared the upper-left port which permits fluid movement from the lower-left port through the annular groove, and out of the upper-left port.

Fluid will continue to flow through these ports until the valve moves back to its original position or moves quite a distance to the left. If the valve moves far enough to the left, number one land closes the lower-right-hand port. Also, the number two land will seal off the fluid from entering through the lower-left-hand port.

Since this value is also a balanced unit, two forces must be present to operate it. For instance, the calibrated spring imposes its force on the end of the large, number three land which attempts to maintain the spool valve in the right-hand position in its

SPOOL VALVE OPERATION

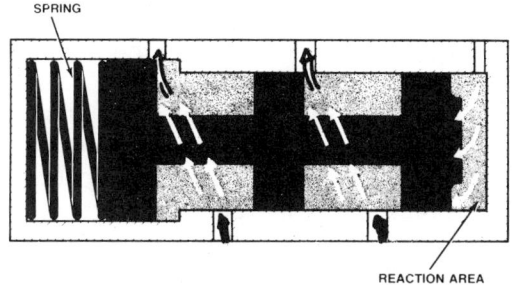

fig. 9-6 The operation of a balanced, spool valve. (Courtesy Chrysler Corp.)

bore. And as previously mentioned, fluid under pressure from the pump enters the upper-right-hand port and fills the cavity behind the number one land.

This hydraulic pressure, when acting on the reaction area of the number one land, will attempt to move the valve against spring tension. It is important to remember that the movement of this valve is dependent upon the product of the reaction area and the applied pressure relative to the opposing force of the spring. The equation for this relationship is: Force (F) equals Pressure (P) times Reaction area (A) or $F = PA$.

spool valve operation

Using the forementioned equation as a reference, it should be easy to see how a spool valve operates. Referring back to Fig. 9-6, the number one land has a reaction area of .5 square inches; and the hydraulic pressure, applied to this area, is 60 psi. The total force applied to this land of the value is equal to pressure (60 psi) times piston area (.5 in.^{2}) or 30 pounds. Now, if land number three has a 30-pound force applied to it by the calibrated spring, the valve will not move in its bore because both forces are equal. The valve, in other words, is now a balanced condition.

If on the other hand, the system pressure increases to 80 psi on the .5 in.^{2} area of the number one land, the valve will move (Fig. 9-6). This movement is the result of increasing the force on the reaction area. The increased force will now be equal to 80 psi (P) times .5 in.^{2} (A) or 40 pounds. Consequently, the force on the reaction area will push the valve over toward the left side of its bore compressing the calibrated spring even further.

As the valve moves to the left, it compresses the spring; this action increases the spring's force on the number three land. When the spring's force reaches 40 pounds, both forces are in balance, and the valve stops moving. If the hydraulic pressure should drop to a value where hydraulic force is less than spring force, the spring will push the valve over to the right in its bore. And, of course, if pressure would continue to increase, the valve would move further to the left until spring force stops it, or the valve bottoms in its bore.

Note also in Fig. 9-5 and 9-6, the diameter of the land nearest the spring is larger than any of the other lands; this diameter is .6 in.^{2}. If pressurized fluid also applies its force against this land, along with the spring's force, this new force produces an additional or secondary reaction area. These combined forces oppose the hydraulic force acting on the primary reaction area.

If the initial spring force on the number three land is 30 pounds and the system also applies a hydraulic force of 20 psi, the total force on the left end of land number three is equal to 30 pounds plus 20 psi (P) times .6 in.^{2} (A) or 42 pounds. Now, to balance this combined effort, hydraulic pressure on the primary reaction area will have to be 42 pounds; and, of course, to move the valve over to the left, pressure on the primary reaction area will have to be higher than that.

The application of fluid pressure to a secondary reaction area of any spool valve produces what is known in hydraulics as a *differential area*. The formation of a differential area on a spool valve occurs any time when opposing lands of the spool valve have pressure applied to them but their areas differ in size. As a result, the ratio of their surface areas and the amount of applied pressure will determine the strength of their relative forces. The land with the larger combination of area and pressure produces the larger differential force. This differential area effect gives the spool valve a compensating action or the ability to move back and forth in its bore in response to variations in pressure at one or more lands. Finally, this compensating action is the means by which a pressure-regulating valve increases system pressure to meet the changing hydraulic system requirements.

pressure regulator design

An actual pressure-regulating valve is much more complex in design than the spool valve just presented. For instance, Fig. 9-7 shows a pressure-regulating spool valve that has four large diameter and two smaller diameter lands. In addition, between each large land

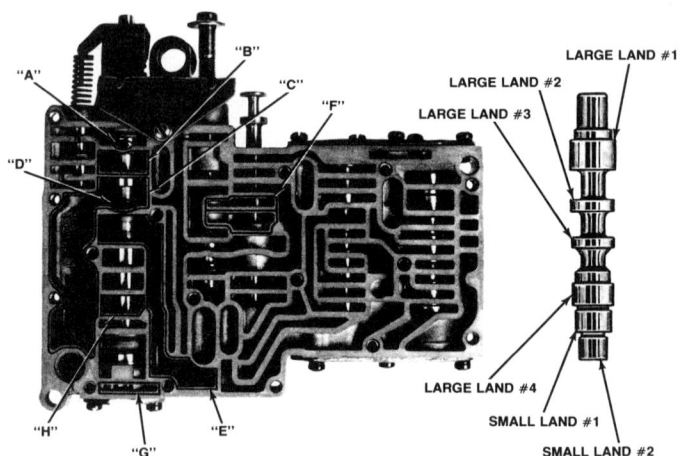

fig. 9-7 A typical, pressure-regulating spool valve. (Courtesy Chrysler Corp.)

is a large annular groove; and two narrow annular grooves separate the fourth, large land and the two, smaller lands.

To keep all the references straight and understandable, this text will number the lands of this pressure regular valve sequentially from the spring, or outermost, end of the valve. For example, the number two diameter land is the second, large land from the spring; the number three, large land is the third, large land from the spring, etc. And with the lands numbered as such, the reader can easily identify the locations of all the annular grooves.

With the numbering sequence in mind, the next step in understanding how this valve operates is to master the functions of the remaining components that are part of the regulating valve train (Fig. 9–4). First, a compression-type spring and bracket that has an adjustment screw will apply a rather large force to the back face of the number one land. This large spring force will try to maintain the valve in the closed position and regulate system pressure to a rather high amount, about 275 psi. Second, on the opposite end of the valve is a line-pressure plug, sleeve, and throttle-pressure plug.

The line-pressure plug assists the primary reaction area in moving the pressure regulating valve against heavy spring tension. Hydraulic pressure applies its force to the left end of this plug and this action forces the plug to move in the sleeve. This plug movement assists the system pressure, on the primary reaction area, to move the valve against the tension of the spring. This combined action regulates pressure to a smaller amount than it would be without the plug's assistance.

The throttle-pressure plug which fits between the line-pressure plug and the regulating valve itself, when activated by pressure, resists any movement of the line pressure plug. By supplying a differential area that offsets or resists the movement of the line pressure plug, system pressure can be compensated, or raised, to meet increased demands. This increased pressure is necessary to provide additional pressure required during an upshift or for locking up the frictional components to prevent slippage under heavy vehicle loads. In other words, the throttle plug, working with the rest of the regulating valve train compensates or adjusts hydraulic pressure to meet the various needs of the transmission.

Some manufacturers install the throttle plug and, if used, the line-pressure plug in a different location. For example, Fig. 9–8 shows a regulator valve with the throttle plug (pressure booster valve) bearing against the spring. The spring in this installation has less tension than the one used in Fig. 9–4, and the pressure booster valve, when moved by hydraulic pressure, increases spring tension. And by increasing spring force, hydraulic pressure in the system will go up accordingly.

pressure regulator valve operation—noncompensated

With the engine operating, the hydraulic pump will rotate creating a void at its intake port (Fig. 9–9). This difference in pressure, between the sump and the pump's inlet, causes fluid to flow up from the sump, through the filter, and into the pump. After the pump applies a force to the fluid, it leaves the pump and enters the hydraulic system circuits.

154 HYDRAULIC PRESSURE CONTROL SYSTEM FUNCTION

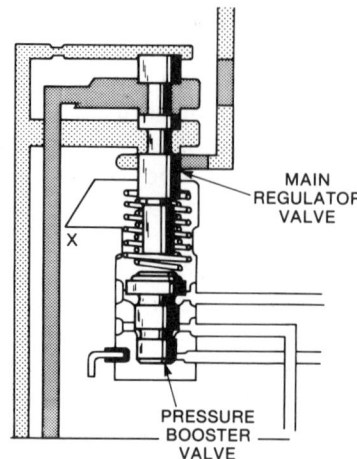

fig. 9–8 A pressure-regulating valve train with the throttle plug (booster valve) located on the spring end of the regulating valve.

One of these circuits routes the fluid to the line-pressure plug and to the end of the small, number two land or primary reaction area. The hydraulic pressure exerted on both of these areas attempts to move the regulator valve against the tension of the spring. But these reaction areas on both the valve and the plug are relatively small, so on initial engine start-up, not much force exerts on the pressure regulator valve to move it very far against the strong tension of the spring.

But the valve does move some initially. This valve movement causes the large, number one land to open a passage to the torque converter. Now, hydraulic fluid under pressure flows to the torque converter and cooling system. In other words, pump pressure does not have to be very great to cause the pressure regulating valve to move and open a hydraulic circuit to the torque converter.

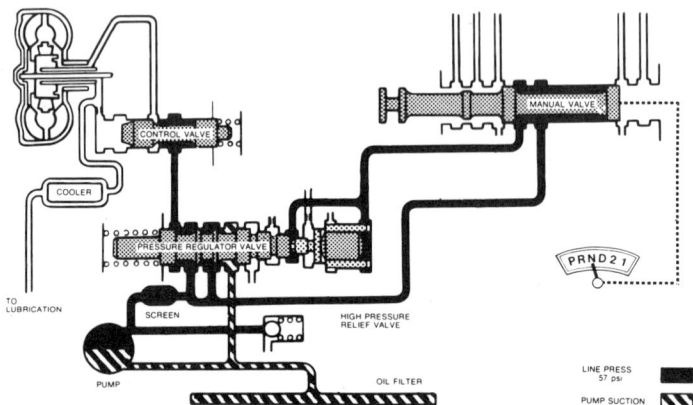

fig. 9–9 Pressure-regulating valve train operation. (Courtesy Chrysler Corp.)

As pump and system pressure continue to increase due to increased pump rotation, hydraulic pressure acting on the line-pressure plug and the primary reaction area will cause the valve to move further toward the spring. As the valve continues to move, the large, number three land opens a passage which leads to the sump. With this port open, the fluid in the annular groove, between the large lands two and three, begins to return to the sump.

Now, as the fluid begins to vent into the sump, the system pressure drops due to this "controlled leak." When the pressure drops, the valve stops its movement toward the spring because the spring and hydraulic forces are in balance. Therefore, hydraulic pressure regulation is just a repetition of the opening and closing of the sump port by the large, number three land; the accompanying "controlled leak" bleeds off excess pressure to the sump.

pressure regulator valve operation—compensated

The previous discussion of pressure regulator valve operation pointed out how the spring's tension regulated the amount of system pressure. In other words, once the pump produced enough pressure to balance spring force and move the valve to the vent position, system pressure would not increase beyond this point. But as previously pointed out, pressure in the system has to increase during certain times. Consequently, the pressure-regulating valve train must have a compensating device, the throttle plug (Fig. 9-4).

As the driver slowly accelerates the engine, the vehicle begins to move, and a special hydraulic pressure signal from the throttle valve enters the passage leading to the regulator's throttle plug (Fig. 9-9). Chapter Eleven will cover the description and operation of the throttle valve system, so for now just remember that this device sends a signal to the throttle plug. And the intensity of this pressure signal will be in proportion to the rpm of the engine or its load.

The presence of the throttle pressure, acting on the large (secondary) reaction area of the throttle plug, forces the line-pressure plug to the right. This action allows the spring to force the valve train to the right which causes the "controlled leak" at the regulator valve's sump port to decrease or stop altogether. As the sump port closes and the leak decreases, the system's pressure must increase in order to push the regulator valve over to the left so that it will be in a regulating cycle again.

The actual amount of pressure increase will be in proportion to the amount of the pressure signal sent from the throttle valve to the throttle plug. At idle and very low engine speeds, this signal is low; therefore, the pressure increase will also be low. But both the signal and system pressure will increase rapidly as the driver opens the throttle. At a given engine speed, the pressure increase stabilizes; this action prevents excessively high and unnecessary pressures from developing in the system. In other words, the throttle valve's pressure signal via the throttle plug will begin to raise system pressure as the driver accelerates the engine, and it will continue to raise system pressure until the engine reaches a given speed. Then, the pressure stabilizes in the system and goes no higher. Of course, the amount of pressure increase and the engine rpm where the pressure reaches its maximum depends on the type of transmission, its hydraulic system requirements, and the type of engine used in the vehicle.

summary

1. Pressure-relief and pressure–regulating valves are devices that bleed off excess system pressure and flow to the sump.
2. A relief valve controls system pressure to a set amount and usually acts as a high-pressure relief valve in a hydraulic system.
3. Manufacturers use two different designs for relief valves, the ball and poppet.
4. Relief valves operate on the balanced valve principle.
5. If the effect of the hydraulic pressure acting on one end of the valve is the same as the spring force on the opposite end of the valve the forces will be in balance and the valve will not move.
6. If the pump is operating at a constant speed and has satisfied system demands for pressure and flow, the relief valve assumes a fixed open position.
7. The pressure-regulating valve controls system pressure when the transmission is operating in a low-torque output phase.
8. The pressure-regulating valve also adjusts system pressure to meet the additional demands placed on the hydraulic system when the transmission is operating in a high-torque output phase.
9. In addition to regulating pressure, the regulating valve also directs pressurized fluid to various transmission components.
10. The spool valve is a cylindrical-shaped device which looks much like a thread spool.
11. Valve lands uncover and cover ports located in the bore in which the valve rides.
12. The annular grooves provide chambers between the lands in which fluid moves from one port to another.
13. The movement of a balanced-type spool valve is dependent upon the product of the reaction area and the applied pressure itself relative to the opposing force of the spring, or force equals pressure times area ($F = PA$).
14. The application of fluid to a secondary reaction area of any spool valve produces what is known in hydraulics as a differential area.
15. Differential area of a spool-regulating valve provides the method of adjusting system pressure to meet various demands.
16. An average pressure-regulating valve has many loads and annular grooves.
17. The line-pressure plugs assist in moving the pressure regulating valve against heavy spring tension.
18. The throttle-pressure plug blocks the movement of the line-pressure plug whenever hydraulic pressure has to increase to meet system demands.

19. As the regulator valve moves open slightly, pressurized fluid enters a passage leading to the torque converter and cooling system.
20. Hydraulic pressure regulation is just a repetition of the opening and closing of the sump port; and the accompanying "controlled leak" bleeds off excess pressure to the sump.
21. The throttle-valve's pressure signal via the throttle plug will begin to raise system pressure as the driver accelerates the engine, and it will continue to raise system pressure until the engine reaches a given speed.

check-up questions

The questions listed below will assist you in determining how well you remember the material contained in this chapter. Read each question carefully before choosing the one or more answers to each item. If you cannot answer a question, review the material in the section of the chapter that covers the question.

1. A device which bleeds off excess system pressure and flow is the _____.
   a. ball valve
   b. poppet valve
   c. relief or regulating valve
   d. transition valve

2. The device that usually protects a transmission against the build-up of extremely high pressures is the _____.
   a. relief valve
   b. spool valve
   c. transition valve
   d. throttle valve

3. The surface of any valve that hydraulic pressure pushes on and attempts to move the valve against spring tension is the _____.
   a. land
   b. groove
   c. port
   d. reaction area

4. If a valve can move in either direction in its bore as a result of forces being applied to both its ends, it is a _____.
   a. balanced valve
   b. transition valve
   c. spool valve
   d. manual valve

158 HYDRAULIC PRESSURE CONTROL SYSTEM FUNCTION

5. A valve spring which has a certain tension is a _____ spring.
   a. compression
   b. calibrated
   c. estimated
   d. adjustable
6. System pressure of a transmission operating in a low torque output phase is between _____.
   a. 200—250 psi
   b. 100—150 psi
   c. 75—100 psi
   d. 50—75 psi
7. The portion of a spool valve that opens and closes port openings is the _____.
   a. lands
   b. grooves
   c. reaction area
   d. spring
8. If the hydraulic pressure, acting on the primary reaction area, is greater than the spring force on the pressure regulating valve, it will _____.
   a. close
   b. open
   c. balance itself
   d. both *a* & *c*
9. The application of pressure to a secondary reaction area of any spool valve produces a _____.
   a. relief area
   b. primary area
   c. differential area
   d. piston area
10. The component of the regulating valve train that assists in moving the valve against spring tension is the _____.
    a. line-pressure plug
    b. throttle plug
    c. adjustment screw
    d. sleeve

11. The device that works with the rest of the regulating valve train to adjust hydraulic pressure is the _____.
    a. adjustment screw
    b. line-pressure plug
    c. throttle plug
    d. sleeve
12. Initial pressure regulator movement opens a port to the _____.
    a. sump
    b. torque converter
    c. reservoir
    d. clutches
13. When the regulator valve moves open to a point where the valve enters the regulatory cycle, a land opens a port to the _____.
    a. clutch
    b. converter
    c. sump
    d. valve circuits

For the answers to these check-up questions, turn to the Appendix located at the back of the text.

10

hydraulic relay valves

As the pressurized fluid leaves the rotating pump, it enters several different hydraulic circuits. A circuit in this case refers to the complete path of the fluid flow including the pressure source, the hydraulic pump. For example, the last chapter explained how a portion of the pump's flow and pressure activated the regulator valve train circuit which, in turn, controlled the system's pressure to a safe operating limit and supplied fluid to the torque converter and cooling system. The rest of the pump's flow enters and fills the various other valve circuits of the hydraulic system. Of these various valve circuits, this chapter will cover the function, design, and operation of the several different flow-control or relay-valve circuits.

function of the valve

Relay valves are devices which direct flow and pressure along a given path or circuit. These valves simply open and close a circuit connecting control (system) pressure to a clutch, servo, or other hydraulic device without restricting the fluid flow or changing its pressure. In other words, these devices are nothing more than manually or hydraulically operated on-off switches.

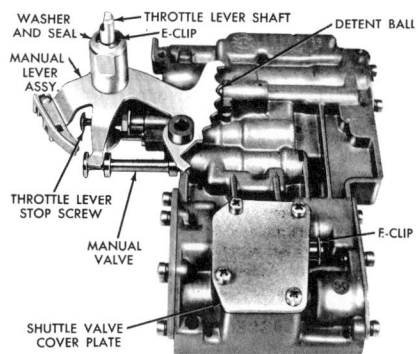

fig. 10-1 The manual valve and lever assembly. (Courtesy Chrysler Corp.)

manual valve function and design

The *manual valve* (Fig. 10-1) is one type of mechanically operated relay valve. Its function, when activated by the driver, is to direct control pressure which will apply the appropriate frictional components necessary to set the vehicle in motion. In other words, this valve will set up the operating conditions within transmission once the driver has moved the gearshift selector lever to a given driving range.

Since the driver mechanically operates this valve, some form of linkage must connect it to the gearshift-selector lever. For example, Fig. 10-1 shows the manual lever arrangement, located on the side of the valve body, that is responsible for actually moving the valve in its bore within the valve body itself. In addition, external linkage of various designs connects this manual lever to the gearshift-selector lever. Consequently, as the driver moves the gearshift-selector lever, this linkage causes the manual lever to move the manual valve in its bore.

Since this manual valve has a spool design, it will have several annular grooves and lands which control port openings. Fig. 10-2 shows a typical manual valve that has two lands of uniform diameter and one of a lesser diameter with annular grooves between the lands. The large groove, between lands one and two, connects the pump and regulator-valve circuits with whatever other driving-range circuits selected by the operator. The smaller groove, between lands two and three, vents to the sump those forward-drive circuits which are not in use.

As the valve moves, the lands of the manual valve open or close ports located in the bore in which it moves; each of these ports connects to a circuit which carries pressurized fluid to a specific frictional component or to another hydraulic valve. For instance, in Fig. 10-2, circuit *A* is the inlet port to the manual valve. This port connects to a circuit leading to the pressure-regulator valve and hydraulic pump. Consequently, this port supplies pressurized fluid to the manual valve and its circuits; and it has to be open no matter what position the manual valve may be in.

If Port *B* is open, it feeds a circuit from the manual valve to the line-pressure plug and to the primary reaction area of the pressure-regulator valve. This pressurized fluid,

162 HYDRAULIC RELAY VALVES

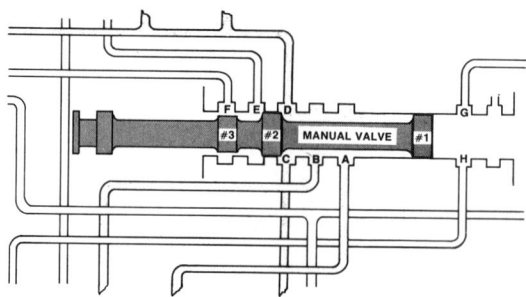

fig. 10-2 The design of a typical manual valve. (Courtesy Chrysler Corp.)

when acting against these two areas of the regulator valve, moves the valve against spring tension to control hydraulic pressure to within safe operating limits. Finally, to regulate hydraulic pressure in all forward driving ranges, the manual valve lands will always keep Port *B* wide open.

Port *C*, if open, supplies fluid pressure to a circuit leading to the governor valve (Fig. 10-3). The governor is a type of balanced spool valve that senses vehicle speed from the transmissions output shaft. The valve sends a hydraulic-speed pressure signal to the shift valves that controls automatic shifting in relation to vehicle speed. Chapter Eleven will cover the construction and operation of this valve and its circuitry in detail.

Port *D* which is open during all forward driving ratios supplies fluid pressure to a circuit leading to a clutch, an accumulator, and related circuits. This pressurized fluid causes the clutch to apply, and the accumulator valve to move in its bore against spring tension. The accumulator, when incorporated into an apply circuit of a friction component, absorbs a portion of this apply pressure which, in turn, controls shift quality. The last section of this chapter will cover the design and operation of this device. Finally, Port *D* also supplies fluid to the throttle and 1-2 shift valves which are necessary to automatically upshift the transmission from first to second ratio under various operating conditions.

If open, Ports *E* and *F* supply fluid pressure to circuits leading to the 2-3 and 1-2 shift valve governor plugs; this action prevents the shift valves from opening. For instance, if Port *E* is open, the 2-3 shift valve will not open because Port *E* pressurizes a circuit leading to a "differential area" on the back face of the governor plug. This action prevents the plug from opening the 2-3 shift valve; as a result, the transmission will not upshift out of second ratio. In other words, Port *E* provides the transmission with a second gear hold capability.

Now, if both Ports *E* and *F* are open, the 2-3 and the 1-2 shift valves will not open. This operation locks the transmission in low gear because both the 1-2 and the 2-3 shift valve governor plugs have pressurized fluid acting on their "differential area." In other words, the transmission cannot upshift out of low gear because the shift valves cannot move to the open position.

When Ports *G* and *H* are open during reverse gear ratio, Port *G* supplies pressure to a circuit leading to the reverse friction components; and Port *H* directs fluid to a circuit

MANUAL VALVE OPERATION

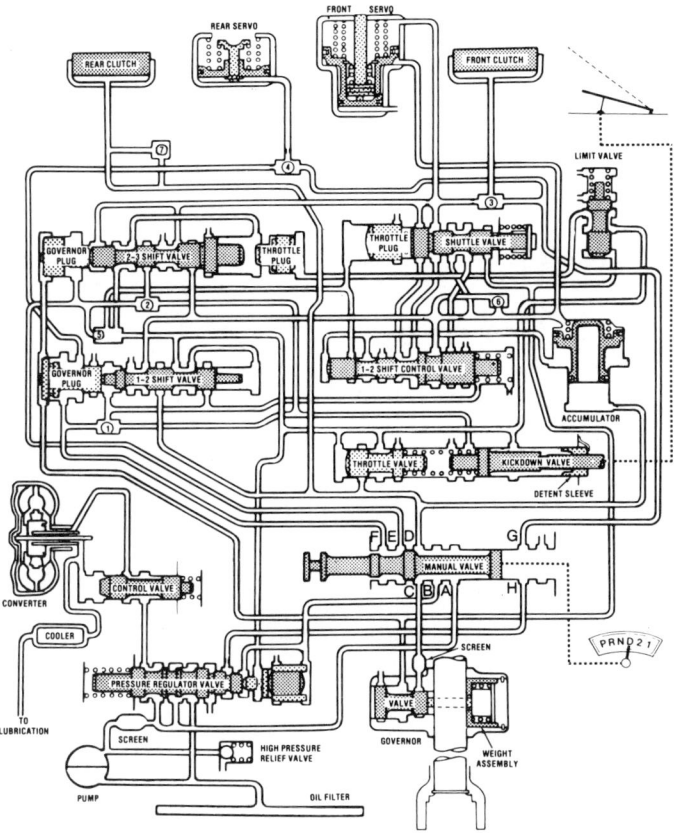

fig. 10-3 A diagram of a manual valve, 1-2 and 2-3 shift valves, throttle valve, and governor circuits. (Courtesy Chrysler Corp.)

back to the pressure-regulator valve train. Now, pressure from the G port applies the friction components necessary for the reverse ratio; and since Port B, of the forward drive circuits, is not open, Port G supplies fluid pressure to the regulator-valve train. This pressure only acts against one reaction area on the regulator valve; therefore, hydraulic pressure in reverse range is higher than it is in the forward driving ranges.

manual valve operation

If the driver places the gearshift-selector lever in reverse range, the manual valve moves to the position shown in Fig. 10-4. The manual valve's land number one now opens Ports G and H, and land number two blocks pressurized fluid to Ports F, E, D, C, and B. Pressurized fluid moves from Port A through the annular groove, between lands one and two, to Port G which supplies the circuit to the friction components with fluid pressure. This action applies the friction components. At the same time, fluid under pressure also moves out of Port H to the pressure-regulator circuit to control hydraulic pressure in

164 HYDRAULIC RELAY VALVES

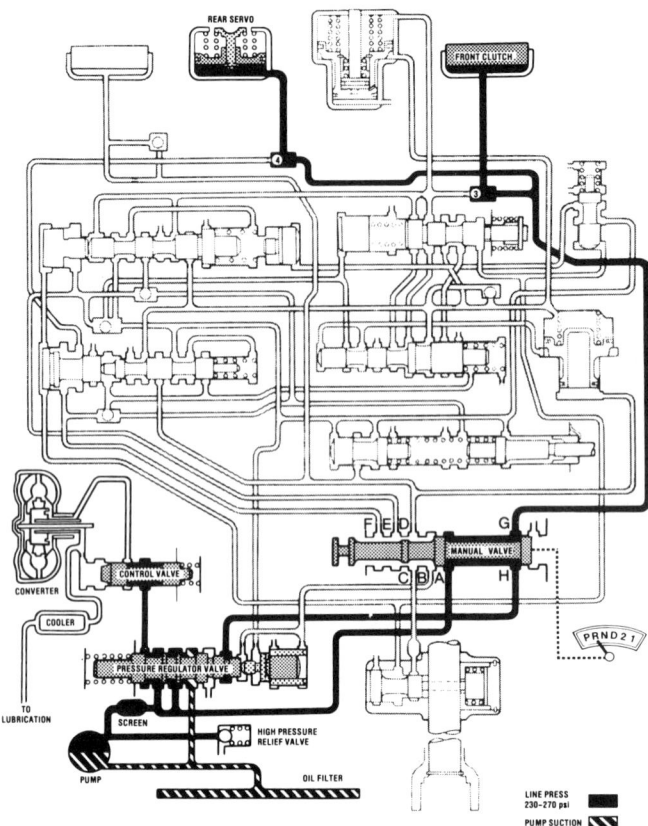

fig. 10–4 A manual valve positioned in reverse-gear ratio. (Courtesy Chrysler Corp.)

reverse range. Finally, since Ports *F, E, D, C,* and *B* are open to the sump via the other annular grooves, any pressurized fluid in the forward drive circuits will vent back to the sump.

When the driver moves the selector lever to manual low, the manual valve assumes a position as shown in Fig. 10–5; the vehicle now can start off in low gear but will not upshift. In this situation, the manual valve's number-two land opens Ports *B, C, D, E,* and *F.* This action permits control pressure from inlet Port *A* to flow through the large annular groove and out of Ports *B, C, D, E,* and *F.* In addition, the number-one land blocks fluid flow to Ports *G* and *H.*

Now, fluid from Port *D* pressurizes the circuits that applies the clutch and band required for low gear and also a supply circuit to the 1–2 shift valve. Port *C* pressurizes a circuit to the governor valve which, along with the fluid sent to the 1–2 shift valve, prepares the transmission for an automatic upshift. But since fluid also flows through Ports *E* and *F* to a circuit leading to a "differential area" of both shift valve governor plugs, the transmission cannot upshift.

Furthermore, with the manual valve positioned in low gear, Ports *G* and *H,* the reverse circuits, are open to the sump. This action permits any remaining pressurized

MANUAL VALVE OPERATION **165**

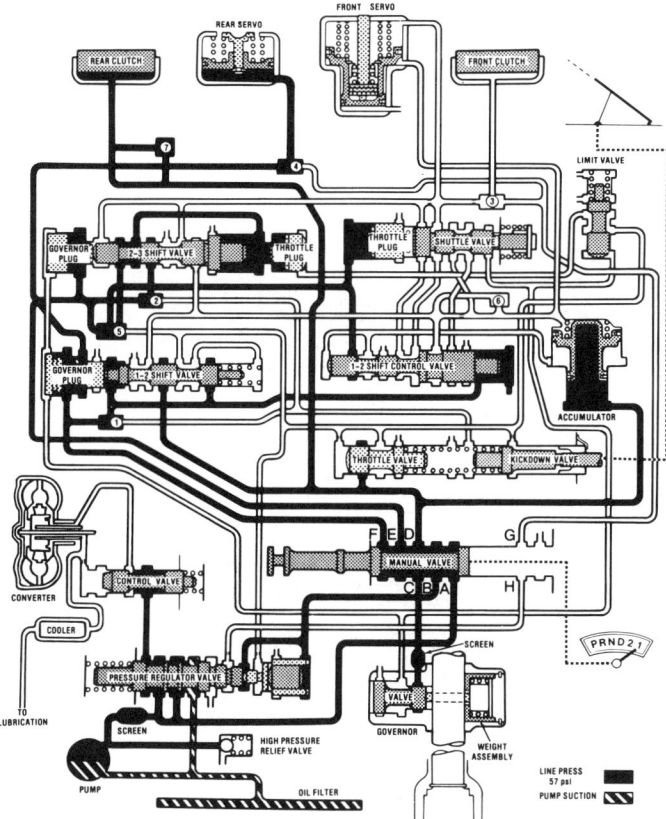

fig. 10–5 A manual valve positioned in low-gear ratio. (Courtesy Chrysler Corp.)

fluid from these circuits to return to the reservoir. With no pressure on the circuits, the frictional components release due to the action of their return springs; the system pressure lowers because Port *H* is open to sump; and Port *B* once again supplies control pressure to the circuits leading to the regulator valve's primary reaction area and the line-pressure plug.

If the driver decides to use the second-gear selector position, the manual valve assumes a position which permits this transmission design to start the vehicle off in low; but the unit will only automatically upshift to second gear (Fig. 10–6). Now, land number two of the manual valve blocks off Port *F*; but it leaves Ports *D, E, B* and *C* open to control pressure. Also, land number one blocks off pressure to Ports *G* and *H* which then remain open to the sump.

In this manual valve position, Port *D* once again pressurizes a circuit which applies the frictional component necessary to set the vehicle in motion in low gear and also pressurizes the 1–2 shift valve circuit. Port *C* supplies fluid to the governor circuit which, along with the pressure sent to the 1–2 shift valve, prepares the transmission for a 1–2 automatic upshift. Therefore, when the vehicle reaches a given road speed, the 1–2 shift valve will open, and the transmission will upshift to second gear.

166 HYDRAULIC RELAY VALVES

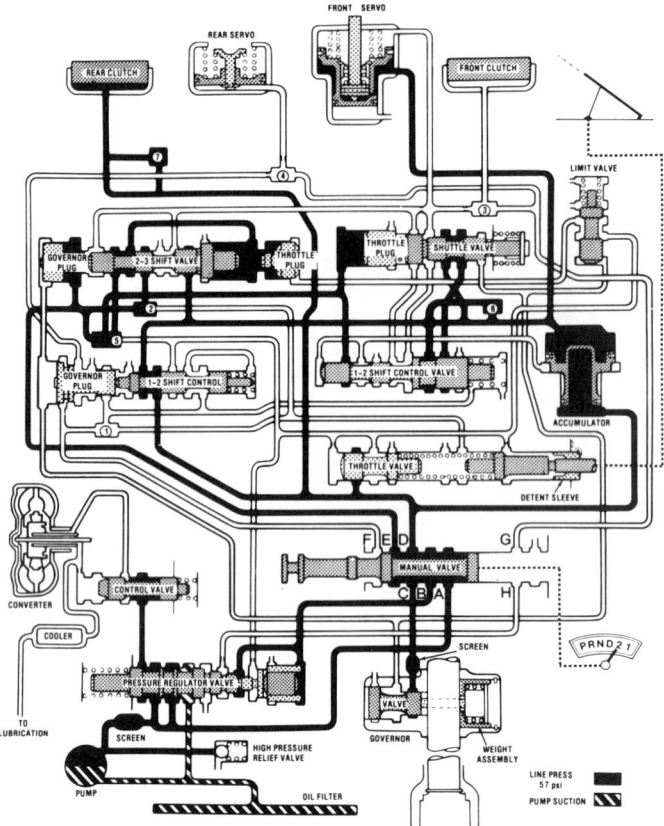

fig. 10–6 A manual valve positioned in second-gear driving range. (Courtesy Chrysler Corp.)

But since Port E is open, fluid under pressure goes to the 2–3 shift valve governor plug to oppose the opening of the 2–3 shift valve. This pressure acts on the backface, "differential area", of the governor plug which balances off any governor pressure on its front face. Consequently, the 2–3 shift valve stays in the off or downshifted position; and the transmission remains in second gear.

The remaining manual valve ports perform the same functions as they did in manual low range. Ports G and H remain open to bleed off the reverse circuits to sump. And Port B supplies fluid pressure to the regulator valve train circuits.

For normal, fully automatic operation, the driver places the selector lever into drive range; this action moves the manual valve to the position shown in Fig. 10–7. In this manual valve position, land number two only opens Ports D, C, and B. Also, land one still blocks off pressure to the reverse Ports G and H.

Control pressure from Port A once again flows through the large annular groove to pressurize Ports D and C. Port D fluid pressure, via a circuit, applies the friction compo-

SHIFT VALVE FUNCTION 167

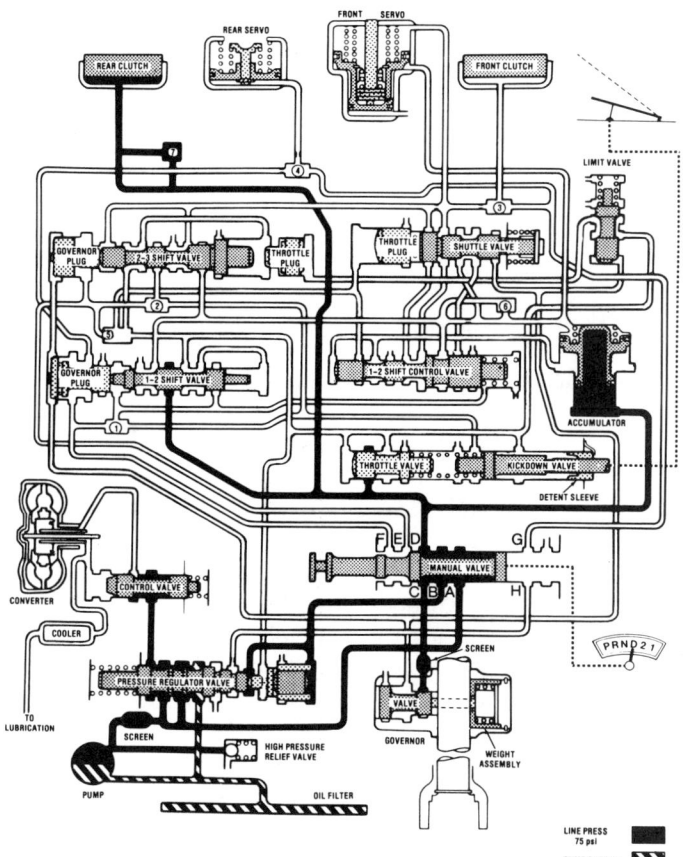

fig. 10-7 A manual valve positioned in the normal, drive range. (Courtesy Chrysler Corp.)

nent necessary to activate the planetary gear train for a low gear ratio; the same port charges the supply circuit to the 1-2 shift valve. Port C provides pressure to the governor which will produce a pressure signal that is responsible for opening both the 1-2 and 2-3 shift valves. The pressure regulator's primary reaction area and its line pressure plug circuits receive fluid pressure from Port B, and Ports G and H remain open to sump. Now, the transmission is set up to automatically upshift from 1-2 and then from 2-3 when the vehicle reaches a given road speed.

shift valve function

Every fully automatic transmission will have one or more shift valves (Fig. 10-8). These balanced spool valves and associated parts are in the hydraulic system for the purpose of making the transmission fully automatic. In other words, the shift valve automatically

168 HYDRAULIC RELAY VALVES

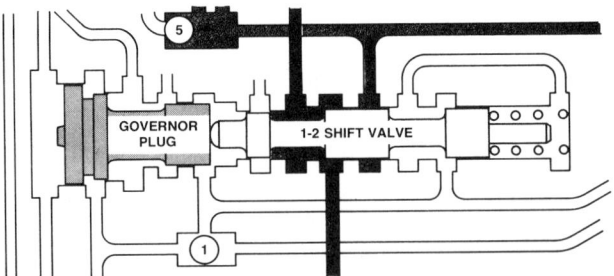

fig. 10-8 A typical shift valve and associated parts. (Courtesy Chrysler Corp.)

controls the upshift and downshift from one gear ratio to another without the driver shifting gears himself.

The shift valves, in order to control the gear ratio changes, just act as on-off hydraulic switches; the number of these shift valves (found in the valve body, hydraulic brain box) depends on the number of forward gear ratios the transmission produces. For example, if the automatic transmission provides the vehicle with two forward speeds, the valve body only contains one shift valve. In this case, the shift valve controls the automatic upshift from low to high and the downshift from high to low. In other words, when this valve is open, control pressure from the manual valve moves through the shift valve to upshift the transmission. But if the valve closes, this position blocks manual valve pressure to the required high gear friction component; consequently, the transmission returns in low ratio.

A three-speed fully automatic transmission has two shift valves (Fig. 10-9). In this situation, the 1-2 shift valve controls the automatic 1-2 upshift and the 2-1 downshift. Whereas, the 2-3 shift valve controls the automatic 2-3 upshift and the 3-2 downshift. And since both of these valves have about the same construction and do operate in much the same manner, this chapter will only cover a 1-2 shift valve and its circuitry.

shift valve train design

A shift valve fits very closely into its bore in the valve body and moves back and forth on a pressurized film of fluid, and the entire shift valve train consists of a calibrated spring, a governor plug, and the shift valve itself (Fig. 10-10). The calibrated spring which bears against one end of the shift valve attempts to keep the valve train in the downshifted (closed) position. Also, located on the opposite end of the shift valve from the spring is a governor plug. This plug has governor pressure acting on its left end; this pressure tries to move the governor plug to the right. And since the governor plug bears against the shift valve, any plug travel will cause the shift valve to move against spring tension.

This governor plug has three lands that have specific functions to perform during the several operating phases of the shift valve train. To make it easy for the reader to locate these lands and see what they do, this text will number them sequentially from left to right. For example, the largest land to the left is number one; and the smallest land to the right is number three.

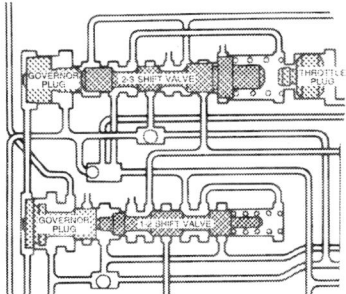

fig. 10-9 The 1-2 and 2-3 shift valves of a three-speed transmission. (Courtesy Chrysler Corp.)

Furthermore, the ports that these lands open and close or from which pressurized fluid flows to these lands will have a letter designation. For instance, beginning at the left side of the plug, the governor-pressure, inlet-port designation is *I*. The *F* port supplies pressure from the manual value that prevents the governor plug from moving in manual low range. Finally, the *J* port is a sump port or is open to the reservoir.

The left end of the large, number-one, governor-plug land is a primary reaction area; this area has a raised button which prevents the governor plug from completely bottoming in its bore. Furthermore, this construction creates a small area, between the bottom of the bore and the governor plug's reaction area, into which governor pressure from Port *I* enters and acts on the primary reaction area. And as previously mentioned, this governor pressure will attempt to move the governor plug and shift valve against spring tension.

The back, inside face of the number-one land is a secondary reaction area or "differential area." If the manual valve is in the manual-low position, fluid pressure from Port *F* acts against this surface. This action pressurizes the surface of the "differential area" and balances off any governor pressure acting on the primary reaction area. As a result, the governor plug and shift valve cannot move against spring tension. Finally, if the 1-2 shift valve train is in the open (upshift) position and the driver positions the manual valve in low, Port *F* pressure, acting on this area, will close the valve train and provide the transmission with a forced (2-1) downshift.

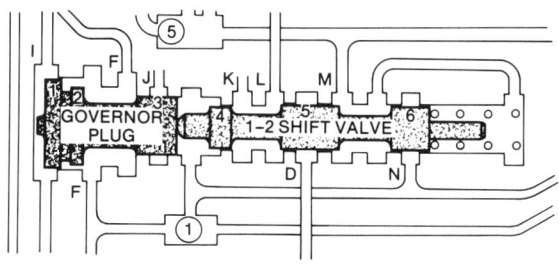

fig. 10-10 A 1-2 shift valve in the closed position. (Courtesy Chrysler Corp.)

In the other forward driving ranges, land number two of the governor plug prevents Port F, manual-valve pressure from passing through the large groove in the governor plug whenever the shift valve train is open. This action temporarily blocks manual valve pressure from the apply circuit of one of the friction components used in manual-low range. Now, if the driver moves the gearshift selector from drive to low, fluid from the lower F port enters the small groove between lands one and two. And since the back face of land one is larger than the face of land two, the pressure acts on the "differential area" which assists the spring in closing the 1–2 shift valve train. As a result, land two now permits manual valve pressure from the lower F port to pass through the large groove; out of the upper F port; and to the apply circuits of the low servo.

Land number three of the governor plug controls the operation of the J sump port. For example, with the manual valve positioned in any other forward driving range but low and with the shift valve train open, Port J is open. This action permits any remaining pressurized fluid in the manual-low apply circuit to bleed off to sump. In other words, the fluid pressure from the manual-low apply circuits vents to the sump via the upper F port; large annular groove; and J port. Finally, if the shift-valve train is in the closed position, land number three completely blocks the J sump port.

The 1–2 shift valve itself has three lands which have the number designations of four, five, and six; and these lands cover and uncover the hydraulic ports required for a 1–2 upshift or a 2–1 downshift. For instance, land four opens the sump port K whenever the 1–2 shift valve is in the (closed) downshift position. The opening of Port K permits the pressurized fluid, used in the second-gear apply circuit, to move back through Port K and vent back to the sump.

Land number five has two distinct functions. First, it controls the fluid flow through Port D which supplies pressure from the manual valve. If the 1–2 shift valve is off, downshift position, this land blocks Port D pressure from reaching the second-gear apply circuits. When the shift valve opens (Fig. 10–11) land five uncovers the D port. This action permits pressurized fluid to pass through the annular groove, between lands four and five, and out the L port to the second-gear apply circuit.

Land five also controls the movement of pressurized fluid through the M port. This land opens the M port whenever the 1–2 shift valve train is off (Fig. 10–10). By opening this port, land five allows throttle pressure to pass through Port M; around the annular groove; through a crossover passage; and to the chamber on the spring end of the 1–2

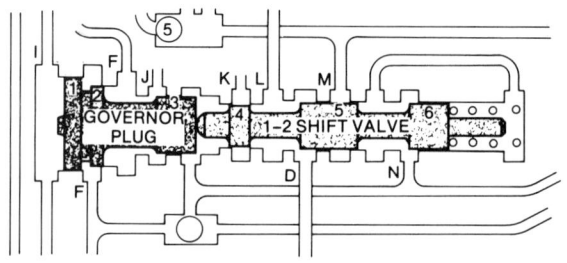

fig. 10–11 A 1–2 shift valve in the open position. (Courtesy Chrysler Corp.)

shift valve. Along with the tension of the spring, this throttle-valve pressure, a pressure signal which is in proportion to engine speed or load, opposes the opening of the 1-2 shift valve train. But as the 1-2 valve opens due to governor pressure on the governor plug (Fig. 10-11) land five blocks off Port "M" which cuts off throttle pressure to the spring end of the shift valve.

Land six also has several functions. For example, it covers and uncovers Port *N*. Port *N*, when opened by land six (Fig. 10-11) acts as a sump port for the trapped throttle pressure behind the shift valve as land five closes the *M* port. In addition, as long as the 1-2 shift valve is open, downshift pressure from the downshift valve can enter through Port *N* and assist the spring in closing the shift valve. This action, of course, would downshift the transmission from 2-1.

Finally, land six also has the force of the spring imposed on its end. The tension (force) of the calibrated spring divided by the area of land six determines how much governor pressure it will take to balance this force and then open the valve which upshifts the transmission. In addition, to limit the travel of the 1-2 shift valve toward the spring, land six has a machined shank on its spring end. This shank prevents the 1-2 shift valve from bottoming in its bore and positions the lands in their proper location whenever the 1-2 shift valve is open.

shift valve operation

When the driver positions the gearshift selector lever into drive range, the manual valve not only directs pressurized fluid to the first-ratio friction components but also to the 1-2 shift valve via the *D* port. Looking at the hydraulic circuit diagram shown in Fig. 10-12, fluid pressure, from the manual valve's *D* port, applies the rear clutch; forces the accumulator valve up in its bore; but deadends at the 1-2 shift valve and throttle valve. In addition, pressurized fluid, from the manual valve's Port *C* flows to the governor valve. Now, the transmission is in first ratio; the vehicle is ready to move; and the circuits which are necessary for the 1-2 automatic upshift have pressurized fluid supplied to them.

As the driver presses on the accelerator and the vehicle begins to move forward, the upshift circuits begin to function. First, throttle pressure, from the throttle valve, enters Port *M*; passes around the annular groove; and flows through the crossover passage to the spring end of the 1-2 shift valve. Now, the 1-2 shift valve has both spring force and throttle pressure acting on its right side holding it over in the left side of its bore.

Of course, the actual amount of throttle pressure will vary with how much the driver depresses the accelerator. For instance, with a light accelerator depression, the throttle pressure will be low. On the other hand, heavy depression of the pedal will bring about high throttle pressure.

As the vehicle's road speed increases over about 5 mph, governor pressure, from the governor valve, flows through Port *I* to the 1-2 shift valve governor plug and attempts to open the valve train. When governor pressure builds up to the point where its force is

172 HYDRAULIC RELAY VALVES

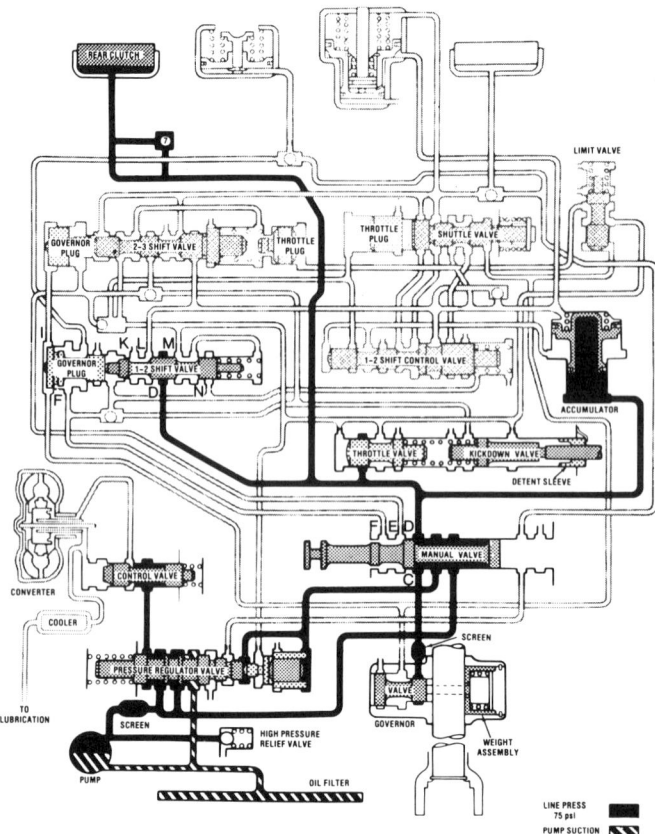

fig. 10-12 A diagram of a drive, first-gear ratio circuit. (Courtesy Chrysler Corp.)

greater than the combined forces of throttle pressure and spring tension, the 1-2 shift valve train will begin to move over to the right (Fig. 10-13). As a result, the valve train is now in the second gear position.

With the valve in this position, land number five of the shift valve closes one port and opens another while land six opens a sump port. Land five closes off the M port; this closure stops throttle pressure from acting on the spring end of the shift valve. The trapped throttle pressure now returns to sump through the N port which land six opened. With the stoppage of throttle pressure to the spring end of the valve, the 1-2 shift valve "snaps" full open rapidly rather than slowly moving into the full open position.

Also as the valve snaps open, the number five land opens the L port. This action permits D fluid to pass through the annular groove, between lands four and five; out of the L port; and to the friction component required for second-ratio operation. This fluid pressure then applies the friction component which upshifts the transmission.

As the vehicle slows to a stop, the 1-2 shift valve train moves back to the first gear position. The 1-2 shift valve moves back in its bore due to a reduction in governor pressure on the governor plug and the force of the calibrated spring acting on the right

SHIFT VALVE OPERATION 173

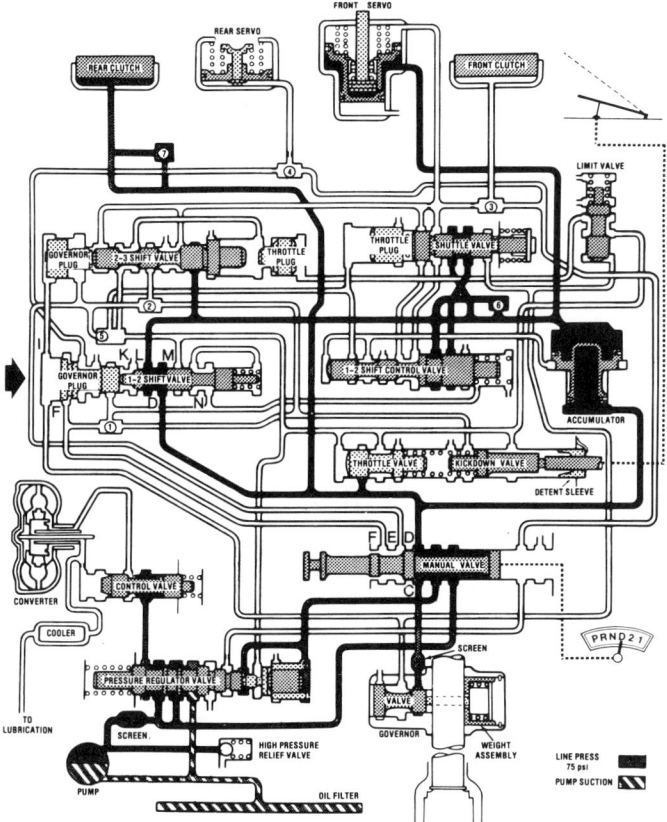

fig. 10-13 A diagram of a drive, second-gear ratio circuit. (Courtesy Chrysler Corp.)

end of the valve train. Now, with the valve train back in the first-gear position, the 1-2 shift hydraulic circuits will cycle back to those shown in Fig. 10-12.

The number five land blocks off fluid pressure to the *L* port, and the number-four land opens the *K* sump port. This action permits the fluid pressure, utilized to apply the band in second gear, to bleed off to sump. As the pressure bleeds off, the band releases; and the transmission downshifts to low gear. The transmission now is ready to start the vehicle off in low ratio.

As previously mentioned, the driver can also force the 1-2 shift valve back by moving the selector lever to the manual low position (Fig. 10-14). This action causes the manual valve to open a port which directs pressure to the 1-2 shift valve lower *F* port. This control pressure, acting on the differential area of the governor plug, offsets the effect of moderate governor pressure on the primary reaction area. Now, the 1-2 shift valve spring pushes the valves back to the closed position. Lastly, since most all of the shift valves open and close in much the same manner, this text will not cover the operation of a 2-3 type shift valve.

174 HYDRAULIC RELAY VALVES

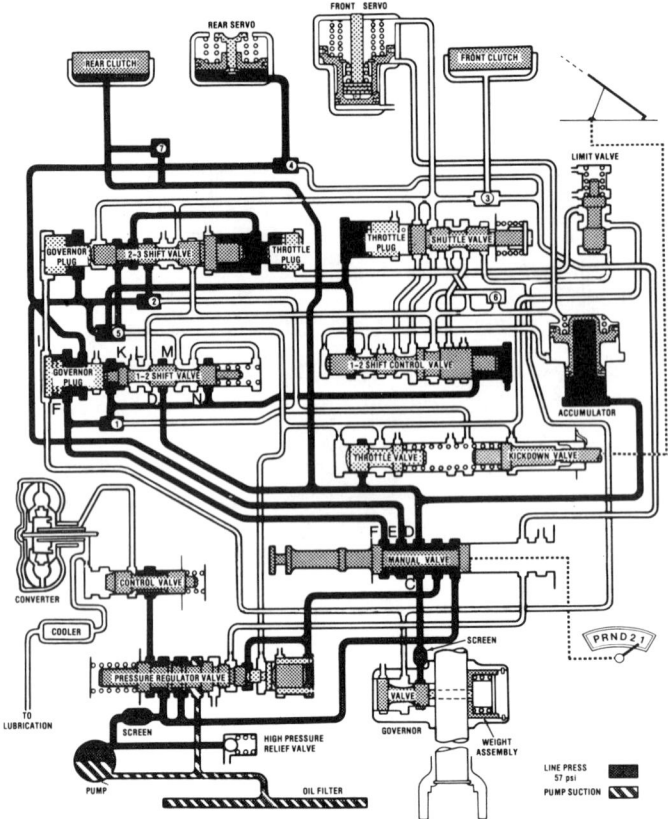

fig. 10–14 A diagram of a manual, low-gear ratio circuit. (Courtesy Chrysler Corp.)

other flow control valves—ball check valve

Most automatic transmissions also have several types of flow-control valves which do not operate by mechanical linkage or by the balanced-valve principle; manufacturers refer to these devices as the check valve and the orifice. The check valve controls fluid flow so that it moves in one direction only, and it plays an important role in directing the various flow patterns used during the different operating phases of the transmission.

The ball check valve, shown in Fig. 10–15, is a good example of this type of device. This valve consists of a steel ball which operates in a bore or cavity. Depending on what the check valve must do in the hydraulic system, the bore will have one or more seats located at the port openings.

If the ball check valve has only one seat, it is a one-way check valve (Fig. 10–15). In this case, the seat is at Port *A* where the fluid will enter; outlet Port *B* has no valve seat. In addition, a valve stop, located between the two ports, prevents the check ball from reaching outlet Port *B*.

OTHER FLOW CONTROL VALVES–BALL CHECK VALVE 175

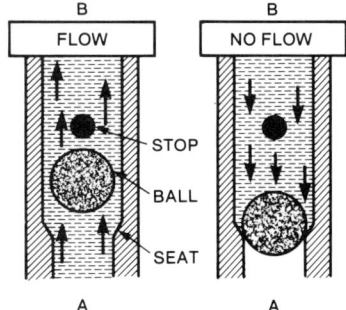

fig. 10–15 A typical one-way, ball-type check valve.

With this arrangement, fluid can move from Port A through Port B but not in the other direction. When fluid enters Port A, it pushes the ball off its seat and against the stop. The fluid then passes around the ball and out of Port B. If fluid attempts to flow in the other direction, from Port B through Port A, no flow occurs because the pressurized fluid forces the ball against the seat.

The two-way check valve, on the other hand, has two seats. This valve design controls pressure sources from two different directions, and pressure from either source can seat or unseat the ball. In other words, the valve will have two pressure inlet ports and one outlet port, but the fluid can only move from one of these inlet ports to the outlet port at any given time.

Fig. 10–16 shows a unit of this design which incorporates a steel ball operating between three ports. Ports A and B are the two pressure inlet sources, and each of these port openings has a seat. Port C is the outlet port and has no seat.

During the operation of this valve, higher pressure entering one inlet source seats the ball and blocks lower pressure from entering and discharging from the outlet Port C. For instance, if pressurized fluid enters Port A, it pushes the ball valve against the seat of

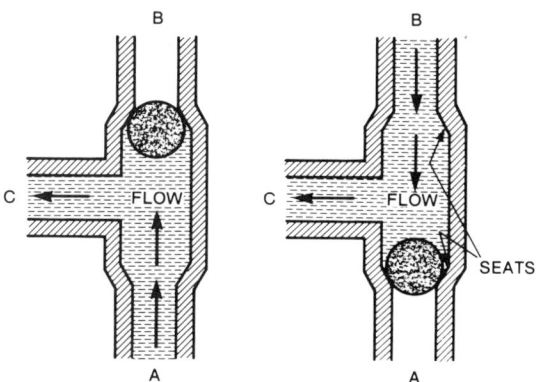

fig. 10–16 A typical two-way, ball-type check valve.

176 HYDRAULIC RELAY VALVES

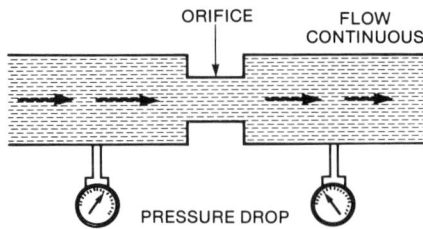

fig. 10-17 Constant flow across an orifice causes a pressure drop.

port B. This action seals off the entrance of any lower pressure from Port B, and only allows the fluid from Port A to pass out of Port C.

But, on the other hand, if fluid under a higher system pressure passes through Port B, it will seat the ball blocking Port A. This action then permits the fluid to flow from Port B to and out of Port C.

orifice

Another simple way of regulating fluid flow and pressure in a hydraulic circuit is the use of an orifice. An orifice is simply a calibrated restriction placed in a hydraulic circuit; this restriction controls fluid flow and pressure build-up. Fig. 10-17 shows an orifice placed in a hydraulic circuit. To also show the effect of the orifice on this hydraulic circuit, the circuit has two hydraulic gauges installed, one on each side of the restriction.

As fluid flows in this circuit, the orifice slows down the flow of fluid by delaying pressure build-up in the circuit downstream from the restriction. This pressure drop occurs because as the fluid attempts to move through the orifice, not all of the flow can move through the restriction at one time. Consequently, pressure builds up in the circuit in front of the orifice.

This difference in pressure between the circuits on both sides of the orifice remains as long as fluid continues to flow through the restriction. But when flow stops through the orifice, pressure equalizes on both of its sides (Fig. 10-18). This situation occurs whenever the hydraulic pressure on the downstream side of the orifice has fully activated the hydraulic unit located there.

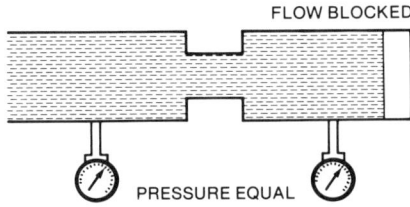

fig. 10-18 When flow stops, the pressure equalizes on both sides of the orifice.

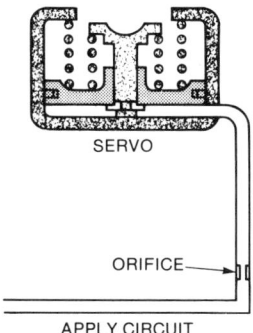

fig. 10-19 An orifice installed in a servo, apply circuit.

Fig. 10-19 shows an example of an orifice installed in a servo apply circuit; this orifice slows down the operation of the servo which cushions the application of the band. By slowing down the fluid flow rate to the servo piston, the orifice permits a back pressure to build up which slows servo piston action. In other words, the orifice causes a cushioning effect of the band application so that the driver does not experience a harsh gear change. But once the servo piston stops moving, full pressure exists on both sides of the orifice that locks the band securely around the drum. Finally, manufacturers also use the orifice to obtain the desired timing between two changing gear ratios. The action of the orifice prevents a lock-up between the ratios or an uncontrolled engine flare-up.

accumulator function and design

The accumulator, like the orifice, is not a valve; but they do both serve a function in the hydraulic system which is quite similar. In other words, neither of these devices actually opens or closes a hydraulic circuit. Instead, the orifice and the accumulator, when in operation, function to cushion the application of a clutch or band. The orifice does this by restricting flow; whereas the accumulator cushions application by absorbing clutch or band apply pressure.

The accumulator assembly consists of a bore, a piston and a return spring. The transmission manufacturer may cast or machine this bore into a detachable housing, the transmission case, or the valve body. In all cases, the bore serves as the guide for the movable piston.

The piston may be a solid plug type, single-diameter piston; a spool type, single-diameter; or a spool type, multiple-diameter. Fig. 10-20, for example, shows a two-diameter piston which operates within a stepped bore in the transmission case. The piston moves in this bore due to the action of hydraulic pressure acting on one or more of its reaction areas or diameters.

The accumulator also has a calibrated return spring. This spring's tension along with whichever reaction area hydraulic pressure acts on are the factors which determine

178 HYDRAULIC RELAY VALVES

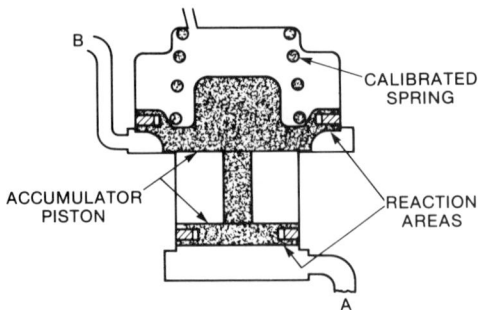

fig. 10–20 The design of a two-diameter, accumulator valve.

how much apply pressure the accumulator will absorb. For instance, if apply pressure acts on the lower, small reaction area, more pressure will be absorbed in order to move the piston against spring tension than if it acted on the larger, upper reaction area.

accumulator operation

For the sake of simplicity in understanding accumulator operation, this text will arbitrarily tie in lower, Port A into a clutch apply circuit and upper, Port B into a servo apply circuit. When the manual valve or a shift valve directs control pressure to the clutch, pressure also flows to Port A. From Port A, control pressure acts against the small diameter end of the piston and pushes it into its bore against spring tension (Fig. 10–21). As this spring compresses with piston movement, pressure will be building up in the clutch assembly. But full application of the clutch by normal pressure cannot take place until the accumulator piston fully seats against the bottom of its bore. In other words, the accumulator temporarily absorbs a portion of the apply pressure sent to the clutch; this absorption of pressure delays and cushions the full application of the clutch until the accumulator piston bottoms.

About the same thing occurs when a band applies if the servo has an accumulator in its apply circuit. Referring back to Fig. 10–21, when pressurized fluid moves in the

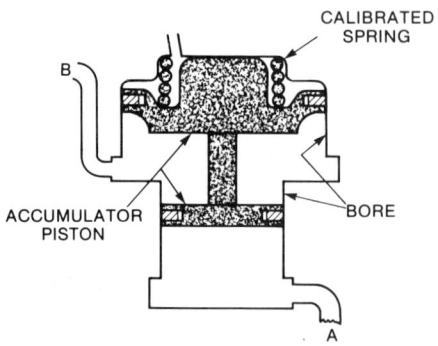

fig. 10–21 Accumulator valve operation.

circuit to activate the servo, it also enters Port *B* of the accumulator. Now the pressure acts on the large diameter of the accumulator piston.

The accumulator piston begins to move within its bore, compressing its spring, as pressure builds up in the servo apply circuit. But full application or band loading will not occur until the accumulator piston bottoms in its bore which normalizes servo apply pressure. Note also that in comparison to the amount the pressure absorbed by the accumulator during clutch application, the absorption is less during band application.

This difference in the amount of pressure absorption is due to the difference in the two piston diameters. In other words, when Port *A* supplies pressure to the smaller diameter land, the piston absorbs a greater pressure to move it against spring tension, whereas the larger diameter land absorbs a lesser amount.

summary

1. Relay valves are devices which direct flow and pressure along a given path or circuit.
2. The manual valve is one type of mechanically operated relay valve.
3. The manual valve connects to the gearshift selector lever through some form of linkage.
4. The manual valve is a spool type with several annular grooves and lands that control port openings.
5. As the manual valve moves, its lands open and close various ports.
6. Every fully automatic transmission will have one or more shift valves.
7. A shift valve automatically controls the upshift and downshift from one gear ratio to another.
8. The number of shift valves, incorporated into the hydraulic system, depends on the number of forward gear ratios the transmission produces.
9. A shift valve fits very closely into its bore in the valve body and moves back and forth on a pressurized film of fluid.
10. A shift valve is a balanced type, and the entire shift-valve train consists of a governor plug, calibrated spring, and the shift valve itself.
11. The calibrated, shift valve spring attempts to keep the shift valve closed.
12. The governor plug has governor pressure acting on it which tries to move the governor plug and shift valve open.
13. The governor plug has a primary and a differential area.
14. The shift valve has lands which cover and uncover the hydraulic ports required for an automatic upshift and downshift.
15. When a shift valve closes, hydraulic pressure is cut off from the upshift, apply circuits.

180 HYDRAULIC RELAY VALVES

16. As the shift valve opens, the shift-valve lands permit fluid flow to the upshift circuits.
17. Governor pressure is a hydraulic signal which is in proportion to vehicle road speed, and this pressure is responsible for opening the shift-valve train.
18. Throttle pressure is a hydraulic signal which is in proportion to engine speed or load, and it is responsible for delaying the upshifts or matching the upshift point to engine load.
19. Most automatic transmissions have several types of flow-control valves which do not operate by mechanical linkage or by the balanced-valve principle.
20. The check valve controls fluid flow so that it moves in one direction only.
21. The ball check valve may have one or more seats and operates in a bore or cavity.
22. The one-way check valve has only one seat.
23. The two-way check valve has two seats.
24. An orifice is a calibrated restriction placed in a hydraulic circuit.
25. An orifice reduces fluid flow in a circuit and creates a back pressure.
26. The accumulator cushions the application of a band or clutch.
27. The accumulator absorbs clutch or servo apply pressure.
28. The accumulator assembly consists of a bore, piston, and a return spring.

check-up questions

The questions listed below will assist you in determining how well you remember the material contained in this chapter. Read each question carefully before choosing the answer to each item. If you cannot answer a question, review the material in the section of the chapter that covers the question.

1. An on-off valve type which directs flow along a given path is the _____.
   a. orifice
   b. accumulator
   c. relay
   d. both a and c
2. The valve the driver activates to set up the operating conditions within the transmission is the _____.
   a. manual valve
   b. accumulator
   c. one-way valve
   d. 1–2 shift valve

3. The portion of a spool valve that opens and closes the port openings is the _____.
   a. grooves
   b. lands
   c. shank
   d. reaction area
4. The valve that is responsible for automatically upshifting the transmission is the _____.
   a. manual valve
   b. orifice
   c. detect valve
   d. shift valve
5. A three-speed fully automatic transmission will have _____.
   a. three shift valves
   b. two shift valves
   c. one shift valve
   d. one shift and one manual valve
6. The component of the shift valve train, mentioned in this chapter, which moves the shift valve against spring tension is the _____.
   a. governor plug
   b. throttle plug
   c. shift valve
   d. calibrated spring
7. The device that produces a pressure signal in proportion to vehicle road speed is the _____.
   a. throttle valve
   b. accumulator valve
   c. shift valve
   d. governor valve
8. An unshift occurs when a shift valve _____.
   a. opens
   b. closes
9. A pressure signal that is in proportion to engine speed or load is _____ pressure.
   a. line
   b. throttle

c. downshift
d. governor
10. The device that controls fluid flow in one direction only is the _____ valve.
   a. manual
   b. check
   c. throttle
   d. governor
11. The device that controls pressure sources from two different directions is the _____ valve.
   a. two-way check
   b. one-way check
   c. orifice
   d. manual
12. A calibrated restriction placed in a hydraulic circuit is called a _____.
   a. valve
   b. ball-check
   c. orifice
   d. obstruction
13. The device which absorbs apply pressure to cushion a band or clutch application is a(n) _____.
   a. orifice
   b. servo
   c. modulator
   d. accumulator

For the answers to these check-up questions, turn to the Appendix located at the back of the text.

11

hydraulic signal devices

As mentioned in the last chapter, fully automatic transmissions require hydraulic-signal devices. These devices are responsible for varying the upshift and downshift sequences of the transmission to meet different conditions. In other words, these signal valves provide the vehicle with shift patterns which efficiently reflect the speed of the vehicle, the load on the engine, or the will of the driver. The valves, found in the hydraulic system, which act as signal units are the governor, throttle, and kickdown valves.

governor function

The *governor* is a balanced valve that senses vehicle speed from the transmission's output shaft (Fig. 11–1). The valve, in turn, sends a hydraulic-speed signal which is in proportion to vehicle speed to the shift valve(s). This signal acts on the shift valve train to open it when the vehicle reaches a predetermined road speed.

    In other words, the governor-valve signal changes as vehicle speed increases. When the vehicle is stationary or below about 10 mph, the governor pressure is zero or very low (Fig. 11–2). From about 10 mph on, the pressure signal increases in intensity until it reaches its maximum amount at high-vehicle speeds.

184 HYDRAULIC SIGNAL DEVICES

fig. 11-1 A single-stage governor assembly mounted on the output shaft.

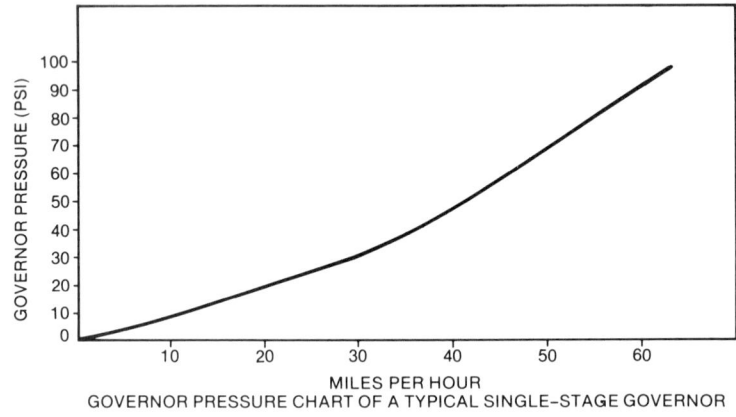

GOVERNOR PRESSURE CHART OF A TYPICAL SINGLE-STAGE GOVERNOR

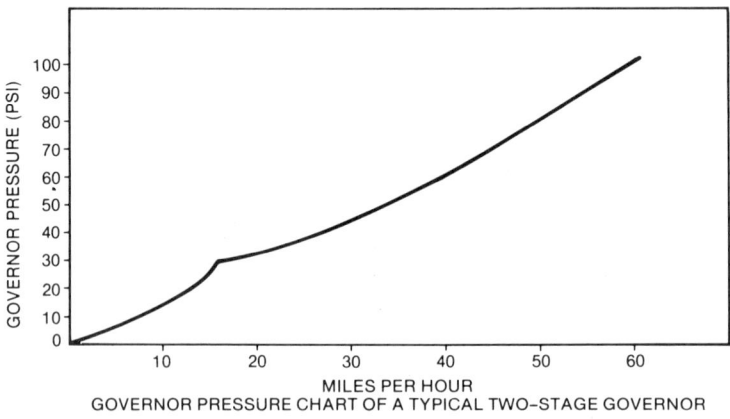

GOVERNOR PRESSURE CHART OF A TYPICAL TWO-STAGE GOVERNOR

fig. 11-2 A typical governor pressure chart for a single and two-stage governor.

SINGLE-STAGE GOVERNOR DESIGN

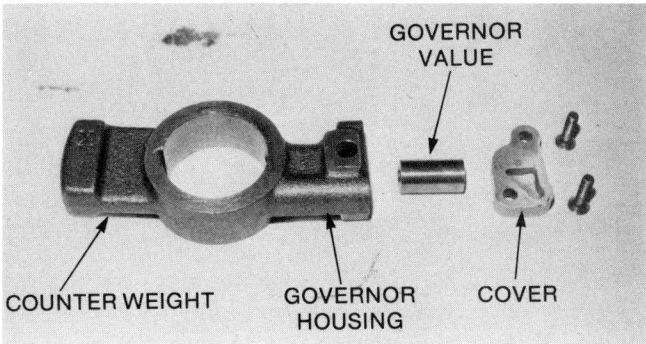

fig. 11-3 The components of a single-stage governor assembly.

The actual amount of governor-pressure signal increase, per mph of vehicle speed, depends on the type of governor used. For instance, a single-stage governor (Fig. 11-2) sends out a pressure signal that steadily increases with each mph of vehicle speed. The two-stage governor, in contrast, produces a pressure signal which rapidly increases at low-vehicle speeds and then slowly continues to increase with vehicle speed until it reaches its maximum intensity.

single-stage governor design

Fig. 11-3 shows a single-stage governor utilized in a two-speed transmission; this unit consists of a housing and governor valve. The governor housing or body attaches to and rotates with the transmission's output shaft. Inside one of the extended sections is a bore for the governor valve. In addition, this bore has two ports machined into it—the inlet and the exhaust. Lastly, the other, extended section forms a counterweight required to balance the rotating-governor body.

The governor valves operates, within the bore of the governor body, by the balanced valve principle (Fig. 11-4). The two forces, attempting to balance each other, are control pressure and centrifugal force. Control pressure attempts to force the valve

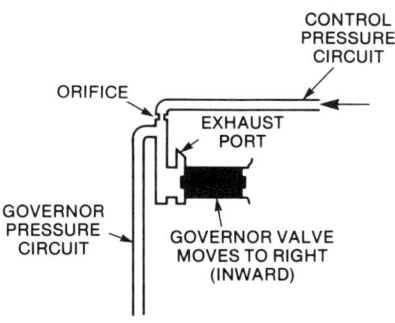

fig. 11-4 Single-stage governor operation with the vehicle stationary.

186 HYDRAULIC SIGNAL DEVICES

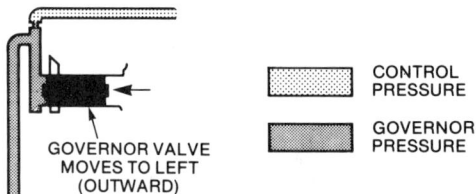

fig. 11-5 Single-stage governor operation with the vehicle moving.

inward in its bore, while centrifugal force, which varies with the rotation of the output shaft tries to move the valve outward in its bore against the force of control pressure. Finally, as these forces move the valve back and forth, the valve opens and closes the exhaust port.

single-stage governor operation

When the vehicle is stationary, with the engine running and the transmission in a forward driving range, the governor valve assumes the position shown in Fig. 11-4. Control pressure, via an orifice, enters the governor body and tries to move the valve inward against centrifugal force. But since the output shaft is stationary, no centrifugal force acts on the valve. Consequently, control pressure forces the valve inward.

This valve movement opens the exhaust port wide open. Now, control pressure bleeds off back to the orifice. As a result, the governor valve produces a zero-pressure signal.

As the vehicle begins to move and pick up speed, the governor valve starts to move outward due to centrifugal force acting on the valve (Fig. 11-5). The centrifugal force attempts to balance the valve against the force of control pressure. Now, as the valve moves, it starts to close off the exhaust port.

With an exhaust port partially restricted, the governor circuit begins to pressurize. The pressure increase is steady as long as the vehicle accelerates. When the governor pressure reaches a given amount, it will open the low-high shift valve to upshift the transmission. But the governor's signal will reach its maximum intensity as centrifugal force moves the governor valve past and seals off the exhaust port. At this point, the vehicle is moving at a high rate of speed; centrifugal force balances control pressure; and the governor valve provides a pressure signal which has the same intensity as control pressure.

two-stage governor design

Fig. 11-6 shows a two-stage governor of a three-speed automatic transmission. This unit consists of a housing, weight assembly, and governor valve. This type of governor housing also attaches to and rotates with the output shaft. In addition, the housing has

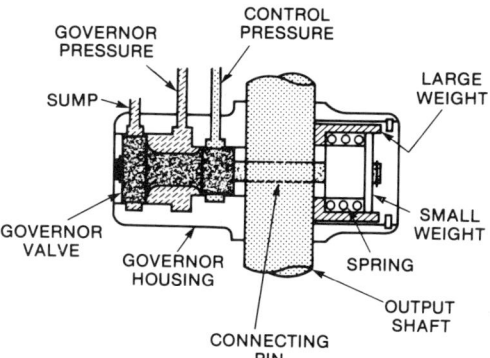

fig. 11-6 The design of a typical two-stage governor assembly.

two bores of different diameters. The large bore forms a guide for the weight assembly, and the governor valve operates in the small bore. Finally, machined into the small bore are three ports: control pressure, governor pressure, and sump.

The weight assembly (Fig. 11-6) consists of a large weight, small weight, and spring. The two weights, acting as a unit, produce adequate governor pressure at low vehicle speeds to produce the 1-2 upshift. In other words, the two weights working together are responsible for the initial rapid rise in governor pressure as the vehicle accelerates from a stationary position; the resulting pressure signal is high enough to open the 1-2 shift valve.

The small weight operates inside a bore in the large weight. At a vehicle speed of about 20 mph, the large weight cannot move any further in its bore, and the small weight takes over the task of increasing governor pressure. Finally, a pin connects the small weight directly to the governor valve so that when centrifugal force acts on the weight assembly, the governor valve will move in its bore.

The location of the governor spring is between the bottom of the small weight and a spring seat machined into the base of the bore in the large weight. The spring's tension will assist centrifugal force in balancing the governor valve against the force of governor pressure. In other words, when governor pressure causes the governor valve to move to the left, the spring compresses; and the small piston moves inward its bore in the large weight. Now, as centrifugal force acts on the small weight, the tension of the spring will assist this force in moving the small weight outward in its bore.

The governor valve, (Fig. 11-6) is a balanced valve with two lands of different diameters and one annular groove. The large land controls the opening and closing of the sump port. Furthermore, the inside face of this large land forms the reaction area upon which governor pressure acts during valve operation.

The small land controls the passage of fluid from the control pressure port to the annular groove. For example, during one phase of governor valve operation, the land position is such that the annular groove connects together the control- and governor-pressure ports. During another phase, the small land blocks the control pressure port; and the groove connects the governor pressure and sump ports together.

two-stage governor operation

Diagram A of Fig. 11-7 shows the position of a two-stage governor valve and weight assembly when the transmission is in a forward driving range, but the vehicle is stationary. The small land blocks the entrance of control pressure to the annular groove. The large land, at this time, opens the sump port that allows any governor pressure remaining in the governor circuits to bleed off to sump via the annular groove.

As the output shaft begins to rotate and the vehicle starts to move forward, the governor weight assembly will start to move outward due to centrifugal force acting on the weights. As the weight assembly moves outward, it pulls the governor valve with it until the small, governor-valve land uncovers the control-pressure port (Diagram B, Fig. 11-7). As the small land uncovers the control-pressure port, it begins to pressurize the governor-pressure port via the annular groove. As a result, governor pressure begins to rapidly increase.

At about 15 to 20 mph, the large governor weight approaches the end of its travel in the governor housing, and the governor valve begins its balancing cycle. The increasing governor pressure begins to act on the reaction area of the large valve land. The force of governor pressure on this land causes the governor valve to momentarily stabilize its movement. This action causes the small weight to move inward, compressing the spring, as the large weight comes to the end of its travel.

As the vehicle continues to increase in road speed, the governor valve moves more inward. The increased output shaft speed causes the small, inner weight, assisted by the spring, to move more outward in its bore within the large weight bringing the governor valve with it. This valve movement causes the small land to open up the control-pressure port even more, which increases governor pressure.

At a very high vehicle speed, the small weight pulls the governor valve to a position that opens the control-pressure port wide open. Now, at this point, control and governor pressure are equal in intensity because control pressure has unrestricted flow to the governor port via the annular groove. Finally, the governor valve will remain in this position as long as the small weight has sufficient centrifugal force acting on it.

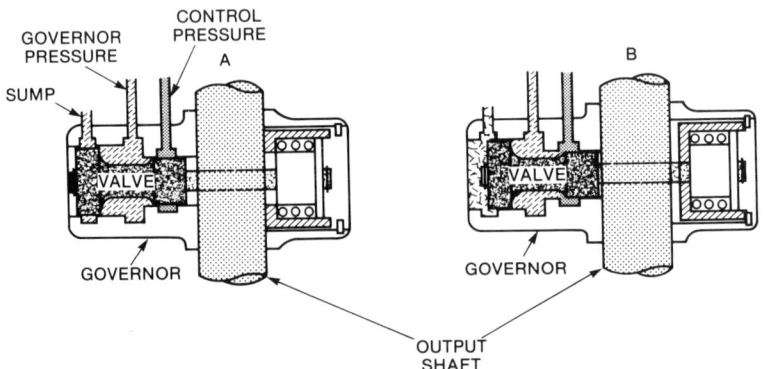

fig. 11-7 The operation of a two-stage governor assembly.

At any point where the vehicle stops accelerating or reaches cruising speed, governor pressure stops increasing. This situation occurs because the governor valve becomes balanced between centrifugal and spring force on one side and governor pressure on the other. In other words, governor pressure, acting on the valve's reaction area, balances the effects of spring tension and centrifugal force on the small weight. As a result, the valve stops any further inward movement which maintains the control-pressure port in a partially restricted condition. Consequently, governor pressure stabilizes to a fixed amount which will be less than that of control pressure.

When the vehicle slows down, governor pressure decreases due to a reduction in centrifugal force. With a reduction in the action of centrifugal force on the weight assembly, governor pressure, acting on the governor-valve's reaction area, immediately pushes the valve outward. This movement permits the large land to open the exhaust port. Of course, the amount of exhaust port opening, along with a resulting reduction in governor pressure, depends on how much centrifugal force, along with spring tension, remains to balance governor pressure on the valve.

In summation, with a double-weight arrangement, the governor provides a rapid rise in governor pressure at low vehicle speeds. This rapid rise in pressure can open the 1–2 shift valve for a rather quick 1–2 upshift. The smaller weight then takes over to gradually increase governor pressure which will be necessary for the 2–3 upshift at moderate to high speeds.

throttle valve function

If governor pressure were the only signal sent to the shift valve(s), it would open the shift valve(s) at the same vehicle road speed each time. The upshifting of the transmission at the same vehicle speed would not be a problem as long as the engine speed and load are always the same at this road speed, but they are not. For example, if the engine is pulling the vehicle up a grade, it has a greater load on it than it would on a level road. Consequently, the engine must operate at a faster rpm in order to carry the additional load. Now, if the transmission upshifts too soon, the engine will not have the lower gear ratios to multiply its torque or be able to operate at the increased rpm necessary to produce high torque output. As a result, the engine will not be able to successfully carry the increased load.

To overcome this problem, the transmission must have some means to sense engine load. To perform this function, the transmission has a throttle valve circuit incorporated into its hydraulic system. This throttle valve produces a pressure signal that is proportional to engine load, and this signal, called throttle valve (TV) pressure, acts on the spring side of the shift valve(s) to assist the spring in opposing governor pressure. Finally, the throttle valve is a balanced valve that has throttle pressure opposing mechanically altered or vacuum-altered spring tension.

throttle valve design—mechanically activated

Fig. 11-8 shows a typical mechanically operated throttle valve train. This train consists of a kickdown valve, spring, and throttle valve which all operate in the same housing bore. The kickdown valve moves in the bore by a mechanical force provided by the driver via the accelerator pedal. In other words, the kickdown valve, by means of external linkage attached to the carburetor, moves in its bore as the driver depresses the accelerator pedal.

The kickdown valve itself performs two functions as it moves within its bore. First, as the driver depresses the accelerator pedal, the valve moves toward the left. This valve motion increases the tension on the spring which fits between the kickdown and throttle valve. This increased spring tension causes the throttle valve to move against throttle pressure. Second, the kickdown valve has a hydraulic function which is to provide the hydraulic system with a downshift pressure signal. The signal, in turn, can downshift the transmission if the vehicle is moving at a reasonable rate of speed.

The spring, in this installation, also serves two purposes. First, in the closed accelerator-pedal position, the initial tension of the spring will maintain the kickdown valve at the end of its bore. Second, since the throttle valve is a balanced unit, the varying spring tension will oppose throttle pressure to determine valve position.

The throttle valve itself has two lands of different length, but they both have the same diameter. The back face of Land *A* forms the reaction area upon which throttle pressure acts to balance the valve against spring force. Furthermore, Land *A* controls the activity of Port *F*. For instance, when the throttle valve cycles to the position where the unit produces no throttle pressure, Land *A* blocks Port *F* which is the control-pressure inlet port.

Land *B* also performs several functions. First of all, spring tension bears against the right-hand face of this land. And second, Land *B* controls the activity of Port *E,* a sump port. For example, as the driver releases foot pressure on the accelerator pedal, Land *B* partially or fully opens the sump port to bleed off pressure in the throttle-valve circuit.

throttle valve operation

If the vehicle is stationary with its engine running at idle rpm, the throttle valve assumes the position as shown in Fig. 11-8. Land *A* blocks control pressure into the valve at Port *F*. Land *B* blocks the sump port *E* and only a slight balancing pressure exists in the throttle valve circuits.

As the driver depresses the accelerator pedal, the linkage moves the kickdown valve to the left. Because the kickdown valve moves inward, the spring, located between the two valves, compresses somewhat and forces the throttle valve to the left. This valve movement permits Land *A* to crack open the control pressure Port *F*.

Control pressure from Port *F* passes around the annular groove and out of Port *D* to become throttle pressure. Now, some of the throttle pressure passes through the

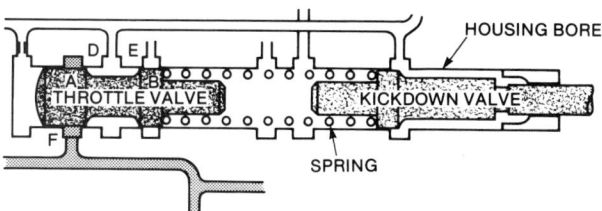

fig. 11–8 The design of a mechanically-operated throttle valve assembly.

orifice and acts on the reaction area of the throttle valve. The pressure, acting on this area, attempts to stabilize valve movement caused by the spring's tension. In other words, the amount of throttle pressure in the circuits and on the reaction area will be whatever it takes to balance the valve against spring tension. Of course, as the operator continues to depress the accelerator pedal, throttle pressure will increase even more in order to balance the valve against the increased spring force.

If at any time the driver depresses the accelerator pedal to the wide-open position, the throttle valve moves as far over to the left as it can (Fig. 11–9). This action permits Land A of the throttle valve to fully open Port F. Now, as much control pressure as possible enters the throttle pressure circuit. In this situation throttle pressure will reach the same intensity as control pressure.

As the driver releases the accelerator pedal so that the engine returns to idle rpm, the throttle valve cycles back to the position as shown in Fig. 11–8. With no outside force on the kickdown valve, the spring pushes it back to the left which also reduces spring force on the throttle valve. Because of this reduced spring force, throttle pressure, acting on the valve's reaction area, immediately pushes the valve to the right. This action causes Land A to block the entrance of control pressure through Port F.

In addition, Land B opens the sump port; and TV pressure begins to bleed off to sump. Pressure rapidly decreases in all the throttle valve circuits until it balances the movement of the valve against the remaining spring force. At this point, the throttle valve will move slightly to the left and close the sump Port E, and the throttle valve train has finished its return cycle to the closed (idle) position. Remember that the amount of throttle pressure from this valve train will always be in proportion to the tension of the spring. If spring tension is weak, TV pressure is low. As spring force increases, TV pressure increases until it reaches the same intensity as control pressure; but it can go no higher.

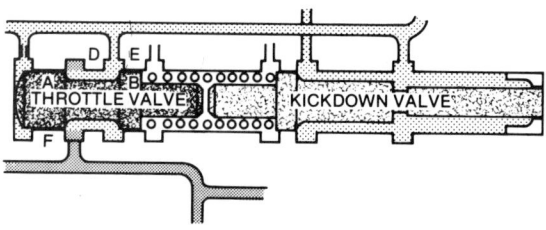

fig. 11–9 The mechanically operated throttle valve in the full-open position.

192 HYDRAULIC SIGNAL DEVICES

design of vacuum-controlled throttle valve trains

Fig. 11-10 shows a typical vacuum-operated throttle-valve train; this valve train consists of a throttle valve, spring, and vacuum-diaphragm assembly. The throttle valve is again a balanced type of spool valve which operates in a special bore located in the transmission case or valve body. Also, inserted into a recess, machined into the right-hand end of the valve, is a push rod that connects the throttle valve to the vacuum diaphragm assembly.

This throttle valve has two lands and one annular groove. Valve Land *A* has two functions. First, it controls the opening and closing of Port *C* which is the control pressure inlet port. Second, the left end of Land *A* forms the reaction area of this throttle valve. In other words, TV pressure, acting on this area, moves the valve against the force of the spring.

Also, note the raised button on the end of Land *A*. This button prevents the valve from completely bottoming in its bore. As a result, when the valve moves to the far left position, a small area remains into which throttle pressure can enter.

On the other hand, Land *B* controls fluid movement through Port *D*, a sump port. For instance, if Land *B* opens Port *D*, throttle pressure bleeds off to the sump. If Land *B* blocks this sump port, throttle pressure can increase in the circuits.

The groove, between Lands *A* and *B*, channels the pressurized fluid from one port to another. For example, when the spring tension forces the throttle valve to the left, fluid passes from Port *C* to Port *E* via the annular groove. But as the valve moves to the right, Land *B* opens the sump port, and Land *A* closes the control pressure port. Throttle pressure now moves from Port *E*, through the annular groove, and out the sump Port *D*.

The vacuum diaphragm assembly consists of a housing, diaphragm, and spring. The manufacturer forms this housing design into two sections using stamped sheet metal. Then after inserting the spring and diaphragm between the two halves, the manufacturer crimps the two halves together.

Each section of this housing also has a port designed into it. The left section has an atmospheric-pressure port which just vents this section to the atmosphere. The other section has a vacuum port which a line connects to the engine's intake manifold.

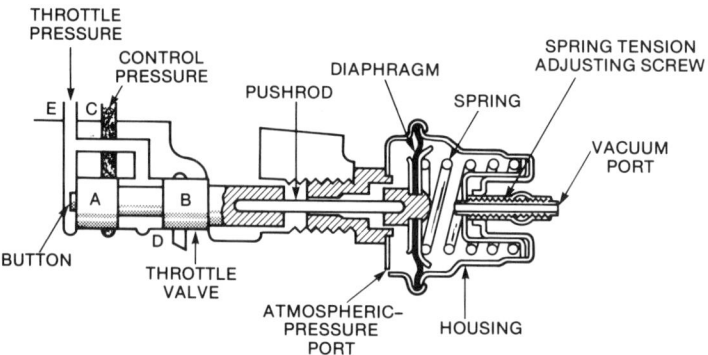

fig. 11-10 A typical vacuum-controlled, throttle-valve train.

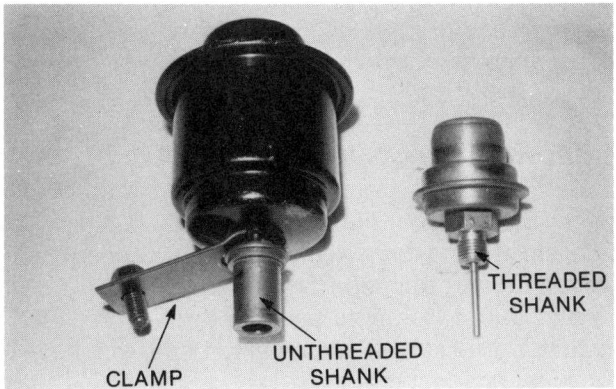

fig. 11-11 The threaded and clamp-on designs of vacuum-diaphragm assemblies.

In addition, designed into the housing is a means of securing the diaphragm assembly to the transmission case. One method, commonly used by manufacturers, is to secure a threaded, machined shank to one end of the sheet metal housing (Fig. 11-11). The threads on this shank mate with threads machined into the transmission case. The other method incorporates the use of an unthreaded shank which has slots machined into it. A U-shaped clamp fits into these slots, and a bolt secures the clamp, shank, and housing on to the transmission case.

The diaphragm is a sealed, flexible piece of material made from chemically treated fabric, rubber, or neoprene (Fig. 11-10). The manufacturer installs and secures the diaphragm inside the housing so that it seals one side of the housing from the other, but it has sufficient flexibility to move back and forth somewhat. Also, fastened to both sides of the diaphragm at its center is a metal piece which is flat on one side but has an extended shank on the other.

The metal piece reinforces the center of the diaphragm so that this section can withstand the two forces applied to it. The two forces, in this case, will be spring tension and throttle pressure. The spring exerts its force on the right side of the diaphragm. To do this, the spring fits between the center of the diaphragm and one end of the housing, and it exerts its force against both these areas.

The second force, applied to the left side of the diaphragm is that of throttle pressure. Throttle pressure, in this situation, first acts on the throttle valve itself which, in turn, applies a force to the push rod. And since the push rod also bears against the center section of the diaphragm, it receives the force of throttle pressure.

As previously mentioned, the diaphragm assembly has a spring installed between the diaphragm and housing. The spring's force works against throttle pressure to balance the throttle valve. In addition, in so much as the spring functions on the vacuum side of the diaphragm, intake-manifold vacuum, acting on the diaphragm, will reduce the spring's tension on the throttle valve. And finally, in some installations, the manufacturer installs an adjustment screw in the housing which can increase or decrease initial spring tension on the diaphragm and the throttle valve. Therefore, by moving this adjustment screw, a mechanic can increase or decrease throttle pressure.

operation of vacuum-controlled throttle valves

Without the diaphragm in operation, the throttle valve is a simple balanced valve with throttle pressure balancing spring force (Fig. 11–10). The spring forces the throttle valve to the left which permits Land *A* to open Port *C*. Now, control pressure passes through the annular groove and out of Port *E* to become throttle pressure. This TV pressure immediately begins to act against the reaction area of the throttle valve and attempts to balance the valve against spring force.

If TV pressure rises too high, it pushes the valve to the right which causes Land *A* to close Port *C*; and Land *B* to crack open sump-part *D*. As the TV pressure begins to bleed off to sump, its force on the reaction area decreases; and the spring pushes the valve to the left which again opens Port *C* and closes Port *D*. Thus, throttle pressure balances the valve against spring force; and the amount of TV pressure which, in this case, is necessary to balance spring force will be as high as control pressure. Consequently, with no vacuum acting on the diaphragm, control pressure and TV pressure have the same intensity.

But as previously mentioned, vacuum on the diaphragm reduces spring force. For example, when the engine is running without a load, intake-manifold vacuum is high. This vacuum is effective against the spring side of the diaphragm, and atmospheric pressure is effective against the opposite side. Therefore, with high engine vacuum, the atmospheric pressure pushes the diaphragm over to the right compressing the spring.

In effect, the high vacuum reduces the force of the spring on the throttle valve and consequently, reduces TV pressure. TV pressure goes down because, with reduced spring force on the throttle valve, throttle pressure on the valve's reaction area pushes it to the right. This action permits Land *A* to block Port *C* and Land *B* to open Port *D*. As a result TV pressure drops to zero or to whatever amount it takes to balance the reduced spring tension.

Now, as the engine is put under a load, its vacuum drops in proportion to the load; and the spring offsets more of the atmospheric pressure's effect on the diaphragm. As a result, the diaphragm and throttle valve have a higher, effective spring force that moves them both back to the left. This new valve position produces a higher throttle pressure in order to balance the valve against the increased spring force.

In effect, the increased spring force pushes the valve far enough toward the left to permit Land *A* to open Port *C* and Land *B* to block Port *D*. Now, TV pressure will increase until its action on the valve's reaction area balances the increased spring tension. In other words, the TV pressure from the valve is inversely proportional to the engine's vacuum. When engine vacuum is high, TV pressure is low; if engine vacuum is low, TV pressure is high (Fig. 11–12). Consequently, TV pressure varies from 0 psi at about 17 to 20 inches of vacuum to whatever control pressure is at zero vacuum.

The diaphragm assembly just described is a noncompensated unit. Noncompensated means that the device has no method of compensating for increases in altitude,

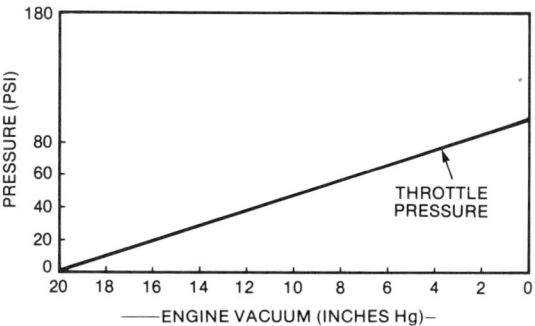

fig. 11–12 A chart of the engine's vacuum effect on throttle-valve pressure.

and altitude changes do affect engine and transmission performance. For example, with an increase in altitude, atmospheric pressure drops while engine vacuum remains relatively unchanged. As a result, the throttle valve train, with a noncompensated diaphragm assembly, produces an increase in TV pressure at higher altitudes.

Higher than normal TV pressure, at this time, causes several changes in transmission operation. First, the increased TV pressure, along with the normal loss in engine power, raises the upshift points too high. Second, higher TV pressure increases the control pressure in the whole system which makes clutch or band operation very harsh. In other words, this higher overall pressure increases the harshness of all upshifts and downshifts of the transmission at high altitudes.

To offset the effects of high altitudes on transmission performance, many manufacturers install an altitude-compensated vacuum-diaphragm unit on their transmissions (Fig. 11–13). Along with the other components of a noncompensated unit, the compensated device has an evacuated bellows attached between the diaphragm and the housing. This bellows is sensitive to atmospheric pressure changes which amount to about one inch Hg. drop for every 1000 feet increase in altitude. In effect, the bellows changes its shape due to the differences in atmospheric pressure.

At sea level, a throttle valve train, using the compensated-diaphragm assembly, produces the same level of TV pressure at any given engine vacuum as the noncom-

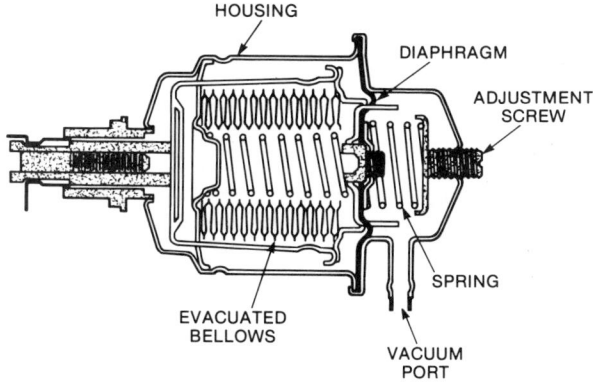

fig. 11–13 An altitude-compensated, vacuum-diaphragm assembly.

pensated valve train; but at higher altitudes, the compensated valve train produces less. This reduction in TV pressure is a direct result of lower atmospheric pressure acting on the bellows. The lower atmospheric pressure has a less crushing effect on the bellows. Consequently, the bellows expands and assists the reduced atmospheric pressure on the diaphragm in decreasing the spring force on the throttle valve. As a result, TV pressure decreases in relation to the increase in altitude to make the shift feel comparable to sea level conditions. In other words, the engine's loss of power at high altitude is offset by a lower TV pressure which causes the transmission shifts to remain as smooth as they were at sea level.

kickdown valve function and design

The manufacturer designs into every fully automatic transmission a valve circuit which permits the driver to downshift the transmission without moving the gear shift lever into a lower driving range. In other words, by activating this circuit, the driver can force the vehicle's transmission into a lower gear ratio for such things as passing another vehicle or climbing a steep grade. The device that actually accomplishes this task is the kickdown valve and its related circuitry. Finally, the two general ways to activate the kickdown valve are mechanical linkage or electricity.

A mechanically operated kickdown valve can operate alone as it does when used in a hydraulic system that has a vacuum-operated throttle valve. Or, the valve can be part of the linkage-activated throttle-valve train. Because both of these valve designs function in much the same way, this text will only cover the latter type. Finally, Fig. 11-14 shows the kickdown and throttle-valve train presented earlier in this chapter.

As previously pointed out, in this valve train, the kickdown valve did two things. First, as throttle linkage moved the valve, it directly increased the spring force which increased TV pressure. Second, as the kickdown valve moved to the end of its travel, it produced a kickdown pressure signal which, at certain road speeds, downshifted the transmission.

To actually produce the signal, the kickdown valve utilizes only one land which must control the fluid movement through three ports. For instance, at any given kickdown valve position, the land permits throttle pressure to enter through port G and fill the groove area to the right of the land itself. In addition, as the valve moves in as far as it can in its bore, the land opens port F, the kickdown pressure port. This action then

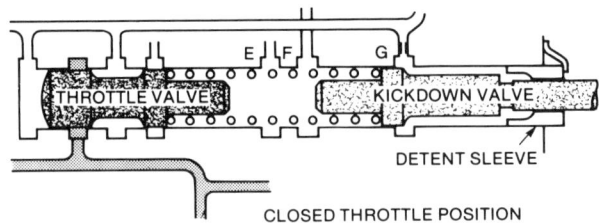

fig. 11-14 The design of a kickdown and throttle-valve train.

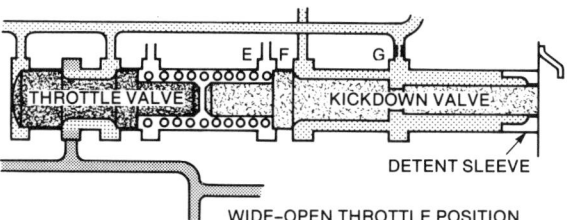

fig. 11-15 The kickdown and throttle valve train in the wide open accelerator-pedal position.

connects ports F and G together. Lastly, as the kickdown valve moves back to the right, the driver has released pressure on accelerator pedal, the land permits sump-port E and kickdown pressure port F to combine but blocks ports E and F from port G.

kickdown valve operation

As the driver accelerates the vehicle, the kickdown valve moves in its bore; and the throttle valve begins to produce TV pressure in its circuits (Fig. 11-14). One of these circuits directs fluid, via an orifice, to Port G. Now, TV pressure enters this port and fills the groove area of the kickdown valve on the right-hand side of its land. At the same time, Port F is open to vent any residual, downshift pressure, through Port E to the sump. This valve and circuit activity continues until the driver fully depresses the accelerator pedal.

If the driver depresses the accelerator pedal to the full open or detent position, the kickdown valve land opens Port F (Fig. 11-15). This valve action permits TV pressure from Port G to move through the groove area, out of Port F, and to the kickdown valve circuit. The pressure which enters this kickdown circuit is kickdown pressure, and the circuit directs this pressure to the spring side of the shift valve(s) where the kickdown pressure will assist the spring's force in moving the shift valve(s) to the downshift position.

Whenever the driver releases foot pressure on the accelerator pedal, the spring forces the kickdown valve to the right. In this position, the valve land prevents fluid from Port G from reaching Port F. Furthermore, the land position is such that Port F fluid pressure begins to vent back to sump via the open Port E. As a result of this reduction in kickdown pressure on the spring end of the shift valve(s), governor pressure will once again open the shift valve(s); and the transmission will upshift.

design of an electrically-operated kickdown valve

The electrically operated kickdown valve performs the exact same function in the hydraulic system as the manual type just described. In other words, this valve train, when the driver pushes the accelerator pedal to the floor, also directs kickdown pressure to the

198 HYDRAULIC SIGNAL DEVICES

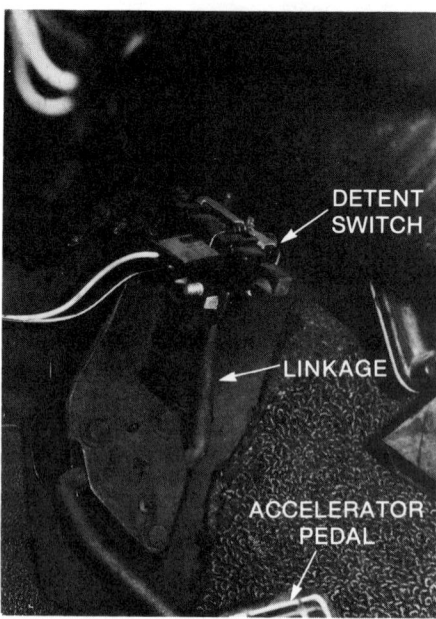

fig. 11-16 A firewall-mounted, electrical detent switch.

shift valves to force them to the downshift position. But the electrically operated kickdown valve train does this task in a slightly different manner, and this system requires more components in order to function.

A typical electrically operated kickdown valve train consists of an electrical detent switch, detent solenoid, hydraulic-detent valve, and detent regulator. The detent switch (Fig. 11-16) usually mounts directly on the side of the carburetor or on the firewall; and the throttle linkage activates the switch when the driver pushes the accelerator pedal all the way down. As the linkage closes the detent switch, it completes an electrical circuit to the detent solenoid.

The detent (kickdown) solenoid is an electrically activated hydraulic valve that controls the amount of control pressure going to the detent valve (Fig. 11-17). This solenoid consists of an electromagnet that has a coil energized by the detent switch. Inside the center of this coil is a spring loaded, movable plunger; the manufacturer machines one end of the plunger to form a valve which controls the activity of a sump port.

At any accelerator-pedal position except fully depressed, the detent switch is open, and the detent-solenoid's electrical circuit is broken. The tension of the plunger spring then forces the plunger down so that its valve contacts a seat which is over the sump port. As a result, line pressure, directed to the detent valve, cannot leak off through the sump port.

DESIGN OF AN ELECTRICALLY-OPERATED KICKDOWN VALVE

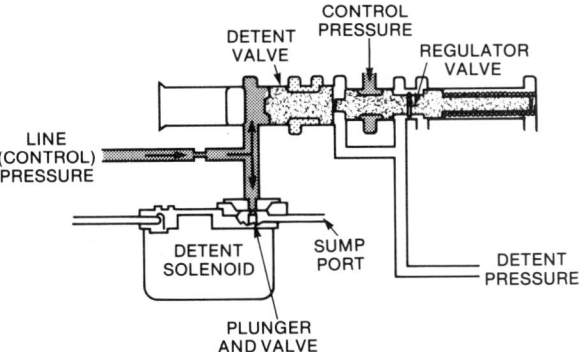

fig. 11-17 The detent solenoid and its circuitry in the deenergized position.

Now, if the driver fully depresses the accelerator pedal, the detent switch closes; and the detent solenoid energizes (Fig. 11-18). The electromagnet pulls the plunger up, compressing its spring; and the valve opens the sump port. As a result, the control pressure, going to the detent valve, bleeds off to the sump.

The primary function of the hydraulic, detent valve is to move the detent-regulator valve against spring tension. As previously pointed out (Fig. 11-17) if the detent switch deenergizes the solenoid, control pressure can build up and act against the left end of the detent valve, its reaction area. This pressure forces both the detent and regulator valves to the right against spring tension. If, on the other hand, the solenoid energizes (Fig. 11-18) control pressure on the detent valve drops, and the spring forces the regulator and detent valves to the left.

The detent regulator valve controls the amount of line pressure which enters the detent (kickdown) pressure circuits, and to do this, this valve has three lands which control three ports. For instance, Land A controls Port D which is the detent-pressure, outlet port. If the regulator valve moves right, Land A blocks this port. But as the valve moves left, the land uncovers Port D.

Land B blocks control pressure entering Port E from reaching Port F. Port E is the place where control pressure enters the regulator valve. Port F is a sump port where detent (kickdown) pressure bleeds off to the sump.

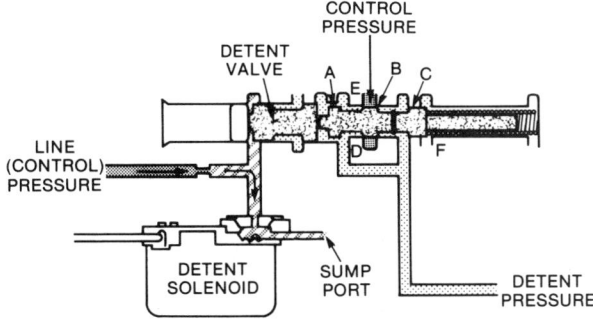

fig. 11-18 The detent solenoid and its circuitry in the energized position.

Finally, Land C controls fluid flow through Port F. For example, whenever the regulator valve moves right (Fig. 11-17) Land C opens the sump Port F which permits detent pressure from Port D to pass through the annular groove, out Port F, and to the sump. If the regulator valve moves left, (Fig. 11-18) Land C blocks Port F, and detent pressure increases in its circuitry.

electrically-controlled kickdown valve operation

At any accelerator-pedal position except wide open, the electrical circuit to the solenoid is open; and the detent-valve train produces no detent pressure to downshift the transmission (Fig. 11-17). In this situation, the detent switch is open which breaks the electrical circuit to the solenoid. The valve, located on the solenoid plunger, blocks off control pressure to the sump which permits line pressure to force the detent valve to the right.

In turn, the detent valve pushes the regulator valve over against spring tension; as a result, the regulator valve produces zero detent pressure. Detent pressure is now zero because Land A blocks control pressure from Port D. Also, Land C opens the sump-port F to Port D which reduces any residual detent pressure to zero.

As the driver moves the accelerator pedal to the fully depressed position, the detent switch energizes the detent solenoid, and detent pressure increases (Fig. 11-18). Because the electrical circuit to the solenoid is complete, the plunger and its valve retract away from the seat covering the sump port. Now control pressure on the end of the detent valve drops which allows the detent-regulator valve spring to force both valves to the left.

As a result of this regulator valve movement, Land A opens Port D, and Land C blocks the sump-port F. Now, control pressure from Port E passes through the annular groove; out of Port D; and to the spring end of the shift valve(s). Detent pressure now has the same intensity as control pressure; and, at certain vehicle speeds, it is high enough to push the shift valve(s) back against governor pressure.

Finally, in both types of kickdown systems, kickdown pressure usually will not be able to downshift the transmission if the vehicle is moving at a very high rate of speed. In other words, the manufacturer provides the transmission with a method of preventing a high speed kickdown either by regulating the intensity of kickdown pressure or by the design of the shift value itself. The manufacturer designs the system this way to protect the engine and transmission from damage which can occur to them from an extremely high speed downshift.

timing valves found in the hydraulic system

Manufacturers of automatic transmission can use several types of timing valves to smooth out the operation of their transmissions. These devices include such things as scheduling valves, shuttle valves, and timing valves. The main function of these valves, when used, is to help control the application and release of the frictional components so that the transmission will smoothly shift under any engine operating load or vehicle speed condition. Because each transmission manufacturer utilizes different types of timing devices, this text will not attempt to cover them in detail. When in doubt as to what a particular valve of this type does in a hydraulic system, refer to the technical manual for that particular automatic transmission.

summary

1. Hydraulic-signal devices are responsible for varying the upshift and downshift sequences of the transmission to meet different conditions.
2. The governor valve develops a pressure signal which is in proportion to road speed.
3. Governor pressure is zero when a vehicle is stationary or below about 10 mph, but then the pressure increases in intensity, with further vehicle acceleration, until it reaches its maximum amount at very high vehicle speeds.
4. A single-stage governor consists of a housing and governor valve.
5. Governor-valve housings attach to the output shaft.
6. Governor valves have two forces acting on them, governor pressure and centrifugal force.
7. A two-stage governor consists of a housing, weight assembly, and governor valve.
8. The weight assembly consists of a large weight, small weight, and spring.
9. A pin connects the small weight to the governor valve. The small weight is responsible for opening the governor valve at vehicle speeds over about 20 mph.
10. The governor spring assists centrifugal force in balancing the governor valve against the force of governor pressure.
11. The two-stage governor valve is a balanced valve with several lands and grooves.
12. The actual intensity of the governor-pressure signal depends on how much centrifugal force is acting on the weight assembly.
13. A two-stage governor produces a rapid rise in governor pressure at low vehicle speeds.
14. The throttle valve produces a pressure signal that is proportional to engine load.
15. A typical mechanically operated throttle valve consists of a kickdown valve, spring, and throttle valve which all operate in the same housing bore.
16. Spring tension on the throttle valve increases or decreases as the driver moves the accelerator pedal.
17. Varying spring tension determines throttle-valve position and throttle-pressure intensity.
18. The typical throttle valve is a balanced unit with several lands which control port activity.

19. The amount of throttle pressure will always be in proportion to the tension of the spring. If spring tension is weak, TV pressure is low. As spring force increases, TV pressure increases until it reaches the same intensity as control pressure; but it can go no higher.
20. A vacuum-controlled throttle valve train consists of a throttle valve, spring, and diaphragm assembly.
21. The vacuum-operated throttle valve itself performs the same functions as the valve used in the mechanically operated throttle valve train.
22. The vacuum-diaphragm assembly consists of a housing, diaphragm, and spring.
23. The housing of the vacuum-diaphragm assembly has an atmosphere and a vacuum port.
24. The diaphragm is a sealed, flexible piece of material.
25. The spring's force works against throttle pressure to balance the throttle valve.
26. The function of the vacuum diaphragm is to reduce spring tension on the throttle valve.
27. With no vacuum acting on the diaphragm, throttle pressure will have the same intensity as control pressure.
28. High vacuum, acting on the diaphragm, reduces the force of the spring on the throttle valve and consequently, reduces TV pressure.
29. Vacuum-diaphragm assemblies can be either compensated or noncompensated.
30. The compensated diaphragm assembly causes the throttle valve to produce lower throttle pressure when a vehicle is operating at altitudes above sea level.
31. The kickdown valve circuit permits the driver to downshift the transmission without moving the gearshift selector lever.
32. The kickdown valve can operate by means of mechanical linkage of electricity.
33. The mechanically operated kickdown valve opens by mechanical linkage as the driver pushes the accelerator pedal to the floor.
34. The electrically operated throttle valve train consists of an electrical-detent switch, detent solenoid, hydraulic-detent valve, and detent regulator.
35. The detent switch which operates by mechanical linkage energizes the solenoid when the driver pushes the accelerator wide open.
36. The solenoid controls the amount of control pressure going to the detent valve's reaction area.
37. The function of the detent valve is to move the regulator valve against spring tension.
38. The detent regulator valve controls the amount of control pressure which enters the detent (kickdown) pressure circuits.
39. At any accelerator pedal position except wide open, the electrical circuit to the solenoid is open, and the detent-valve train produces no detent pressure to downshift the transmission.

40. As the driver moves the accelerator pedal to the fully depressed position, the detent switch energizes the detent solenoid; and the detent pressure increases.
41. Manufacturers use several types of timing valves to smooth out the operation of their transmissions.

check-up questions

The questions listed below will assist you in determining how well you remember the material contained in this chapter. Read each question carefully before choosing the answer to each item. If you cannot answer a question, review the material in the section of the chapter that covers the question.

1. The valve which produces a hydraulic signal in proportion to vehicle speed is the _____.
   a. throttle valve
   b. kickdown valve
   c. detent valve
   d. governor

2. The output shaft of the transmission drives the _____ assembly.
   a. detent valve
   b. kickdown valve
   c. governor valve
   d. throttle valve

3. In a two-stage governor, centrifugal force acts on the _____.
   a. weight assembly
   b. governor valve
   c. spring
   d. connecting pin

4. The type of governor which produces a rapid rise in governor pressure at low vehicle speeds is the _____.
   a. single-stage
   b. two-stage
   c. three-stage
   d. both a and c

5. The valve that produces a pressure signal which is in proportion to engine load is the _____.
   a. governor valve
   b. kickdown valve

204 HYDRAULIC SIGNAL DEVICES

   c. throttle valve
   d. detent valve
6. In the throttle valve design discussed in this chapter the component directly moved by throttle linkage was the _____.
   a. detent valve
   b. kickdown valve
   c. throttle valve
   d. spring
7. In throttle valve systems, the amount of throttle pressure always varies with _____.
   a. spring tension
   b. road speed
   c. manual valve position
   d. detent pressure
8. In a vacuum-operated throttle valve system, the diaphragm functions to _____ spring tension on the throttle valve.
   a. decrease
   b. increase
   c. remove
   d. stabilize
9. With zero vacuum on the diaphragm, TV pressure will be _____.
   a. low
   b. moderate
   c. zero
   d. the same as control pressure
10. At engine idle speed, the vacuum-operated throttle valve will produce _____ TV pressure.
    a. high
    b. low
    c. zero
    d. moderate
11. The vacuum diaphragm assembly, designed to operate the throttle valve effectively at both sea level and high altitudes, is the _____.
    a. modulated type
    b. noncompensated type
    c. compensated type
    d. adjusted type

12. The valve circuit which permits the driver to downshift the transmission without moving the selector lever is the _____.
    a. throttle
    b. governor
    c. manual
    d. kickdown
13. The kickdown valve produces its signal as the driver moves the accelerator pedal _____.
    a. partially open
    b. halfway open
    c. full open
    d. to the idle position
14. The component of the electrically operated kickdown valve train that bleeds off control pressure to the detent valve is the _____.
    a. regulator valve
    b. spring
    c. detent switch
    d. detent solenoid
15. As the driver fully depresses the accelerator pedal, the detent solenoid's plunger _____.
    a. remains stationary
    b. retracts away from the sump port
    c. extends toward the sump port
    d. vibrates

For the answers to these check-up questions, turn to the Appendix located at the back of the text.

12

hydraulic system sealing devices — their function

The purpose of the various kinds of sealing devices found within the automatic transmission, is to control the amount of external and internal leakage of hydraulic fluid. External leakage, fluid which leaks to the outside of the transmission itself, is very obvious to the vehicle owner because of the oily spots left on his driveway or garage floor. Not only is this type of leakage an annoyance in that the leak creates a messy clean-up job, but it also forces the owner to check and add fluid to the transmission on a regular basis.

On the other hand, internal leakage, the excessive loss of pressurized fluid from a sealed component inside the transmission case, may develop over a period of time. Consequently, the driver may not become aware of it until the transmission really begins to malfunction. In other words, the operator may feel the transmission slipping a little bit, on initial engagement or during an upshift, because of this internal leakage; but he will usually tolerate these conditions as long as the vehicle continues to move to avoid the high cost of repair.

leakage control—a large task

The control of external and internal fluid leaks is a large undertaking for the automatic transmission manufacturer for three reasons. First, in order for the pressurized fluid to lubricate or activate the various transmission components, it has to, in many cases,

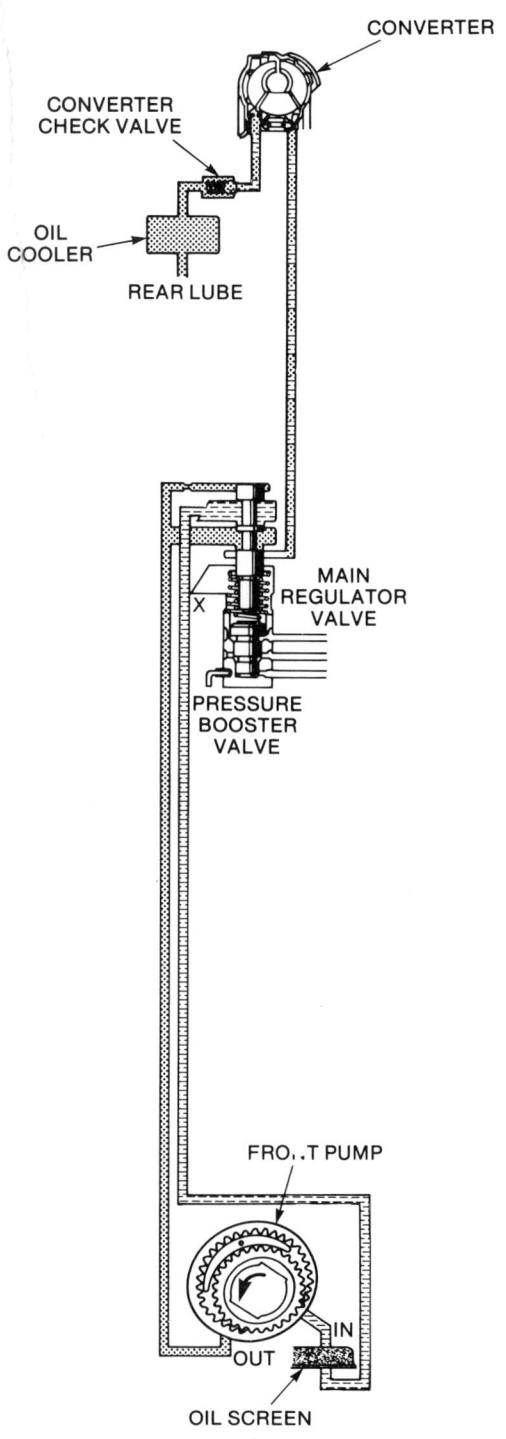

fig. 12-1 The rear lubrication system of a typical transmission.

208 HYDRAULIC SYSTEM SEALING DEVICES–THEIR FUNCTION

travel some distance and through various components before reaching its final destination. For example, within one model of automatic transmission, (Fig. 12-1) the pressurized fluid moves quite far before reaching the rear lubrication system. As in all hydraulic systems, initial fluid movement is from the sump to the pump. The pump applies a force to the fluid and causes pressure and flow to the regulator valve. From the regulator valve, the fluid moves into and then out of the torque converter.

As the fluid leaves the converter, it passes through the converter out the check valve and enters the cooler circuit. The fluid now flows through the external line to the transmission cooler inside the radiator. After passing through the cooler, the fluid enters a return line connected to the rear lubrication system of the transmission.

In order to prevent external or internal leakage of this pressurized fluid moving toward the rear lubrication system, the manufacturer utilizes many sealing devices. For this particular circuit, a total of about six devices are necessary to control the leakage. Of course, the complete transmission requires a great deal more, usually about twenty for the average unit.

The second factor that makes sealing a problem is the high temperatures under which certain components operate; these high temperatures prevent the use of certain excellent seal designs. For instance, synthetic rubber seals will deteriorate faster if subjected to high temperatures. This high-temperature deterioration is one of the reasons why manufacturers use metal, sealing rings instead of synthetic seals in various locations within the transmission (Fig. 12-2). The metal ring does not check fluid leakage as well as the synthetic seal in most cases, but it can function in areas of high temperature without failing.

The last sealing difficulty arises due to the fact that while some sealed parts do not move, others will have a rotary or reciprocating (back and forth) motion. In other words, the two sealed components may have relative motion between them. If the two parts, for example, are stationary with a seal between them, the sealing task is less difficult. For this type of installation, manufacturers use some form of static seal which provides a positive seal to prevent any leakage between the joined parts.

But on the other hand, rotary or reciprocating motions between sealed components does present a real sealing problem. The sealing devices in this situation must control leakage when the parts are moving and even when they are stationary. The manufacturer uses a form of dynamic seal to check fluid leakage in these types of installations. These dynamic seals can provide a positive seal, but in some cases the seal allows a

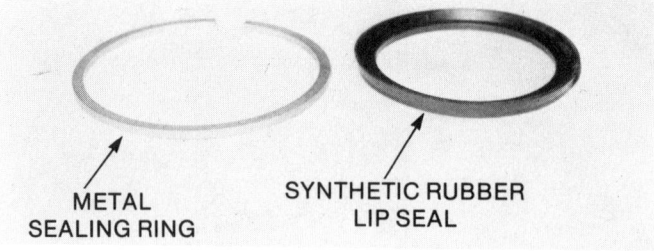

fig. 12-2 A synthetic rubber lip seal and a metal sealing ring.

controlled leak for lubrication purposes. Manufacturers classify these latter seals as the nonpositive type.

static sealing devices—gaskets

The types of sealing devices utilized in static applications are the gasket, lathe-cut, and the O-ring seals. A *gasket* is a device that fills in the space between two machined surfaces to provide a tight seal between them. The gasket, in this situation, prevents leakage by filling in the surface irregularities found on the mating surfaces of each part. These surface irregularities would otherwise form passageways which the fluid could follow to create a leak between the two components.

The gasket manufacturer uses several types of material to produce gaskets. The most common materials are: paper, cork, or a composition material of compressed particles of paper, cork, plastic or other synthetic material. Finally, the three common areas of the automatic transmission where the manufacturer utilizes these materials for gaskets are at the fluid pan, front pump, and valve body.

The pan gasket (Fig. 12-3) fits between the bottom of the transmission case and the pan to prevent external leakage. The gasket material used in this type of installation is cork or a composition material. Furthermore, the gasket is generally about $1/16$ to $1/8$ inch thick, and it easily compresses as the installer tightens the pan bolts.

Because of the flexibility of the material used and its thickness, pan gaskets do a rather good job of sealing even under less than ideal mating surface conditions. For example, poor mating surface conditions occur when the pan itself becomes somewhat distorted. The pan which is usually formed of sheet metal will easily distort if it contacts some object in the road or if the mechanic overtightens its attaching bolts. Of course, if pan distortion is excessive, the gasket will not seal and replacement of the pan is necessary.

A paper or composition, paper-base gasket also fits between the body of the hydraulic pump and the transmission case. This gasket performs two functions (Fig. 12-4). First, like the pan gasket, it takes up the space between the two mating surfaces to prevent static leakage. But in this type of installation, the leakage would be internal because the pump has a second seal that controls any external leaks. Second, open

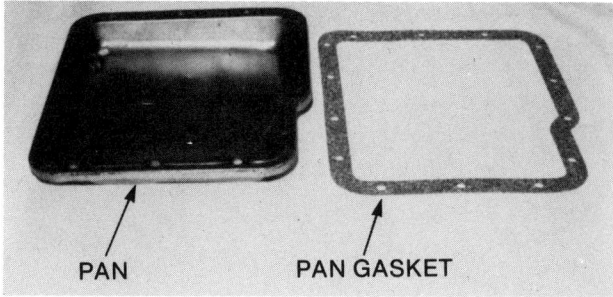

fig. 12-3 A pan gasket and fluid pan.

210 HYDRAULIC SYSTEM SEALING DEVICES—THEIR FUNCTION

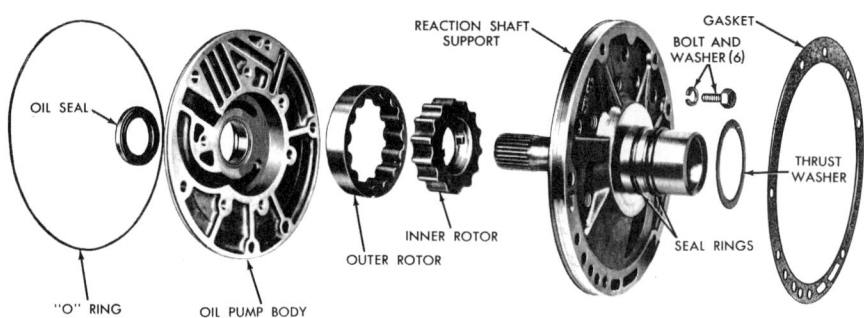

fig. 12–4 A typical hydraulic pump and case gasket. (Courtesy Chrysler Corp.)

holes in the gasket form channels for the fluid as it moves from the case to the pump and back.

Manufacturers also use the paper-type gaskets between the separator plate and the valve body (Fig. 12–5). These gaskets also check leakage caused by surface irregularities, but at the same time, the large number of openings in the gaskets direct the flow of fluid from one valve-body half, through the separator plate, and to the different circuits found in the other valve-body half. Therefore, in many installations, a gasket is necessary on each side of the separator plate. But on some valve bodies, where leakage is not a problem, the manufacturer will install only one gasket while in other designs no gasket is necessary at all.

The manufacturer, as mentioned earlier, may use the same transmission with several engine types. To mate the transmission with the engine, one of the things the manufacturer does in many cases is to install different design gaskets and separator plates between the valve body halves. One design, for example, blocks off specific circuits between the valve-body halves while another type may open these circuits and block still others (Fig. 12–6). Consequently, the mating of the proper gasket to the valve

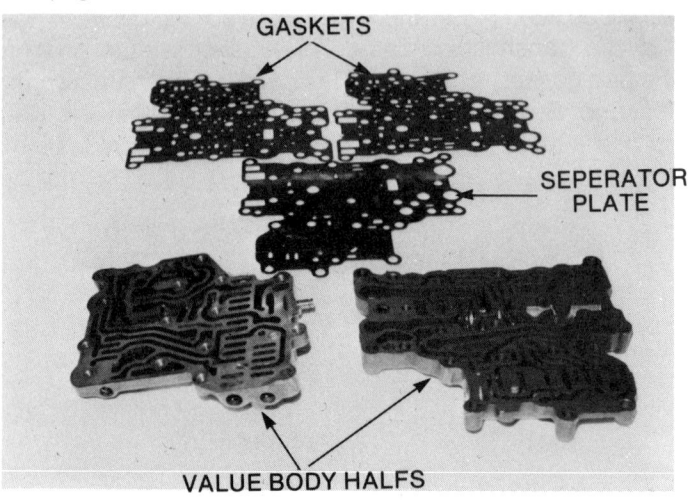

fig. 12–5 The halves of a valve body, its gaskets, and separator plate.

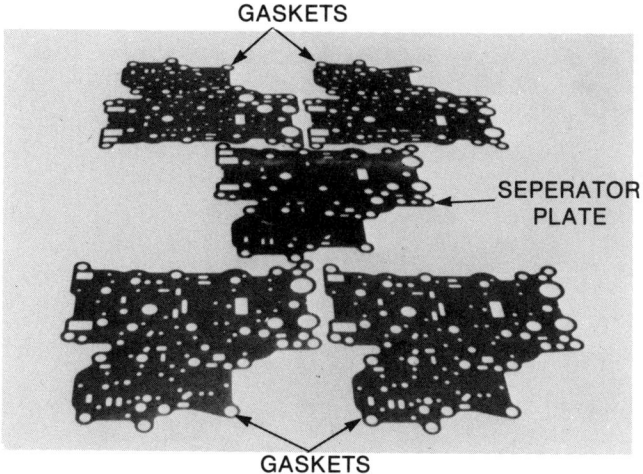

fig. 12-6 Different types of gaskets for the same valve body.

body is of utmost importance. If a mechanic should install the wrong gaskets or place them in the wrong location, the transmission will malfunction or not operate at all.

lathe-cut seals

The second type of static sealing device is the *square- or lath-cut seal,* formed from a synthetic rubber, Neoprene. This material, used extensively by manufacturers, is not as brittle as pure rubber. Furthermore, the Neoprene can withstand more heat and contact with various chemicals much better than a pure rubber seal.

The square-cut seal is circular in shape with a square cross section (Fig. 12-7). To produce this design, the manufacturer generally molds this seal type into a tube shape and then cuts it into individual rings on a lathe. The seal now has the correct diameter and width to fit properly into a groove cut into one of the components it will seal.

In order to provide positive leakage control, the square-cut seal depends on a squeezing or compressing action. If, for example, a manufacturer utilizes this seal to check external leakage of a hydraulic pump, the size of the seal and the case bore diameter determine the extent of seal compression. In this installation, the seal is larger

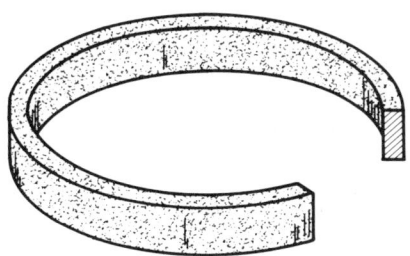

fig. 12-7 A lathe-cut seal.

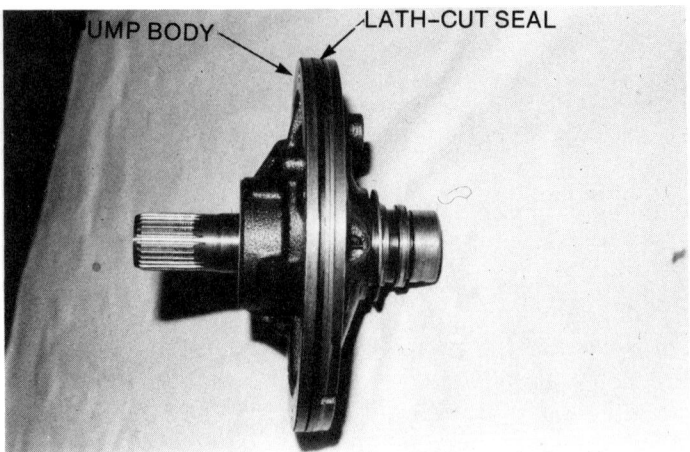

fig. 12-8 A lathe-cut seal installed in a groove cut into the pump body.

in diameter than its bore in the transmission case, and it fits rather snugly into a groove cut into the outer circumference of the pump body (Fig. 12-8).

As the installer pushes the pump assembly into its bore in the transmission case, the seal has to compress somewhat down into the groove in order for the pump to enter the bore (Fig. 12-9). With the pump in place, the natural tendency of the compressed seal is now to return to its original shape. As a result of this seal elasticity, the inner and outer circumferences of the seal provide a positive control of fluid leakage at its contact areas. In other words, the seal prevents leakage between its outer circumference and the case bore and also at its inner circumference and the groove in the pump body.

o-ring seals

The *O-ring* is another form of static seal which, by its design, provides positive leakage control. The seal manufacturer also molds this device in a tube or round shape, but the finished seal has a circular cross section (Fig. 12-10). Also, by being larger in diameter

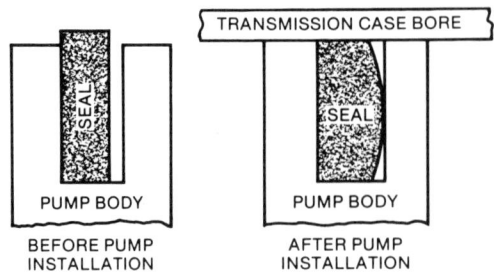

fig. 12-9 A lathe-cut seal before and after being compressed into its groove.

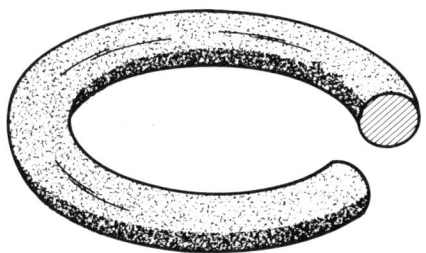

fig. 12–10 An O-ring seal.

than its bore, this seal functions by a compressing action in a manner similar to the lathe-cut seal.

Fig. 12–11 shows an O-ring used on a front-pump assembly; this seal will also control external leakage. The seal in this installation also fits into a groove in the pump body. Also, the groove itself is not as deep as the thickness of the seal. As a result, the seal protrudes above the surface of the groove and pump body.

As the transmission assembler inserts the pump into its bore in the transmission case, the O-ring has to compress slightly to allow the pump to enter the bore. The compression of the seal squeezes or packs it into the groove in the pump body. As a result, the O-ring forms a positive seal between the pump body and its bore in the transmission case (Fig. 12–12).

dynamic sealing devices

As previously mentioned, dynamic sealing devices must check leakage at installations in which one or both components are moving. In applications such as these, the sealing device may provide a positive seal while in others a nonpositive type of sealing is all that is necessary. A nonpositive seal will allow a certain amount of controlled leakage for

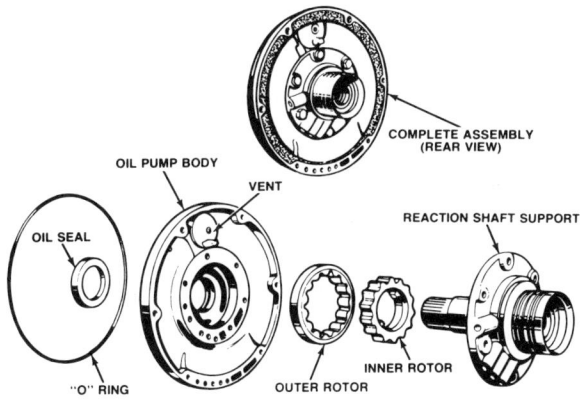

fig. 12–11 An O-ring seal used with a front pump assembly. (Courtesy Chrysler Corp.)

214 HYDRAULIC SYSTEM SEALING DEVICES–THEIR FUNCTION

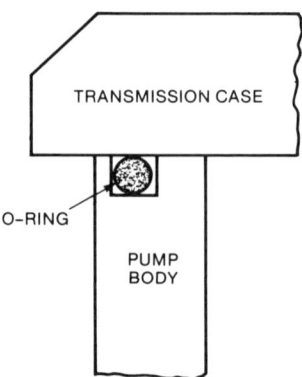

fig. 12–12 An O-ring seal compressed into its groove by installation of the pump.

lubrication purposes. The seal designs which are both static as well as dynamic are the lathe-cut and O-ring; the seals which are primarily dynamic are the lip and metal-clad seals, the metal ring, and the Teflon seal.

dynamic lathe-cut seals

Fig. 12–13 displays two lathe-cut seals installed on a clutch piston. In this installation, the square-cut seals will provide a positive control of leakage at both the inner and outer circumferences of the piston. Furthermore, in this application, the seals control this leakage as the piston moves back and forth in its bore in the transmission case.

As in a static application, a slight compression of these clutch seals causes them to form a dynamic, positive seal. To accomplish this compressing action, the manufacturer

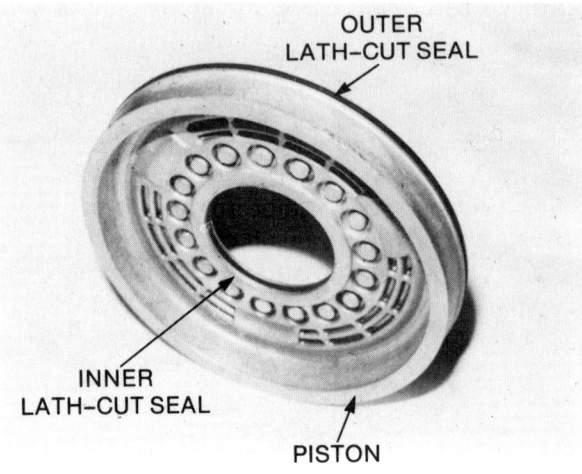

fig. 12–13 Dynamic lathe-cut seals installed on a clutch piston.

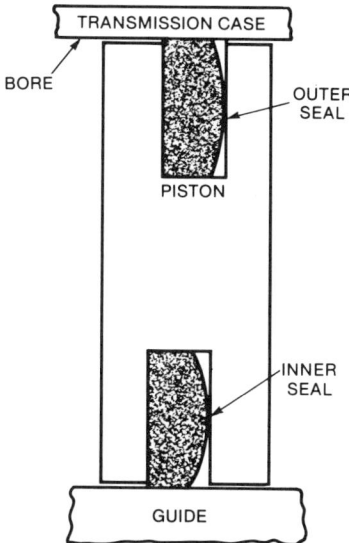

fig. 12–14 Lathe-cut seals compressed into their grooves in the clutch piston.

makes the large, outer-seal's outside diameter larger than the diameter of its bore in the transmission case. On the other hand, the inside circumference of the inner seal is smaller than the outer circumference of the piston guide built into the transmission case. Finally, both of these seals fit into outer and inner grooves machined into the piston.

As the mechanic installs the piston into its bore and over its guide, both seals must compress slightly into their respective grooves (Fig. 12–14). The reaction force of this compression tries to return the seals to their original shape. As a result, the seals provide a positive control of fluid leakage at all their contact surfaces. Finally, this sealing action occurs with the piston stationary or with it moving back and forth.

dynamic o-ring seals

The O-ring seal, when installed in a reciprocating, dynamic application, also provides a positive seal. But manufacturers only use this type of seal for clutch pistons and servos which have a short stroke or back and forth motion. The reason for this is that the O-ring tends to roll or twist if subjected to much reciprocating motion. Consequently, this tendency to roll limits its dynamic applications to parts with small movements in order to prevent damage to the seal.

Fig. 12–15 illustrates an O-ring installed in a dynamic application. The O-ring in this installation fits into a groove in a movable component. During the installation of this part into its bore, the difference in bore diameter and seal size squeezes the seal into its groove that causes a positive seal at two locations.

As the component moves in its bore, the motion forces the O-ring against one side of its groove (Fig. 12–16). This action also packs the seal against this corner of the

216 HYDRAULIC SYSTEM SEALING DEVICES–THEIR FUNCTION

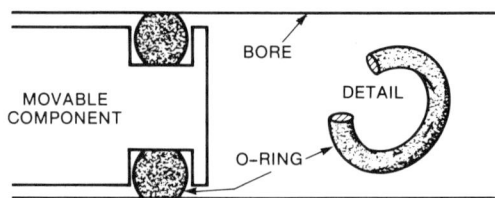

fig. 12–15 An O-ring seal installed in a dynamic application.

groove. As a result, the O-ring now controls leakage at three locations: at its top, bottom, and one side; and it is capable of withstanding very high pressure without leaking.

If the part moves in the other direction, the motion moves the seal in the opposite direction (Fig. 12–17). This action then packs the seal against the other side of the groove and seals it against leakage. In other words, the O-ring has the ability to provide sealing action on three sides no matter which direction the part moves.

As previously mentioned, the O-ring cannot tolerate excessive reciprocating motion; it also will not function where rotational forces exist. Under rotary conditions, the O-ring cannot seat properly in its groove. As a result, the seal will not be able to control leakage at its contact points.

dynamic lip seals

The design of the *synthetic lip seal* is such that it can function in applications where both reciprocating and rotary motions are present (Fig. 12–18). The lip seal, like the O-ring and square-cut seals, is circular in shape. But this molded-seal design has an extended lip that is larger in diameter than the bore it fits into. Therefore, in order for the lip of this seal to enter the bore, it must deflect or compress downward somewhat; as the lip attempts to return to its original shape, it applies a tension against the wall of the bore.

Fig. 12–19 illustrates a lip seal properly installed in a groove located in the other circumference of a clutch piston; in this installation, the seal controls leakage in two ways. First, as previously stated, the lip imposes tension on the bore wall due to its elasticity. Second, as hydraulic pressure activates the piston, it also applies a force on the lip that presses it even harder against the bore (Fig. 12–20).

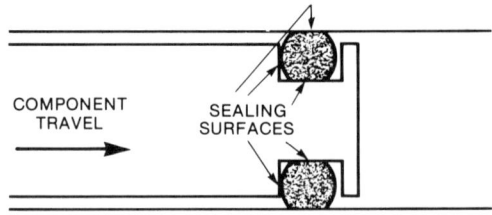

fig. 12–16 The O-ring seal forced against one side of its groove by component movement in one direction.

METAL-CLAD LIP SEALS 217

fig. 12–17 The O-ring seal forced against the other side of its groove by component movement in the opposite direction.

In order for the lip seal to function in a dynamic application, the lip must always face toward the pressure source. If it does not, the hydraulic pressure will not be able to force the force the lip against the wall of the bore. In fact, the pressure will deflect the seal away from the bore wall, and a large leak will result. Consequently, it is very important that the mechanic install this seal with the lip facing in the proper direction.

metal-clad lip seals

The automatic transmission manufacturer uses the *metal-clad lip seal* in several dynamic applications to control external leakage. For example, the extension housing will have one of these seal types pressed into its end (Fig. 12–21). The seal in this application provides a positive seal between the housing and the revolving slip-yoke section of the drive shaft. The front pump will also have a metal-clad seal pressed into it. This seal controls leakage between the revolving converter hub and the pump body. Finally, in some transmissions, this metal-clad device produces a seal where the shifter shaft enters the transmission case.

The design of the metal-clad seal is such that it can control two types of leakage at the same time. The simple metal-clad seal is nothing more than a lip seal bonded to a circular, metal shell (Fig. 12–22). The shell is larger in diameter than the bore it fits into, and in some cases, the manufacturer coats the shell's outer circumference with a sealing material such as rubber or resin. And because of the differences in diameter

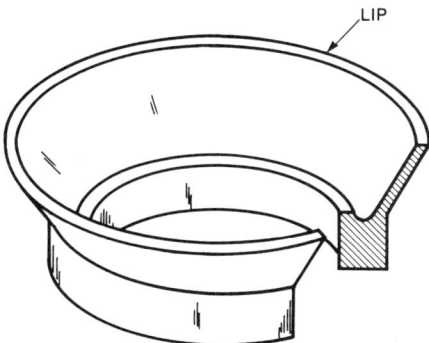

fig. 12–18 A typical lip seal.

218 HYDRAULIC SYSTEM SEALING DEVICES–THEIR FUNCTION

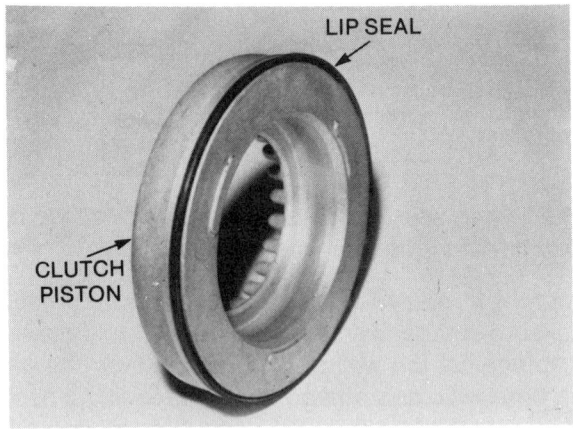

fig. 12-19 A lip seal installed in its groove in a clutch piston.

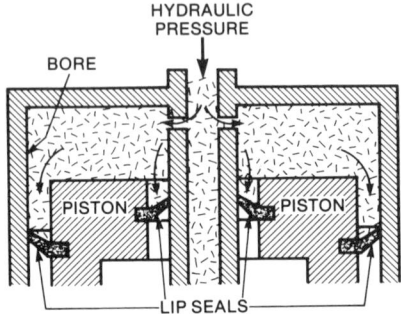

fig. 12-20 Hydraulic pressure acting on the lip seal forces the lip tightly against the bore.

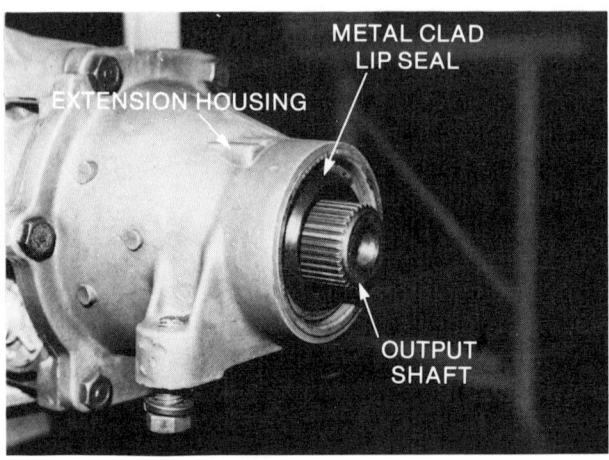

fig. 12-21 A metal-clad seal installed in an extension housing.

METAL-CLAD LIP SEALS 219

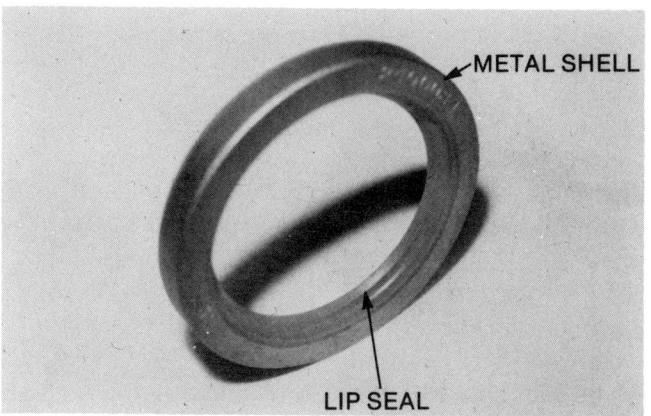

fig. 12-22 The design of a typical metal-clad seal.

between the shell and its bore, the mechanic must press or drive the seal into position. This interference fit, in addition to the sealing compound when used, prevents a static leak between the bore wall and the seal's shell.

The synthetic rubber lip section of the seal must control both static and dynamic leakage, and the actual lip design varies with different seal applications. For instance, a shifter-shaft seal will usually have a single lip that has no garter spring (Fig. 12-23). With the seal installed, the lip faces toward the fluid source; the bonded-lip's elasticity prevents both static and dynamic leakage between the shaft and the seal's shell.

Because the front-pump metal-clad seal has a harder sealing task to perform, its lip has a garter spring under it (Fig. 12-24). This spring helps to keep the lip pressed against the converter hub. In other words, the spring assists the elasticity of the lip in controlling leakage at the place where the converter enters the pump.

To stop the entrance of foreign material such as dust, dirt, or moisture from entering the seal area, some metal-clad seals will have a double-lip and a garter spring (Diagram A of Fig. 12-25). The transmission manufacturer installs these double-lip seals at locations such as the front pump and extension housing. With this seal design, the spring-loaded, primary lip controls fluid leakage while the non-spring-loaded, secondary lip prevents the entrance of foreign matter.

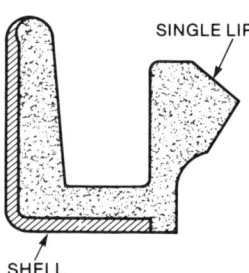

fig. 12-23 A metal-clad seal with a single lip and no garter spring.

220 HYDRAULIC SYSTEM SEALING DEVICES–THEIR FUNCTION

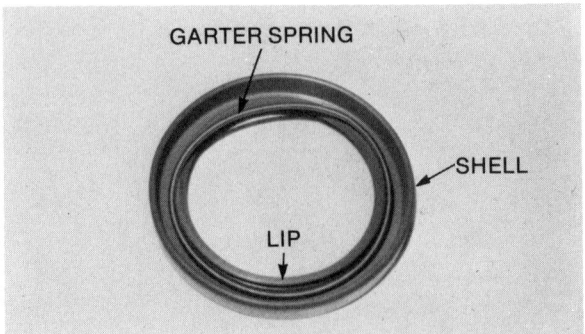

fig. 12–24 Metal-clad seal with a single lip and a garter spring.

In some extension housing applications, the metal-clad seal will have a spring-loaded, primary lip; but it will utilize a packing material instead of a secondary lip (Diagram B of Fig. 12–25). In this design, the packing serves the same function as the secondary lip. The packing used in many cases is a felt material that fits into a groove made into the metal shell.

Fig. 12–26 shows another type of extension housing seal with a dust boot. This seal also has a spring-loaded primary lip to control fluid leakage and a secondary lip to stop the entrance of foreign matter to the seal area. In addition, this seal has a dust boot attached to the shell. This synthetic boot has a ring that resembles a lathe-cut seal molded into its end. This sealing ring also encircles the slip-yoke to provide extra protection against the entrance of foreign material to the seal area.

In many metal-clad seals, the manufacturers use supplemental sealing devices to control fluid leakage. As previously mentioned, with the lip facing the direction of the fluid source, the elasticity of the lip and, in many cases, the garter spring regulate the amount of fluid leakage. But in some installations, these two methods are not sufficient to control leakage within acceptable limits.

To provide the seal with additional control of fluid leakage, the manufacturer will mold ribs or depressions on the outside lip surface (Fig. 12–27). The function of these

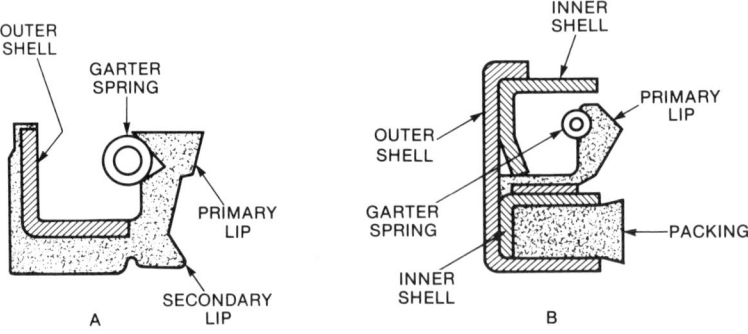

fig. 12–25 Metal-clad seal with double lip or packing plus a garter spring.

METAL-CLAD LIP SEALS **221**

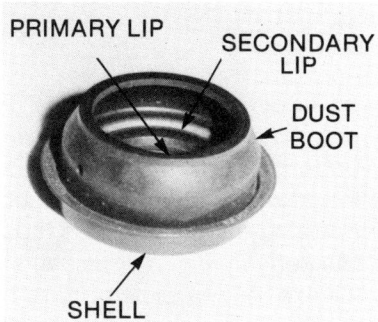

fig. 12–26 A metal-clad seal with a dust boot.

supplemental devices is to direct the fluid away from the seal surface or back toward its source. In other words, these devices direct some of the fluid away from the lip-contact surface; normal-lip elasticity, in addition to the tension of the garter spring, will then be able to control the fluid leakage even under less than ideal conditions.

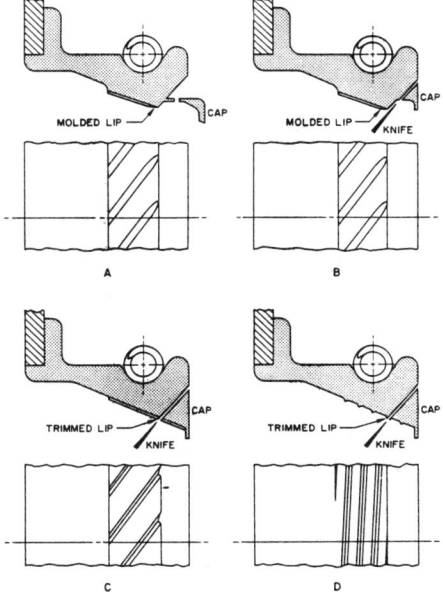

fig. 12–27 Supplemental sealing devices. The seals shown in (A) and (B) have a molded lip. The excess material is removed by tearing the cap from the molded part in (A) and by a knife in (B). The helical ribs in both designs terminate at the contact point of the static lip. Seals shown in (C) and (D) are trimmed up seals; that is, a knife trimming operation forms the contact lip as the excess material is removed. The helical ribs protrude at the contact point and must be compressed to prevent the seal from leaking when the shaft is not rotating prior to initial operation. (Reprinted with permission from the SAE handbook, © 1978 Society of Automotive Engineers, Inc.)

metal sealing rings

Metal sealing rings, when used in dynamic applications, have two primary functions. First, as previously stated, manufacturers use metal rings (Fig. 12-28) to control fluid leakage at locations where high temperatures are present. Second, the rings can provide adequate sealing of rotating shafts which carry pressurized fluid to various components; but they do permit some leakage that lubricates the shaft journals and bushings as needed. In other words, these sealing rings act as dams to direct fluid pressure from oil passages in the shaft to, for example, a clutch drum, but allow some seepage for lubrication.

The metal sealing ring has about the same design and construction as the common engine piston ring. The manufacturer forms these rings primarily from grey cast-iron, but for some transmission component applications, they also use aluminum. In addition, the iron sealing rings have a surface coating of Phosphate or Oxide; or, occasionally the coating will be a metallic plating such as tin or chrome. Finally, the original process used to manufacture the ring is such that it gives the ring elasticity. In other words, the metal ring can, after being compressed, return to its original shape. As a result, the ring presses against the bore wall with a given amount of tension that is necessary to control leakage at this point.

Manufacturers also produce these metal sealing rings with two types of joint ends—the butt and the lock. The butt-joint design is such that when the ring is in its bore, a small clearance exists between its ends. This clearance compensates for heat expansion of the ring and permits some fluid leakage past the joint for lubrication. Consequently, the manufacturer will install this ring type in high-temperature locations where leakage is not a problem or where the leakage is necessary for component lubrication.

The lock-joint design, on the other hand, has small tangs which holds the ends of the ring together or in partial compression. But the design of the tangs is such that they do permit some ring tension on the bore wall and at the same time allow for heat expansion of the ring. The transmission manufacturer will utilize this ring design for two reasons: first, to reduce the leakage past the ends of the rings after their installation; second, the lock joint holds the ring in compression enough so that the mechanic can install the component the ring fits on into a blind bore without breaking the ring.

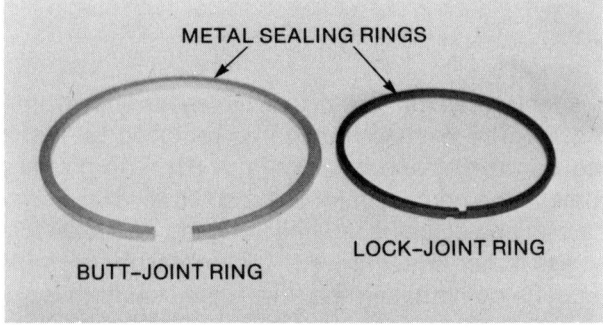

fig. 12-28 Metal sealing rings with butt and lock joints.

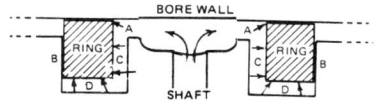

fig. 12-29 The metal sealing ring installed on a stationary shaft. (© Research, El Monte, California)

Fig. 12-29 illustrates two iron sealing rings, installed on a stationary shaft, on either side of a fluid passage; the rings, in this installation, must control leakage between the stationary shaft and rotating bore wall. The elasticity of the ring must be great enough to initially control fluid leakage at Point A long enough for the fluid pressure to move the ring against the B side of the groove. This ring action allows pressurized fluid to flow down area C, between the side of the ring and groove, and to the underside of Ring D.

The fluid pressure, now acting on the underside of Ring D, forces the ring tightly against the bore wall. This action causes the metal ring to seal leakage at Point A. In addition, since the combined forces of fluid pressure and ring elasticity keep it in contact with the bore wall, the ring rotates with the bore as required. Of course, the metal rings used on a reciprocating servo or accumulator piston do not rotate.

teflon seals

Some automatic transmission manufacturers utilize Teflon or a similar plastic material instead of metal rings in some dynamic applications. These nonmetallic seals serve the same function as the metal rings and operate in much the same manner. This seal type does an excellent job of sealing when working properly, and it provides a cost reduction for the manufacturer during the original assembly of the transmission.

But nonmetallic seals are vulnerable to scratching and impregnation by metal particles. The scratches prevent sealing at the outside diameter of the seal. The particle impregnation, on the other hand, prevents a seal at Point B side of the groove (Fig. 12-29) and often makes the ring too tight in its groove. For these reasons, most transmission rebuilders replace the Teflon seals with metal rings during an overhaul.

summary

1. The purpose of the various kinds of sealing devices found within the automatic transmission is to control the amount of external and internal leakage of hydraulic fluid.
2. External leakage is fluid loss to the outside of the transmission.
3. Internal leakage is the excessive loss of pressurized fluid from a sealed component inside the transmission case.
4. The control of leakage is a large undertaking for the automatic transmission manufacturer.

5. The distance the fluid has to travel and the number of parts it moves through make sealing a problem.
6. High temperatures also make sealing a problem.
7. The sealing of moving parts is more difficult than the sealing of stationary ones.
8. A gasket is a static device that fills in the space between two machined surfaces to provide a tight seal between them.
9. Manufacturers make gaskets out of paper, cork, or a composition material.
10. Gaskets may have holes which permit fluid to move from one part to another.
11. Manufacturers use gaskets at such locations as the pan, front pump, and valve body.
12. Lathe-cut, O-rings, and lip seals are now made of Neoprene, a synthetic rubber.
13. Manufacturers use the lathe-cut seal in both static and dynamic applications. This device depends on a compressing action in order to provide a positive seal.
14. The O-ring seal also functions in both static and some dynamic applications, in much the same manner as the lathe-cut seal, and provides a positive seal.
15. Lip seals can function in applications where both reciprocating and rotary motions are present.
16. Manufacturers use the metal-clad seal in several locations to control external leakage.
17. Metal-clad seals control both static and dynamic leakage.
18. Some metal-clad seals have a garter spring that assists the lip in checking fluid leakage.
19. Some metal-clad seals have a second lip or other device which prevents the entrance of foreign matter into the seal area.
20. Metal rings function well in high-temperature areas but do not provide positive sealing.
21. The metal sealing ring has about the same design and construction as the common piston ring used in an engine.
22. The metal sealing ring may have a butt or lock joint.
23. Manufacturers also install Teflon rings instead of metal rings in some dynamic applications.

check-up questions

The questions listed below will assist you in determining how well you remember the material contained in this chapter. Read each question carefully before choosing the answer to each item. If you cannot answer the question, review the material in the section of the chapter that covers the question.

1. The average automatic transmission will have about _____ sealing devices.
   a. 6
   b. 12
   c. 18
   d. 20
2. High temperatures will deteriorate _____ seals.
   a. cast-iron
   b. aluminum
   c. synthetic rubber
   d. both *a* and *c*
3. The gasket provides a positive seal in _____ sealing applications.
   a. static
   b. dynamic
   c. both *a* and *b*
   d. no
4. Lathe-cut seals provide positive sealing in _____ applications.
   a. no
   b. dynamic
   c. static
   d. both *b* and *c*
5. The seal that is circular in shape with a round cross section is the _____.
   a. lathe-cut
   b. O-ring
   c. lip
   d. metal
6. The seals which control fluid leakage due to a squeezing action of the entire seal are the _____.
   a. square-cut and metal
   b. metal and Teflon
   c. O-ring and square-cut
   d. lip and O-ring
7. Which seal type does not operate well in all dynamic applications?
   a. lip
   b. metal
   c. O-ring
   d. lathe-cut

8. The seal that utilizes hydraulic pressure to help it in providing a better control of leakage is the _____.
   a. lip
   b. lathe-cut
   c. gasket
   d. O-ring
9. The seal design that uses the garter spring is the _____.
   a. lip
   b. metal-clad
   c. gasket
   d. O-ring
10. The secondary lip, found on many metal-clad seals, controls the entrance of _____ to the seal area.
    a. fluid
    b. foreign material
    c. air
    d. both A and B
11. Metal sealing rings provide _____ sealing.
    a. nonpositive
    b. positive
    c. no
    d. extra
12. In some applications, the manufacturer will install a(n) _____ seal instead of a metal one.
    a. O-ring
    b. square-cut
    c. Teflon
    d. lip

For the answers to these check-up questions, turn to the Appendix located at the back of the text.

13

hydraulic system diagrams – their function

For the purpose of trouble-shooting a malfunctioning automatic transmission, the hydraulic-system diagram is a very useful tool because it provides the repairman with a great deal of useful information. For instance, a hydraulic-system chart shows him all the different circuits of the transmission's hydraulic system (Fig. 13–1). Of course, the drawing is a graphic representation of all the circuits the manufacturer machines into the transmission, and for practical reasons is not a scale drawing.

If the schematic were to be a scale drawing, as to the length and direction of each circuit, the diagram would be quite large and more difficult to interpret. Consequently, the chart shows the mechanic that a transmission has a certain circuit, but it will not inform him of the circuit's actual length or direction. This, of course, makes the diagram of little use to the mechanic in actually locating a given circuit in the transmission itself.

The hydraulic-system chart also contains all the valves utilized in the hydraulic system, but the diagram, in this case, displays these valve trains in great detail. For example, Fig. 13–2 is a partial illustration of a diagram showing a complete valve train with all its related components. This drawing clearly indicates the number of lands, grooves, and reaction areas of the valve plus all the port openings and circuits which the lands control. Finally, for the sake of simplicity, the charts usually show each valve train in either its closed or fully open position. The only exception to this general rule is in the

228 HYDRAULIC SYSTEM DIAGRAMS–THEIR FUNCTION

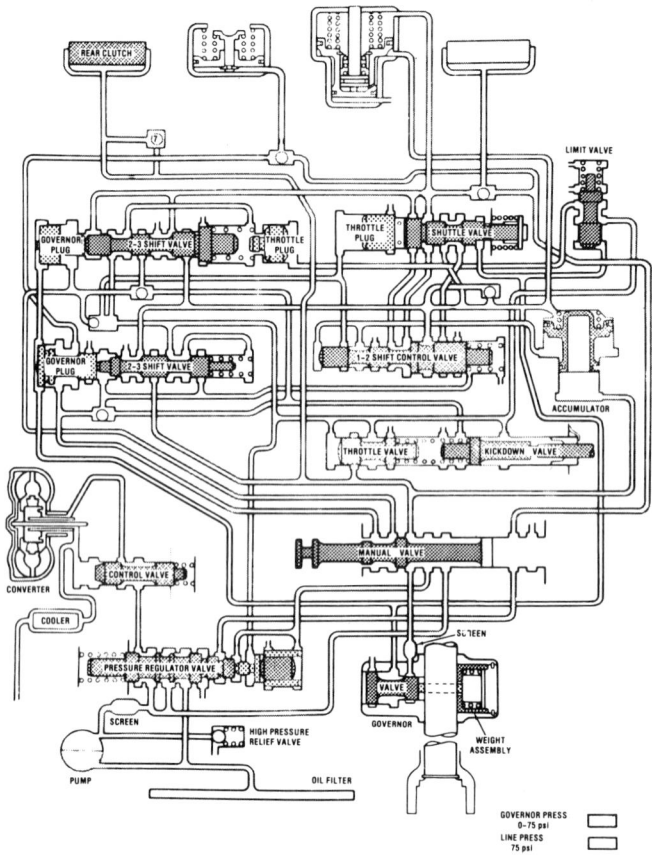

fig. 13-1 A typical hydraulic system diagram. (Courtesy Chrysler Corp.)

case of regulating-type valves which a chart usually pictures closed or in their regulating cycle position.

In addition, a complete diagram will illustrate the hydraulic pump and its related circuitry (Fig. 13-3). This section of the schematic will show in most cases the type of pump employed by the hydraulic system, gear, rotor, or vane; the various port openings to the pump; and the various circuits leading to and away from the pump. Furthermore, this portion of the chart shows, but not in great detail, the sump and inlet screen or filter of the system.

The last items, displayed on most hydraulic charts, are the hydraulically operated units (Fig. 13-4). In other words, a schematic usually shows all the band servos and clutch pistons necessary to apply the frictional components which control the operation of the planetary gear train. And due to the complexity in design and operation of most servos over the clutch pistons, the drawings usually illustrate the servos in great detail but not the clutch pistons. Lastly, as in the case of the valve trains, the chart shows the hydraulically operated units in a single position—either off or in their fully applied position.

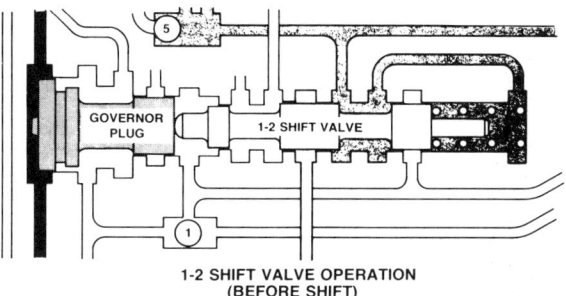

fig. 13–2 A diagram of a shift-valve train. (Courtesy Chrysler Corp.)

symbols used on diagrams

Before a technician can interpret a hydraulic diagram, he must understand the symbols used on that particular schematic. Many transmission manufacturers use the same symbols or marks to represent certain devices and circuits on hydraulic charts while others utilize their own symbols which, of course, will only relate to their schematics. Therefore, the mechanic must know the standard symbols and at the same time, be aware of and look for any special marks a given manufacturer may use.

The standard symbols, used extensively by the industry, are those which represent the circuit and the orifice. The symbol for a circuit is nothing more than two parallel lines which run from one hydraulic component to another (Fig. 13–5). And as previously stated, these parallel lines do not necessarily represent the length or direction a circuit

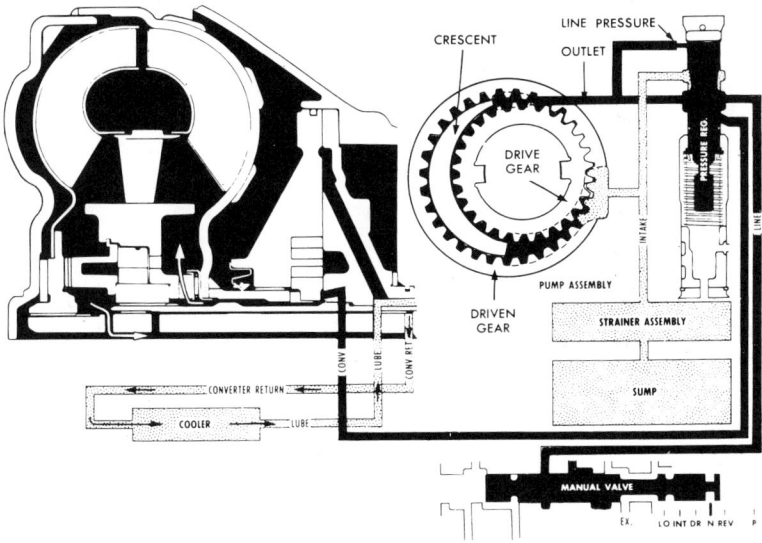

fig. 13–3 A drawing of a pump circuit. (Courtesy Hydra-matic Division of General Motors Corp.)

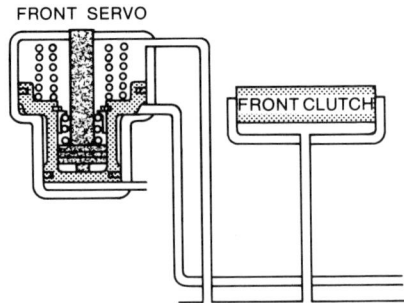

fig. 13–4 A diagram of several hydraulically operated units.

follows within the transmission itself. In other words, all these marks show is that a circuit does connect one unit to another.

Fig. 13–6 shows the symbol for the orifice. This mark, a restriction, appears in the circuit leading to the component affected by the action of the orifice. In the above-mentioned figure, the orifice is in the circuit to slow down the operation of an accumulator.

There is not a standard symbol for any valve in the hydraulic system. Instead, each manufacturer uses a drawing of the valve itself. The reason for this action is that each different transmission design utilizes a certain number of special valves which perform certain tasks in that particular unit. Consequently, there can be no one symbol to represent any valve for all hydraulic diagrams.

Fig. 13–7 illustrates a typical drawing of a 2–3 shift valve train as it will appear on the hydraulic diagram. Note that this drawing shows the total valve train with its individual components. Also, note that all valve lands, grooves, and port openings are clearly visible. Furthermore, to make it easier for the mechanic to locate the valve train on the complete diagram, the draftsman prints the name of each valve and, in some cases, its major components on or to one side of the valve itself.

Finally, there are not any standard symbols for the hydraulic pump, torque converter, and the hydraulically operated units. All manufacturers use drawings to indicate

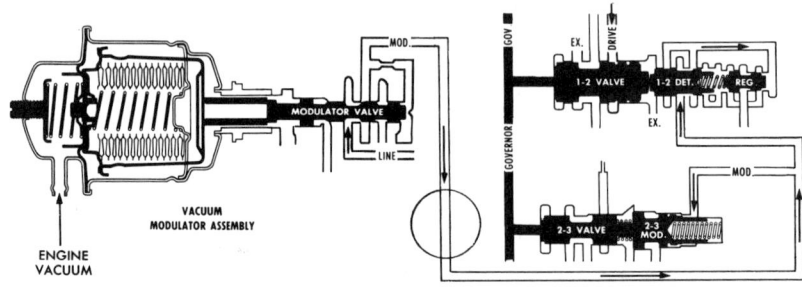

fig. 13–5 The two parallel lines within the circle represent the standard symbol for a circuit. (Courtesy Hydra-matic Division of General Motors Corp.)

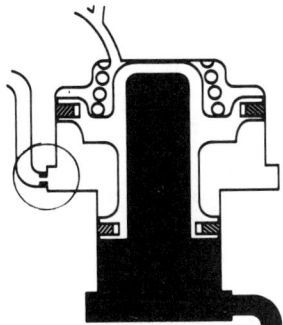

fig. 13–6 The mark, a circuit restriction, within the circle represents the standard symbol of an orifice. (Courtesy Chrysler Corp.)

these units on their respective diagrams, and the complexity of the component determines how accurate the line drawing is. For example, Fig. 13–8 shows a line drawing of a servo. Note the detail in this illustration. This detailed drawing will make it easy for the mechanic to trouble shoot the unit if it happens to malfunction.

circuit codes

Because the hydraulic schematic incorporates all the transmission's many pressurized circuits, a mechanic would have a difficult, if not impossible time, tracing a particular circuit if the manufacturer did not code the circuits in some manner. Circuit codes are the means by which the draftsman designates one pressurized circuit from another. And the two most common codes used for this purpose are the color and the pattern types.

The color-coded diagram is one in which the manufacturer uses a given color to represent the type of pressurized-fluid flow in a particular circuit. Fig. 13–9 illustrates an example of typical color codes displayed in small boxes at the bottom of a hydraulic chart. In this particular example, blue is the color for line or control pressure; blue and white are the colors used for pump suction; converter pressure is yellow; and yellow-white are the colors utilized for the lubrication circuits.

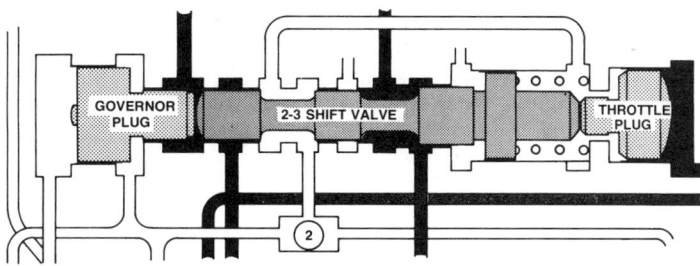

fig. 13–7 A drawing of a 2–3 shift-valve train. (Courtesy Chrysler Corp.)

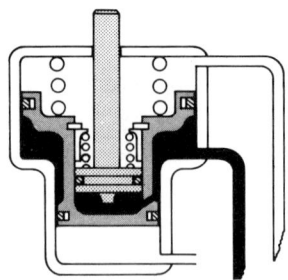

fig. 13–8 A typical drawing of a servo assembly. (Courtesy Chrysler Corp.)

Also note in Fig. 13-9 the pressure specifications next to the color-coded boxes. These specifications, when given, inform the technician of how much pressure should be in each circuit during a given phase of transmission operation represented by the schematic. For example, in this diagram of reverse-ratio, line-pressure regulation, the pressure specifications are: line 230–270 psi, converter 10–75 psi, and lubrication 5–30 psi. In many cases, these specifications are not on the diagram itself but are on tables located in another area of the service manual. Finally, the technician should use these specifications as a guide when pressure testing the transmission for circuit malfunctions.

Note that Fig. 13-9 also shows two special symbols located above the color-coded boxes. These symbols represent a circuit vent and a circuit that is not in use. Some manufacturers use the vent symbol for both, but when they do, the draftsman will print the word "vent" or "exhaust" near the symbol to differentiate the vented circuit from a circuit that is not in use.

Fig. 13–10 shows the coding section of a hydraulic chart that has the pattern method of designating the different pressures found in the various circuits. Note with this type of coding, different combinations of line or dot patterns represent control, lubrica-

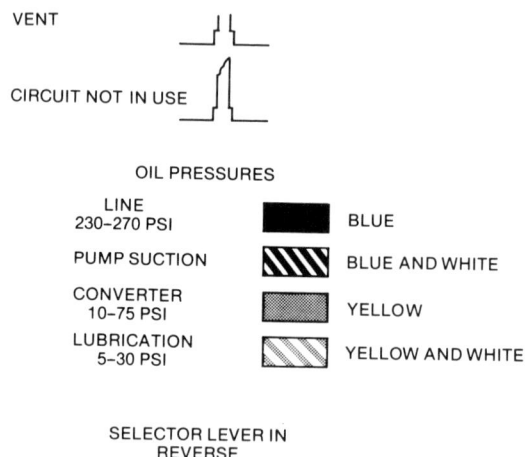

fig. 13–9 Color code chart used on a typical schematic.

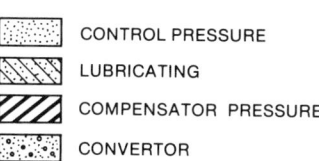

X EXHAUST

fig. 13-10 The pattern codes found on a typical hydraulic chart.

tion, compensating, and converter pressures. Also, this diagram has no pressure specifications printed next to the coded boxes.

Also, note in this illustration, the letter *X* and the word "exhaust", placed next to the symbol. The letter *X* when placed next to this symbol anywhere on this diagram, means that the port opening is an exhaust or vent for that particular circuit. Finally, referring back to Fig. 13-9, note that this diagram has a different symbol for a vented circuit. These two different symbols used in Figs. 13-9 and 13-10 are good examples of the manner in which manufacturers code their own diagrams. Therefore, it is important that the technician check for these special marks before attempting to interpret the schematic.

Finally, to make it easier for the mechanic to locate a hydraulic problem that occurs in a particular driving range, the manufacturers will usually produce a single hydraulic schematic for each operating range of the transmission. In other words, the manufacturer makes a diagram for each forward-drive range, neutral and park, in addition to reverse range. Each of these charts will only show the mechanic what is occurring in the hydraulic system during that one particular phase of operation. By excluding from the diagram the codes of circuits which are not now in use, the mechanic can more easily follow the diagram and locate the malfunctioning component.

valve definitions

In order to assist the mechanic in interpreting the hydraulic diagram of an automatic transmission, its manufacturer will usually devote a section of the transmission service manual to define the various valves used in the hydraulic system. In some manuals, the diagrams will precede these valve definitions, while in other books the definitions will precede the hydraulic schematics—a much better practice. The following valve definitions are typical of those found in an average service manual, and these definitions will assist you in understanding the schematics which are to follow:

high-pressure relief valve: A safety valve that will protect the hydraulic system from an accidental build-up of excessively high-system pressure.

pressure regulating valve: This valve regulates the pressure of the pump's output and supplies the basic fluid pressure necessary to operate the transmission.

control valve: This valve controls both the flow and pressure into and out of the torque converter.

manual valve: The driver, by means of mechanical linkage, activates this valve; the valve, in turn, sets up the operating conditions of the transmission.

governor valve: It is a balanced valve that senses vehicle speed from the transmission's output shaft; the valve then sends a hydraulic speed signal to the shift valves that control gear shifting in relation to vehicle speed.

throttle valve: This valve produces a pressure signal that is in proportion to engine speed or load; this signal acts on the shift valves to control shifting in relation to engine load or speed.

kickdown valve: A valve activated by full depression of the throttle pedal; kickdown pressure from this valve will then cause the shift valve(s) to close which downshifts the transmission.

1–2 and 2–3 shift valve trains: These valves trigger the automatic shifts, in response to governor and throttle signals, by directing pressurized fluid to the appropriate band or clutch that, in turn, causes the shift to occur.

1–2 shift control valve: This valve aids in controlling the quality of the 1–2 upshift; it also aids in the timing and quality of the various 3–2 kickdown ranges.

accumulator: The accumulator controls shift quality by absorbing the apply pressure of the rear clutch or front band.

shuttle valve train: This valve helps to control the rate of front servo apply pressure during part-to-full throttle, 2–3 upshift and a kickdown from 3–2.

limit valve: This valve prevents a part-throttle 3–2 downshift at high-vehicle speeds.

interpreting the diagrams

To be successful in interpreting a hydraulic diagram, the technician should follow several easy steps. First, locate the diagram that represents the operating phase of the transmission where the malfunction occurs. For instance, if the transmission will not upshift from first to second, in the normal drive range, the mechanic should study the drive, 1–2 upshift chart. Some manufacturers will also refer to this operating phase as the second gear *D* range. Finally, it may also be necessary for the mechanic to look at the drive, first gear circuit chart to see the position of the various valves which prepare the transmission for the automatic upshift.

Second, take note of the special symbols and codes located on the diagram itself. In Fig. 13–11, the codes which represent the various pressures, are in the form of different line or dot patterns. For example, a solid dark line represents line or control pressure. Pump suction is a series of diagonal lines; governor pressure is a series of straight lines; throttle pressure is a series of dots; 1–2 shift control pressure is a series of Xs; converter pressure is a series of wide, diagonal lines; and lubrication pressure is a series of wide, straight lines. Finally, note that this diagram has the pressure specifications for each circuit that the mechanic can use when checking the various operating pressures in the circuitry.

INTERPRETING THE DIAGRAMS **235**

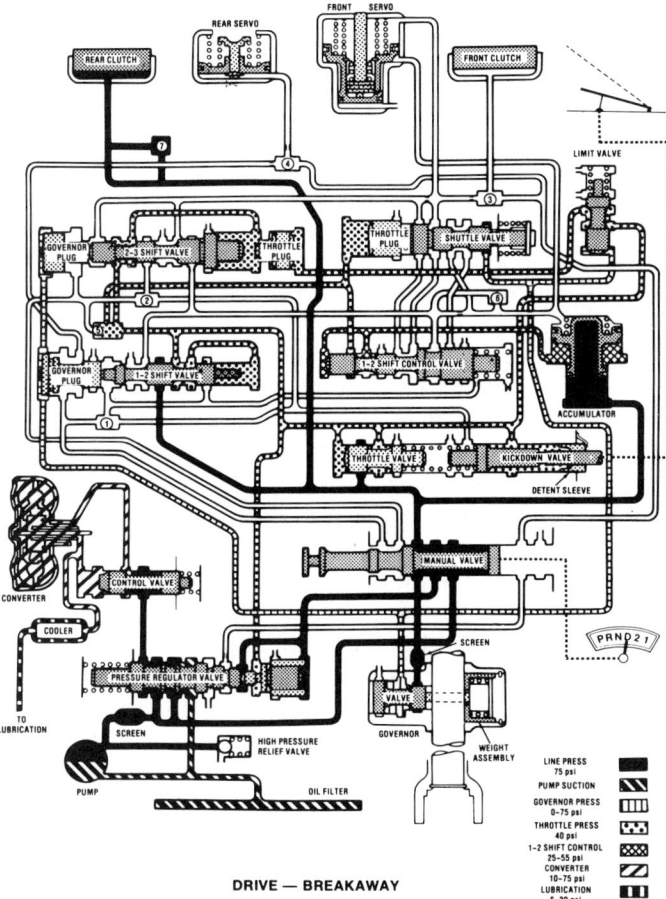

fig. 13-11 A complete drive, first-ratio hydraulic schematic. (Courtesy Chrysler Corp.)

Now that all the codes are understood, the next step is to study the chart to locate the fluid source and then follow the fluid flow through each of the various circuits. Looking at Fig. 13-11, note the diagonal lines which refer to the fluid source, beginning at the filter and moving to the suction side of the pump. As the fluid leaves the pressure side of the pump, the code changes to a solid, dark line that represents control pressure.

As the pressurized fluid leaves the pump, it takes two passages, each leading to a valve. One of these passages directs fluid pressure to the relief valve that protects the system against uncontrolled high pressure. This valve is shown in the closed position that stops any pressure leakage to the sump at this time.

The other passage leads to several ports of the pressure-regulating valve. Upon initial opening of the regulator valve, pressurized fluid from one of these ports will pass through the regulator valve and enter a circuit leading to the torque converter control valve. As the regulator valve begins to control pressure, the pressurized fluid from the other port will pass through a groove in the valve and return to the suction side of the pump.

The pressurized fluid leaving the torque-converter control valve becomes converter pressure (wide diagonal lines on the schematic). This fluid moves through the converter but maintains a sufficient level in the converter so that it can function at all times. Now as the fluid leaves the converter, it passes through an orifice and acts on the reaction area of the control valve.

The fluid pressure, acting on this reaction area, causes the valve to regulate converter pressure. If converter pressure reaches a predetermined amount, its force on the reaction area moves the control valve to the right. This action permits a land of the control valve to block the converter pressure port which results in a reduction of converter pressure.

The pressurized fluid leaving the converter also enters a circuit leading to the cooler. As this fluid enters the cooler, it becomes lubrication pressure (a series of wide, straight lines on the diagram). This fluid then passes through the cooler and enters a circuit that terminates at the transmission's lubrication system.

Looking back at the regulator valve again, note that the circuit that feeds the two ports of the regulator valve also connects to the manual valve. This circuit supplies the manual valve with the line pressure necessary to set up the operating conditions of the transmission as the driver moves the gearshift selector lever to various positions. Also, note that in this manual-valve position, line pressure enters a port that routes fluid back through a circuit to two restricted ports of the regulator-valve train.

The fluid entering the one port acts on the valve's primary reaction area; the fluid entering the other port acts on the line-pressure plug. If the combination of these fluid pressures, acting on these two areas is high enough, they will move the regulator valve against the force of the calibrated spring. This action causes a regulator-valve land to open a port to the suction side of the pump that reduces line pressure to a maximum of 75 psi.

With the manual valve in the drive position, pressurized fluid also enters a circuit leading to the governor valve. And since the vehicle is in motion, the governor valve produces governor pressure that is in proportion to vehicle speed. In other words, the governor valve produces a varying pressure of between 6 and 75 psi.

From the governor valve, governor pressure enters a branched circuit leading to four valves. The left branch carries governor pressure to both the 1–2 and 2–3 shift valves. This pressure will open the shift valves when it reaches a predetermined value. Note that in this diagram governor pressure has not opened the 1–2 shift valve against the force of its spring.

The right-hand branch carriers governor pressure to the limit valve and shuttle valve. The governor pressure acts on the bottom face of the lower, limit-valve land and attempts to move the valve against spring force. If the limit valve bottoms in its bore due to the action of governor pressure, throttle pressure is cut off to the 2–3 shift-valve throttle plug.

The governor pressure, acting on the shuttle valve's reaction area, assists the shuttle valve spring in retarding the shuttle valve's movement in its bore. With high throttle pressure acting on the throttle plug, the shuttle valve moves over to the right, compressing its spring. But as governor pressure increases with road speed, it along with the spring's force will resist the action of throttle pressure until it reaches a given value.

If the shuttle valve bottoms in its bore due to high throttle pressure, the valve opens a bypass circuit for the front-servo apply circuit. In this situation, front servo apply pressure bypasses the orifice, and the servo applies faster. If, on the other hand, throttle pressure is low, governor pressure and spring force will move the valve to the left closing the bypass circuit.

Also, with the manual valve positioned in the drive position, fluid enters circuits leading to the accumulator, rear clutch, 1-2 shift valve, and throttle valve. The pressurized fluid, acting on the accumulator circuit, causes the accumulator piston to move in its bore against spring force. At this same time, fluid pressure acts on and attempts to apply the rear clutch. But because of accumulator action, the rear clutch will not fully apply until the accumulator piston bottoms in its bore. This action, of course, cushions clutch application.

Line pressure from the manual valve also charges a circuit to the 1-2 shift valve. But since the 1-2 shift valve is now off (closed), the fluid pressure deadends at the valve. In other words, a land of the 1-2 shift valve blocks line pressure at this point thus preventing the pressure from charging the second-gear circuit.

Finally, an open port at the manual valve charges a circuit to the throttle valve with line pressure. Remember, that the throttle valve produces a pressure signal from this line pressure that is in proportion to engine speed or load. And a circuit from the throttle valve carries this signal to the spring end of both the 1-2 and 2-3 shift valves where it assists the valve spring in controlling the shift points by resisting shift-valve opening. Lastly, as previously mentioned, throttle pressure also goes to the shuttle valve and 1-2 shift control valve trains.

Now, look at the diagram of drive-second, Fig. 13-12, and note what has occurred in the hydraulic system to cause the upshift from low to second. Governor pressure, acting on the 1-2 governor plug, has moved the 1-2 shift valve train to the open position against the effects of throttle pressure and spring force. This valve movement blocks throttle pressure to the spring end of the 1-2 shift valve and opens a circuit through the shift valve to apply the front servo.

The servo-apply pressure, leaving the 1-2 shift valve, performs several functions. First, it charges a circuit leading to the 2-3 shift valve. The fluid in this circuit deadends at the 2-3 shift valve because the valve is now in the closed position, but when the valve opens, this pressure will upshift the transmission into third ratio.

Second, the open 1-2 shift valve supplies pressure and flow to a circuit leading to the accumulator and front servo. The fluid under pressure first passes through an orifice before reaching the accumulator; the orifice slows accumulator and servo operation. The pressurized fluid then enters the accumulator to assist the spring in pushing the piston down against the line pressure below the piston. At this same time, pressurized fluid will begin to move the servo piston in its bore; but the servo will not tighten the band firmly around the drum until the accumulator piston bottoms in its bore. In other words, the action of the accumulator cushions band application.

Also to assist in cushioning band application even more, the 1-2 shift control valve

238 HYDRAULIC SYSTEM DIAGRAMS–THEIR FUNCTION

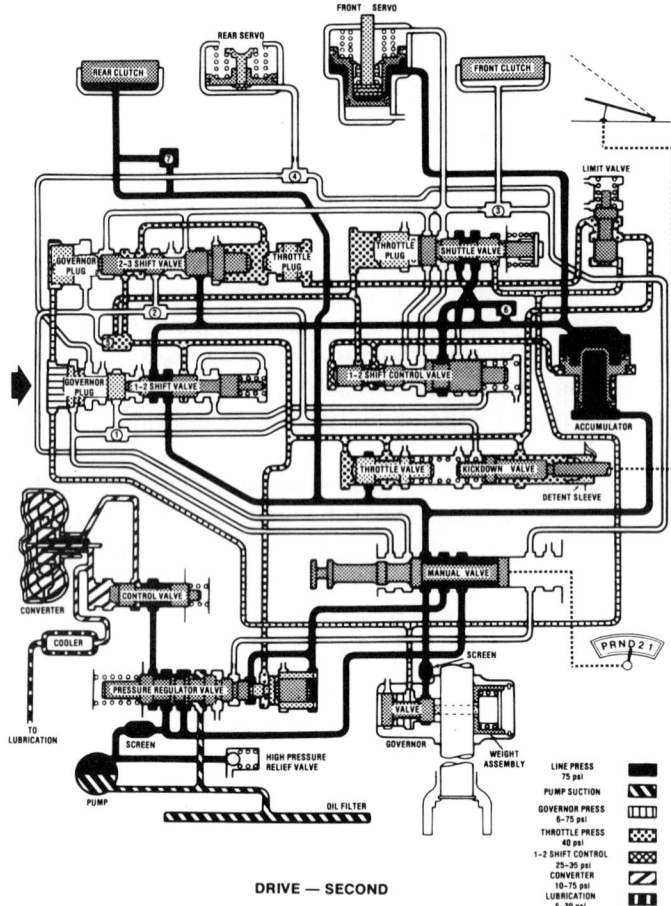

fig. 13-12 A complete drive, second-ratio hydraulic schematic. (Courtesy Chrysler Corp.)

supplies 1-2 shift control or a modulated throttle pressure to the middle land of the accumulator piston. This pressure controls the kickdown servo apply pressure necessary to activate the kickdown and accumulator pistons during the 1-2 upshift. Therefore, the 1-2 shift control valve improves the quality of the 1-2 upshift or cushions the band application.

trouble-shooting malfunctions using hydraulic diagrams

Hydraulic schematics can be of practical assistance to a mechanic in trouble-shooting a malfunctioning transmission. For example, if the unit will not automatically upshift from first to second, the first thing the mechanic should try to determine from the diagram(s) is what valve(s) the hydraulic system utilizes to upshift the transmission. In Fig. 13-12, the diagram indicates the valve train that actually upshifts the transmission is the 1-2 shift valve. This valve, when opened, directs pressure to the front servo that applies the band.

The next thing to consider is the forces the hydraulic system uses to control this valve's operation. In the case of the 1-2 shift valve, governor pressure opens the valve in opposition to the valve's spring and throttle pressure. In other words, the governor pressure *must* be high enough to overcome the tension of the spring and throttle pressure or the 1-2 shift valve will not open.

Consequently, one of the possible problems that may cause the transmission to not automatically upshift from first to second is a malfunctioning governor. Referring back to the diagram in Fig. 13-12, note that the governor in this transmission has a screen in its inlet circuit. If this screen becomes clogged, the governor will not receive control pressure from the manual valve; and as a result, it will malfunction and not produce governor pressure. Of course, the governor would also malfunction if its valve or weight assembly sticks in its bore in the governor housing. Finally, to determine if the governor is at fault, always refer to the procedure outlined in the transmission service manual for testing governor operation. This procedure will vary from one type of transmission to another.

A second possible reason why the shift valve will not open is high throttle pressure. Excessively high throttle pressure may be the result of, in the case of the mechanically operated unit, linkage that is out of adjustment or the throttle valve is stuck. If, on the other hand, the transmission has a vacuum-operated unit, the cause may be a ruptured diaphragm, vacuum leak, or a stuck valve. But no matter what the cause, high throttle pressure assists the shift valve spring in preventing governor pressure from opening the shift valve. Finally, to test and or adjust the throttle valve, always refer to the service manual for the correct procedure to follow. These procedures also differ from one transmission to another.

If both the governor and throttle valves are functioning according to specifications but the transmission will not upshift, the shift valve may be stuck in its bore. In this situation, governor pressure will not be able to open it, and the servo apply circuit will not receive pressurized fluid. Before tearing down the valve body to check for a jammed 1-2 shift valve, always check the service manual first to determine if it is possible to test for servo apply pressure. If a test is possible, always check servo apply pressure first because if the pressure is normal but the transmission still will not upshift, the problem is *not* in the shift valve train at all.

For example, if the servo receives apply pressure but the transmission still will not upshift, the band itself may be out of adjustment or worn out. In this case, the hydraulic system is doing its job, but the band is just not holding. And since the band does not hold the planetary, gear-train member necessary for second-gear operation, the planetary-gear train remains in first ratio.

These hydraulic diagrams can save the technician a great deal of time and effort in trying to determine transmission malfunctions. If the mechanic takes a few moments to consider what is taking place in the hydraulic system during the time the malfunction occurs and then performs whatever tests are necessary to verify component operation, he will be able to pinpoint the problem in the transmission and not waste time guessing or using the trial and error method of trouble-shooting.

summary

1. For the purpose of trouble-shooting a malfunctioning automatic transmission, the hydraulic-system diagram is a very useful tool because it provides the repairman with a great deal of useful information.
2. If the schematic were to be a scale drawing as to the length and direction of each circuit the diagram would be quite large and more difficult to interpret.
3. The hydraulic-system chart contains the pump circuit, all the valve circuits, the torque converter, and all the hydraulically operated units.
4. Before a technician can interpret a hydraulic diagram, he must understand the symbols used on that particular schematic.
5. The standard symbols, used extensively by the industry, are those which represent the circuit and the orifice.
6. There is not a standard symbol for any valve in the hydraulic system; instead, each manufacturer uses a drawing of the valve itself.
7. There are also no standard symbols for the hydraulic pump, torque converter, and the hydraulically operated units.
8. Because the hydraulic schematic incorporates all the pressurized circuits of the transmission, a mechanic would have a hard time tracing a particular circuit if the manufacturer did not code the circuits in some manner.
9. The color-coded diagram is one in which the manufacturer uses a given color to represent the type of pressurized-fluid flow in a particular circuit.
10. The pattern-coded diagram is one in which the manufacturer uses different combinations of line and dot patterns to represent the type of pressurized-fluid flow in a given circuit.
11. In order to assist the mechanic in interpreting the hydraulic diagram of an automatic transmission, its manufacturer will usually devote a section of the service manual to define the various valves used in the hydraulic system.
12. The first thing a mechanic should do when using a diagram to troubleshoot a problem is locate the chart that covers the operating phase of the transmission where the malfunction occurs.
13. When interpreting a schematic, the mechanic should take note of the special symbols and codes located on the drawing.
14. With all the codes understood, the next step in mastering the schematic is to locate the fluid source and then follow the fluid flow through each of the various circuits.
15. The first thing the mechanic should do when using the diagram to troubleshoot a transmission malfunction is to determine from the chart which valves are necessary to operate the unit during the phase of operation where the trouble occurs.
16. The next step is to test, if at all possible, each valve and circuit, one at a time, to determine exactly where the problem originates.

17. Hydraulic diagrams can save the technician a great deal of time and effort in locating transmission malfunctions.

check-up questions

The questions listed below will assist you in determining how well you remember the material contained in this chapter. Read each question carefully before choosing the answer to each item. If you cannot answer a question, review the material in the section of the chapter that covers the question.

1. The portion of the hydraulic schematic which is not drawn to scale is the _____.
    a. valves
    b. orifices
    c. circuits
    d. codes

2. The hydraulic charts usually show the _____ valve in its part-open position.
    a. regulator
    b. shift
    c. accumulator
    d. manual

3. The standard symbols on hydraulic charts are those representing the _____ and the _____.
    a. valve, circuit
    b. orifice, circuit
    c. orifice, mechanically operated unit
    d. mechanically operated unit, torque converter

4. Two parallel lines represent the _____.
    a. circuit
    b. orifice
    c. valve
    d. torque converter

5. To assist the mechanic in following a given circuit on the schematic, the circuits have special _____.
    a. symbols
    b. valves
    c. marks
    d. codes

242 HYDRAULIC SYSTEM DIAGRAMS–THEIR FUNCTION

6. Usually a section of the service manual will contain _____ which will help the mechanic interpret the hydraulic chart.
   a. valve definitions
   b. an index
   c. pressure specifications
   d. only one chart

7. When studying a schematic, first locate the fluid _____.
   a. valve
   b. source
   c. regulator
   d. type

8. If the transmission will not upshift from first to second, check the chart for the _____ that upshifts the unit.
   a. band
   b. clutch
   c. valve
   d. both a and b

9. Before disassembling a valve body for a stuck valve, check the service manual to see if a _____ should be performed to verify the valve's condition.
   a. special inspection
   b. test
   c. alignment
   d. both a and c

10. If the hydraulic system checks out according to factory specifications but still malfunctions, the problem is most likely _____.
    a. a defective clutch
    b. a defective band
    c. a defective governor
    d. either a or b

For the answers to these check-up questions, turn to the Appendix located at the back of the text.

14

operation of the transmission

Up to this point, this text has covered the design and operation of the many individual components of an automatic transmission. The time has now come to put all this information together and see how all the components operate simultaneously to produce the various ratios of a two- and three-speed automatic transmission. The two transmissions whose operation this chapter will cover with the General Motors T-300 and the Chrysler Torqueflite. To make it easier for the reader to follow the operation of these units, this section will first present a brief description of each transmission and then cover its operation.

description of a T-300 transmission

The T-300 automatic transmission (Fig. 14-1) is a unit that has a three-member torque converter combined with a two-speed compound planetary gear train. To operate the compound-planetary gear train, the transmission utilizes a forward and reverse clutch in addition to a low band. The gearshift selector positions for this unit are: park (P), neutral (N), drive (D), low (L), and reverse (R).

244 OPERATION OF THE TRANSMISSION

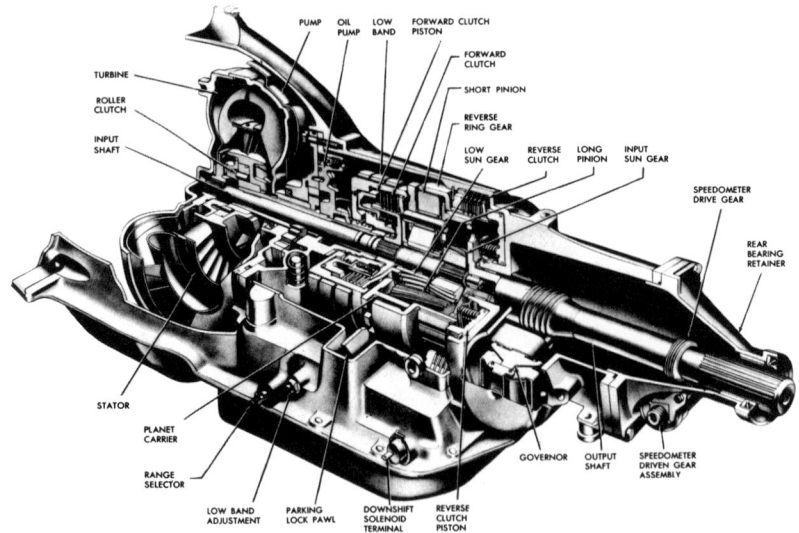

fig. 14-1 A T-300 Automatic Transmission. (Courtesy Buick Division of General Motors)

converter

The T-300 torque converter attaches to the engine's crankshaft and serves as a hydraulic coupling that connects engine torque to the input shaft of the transmission. The converter will multiply engine torque whenever vehicle operating conditions demand greater torque than the engine alone can produce. In addition, at normal road load conditions and at higher speeds, the converter acts as an efficient fluid coupling.

The converter has three main components, the pump, turbine, and variable or fixed stator. The converter's pump attaches to and rotates with the engine-driven converter housing. The rotating pump (impeller) functions as a centrifugal pump, picking up fluid at its center and discharging the fluid at its curved rim. As a result, the pump discharges fluid into the converter's turbine.

The converter's turbine splines to and drives the transmission's input shaft. The function of the turbine is to absorb the energy from the fluid supplied to it by the pump and convert it to rotary motion. In other words, the turbine converts fluid energy into torque and transmits this torque to the input shaft.

The stator, whether it be variable or fixed-blade design, fits between the turbine and pump; it mounts and operates on an overrunning clutch. The function of the stator blades, when the overrunning clutch locks the stator assembly to the case, is to redirect the fluid flow from the turbine to the pump during the torque multiplication phase of the converter. During the coupling phase of converter operation, the overrunning clutch permits the stator assembly to freewheel so that its blades will not interfere with the flow of fluid between the turbine and pump (impeller).

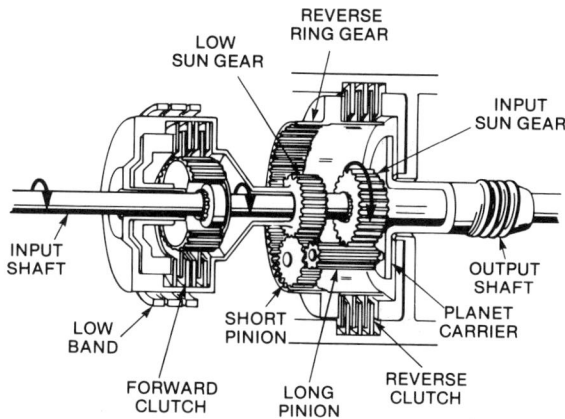

fig. 14-2 The planetary gear train of a T-300 transmission.

planetary gear train

The compound-planetary gear train of the T-300 transmission consists of an input sun gear, long and short pinions which attach to a common carrier, low sun gear, and a reverse ring gear (Fig. 14-2). The input shaft splines to and drives the input sun gear in a clockwise direction. The input sun gear meshes with the three long pinions and drives these pinions counterclockwise.

The short pinions are in mesh with the long pinions, the low sun gear, and the reverse ring gear. The long pinions, when rotating, drive these short pinions clockwise. If the low sun gear is free to revolve, the short pinions will turn it counterclockwise. Finally, the short pinions will also spin the reverse ring gear in a clockwise direction if the ring gear is free to rotate.

Holding of either the low sun gear or reverse ring gear determines whether the carrier and output shaft turn in a forward or backward direction. For instance, if the low sun gear is stationary, with the input sun gear rotating, the short pinions walk the carrier around the held low sun gear in a clockwise direction. Whereas, when the reverse ring gear is stationary, with the low sun gear driving, the short pinions walk the carrier around the held ring gear in a backwards direction.

Finally, if the input shaft drives both the input and low sun gear, the planetary gear train is in direct drive. The planetary gear train locks up or rotates as a solid unit because the long and short pinions cannot rotate in opposite directions as they normally do. As a result, the input shaft and carrier turn at the same speed.

forward clutch

The forward clutch is a multiple-disc, wet-type clutch applied in direct drive (Fig. 14-3). When the hydraulic system activates this clutch, it connects the low sun gear to the input shaft. As a result, the sun gear revolves at input shaft speed.

246 OPERATION OF THE TRANSMISSION

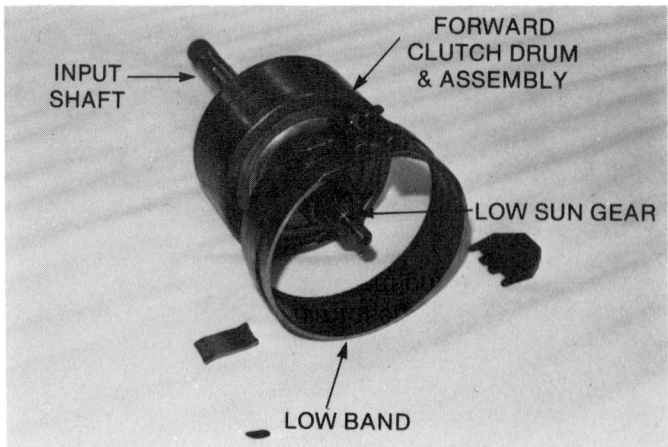

fig. 14-3 The forward clutch and low band of the T-300 transmission.

low band

The hydraulic system applies the low band in low ratio (Fig. 14-3). The band itself surrounds the forward clutch drum. And when the servo applies the band, it stops any rotation of the drum. Consequently, the low sun gear, attached to the forward clutch drum, stops turning. In other words, the low band locks the sun gear to the transmission case.

reverse clutch

This transmission utilizes a multiple-disc, wet-type clutch to reverse the direction of the carrier and output shaft (Fig. 14-4). This stationary type clutch has components which fit inside the back section of the transmission case, and when the hydraulic system directs pressurized fluid to the reverse-clutch piston, it, in turn, locks all the clutch plates together. And because the reverse-ring gear splines to the friction plates, the ring gear stops turning or is stationary. This action, as previously mentioned, will reverse the direction of the carrier and output shaft.

function of hydraulic system components

hydraulic pump: A positive-displacement, gear-type pump supplies pressurized fluid to fill the converter, engage the forward and reverse clutches, apply and release the low band, and feed the lubrication system (Fig. 14-5).

pressure regulating valve: This valve adjusts control (line) pressure to meet the demands placed on the hydraulic system. But at the same time, this valve regulates pressure so that it does not exceed a safe operating limit.

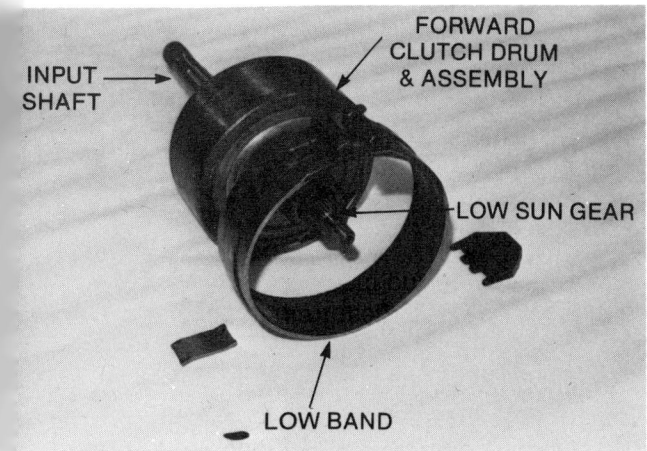

The forward clutch and low band of the T-300 transmission.

...ulic system applies the low band in low ratio (Fig. 14–3). The band itself ... the forward clutch drum. And when the servo applies the band, it stops any ... the drum. Consequently, the low sun gear, attached to the forward clutch ... turning. In other words, the low band locks the sun gear to the transmission

clutch

...smission utilizes a multiple-disc, wet-type clutch to reverse the direction of the ...d output shaft (Fig. 14–4). This stationary type clutch has components which fit ... back section of the transmission case, and when the hydraulic system directs ...ed fluid to the reverse-clutch piston, it, in turn, locks all the clutch plates to-...nd because the reverse-ring gear splines to the friction plates, the ring gear ...ning or is stationary. This action, as previously mentioned, will reverse the ... of the carrier and output shaft.

...n of hydraulic system components

...raulic pump: A positive-displacement, gear-type pump supplies pressurized fluid to fill the converter, engage the forward and reverse clutches, apply and release the low band, and feed the lubrication system (Fig. 14–5).

...ssure regulating valve: This valve adjusts control (line) pressure to meet the demands placed on the hydraulic system. But at the same time, this valve regulates pressure so that it does not exceed a safe operating limit.

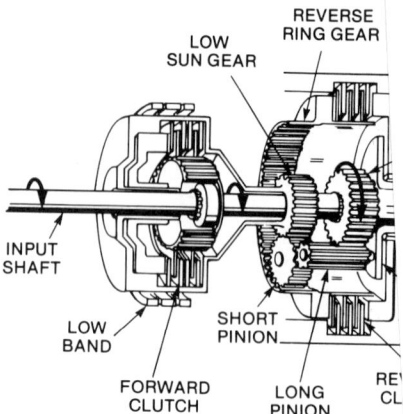

fig. 14-2 The planetary gear train of a T

planetary gear train

The compound-planetary gear train of the T-300 trans gear, long and short pinions which attach to a comm reverse ring gear (Fig. 14-2). The input shaft splines to a clockwise direction. The input sun gear meshes with th these pinions counterclockwise.

The short pinions are in mesh with the long pini reverse ring gear. The long pinions, when rotating, drive the low sun gear is free to revolve, the short pinions will the short pinions will also spin the reverse ring gear in gear is free to rotate.

Holding of either the low sun gear or reverse ring carrier and output shaft turn in a forward or backward di sun gear is stationary, with the input sun gear rotating, th around the held low sun gear in a clockwise direction. W gear is stationary, with the low sun gear driving, the short the held ring gear in a backwards direction.

Finally, if the input shaft drives both the input and lo train is in direct drive. The planetary gear train locks up or the long and short pinions cannot rotate in opposite direct result, the input shaft and carrier turn at the same speed

forward clutch

The forward clutch is a multiple-disc, wet-type clutch appl When the hydraulic system activates this clutch, it connect shaft. As a result, the sun gear revolves at input shaft sp

FUNCTION OF HYDRAULIC SYSTEM COMPONENTS **247**

fig. 14–4 The reverse clutch of the T-300 transmission.

manual-shift control valve: Mechanical linkage connects this valve to the gearshift control lever. When the driver moves the gearshift control lever, the manual-shift control valve routes pressurized fluid to the devices which govern the operation of the transmission.

governor: The governor produces a pressure signal that is in proportion to vehicle speed. This signal, when high enough, moves the shift valve to the open position against spring tension.

shift and shift control valves: These valves operate together in the same bore within the valve body. These valves interpret fluid pressures from the governor and vacuum modulator valves; and at the proper time, the valves move and cause an automatic upshift from low to direct drive or from direct drive back to low.

vacuum modulator and valve: The vacuum modulator and valve assembly is a device that produces a pressure signal (modulator pressure) that is in proportion to the engine's load. A bellows, built into the diaphragm assembly, lowers this modulator pressure at altitudes above sea level. Modulator pressure acts against the pressure-regulator boost valve to increase hydraulic pressure under high torque conditions, and it also acts on the spring end of the shift-control valve to match the upshift point to engine-load conditions.

modulator limit valve: The modulator limit valve is a pressure regulator type valve that controls the point at which a wide-open throttle upshift will occur.

detent valve: A solenoid operates this two-position valve to provide a wide-open throttle downshift if the vehicle's speed is low enough.

high-speed downshift timing valve: This valve, located in the valve body, controls the rate of low-servo application at high vehicle speeds.

248 OPERATION OF THE TRANSMISSION

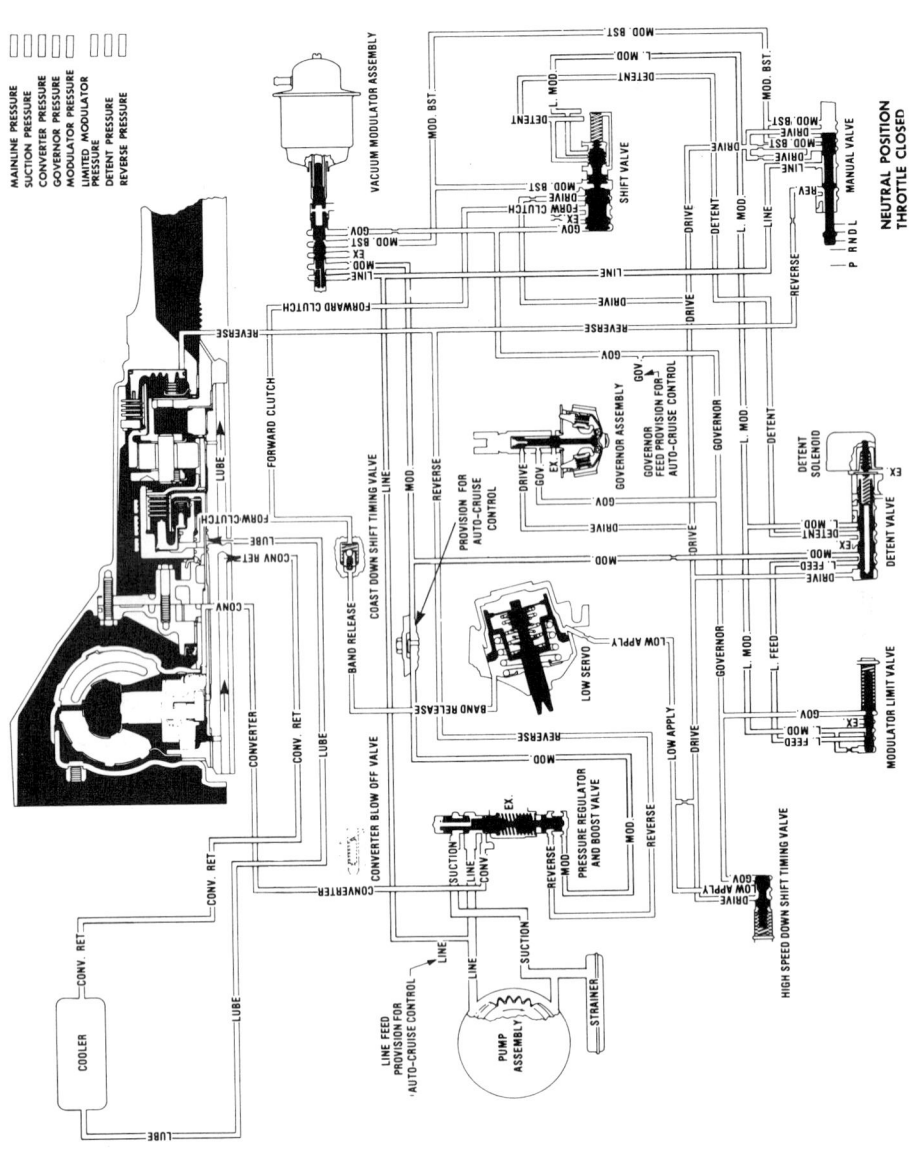

fig. 14-5 A T-300 hydraulic schematic showing all system components. (Courtesy Buick Division of General Motors)

FUNCTION OF HYDRAULIC SYSTEM 249

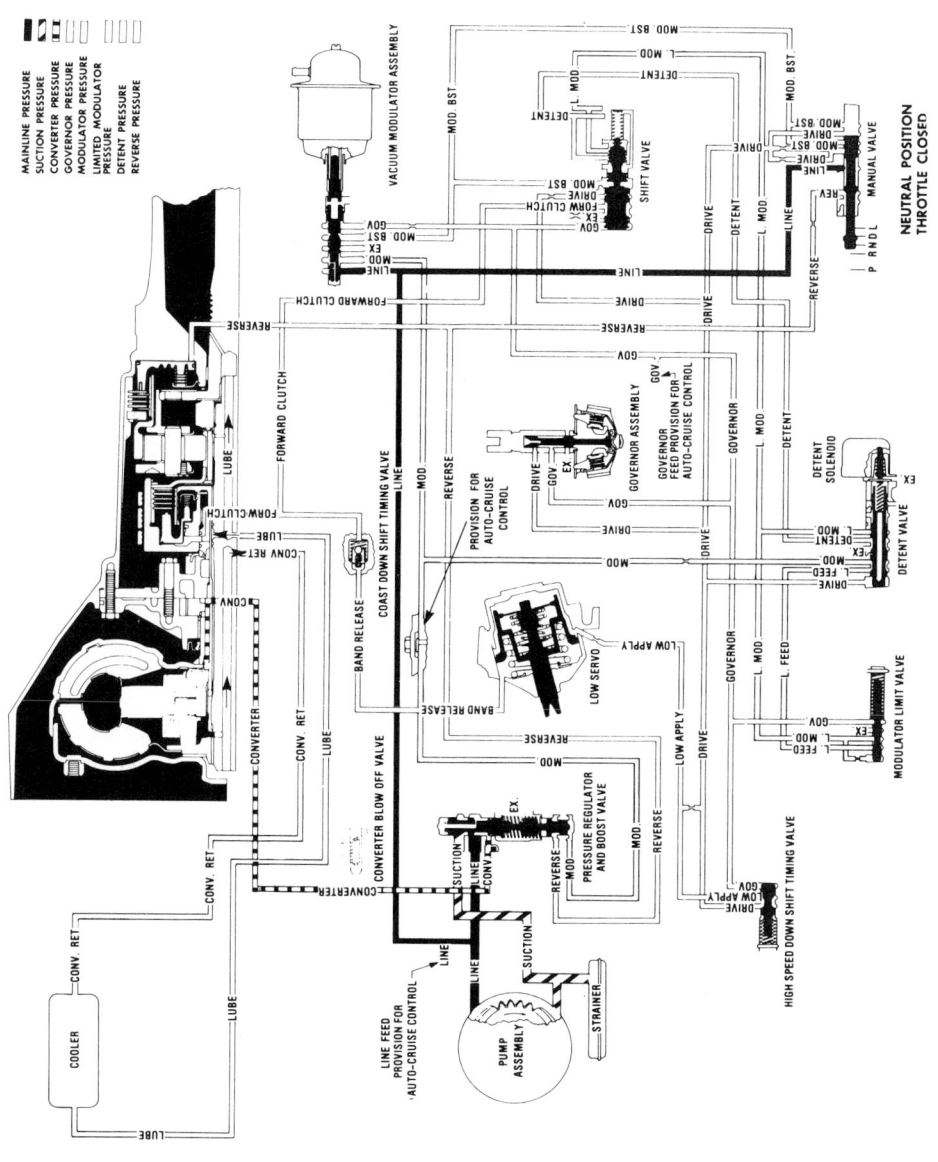

fig. 14-6 A T-300 hydraulic schematic with the manual valve in neutral or park. (Courtesy Buick Division of General Motors)

coast, downshift timing valve: This valve cushions the initial engagement of the low band whenever the vehicle coasts down to a speed low enough to permit the transmission to automatically downshift.

stator control valve (when used): The function of this valve is to control the high or low angle position of the variable stator blades. Spring tension and the action of an electrical solenoid control the operation of this valve.

T-300 operation

neutral or park—hydraulic operation

Fig. 14–6 illustrates the condition of the hydraulic system with the engine running at an idle rpm and the gearshift selector lever in neutral or park. When the driver first starts the engine, pressurized fluid enters the main pressure regulator valve assembly between the first and second lands; it then flows through interconnecting drilled holes in the valve to the end of land three, the primary reaction area. This pressurized fluid moves the valve against spring tension to open the port that directs fluid to the converter, fluid cooler, and finally to the lubrication system of the transmission.

As system pressure increases, the pressurized fluid, acting on the pressure-regulator's primary reaction area, continues to move the valve against spring force. This further movement of the regulating valve opens a port that allows mainline pressure to vent to the suction side of the pump. The opening of this sump port regulates system pressure to a predetermined amount. Finally, with the engine idling, the vacuum-modulator valve circuit has no effect on the regulator valve. Consequently, system pressure stabilizes at the amount determined by the regulator spring.

From the regulator valve, pressurized fluid enters a circuit leading to the modulator valve and manual valve. Because the engine at this time is producing high vacuum, the modulator valve cycles to a position that blocks control pressure to the modulator circuit. The manual valve is also now in a position that blocks control pressure to all hydraulically operated units. As a result, the planetary gear train will not transmit torque or is in neutral.

neutral or park—powerflow

With the gearshift-selector lever in neutral position, the output shaft receives no driving torque but is free to revolve. Both of the clutches and the low band are off, in the released position (Fig. 14–7). Consequently, there is no holding planetary member, and as the input sun gear revolves with the turbine and input shaft, all the planet pinions are free to spin around their own axis. The end result is that the planet carrier and output shaft will not revolve because there is no holding member.

DRIVE, LOW-RANGE–HYDRAULIC OPERATION 251

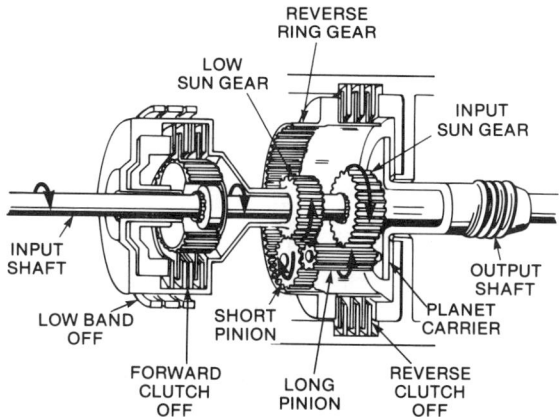

fig. 14–7 The powerflow of a T-300 transmission in neutral or park.

With one exception, the powerflow in park is the same as it is in neutral. In the park selector position, a parking pawl engages with the heavy teeth spaced around the front face of the planetary carrier. This action locks the carrier and output shaft to the transmission case, so the vehicle cannot roll down a grade.

drive, low-range—hydraulic operation

Fig. 14–8 shows the condition of the hydraulic system with the engine running at idle speed and the gearshift-selector lever in the drive position. At this time, line pressure remains the same as it was in neutral and park. In addition, line pressure, from the regulator valve, passes through the manual valve and charges the circuits to the governor valve, detent valve, high-speed downshift timing valve, shift valve, and low servo. The hydraulic pressure on the low-servo piston moves the piston in its bore so that it applies the band around the forward clutch drum.

As the driver accelerates the engine to set the vehicle in motion, line pressure increases due to the action of the modulator valve. Control pressure, directed to the modulator valve, enters the port between the first and second valve lands. And since engine vacuum drops during acceleration, the vacuum-modulator diaphragm spring now tends to keep the valve toward the bottom of its bore. In this valve position, pressurized fluid moves through a drilled passage in the valve to the space between its reaction area on the end of land one and the bottom of the bore.

Fluid pressure on the primary reaction area tends to move the valve against the force of its spring. This action regulates the amount of modulator pressure leaving the valve. The regulated modulator pressure leaving the valve goes to the regulator boost valve, shift control valve, modulator limit valve, and detent valve.

Modulator pressure now applies a force to the first land of the boost valve and causes it to move in its bore. As the boost valve moves, it contacts the pressure

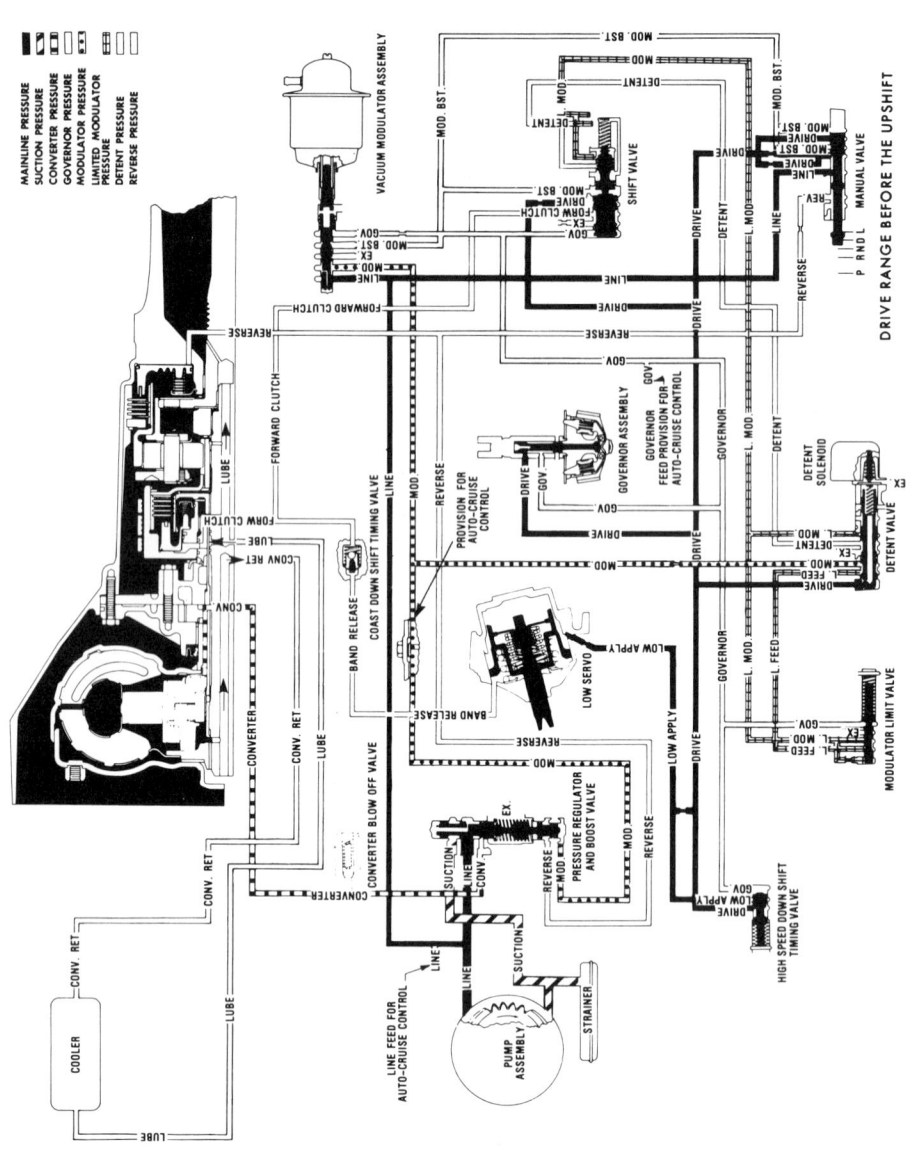

fig. 14-8 A T-300 hydraulic schematic with the manual valve in drive range. (Courtesy Buick Division of General Motors)

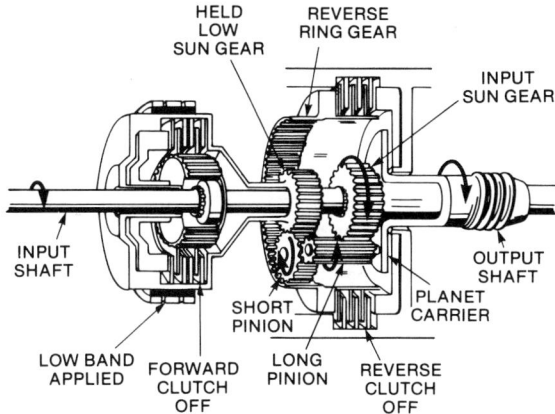

fig. 14-9 The powerflow of a T-300 transmission in drive, first ratio.

regulator valve and causes it to move also. The action of the boost valve combined with normal spring tension of the pressure-regulator valve results in an increase in control pressure as the vehicle accelerates.

drive, low-range—powerflow

With the gearshift-selector lever in drive, the transmission starts the vehicle moving in low reduction as the driver presses down on the accelerator pedal (Fig. 14-9). The forward clutch is now off, and the servo applies the low band around the outside diameter of the foward-clutch drum that holds the low sun gear stationary.

With the low sun gear held stationary and the input shaft driving the input sun gear clockwise, the long planet pinions rotate counterclockwise. Now, the long pinions force the short pinions to turn clockwise. The short pinions then walk the planet carrier and output shaft around the low sun gear in a clockwise direction but at a slower speed than the input sun gear is turning.

drive, direct—drive hydraulic operation

Fig. 14-10 illustrates the condition of the hydraulic system as the transmission automatically upshifts from low to direct drive. The actual upshift cycle to direct drive is dependent upon vehicle speed and throttle opening. But when the upshift does occur, the low band releases and the forward clutch applies.

Now, referring back to Fig. 14-8, note that the shift and shift-control valves are in the closed position. During this period of operation, spring tension and the low modulator pressure exerted on the end of the shift control valve holds the shift valve in the closed position. With the shift valve in this position, pressurized fluid cannot reach the high clutch or the spring side of the low-servo piston.

254 OPERATION OF THE TRANSMISSION

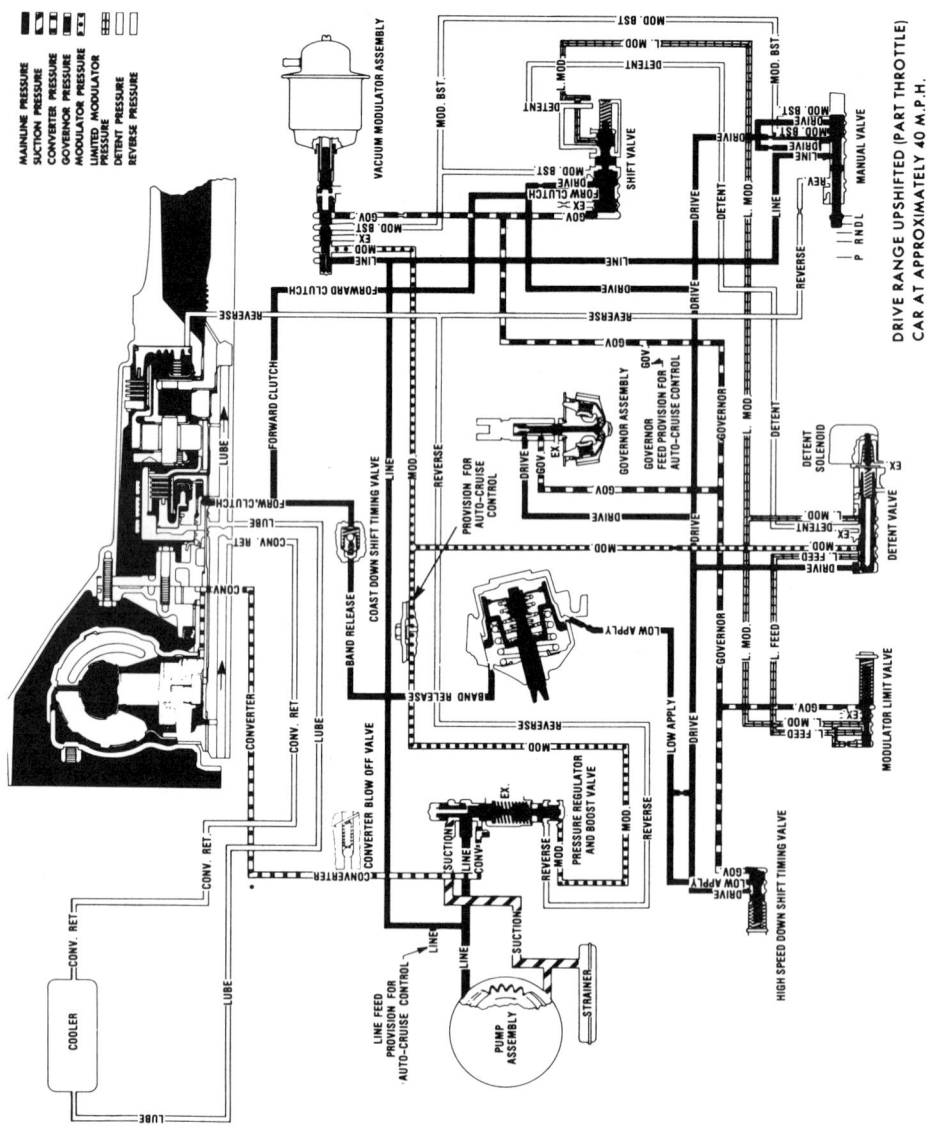

fig. 14-10 A T-300 hydraulic schematic with the transmission upshifted into direct drive. (Courtesy Buick Division of General Motors)

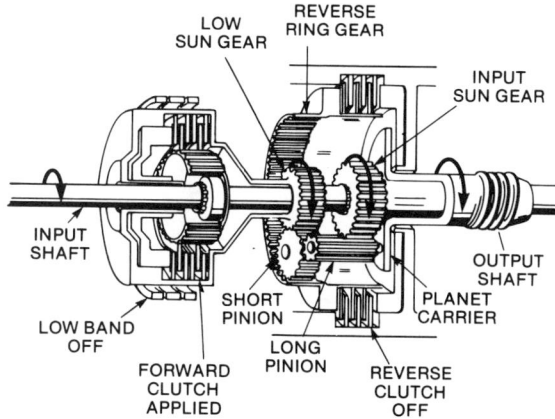

fig. 14-11 The powerflow of a T-300 transmission in direct drive.

When the correct relationship between vehicle speed and throttle opening occurs, governor pressure, acting against the first land of the shift valve, overcomes spring tension and the force of regulated modulator pressure against the shift-control valve and moves both valves to the right (Fig. 14-10). With the valves in this position, fluid under system pressure moves to apply the forward clutch piston and release the low-servo piston. Finally, to assure a positive engagement of the clutch and release of the band, line pressure has increased due to the action of modulator pressure on the regulator's boost valve; but line pressure will decrease once again as engine rpm stabilizes after the upshift occurs.

drive, direct—powerflow

When the transmission upshifts to direct drive (Fig. 14-11) the input shaft drives both the input and low sun gear in a clockwise direction. The forward clutch connects the low sun gear to the input shaft during this ratio. Now, since the sun gears try to spin the long and short pinions in the same direction, the pinions lock up and the entire gear train rotates as a solid unit. In other words, the input and output shafts turn at the same speed.

reverse ratio—hydraulic operation

Fig. 14-12 illustrates the action within the hydraulic system when the driver moves the gearshift-selector lever into reverse. Pressurized fluid from the manual valve moves through a circuit to apply the reverse clutch. At the same time, control pressure also enters a port between lands one and two of the regulator's boost valve.

This control pressure applies a force to the second land of the boost valve causing it to move in its bore. As the boost valve moves, it contacts the pressure regulator valve. This movement of the boost valve, along with spring force, raises control pressure to meet the pressure demands of reverse operation.

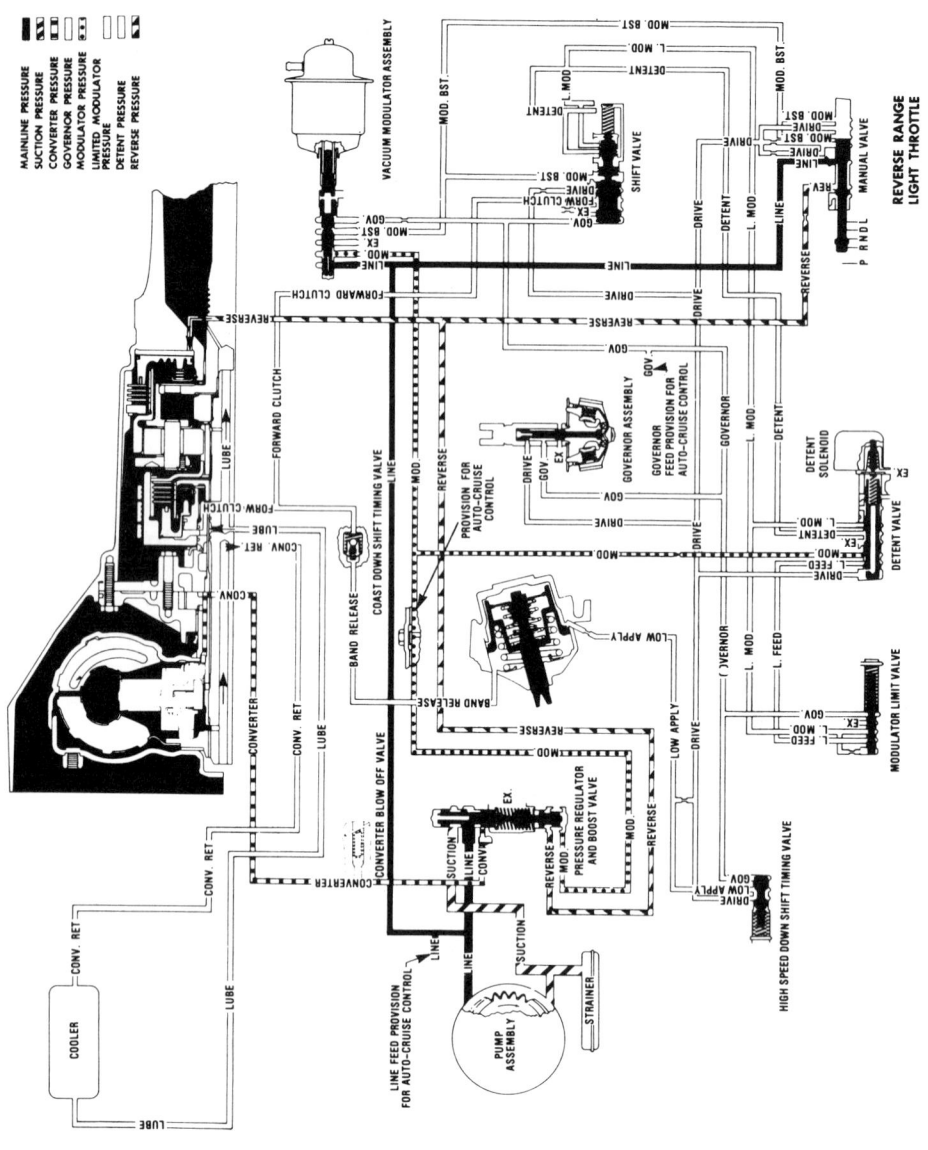

fig. 14–12 A T-300 hydraulic schematic with the manual valve in the reverse position. (Courtesy Buick Division of General Motors)

DESCRIPTION OF THE TORQUEFLITE TRANSMISSION 257

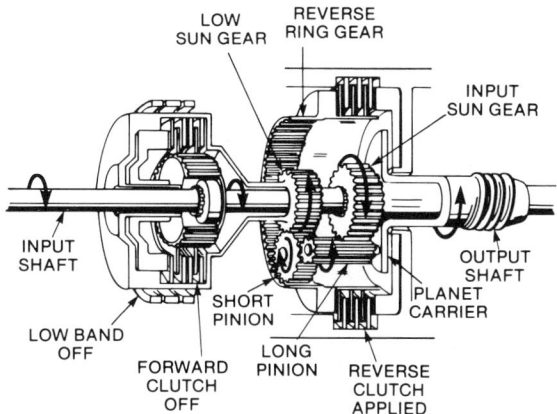

fig. 14-13 The powerflow of a T-300 transmission in reverse.

As the driver accelerates the engine, control pressure increases even higher due to the action of the modulator valve. When engine vacuum drops during acceleration, the vacuum modulator tends to keep the modulator valve toward the bottom of its bore. In this valve position, pressurized fluid passes through a drilled passage in the valve to the area between land one and the base of the bore. This fluid pressure, acting on land one, moves the valve against the force of its spring to regulate modulator pressure to a higher value before it leaves the valve.

Now, this increased pressure passes through a circuit to the boost valve. The pressure acts on land one of the boost valves causing the valve to move up. As a result, modulator pressure on land one and reverse apply pressure on land two combine with regulator-valve spring force to increase control pressure for reverse operation.

reverse ratio—powerflow

During the reverse gear ratio, the input shaft drives the input sun gear clockwise; and the reverse clutch holds the reverse ring gear stationary (Fig. 14-13). Since the input sun gear spins clockwise, it drives the long pinions counterclockwise. The long pinions, in turn, rotate the short pinions clockwise. And because the ring gear is stationary, the short pinions walk around inside the ring gear pulling the planet carrier and output shaft with them. This action imparts a reverse motion to the output shaft and a reduction in speed between the input and output shafts.

description of the torqueflite transmission

The Chrysler Torqueflite transmission (Fig. 14-14), is a unit that combines a three-member torque converter with a Simpson design three-speed planetary gear train. Also, to operate the Simpson gear train, the transmission utilizes two multiple disc clutches,

258 OPERATION OF THE TRANSMISSION

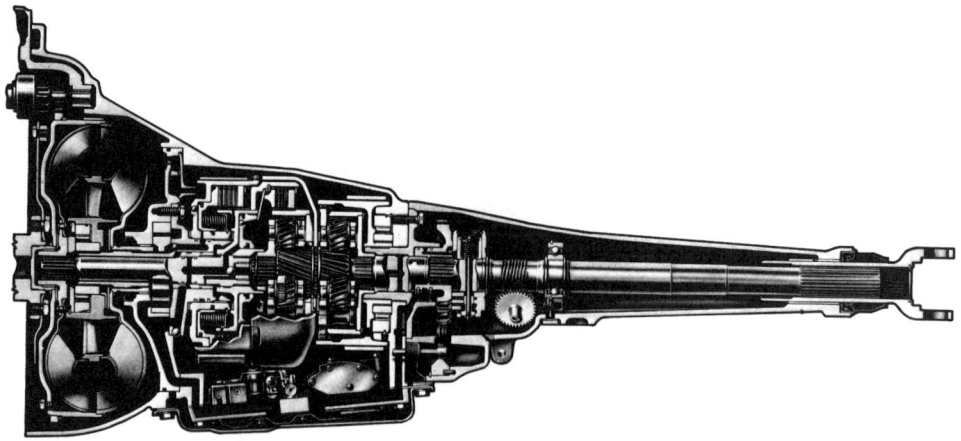

fig. 14-14 The Chrysler Torqueflite Transmission. (Courtesy Chrysler Corp.)

an overrunning clutch, and two servo-operated bands. And finally, the gearshift-selector positions for this transmission are: park (P), neutral (N), drive (D), manual second (2), and manual low (1).

converter

The Torqueflite converter also attaches to the engine crankshaft through a flexible driving plate and serves as a hydraulic coupling that connects engine torque to the input shaft of the transmission. This three-member converter operates in much the same manner as the T-300 converter to multiply engine torque when vehicle operating conditions demand greater torque than the engine can produce, but this unit utilizes fixed stator blades. Furthermore, this converter also acts as an efficient fluid coupling at normal road load conditions and at high speeds. Lastly, some Torqueflite transmissions now utilize a lock-up, three-member converter. In this particular converter, the turbine operates at impeller speed during the coupling phase of converter operation.

planetary gear train

The Torqueflite planetary gear train consists of two simple planetary gearsets connected together by a common sun gear (Fig. 14-15). The front unit consists of an annulus (ring) gear and carrier. The rear clutch assembly, when activated, connects the front unit annulus to the input shaft. Therefore, the annulus gear is the driving member of the front planetary gearset. The front carrier is the output member of the front gear set because it splines directly to the output shaft.

The common sun gear can be a driving- or stationary-planetary member. This gear connects to the front (reverse and high) clutch drum through a driving shell. If the clutch activates, the input shaft drives the sun gear clockwise.

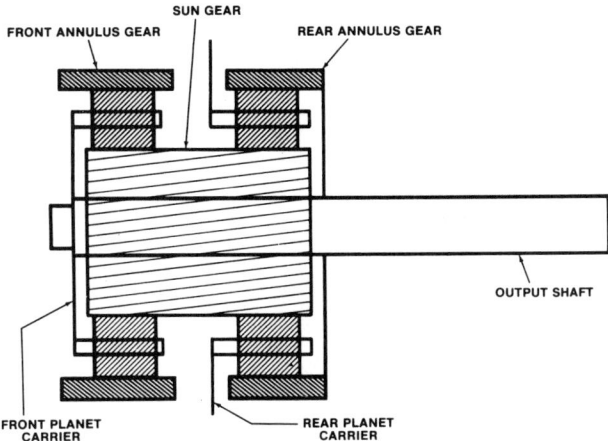

fig. 14-15 The complete Torqueflite Simpson planetary gear train. (Courtesy Chrysler Corp.)

In addition, a servo-operated band encircles the front clutch drum. If the hydraulic system applies the servo, the band will stop drum rotation. As a result, the drum, via the driving shell, holds the common sun gear stationary.

The rear planetary gearset consists of an annulus (ring) gear and a carrier. The annulus gear of this gearset is the output member because it splines to the output shaft. The carrier is the reaction (stationary) member. It attaches to a drum held, either by an overrunning clutch, a band, or a combination of the two, to the transmission case.

clutches

The rear-clutch assembly is a multiple-disc unit that transmits torque from the input shaft to the front annulus gear (Fig. 14-16). The hydraulic system activates this clutch in all forward driving ratios. And as a result, the front annulus gear rotates at input shaft speed and supplies torque to the front planetary gearset.

The front clutch assembly is also a multiple-disc type. But the hydraulic system activates this clutch assembly in reverse and direct drive only. When the clutch does apply, it connects the common sun gear, via the driving shell, to the input shaft (Fig. 14-17).

Finally, an overrunning-mechanical clutch holds the low-reverse drum against counterclockwise rotation in drive, first ratio and also in manual low (Fig. 14-18). This overrunning clutch fits in the back of the transmission case and splines to the low-reverse drum. When planetary gear train action forces the rear planet carrier and low-reverse drum to turn counterclockwise, the overrunning clutch locks them to the transmission case. But the overrunning clutch permits free rotation of the rear planet carrier and low-reverse drum in a clockwise direction.

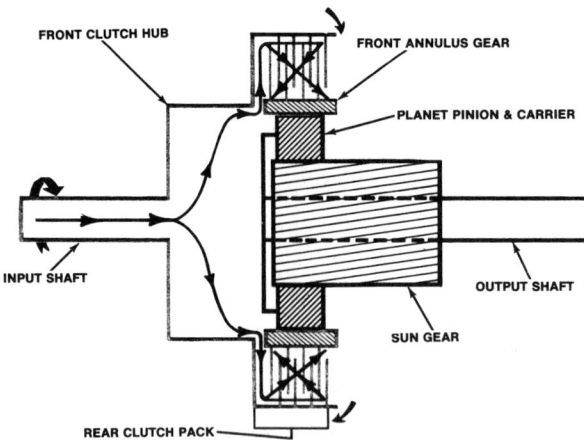

fig. 14–16 The rear clutch connects the front annulus gear to the input shaft. (Courtesy Chrysler Corp.)

bands

The Torqueflite transmission uses two friction bands, a front band—commonly called the kickdown band, and a low-reverse band. Fig. 14–19 shows the kickdown band used in this installation. The task of this band is to hold the common sun gear stationary in second ratio. The band itself actually applies on the surface of the front clutch retainer (drum) that, in turn, locks to the sun gear driving shell. As a result, the sun gear stops any rotation and becomes a reaction member for the front planetary gearset.

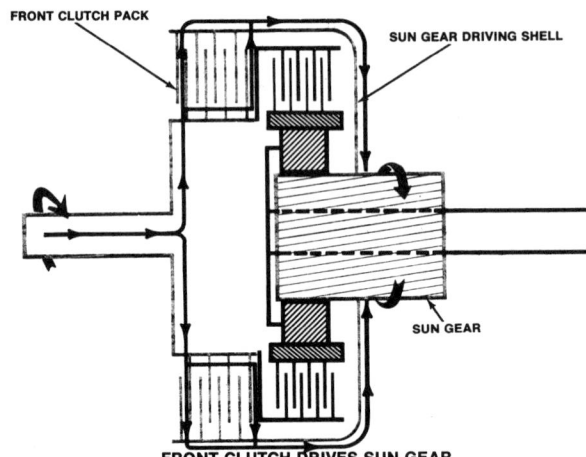

fig. 14–17 The front clutch connects the common sun gear to the input shaft. (Courtesy Chrysler Corp.)

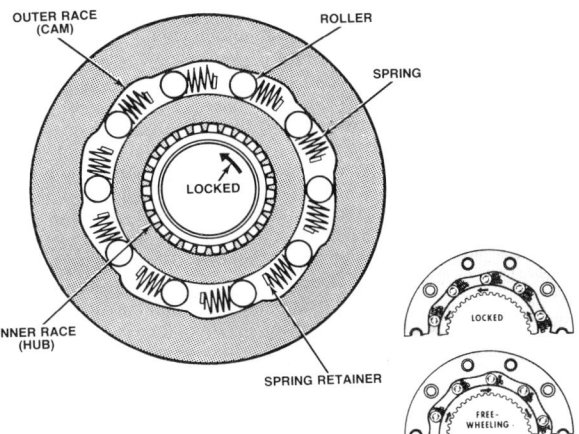

fig. 14-18 The overrunning clutch assembly of a Torqueflite transmission. (Courtesy Chrysler Corp.)

The function of the low-reverse band is to hold the rear planet carrier stationary (Fig. 14-20). To perform this function in manual low and reverse, the band surrounds the low-reverse drum. The low-reverse drum locks into the rear planet carrier. Now, if the band tightens around the low-reverse drum, it and the rear planet carrier will stop turning; and the carrier becomes the reaction member of the rear planetary gearset.

function of hydraulic system components

hydraulic pump: A positive-displacement, rotor-type pump (Fig. 14-21) supplies pressurized fluid to fill the converter, engage the front and rear clutches, apply the bands, and feed the lubrication system.

high-pressure relief valve: A safety valve that will protect the hydraulic system from an accidental build-up of excessively high system pressure.

pressure-regulating valve: This valve regulates the pressure of the pump's output and supplies the basic fluid pressure necessary to operate the transmission.

control valve: This valve controls both the flow and pressure into and out of the torque converter.

manual valve: The driver, by means of mechanical linkage, activates this valve; the valve, in turn, sets up the operating conditions of the transmission.

governor valve: It is a balanced valve that senses vehicle speed from the transmission's output shaft; the valve then sends a hydraulic speed signal to the shift valves to control gearshifting in relation to vehicle speed.

262 OPERATION OF THE TRANSMISSION

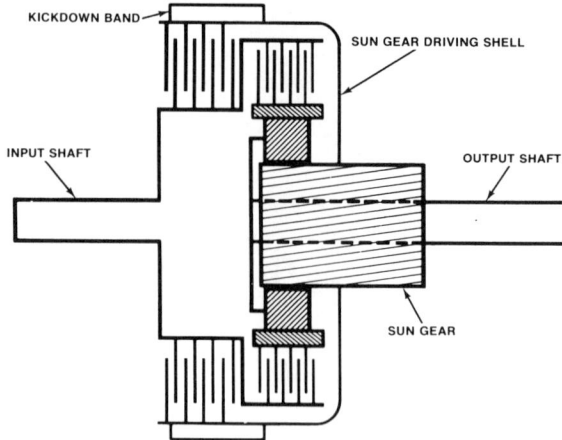

fig. 14–19 The kickdown band surrounds the front clutch retainer and when applied, holds the sun gear stationary. (Courtesy Chrysler Corp.)

throttle valve: This valve produces a pressure signal that is in proportion to engine speed or load; this signal acts on the shift valves to control shifting in relation to engine load or speed.

kickdown valve: A valve activated by full depression of the throttle; kickdown pressure, from this valve, will then cause the shift valve(s) to close which downshifts the transmission.

1–2 and 2–3 shift-valve trains: These valves trigger the shifts, in response to

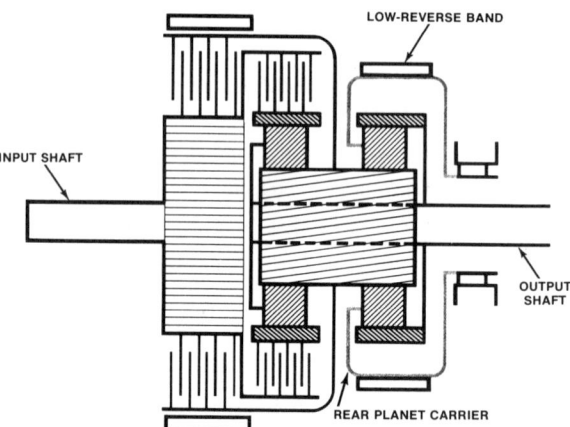

fig. 14–20 The low-reverse band surrounds the low-reverse drum and when applied, holds the rear-planet carrier stationary. (Courtesy Chrysler Corp.)

FUNCTION OF HYDRAULIC SYSTEM COMPONENTS 263

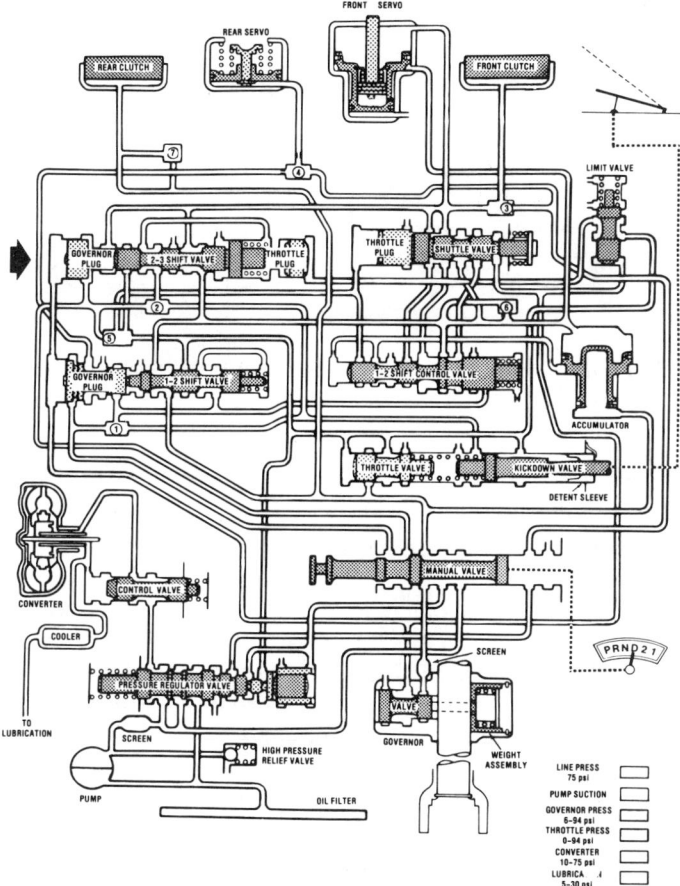

fig. 14–21 A Torqueflite hydraulic schematic showing all system components. (Courtesy Chrysler Corp.)

governor and throttle signals, by directing pressurized fluid to the appropriate band or clutch that, in turn, causes the shift to occur.

accumulator: The accumulator controls shift quality by absorbing the apply pressure of the rear clutch or front band.

shuttle-valve train: This valve helps to control the rate of front-servo apply pressure during part-to-full throttle, 2–3 upshift and a kickdown from 3–2.

limit valve: This valve prevents a part-throttle 3–2 downshift at high-vehicle speeds.

1–2 shift control valve: This valve aids in controlling the quality of the 1–2 upshift; it also aids in the timing and quality of the various 3–2 kickdown ranges.

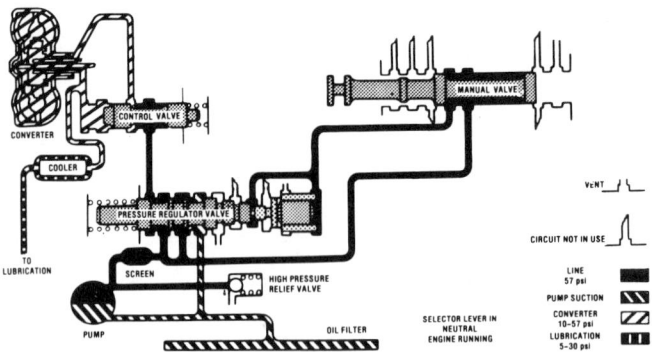

fig. 14–22 A Torqueflite hydraulic schematic with the manual valve in neutral. (Courtesy Chrysler Corp.)

torqueflite operation

netural and park—hydraulic operation

Fig. 14–22 illustrates what is taking place in the hydraulic system with the engine operating at idle rpm and the gearshift selector in neutral. The fluid first moves from the pan, through the filter, and to the suction side of the pump. After the pump pressurizes the fluid, it enters a branched circuit; one branch leads to the high-pressure relief valve. The other branch leads to the pressure-regulating valve.

After passing through a screen, the pressurized fluid enters two ports of the regulating valve and then moves through a circuit to the manual valve. With the manual valve in the neutral position, the fluid passes through the large groove and enters a circuit leading to the line-pressure plug and primary reaction area of the pressure-regulating valve. The pressure, acting on these areas, moves the regulating valve against spring tension.

When the regulating valve initially moves, large, number-one land uncovers a port leading to the control valve. Now, pressurized fluid can pass through the annular groove, between lands one and two of the regulating valve, to the open control valve. From the control valve, fluid enters the torque converter, cooler, and lubrication circuits.

The pressurized fluid leaving the converter acts on a reaction area of the control valve. This fluid pressure tends to move the control valve against spring tension. As a result, the control valve moves in its bore and regulates converter pressure and flow.

As system pressure continues to increase, the regulator valves moves further against the tension of the spring. Further movement of the valve permits large, number-three land to open a circuit to the suction side of the pump. Consequently, pump pressure, in the groove between lands two and three, begins to leak off to the sump. This controlled leak regulates the pressure in the system to about 57 psi. If, on the otherhand, the gearshift-selector lever is in the park position, line pressure will decrease (Fig. 14–23). The difference in system pressure between neutral and park is due mainly to the

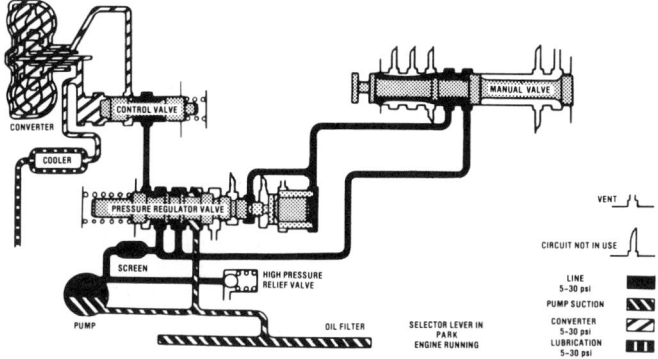

fig. 14-23 A Torqueflite hydraulic schematic with the manual valve in park. (Courtesy Chrysler Corp.)

position of the manual valve. As the manual valve moves into the park position, its two large lands shift position in the bore. This valve position allows fluid to come between one large land and another land of a smaller dimension.

Since the size of the bore remains the same, the fluid leaks past the smaller land, out of the valve body, and returns back to the sump. And because some fluid is flowing, pressure cannot build up as high as it did in neutral. In other words, the leak causes a reduction in pressure in the park operating range.

neutral and park—powerflow

With the gearshift-selector lever in the neutral position, the output shaft is free to turn but receives no driving torque from the engine. Since both of the friction clutches are off or in their release position (Fig. 14-24), there is no driving planetary member for either

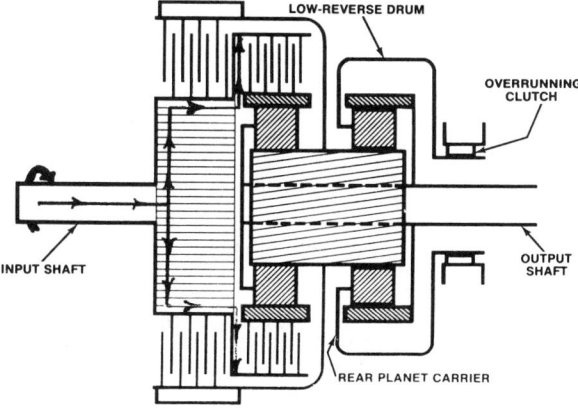

fig. 14-24 The powerflow of a Torqueflite transmission in neutral or park. (Courtesy Chrysler Corp.)

266 OPERATION OF THE TRANSMISSION

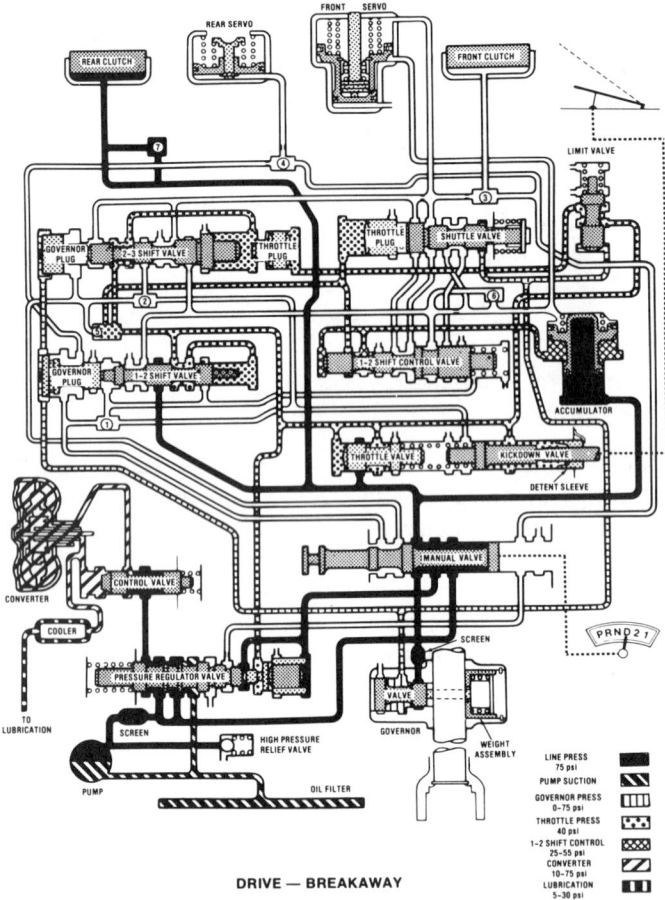

fig. 14-25 A hydraulic schematic of a Torqueflite transmission in the drive-breakaway range. (Courtesy Chrysler Corp.)

gearset. The input shaft can rotate the rear clutch retainer (drum), but the powerflow ceases at this point.

In the park selector-lever position, a lever engages with the parking gear on the output shaft. This action locks the output shaft to the transmission case. This locking arrangement prevents the vehicle from rolling down an incline due to its weight.

drive, breakaway—hydraulic operation

Fig. 14-25 shows what occurs within the hydraulic system whenever the driver places the gearshift-selector lever into drive. Now, with the engine running at idle, the control of line pressure, converter feed, fluid cooling, and transmission lubrication is the same as it was in neutral. But since the manual valve has moved, it now opens several ports.

One of the ports pressurizes a circuit to the governor. And when the vehicle begins to move, the governor valve will produce a pressure signal that is in proportion to vehicle speed. Finally, circuits direct this pressure signal to both shift valves, limit valve, and shuttle valve.

The remaining, uncovered manual valve port pressurizes circuits to the 1-2 shift valve, rear clutch, accumulator, and throttle valve. The pressurized fluid, directed to the 1-2 shift valve, will upshift the transmission when the valve opens; but at this time the shift valve blocks the circuit to the second-gear apply circuit.

The fluid pressure directed to the rear clutch begins to apply the clutch. But the accumulator absorbs some of the clutch's apply pressure, and the rear clutch will not fully apply until the accumulator piston bottoms in its bore against the force of its spring. This accumulator action cushions the initial application of the rear clutch.

The last circuit, charged by the open manual valve port, is to the throttle valve. The throttle valve will develop a signal from this pressure that is in proportion to engine speed or load, and this signal increases as the driver depresses the accelerator pedal. Lastly, circuits carry this throttle pressure to the pressure regulator, shift valves, shuttle valve, 1-2 shift control valve, kickdown valve, and limit valve.

Throttle pressure acts on the pressure-regulator valve to increase line pressure during acceleration in preparation for the upcoming shift. This throttle pressure reacts on the large land of the throttle plug located between the line-pressure plug and the regulator valve. The pressure causes the throttle plug to resist the movement of the line-pressure plug. As a result, line pressure on the line-pressure plug and the small, regulator-land two must increase to move the valve against spring force. This action increases control pressure as engine speed goes up and the vehicle accelerates.

drive, breakaway–powerflow

With the gearshift-selector lever placed in drive, the transmission is in the drive-breakaway or first ratio phase of operation (Fig. 14-26). As previously mentioned, the hydraulic system now activates the rear clutch that connects the input shaft to the front

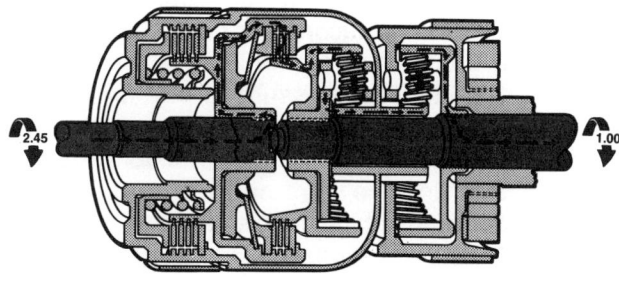

POWER FLOW IN DRIVE BREAKAWAY

fig. 14-26 The powerflow of a Torqueflite transmission in drive-breakaway. (Courtesy Chrysler Corp.)

annulus (ring) gear. The input shaft drives the front annulus gear clockwise at turbine speed.

Since the weight of the vehicle is on the output shaft, it will not turn at this time. Consequently, the front planet carrier and rear annulus gear are also momentarily stationary. This action causes the front annulus gear to drive the front pinions clockwise on their support pins.

The front pinions which are momentarily idling rotate the sun gear counterclockwise; and the sun gear rotation forces the rear planet pinions to spin clockwise. Now, with the weight of the vehicle imposed on the rear annulus gear, the rear pinion rotation on the annulus gear forces the rear planet carrier to revolve counterclockwise.

But the rear planet carrier locks into the low-reverse drum that splines to the inner race of the overrunning clutch. Now, any counterclockwise rotation of the rear carrier and low-reverse drum causes the overrunning clutch to lock up. And with the clutch locked up, the rear planet carrier is stationary. This action results in a torque transfer from the rear planet pinions to the rear annulus gear and the output shaft.

This output shaft rotation also forces the front carrier to turn at the same speed and in the same direction as the output shaft. Consequently, the front annulus gear and carrier are both turning clockwise, but the front carrier is spinning at a slower speed than the annulus gear. The actual gear ratio, in this situation, between the input and output shafts is the result of a combination of ratios provided by the front and rear planetary gearsets.

drive, second–hydraulic operation

Fig. 14–27 illustrates the condition of the hydraulic system when the transmission automatically upshifts from breakaway to second. During this phase of hydraulic operation, governor pressure has now overcome the effects of spring force and throttle pressure on the 1–2 shift valve; and the valve opens. Now, control pressure passes through the groove and pressurizes the second-gear apply circuit.

A branch of this second-gear apply circuit terminates at the 2–3 shift valve. A land of the 2–3 shift valve blocks the fluid pressure, at this time, from the third-gear apply circuit. In other words, this part of the second-gear apply circuit just supplies the fluid necessary to complete the 2–3 upshift when the 2–3 shift valve opens.

After supplying the 2–3 shift valve, pressurized fluid follows the circuit to the accumulator and finally to the front servo. This fluid under pressure first passes through an orifice before proceeding to the accumulator; then, it enters the circuit leading to the spring end of the accumulator and the front servo. The fluid pressure entering the accumulator will assist the spring in pushing the piston down against line pressure that is below the piston. At the same time, pressurized fluid begins to move the servo piston in its bore. But the servo will not tighten the band firmly around the drum until the accumulator piston bottoms in its bore. This accumulator action cushions band application.

Also, to further cushion band application under certain throttle settings, the 1–2 shift control valve supplies 1–2 shift control or modulated throttle pressure to the middle

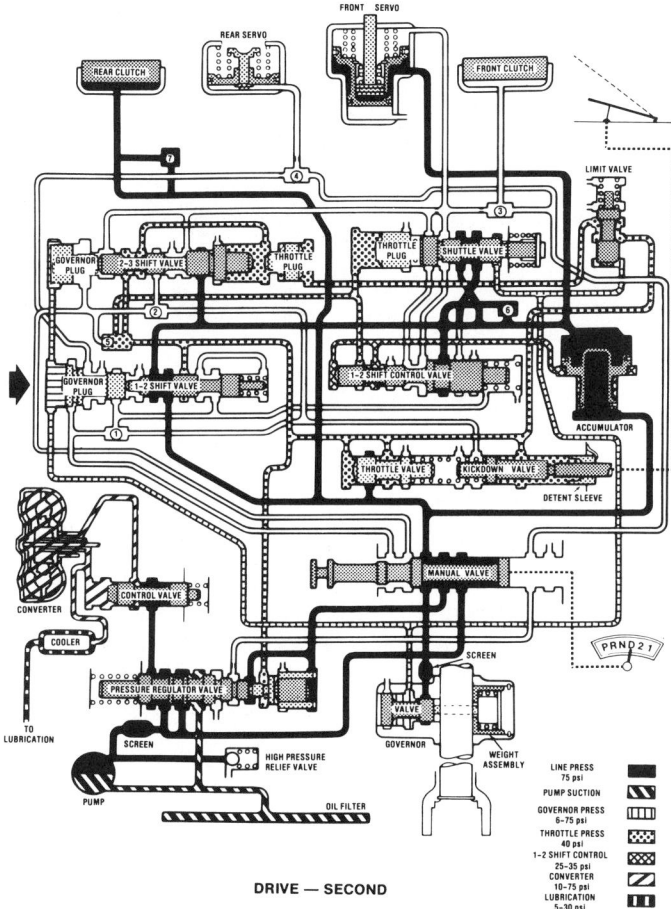

fig. 14-27 A hydraulic schematic of a Torqueflite transmission in the drive-second range. (Courtesy Chrysler Corp.)

land of the accumulator piston. This pressure controls the kickdown servo apply pressure necessary to activate the kickdown servo and accumulator pistons during the 1–2 upshift. As a result, the 1–2 shift control valve improves the quality of the 1–2 upshift or cushions the shift point even more.

drive, second—powerflow

In drive, second ratio, the transmission makes the upshift by keeping the rear clutch applied and also by activating the front servo that applies the kickdown band (Fig. 14–28). The kickdown band holds the front clutch retainer that locks to the sun gear driving shell. As a result, the sun gear is stationary or locked to the transmission case.

270 OPERATION OF THE TRANSMISSION

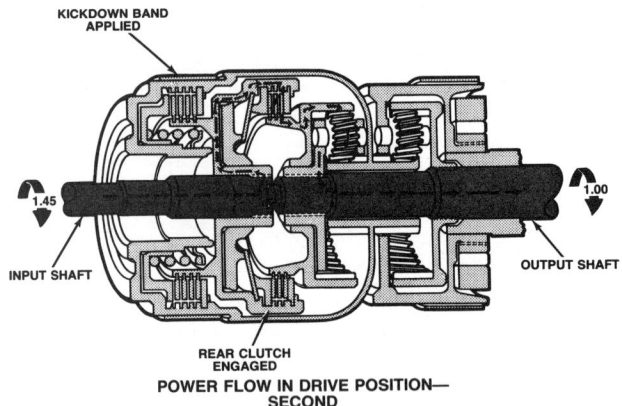

fig. 14-28 The powerflow of a Torqueflite transmission in drive position, second ratio. (Courtesy Chrysler Corp.)

Since the rear clutch is still on, the input shaft drives the front annulus gear clockwise at input shaft speed. Because the sun gear is now stationary, the annulus rotation causes the planet pinions of the front unit to turn clockwise. The pinions, in turn, walk the carrier around the held sun gear in a clockwise direction. This action transmits torque to the output shaft that splines directly to the front planet carrier. Note that in this gear ratio, the front planetary gearset alone produces the reduction and torque multiplication.

drive, third—hydraulic operation

Fig. 14-29 shows what takes place in the hydraulic system when the upshift occurs from second to third ratio. During this phase of operation, governor pressure has overcome the effects of spring force and throttle pressure on the 2-3 shift valve, and the valve has opened. Now, control pressure from the 1-2 shift valve circuit passes through a groove in the shift valve and pressurizes the third-gear apply circuit.

Pressurized fluid now flows to the shift-valve land between the governor plug and the 2-3 shift valve, to the release side of the servo, and to the front clutch. The pressurized fluid passes through an orifice before entering the release side of the servo. This pressure, assisted by the servo spring, pushes the servo piston to the base of its bore releasing the band.

At the same time, 2-3 shift valve pressure acts on the back face of the large, shuttle-valve land. This pressure moves the shuttle valve to the left against throttle pressure on the throttle plug. As a result, front-clutch apply pressure moves through the shuttle valve to the middle groove of the 1-2 shift control valve.

The fluid entering the 1-2 shift control valve acts on the inside face of the large, number-two land and moves the control valve to the right compressing its spring. This action results in two different situations occurring at the time of this valve's movement. First, 1-2 shift control pressure to the accumulator drops to zero due to the opening of a

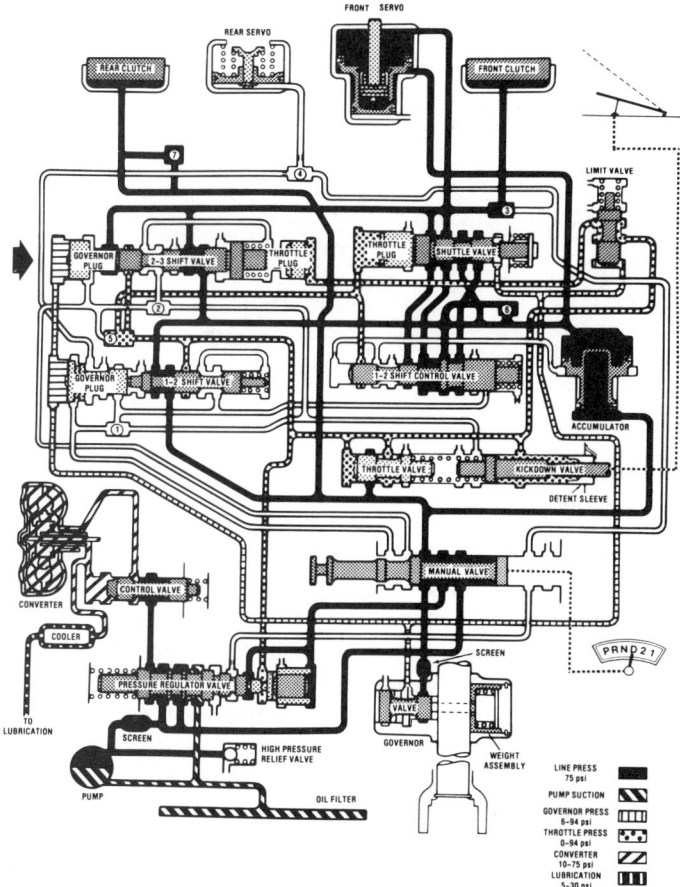

fig. 14-29 A hydraulic schematic of a Torqueflite transmission in drive, high gear. (Courtesy Chrysler Corp.)

passage to the sump. Second, land one of the 1-2 shift control valve blocks the supply pressure from the kickdown valve. Now, the valve is ready to aid in controlling the quality of the 3-2 kickdown downshift if and when it should occur.

Finally, the fluid pressure after entering the front servo's release side and shuttle valve passes through another orifice and enters the front clutch. This pressure applies the front clutch. Now, with the front band released and the front clutch applied, the transmission is in third ratio.

drive, third—powerflow

As previously stated, when the 2-3 shift valve opens, the front band releases and the front clutch applies (Fig. 14-30). But the rear clutch, during this time, remains applied. With the application of the front clutch, the input shaft now drives the front clutch retainer

272 OPERATION OF THE TRANSMISSION

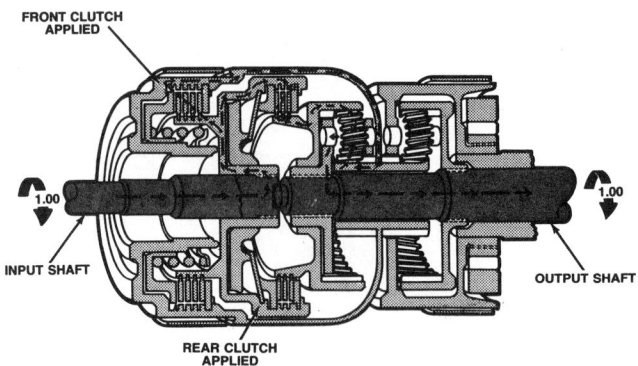

fig. 14-30 The powerflow of a Torqueflite transmission in high gear. (Courtesy Chrysler Corp.)

that locks to the driving shell. The driving shell, in turn, turns the sun gear at input shaft speed. And finally, since the rear clutch is still on, the input shaft still drives the front annulus gear clockwise at input shaft speed.

Remember from the discussion in Chapter Two that whenever the input shaft drives any two members of a planetary gear train in the same direction and at the same speed, direct drive results. In other words, when the two members rotate at the same speed and direction, the gear train locks up and turns as a unit.

This lock-up condition results from the fact that the front and rear planet pinions cannot turn at all in direct drive. The only rotation is the input shaft and the output shaft. The remaining parts just spin as one common unit.

reverse—hydraulic operation

Fig. 14-31 illustrates the condition of the hydraulic system when the driver places the gearshift-selector lever into Reverse. With the manual valve moved into this position, it directs pressurized fluid to a circuit to the front clutch and rear servo. This pressure applies the front clutch and rear band.

At the same time, pressurized fluid is now cut off to the line-pressure plug and primary reaction area of the regulator valve. This action would normally permit control pressure to increase to the maximum amount. But reverse apply pressure, from the manual valve also moves to the reaction area located on the small, number-one land of the regulator valve.

This reaction area is much smaller than the combined reaction areas of land two and the line-pressure plug. As a result, more system pressure is necessary on this smaller reaction area in order to move the valve far enough to regulate line pressure. Therefore, line pressure in reverse range is between 230 and 270 psi.

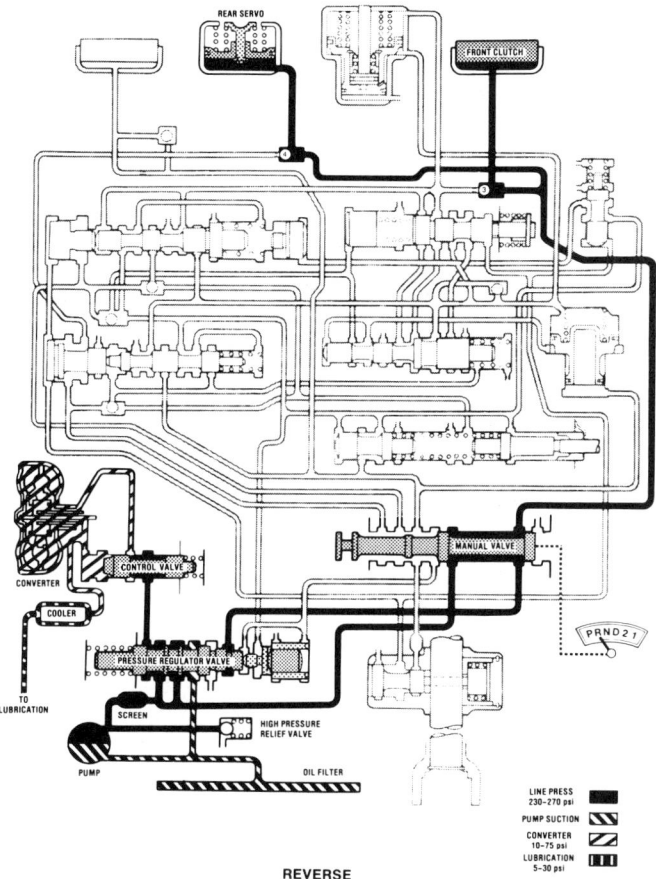

fig. 14-31 A hydraulic schematic of a Torqueflite transmission in reverse. (Courtesy Chrysler Corp.)

reverse—powerflow

As previously mentioned, in reverse, the hydraulic system activates the front clutch and rear band. As a result, the input shaft drives the sun gear clockwise at input shaft speed. Also, the rear band holds the rear planet carrier stationary (Fig. 14-32).

As the input shaft drives the sun gear clockwise, it turns the rear planet pinions counterclockwise on their support pins. Since the carrier is stationary, the pinions, in turn, rotate the rear annulus gear. Consequently, the annulus gear that splines to the output shaft now spins counterclockwise.

In reverse, the rear planetary gearset alone handles the transmission of torque. There is input to the front unit through the sun gear, but no other member is stationary. Therefore, torque through the front unit cannot occur. In other words, the front planetary gears just idle during the reverse stage of transmission operation.

274 OPERATION OF THE TRANSMISSION

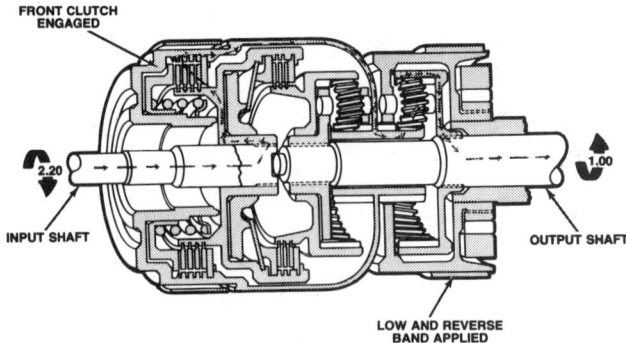

fig. 14-32 The powerflow of a Torqueflite transmission in reverse. (Courtesy Chrysler Corp.)

summary

1. This chapter covers the operation of the T-300 and the Torqueflite transmissions.
2. The T-300 automatic transmission is a unit that has a three-member torque converter combined with a two-speed compound-planetary gear train.
3. The T-300 torque converter attaches to the engine's crankshaft and serves as a hydraulic coupling that connects engine torque to the input shaft of the transmission.
4. The T-300 converter also multiplies torque and acts as an efficient fluid coupling.
5. The T-300 compound-planetary gear train consists of an input sun gear, long and short pinions which attach to a common carrier, low sun gear, and a reverse ring gear.
6. The T-300 forward clutch connects the low sun gear to the input shaft.
7. The T-300 low band holds the low sun gear stationary.
8. The T-300 reverse clutch holds the reverse ring gear stationary.
9. The T-300 hydraulic system consists of a hydraulic pump; pressure-regulating valve; manual-shift control valve; governor; shift- and shift-control valves; vacuum modulator and valve; modulator limit valve; detent valve; high-speed downshift timing valve; coast, downshift timing valve; and the stator control valve.
10. When the T-300 is in neutral or park, the regulator valve spring controls system pressure, and the manual control valve lands block fluid pressure to the hydraulically operated units.
11. With the T-300 in neutral, the input shaft can drive the input sun gear but there is no holding member; consequently, the output shaft receives no driving torque. Furthermore, in park, a parking pawl locks the output shaft to the transmission case.
12. With the selector lever of the T-300 in drive, the manual valve directs fluid to the detent valve, high-speed downshift timing valve, shift valve, and low servo that

SUMMARY

applies the band. Hydraulic pressure, at this time is under the control of the regulator valve and modulator valve.

13. When the T-300 is in drive, low ratio, the input sun gear is the driving member; the low sun gear is the holding member; and the carrier is the output member.
14. When the shift control valve opens, the T-300 upshifts from low to direct because the shift valve directs fluid to release the low band and apply the forward clutch.
15. Direct drive in the T-300 results from the input shaft driving both the input and low sun gears in the same direction and at the same speed.
16. When the driver places the selector lever into reverse, the manual valve directs fluid to apply the reverse clutch and to the regulator, boost valve that raises control pressure.
17. When the T-300 is in reverse, the input sun gear is the driving member; the ring gear is the holding member; and the carrier is the output member.
18. The Torqueflite transmission is a unit that combines a three-member torque converter with a Simpson design three-speed planetary gear train.
19. The Torqueflite converter operates in much the same manner as the T-300 converter, but some Torqueflites now utilize a lock-up converter in which the turbine locks to the housing during the coupling phase of converter operation.
20. The Torqueflite planetary gear train consists of two simple planetary gearsets connected together by a common sun gear.
21. The rear clutch of the Torqueflite connects the input shaft to the front annulus; the front clutch connects the input shaft to the sun gear; and the overrunning clutch holds the rear planet carrier to the transmission case.
22. The kickdown band holds the sun gear stationary, and the rear band holds the rear planet carrier stationary.
23. The Torqueflite hydraulic system consists of a hydraulic pump, high-pressure relief valve, pressure-regulating valve, control valve, manual valve, governor valve, throttle valve, kickdown valve, 1-2 and 2-3 shift valves, accumulator, shuttle-valve train, limit valve, and 1-2 shift control valve.
24. When a Torqueflite transmission is in neutral, the regulator's primary reaction area and line-pressure plug receive pressure from the manual valve; this pressure, on these two areas, moves the regulator valve against spring tension.
25. With the selector lever of the Torqueflite in park, hydraulic pressure will decrease due to the controlled leak at the manual valve.
26. In neutral or park, the output shaft of the Torqueflite receives no driving torque because the input shaft drives none of the planetary members.
27. When the Torqueflite is in drive, the control of line pressure, converter feed, fluid cooling, and transmission lubrication is the same as it is in neutral; but the manual valve now opens several ports.
28. These ports direct pressurized fluid to the governor, 1-2 shift valve, rear clutch, accumulator, and throttle valve.

29. Fluid pressure on the accumulator and rear clutch circuits applies the rear clutch that is necessary for first ratio.
30. Throttle pressure in the drive range increases line pressure and delays the upshift so that it matches the speed or load on the engine.
31. In drive, breakaway, the front annulus gear is the driving planetary member; the rear planet carrier is the held member; and the rear annulus gear and front carrier are the output members.
32. As the 1–2 shift valve opens the Torqueflite upshifts from breakaway to second.
33. When the valve opens, it pressurizes the circuits leading to the 2–3 shift valve, accumulator, and front servo.
34. In drive, second ratio, the front annulus gear is the driving planetary member; The sun gear is the held member; and the front carrier is the output member.
35. As the 2–3 shift valve opens, the Torqueflite upshifts to third ratio.
36. The 2–3 shift valve, when open, pressurizes a circuit to the release side of the servo and the front clutch.
37. This pressure releases the front band and applies the front clutch.
38. When the Torqueflite is in third (direct) ratio, the input shaft drives both the front annulus and the sun gear which causes the pinions to lock up; this action causes the entire planetary gear train to revolve as a solid unit.
39. In reverse, the manual valve directs fluid pressure to the front clutch and rear servo. Also, it cuts off pressure to the regulator valve's primary reaction area and line-pressure plug but opens a circuit to a smaller reaction area on the regulator valve. This action raises control pressure needed for reverse operation.
40. In reverse, the sun gear is the driving planetary member; the rear carrier is the held member, and the rear annulus is the output member.

check-up questions

The questions listed below will assist you in determining how well you remember the material contained in this chapter. Read each question carefully before choosing the answer to each item. If you cannot answer a question, review the material in the section of the chapter that covers the question.

1. The T-300 transmission utilizes a _____ planetary gear train.
    a. simple
    b. Simpson
    c. compound
    d. complex

2. In the T-300 planetary gear train, the output member is the _____.
   a. carrier
   b. ring gear
   c. low sun gear
   d. pinions
3. The function of the reverse clutch of the T-300 transmission is to hold the _____.
   a. low sun gear
   b. carrier
   c. pinions
   d. ring gear
4. The valve that sets up the operating conditions of the T-300 transmission is the _____.
   a. governor
   b. manual-shift control
   c. shift and shift control
   d. modulator
5. The modulator valve will not raise control pressure when the engine is operating at _____.
   a. idle
   b. half throttle
   c. three-fourths throttle
   d. full throttle
6. When the T-300 transmission is in drive, low range, the _____ receives control pressure.
   a. reverse clutch
   b. forward clutch
   c. low servo
   d. both b and c
7. The driving planetary member of the T-300 transmission in all ranges is the _____.
   a. low sun gear
   b. input sun gear
   c. carrier
   d. ring gear

278 OPERATION OF THE TRANSMISSION

8. As the _____ opens, the T-300 transmission upshifts to direct drive.
   a. shift valve
   b. governor
   c. throttle
   d. modulator

9. The holding planetary member in reverse is the _____.
   a. ring gear
   b. carrier
   c. pinions
   d. low sun gear

10. The Torqueflite transmission uses a _____ planetary gear train.
    a. compound
    b. complex
    c. Simpson
    d. simple

11. The Torquflite converter in which the turbine operates at impeller speed during the coupling phase is the _____.
    a. variable-pitch design
    b. four-member design
    c. solid design
    d. lock-up design

12. Within the Torqueflite transmission, the kickdown bands holds the _____.
    a. front annulus
    b. front carrier
    c. rear annulus
    d. sun gear

13. The valve that protects the system from an accidental build-up of high pressure is the _____.
    a. governor
    b. orifice
    c. high-pressure relief
    d. throttle

14. In neutral and park ranges of the Torqueflite, the manual valve directs fluid to the primary reaction area and the _____ of the regulator valve.
    a. line-pressure plug
    b. throttle plug

c. governor plug
d. modulator plug

15. The clutch that the Torqueflite uses in second ratio is the _____.
    a. overrunning
    b. front
    c. rear
    d. both *a* and *c*

16. The overrunning clutch is effective in _____.
    a. first
    b. second
    c. third
    d. reverse

17. The valve that opens to upshift the Torqueflite from second to third is the _____.
    a. governor
    b. 1–2 shift
    c. 2–3 shift
    d. throttle

18. The driving planetary member of the Torqueflite planetary gear train in second is the _____.
    a. front annulus
    b. rear annulus
    c. sun gear
    d. front carrier

19. The planetary gear train is in direct drive because the _____ cannot turn.
    a. pinions
    b. sun gear
    c. front carrier
    d. rear carrier

20. The driving member during reverse operation of the Torqueflite is the _____.
    a. front annulus
    b. front carrier
    c. rear annulus
    d. sun gear

For the answers to these check-up questions, turn to the Appendix located at the back of the text.

appendix

answers to chapter one check-up questions

1. a
2. c
3. a
4. d
5. b
6. c
7. d
8. b
9. a
10. d

answers to chapter two check-up questions

1. c
2. a
3. a

ANSWERS TO CHECK-UP QUESTIONS 281

4. b
5. d
6. a
7. c
8. b
9. b
10. a
11. d
12. c
13. b
14. a
15. d
16. a
17. c
18. b
19. c
20. a

answers to chapter three check-up questions

1. c
2. a
3. c
4. b
5. d
6. c
7. b
8. a
9. c
10. d
11. a
12. c

answers to chapter four check-up questions

1. d
2. a
3. b
4. c
5. b
6. a
7. b
8. d
9. d
10. b
11. c
12. a
13. c
14. b
15. c
16. a
17. c
18. a
19. b
20. c

answers to chapter five check-up questions

1. c
2. a
3. b
4. b
5. d
6. a
7. d
8. c
9. b
10. d

answers to chapter six check-up questions

1. b
2. a
3. d
4. c
5. d
6. a
7. a
8. c
9. d
10. a
11. a
12. b

answers to chapter seven check-up questions

1. c
2. a
3. b
4. a
5. c
6. a
7. a
8. a
9. b
10. c
11. a
12. c
13. a

answers to chapter eight check-up questions

1. c
2. a
3. b

4. a
5. d
6. b
7. a
8. b
9. d
10. a
11. b
12. a
13. b

answers to chapter nine check-up questions

1. c
2. a
3. d
4. a
5. b
6. d
7. a
8. b
9. c
10. a
11. c
12. b
13. c

answers to chapter ten check-up questions

1. c
2. a
3. b
4. d
5. b
6. a
7. d

8. a
9. b
10. b
11. a
12. c
13. d

answers to chapter eleven check-up questions
1. d
2. c
3. a
4. b
5. c
6. b
7. a
8. a
9. d
10. c
11. c
12. d
13. c
14. d
15. b

answers to chapter twelve check-up questions
1. d
2. c
3. a
4. d
5. b
6. c
7. c
8. a
9. b

10. b
11. a
12. c

answers to chapter thirteen check-up questions

1. c
2. a
3. b
4. a
5. d
6. a
7. b
8. c
9. b
10. d

answers to chapter fourteen check-up questions

1. c
2. a
3. d
4. b
5. a
6. c
7. b
8. a
9. a
10. c
11. d
12. d
13. c
14. a
15. c
16. a

17. c
18. a
19. a
20. d

index

a acceleration, 64–65, 155, 171, 186, 188, 190–191, 197–200
  Torqueflite transmission, 267
  T-300 transmission, 251, 253, 257
  and torque, 4–5, 8–9
accumulator, 162, 177–179, 234, 237–238
  torqueflite transmission, 263, 267–270
accumulator valve, 171
additives, fluid, 43–44
adjustment screw, 148, 153, 193–194
air-cooled system, fluid, 47–48
altitude-compensated vacuum-diaphragm, 195–196
American Motors:
  fluid, 46–47
anchor, 104–105
annular groove, 150
  governor valve, 187–188
  manual valve, 161, 163–164
  pressure-regulating valve, 150, 153, 155
  shift valve, 171–172
  throttle valve, 190, 192, 194
annulus gear, *see* ring gear
antifoam additives, fluid, 43
applied band, 178–179, 237–238, 251, 253
applied clutch, 90–91, 162, 171, 178, 237, 253, 267, 269, 271–272
AQ (Armour Qualification) number, fluid, 45
ATF (automatic transmission fluid), *see* fluid
atmospheric pressure, 194–196
automatic transmission:
  advantages, 9
  functions, 2
  operation, 243–279
automatic transmission fluid, *see* Fluid
auxiliary cooler, fluid, 49
axle drive, 7–8

b balanced valve principle, 147–148
ball check valve, 86–87, 92–93, 125–126, 147–148, 174–176
band, 237–238
  coast condition, 98
  design, 104–107
  function, 102–104
  malfunctioning, 239
  operation, 41, 107–108
  in Simpson gear train, 32–33
  slippage, 43
  Torqueflite transmission, 258–262, 268–269, 271–273
  T-300 transmission, 243, 246, 251, 253, 255
band adjustment, 103–105, 112–114
bellows, of compensated vacuum-diaphragm, 195–196
boost valve, 251, 253, 255, 257
breakaway, 266–268
bronze friction lining, 88–89
bushing, 77
butt-joint design, of metal sealing ring, 222

c calibrated spring, 149–151, 168, 171–172, 177
cam and roller overrunning clutch, 96–97
centrifugal force, 62, 185–189
check valves:
  ball type, 86–87, 92–93, 125–126, 147–148, 174–176
  poppet type, 147–148
Chrysler Corporation:
  fluid, 46–47
  Torqueflite transmission, 257–274

C-J fluid, 46
cleaning of parts by fluid, 42
clutch, 56–57, 85–101, 162, 171, 237
  accumulator operation, 178
  function, 85
  operation, 41
  in Simpson gear train, 29, 31, 34
  slippage, 43
  Torqueflite transmission, 257–261, 267–273
  T-300 transmission, 243, 245, 246, 253, 255, 257; *see also* applied clutch; multiple disc clutch; primary clutch; overrunning clutch; roller clutch; secondary clutch; stationary clutch
clutch hub, 90, 92–95
coast condition, 98, 250
coefficient of friction, 44
color-coded diagram, 231–232
compensated pressure regulator valve operation, 155–156
composition material:
  friction lining, 88–89, 105
  gaskets, 209
compound planetary gear train, 23–28
compression ratio, 3
compression spring, 86, 93, 109–112, 153
confined fluid, 121–122
controlled leak, 155
controlled-load servo, 110–111
control pressure, 149, 255, 257, 267–268, 270
control valve, 233, 236
  Torqueflite transmission, 261, 264, 270
converter, torque, *see* Torque converter
cooling systems, 41, 47–50
cork gasket, 209
corrosion, effect on fluid on, 43–44
coupling devices, 56–58
coupling phase, 64–66, 69–70, 73
crankshaft, 3
cruise condition, 8, 149, 189
C-6 transmission, 93

d dacron filter, 142
damping, by torque converter, 72–74
detent regulator, 198–200
detent solenoid, 198–200
detent switch, 198–200
detent valve, 198–199, 247
dexron fluid, 45–47, 91
diaphragm, of vacuum-controlled throttle valve, 192–194
diaphragm spring, of primary clutch, 86
differential area, 152–153
direct drive, 18–19, 23–25, 27, 33, 272
  Torqueflite transmission, 259
  T-300 transmission, 253–255
disc clutch, 85–95, 98, 102–103, 245–246, 257, 259
downshift pressure signal, of kickdown valve, 190
drive, 149, 235–238
  manual shift positioned in, 166–167
  Torqueflite transmission, 258–259, 266–272
  T-300 transmission, 243, 251–255
  see also direct drive; low gear; second gear; third gear
drive gear, of gear pump, 134–136
driven friction plate, 88, 90–92
driven gear, of gear pump, 134–136
drive plate, 58, 77–78, 87–92
drive wheels, spinning of, 56

288

INDEX 289

e

driving shell, 272
dual band, *see* Split band
dynamic sealing devices, 208, 213–223

electrically-operated kickdown valve, 197–200
energy, 50–51
engine load, and TV pressure, 189, 194
engine vacuum, and TV pressure, 194–195
extension housing, of metal-clad lip seal, 217, 220

f

filter, hydraulic pump, 142
first position, *see* Low gear
flex drive plate, 77–78
fluid (automatic transmission fluid, or ATF), 40–55
    in band operation, 107–108
    in clutch assembly, 90–92
    confined fluid, pressure on, 121–122
    cooling, 47–50
    direction by pressure-regulating valve, 149
    energy, 50–51
    force, 51–52
    and friction linings, 90, 105
    functions, 40–43
    physical characteristics, 119–120
    pressure, 51–52
    sealing devices, 206–226
    structure, 43–45
    types, 44–47
fluid coupling, 58–61
fluid momentum, 51
fluid movement, in diagrams, 235–237
fluid pan reservoir, 141
foam, fluid, 43
force, 13–16, 120–122
    centrifugal, 62, 185–189
    fluid, 51–52
    in hydraulic jack, 124
    see also Spring force
force multiplication, 122–123
Ford Motor Company:
    fluids, 45–46
forward clutch, of T-300 transmission, 243–246, 253, 255
forward drive, 23, 25, 28, 34
    governor position, 188
    hydraulic pressure regulation, 162
    shift valves, 168, 170
    Torqueflite transmission, 259
friction, 42–45
    band-to-drum, 108
    as a force, 120
    in primary clutch, 90–91
friction linings, 72, 88–89, 105
friction plate, 88–92, 94–95
front clutch, of Torqueflite transmission, 259–260, 269, 271–273
front-clutch apply pressure, 270
front pump, 139–140
    seals, 213, 217
    stationary stator support, 67–68
front-servo apply circuit and pressure, 237
fuel economy:
    with lock-up converter, 70
    and ring and pinion ratios, 8
fulcrum, *see* Lever and fulcrum

g

gas, 119
gasket, 209–211
gear, construction and design, 12–39
gear pump, 133–137
gear ratio, 6–8, 17
    compound planetary gear train, 24–28
    shift valve control, 168
    simple planetary gearset, 18–23
    Simpson gear train, 31–34

gearset, simple planetary, *see* planetary gearset, simple
gearshift selector, 161
    Torqueflite transmission, 258
    T-300 transmission, 243
gear train, planetary, *see* Planetary gear train
General Motors:
    fluid, 46–47
    T-300 transmission, 243–257
    T-400 transmission, 112
governor, 163, 165, 183–189
    malfunctioning, 239
    T-300 transmission, 247
governor housing, 185–186
governor plug, 162, 168–171, 173
governor pressure, 168–169, 171–173, 234, 236–237, 239
    Torqueflite transmission, 268, 270
    T-300 transmission, 255
governor spring, 187
governor valve, 162, 164, 171, 185–189, 234, 236
    Torqueflite transmission, 261, 267
governor weight assembly, 187–189
gravity, 120

h

heat:
    carrying of, by fluid, 41
    effect on fluid, 43–44, 48–49
high gear, 8, 24–25
high-pressure relief valve, 233
    Torqueflite transmission, 261, 264
high-speed downshift timing valve, 247
horsepower, 3
hydraulic circuits, 160, 229–237
hydraulic diagrams, 227–242
hydraulic jack, 124–126, 131–132
hydraulic lever, 120, 124
hydraulic pressure, 51–52, 121–122
    control system, 146–159
    hydraulic jack, 124–125
    primary clutch operation, 90–92
    servo piston return, 112
    stationary clutch, 94–95
    transmission by fluid, 41
hydraulic pump, 78, 131–145
    capacity, 138–139
    diagrams, 228, 235
    displacement, 138
    efficiency, 139
    filter, 142
    gear pump, 134–137
    hydraulic jack, 124–126
    multiple systems, 139–141
    reservoir, 141
    rotary pump, 132–133
    rotor pump, 137–138
    Torqueflite transmission, 261
    T-300 transmission, 246
    vent, 142
hydraulics, 118–130
hydraulic signals, 41, 183–205
    governor, 183–189
    kickdown valve, 196–200
    throttle valve, 189–196
    timing valve, 200–201
hydraulic systems, 124–126
    diagrams, 227–242
    pressure control, 146–159
    sealing devices, 206–226
hydrodynamics, 118
hydrostatics, 118–120

i

idle, 4, 7, 56, 63, 155
    compound planetary gear train, 26, 28
    simple planetary gearset, 19
    Simpson gear train, 30–31, 34
    throttle valve position, 191

idle *(Contd.)*
    torque converter design, 75
    Torqueflite transmission, 264, 266
    T-300 transmission, 250–251
impeller, of torque converter, 7, 40–41, 57–60, 64–66, 71
    in coupling phase, 69
    fluid energy, 51
    fluid motions produced by, 61–64
    slippage, 64, 66
    T-300 transmission, 244
input piston, 122–123
input shell, 102
internal gear, of planetary gear train, *see* Ring gear
iron sealing rings, 222–223
IX gear hydraulic pump, 133–137

j   jack, 123–126, 131–132

k   kickdown band, of Torqueflite transmission, 260, 262, 269
    kickdown pressure, 197
    kickdown valve, 190–191, 196–200, 234, 238
        Torqueflite transmission, 262, 267, 271
    kinetic energy, 50–51

l   land, valve, *see* valve land
    lathe-cut seal, 211–212, 214–215
    leakage, fluid, control of, 206–226
    lever, hydraulic, 120, 124
    lever and fulcrum, 13–16
    limit valve, 234, 236
        Torqueflite transmission, 263, 267
    line pressure, 234, 236–237
        Torqueflite transmission, 264–265, 267–268, 272
        T-300 transmission, 251
    line-pressure plug, 153–155, 267
    lip seals, 216–221
    liquid, 119
    load check valve, 125–126
    lock-joint design, of metal sealing ring, 222
    lock-up condition, of gear train, 33, 273
    lock-up torque converter, 70–73, 258
    low band, 243, 246, 253
    low gear (first position), 7, 24, 26, 31, 34, 149, 162, 164–165, 170–174
        Torqueflite transmission, 258–259, 261, 267
        T-300 transmission, 243, 251, 253
    low-reverse band, 260–262
    low-servo piston, 255
    lubrication, 40–55, 207
    lubrication pressure, 234, 236

m   manual low, Torqueflite transmission, 258–259, 261
    manual second, Torqueflite transmission, 258
    manual valve, 161–167, 171, 173, 234, 236–237
        Torqueflite transmission, 261, 264–267, 272
        T-300 transmission, 247, 250, 252, 255
    mechanical advantage, 14
    mechanical overrunning clutch, 95–98
    metal seals, 208, 217–223
    modulator pressure, 247
        T-300 transmission, 251, 255, 257
    modulator valve, 247
        T-300 transmission, 250–251, 257
    molecule, 119
    multiple-disc clutch, 85–95, 98, 102–103
        Torqueflite transmission, 257, 259
        T-300 transmission, 245–246
    multiple hydraulic pump system, 139–141

n   needle valve, 125–126
    neoprene, for lathe-out seals, 211

neutral, 56, 64
    control pressure, 149
    Simpson planetary gear train, 34
    Torqueflite transmission, 258, 264–266
    T-300 transmission, 243, 250–251
noncompensated pressure regulator valve operation, 153–155
noncompensated vacuum-diaphragm assembly, 194–195
nonpositive seal, 209

o   one-way check valve, 174–175
    orifice, 176–177
        symbol in diagram, 230–231
    O-ring seal, 212–217
    output piston, 52, 122–123, 125–126
    overdrive, 6, 19–20, 23
    overheating, of fluid, 48
    overrunning clutch, 67–68, 95–98, 102–103
        Torqueflite transmission, 258–259, 261, 268
        T-300 transmission, 244
    oxidation, of fluid, 43, 48–49

p   pan gasket, 209
    paper filter, 142
    paper gasket, 209–210
    park, 56, 64, 149
        Torqueflite transmission, 258, 264–266
        T-300 transmission, 243, 250–251
    Pascal's Law, 120, 122
    piston, 52, 120, 122–123, 125–126
        accumulator, 177–179
        clutch, 86, 90–95, 214–215, 228
        lock-up converter, 71–73
        servo, 104–105, 107–112, 255, 268–270
    piston engine:
        horsepower, 3
        torque, 3–5
    piston hydraulic pump, 131–132
    piston plug, spring-loaded, 110
    piston travel, 123–124
    planetary gearset, 6
        simple, 18–23, 28
    planetary gear train, 6, 18–19
        compound, 23–28
        Simpson, 28–34
        Torqueflite transmission, 257–259
        T-300 transmission, 234, 245
    planet carrier, 18–34
        Torqueflite transmission, 258–259, 261, 268, 270, 273
        T-300 transmission, 245, 250–251, 253, 257
    planet pinion, 18–34
        Torqueflite transmission, 268, 270, 273
        T-300 transmission, 245, 253, 257
    poppet relief valve, 147–148
    positive-displacement (positive-delivery) pump, 138
    positive seal, 208
    powerflow, 16, 28
        Torqueflite transmission, 265–273
        T-300 transmission, 250–251, 255, 257
    power train, 1–2
    pressure, 121
        see also atmospheric pressure; hydraulic pressure
    pressure-regulating valve, 146, 149–156, 233, 235–236
        Torqueflite transmission, 264, 267, 272
        T-300 transmission, 246, 250–251, 253, 255
    pressure-relief valve, 146–149, 233, 235
        Torqueflite transmission, 261, 264
    primary clutch, 86–92
    primary planet pinion, 26–28
    primary sun gear, 25–27
    pump, hydraulic, *see* hydraulic pump
    push starting, of vehicle with rear pump, 140–141

INDEX

r Ravigneau planetary gear train, 23
reaction area:
   of detent valve, 199
   of governor valve, 187-189
   of pressure-regulating valve, 150-155
   of shift valve, 169
   of throttle valve, 190-192, 194
reaction plate, of stationary clutch, 94
rear clutch, 171, 237
   Torqueflite transmission, 259-260, 267, 269-272
rear hydraulic pump, 139-141
regulator boost valve, 251, 253, 255, 257
regulator valve, 146, 149-156, 233, 235-236
   Torqueflite transmission, 264, 267, 272
   T-300 transmission, 246, 250-251, 253, 255
relay valve, 160-182
   ball check valve, 174-176
   manual valve, 161-167
   shift valve, 167-173
   see also accumulator; orifice
relief valve, 146-149, 233, 235
   Torqueflite transmission, 261, 264
reservoir (sump), 124-126, 141
reservoir check valve, 125-126
return line, of hydraulic jack, 124
return spring:
   accumulator, 177
   servo piston, 109-112
reverse apply pressure, 272
reverse clutch, 243, 246, 255, 257
reverse gear, 6, 20, 22-26, 28, 33-34, 149, 162-164
   Torqueflite transmission, 259, 272-274
   T-300 transmission, 243, 255-257
reverse ring gear, 245, 257
ring and pinion gears, 7, 8
ring gear, 18-34, 78-79, 94-95
   Torqueflite transmission, 258-259, 268, 270, 272-273
   T-300 transmission, 245, 257
roller clutch, 96-97
rotary fluid motion, 61-63, 69
rotary pump, 131-133
rotor pump, 132-133, 137-138

s scoring, 44
sealing devices, 42, 206-226
   gasket, 209-211
   lathe-cut seal, 211-212, 214-215
   lip seal, 216-221
   metal sealing ring, 222-223
   O-ring seal, 212-217
   Teflon seal, 223
secondary clutch, 86, 92-93
secondary planet pinion, 26-28
secondary sun gear, 26-28
second gear, 27, 32-33
   hold capability, 162
   manual valve in, 165-166
   shift valve operation, 172-173
   Torqueflite transmission, 258, 260, 268-270
second-gear apply circuit, 268
self-energizing action, of band, 106-107
servo, 109-112, 237
   accumulator operation, 178-179
   diagrams, 228, 231-232
   movement, 103
   Torqueflite transmission, 269-270
servo apply circuit, 177
servo apply pressure, 237-238
   testing, 239
servo housing, 109
servo piston, 104-105, 107-112
   Torqueflite transmission, 268-270
   T-300 transmission, 255
servo struct, 104-105

shaft torque, 14-16
shift control pressure, 234, 238
shift control valve, 234, 237-238
   Torqueflite transmission, 263, 267-271
   T-300 transmission, 247, 253, 255
shift valve, 162-173, 234, 236-239
   diagrams, 229-231
   Torqueflite transmission, 262-263, 267-268, 270-271
   T-300 transmission, 247, 253, 255
shuttle valve, 234, 236-237
   Torqueflite transmission, 263, 267, 270
signal devices, *see* hydraulic signals
simple planetary gearset, 18-23, 28
Simpson gear train, 28-34
   Torqueflite transmission, 257
single-stage governor, 184-186
six-cylinder engine, band, 105-106
sliding speed, 44
slippage, 43
sludge, in fluid, 43
snap ring, 86, 93
solid, 119
solid band, 104-105
speed of engine:
   and hydraulic pressure regulation, 155
   increase, 19-20
   reduction, 21-23, 32
   and shift valve operation, 171
speed ratio, of torque converter, 7
speed signals, by governor, 183, 185-186, 188-189
spline, 29
split band, 106-107
split guide ring, of impeller, 58
spool valve, 150-152
sprag clutch, 97-98
spring:
   calibrated, 149-151, 168, 171-172, 177
   compression, 86, 93, 153
   damper, 72-73
   governor, 187
   return, of servo piston, 109-112
   throttle valve train, 190, 192-193
spring force, 121
   pressure-relief valve, 147-148
   shift valve, 171
   spool valve, 150-153
   throttle valve, 191, 193-194
spring-loaded piston plug, 110
spring-loaded poppet valve, 147-148
square-cut seal, 211-212, 214-215
stall, 56, 75
standard duty servo, 109-110
starter ring gear, 78-79
start-up, 64
static seal, 208-213
stationary clutch, 86, 92-95
stationary vehicle, 64-65, 149, 186, 188, 190
stator, 9, 57, 66-71
   blade angle, and torque capacity, 74-75
   coupling phase, 69-70
   Torqueflite transmission, 258
   torque increase, 67-69
   T-300 transmission, 244
   variable-pitch, 75-77
stator control valve, 250
stator support, 67-68, 134-136
stopping of vehicle, 172
suction line, of hydraulic jack, 124
sump, *see* Reservoir
sun gear, 18-34
   Torqueflite transmission, 258-260, 268-270, 272-273
   T-300 transmission, 245-246, 253, 255, 257
symbols, in hydraulic diagrams, 229-231, 234
synthetic lip seal, 216-217
synthetic-rubber seal, 208, 211

t Teflon seals, 223
temperature:
    effect on fluid, 43–44, 48–49
    effect on seal design, 208
third gear, 27–28, 33
    Torqueflite transmission, 270–272
third-gear apply circuit, 270
three-speed transmission, 168–169
throttle plug, 153–155, 267
throttle valve, 3–5, 155, 162–163, 171, 189–197, 234, 237
    testing and adjusting, 239
    Torqueflite transmission, 262, 267
throttle valve housing, 192–193
throttle valve (TV) pressure, 189–197, 234, 236–239
    shift valve control, 170–172
    Torqueflite transmission, 267–270
timing valve, 200–201
torque, 2–6, 8
    conservation of, in multiple pump system, 140
    shaft torque, 14–16
    transmission by ATF, 40–41
torque converter, 5, 7–9, 40–41, 56–84
    advantages of, 74
    air-cooled system, 48
    combination low and high capacity, 75–76
    coupling operation, 64–66, 69–70
    efficiency, 7
    fluid coupling design, 58–61
    fluid energy, 51
    fluid motions produced by impeller, 61–64
    installation, 77–78
    lock-up converter, 70–73
    size, and torque capacity, 74–75
    Torqueflite transmission, 257–258
    T-300 transmission, 243–244
torque converter pressure, 234, 236
Torqueflite transmission, of Chrysler Corporation, 257–274
torque multiplication, 5, 13–17, 21–22, 32, 66–69, 73
torque ratio, 8–9
torque reduction, 19–20
towing, of vehicle without rear pump, 141
transmission pan, 50
trouble-shooting, using hydraulic diagrams, 238–239
T-300 transmission, of General Motors, 243–257
T-400 transmission, of General Motors, 112
turbine, of torque converter, 7, 41, 57–61, 64–66
    coupling phase, 69
    fluid energy, 51
    lock-up converter, 70–73

turbine, of torque converter *(Contd.)*
    slippage, 64, 66
    total turbine torque, 69
    T-300 transmission, 244
TV pressure, *see* throttle valve pressure
two-diameter accumulator piston, 177–178
two-land piston, 111
two-speed transmission, 168
two-stage governor, 184–189
two-way check valve, 175
Type A fluid, 45–46
Type F fluid, 44–46, 91

u upshift, 149

v vacuum-controlled throttle valve train, 192–196
vacuum modulator, 247, 250–251, 257
valve, 125–126, 233–234, 246–247, 250, 261–263
    balanced valve principle, 147
    diagrams, 227–228, 230, 235–237
    diagrams, use of, in finding malfunctions, 238–239
    pressure-relief and regulation, 146–156
    relay, 160–179
    signal devices, 183–201
    see also annular groove; valve land; and names of specific valves
valve land, 150
    detent regulator valve, 199–200
    governor plug of shift valve, 168–169
    governor valve, 187–189
    kickdown valve, 196–197
    manual valve, 161, 163–166
    pressure-regulating valve, 150–155
    shift valve, 170–172
    throttle valve, 190–192, 194
variable-pitch stator, 75–77
varnish, 43
V-eight engine, band, 105–106
vent, 142, 232–233
vent line, of hydraulic jack, 124
viscosity, 43–44
viscous friction, 42
vortex fluid motion, 62–63, 65–66, 68–69

w water-cooled system, for fluid, 47–50
wire mesh filter, 142